DECISIONS
on the
RULES OF GOLF

Official Rulings on over 1,000 Golf Situations

D0124484

By the
United States Golf Association®
and
The Royal and Ancient Golf Club
of St. Andrews, Scotland

TRIUMPH BOOKS
Chicago

International Standard Book Number: 1-880141-21-3

For more information on the USGA®, contact:

United States Golf Association®
Golf House
Far Hills, New Jersey 07931

This book is available in quantity at special
discounts for your group or organization. For further
information contact:

Triumph Books
644 South Clark Street, Suite 2000
Chicago, IL 60605
(312) 939-3330
Fax (312) 663-3557

Cover design and illustrations by:
Mark Anderson Design, Chicago, Illinois

Typography by: Photo Composition Service/
BookComp, Grand Rapids, Michigan

Printed in the United States of America

CONTENTS

INDEX i-1
I. ETIQUETTE 1
II. DEFINITIONS 3
III. THE RULES OF PLAY .11

The Game

1. The Game 11
2. Match Play 27
3. Stroke Play 49

Clubs and the Ball

4. Clubs 61
5. The Ball 75

Player's Responsibilities

6. The Player 81
7. Practice 111
8. Advice; Indicating Line of Play 119
9. Information as to Strokes Taken 129

Order of Play

10. Order of Play 139

Teeing Ground

11. Teeing Ground 147

Playing the Ball

12. Searching for and Identifying Ball 155
13. Ball Played as It Lies; Lie, Area of
    Intended Swing and Line of Play;
    Stance 161
14. Striking the Ball 197
15. Playing a Wrong Ball 211

The Putting Green

16. The Putting Green 227
17. The Flagstick 245

Ball Moved, Deflected or Stopped

18. Ball at Rest Moved 255
19. Ball in Motion Deflected or Stopped 291

Relief Situations and Procedure

20. Lifting, Dropping and Placing;
    Playing from Wrong Place 305
21. Cleaning Ball 339
22. Ball Interfering with or Assisting
    Play 343
23. Loose Impediments 347
24. Obstructions............................357
25. Abnormal Ground Conditions and
    Wrong Putting Green 379
26. Water Hazards (Including Lateral
    Water Hazards) 409
27. Ball Lost or Out of Bounds;
    Provisional Ball 429
28 Ball Unplayable 453

Other Forms of Play

29. Threesomes and Foursomes 463
30. Three-Ball, Best-Ball and Four-Ball
    Match Play 471
31. Four-Ball Stroke Play 487
32. Bogey, Par and Stableford
    Competitions 493

Administration

33. The Committee 499
34. Disputes and Decisions 543

APPENDIX I: LOCAL RULES;
  CONDITIONS OF THE COMPETITION 553

APPENDIX II: DESIGN OF CLUBS 565

APPENDIX III: THE BALL 569

APPENDIX IV: MISCELLANEOUS 571

MISCELLANEOUS DECISIONS................573

DECISIONS APPLICABLE ONLY IN THE
  UNITED STATES OF AMERICA 573

PRINCIPAL CHANGES SINCE 1992............579

INTRODUCTION

Each year, the United States Golf Association and the Royal and Ancient Golf Club of St. Andrew's, Scotland receive thousands of phone calls and letters regarding clarification of the Rules of Golf. In order to help millions of golfers around the world better understand how these detailed Rules are applied and interpreted, the USGA and R&A developed the comprehensive *Decisions on the Rules of Golf*. The topics of Etiquette, Definitions, and the Rules of Play are discussed at length. The format is geared towards questions and answers and is designed to be used as a reference at home, or right on the golf course.

Since 1951 the USGA and R&A have been meeting regularly in order to establish a uniform code of Rules. *Decisions on the Rules of Golf* is the result of these meetings. However, each year brings about a whole new round of questions not specifically addressed in the *Rules of Golf*. Committees meet from both organizations to discuss these new questions — anything from water hazards, and points of relief, to how to play a ball near a dead elk — and arrive at a decision with which both the USGA and R&A agree. *Decisions on the Rules of Golf* is amended every year in order to keep up on the ever evolving game of golf.

The partnership of the USGA and the R&A has worked to further the understanding and enjoyment of the game of golf. With their official expertise, golf enthusiasts can rest assured that even the most unusual situation can be addressed. Whether it's a question of casual water, loose impediments, or line of play, no answer is out of bounds.

INDEX

ABNORMAL GROUND CONDITIONS —
See "BURROWING ANIMAL," "CASUAL
WATER" and "GROUND UNDER REPAIR"

ADDRESSING THE BALL
After ball addressed on putting green ball moved in removal of loose impediment	18-2c/2
Ball addressed; club breaks on downswing; swing stopped but clubhead falls and moves ball	14/4
Ball dropped in improper manner moves when addressed; player then lifts ball and drops it in proper manner	20-2a/4
Ball falls into hole after being addressed	18-2b/10
Ball in rough moves downward when addressed; ball will not remain at rest when replaced	20-3d/3
Ball moved by another ball after being addressed	18-2b/11
Ball moves after address and comes to rest out of bounds	18-2b/9
Ball moves after address and is stopped by player's club	18-2b/12
Ball moves after being addressed in hazard without club	18-2b/2
Ball moves after player addresses it and then steps away	18-2b/7
Ball moves after player grounds club but before stance completed	18-2b/4
Ball moves after stance taken but before address	18-2b/1
Ball moves while player in process of addressing it in bunker	18-2b/3
Ball moving in water hazard after address	14-6/1
Order of play in foursome match if player accidentally moves ball after address	29-1/5
Original ball out of bounds; ball played under stroke-and-distance procedure falls off tee at address	11-3/3
Placing clubhead on ground in front of ball when addressing	18/5
Player addresses ball, steps away, lifts ball and replaces it; ball then moves	18-2b/8
Provisional ball moves after being addressed	15/7
Stroke misses ball which is then accidentally knocked off tee after being addressed	11-3/1
When ball addressed in bunker	13-4/23
When club grounded in grass	18-2b/5
When player who putts "side-saddle" has addressed ball	18/6
Whether ball addressed if stance taken and club rested on heather	18-2b/6

ADHESIVE TAPE
  Applying to golf glove   14-3/8
  Binding fingers together   14-3/8

ADVICE
  Absent partner gives advice before joining
    four-ball match   30-3a/2
  Asking advice when play suspended   8-1/20
  Between rounds in 36-hole match   8-1/19
  Club selection -
    After player has played to green he asks
      opponent or fellow-competitor what club
      he used in playing to green   8-1/7
    Asking opponent or fellow-competitor what
      club he used at previous hole   8-1/6
    Comment about club selection after stroke 8-1/8
    Double caddie informs one employer about
      club used by other   8-1/12
    Looking into another player's bag to
      determine club used   8-1/10
    Misleading statement about club selection 8-1/9
    Removing towel covering another player's
      clubs to determine club used   8-1/11
  Distance -
    Asking if distance marker accurate   8-1/3
    Inquiring as to distance from certain object
      to green   8-1/2
    Seeking information about length of hole   8-1/1
  Given on request; penalties in various forms of
    play   8-1/25
  Instruction -
    Caddie swings club to show player how to
      play shot   8-1/15
    Competitor, after finishing hole,
      demonstrates to fellow-competitor
      how to play shot   8-1/14
    Player giving opponent or fellow-competitor
      instruction during round   8-1/13
  Player putting for half is given advice by
    opponent   2-2/1
  Player who has not yet played seeks advice
    from player who has finished round   8-1/18
  Request for advice made in error to opponent's
    caddie withdrawn before advice given   8-1/17
  Seeking information on whereabouts of
    another player's ball   8-1/5
  Suggesting to competitor that he declare his
    ball unplayable   8-1/16
  Team competition -
    Advice given by team coach or captain   8-1/24
    Advice given by team mate in another group
      in stroke play   8-1/21
    Condition stipulates who is authorized to
      give advice   8/1

ADVICE (Continued)
  Team competition (Continued)
    Player's team mate in gallery hits ball to
      green to show player whether green will
      hold 8-1/23
    Team mates playing as fellow-competitors
      exchange advice 8-1/22
    Whether team captain who is authorized to
      give advice may be required to keep off
      putting greens 8-2b/4

AGREEMENT TO WAIVE RULES
  Player who has reached third round of match
    play disqualified for agreeing to waive Rules
    in first-round match 33/2
  Time limit on applying penalty for agreeing to
    waive Rules in match play 1-3/8
  Whether agreement to waive Rules occurs if -
    Competitor refuses Committee member's
      request to lift ball assisting fellow-
      competitor 22/7
    Competitor requests that ball in position to
      assist him should not be lifted 22/6
    Competitors in stroke play agree to play out
      of turn but not for purpose of giving one
      of them an advantage 10-2c/2
    Discontinued match replayed in error
      instead of being resumed from where play
      stopped 2-3/5
    Handicap stroke given at incorrect hole in
      error 6-2a/2
    Marker attests wrong score knowingly and
      competitor aware score wrong 1-3/6
    Marker attests wrong score knowingly but
      competitor unaware score wrong 6-6a/5
    Match decided by wrong form of play by
      agreement 33-1/4
    Penalty not applied because players unaware
      penalty incurred 1-3/5
    Player and opponent or fellow-competitor
      agree to repair spike marks on one
      another's line of putt 1-3/3
    Player disregards breach of Rules by
      opponent 2-5/1
    Players agree not to tee off in prescribed
      order to save time 1-3/1
    Players agree that side losing after 18 holes
      of 36-hole match will concede match 1-3/7
    Players agree to concede short putts 1-3/2
    Players fail to apply known penalty 1-3/4
    Players unable to resolve Rules problem
      agree to consider hole halved 2-1/1
    Two holes purposely omitted in match 2-3/3
    Wrong form of play used in match play
      event 6-1/1

ANTS
Ant hill; status   23/5
Local Rule treating ant hills as ground under
  repair   33-8/22

AREA OF INTENDED SWING
Improved by -
  Bending boundary fence   13-2/18
  Bending grass in removal of loose
    impediments   13-2/13
  Bending shrub in water hazard   13-4/28
  Breaking branch; area of swing finally used
    not affected by branch   13-2/24
  Breaking branch interfering with back-swing
    on teeing ground   13-2/14
  Breaking branch on backswing; swing
    discontinued when branch broken   13-2/14.5
  Breaking stake supporting tree in attempt to
    remove it   13-2/16
  Knocking down leaves with practice swing   13-2/22
  Moving growing or fixed object situated out
    of bounds   13-2/19
  Moving natural object to determine whether
    it is loose   13-2/26
  Pressing down divot in divot hole behind
    ball   13-2/6
  Pushing back fence off course which leans
    across boundary   13-2/20
  Removing boundary stake   13-2/17
  Removing immovable obstruction   13-2/15
  Repairing pitch-mark made by ball on
    previous stroke   13-2/21
  Replacing or removing undetached divot   13-2/5
  Shaking water from tree branch interfering
    with backswing   13-2/23
Meaning of term in immovable obstruction
  Rule   24-2a/2
Position of ball worsened when obstruction
  removed; player replaces obstruction   13-2/15.5
Whether removal of dew from behind ball
  improves area of intended swing   13-2/35

**ARTIFICIAL DEVICES and UNUSUAL
EQUIPMENT**
Whether Rule prohibiting artificial devices is
breached if -
  Adhesive tape applied to golf glove   14-3/8
  Adhesive tape used to bind fingers together   14-3/8
  Artificial limb utilized   14-3/15
  Ball held in hand against grip when putting   14-3/6
  Booklet providing distances to hole from
    various points used   14-3/5
  Club used as plumb-line   14-3/12
  Compass used during round   14-3/4
  Device which emits click if swing timed
    properly used   14-3/10

ARTIFICIAL DEVICES and UNUSUAL
EQUIPMENT (Continued)
  Whether Rule prohibiting artificial devices is
    breached if (Continued)
      Distance meter attached to golf cart   14-3/1
      Elastic bandage worn on right wrist and
        hand because of injury   14-3/7
      Electronic instrument used to find ball   14-3/14
      Golf ball warmer or hand warmer used   14-3/13
      Instructional material used   14-3/16
      Pencil or score card used to assist in gauging
        distance   14-3/2
      Player putts with one hand and steadies
        himself with club held in other hand   14-3/9
      Player with injured right wrist inserts left
        thumb under elastic bandage on right
        wrist and hand   14-3/7
      Plumb-line used   14-3/11
      Standard spectacles and field glasses used   14-3/3

ARTIFICIAL OBJECT — See
  "OBSTRUCTIONS"

ASSISTANCE
  Ball assisting play — See "BALL: Assisting
    play"
  Ball mark in position to assist opponent   16-1c/2
  Ball-marker in position to assist another player   20-1/11
  Caddie shields player from sun during stroke   14-2/3
  In removing large loose impediment   23-1/3
  Player aligns partner's club before stroke   14-2/1
  Player plays away from hole to assist partner   30-3f/6
  Putting out after concession of stroke; act
    assists partner   2-4/6
  Umbrella held over player's head during
    stroke   14-2/2

BALL
  Abandoned ball -
    Player plays stroke at part of abandoned ball
      which had broken into pieces   15/3
    Status   24-1/2
  Adhering to face of club after stroke   1-4/2
  Assisting play -
    Assisting ball lifted by opponent replaced
      on request; player's ball then strikes
      opponent's ball and opponent lodges
      claim   22/5
    Ball assisting fellow-competitor on putting
      green; procedure for Committee member
      if competitor does not lift ball   22/7
    Competitor not given opportunity to lift ball
      assisting fellow-competitor   3-4/1
    Competitor requests that ball in position to
      assist him should not be lifted   22/6

BALL (Continued)
Assisting play (Continued)

Request to lift ball assisting partner not
  honored 30-3f/11
Blown into hole by competitor 3-2/2
Cleaning -
  Ball lifted without authority and cleaned ... 18-2a/13
  Ball thought to be unfit for play lifted
    under another Rule and cleaned; ball then
    determined to be unfit for play 5-3/6
  Position of ball lifted for identification not
    marked, intention to lift not announced
    and ball cleaned beyond extent necessary
    to identify it 21/4
  Removal of insect on ball 23-1/5
  Removing grass adhering to ball 21/2
  Removing lime from ball 21/1
  Rubbing ball on putting green for cleaning
    purposes 16-1d/5
  When ball may be cleaned or substituted
    after play has been discontinued 6-8c/1
  Whether ball cleaned through act of caddie
    throwing it to player 21/3
Club thrown at ball 1-2/4.5
Competitor's ball played from putting
  green touches but does not move ball of
  fellow-competitor lying on green 19-5/4
Condition requiring use of ball on List of
  Conforming Golf Balls -
  Ball not on List played as provisional ball .. 5-1/3
  Penalty for breach 5-1/2
Deflected or stopped -
  Attendant removes flagstick whereupon
    knob falls from top of flagstick and
    deflects ball 17/9
  Ball played from spot where original ball
    deflected out of bounds by maintenance
    vehicle 20-7/1
  Ball strikes edge of hole-liner and bounces
    out of hole 16/5
  Ball strikes hole-liner pulled out with
    flagstick 17/8
  Breaks into pieces as a result of striking
    paved cart path 5-3/4
  By a ball at rest -
    After player putts opponent or fellow-
      competitor drops his ball; player's
      ball strikes opponent's or fellow-
      competitor's ball after it is at
      rest 19-5/1.5
    Competitor not given opportunity to lift
      ball assisting fellow-competitor; fellow-
      competitor's ball strikes competitor's
      ball 3-4/1

BALL (Continued)
  Deflected or stopped (Continued)
    By a ball at rest (Continued)

        Competitor's ball played from putting
          green strikes ball on green belonging to
          competitor playing in another group   19-5/2
        Competitor's ball played on putting
          green deflected by balls of two
          fellow-competitors   19-5/3
        Original ball strikes second ball or vice
          versa   3-3/7
        Player lifts his ball on putting green and
          sets it aside; opponent's or fellow-
          competitor's ball played from green
          subsequently strikes player's ball   19-5/1
        Provisional ball strikes original ball   18-5/2
        Provisional ball struck by original ball   19-5/5
      By another ball in motion -
        Ball dropped on putting green by
          opponent or fellow-competitor falls on
          player's moving ball   19-5/1.7
        Ball in motion after stroke on putting
          green deflected by ball played at another
          hole   19-1/10
        By clubs belonging to different side but
          carried in same bag   19-2/5
        By golf cart shared by two players   19/1
      By opponent accidentally -
        Ball strikes opponent standing out of
          bounds and comes to rest out of bounds   19-3/1
        Dropped ball deflected by opponent   19-3/2
      By outside agency -
        Ball played from putting green deflected
          into hole by moving outside agency;
          stroke not replayed   19-1/3
        Ball played from spot where original ball
          deflected out of bounds by maintenance
          vehicle   20-7/1
        By direction post   19-1/1
        By dog on putting green after stroke from
          off green   19-1/6
        By dog on putting green after stroke on
          green   19-1/7
        By stroke of player in another group   19-1/2
        Deliberately by spectator on putting green   19-1/4
        Deliberately by spectator through the
          green   19-1/4.1
        Deliberately on putting green by
          fellow-competitor   19-1/5
      By player, partner, caddie or equipment -
        Ball falls on club face after stroke and
          sticks to mud thereon   14-4/1
        Ball moves after address and is stopped
          by player's club   18-2b/12

BALL (Continued)
  Deflected or stopped (Continued)
    By player, partner, caddie or equipment
      (Continued)
      Ball popped up swung at in disgust and
        hit | 14/6
      Ball strikes pipeline and on rebound is
        deflected by face of club | 14-4/2
    By competitor's golf bag and then his caddie | 19-2/7
    By player's club; player removes club and
      ball rolls away | 19-2/1.5
    By player's foot; ball moves when foot
      removed | 19-2/1
    By player's golf cart being pulled by
      opponent or fellow-competitor | 19-2/6
    Caddie stops dropped ball before it comes
      to rest; when penalty incurred | 20-2c/4
    Player putts with one hand and catches ball
      in hole with other hand | 1-2/5
    Player's ball strikes own caddie and comes
      to rest out of bounds | 19-2/2
    Player's ball strikes own caddie standing out
      of bounds -
      Ball comes to rest on course | 19-2/3
      Ball comes to rest out of bounds | 19-2/4
    Local Rule for ball deflected by power line | 33-8/13
    Local Rule for ball deflected by sprinkler
      head | 33-8/12
    Tee marking position of player's ball deflects
      opponent's ball | 20-1/17
  Dropping and re-dropping -
    Ball dropped at wrong place and played —
      See "PLAYING FROM WRONG PLACE"
    Ball dropped from casual water in bunker at
      point of maximum relief rolls elsewhere | 25-1b/6
    Ball dropped from ground under repair area
      rolls to position where area interferes with
      stance; whether re-drop required | 20-2c/0.5
    Ball dropped in area where original ball lost;
      ball then played | 27-1/3
    Ball dropped in improper manner and in
      wrong place | 20-2a/3
    Ball dropped in improper manner moves
      when addressed; player then lifts ball and
      drops it in proper manner | 20-2a/4
    Ball dropped third time when placement
      required after second drop | 20-2c/2
    Ball dropped twice each time rolls to position
      where there is interference by condition;
      circumstances under which ball not placed | 24-2b/9.5
    Ball dropped under unplayable ball
      Rule comes to rest in original position
      or another position at which ball is
      unplayable | 28/3
    Ball dropped when required to be placed
      or placed when required to be dropped;
      correction of error | 20-6/1

BALL (Continued)

Dropping and re-dropping (Continued)

Ball lifted without authority dropped instead
of being replaced   18-2a/9

Ball mistakenly substituted when dropped;
correction of error   20-6/3

Ball moved in measuring to determine if
re-drop required   20-2c/6

Ball played from bunker is out of bounds
or lost; player smooths footprints before
dropping another ball in bunker   13-4/37

Ball rolls towards hole when dropped at
spot from which previous stroke played   20-2c/1.5

Caddie holds back tree branch to prevent
branch from deflecting dropped ball   20-2a/5

Caddie stops dropped ball before it comes
to rest; when penalty incurred   20-2c/4

Changing relief option after ball dropped in
a wrong place   20-6/2

Changing relief option when re-dropping
required   20-2c/5

Divots replaced and pressed down in area in
which ball is to be dropped   13-2/4.5

Dropped ball accidentally deflected by
opponent or his caddie   19-3/2

Dropped ball embeds   25-2/2

Procedure if ball again embeds when
re-dropped   25-2/2.5

Dropped ball never strikes ground   20-2b/1

Dropped ball rolling out of prescribed
dropping area   20-2c/1

Dropped ball rolls into pitch-mark from
which lifted   25-2/3

Dropped ball strikes glove used as indicating
mark   18/9

Dropped ball strikes tree branch then
ground; whether re-drop required   20-2c/1.3

Local Rule permitting re-dropping or placing
when dropped ball embeds in bunker   33-8/28

Original ball found within five-minute
search period after another ball dropped   27-1/2

Penalty when ball dropped in other than
prescribed manner   20-2a/1

Permissible dropping area so narrow player
has difficulty dropping within it   26-1/19

Pitch-mark in dropping area repaired before
ball dropped   13-2/10

Placing ball instead of dropping when
obvious dropped ball will roll into hazard,
etc.   20-2c/3

Placing ball on bank of water hazard instead
of dropping to prevent ball rolling into
water   26-1/10

Player distracted by ball accidentally
dropped by another player mis-hits ball   1-4/1

BALL (Continued)
  Dropping and re-dropping (Continued)
    Player's ball moved by ball accidentally
      dropped by opponent or fellow-competitor   18/7.5
    Procedure for dropping in Ball Drop   33-8/34
    Removal of loose impediments from area in
      which ball to be dropped   23-1/6
    Removing sand or loose soil from dropping
      area   13-2/11
    Spinning ball when dropping   20-2a/2
    Who drops ball in foursome competition   29/4
  Embedded -
    Ball on steep bank driven straight into
      ground   25-2/6
    Bounces out of its pitch-mark and spins back
      into it   25-2/1
    Completely embedded in lip of bunker   13/4
    Dropped ball embeds   25-2/2
      Procedure if ball again embeds when
        re-dropped   25-2/2.5
    Dropped ball rolls into pitch-mark from
      which lifted   25-2/3
    In grass bank or face of bunker   25-2/5
    In ground under repair in closely mown area   25-2/4
    In side of hole; all of ball below lip of hole   16/2
    In side of hole; all of ball not below lip of
      hole   16/3
    Lifting ball to determine whether it is
      embedded   25-2/7
    Lifting in hazard to determine whether unfit
      for play   5-3/5
    Local Rule permitting re-dropping or placing
      when dropped ball embeds in bunker   33-8/28
  Exchanging -
    Ball changed during play of hole to aid
      identification   15/6.5
    Ball mistakenly substituted when dropped;
      correction of error   20-6/3
    Ball not unfit for play deemed unfit and
      another ball substituted   5-3/3
    Balls inadvertently exchanged by competitors
      at unknown place   15-1/2
    Balls inadvertently exchanged by players
      after one ball struck and moved the other   15-1/2.5
    Balls inadvertently exchanged by players
      between holes   15-1/1
    Competitor mistakenly substitutes another
      ball on putting green; error discovered
      after stroke played from next teeing
      ground   15-1/8
    Competitor who lifts his ball and fellow-
      competitor's ball inadvertently exchanges
      balls when replacing them   15-1/9

BALL (Continued)
  Exchanging (Continued)
    Competitor's ball lifted without authority
      by fellow-competitor's caddie who
      subsequently substitutes another ball
      which competitor plays   20-1/5
    Place at which exchange took place unknown   15-1/3
    Player mistakenly substitutes another ball
      on putting green; error discovered before
      stroke played   15-1/7
    Player substitutes another ball on putting
      green because original ball thrown to
      caddie for cleaning came to rest in lake   15-1/6
    Players inadvertently exchange balls
      recovered from water hazard   15-1/4
    When ball may be substituted after play has
      been discontinued   6-8c/1
  Exerting influence on — See "EXERTING
    INFLUENCE ON BALL"
  Falls on club face after stroke and sticks to
    mud thereon   14-4/1
  Found in immovable obstruction but not
    immediately recoverable   24-2b/4.5
  Holding ball in hand against grip when
    putting   14-3/6
  Holed or holing out — See "HOLED OR
    HOLING OUT"
  Identifying -
    Ball changed during play of hole to aid
      identification   15/6.5
    Ball dislodged from tree for identification
      purposes by shaking tree or throwing club   18-2a/27
    Ball in tree identified but not retrieved   27/14
    Ball in tree visible but not identifiable   27/15
    Caddie on own initiative lifts ball for
      identification   18-2a/14
    Identification of ball through testimony of
      spectator   27/12
    Identifying ball by brand and number only   12-2/1
    Player unable to distinguish his ball from
      another ball   27/10
    Position of ball lifted for identification not
      marked, intention to lift not announced
      and ball cleaned beyond extent necessary
      to identify it   21/4
    Provisional ball not distinguishable from
      original ball   27/11
    Refusal to identify ball   27/13
    Touching and rotating half-buried ball in
      hazard for identification purposes   12-2/3
    Touching and rotating half-buried ball in
      rough for identification purposes   12-2/2
    Two balls lie together in hazard and neither
      is identifiable   1-4/6

BALL (Continued)
  Identifying (Continued)

    Unidentifiable ball played in water hazard
      and lost   26/5
    When necessary to find and identify ball
      declared unplayable   28/1
  Interfering with play -
    Abandoned ball interferes with play   24-1/2
    Ball accidentally kicked by player asked to
      lift it due to interference   22/4
    Interfering ball in bunker lifted; lie altered
      by another player's stroke   20-3b/1
    Mental interference by another ball   22/1
    Player claims that another ball lying 30
      yards away interferes with his play   22/2
    Player requested to lift ball due to
      interference plays out of turn instead   10-1c/2
    Player requests another player to lift his ball
      in absence of reasonable possibility ball
      might interfere   22/3
    Two balls lie together in hazard and neither
      is identifiable   1-4/6
  Lie of — See also "AREA OF INTENDED
  SWING"
    Altered -
      Ball moved accidentally and original lie
        altered; player places ball in wrong
        place and plays   18-2a/21.3
      By pitch-mark made by partner's,
        opponent's or fellow-competitor's ball   13-2/8
      By removal of gallery-control stake   20-3b/3
      By tractor   20-3b/4
      Lie in bunker altered by another player
        taking his stance   20-3b/2
      Lie of ball embedded in hazard altered
        when ball lifted to determine whether
        unfit for play   5-3/5
      Lie of ball to be replaced altered and
        spot where ball originally lay not
        determinable   20-3b/5
      Lie of lifted ball in bunker altered by
        another player's stroke   20-3b/1
      Partner's, opponent's or fellow-
        competitor's divot comes to rest near
        player's ball in bunker   13-4/18
      Pine cone falls from tree and comes to rest
        behind ball lying in bunker   13-4/18.5
      Player's lie affected by sand from partner's,
        opponent's or fellow-competitor's stroke
        from bunker   13-2/8.5
      When player presses oscillating ball into
        surface of putting green   18-2a/6
      Worsened when obstruction removed;
        player replaces obstruction   13-2/15.5

BALL (Continued)
  Lie of (Continued)
    Improved -
      By bending grass in removal of loose
        impediments   13-2/13
      By breaking off grass behind ball on teeing
        ground   13-2/3
      By pressing down irregularities on tee
        when ball in play   13-2/2
      By pressing down replaced divot   13-2/6
      By removing sand behind ball through the
        green with backswing   13-2/9
      By replacing or removing undetached
        divot   13-2/5
      When greenkeeping staff member rakes
        bunker   13-2/4
  Lifting — See also "BALL: Moved or moving"
    Ball lifted and dropped away from boundary
      stake under obstruction Rule   18-2a/3
    Ball falling off tee when stroke just touches
      it is picked up and re-teed   18-2a/2
    Ball lifted and dropped away from movable
      obstruction   18-2a/4
    Ball lifted from putting green in mistaken
      belief it is wrong ball   20-1/1
    Ball lifted without authority and cleaned   18-2a/13
    Ball lifted without authority dropped instead
      of being replaced   18-2a/9
    Ball marked and lifted by opponent without
      player's authority; player lifts ball-marker,
      claims hole and opponent disputes claim   20-1/3
    Ball moved by wind lifted and replaced   18-2a/7
    Ball on putting green lifted because player
      feared ball might move   16-1b/1
    Ball overhanging hole is lifted, cleaned and
      replaced; ball then falls into hole   16-2/0.5
    Ball played from ground under repair picked
      up and relief taken under ground under
      repair Rule   18-2a/8
    Ball putted from wrong place lifted and
      putted from right place   20-7b/2
    Ball resting against flagstick lifted before
      being holed   17-4/1
    Others in four-ball match pick up mistakenly
      believing player won hole   30-3f/3
    Ball wrongly thought to be out of bounds
      lifted; competitor proceeds under Rule
      27-1   18-2a/11
    Caddie lifts ball in water hazard without
      player's authority   26-1/9
    Caddie on own initiative lifts ball considering
      it unplayable   18-2a/15
    Caddie on own initiative lifts ball for
      identification   18-2a/14

BALL (Continued)
Lifting (Continued)

Competitor who lifts his ball and fellow-
   competitor's ball inadvertently exchanges
   balls when replacing them   15-1/9
Competitor's ball lifted without authority by
   fellow-competitor   20-1/4
Competitor's ball lifted without authority
   by fellow-competitor's caddie who
   subsequently substitutes another ball
   which competitor plays   20-1/5
Competitor's ball picked up by fellow-
   competitor at competitor's request   18-2a/16
Dropped ball lifted and re-dropped when
   it should have been played as it lay; ball
   then lifted again and placed   18-2a/10
Fellow-competitor lifts competitor's ball and
   sets it aside; competitor plays ball from
   where set aside   15-3/3
Knocking ball aside after marking position
   instead of lifting   20-1/22
Lifting ball in play but still within teeing
   ground   11-3/2
Loose impediment affecting lie moved when
   ball lifted   23-1/7
Loose impediment affecting lie removed
   while ball lifted   23-1/8
Opponent's caddie lifts player's ball after
   player claims another ball   18-3b/4
Opponent's caddie lifts player's ball which
   may or may not have been out of bounds   18-3b/5
Player concedes match due to misconception
   as to opponent's score at last hole and
   picks up ball   2-4/14
Player entitled to relief from condition lifts
   ball; player then replaces ball and plays it
   from original position   18-2a/12
Player lifts ball in mistaken belief that next
   stroke conceded   2-4/3
Player lifts ball, sets it aside and plays it
   from where set aside   15/4
Player lifts ball without authority due to
   misunderstanding Committee member's
   instructions   34-3/3.5
Player lifts his ball on putting green and sets
   it aside; opponent's or fellow-competitor's
   ball played from green subsequently
   strikes player's ball   19-5/1
Player's ball lifted by opponent without
   authority   20-1/2
In four-ball match   30-3f/10
Position of ball lifted for identification not
   marked, intention to lift not announced
   and ball cleaned beyond extent necessary
   to identify it   21/4

BALL (Continued)
  Lifting (Continued)

Provisional ball lifted in erroneous belief original ball is in bounds	27-2b/8
Provisional ball lifted subsequently becomes ball in play	27-2b/9
To determine whether it is embedded	25-2/7
To determine whether it lies in burrowing animal hole	25/21
Whether player himself must lift ball	20-1/0.5

  Lost — See "LOST BALL"
  Lying in or touching hazard — See "HAZARD"
  Marking position when lifting -

Ball moved by ball-marker dropped accidentally by player	20-1/15
Ball moved in removing ball-marker after replacing ball	20-3a/1
Ball-marker in position to assist another player	20-1/11
Ball-marker lifted by outside agency	20-1/9
Ball-marker lifted by player who mistakenly believes he has won hole	20-1/8
Ball-marker moved accidentally by player	20-1/5.5
Ball-marker moved accidentally by player in process of marking position of ball	20-1/6
Ball-marker moved by opponent's caddie accidentally	20-1/7
Ball-marker moved off green by wind or casual water	20-1/10
Knocking ball aside after marking position instead of lifting	20-1/22
Marking position of ball by scratching line on putting green	20-1/16
Marking position of ball with toe of club	20-1/12
Placing ball-marker to side	US/20-1/100
Placing object marking position of ball other than behind ball	20-1/19
Player places ball-marker approximately two inches behind ball	20-1/20
Position of ball lifted for identification not marked, intention to lift not announced and ball cleaned beyond extent necessary to identify it	21/4
Position of ball marked before obstruction removed; ball moves when ball-marker removed	24-1/5
Position of ball marked with daisy	20-1/18
Position of ball not marked but player able to replace ball because of adjacent blemish	20-1/21
Rotating ball on putting green without marking position	18-2a/33
Tee marking position of player's ball deflects opponent's ball	20-1/17

BALL (Continued)

Marking position when lifting (Continued)

Whether lifting opponent's ball-marker is
concession of next stroke   2-4/5

Wrong information causes opponent to lift
his ball-marker   9-2/5

Moved or moving — See also "BALL: Lifting"

After address — See "ADDRESSING THE
BALL"

After loose impediment touched -

After ball addressed on putting green ball
moved in removal of loose impediment   18-2c/2

By foot during removal of loose
impediment on green   18-2c/1

Loose impediments within one club-length
removed; ball lifted and replaced; ball
moves before address   18-2c/3

After player grounds club but before stance
completed   18-2b/4

After player takes several practice swings
near ball and touches grass behind ball   18-2a/30

After replacement on putting green but
before ball-marker removed   20-4/1

Ball moves prior to address and is
accidentally stopped by player's club;
player removes club and ball rolls away   19-2/1.5

By another ball -

After being addressed   18-2b/11

By wrong ball played by opponent   18-5/1

Competitor's ball played from putting
green moves ball on green belonging to
competitor playing in another group   19-5/2

Opponent's ball knocked away by player
after concession moves player's ball   18-2a/18

Original ball strikes second ball or vice
versa   3-3/7

Original ball struck by provisional ball   18-5/2

Player mistakenly places opponent's or
fellow-competitor's ball at spot from
which his ball moved   15-1/2.5

Player's ball moved by ball accidentally
dropped by opponent or fellow-
competitor   18/7.5

Provisional ball struck by original ball   19-5/5

By cart shared by two players   18/8

By fellow-competitor -

Ball resting against flagstick moves away
from hole when flagstick removed by
fellow-competitor   17-4/3

Competitor's ball knocked out of bunker
by fellow-competitor's stroke at own
ball   18-4/2

Competitor's ball played by fellow-
competitor in bunker not replaced   18-4/1

BALL (Continued)
  Moved or moving (Continued)
    By fellow-competitor (Continued)

Fellow-competitor's ball knocked from lip
  of hole by competitor not replaced   3-2/1
By opponent, caddie or equipment -
  Ball resting against flagstick moves away
    from hole when opponent removes
    flagstick   17-4/3
  By opponent in playing his own ball   18-3b/1
  By stone dislodged by opponent's stroke   18-1/8
  Caddie shared by opponents' side in
    four-ball match moves player's ball   30/2
  Opponent's stroke disturbs bushes causing
    player's ball to move   18-3b/2
  Stepped on by opponent's caddie   18-3b/3
By outside agency -
  Ball in plastic bag moves when bag blown
    to new position by wind   18-1/7
  Ball visible from tee disappears while play
    suspended   18-1/2
  By blowing tumbleweed   18-1/6
  By stone dislodged by partner's or
    opponent's stroke   18-1/8
  Kicked away from hole by spectator
    attending flagstick   18-1/10
  Knocked down from tree   18-1/9
  Lost ball treated as moved by outside
    agency in absence of reasonable
    evidence to that effect   27-1/2.5
  Player unaware ball moved by outside
    agency does not replace ball   18-1/3
  Spectator says ball was moved by outside
    agency but player not sure   18-1/4
  Stolen from unknown spot   18-1/5
  Treating ball as moved by outside agency
    rather than lost   18-1/1
By player, partner, caddie or equipment -
  Ball stopped by player's foot moves when
    foot removed   19-2/1
  Blown into hole by competitor and not
    replaced and holed out   3-2/2
  By backward movement of club after
    stroke misses; ball comes to rest out of
    bounds   18-2a/22
  By ball-marker dropped accidentally by
    player   20-1/15
  By flagstick accidentally dropped on ball   18-2a/24
  By foot during removal of loose
    impediment on putting green   18-2c/1
  By partner in playing his own ball   30-3f/9
  By player in playing wrong ball   18-2a/21
  By practice swing prior to tee shot   18-2a/19
  By practice swing when ball in play   18-2a/20

BALL (Continued)
  Moved or moving (Continued)
    By player, partner, caddie or equipment
      (Continued)
      By putter dropped by player approaching
        ball to lift it 20-1/14
      By putter instinctively thrown by player ... 1-2/4.5
      By stone dislodged by partner's stroke ... 18-1/8
      Club breaks during downswing; swing
        stopped but clubhead falls and moves
        ball 14/4
      Dislodged from tree -
        Circumstances in which player not
          penalized 18-2a/27
        Circumstances in which player
          penalized 18-2a/28
        Replacement of ball not possible 18-2a/29
        When player climbs tree to play stroke 18-2a/26
      In measuring to determine if re-drop
        required 20-2c/6
      In removing ball-marker after replacing
        ball 20-3a/1
      Kicked by player asked to lift it due to
        interference 22/4
      Knocked from lip of hole in disgust 18-2a/23
      Opponent's ball knocked away by player
        after concession moves player's ball ... 18-2a/18
      Original lie altered in process; player
        places ball in wrong place and plays ... 18-2a/21.3
      Oscillating ball pressed into surface of
        putting green 18-2a/6
      Player jumps close to hole to cause ball to
        drop and ball drops 1-2/4
      Player who misses tee shot tees ball lower
        before playing next stroke 18-2a/1
      Position of ball marked before obstruction
        removed; ball moves when ball-marker
        removed 24-1/5
      Rake thrown into bunker before stroke
        moves ball 13-4/21
      Spot where ball originally lay not
        determinable; player places ball instead
        of dropping it 18-2a/21.5
      Striking at tree branch to move ball lodged
        higher in branch 14/7
      Towel dropped by player is blown onto
        and moves ball 18-2a/17
    By wind after being replaced at rest 18-1/12
    By wind or casual water while play
      suspended 18-1/11
    By wind; player replaces it 18-2a/7
    Caddie shared by members of opposite sides
      in four-ball match moves ball 30/1
    Falls into bunker when person walks nearby 18/10

BALL (Continued)

Moved or moving (Continued)

Moving in relation to ground but not in
relation to fork of tree in which lodged   18/3
Moving vertically downwards   18/1
Oscillates during address   18/2
When ball moved is deemed to be
"immediately recoverable"   18/11
Overhanging hole — See "PUTTING GREEN:
Ball overhanging hole"
Placing and replacing -
Ball dropped twice each time rolls to position
where there is interference by condition;
circumstances under which ball not placed   24-2b/9.5
Ball dropped when required to be placed
or placed when required to be dropped;
correction of error   20-6/1
Ball lifted without authority dropped instead
of being replaced   18-2a/9
Ball moved in removing ball-marker after
replacing ball   20-3a/1
Ball placed at wrong place and played —
See "PLAYING FROM WRONG PLACE"
Ball replaced on putting green but ball-
marker not removed; ball then moves   20-4/1
Lie of ball to be placed or replaced altered -
Lie of lifted ball in bunker altered by
another player's stroke   20-3b/1
Spot where ball originally lay not
determinable   20-3b/5
When embedded ball in hazard lifted to
determine whether unfit for play   5-3/5
When player presses oscillating ball into
surface of putting green   18-2a/6
Placed ball fails to remain on spot -
Ball dislodged from tree by player; ball
fails to remain on correct spot when
replaced   18-2a/29
Ball in bunker moves closer to hole when
obstruction removed and ball will not
remain at rest when replaced; all other
parts of bunker are nearer hole   20-3d/2
Ball in rough moves downward when
addressed; ball will not remain at rest
when replaced   20-3d/3
Ball overhanging hole is lifted, cleaned
and replaced; ball then falls into hole   16-2/0.5
Ball rolls into hole   20-3d/1
Placing ball instead of dropping when
obvious dropped ball will roll into hazard,
etc.   20-2c/3
Placing ball on bank of water hazard instead
of dropping to prevent ball rolling into
water   26-1/10

BALL (Continued)
  Placing and replacing (Continued)

    Player returns ball to spot from which lifted
      by rolling it with putter 16-1d/3
    Spot where ball to be placed not
      determinable -
      Ball dislodged from tree by player; spot
        where ball lay not determinable 18-2a/29
      Ball lodged in tree knocked down from
        unknown place by outside agency 18-1/9
      Ball-marker lifted by outside agency 20-1/9
      Ball-marker moved accidentally by player 20-1/5.5
      Ball-marker moved accidentally by player
        in process of marking position of ball 20-1/6
      Ball-marker moved off green by wind or
        casual water 20-1/10
      Ball moved accidentally; spot where ball
        originally lay not determinable; player
        places ball instead of dropping it 18-2a/21.5
    Trademark aimed along line of putt when
      ball replaced 20-3a/2
    Whether player himself must place or
      replace ball 20-3a/0.5
  Player finds ball and hits it to player who lost
    it 7-2/5.5
  Playing from wrong place — See "PLAYING
    FROM WRONG PLACE"
  Playing moving ball -
    Ball moving during backswing struck while
      still moving 14-5/1
    Ball moving in water in water hazard played
      while moving 14-6/1
  Provisional ball — See "PROVISIONAL BALL"
  Removal of loose impediments from spot on
    which ball to be placed 23-1/6.5
  Searching for — See "LOST BALL"
  Status of ball not on List of Conforming Golf
    Balls US/5-1/101
  Status of ball to be removed from List of
    Conforming Golf Balls US/5-1/102
  Status of original ball if another ball played
    under stroke-and-distance procedure 27/17
  Striking — See "BALL: Deflected or stopped"
    and "STRIKING THE BALL"
  Touching -
    Accidentally in removing loose impediment ... 18-2a/31
    Accidentally with club in hazard 13-4/12
    Holding in place while removing obstruction .. 24-1/4
    Rotating half-buried ball in hazard for
      identification purposes 12-2/3
    Rotating half-buried ball in rough for
      identification purposes 12-2/2
    Rotating on putting green without marking
      position 18-2a/33

BALL (Continued)
  Touching (Continued)

    With fir cone or stick to prevent movement
       when loose impediment removed   18-2a/32
  Two balls in play simultaneously at different
    holes   1-1/1
  Unfit for play -
    Ball declared unfit for play played at later
      hole   5-3/2
    Ball embedded in hazard lifted to determine
      whether unfit for play   5-3/5
    Ball not unfit for play deemed unfit   5-3/3
    Ball thought to be unfit for play lifted
      under another Rule and cleaned; ball then
      determined to be unfit for play   5-3/6
    Breaks into pieces as a result of striking
      paved cart path   5-3/4
    Opponent disputes player's claim that ball
      is unfit for play   2-5/14
    Player lifts ball on putting green, throws ball
      into lake and then announces that ball is
      unfit for play   5-3/3.5
    Whether ball unfit for play if player claims
      it is internally damaged   5-3/1
  Unplayable -
    After declaring ball unplayable and lifting it,
      player discovers ball was in ground under
      repair   28/13
    At base of cliff; player wishes to drop within
      two club-lengths of point above ball   28/12
    Ball declared unplayable dropped in ground
      under repair from which play prohibited;
      ball then dropped under ground under
      repair Rule   25-1b/14.5
    Ball declared unplayable in water hazard is
      dropped in hazard and played   20-7/2
    Ball declared unplayable; place from which
      previous stroke played is nearer hole   28/8
    Ball declared unplayable through the green
      dropped in hazard   28/4
    Ball dropped under unplayable ball
      Rule comes to rest in original position
      or another position at which ball is
      unplayable   28/3
    Ball in bunker deemed unplayable dropped
      in bunker and played; ball then discovered
      to be wrong ball   15/14
    Ball in tree identified but not retrieved
      declared unplayable   27/14
    Ball lying on grass-covered ground within
      bunker declared unplayable   28/9
    Caddie on own initiative lifts ball considering
      it unplayable   18-2a/15
    Changing relief option after ball dropped in
      a wrong place   20-6/2

BALL (Continued)
  Unplayable (Continued)

Changing relief option when re-dropping required	20-2c/5
Dropped outside bunker under option requiring drop in bunker	28/10
In tree; ball dislodged by shaking tree or throwing club	18-2a/27
In tree; player opts to drop within two club-lengths	28/11
Obstruction interferes but ball unplayable due to other condition	24-2b/16
Player declares first ball from tee unplayable, abandons provisional ball and claims he is lying three with third ball	28/2
Player misses ball and declares it unplayable	28/7
Player plays second shot, declares ball unplayable and returns to tee	28/6
Provisional ball serving as ball in play if original ball unplayable	27-2/1
Regression under unplayable ball Rule	28/5
Suggesting to competitor that he declare his ball unplayable	8-1/16
When necessary to find and identify ball declared unplayable	28/1
Wrong ball declared unplayable, dropped within two club-lengths and played before error discovered	28/15
Wrong ball declared unplayable played under stroke-and-distance procedure; original ball then found	28/14
Wrong ball dropped under unplayable ball Rule but not played	15/13
Use of ball not conforming with prescribed specifications	5-1/1
Warming ball with golf ball warmer or hand warmer	14-3/13

BALL DROP

Establishing on hole with island green	33-2a/10
Establishment on green side of water hazard for use when ball fails to clear hazard	33-8/2
Procedure for dropping	33-8/34

BALL MARKER — See "BALL: Marking position when lifting"

BANDAGE

Elastic bandage on wrist used as aid in gripping	14-3/7
Use of elastic bandage by player with injured wrist	14-3/7

BIRD'S NEST

Interferes with stroke	1-4/9

BOGEY COMPETITIONS
Competing simultaneously in bogey
competition and stroke play competition — 32-1/1
Omitting holes in bogey competition — 32-1/2

BOUNDARY — See "OUT OF BOUNDS"

BRIDGE
Ball lying on bridge over deep hollow — 24-2b/11
Grounding club on bridge in water hazard — 13-4/30

BUNKER — See "HAZARD"

BURROWING ANIMAL
Ball enters burrowing animal hole in bounds
and comes to rest out of bounds — 25-1b/24
Ball enters burrowing animal hole in bunker
and comes to rest underneath putting green — 25-1b/25
Ball enters burrowing animal hole out of
bounds and comes to rest in bounds — 25-1b/23
Ball found in burrowing animal hole after
five-minute search — 27/7
Ball lies on mound made by burrowing animal;
unreasonable to play stroke due to bush — 25-1b/19
Cast of burrowing animal interferes
with sideways stroke; when relief granted — 25-1b/22
Cast of burrowing animal interferes with
stroke towards green; tree prevents such
stroke — 25-1b/21
Clarification of "point on the course nearest to
where the ball lies" — 25-1b/1
Diagrams illustrating "point on the course
nearest to where the ball lies" — 25-1b/2
Holes made by non-burrowing animals; status — 25/20
Improving line of play when taking relief from
burrowing animal hole — 25-1b/3
Lifting ball to determine whether it lies in
burrowing animal hole — 25/21
Molehills swept flat; status — 25/23
Player entitled to relief from burrowing animal
hole lifts ball; player then replaces ball and
plays it from original position — 18-2a/12
Player unable physically to determine "nearest
point" — 24-2b/3.5
Stance interfered with by burrowing animal
hole; unreasonable to play stroke because of
other condition — 25-1b/20
Touching mound made by burrowing animal
with backswing in bunker — 13-4/5
What constitutes burrowing animal — 25/19
Whether crawfish is burrowing animal — 25-1b/18
Whether salamander is burrowing animal — 25/22

CADDIE
Acts which caddie may perform — 6-4/10

CADDIE (Continued)

Ball thrown into bounds by outside agency and
  played; caddie aware of action of outside
  agency   15/9
Casts shadow to indicate line of putt   8-2b/1
Changing caddies during round   6-4/7
Competitor withdraws during round and
  carries fellow-competitor's clubs for
  remainder of round   6-4/9
Competitor's caddie practices on or tests
  putting green surfaces of the course before
  stroke play round   7-1b/5
Condition banning use of caddies   33-1/10
Condition restricting player in choice of caddie   33-1/11
Double caddie -
  Caddie shared by members of opposite sides
    in four-ball match moves ball   30/1
  Caddie shared by opponents' side in
    four-ball match moves player's ball   30/2
  Informs one employer about club used by
    other   8-1/12
  Meaning of "specific directions" in Definition
    of "Caddie"   6-4/1
  Status of carts pulled by double caddie   6-4/6
Gives player's clubs to another caddie or
  friend to carry while he returns to tee with
  player's glove   6-4/4.5
Hires boy to carry all of player's clubs except
  putter   6-4/4
Holding back tree branch to prevent branch
  from deflecting dropped ball   20-2a/5
Lifting ball -
  In water hazard without player's authority   26-1/9
  On own initiative considering ball
    unplayable   18-2a/15
  On own initiative for identification   18-2a/14
Opponent's caddie lifts player's ball after
  player claims another ball   18-3b/4
Opponent's caddie lifts player's ball which
  may or may not have been out of bounds   18-3b/5
Player in competition caddies for another
  player in same event   6-4/8
Player whose clubs are transported on
  motorized golf cart hires individual to
  perform all other functions of a caddie   6-4/3
Player's ball strikes own caddie -
  Ball comes to rest out of bounds   19-2/2
  Caddie is standing out of bounds and ball
    comes to rest on course   19-2/3
  Caddie is standing out of bounds and ball
    comes to rest out of bounds   19-2/4
Roughens surface of putting green but player
  does not benefit   16-1d/6
Shielding player from sun during stroke   14-2/3

CADDIE (Continued)

Status of individual who transports player's clubs on motorized golf cart or trolley	6-4/2.5
Stops dropped ball before it comes to rest; when penalty incurred	20-2c/4
Swinging club to show player how to play shot	8-1/15
Umbrella carrier employed in addition to caddie	6-4/5
Who may serve as caddie	6-4/2
Wrong information given by caddie	9-2/2

CAR

Status of parked car	24/8

CART

Ball deflected or stopped by cart shared by two players	19/1
Ball deflected or stopped by player's golf cart being pulled by opponent or fellow-competitor	19-2/6
Ball moved by cart shared by two players	18/8
Breach of condition prohibiting carts	33-1/9
Discontinuing play due to inoperable motorized cart	6-8a/4
Distance meter attached to cart	14-3/1
Excess club declared out of play before round and placed on floor of cart	4-4c/1
Local Rule for events in which motorized carts permitted	33-8/4
Player whose clubs are transported on motorized golf cart hires individual to perform all other functions of a caddie	6-4/3
Status of carts pulled by double caddie	6-4/6
Status of individual who transports player's clubs on motorized golf cart or trolley	6-4/2.5
Whether use of carts permitted in competition	33-1/8

CASUAL WATER

Ball in casual water difficult to retrieve	25-1/1
Ball in casual water within ground under repair	25-1b/11
Ball lost in either water hazard or casual water overflowing hazard	1-4/7
Ball moved by casual water while play suspended	18-1/11
Clarification of "point on the course nearest to where the ball lies"	25-1b/1
Covering teeing ground	25-1b/4
Diagrams illustrating "point on the course nearest to where the ball lies"	25-1b/2
Improving line of play when taking relief	25-1b/3
In bunker — See "HAZARD: Casual water in bunker"	
Meaning of "reasonable evidence" that ball lost in casual water	25-1c/1

CASUAL WATER (Continued)

Mistaken for water hazard -
  Original ball played under water hazard
    Rule   25-1b/12
  Substituted ball played under water hazard
    Rule   25-1b/13
Mopping up casual water on line of play   13-2/34
Nearest point of relief from cart path is in
  casual water; nearest point of relief from
  casual water is back on cart path   1-4/8
Pitch-mark in which ball lies is filled with
  casual water   25/3
Player entitled to relief from casual water lifts
  ball; player then replaces ball and plays it
  from original position   18-2a/12
Player unable physically to determine "nearest
  point"   24-2b/3.5
Putting green -
  Ball-marker moved off green by casual water   20-1/10
  Brushing aside or mopping up on line of
    putt   16-1a/1
  Hole surrounded   33-2d/2
  Intervenes between ball off green and hole   25-1a/2
  Nearest relief is off green   25-1b/10
  Removal by Committee   33/1
  Scooping from hole   16-1a/4
  Visible when player walks beside line of
    putt but not visible elsewhere   25/5
  Whether player entitled to relief for
    intervention if ball is on green and nearest
    point of relief is off green   25-1b/10.5
Soft, mushy earth; status   25/1
Water visible as result of undue effort with
  feet; status   25/4
Whether overflow from water hazard is casual
  water   25/2

CLAIMS AND DISPUTES

Ball marked and lifted by opponent without
  player's authority; player lifts ball-marker,
  claims hole and opponent disputes claim   20-1/3
Breach of 14-club rule discovered after match
  concluded but before results officially
  announced   2-5/5.5
Procedure for a valid claim   2-5/2
Determination of honor at hole following
  disputed hole   10-1a/2
Dispute as to whether competitor played from
  outside teeing ground   34-3/4
Doubt whether ball moved by outside agency;
  opponent lodges claim   18-1/4
Extra stroke taken by mistake in handicap
  match; status of late claim   2-5/13
In foursome side drives for three holes in
  wrong order and then claim is made   29-2/2
Invalid claim not disputed   2-5/5

CLAIMS AND DISPUTES (Continued)

Match discontinued by agreement due to
rain; one player subsequently wishes to
resume; opponent refuses on ground course
unplayable and makes claim 6-8a/6

Opponent disputes player's claim that ball is
unfit for play 2-5/14

Player accepting erroneous claim disputes it
after result announced 2-5/10

Player agreeing with opponent that hole was
halved later realizes he has won hole; player
then makes claim 2-5/9

Player concedes hole on basis of invalid claim 2-4/12

Player concedes match after winning it when
opponent lodges invalid claim regarding
strokes taken 2-4/15

Player lifts ball before holing out; opponent
then picks up his ball claiming player loses
hole 2-5/3

Player omits penalty stroke when advising
opponent as to score for hole; error
discovered after match conceded by
opponent; opponent lodges claim 9-2/10

Player plays partner's ball; error discovered
after opponents have played next strokes;
claim then made 30-3d/3.5

Player wins hole with own ball after playing
wrong ball; opponent lodges belated claim 2-5/4

Player wins hole with wrong ball and partner
picks up; error discovered at next hole;
opponents claim hole 30-3d/2

Player wins hole with wrong ball; error
discovered at next hole; opponent claims
previous hole 9-2/8

Player with lost ball concedes hole; ball then
found in hole and player claims hole 2-4/11

Players mistakenly believe match is all square
after 18 holes and play extra hole without
claim being made 2-5/6

Player's obligation re lodging claim 2-5/1

Players on opposite sides exchange balls
during play of hole and their partners pick
up; error discovered at next hole and claim
made 30-3d/3

Players under impression match is over later
realize it was all square 2-3/1

Rightful winner of match makes no claim and
agrees to play extra holes 2-5/7

Second ball played in match play; no claim
made 3-3/9

Status of valid claim if players accept wrong
ruling from someone not on Committee and
continue match 2-5/8

Valid timely claim made after concession of
match 2-4/16

CLAIMS AND DISPUTES (Continued)

Wrong handicap used in match by mistake; error discovered after result officially announced; status of claim by opponent   6-2a/5

Wrong information given after play of last hole; claim made after result announced   2-5/11

CLEANING BALL — See "BALL: Cleaning"

CLUB

Attachment to grip or shaft of club of player with artificial arm   14-3/15

Ball moved by putter dropped by player approaching ball to lift it   20-1/14

Ball moves after address and is stopped by player's club   18-2b/12

Ball moves prior to address and is accidentally stopped by player's club; player removes club and ball rolls away   19-2/1.5

Ball strikes pipeline and on rebound is deflected by face of club   14-4/2

Breaking during swing -

   Club breaks during backswing; swing completed and ball missed   14/2

   Club breaks during downswing; swing completed but misses ball; clubhead falls and moves ball   14/5

   Club breaks during downswing; swing stopped short of ball; clubhead falls and moves ball   14/4

   Clubhead separates from shaft on downswing   14/3

Club thrown at ball   1-2/4.5

Club to be used in measuring club-length   20/1

Competitor changes weight of club during round; breach discovered after competition closed   34-1b/4

Face -

   Applying chalk   4-3/1

   Applying saliva   4-3/2

   Ball adhering to face of club after stroke   1-4/2

   Ball falls on club face after stroke and sticks to mud thereon   14-4/1

   Clubface markings; groove spacing   US/4-1/100

Grounding -

   Ball moves after player grounds club but before stance completed   18-2b/4

   When club grounded in grass   18-2b/5

Head -

   Applying material to top of head to reduce glare   4-2/1

   Material in head of metal wood club broken away from shell   4-1/2

   Playing stroke with back of clubhead   14-1/1

   Striking ball with bottom of clubhead   14-1/2

CLUB (Continued)

Intent to strike ball ceases during down-swing; club not stopped but path of clubhead altered to avoid striking ball — 14/1.5

Marking position of ball with toe of club — 20-1/12

Marking position of hole with club — 17-3/6

Modifying penalty for holing short putt with club whose playing characteristics changed other than in normal course of play — 4-2/1.5

Non-conforming club carried but not used — 4-1/1

Placed on ground to align feet — 8-2a/1

Player aligns partner's club before stroke — 14-2/1

Player holds club with left hand and moves ball by striking shaft with other hand — 14-1/6

Player putts with one hand and steadies himself with club held in other hand — 14-3/9

Player returns to tee to retrieve forgotten club — 6-7/1

Playing characteristics changed while play suspended; error discovered before play resumed — 4-2/2

Putting with wrong end of putter — 14-1/3

Stopped on downswing by agency other than player — 14/1

Using as cane to enter or leave hazard when ball lies in hazard — 13-4/3.5

Using as plumb-line — 14-3/12

Using more than one club to make stroke — 14-1/7

CLUBS

Ball deflected by clubs belonging to different side but carried in same bag — 19-2/5

Maximum of fourteen -
Borrowing partner's putter — 4-4b/1

Breach of 14-club rule discovered after match concluded but before result officially announced — 2-5/5.5

Breach of 14-club Rule in stroke play discovered at 8th hole; where penalty strokes applied — 4-4a/17

Carrying weighted training club — 4-4a/14

Changing clubs because of wet grips — 4-4a/1

Changing clubs between rounds in 36-hole match — 4-4a/8

Clarification of match play penalty — 4-4a/16

Club broken due to habit of hitting head of club on ground — 4-4a/5

Club broken while used as cane — 4-4a/3

Competitor who misplaces putter borrows fellow-competitor's putter — 4-4a/19

Competitor withdraws during round and puts his clubs in fellow-competitor's bag — 4-4a/10

Excess club declared out of play before round and placed on floor of golf cart — 4-4c/1

Excess club discovered before player plays from 2nd tee but after opponent or fellow-competitor has played — 4-4a/18

CLUBS (Continued)
Maximum of fourteen (Continued)
Excess club put in player's golf bag after player has counted his clubs at 1st tee; error discovered after player has started round   4-4a/13

Fellow-competitor's club put in competitor's bag by mistake during round used unintentionally by competitor   4-4a/12

Partners' clubs carried in one bag   4-4a/11

Player starting with 13 clubs breaks putter in anger and replaces it   4-4a/4

Replacement of club broken on practice ground while play suspended   4-4a/6.5

Replacement of club lost during round   4-4a/6

Replacing club for stroke play play-off   4-4a/9

Replacing club when grip becomes loose during round   4-4a/2

Retrieving another player's lost club   4-4a/15

When club is considered added   4-4a/7

COMMITTEE
Alteration of handicap stroke table   33-4/1

Authority to deem artificial limb to be artificial device   14-3/15

Authority to waive or modify disqualification penalty   33-7/1

Ball assisting fellow-competitor on putting green; procedure for Committee member if competitor does not lift ball   22/7

Conditions — See "CONDITIONS OF COMPETITION"

Defining bounds and margins — See "COURSE: Defining bounds, margins, etc."

Direction posts; recommendation reinstallation   33/4

Displaying at tee map of putting green indicating hole position   33/6

Disqualification penalty; waiving, modifying or imposing — See "PENALTY"

Distance markers; installation by Committee   33/5

Dividing double green   25-3/1

Error -
Competitor wins competition with handicap which was incorrect due to Committee error; error discovered several days later   6-2b/3

Correction of incorrect decision   34-3/1

Disqualification penalty wrongly applied to winner of event; error discovered after two other competitors play off for first place   34-1b/5

Failure to advise competitors where to return cards   6-6b/4

Failure to indicate hole numbers on teeing grounds   11-5/2

Misapplication of handicap affects match play draw   33-5/3

COMMITTEE (Continued)
  Error (Continued)
    Omission of penalty strokes when score
      returned is due to incorrect ruling 34-3/1
    Play of wrong ball not rectified on advice of
      Committee member 33-7/5
    Player proceeds on basis of incorrect ruling .. 34-3/3
    Winner's score not posted due to Committee
      error 34-1b/6
    Wrong form of play used due to Committee
      error 6-1/1
    Wrong handicap applied by Committee
      results in player not receiving prize 33-5/2
    Wrong handicap used due to Committee
      misinformation 33-1/12
  Guidelines on whether to cancel round 33-2d/1
  Intervention in match play US/34-3/100
  Intervention in match play when search for
    lost ball exceeds five minutes US/34-3/101
  Member of Committee finds player's original
    ball; player prefers to continue with
    provisional ball 27-2/2
  Player claiming danger from lightning refuses
    to resume play when resumption ordered by
    Committee 6-8b/5
  Player lifts ball without authority due to
    misunderstanding Committee member's
    instructions 34-3/3.5
  Preventing ball from being carried out of
    bounds by flow of water in water hazard .. 26-1/7
  Procedure for Committee if -
    Casual water covering teeing ground 25-1b/4
    Dispute as to whether competitor played
      from outside teeing ground 34-3/4
    Hole surrounded by casual water 33-2d/2
    Match play finalists both disqualified 33/3
    Player who has advanced in match play is
      disqualified for wrong score in qualifying
      round 34-1b/8
    Player who has reached third round of
      match play disqualified for agreeing to
      waive Rules in first-round match 33/2
    True state of match not determinable 34-3/5
  Reducing number of holes of stipulated round
    after play has commenced 33-1/2
  Reducing number of holes of stroke play
    competition during the competition 33-1/2
  Removal of casual water on putting green by
    Committee 33/1
  Retrospective appointment of marker by
    Committee 33-1/5
  Second ball played despite adverse ruling by
    Committee member 3-3/2

COMMITTEE (Continued)

Second ball played without announcing
intention to invoke Rule 3-3 and failing to
report facts to Committee — 3-3/6.5

Starting players from 1st and 10th tees — 33-1/3

Time of starting; all competitors must be
present — 6-3a/2

Use of attachment to flagstick to indicate
position of hole on green — 17/1

Use of different colored flags to indicate
position of hole on green — 17/2

CONCESSION — See also "DEFAULT"

Fellow-competitor lifts competitor's ball
conceding next stroke in stroke play play-off — 18-4/3

Hole — See "HOLE: Concession of"

Match -

Agreement that side losing after 18 holes of
36-hole match will concede match — 1-3/7

Conceding match to avoid disqualification — 2-3/4, 33-1/6

Player concedes match after winning it when
opponent lodges invalid claim regarding
strokes taken — 2-4/15

Player concedes match due to misconception
as to opponent's score at last hole — 2-4/14

Player in erroneous belief match is over
shakes opponent's hand and picks up
opponent's ball — 2-4/17

Player omits penalty stroke when advising
opponent as to score for hole; error
discovered after match conceded by
opponent — 9-2/10

Player's conscious failure to correct
opponent's misunderstanding of state
of match results in opponent conceding
match when in fact player is dormie — 9-2/12

Valid timely claim made after concession of
match — 2-4/16

Next stroke in match play — See "PUTTING
GREEN: Conceding opponent's next stroke"

CONDITIONS OF COMPETITION

Agreement to waive condition — 1-3/7

Altering conditions after competition starts — 33-1/1

Caddies -

Banning — 33-1/10

Restriction on caddies — 33-1/11

Condition requiring use of ball on List of
Conforming Golf balls -

Ball not on List played as provisional ball — 5-1/3

Penalty for breach — 5-1/2

Condition stipulates who is authorized to give
advice in team competition — 8/1

Form of play -

Wrong form used by agreement of players — 33-1/4

Wrong form used due to Committee error — 6-1/1

CONDITIONS OF COMPETITION (Continued)
  Form of play (Continued)

    Wrong form used intentionally by players   6-1/1
    Wrong form used unintentionally by players 6-1/1
  Golf carts -
    Breach of condition prohibiting   33-1/9
    Use when condition does not prohibit   33-1/8
  Handicap allowance -
    Wrong allowance used by mistake in match 6-2a/6
    Wrong allowance used due to Committee
      misinformation   33-1/12
  Making competitors responsible for adding
    scores   33-1/7
  Number of holes of stroke play competition;
    Committee alteration during the competition 33-1/2
  Players exclude operation of condition   1-3/7
  Prohibiting employment of umbrella carrier 6-4/5
  Requirement that alteration on score card be
    initialled   6-6a/6
  Stipulated round -
    Committee authority to start players from
      1st and 10th tees   33-1/3
    Player's responsibility to know   11-5/2

COURSE
  Course record   Misc./1
  Defining bounds, margins, etc. - Ground under
    repair — See "GROUND UNDER REPAIR"
    Out of bounds — See "OUT OF BOUNDS"
  Stone serving as part of drain in bunker;
    suggested procedure   24/7
  Water hazards and lateral water hazards —
    See "WATER HAZARD"
  Unplayable -
    Casual water covering teeing ground   25-1b/4
    Competitor refuses to start or picks up
      because of weather conditions; round
      subsequently cancelled because course
      unplayable   33-2d/3
    Guidelines on whether to cancel round   33-2d/1
    Hole surrounded by casual water   33-2d/2
    Match begun in ignorance that course closed 33-2d/4
    Reducing number of holes of stroke
      play competition because course
      unplayable   33-1/2

DANGEROUS SITUATION
  Danger from fire-ants   33-8/22
  Rattlesnake or bees interfere with play   1-4/10

**DECISION — See "COMMITTEE" and
"REFEREE"**

DEFAULT
  Defaulting player plays informal match with
    opponent and wins   2-4/18

DEFAULT (Continued)
Player unable to meet match play schedule defaults; schedule then changed and player requests reinstatement — 2-4/20
Winner of match wishes to default to beaten opponent — 2-4/19

DELAY, UNDUE — See "UNDUE DELAY"

DEW
Removing from behind or to side of ball or from line of play — 13-2/35
Removing from line of putt — 16-1a/3

DIRECTION POSTS
Ball deflected by post — 19-1/1
Recommendation re installation — 33/4

DISCONTINUANCE OF PLAY — See also "SUSPENSION OF PLAY"
Because hole-liner not sunk deep enough — 16/4
Because of weather conditions; round subsequently cancelled — 33-2d/3
Due to inoperable motorized cart — 6-8a/4
Due to physical problem — 6-8a/3
Due to raised or sunken hole plug on line of putt — 16-1c/3
Local Rule for suspension of play due to dangerous situation — US/33-8/1(
Local Rule permitting competitors to discontinue play by agreement in bad weather — 33-8/5
Match discontinued by agreement due to rain; one player subsequently wishes to resume; opponent refuses although course playable — 6-8a/5
Match discontinued by agreement due to rain; one player subsequently wishes to resume, opponent refuses on ground course unplayable — 6-8a/6
Player returns to tee to retrieve forgotten club — 6-7/1
Replaying match when play discontinued instead of resuming from where play stopped — 2-3/5
Taking shelter while waiting to play — 6-8a/2
Watching television for 45 minutes after nine holes — 6-8a/1
When ball may be cleaned or substituted after play has been discontinued — 6-8c/1

DISPUTES — See "CLAIMS AND DISPUTES"

DISTANCE
Asking if distance marker accurate — 8-1/3
Booklet providing distances to holes from various points — 14-3/5
Gauging with pencil or score card — 14-3/2

DISTANCE (Continued)
Inquiring as to distance from certain object to green — 8-1/2
Markers to indicate distances to the green — 33/5
Seeking information about length of hole — 8-1/1
Use of distance meter — 14-3/1

DIVOT
Divots replaced and pressed down in area in which ball is to be dropped — 13-2/4.5
Partner's, opponent's or fellow-competitor's divot comes to rest near player's ball in bunker — 13-4/18
Replacing divot in divot hole behind ball — 13-2/6
Replacing or removing undetached divot — 13-2/5
When divot replaced — 13-2/7

DOUBT AS TO PROCEDURE — See "STROKE PLAY: Doubt as to procedure"

DRAINPIPE
Ball in drainpipe under course; entrance to drainpipe is out of bounds — 24-2b/12
Ball lost in underground drainpipe — 24-2c/1

DROPPING BALL — See "BALL: Dropping and re-dropping"

EMBEDDED BALL — See "BALL: Embedded"

EQUIPMENT
Explanation of "any ball he has played" — 18/7
Status as equipment of golf cart shared by two players — 18/8, 19/1
Status as equipment of golf carts being pulled by double caddie — 6-4/6
Towel dropped by player is blown onto and moves ball — 18-2a/17
Unusual equipment — See "ARTIFICIAL DEVICES AND UNUSUAL EQUIPMENT"
Whether glove used as indicating mark is equipment — 18/9

EQUITY
Situations in which decision made in equity -
Advice -
No action taken to stop team captain giving advice without authority — 8-1/24
No action taken to stop team mate's irregular procedure — 8-1/23
Ball adhering to club face after stroke — 1-4/2
Ball deflected by player's golf cart being pulled by opponent or fellow-competitor without player's knowledge — 19-2/6
Ball dislodged from tree by player; replacement of ball not possible — 18-2a/29

EQUITY (Continued)
  Situations in which decision made in equity
    (Continued)
    Ball moved in measuring to determine if
      re-drop required   20-2c/6
    Dangerous situation -
      Danger from fire-ants   33-8/22
      Rattlesnake or bees interfere with play   1-4/10
    Divots replaced and pressed down in area in
      which ball is to be dropped   13-2/4.5
    Extension of line of play affected when
      opponent or fellow-competitor creates
      footprints in bunker   13-2/29.5
    Hazard -
      Ball dropped from casual water in
        bunker at point of maximum relief rolls
        elsewhere   25-1b/6
      Ball in bunker moves closer to hole when
        obstruction removed and ball will not
        remain at rest when replaced; all other
        parts of bunker are nearer hole   20-3d/2
      Ball lost in either water hazard or casual
        water overflowing hazard   1-4/7
      Lie in bunker altered by another player
        taking his stance   20-3b/2
      Partner's, opponent's or fellow-
        competitor's divot comes to rest near
        player's ball in bunker   13-4/18
      Two balls lie together in hazard and
        neither is identifiable   1-4/6
    Lie of ball-
      Affected by pitch mark made by another
        player's ball after player's ball came
        to rest   13-2/8
      Affected by sand from partner's,
        opponent's or fellow-competitor's
        stroke from bunker   13-2/8.5
      Altered by removal of gallery-control
        stake   20-3b/3
      Altered by tractor   20-3b/4
      Altered in bunker by another player
        taking his stance   20-3b/2
      Ball lifted to determine whether
        embedded   25-2/7
      Ball lifted to determine whether it lies
        in burrowing animal hole   25/21
      Bird's nest interfering with stroke   1-4/9
    Line of play
      Extension of line of play affected when
        opponent or fellow-competitor creates
        footprints in bunker   13-2/29.5
    Loose impediments -
      Loose impediment affecting lie moved
        when ball lifted   23-1/7

EQUITY (Continued)
Situations in which decision made in equity
(Continued)
Loose impediments (Continued)

Loose impediment affecting lie removed while ball lifted	23-1/8
Removal of obstruction in hazard would move loose impediment	1-4/5

Obstruction -
Nearest point of relief from cart path is in casual water; nearest point of relief from casual water is back on cart path	1-4/8
Opponent or fellow-competitor removes obstruction affecting player's play	24/16
Original and second balls dropped in wrong place and played	3-3/5.5

Out of bounds -
Ball thrown into bounds by outside agency and played; neither player nor his caddie aware of action of outside agency	15/10
Open gate in boundary fence interferes with swing	27/18

Outside agency -
Ball deliberately deflected or stopped on putting green by fellow-competitor	19-1/5
Ball deliberately deflected or stopped on putting green by spectator	19-1/4
Ball deliberately deflected or stopped through the green by spectator	19-1/4.1
Ball lodged in tree knocked down by outside agency	18-1/9
Ball stolen by outside agency from unknown spot	18-1/5

Penalty -
Caddie shared by opponents' side in four-ball match moves player's ball	30/2
Player who has advanced in match play disqualified for wrong score in qualifying round	34-1b/8
Player who has reached third round of match play disqualified for agreeing to waive Rules in first-round match	33/2
Player distracted by ball dropped by another player mis-hits ball	1-4/1
Player in anger strikes ball played by player in following group	1-4/4
Playing characteristics of club changed while play suspended; error discovered before play resumed	4-2/2
Provisional ball not distinguishable from original ball	27/11

Putting green -
Ball-marker moved by opponent's caddie accidentally	20-1/7

EQUITY (Continued)
  Situations in which decision made in equity
    (Continued)
    Putting green (Continued)
      Flagstick stuck into green some distance
        from hole by practical joker   1-4/3
      Player concedes opponent's next stroke
        and plays before opponent has
        opportunity to lift ball   2-4/8
      Player lifts ball in mistaken belief next
        stroke conceded   2-4/3
      Player lifts opponent's ball-marker in
        mistaken belief he has won hole   2-4/5
      Player plays away from hole to assist
        partner   30-3f/6
      Player putts out after concession of stroke;
        act assists partner   2-4/6
      Player's ball strikes flagstick deliberately
        left in hole by opponent or fellow-
        competitor attending flagstick   17-3/2
    Teeing ground -
      Competitors estimate area of teeing
        ground when one tee-marker missing   11-4b/2
      Determination of honor at hole following
        disputed hole   10-1a/2
    Wrong ball -
      Hole at which played unknown   15-1/3

EXERTING INFLUENCE ON BALL
  Whether the Rule prohibiting exerting
    influence on ball is breached if -
    Ball deliberately deflected or stopped on
      putting green by fellow-competitor   19-1/5
    Ball lifted on putting green placed ahead
      of ball-marker and then moved back to
      original position   16-1a/17
    Ball mark in position to assist opponent
      repaired by player   16-1c/2
    Ball overhanging hole knocked away by
      opponent before player determines status   16-2/2
    Ball popped up swung at in disgust   14/6
    Caddie holds back tree branch to prevent
      branch from deflecting dropped ball   20-2a/5
    Caddie stops dropped ball before it comes
      to rest   20-2c/4
    Competitor sanctions repair of spike damage
      on his line of putt by fellow-competitor   13-2/36
    Flagstick is adjusted to more favorable
      position   17/4
    Flagstick lying on putting green removed
      by player to prevent another player's ball
      from striking it   1-2/3
    Line of putt altered purposely by opponent
      or fellow-competitor by stepping on it   1-2/1
    Line of putt is shielded from wind   1-2/2

EXERTING INFLUENCE ON BALL (Continued)
  Whether the Rule prohibiting exerting
    influence on ball is breached if (Continued)
    Line of putt stepped on accidentally by
      opponent or fellow-competitor   16-1a/13
    Loose impediments affecting player's play
      removed by opponent or fellow-competitor   23-1/10
    Loose impediments brushed along line of
      putt rather than to side   16-1a/10
    Object marking position of ball is placed in
      front of ball   20-1/9
    Opponent or fellow-competitor attending
      flagstick for player deliberately fails to
      remove it   17-3/2
    Player jumps close to hole to cause ball to
      drop   1-2/4
    Player leaves putt short and instinctively
      throws putter at ball   1-2/4.5
    Player putts with one hand and catches ball
      in hole with other hand   1-2/5
    Player removes loose impediment affecting
      opponent's lie in hazard   1-2/6
    Player repairs hole after holing out but
      before opponent, fellow-competitor or
      partner holes out   1-2/3.5
    Player replaces loose impediments removed
      by opponent or fellow-competitor   23-1/10
    Shadow is cast on ball overhanging ball   16-2/3

FLAGSTICK
  Adjustment; player's rights   17/4
  Attachment to indicate position of hole on
    green   17/1
  Attended -
    Attendant removes flagstick and holds it
      upright behind hole; end of flagstick
      touches green   17-1/4.5
    Attendant removes flagstick whereupon
      knob falls from top of flagstick and
      deflects ball   17/9
    Attendant stands behind hole   17-1/4
    Ball at rest kicked away from hole by
      spectator attending flagstick   18-1/10
    By partner without express authority of
      player; ball strikes flagstick or partner   17-3/4
    By referee, observer or marker at player's
      request   17-1/3
    Flag struck by ball when flagstick attended   17-3/5
    Hole-liner pulled out by flagstick attendant
      and ball falls into unlined hole   17/7
    Opponent or fellow-competitor attending
      flagstick for player fails to remove it;
      player's ball strikes flagstick   17-3/2
    Opponent or fellow-competitor declines to
      attend flagstick   17-1/2

FLAGSTICK (Continued)
  Attended (Continued)

Player attending flagstick for opponent
  struck by ball of opponent's partner who
  played out of turn — 30-3f/5
When one who "stands near the hole" is
  deemed to be attending — 17-1/1
Ball lodged in flag — 17/6
Ball moved by flagstick accidentally dropped
  on ball — 18-2a/24
Ball resting against -
  Lifted before being holed — 17-4/1
    Others in match pick up mistakenly
     believing player won hole — 30-3f/3
  Moves away from hole when flagstick
    removed by opponent or fellow-
    competitor — 17-4/3
  Putt conceded and ball removed before
    player can remove flagstick — 17-4/2
Ball strikes flagstick lying on green — 17-3/3
Ball strikes hole-liner pulled out with flagstick — 17/8
Different colored flags used to indicate position
  of hole on green — 17/2
Flagstick lying on putting green removed by
  player to prevent another player's ball from
  striking it — 1-2/3
Holding flagstick with one hand and putting
  with other hand — 17-1/5
Holing out without ball touching flagstick — 17-3/1
Local Rule prohibiting removal of flagstick — 33-8/10
Local Rule waiving penalty for ball striking
  unattended flagstick — 33-8/11
Marking position of hole with club — 17-3/6
Stuck into green some distance from hole by
  practical joker — 1-4/3
Tapered or of varying diameters — 17/3

FOUR-BALL MATCH PLAY
Absent partner gives advice before joining
  match — 30-3a/2
Absent partner joins match during play of hole — 30-3a/1
Advice given on request of opponent — 8-1/25
Caddie shared by members of opposite sides
  moves ball — 30/1
Caddie shared by opponents' side moves
  player's ball — 30/2
Determination of handicap allowances if one
  player unable to compete — 30-3a/3
Determination of honor in match in which
  points awarded for both better-ball and
  aggregate scores — 30/3
Flagstick attended by partner without express
  authority of player; ball strikes flagstick or
  partner — 17-3/4

FOUR-BALL MATCH PLAY (Continued)

Hitting sand in bunker with club after failing to extricate ball; partner's ball in same bunker — 30-3f/2

Player after picking up drops ball where partner's ball lies and plays practice stroke — 30-3f/7

Player attending flagstick for opponent struck by ball of opponent's partner who played out of turn — 30-3f/5

Player disqualified for next hole plays that hole — 30-3f/8

Player lifts loose impediment in bunker when his ball and partner's ball in bunker — 30-3f/1

Player plays away from hole to assist partner — 30-3f/6

Player plays partner's ball; act assists partner — 30-3d/1

Player plays partner's ball; error is discovered after opponents have played next strokes — 30-3d/3.5

Player plays practice putt after he and partner have holed out but before opponents hole out — 30/6

Player putting first when partner farther from hole stands on partner's or opponent's line of putt — 30-3c/1

Player touches putting green in pointing out line for putting for partner and incidentally touches own line of putt — 30/2.5

Player who has holed out touches partner's line of putt — 1-2/3.5

Player who walks off green under mistaken impression partner halved hole returns and putts for half — 30/4

Player wins hole with wrong ball and partner picks up; error discovered at next hole — 30-3d/2

Player with putt for half picks up in error at suggestion of opponent based on misunderstanding — 30/5

Player's ball lifted without authority by opponent — 30-3f/10

Player's ball moved by partner in playing his own ball — 30-3f/9

Player's ball resting against flagstick lifted before being holed; others in match pick up mistakenly believing player won hole — 30-3f/3

Players on opposite sides exchange balls during play of hole and their partners pick up; error discovered at next hole — 30-3d/3

Putting out after concession of next stroke; act assists partner — 2-4/6

Request to lift ball that might assist partner not honored — 30-3f/11

Side plays out of turn from tee; opponents require one member of side to replay but not other — 30-1/1

Waiving turn to putt — 30-3c/2

FOUR-BALL MATCH PLAY (Continued)
Wrong information given by player out of
contention   30-3f/4

FOUR-BALL STROKE PLAY
Breach of 14-club Rule discovered at 8th hole;
where penalty strokes applied   4-4a/17
Competitor after picking up drops ball where
partner's ball lies and plays practice stroke   30-3f/7
Competitor lifts loose impediment in bunker
when his ball and partner's ball are in
bunker   31-8/1
Competitor plays away from hole to assist
partner   30-3f/6
Competitor who has holed out touches
partner's line of putt   1-2/3.5
Flagstick attended by partner without express
authority of competitor; ball strikes flagstick
or partner   17-3/4
Score -
  Competitor records score for hole not
  completed   31-7a/1
  Gross score of partner with better net score
  omitted from card   31-4/1
  Lower gross score attributed to wrong
  partner   31-7a/2
  Side's scores transposed at a hole in
  handicap competition but not to side's
  advantage   32-2a/1

FOURSOMES
Ball played from outside teeing ground in
match   29-1/1
Both player and partner drive at same tee   29-1/9
Changing partners after driving from first tee   29/1
Competitor plays from outside teeing ground
in stroke play; partner replays stroke   29-1/2
Competitor records incorrect handicap for
partner in stroke play competition; error
discovered after competition closed   6-2b/2.5
Competitors fail to record individual handicaps
on score card   6-2b/4
Dropping ball in foursome competition   29/4
Hitting sand in bunker with club after failing
to extricate ball; foursome match   29/5
Mixed foursome in which different tees used
by men and women; tee shot out of bounds   29/2
Order of play if player accidentally moves ball
after address   29-1/5
Order of play in stroke play when wrong ball
played   29-1/8
Penalty in "Pinehurst" foursome not related to
ball holed out   US/29/100
Player in foursome match practices putts on
previous green after partner has driven from
next tee   29/3

FOURSOMES (Continued)

Player misses ball accidentally when making stroke 29-1/6

Player misses ball purposely so partner would play ball over water 29-1/7

Players by mistake play on four-ball rather than foursome basis 6-1/1

Provisional ball played by wrong member of side 29-1/4

Side drives for three holes in wrong order and then claim is made 29-2/2

Signing of score card in foursome stroke play 29/6

Who plays provisional ball 29-1/3

Wrong partners drive for both sides in match 29-2/1

FROST

Removing from behind or to side of ball or from line of play 13-2/35

Removing from line of putt 16-1a/3

FRUIT

Ball embedded in fruit 23/10

Fruit skins; status 23/4

Half-eaten pear; status 23/3

GLOVE

Applying adhesive tape 14-3/8

Used as indicating mark; ball strikes glove 18/9

GOLF CART — See "CART"

GRASS

Ball moves after player takes several practice swings near ball and touches grass behind ball 18-2a/30

Ball outside ground under repair but high grass within area interferes with swing 25-1a/1

Bending grass in removal of loose impediments 13-2/13

Breaking off grass behind ball on teeing ground 13-2/3

Grass-covered ground within bunker; status 28/9

Grass cuttings; status 25/11

Raised tuft of grass on line of putt brushed to determine whether it is loose 16-1a/11

Removing grass adhering to ball 21/2

Touching grass with practice swing in hazard 13-4/4

When club grounded in grass 18-2b/5

GRIP

Attachment to grip of club of player with artificial arm 14-3/15

Binding fingers together with tape to aid in gripping 14-3/8

Changing clubs because of wet grips 4-4a/1

Holding ball in hand against grip when putting 14-3/6

Replacing club when grip becomes loose during round 4-4a/2

GROUND UNDER REPAIR — **See also
"HOLE MADE BY GREENKEEPER" and
"MATERIAL PILED FOR REMOVAL"**

After declaring ball unplayable and lifting it,
   player discovers that ball was in ground
   under repair   28/13

Ball declared unplayable dropped in ground
   under repair from which play prohibited;
   ball then dropped under ground repair Rule   25-1b/14.5

Ball dropped and played under ground
   under repair Rule in absence of reasonable
   evidence original ball lost in ground under
   repair   25-1c/2

Ball dropped from ground under repair area
   rolls to position where area interferes with
   stance; whether re-drop required   20-2c/0.5

Ball embedded in ground under repair in
   closely mown area   25-2/4

Ball equidistant from two points which meet
   requirements of ground under repair Rule   25-1b/16

Ball in casual water within ground under
   repair   25-1b/11

Ball in ground under repair thought to be unfit
   for play lifted and cleaned   5-3/6

Ball lost in tree in ground under repair   25/10

Ball outside ground under repair but high
   grass within area interferes with swing   25-1a/1

Ball played from ground under repair picked
   up and relief taken under ground under
   repair Rule   18-2a/8

Ball played in ground under repair area lost in
   same area   25-1c/3

Ball played under Rule for ball lost in ground
   under repair after another ball played under
   stroke-and-distance procedure   15/8

Bunker totally under repair   25/13

Clarification of "point on the course nearest to
   where the ball lies" in ground under repair
   Rule   25-1b/1

Crossing over obstruction in obtaining relief
   from ground under repair   25-1b/14

Declaring area as ground under repair during
   competition round   33-2a/2

Diagrams illustrating "point on the course
   nearest to where the ball lies" in ground
   under repair Rule   25-1b/2

Improving line of play when taking relief from
   ground under repair   25-1b/3

Local Rule — See "LOCAL RULE: Ground
   under repair"

Measuring across ground under repair in
   obtaining relief   25-1b/15

Obstruction in ground under repair interferes
   with player's swing   24-2b/10

Order of play when two balls lie in ground
   under repair and both players take relief   10/1

GROUND UNDER REPAIR (Continued)

Pine needles piled for removal interfere with line of play after ball dropped away — 25-1b/17

Player entitled to relief from ground under repair lifts ball; player then replaces ball and plays it from original position — 18-2a/12

Player unable physically to determine "nearest point" — 24-2b/3.5

Referee's authority to declare ground under repair — 34-2/1

Status as ground under repair of -
Aeration holes — 25/15
Cracks in earth — 25/12
Damage to line of putt caused by fellow-competitor's caddie — 16-1a/14
Extensive damage due to heavy rain and traffic — 33-2a/3
Fallen tree attached to stump — 25/9
Fallen tree in process of being removed — 25/7
Grass cuttings — 25/11
Hole made by non-burrowing animal — 25/20
Hole of removed stake defining water hazard — 25/18
Hole on putting green not in use — 16/7
Old hole plug sunk or raised on line of putt — 16-1c/3
Rut made by tractor — 25/16
Sunken hole plug — 25/17
Tree stump — 25/8
Water hazard under repair — 33-2a/5

GROUPINGS

Competitors determining own groupings — 33-3/3
Groupings for stroke play play-off — 33-3/4

HANDICAP

Match play -
Determination of handicap allowances in four-ball match if one player unable to compete — 30-3a/3
Determination of honor — 10-1a/1
Extra stroke taken by mistake; error discovered several holes later — 2-5/13
Failure to determine handicaps prior to start of match — 6-2a/1
Handicap stroke claimed after hole conceded — 6-2a/4
Handicap stroke given at incorrect hole in error — 6-2a/2
Handicap stroke wrongly claimed at hole; error discovered before hole completed — 6-2a/3
How to settle tie — 33-6/1
Misapplication of handicap affects draw — 33-5/3
Player uses established handicap but handicap too high due to player's failure to observe provision of handicap system — US/6-2a/10
Wrong handicap allowance used — 6-2a/6

HANDICAP (Continued)
 Match play (Continued)
  Wrong handicap used by mistake; error
   discovered after result officially announced 6-2a/5
  Wrong handicap used due to Committee
   misinformation 33-1/12
 Minus or zero net score 2-1/2
 Stroke play -
  Competitor disqualified from handicap
   event claims gross prize 33-1/13
  Competitor records incorrect handicap for
   partner in foursome competition; error
   discovered after competition closed 6-2b/2.5
  Competitor wins competition with handicap
   which was incorrect due to Committee
   error; error discovered several days later 6-2b/3
  Competitors in foursome competition fail to
   record individual handicaps on score card 6-2b/4
  Determination of honor 10-2a/1
  How to settle tie 33-6/2
  Wrong handicap applied by Committee
   results in player not receiving prize 33-5/2
  Wrong handicap knowingly used; error
   discovered after competition closed 6-2b/2
  Wrong handicap used by mistake; error
   discovered after competition closed 6-2b/1
 Stroke table -
  Alteration by Committee 33-4/1

HAZARD — See also "WATER HAZARD"
 Ball believed to be lost in bunker; competitor
  drops another ball in bunker and plays it;
  original ball then found outside bunker 20-7b/3
 Ball declared unplayable through the green
  dropped in hazard 28/4
 Ball embedded -
  Completely in lip of bunker 13/4
  In grass bank or face of bunker 25-2/5
  Lifting to determine whether unfit for play 5-3/5
 Ball enters burrowing animal hole in bunker
  and comes to rest underneath putting green 25-1b/25
 Ball knocked out of bunker by fellow-
  competitor's stroke at own ball not replaced 18-4/2
 Ball moved accidentally by player in playing
  wrong ball 18-2a/21
 Ball on edge of bunker overhanging sand 13/3
 Ball touched accidentally with club in hazard
  but not moved 13-4/12
 Ball unplayable in bunker -
  Ball lying on grass-covered ground in
   bunker declared unplayable 28/9
  Dropped in bunker and played; ball then
   discovered to be wrong ball 15/14
  Dropped outside bunker under option
   requiring drop in bunker 28/10

HAZARD (Continued)

Bunker totally under repair — 25/13

Casual water in bunker -
 Ball dropped at point of maximum relief
  rolls elsewhere — 25-1b/6
 Ball to be dropped in bunker dropped
  outside bunker and rolls into bunker — 25-1b/7
 Explanation of "maximum available relief" — 25-1b/5
 Options when bunker completely covered
  by casual water — 25-1b/8
 Player who invokes first option of relief Rule
  then wishes to invoke second option — 25-1b/9

Competitor's ball played by fellow-competitor
 in bunker not replaced — 18-4/1

Lie altered in bunker -
 By another player taking his stance — 20-3b/2
 Lie of lifted ball altered by another player's
  stroke — 20-3b/1

Local Rule — See "LOCAL RULE: Bunker"
 and "LOCAL RULE: "Water Hazard"

Loose impediment -
 Accidentally moving — 13-4/13
 Ball moves when loose impediment removed — 13-4/15
 Ball outside bunker; stone in bunker on line
  of play pressed down or removed — 13-2/31
 Bunker covered by leaves; player touches
  leaves during backswing — 13-4/33
 Club touches partially embedded pine
  needle on backswing in bunker — 13-4/32
 Competitor lifts loose impediment in bunker
  when his ball and partner's ball in bunker — 31-8/1
 Partner's, opponent's or fellow-competitor's
  divot comes to rest near player's ball in
  bunker — 13-4/18
 Pine cone falls from tree and comes to rest
  behind ball lying in bunker — 13-4/18.5
 Player accidentally kicks pine cone into
  bunker and picks it up — 13-4/14
 Player lifts loose impediment in bunker
  when his ball and partner's ball in bunker — 30-3f/1
 Player removes loose impediment affecting
  opponent's lie in hazard — 1-2/6
 Removal of loose impediment in water
  hazard covering wrong ball — 13-4/16
 Removal of obstruction in hazard would
  move loose impediment — 1-4/5
 Removed from water hazard; player then
  decides not to play from hazard — 13-4/17
 Stone serving as part of drain in bunker — 24/7

Obstruction -
 Ball in bunker moves closer to hole when
  obstruction removed and ball will not
  remain at rest when replaced; all other
  parts of bunker are nearer hole — 20-3d/2
 Ball lying on obstruction in bunker — 13/5

HAZARD (Continued)
  Obstruction (Continued)
    Clarification of relief procedure from
      obstruction in bunker   24-2b/5
    Removal of obstruction in hazard would
      move loose impediment   1-4/5
    Stone serving as part of drain in bunker   24/7
    Whether rakes should be placed in or
      outside bunkers   Misc./2
  Player concedes hole after which it is
    discovered that opponent's last stroke was
    played with a wrong ball from a hazard   2-4/9.5
  Sand spilling over margin of bunker   13/1
  Searching for ball -
    Ball covered by sand in bunker removed
      from buried lie during search   12-1/2
    Searching with clubhead for ball covered by
      sand in bunker   12-1/1
    Top of ball in hazard covered by leaves but
      part of ball visible from another angle   12-1/3
  Smoothing irregularities in bunker -
    After ball played out of bunker; ball later
      returns to smoothed area   13-4/38
    After playing out of turn in match play;
      opponent then recalls stroke and player
      must drop ball in smoothed area   13-4/39
    After stroke but before ball extricated   13-4/36
    Ball played from bunker is out of bounds
      or lost; player smooths footprints before
      dropping another ball   13-4/37
    Creating and then smoothing footprints on
      line of play   13-2/29
    Greenkeeping staff member rakes bunker
      when player's ball lies therein   13-2/4
    Irregularities are situated between ball and
      hole   13-2/28
    Player preparing to play from bunker
      requests another player who has just
      played from bunker to smooth his
      footprints   13-4/19
    Smoothing footprints made in search for ball
      in bunker before playing stroke from
      bunker   13-4/11
  Stance -
    Ball moves after stance taken without club   18-2b/2
    Ball moves while player in process of taking
      stance   18-2b/3
    Knocking down side of bunker to get level
      stance   13-3/3
    Lie in bunker altered by another player
      taking his stance   20-3b/2
    Player in bunker takes firm stance and then
      smooths footprints when he decides to
      play different type shot   13-4/27
    Stance in bunker taken without club   13-4/24

HAZARD (Continued)

Stance (Continued)

Taking firm stance in bunker some distance
from where ball lies in bunker to simulate
next stroke 13-4/25

Taking stance in bunker and then changing
clubs 13-4/26

When stance taken in bunker 13-4/23

Testing conditions -

Ball played from bunker is out of bounds
or lost; player tests condition of bunker
before dropping another ball 13-4/37

Testing condition of bunker before deciding
whether to play through it 13-2/30

Whether sticking rake handle in sand in
bunker constitutes testing 13-4/22

Touching grass with club in practice swing 13-4/4

Touching ground -

Ball played from bunker onto grass bank;
player hits sand with club; ball then rolls
back into bunker 13-4/35.5

During backswing 13-4/31

Grounding club on bridge in water hazard 13-4/30

Grounding club outside water hazard when
playing stroke at ball in hazard 13-4/29

Grounding club, removing leaves and
improving area of intended swing in
water hazard 13-4/28

Hitting sand in bunker with club after failing
to extricate ball 13-4/35

Foursome match 29/5

Partner's ball in same bunker 30-3f/2

Leaning on club in bunker while waiting to
play 13-4/2

Rake handle stuck in bunker before stroke 13-4/22

Rake thrown into bunker before stroke 13-4/21

Touching bare earth wall of bunker on
backswing 13-4/34

Touching mound made by burrowing animal
with backswing in bunker 13-4/5

Umbrella or rake placed in bunker before
stroke 13-4/20

Using cane or club to enter or leave hazard
when ball lies in hazard 13-4/3.5

When ball lies outside hazard 13-4/1

When club grounded in grass 18-2b/5

Whether touching solidly embedded stone
with club during backswing constitutes
touching ground 13-4/6

With several practice swings 13-4/3

Tree in bunker; status 13/2

Two balls lie together in hazard and neither is
identifiable 1-4/6

HOLE

Aeration holes; status   25/15
     Local Rule   33-8/32
Attachment to flagstick to indicate position of
    hole on green   17/1
Ball blown into hole by competitor   3-2/2
Ball embedded in side of hole -
    All of ball below lip of hole   16/2
    All of ball not below lip of hole   16/3
Ball falls into hole after being addressed   18-2b/10
Ball knocked from lip of hole in disgust   18-2a/23
Ball overhanging — See "PUTTING GREEN:
    Ball overhanging hole"
Completing hole in match play after result of
    hole decided   7-2/6
Concession of -
    Handicap stroke claimed after hole conceded   6-2a/4
    Implied concession of hole withdrawn   2-4/13
    Player concedes hole after which it is
      discovered opponent had played wrong
      ball   2-4/9
    Player concedes hole after which it is
      discovered opponent's last stroke was
      played with a wrong ball from a hazard   2-4/9.5
    Player concedes hole after which opponent
      plays wrong ball   2-4/10
    Player concedes hole on basis of invalid
      claim   2-4/12
    Player concluding he played wrong ball
      when opponent misread number on
      player's ball concedes hole   9-2/11
    Player with lost ball concedes hole; ball then
      found in hole   2-4/11
Cutting hole on slope   16/6
Damaged; procedure for player   16-1a/6
Different colored flags used to indicate position
    of hole on green   17/2
Halved -
    Player agreeing with opponent that hole
      halved later realizes he has won hole   2-5/9
    Player incorrectly believing he has won
      a hole lifts opponent's ball-marker;
      opponent had putt for half   2-4/5
    Player putting for half is given advice by
      opponent   2-2/1
    Player reporting wrong score causes
      opponent with chance for half to pick up   9-2/6
    Players unable to resolve Rules problem
      agree to consider hole halved   2-1/1
    Whether hole halved if neither player in
      match holes out   2-5/3
Hole-liner -
    Ball strikes edge of hole-liner and bounces
      out of hole   16/5
    Ball strikes hole-liner pulled out with
      flagstick   17/8

HOLE (Continued)

Hole-liner (Continued)

Not sunk deep enough — 16/4

Pulled out by flagstick attendant and ball falls into unlined hole — 17/7

Holes relocated and/or tee-markers moved during stroke play round — 33-2b/1

Made by burrowing animal — See "BURROWING ANIMAL"

Map of putting green indicating hole position displayed at tee — 33/6

Marking position with club — 17-3/6

Omitted in match -

Inadvertently; error discovered after match concluded — 2-3/2

Purposely — 2-3/3

Placed ball rolls into hole — 20-3d/1

Play suspended during play of hole -

Competitors discontinue play immediately but then complete hole before Committee orders resumption of play — 6-8b/1

Completion of hole by one competitor in group — 6-8b/3

Options if one competitor in group has played from tee — 6-8b/2

Options if Local Rule for suspension of play due to dangerous situation in effect — US/33-8/102

Player plays away from hole to assist partner — 30-3f/6

Player putts with one hand and catches ball in hole with other hand — 1-2/5

Player repairs hole after holing out but before opponent, fellow-competitor or partner holes out — 1-2/3.5

Playing out of sequence in match — 2-3/4

Scooping casual water from hole — 16-1a/4

Status if neither player in match completes hole — 2-5/3

Surrounded by casual water — 33-2d/2

Touching inside edge — 16-1a/5

Two holes on each green of nine-hole course — 16/7

When play of hole over — 7-2/1

HOLE MADE BY GREENKEEPER

Explanation of term in Definition of "Ground Under Repair" — 25/14

Status as hole made by greenkeeper of -

Aeration holes — 25/15

Hole of removed stake defining water hazard — 25/18

Hole on putting green not in use — 16/7

Rut made by tractor — 25/16

Sunken hole plug — 25/17

HOLE PLUG

Old hole plug sunk or raised on line of putt — 16-1c/3

HOLE PLUG (Continued)
    Spike mark on line of putt pressed down when
      player repairs old hole plug   16-1a/16.5
    Status of sunken hole plug   25/17

HOLED OR HOLING OUT
    Failure to hole out; stroke play — See
      "STROKE PLAY: Failure to hole out"
    Holing out without ball touching flagstick   17-3/1
    Local Rule for temporary putting green waives
      requirement to hole out   33-8/1
    Player discovers original ball in hole after
      searching five minutes and then continuing
      play with provisional ball   1-1/3
    Player discovers own ball in hole after playing
      wrong ball   1-1/4
    Player unaware he has holed out puts
      another ball into play   1-1/2
    Player with lost ball concedes hole; ball then
      found in hole   2-4/11
    Whether ball holed if -
      Ball embedded in side of hole -
        All of ball below lip of hole   16/2
        All of ball not below lip of hole   16/3
      Ball falls into hole after being addressed   18-2b/10
      Placed ball rolls into hole   20-3d/1
      Player holes short putt and allegedly
        removes ball from hole before it is at rest   16/5.5

HONOR
    At hole following disputed hole   10-1a/2
    In four-ball match in which points awarded
      for both better-ball and aggregate scores   30/3
    In handicap match   10-1a/1
    In handicap Stableford competition   32-1/3
    In handicap stroke play   10-2a/1

**IDENTIFYING BALL — See "BALL:
Identifying"**

**INFORMATION AS TO STROKES TAKEN —
See also "WRONG INFORMATION"**
    Player concedes match after winning it when
      opponent lodges invalid claim regarding
      strokes taken   2-4/15
    Player omits penalty stroke when advising
      opponent as to score for hole; error
      discovered after match conceded by
      opponent   9-2/10
    Player reporting wrong score causes opponent
      with chance for half to pick up ball   9-2/6
    Player reports wrong score for hole; error
      discovered several holes later   9-2/9
    Withholding information on strokes taken until
      opponent's turn to play   9-2/4

INSECTS
Danger from bees 1-4/10
Danger from fire-ants 33-8/22
Removal of insect on ball 23-1/5

LATERAL WATER HAZARD — See "HAZARD" and "WATER HAZARD: Lateral"

LEAVES
Bunker covered by leaves; player touches
    leaves during backswing 13-4/33
Knocking down leaves with practice swing ... 13-2/22
Local Rule for accumulations of leaves in
    bunkers 13-4/33
Local Rule providing relief from accumulations
    of leaves through the green 33-8/31
Top of ball in hazard covered by leaves but
    part of ball visible from another angle 12-1/3

LIE OF BALL — See "BALL: Lie of"

LIFTING BALL — See "BALL: Lifting"

LIGHTNING
Player claiming danger from lightning refuses
    to resume play when resumption ordered by
    Committee 6-8b/5
Local rule for suspension of play for dangerous
    situations US/33-8/102

LINE OF PLAY — See also "PUTTING GREEN: Line of Putt"
Affected by pitch-mark made by partner's,
    opponent's or fellow-competitor's ball 13-2/8
Ball mark partially on and partially off putting
    green is on line of play 16-1c/1.5
Ball outside bunker; stone in bunker on line of
    play pressed down or removed 13-2/31
Bending grass in removing loose impediments
    improves line of play 13-2/13
Boundary post on line of play removed but
    replaced before stroke 13-2/25
Competitor sanctions repair of spike damage
    on his line of putt by fellow-competitor 13-2/36
Creating and then smoothing footprints in
    bunker on line of play 13-2/29
Extension affected when opponent or fellow-
    competitor creates footprints in bunker 13-2/29.5
Greenkeeping staff member rakes bunker and
    improves player's line of play 13-2/4
Improving by mopping up casual water 13-2/34
Improving by removing part of fence 13-2/32.5
Improving by removing stone from wall 13-2/32
Improving when taking relief from abnormal
    ground condition 25-1b/3

LINE OF PLAY (Continued)

Indicating -
  Caddie touches putting green to indicate line
    of play before player chips from off green 8-2b/3
  Club placed on ground to align feet 8-2a/1
  Object placed beside or behind ball to
    indicate line of play 8-2a/2
Local Rule giving line-of-sight relief from
  protective fence near line of play 33-8/18
Local Rule providing line-of-sight relief from
  irrigation-control boxes 33-8/17
Opening barn doors to play shot through barn 24-2b/15
Outside agency removes immovable
  obstruction on player's line of play 13-2/33
Pine needles piled for removal interfere with
  line of play after ball dropped away 25-1b/17
Relief from obstruction incidentally gives relief
  from intervention on line of play 24-2b/7
Removing dew from line of play 13-2/35
Smoothing irregularities in bunker situated
  between ball and hole 13-2/28
Testing condition of bunker before deciding
  whether to play through it; act improves line
  of play 13-2/30
Window of clubhouse opened and ball played
  through window 24-2b/14

LOCAL RULE

Aeration holes 33-8/32
Allowing competitors to discontinue play by
  agreement in bad weather 33-8/5
Ant hills; treating as ground under repair 33-8/22
Ball deflected -
  By power line 33-8/13
  By sprinkler head 33-8/12
Ball drop; procedure for dropping 33-8/34
Bunker -
  For face of bunker comprising stacked turf 33-8/39
  Permitting re-dropping or placing when
    dropped ball embeds 33-8/28
  Providing relief from accumulation of leaves 13-4/33
  Providing relief from damage caused by
    children 33-8/9
  Providing relief without penalty from
    flooded bunker 33-8/27
  When bunker adjacent to lateral water
    hazard US/33-8/100
Dangerous situations; Local Rule for
  suspension of play US/33-8/102
Flagstick -
  Prohibiting removal 33-8/10
  Waiving penalty for ball striking unattended
    flagstick 33-8/11
Golf cart -
  For events in which motorized carts
    permitted 33-8/4

LOCAL RULE (Continued)

Ground under repair -
Altering relief procedure   33-8/26
Denying relief from ground under repair
   during play of particular hole   33-8/23
Treating ant hills as ground under repair   33-8/22
When ground under repair is adjacent to
   artificially-surfaced cart path   33-8/25

Leaves -
Providing relief from accumulation in
   bunker   13-4/33
Providing relief from accumulation through
   the green   33-8/31

Lightning-
Local Rule for suspension of play   US/33-8/102

Obstruction -
Providing line-of-sight relief from irrigation-
   control boxes   33-8/17
Providing line-of-sight relief from protective
   fence near line of play   33-8/18

Out of bounds -
Deeming ball in bounds until beyond
   boundary wall   33-2a/16
Deeming interior boundary fence to be
   obstruction   33-8/14
Deeming out of bounds ball which crosses
   boundary but comes to rest on course   33-8/38
Treatment of boundary stakes having no
   significance in play of hole being played   24/5
When public road dividing course is defined
   as out of bounds   27/20

Putting green -
Prohibiting practice during round;
   competitor practices on last green after
   holing out   33-8/6
Providing relief from edging grooves around
   green   33-8/24
Providing relief from mushrooms on line of
   putt   16-1a/15
Requiring player to play out of turn   33-8/7
Temporary - Waiving requirement to hole
   out   33-8/1
Wrong - Prohibiting dropping ball on apron   33-8/33

Road or path -
Permitting relief on specified side of paved
   path   33-8/19
Providing relief from unsurfaced road for
   tee shot only   33-8/20
Recommendation when ground under repair
   adjacent   33-8/25
When public road dividing course is defined
   as out of bounds   27/20

Rough; treating as lateral water hazard   33-8/35

Second ball -
Allowing in match play   33-8/3

LOCAL RULE (Continued)

Sportsmanship code; assessing penalty for
  breach — US/33-8/10

Stakes -
  Deeming all stakes on course to be
    immovable obstructions — 33-8/16
  For boundary stakes having no significance
    in play of hole being played — 24/5
  Providing relief from immovable water
    hazard stake for ball lying in water hazard — 33-8/15

Trees -
  Providing protection for young trees — 33-8/30
  Providing relief from tree nursery — 33-8/29
  Providing relief from tree roots — 33-8/8

Water hazard -
  Allowing drop in hazard behind point where
    ball lies unplayable in hazard — 33-8/37
  Allowing drop on green side when ball fails
    to clear hazard — 33-8/2
  Allowing drop opposite spot where ball
    comes to rest in lateral water hazard — 26-1/20
  For lateral water hazard with bunker
    adjacent — US/33-8/10(
  For part of lateral water hazard where
    impossible to drop not nearer hole — 33-2a/9
  Giving free relief — 33-8/36
  Island green — 33-2a/10
  Providing relief from immovable water
    hazard stake for ball lying in hazard — 33-8/15
  When pond is water hazard from men's tee
    and lateral from women's tee — 33-2a/6

LOOSE IMPEDIMENTS

Assistance in removing large loose impediment — 23-1/3
Ball touched accidentally in removing loose
  impediment — 18-2a/31
Ball touched with fir cone or stick to prevent
  movement when loose impediment removed — 18-2a/32
Bending grass in removal of loose impediment — 13-2/13
Breaking off part of large loose impediment — 23-1/4
Competitor seeks help from fellow-competitor
  in removing loose impediment to avoid
  penalty — 33-7/7
Determining whether natural object interfering
  with area of intended swing is loose
  impediment — 13-2/26
Hazard — See "HAZARD: Loose Impediment"
Large stone removable only with much effort — 23-1/2
Loose impediment affecting lie moved when
  ball lifted — 23-1/7
Loose impediment affecting lie removed while
  ball lifted — 23-1/8
Loose impediments within one club-length
  removed; ball lifted and replaced; ball moves
  before address — 18-2c/3
Meaning of "solidly embedded" in Definition — 23/2

LOOSE IMPEDIMENTS (Continued)

Means by which loose impediments may be removed — 23-1/1

Pine needles piled for removal interfere with line of play after ball dropped away — 25-1b/17

Putting green -

  After ball addressed ball moved in removal of loose impediment — 18-2c/2

  Ball moved accidentally by foot during removal of loose impediment — 18-2c/1

  Brushed along line of putt rather than to side — 16-1a/10

  Brushing off line of putt with palm of hand — 16-1a/9

  Determining whether natural object on line of putt is loose impediment — 16-1a/11

  Player repairs depression on line of putt created when partially embedded acorn removed — 16-1a/7

  Removed from line of putt with cap or towel — 16-1a/8

Removal from area in which ball to be dropped — 23-1/6

Removal from spot on which ball to be placed — 23-1/6.5

Removal of loose impediments affecting player's play — 23-1/10

Removal of loose impediment lying out of bounds — 23-1/9

Replacement of loose impediments removed by opponent or fellow-competitor — 23-1/10

Status as loose impediment of -

  Aeration plugs — 23/12

  Ant hill — 23/5

  Clod of earth — 23/13

  Dead land crab — 23/6

  Embedded acorn — 23/9

  Fallen tree — 23/7

  Fruit in which ball embedded — 23/10

  Fruit skins — 23/4

  Grass adhering to ball — 21/2

  Grass cuttings — 25/11

  Gravel used to surface road — 23/14

  Half-eaten pear — 23/3

  Insect on ball — 23-1/5

  Loose soil remaining when molehill swept flat — 23/11

  Moss in tree and on ground — 13-2/37

  Partially embedded pine needle in hazard — 13-4/32

  Snake — 18/4

  Undetached divot — 13-2/5

  Worm partially underground — 23/8

When loose impediment transformed into obstruction — 23/1

LOST BALL — See also "BALL: Identifying"

Ball believed lost found in hole after player has searched five minutes and then continued play with provisional ball — 1-1/3 i-58

LOST BALL (Continued)

Ball believed to be lost in bunker; competitor
  drops another ball in bunker and plays it;
  original ball then found outside bunker — 20-7b/3

Ball covered by sand in bunker removed from
  buried lie during search — 12-1/2

Ball declared lost is found before another ball
  put into play — 27/16

Ball dropped in area where original ball lost;
  ball then played — 27-1/3

Ball found after search exceeding five minutes
  is then played — 27/8

Ball found in burrowing animal hole after
  five-minute search — 27/7

Ball lost in tree in ground under repair — 25/10

Ball lost in underground drainpipe — 24-2c/1

Ball played from bunker is lost; player tests
  condition of bunker or smooths footprints
  before dropping another ball — 13-4/37

Ball played in ground under repair area lost in
  same area — 25-1c/3

Ball played out of turn from tee abandoned
  and another ball played in proper order;
  whether original ball is lost — 10-2c/1

Ball played under Rule for ball lost in ground
  under repair after another ball played under
  stroke-and-distance procedure — 15/8

Committee intervention in match play when
  search exceeds five minutes — US/34-3/1

Competitor plays wrong ball and loses it; ball
  may have been fellow-competitor's ball — 15-3/1

Electronic device used to find ball — 14-3/14

Original ball found and played after another
  ball put into play — 15/5

Original ball found within five-minute search
  period after another ball dropped — 27-1/2

Original ball found within five-minute search
  period after another ball teed — 27-1/1

Player directs caddie not to search for his ball
  until others can assist — 27/1

Player searching for ball mistakes his ball for
  opponent's — 27/5

Player unable to find his ball because another
  player played it — 27/6

Player with lost ball concedes hole; ball then
  found in hole — 2-4/11

Searching for lost ball after putting another
  ball into play — 27/9

Searching ten minutes for lost ball — 6-7/2

Searching with clubhead for ball covered by
  sand in bunker — 12-1/1

Smoothing footprints made in search for ball
  in bunker before playing stroke from bunker — 13-4/11

Time permitted for search for lost ball after
  wrong ball played — 27/2

LOST BALL (Continued)

Time permitted for search for original ball and
provisional ball   27/4

Time permitted for search when lost ball found
and then lost again   27/3

Treated as moved by outside agency in absence
of reasonable evidence to that effect   27-1/2.5

Treating ball as moved by outside agency
rather than lost   18-1/1

Whether original ball is lost if another ball
played under stroke-and-distance procedure   27/17

MARKER

Competitor and marker sign score card in
wrong places   6-6b/1

Competitor plays several holes without marker   6-6a/2

Flagstick attended by marker   17-1/3

Hole scores entered in wrong boxes; marker
corrects error by altering hole numbers on
card   6-6a/3

Hole scores for first nine holes recorded in
boxes for second nine and vice versa   6-6d/3

Lone competitor appoints own marker   6-6a/1

Marker attests wrong score knowingly -
Competitor aware score wrong   1-3/6
Competitor unaware score wrong   6-6a/5

Marker disappears with competitor's score
card   6-6b/6

Marker not appointed by Committee signs
cards   6-6b/5

Marker refuses to sign competitor's card after
dispute resolved in favor of competitor   6-6a/4

Retrospective appointment of marker by
Committee   33-1/5

Score corrected by competitor after marker
leaves area in which card returned   6-6b/7

MATCH PLAY

Advice between rounds in 36-hole match   8-1/19

Ascertaining whereabouts of opponent's ball
before playing   9-2/16

Changing clubs between rounds in 36-hole
match   4-4a/8

Claims — See "CLAIMS AND DISPUTES"

Committee intervention   US/34-3/100
When search for lost ball exceeds five
minutes   US/34-3/101

Completing hole after result decided   7-2/1.5

Concession of hole — See "HOLE: Concession
of"

Concession of match — See "CONCESSION:
Match"

Concession of next stroke — See "PUTTING
GREEN: Conceding opponent's next stroke"

Conscious failure to correct opponent's
misunderstanding of state of match   9-2/12

MATCH PLAY (Continued)

Default — See "DEFAULT"

Determination of handicap allowances in
four-ball match if one player unable to
compete 30-3a/3

Determination of honor in handicap match 10-1a/1

Finalists both disqualified 33/3

Halved hole — See "HOLE: Halved"

Hole inadvertently omitted in match; error
discovered after match concluded 2-3/2

Hole not completed by either player 2-5/3

How to settle tie in handicap match 33-6/1

Local Rule allowing play of second ball 33-8/3

Match begun in ignorance that course closed .. 33-2d/4

Match decided by wrong form of play by
agreement 33-1/4

Misapplication of handicap affects draw 33-5/3

Nassau match -
Player who wins first nine holes withdraws
during second nine US/2-3/

One player in match competes concurrently in
stroke play competition 33-1/6

Player reporting wrong score causes opponent
with chance for half to pick up 9-2/6

Player unable to resume suspended match at
scheduled time 6-8b/4

Player who has advanced in match play is
disqualified for wrong score in qualifying
round 34-1b/8

Player who has reached third round of match
play disqualified for agreeing to waive Rules
in first-round match 33/2

Players decide method of settling tie when
Committee fails to do so 33-6/4

Players in singles match accompanied by third
party 2/1

Players mistakenly believing match is all
square after 18 holes play extra hole without
claim being made 2-5/6

Players unable to resolve Rules problem agree
to consider hole halved 2-1/1

Players under impression match is over later
realize it was all square 2-3/1

Postponement of final match due to injury of
player 6-3a/1

Replaying match when play discontinued
instead of resuming from where play
stopped 2-3/5

Rightful winner of match makes no claim and
agrees to play extra holes 2-5/7

Second ball played 3-3/9

Three holes played out of sequence in match .. 2-3/4

True state of match not determinable 34-3/5

Two holes purposely omitted in match 2-3/3

MATCH PLAY (Continued)

Whether disqualified player entitled to prize
won prior to disqualification 33/7

Wrong form of play used 6-1/1

Wrong score in qualifying round discovered
during match play 34-1b/7

MATERIAL PILED FOR REMOVAL

Pine needles piled for removal interfere with
line of play after ball dropped away 25-1b/17

Status as material piled for removal of -
Fallen tree in process of being removed 25/7
Grass cuttings 25/11
Tree stump 25/8

MEASURING

Ball moved in measuring to determine if
re-drop required 20-2c/6

Club to be used in measuring club-length 20/1

Distance meter attached to golf cart 14-3/1

MOSS

Status of moss in tree and on ground 13-2/37

**NATURAL OBJECTS — See "LOOSE
IMPEDIMENTS"**

OBSERVER

Flagstick attended by observer 17-1/3

OBSTRUCTIONS

After relief taken from obstruction for stroke
towards green, obstruction interferes with
stance for necessary sideways stroke 24-2b/9.5

Artificially-surfaced road or path; what
constitutes 24/9

Ball lying on obstruction in bunker 13/5

Direction posts; suggestion re installation 33/4

Immovable -
After relief from obstruction second
obstruction interferes 24-2b/9

Area of intended swing improved by
removing obstruction 13-2/15

Ball bounces across obstruction after drop ... 24-2b/13

Ball found in immovable obstruction
but not immediately recoverable 24-2b/4.5

Ball in drainpipe under course; entrance to
drainpipe is out of bounds 24-2b/12

Ball lost in underground drainpipe 24-2c/1

Ball lying on elevated obstruction 24-2b/11
dropped away; ball rolls to position
where player would have to stand on
obstruction; whether re-drop required ... 20-2c/0.5

Bridge in water hazard; whether grounding
club permissible 13-4/30

Clarification of "point on the course nearest
to where the ball lies" in relief Rule 24-2b/3

OBSTRUCTIONS (Continued)
Immovable (Continued)

Clarification of relief procedure from
obstruction in bunker   24-2b/5

Club used to determine "nearest point" not
used for next stroke   24-2b/4

Crossing over obstruction in obtaining relief
from ground under repair   25-1b/14

Diagrams illustrating "point on the course
nearest to where the ball lies"   25-1b/2

Dropped ball rolling out of prescribed
dropping area   20-2c/1

Dropping from rough to fairway in obtaining
relief   24-2b/8

Exposed water pipe adjacent and parallel to
boundary fence; suggested treatment   33-2a/1

Improving line of play by removing part of
fence   13-2/32.5

Improving line of play by removing stone
from wall   13-2/32

Local Rule — See "LOCAL RULE:
Obstruction" and "LOCAL RULE: Road
or path"

Meaning of "area of his intended swing" in
relief Rule   24-2a/2

Mental interference   24-2a/1

Nearest point of relief from cart path is in
casual water; nearest point of relief from
casual water is back on cart path   1-4/8

Obstruction in ground under repair interferes
with player's swing   24-2b/10

Obstruction interferes but ball unplayable
due to some other condition   24-2b/16

Obstruction interferes with abnormal
stroke; abnormal stroke not reasonable in
circumstances   24-2b/18

Obstruction interferes with abnormal
stroke; abnormal stroke reasonable in
circumstances   24-2b/17

Opening barn doors to play shot through
barn   24-2b/15

Outside agency removes immovable
obstruction on player's line of play   13-2/33

Player entitled to relief lifts ball; player then
replaces ball and plays it from original
position   18-2a/12

Player unable physically to determine
"nearest point"   24-2b/3.5

Relief from obstruction incidentally results
in relief from boundary fence   24-2b/6

Relief from obstruction interfering with
swing incidentally gives relief from
intervention on line of play   24-2b/7

Stake supporting tree broken in attempt to
remove it   13-2/16

OBSTRUCTIONS (Continued)
  Immovable (Continued)

Status of movable part of drainage hose — 24-2b/15.3

Stroke at ball not reasonable due to interference by obstruction and casual water — 24-2b/19

Window of clubhouse opened and ball played through window — 24-2b/14

  Movable -

Ball in bunker moves closer to hole when obstruction removed and ball will not remain at rest when replaced; all other parts of bunker are nearer hole — 20-3d/2

Ball in plastic bag moves when bag blown to new position by wind — 18-1/7

Ball lifted and dropped away from movable obstruction — 18-2a/4

Holding ball in place while removing obstruction — 24-1/4

Movable obstruction defined — 24-1/1

Position of ball marked before obstruction removed; ball moves when ball-marker removed — 24-1/5

Position of ball worsened when obstruction removed; player replaces obstruction — 13-2/15.5

Removal of obstruction in hazard would move loose impediment — 1-4/5

Whether rakes should be placed in or outside bunker — Misc./2

Opponent or fellow-competitor removes obstruction affecting player's play — 24/16

  Status as obstruction of -

Abandoned ball — 24-1/2

Angled supports or guy wires supporting boundary fence — 24/2

Boundary stakes having no significance in play of hole being played — 24/5

Concrete bases of boundary fence posts — 24/3

Displaced boundary stake — 33-2a/20

Flagstick lying on putting green — 1-2/3

Gate in boundary fence — 27/18

Half-eaten pear — 23/3

Immovable artificial object situated out of bounds — 24-2b/21

Line on ground consisting of lime — 24-2b/20

Movable artificial object lying out of bounds — 24-1/3

Parked car — 24/8

Part of boundary fence within boundary line — 24/4

Part of fence off course which leans across boundary — 13-2/20

Paved area — 24/10

Stile attached to boundary fence — 24/1

Stone broken away from retaining wall in water hazard — 24/6

Stone serving as part of drain in bunker — 24/7

OBSTRUCTIONS (Continued)
Status as obstruction of (Continued)

Tee-markers	11-2/1
Tree basin	33-2a/10.5
Turf raised by underground pipe	24/14
Wooden planks	24/11
Wooden or earthen steps	24/12
When loose impediment transformed into obstruction	23/1

ORDER OF PLAY
Honor — See "HONOR"

In foursome match if player accidentally moves ball after address	29-1/5
In foursome stroke play when wrong ball played	29-1/8
Playing out of turn — See "PLAYING OUT OF TURN"	
Procedure for referee in determining ball farther from hole	10-1b/1
Waiving turn to putt in four-ball match	30-3c/2
When two balls are lost in lateral water hazard	10/3
When two balls lie in ground under repair and both players take relief	10/1
When two balls lie in lateral water hazard and both players take relief	10/2

OUT OF BOUNDS

Ball enters burrowing animal hole in bounds and comes to rest out of bounds	25-1b/24
Ball enters burrowing animal hole out of bounds and comes to rest in bounds	25-1b/23
Ball in drainpipe under course; entrance to drainpipe is out of bounds	24-2b/12
Ball moved accidentally by backward movement of club after stroke misses; ball comes to rest out of bounds	18-2a/22
Ball moved into bounds by flow of water in water hazard	26-1/8
Ball moved out of bounds by flow of water in water hazard	26-1/7
Ball moves after address and come to rest out of bounds	18-2b/9
Ball played from bunker is out of bounds; player tests condition of bunker or smooths footprints before dropping another ball	13-4/37
Ball played from outside teeing ground goes out of bounds	11-4b/6
Ball played from spot where original ball deflected out of bounds by maintenance vehicle	20-7/1
Ball played out of bounds from wrong teeing ground not recalled	11-5/3
Ball strikes opponent standing out of bounds and comes to rest out of bounds	19-3/1

OUT OF BOUNDS (Continued)

Ball thrown into bounds by outside agency
and played —
  Caddie aware of action of outside agency   15/9
  Neither player nor his caddie aware of
     action of outside agency   15/10
Ball wrongly thought to be out of bounds
  lifted; competitor proceeds under Rule 27-1   18-2a/11
Fence defining -
  Angled supports or guy wires supporting
     fence; status   24/2
  Concrete bases of boundary fence posts;
     status   24/3
  Establishing boundary line inside fence on
     property line   33-2a/15
  Exposed water pipe adjacent and parallel to
     fence; suggested procedure   33-2a/1
  Gate in fence; status   27/18
  Improving position of ball by bending fence   13-2/18
  Moving ball lying against fence by striking
     other side of fence   14-1/5
  Part of fence within boundary line; status   24/4
  Relief from immovable obstruction
     incidentally results in relief from fence   24-2b/6
  Stile attached to boundary fence; status   24/1
  When ball inside boundary fence is out of
     bounds   27/19
Improving area of intended swing by moving
  growing or fixed object situated out of
  bounds   13-2/19
Interference by immovable artificial object
  situated out of bounds   24-2b/21
Internal boundary between holes; whether
  permissible   33-2a/12
Internal out of bounds applying to stroke from
  teeing ground only   33-2a/14
Local Rule — See "LOCAL RULE: Out of
  bounds"
Movable artificial object lying out of bounds;
  status   24-1/3
Opponent's caddie lifts player's ball which
  may or may not have been out of bounds   18-3b/5
Original ball and provisional ball found out of
  bounds   27-2c/4
Original ball out of bounds; ball played under
  stroke-and-distance procedure falls off tee at
  address   11-3/3
Part of fence off course leans across boundary
  and interferes with swing   13-2/20
Player's ball strikes own caddie and comes to
  rest out of bounds   19-2/2
Player's ball strikes own caddie standing out
  of bounds and comes to rest on course   19-2/3
Player's ball strikes own caddie standing out
  of bounds and comes to rest out of bounds   19-2/4

OUT OF BOUNDS (Continued)

Provisional ball used as second ball when not
determinable whether original ball is out of
bounds 3-3/1

Public road defined as out of bounds divides
course; status of ball crossing road 27/20

Removal of loose impediment lying out of
bounds 23-1/9

River forming part of course boundary; how
to define 33-2a/11

Stakes or posts defining — See "STAKES:
Defining out of bounds"

Stroke played with ball lying out of bounds 15/6

Tee decreed to be in bounds for tee shot and
out of bounds thereafter 33-2a/13

Tee shot out of bounds in mixed foursome
in which different tees used by men and
women 29/2

Teed ball missed then hit out of bounds 20-5/1

Wrong ball found out of bounds played under
stroke-and-distance procedure; original ball
then found in bounds 15/12

Wrong ball hit out of bounds; another ball
played under Rule 27-1; original ball then
found nearby 15/11

OUTSIDE AGENCY

Ball deflected or stopped by — See "BALL:
Deflected or stopped by outside agency"

Ball-marker lifted by outside agency 20-1/9

Ball moved by — See "BALL: Moved by
outside agency"

Ball thrown into bounds by outside agency
and played 15/9, 15/10

Removes immovable obstruction on player's
line of play 13-2/33

Removes movable obstruction which worsens
position of ball 13-2/15.5

When snake is outside agency 18/4

PENALTY

Advice given on request; penalties in various
forms of play 8-1/25

Breach of 14-club Rule in stroke play
discovered at 8th hole; where penalty strokes
applied 4-4a/17

Clarification of penalty for breach of 14-club
Rule in match play 4-4a/16

Condition requiring use of ball on List of
Conforming Golf Balls; penalty for breach ... 5-1/2

Disqualification penalty -

Competitor disqualified from handicap
event claims gross prize 33-1/13

Competitor seeks help from fellow-
competitor to avoid penalty 33-7/7

Discovered after competition closed -

PENALTY (Continued)
Disqualification penalty (Continued)
Discovered after competition closed
(Continued)
Competitor changed weight of club during
round   34-1b/4
Competitor correctly advised by fellow-
competitor that he had incurred
a penalty disagrees with fellow-
competitor and fails to include penalty
in his score   34-1b/1.5
Competitor failed to countersign card   34-1b/2
Competitor records incorrect handicap
for partner in foursome stroke play
competition   6-2b/2.5
Omission of penalty stroke when score
returned   34-1b/1
Play of wrong ball in stroke play not
rectified   34-1b/3
Wrong handicap knowingly used in stroke
play   6-2b/2
Wrong handicap used in stroke play by
mistake   6-2b/1
Finalists both disqualified   33/3
Imposing; whether justified -
Competitor repeatedly replaces ball nearer
hole on green   33-7/6
Competitors play two holes not included
in stipulated round   3/2
Marker attests wrong score knowingly   6-6a/5
Player alters teeing ground by relocating
tee-marker   11-2/2
Player fails to correct opponent's
misunderstanding as to state of match   9-2/12
Player knowingly gives incorrect
information on Rules   9/1
Player refuses to identify his ball   27/13
In play-off   3/1
Modifying or waiving -
Authority to waive or modify   33-7/1
Whether justified -
Competitor plays one practice stroke on
course before stroke play round   7-1b/1
Competitor practices on course after
qualifying round and is subsequently
in play-off on same day   7-1b/3
Competitor practices on course between
rounds in stroke play   7-1b/2
Competitor returns wrong score   33-7/4
Competitor unaware of penalty returns
wrong score   33-7/4.5
Competitor's failure to sign card
blamed on lack of time provided by
Committee   33-7/3
Failure to hole out in stroke play   33-7/2

PENALTY (Continued)
  Disqualification penalty (Continued)
    Modifying or waiving (Continued)
      Non-conforming club carried but not used — 4-1/1
      Play of wrong ball not rectified on advice of Committee member — 33-7/5
      Play suspended by Committee; competitor does not resume play at time ordered by Committee — 6-8b/6
      Player holes short putt with club whose playing characteristics changed other than in normal course of play — 4-2/1.5
      Player plays one stroke with non-conforming ball — 5-1/1
      Players agree not to tee off in prescribed order to save time — 1-3/1
    Player who has advanced in match play is disqualified for wrong score in qualifying round — 34-1b/8
    Player who has reached third round of match play disqualified for agreeing to waive Rules in first-round match — 33/2
    Whether disqualified player entitled to prize won prior to disqualification — 33/7
    Wrongly applied to winner of event; error discovered after two other competitors play off for first place — 34-1b/5
  Failure of players to apply known penalty — 1-3/4
  Imposition of penalty by referee after any player in match has played from next tee — 2-5/12
  Multiple penalty; whether applicable if -
    Ball changed during play of hole to aid identification — 15/6.5
    Ball declared unplayable in water hazard is dropped in hazard and played — 20-7/2
    Ball dropped in improper manner and in wrong place — 20-2a/3
    Ball in hazard moves when loose impediment removed — 13-4/15
    Ball lifted without authority and cleaned — 18-2a/13
    Ball moved accidentally and original lie altered; player places ball in wrong place and plays — 18-2a/21.3
    Ball moved accidentally; spot where ball originally lay not determinable; player places ball instead of dropping it — 18-2a/21.5
    Ball moves after address and is stopped by player's club — 18-2b/12
    Ball moves prior to address and is accidentally stopped by player's club; player removes club and ball rolls away — 19-2/1.5
    Ball putted from wrong place lifted and putted from right place — 20-7b/2

PENALTY (Continued)

Multiple penalty; whether applicable if
(Continued)

Ball stopped by player's foot moves when
foot removed 19-2/1

Ball strikes competitor's golf bag and then
his caddie 19-2/7

Caddie lifts ball for identification without
authority and without intentions being
announced 18-2a/14

Competitor plays from outside teeing
ground in foursome stroke play; partner
replays stroke 29-1/2

Competitor's ball played on putting
green deflected by balls of two fellow-
competitors 19-5/3

Dropped ball lifted and re-dropped when
it should have been played as it lay; ball
then lifted again and placed 18-2a/10

Ground in hazard touched with several
practice swings 13-4/3

In hazard club grounded, leaves removed
and area of intended swing improved 13-4/28

Loose impediment removed from water
hazard; player then decides not to play
from hazard 13-4/17

Player who moves ball in breach of Rule
18-2a and alters lie in process does not
proceed under Rule 20-3b 18-2a/6

Player's ball strikes own caddie and comes
to rest out of bounds 19-2/2

Player's ball strikes own caddie standing
out of bounds and comes to rest out of
bounds 19-2/4

Position of ball lifted for identification not
marked, intention to lift not announced
and ball cleaned beyond extent necessary
to identify it 21/4

Stroke played with ball lying out of bounds 15/6

Two different wrong balls played between
strokes with ball in play 15-3/2

Omission of penalty stroke when score
returned 34-1b/1

Omission of penalty strokes when score
returned is due to incorrect ruling 34-3/1

Players in match unaware penalty incurred 1-3/5

Time limit on applying penalty for agreeing to
waive Rule in match play 1-3/8

PHYSICAL PROBLEM

Artificial limbs 14-3/15

Discontinuing play due to physical problem 6-8a/3

Postponement of final match due to injury of
player 6-3a/1

Use of elastic bandage by player with injured
wrist 14-3/7

PITCH-MARK

Area of intended swing improved by repairing
pitch-mark made by ball on previous stroke   13-2/21

Ball bounces out of its pitch-mark and spins
back into it   25-2/1

Dropped ball rolls into pitch-mark from which
lifted   25-2/3

Pitch-mark filled with casual water   25/3

Pitch-mark in dropping area repaired before
ball dropped   13-2/10

Player's lie or line of play affected by
pitch-mark made by partner's, opponent's
or fellow-competitor's ball   13-2/8

**PLACING AND REPLACING BALL — See
"BALL: Placing and replacing"**

PLAYING FROM WRONG PLACE

Ball believed to be lost in bunker; competitor
drops another ball in bunker and plays it;
original ball then found outside bunker   20-7b/3

Ball declared unplayable in water hazard is
dropped in hazard and played   20-7/2

Ball dropped in area where original ball lost;
ball then played   27-1/3

Ball dropped in improper manner and in
wrong place   20-2a/3

Ball dropped in wrong place and played; Rule
3-3 then invoked and second ball dropped
in right place; both balls played out   3-3/3

Ball dropped in wrong place but not played;
Rule 3-3 then invoked and second ball
dropped in right place; both balls played out   3-3/4

Balls dropped outside bunker under option
of unplayable ball Rule requiring drop in
bunker   28/10

Ball knocked out of bunker by fellow-
competitor's stroke at own ball not replaced   18-4/2

Ball moved accidentally and original lie
altered; player places ball in wrong place
and plays   18-2a/21.3

Ball played from spot where original ball
deflected out of bounds by maintenance
vehicle   20-7/1

Ball putted from wrong place lifted and putted
from right place   20-7b/2

Ball replaced at wrong place on putting green
and holed   20-7b/1

Casual water mistaken for water hazard;
original ball played under water hazard
Rule   25-1b/12

Competitor's ball played by fellow-competitor;
competitor substitutes another ball at wrong
place, plays it and then abandons it and
plays out original ball from right place   20-7b/5

PLAYING FROM WRONG PLACE (Continued)

Example of serious breach of lateral water hazard Rule — 26-1/21

Fellow-competitor lifts competitor's ball and sets it aside; competitor plays ball from where set aside — 15-3/3

Guidelines for determining which ball counts when player proceeds under Rule 3-3 — 3-3/0.5

Penalty for repeatedly replacing ball nearer hole on green — 33-7/6

Player plays from wrong place on basis of incorrect ruling — 34-3/3

Player plays second shot, declares ball unplayable and returns to tee — 28/6

Point where ball last crossed margin of lateral water hazard determined and ball dropped and played; point then proves to be wrong point — 26-1/17

Procedure if both original and second balls dropped in wrong place and played — 3-3/5.5

Water hazard treated as lateral water hazard — 26-1/11

Whether score with second ball counts if ball dropped in wrong place and played — 3-3/5

PLAYING OUT OF TURN

Ball played out of turn from tee abandoned and another ball played in proper order — 10-2c/1

Competitor objects to fellow-competitor putting out of turn — 10-2b/1

Competitors in stroke play agree to play out of turn but not for purpose of giving one of them an advantage — 10-2c/2

Local Rule requiring players to play out of turn on putting green — 33-8/7

Player plays out of turn from tee in three-ball match; one opponent requests replay and other does not — 30-2/1

Player requested to lift ball due to interference plays out of turn instead — 10-1c/2

Player smooths irregularities in bunker after playing out of turn in match play; opponent then recalls stroke and player must drop ball in smoothed area — 13-4/39

Player wishing to render original ball lost plays provisional ball out of turn — 27-2b/1

Players in match agree not to tee off in prescribed order — 1-3/1

Request for player to replay stroke played out of turn withdrawn after opponent plays — 10-1c/1

Side plays out of turn from tee; opponents require one member of side to replay but not other — 30-1/1

PLAY-OFF

Competitor in sudden-death play-off gives wrong information — 9-2/17

PLAY-OFF (Continued)
Determining winner and positions in stroke
play play-off   33-6/3
Disqualification in play-off   3/1
Fellow-competitor lifts competitor's ball
conceding next stroke in stroke play play-off   18-4/3
Groupings for stroke play play-off   33-3/4
Replacing club for stroke play play-off   4-4a/9
Score cards in sudden-death play-off   33-5/1

PLUMB-LINE
Club used as plumb-line   14-3/12
Using during round   14-3/11

POWER LINES
Local Rule for ball deflected by power line   33-8/13

PRACTICE
Before or between rounds -
Competitor practices putting on 18th green
immediately after finishing first round
of stroke play competition played over
consecutive days   7-2/8
Competitor practices putting on 3rd green
after finishing hole during first round of
36-hole stroke play competition   7-1b/7
Competitor who practices on competition
course after qualifying round subsequently
is in play-off on same day   7-1b/3
Competitor's caddie practices on or tests
putting green surfaces of the course before
stroke play round   7-1b/5
One practice stroke played on course before
stroke play round   7-1b/1
Stroke play over 54 holes on consecutive
days; second round cancelled and
competitor practices on course following
cancellation   7-1b/6
Stroke play over 36 holes on two courses;
player completes first round, practices on
same course and is later in play-off on
that course   7-1b/4
Waiving penalty for practice on course
between rounds   7-1b/2
During round -
Completing hole in match play after result
of hole decided   7-2/1.5
Hitting plastic ball before playing ball in
play   7-2/4
Hitting practice range ball back to range;
when stroke is practice stroke   7-2/5
In anger player hits ball played by player
in following group; whether stroke is
practice stroke   1-4/4

PRACTICE (Continued)
 During round (Continued)
  In four-ball player disqualified for next hole
   plays that hole; whether strokes played on
   that hole were practice strokes — 30-3f/8
  Local Rule prohibits practice during round
   on putting green of hole last played;
   competitor practices on last green after
   holing out — 33-8/6
  Player after picking up drops ball where
   partner's ball lies and plays practice stroke — 30-3f/7
  Player finds ball and hits it to player who
   lost it; whether stroke is practice stroke — 7-2/5.5
  Player in foursome match practices putts on
   previous green after partner has driven
   from next tee — 29/3
  Player plays practice putt after he and
   partner have holed out but before
   opponents hole out — 30/6
  Player practices putting off green while
   waiting to putt — 7-2/3
  Putting on fairway while waiting to play to
   green — 7-2/2
  When play of hole over — 7-2/1

PRACTICE SWING
 Ball in play moved accidentally by practice
  swing — 18-2a/20
 Ball moved accidentally by practice swing
  prior to tee shot — 18-2a/19
 Ball moves after player takes several practice
  swings near ball and touches grass behind
  ball — 18-2a/30
 Dislodges concealed ball — 7-2/7
 Knocking down leaves with practice swing — 13-2/22
 Touching grass with club in practice swing in
  hazard — 13-4/4
 Touching ground in hazard with several
  practice swings — 13-4/3

PRIZE
 Competitor disqualified in handicap event
  claims gross prize — 33-1/13
 Whether player disqualified in match play
  event entitled to prize won prior to
  disqualification — 33/7

PROVISIONAL BALL
 Announcement — 27-2a/1
 Condition requiring use of ball on List of
  Conforming Golf Balls; ball not on List
  played as provisional ball — 5-1/3
 Continuation of play with provisional ball
  without searching for original ball — 27-2b/1
 Lifted in erroneous belief original ball is in
  bounds — 27-2b/8

PROVISIONAL BALL (Continued)

Lifted; subsequently becomes ball in play   27-2b/9

Member of Committee finds player's original ball; player prefers to continue with provisional ball   27-2/2

Moves after being addressed   15/7

Not distinguishable from original ball   27/11

Original ball and provisional ball found out of bounds   27-2c/4

Original ball found; player wishes to ignore it and continue play with provisional ball   27-2c/2

Original ball is beyond provisional ball; player searches briefly for original ball, plays provisional ball and then finds original ball   27-2b/3

Original ball played after provisional ball played from point nearer hole than original ball is likely to be   27-2b/5

Original ball struck by provisional ball   18-5/2

Play of a second provisional ball   27-2a/4

Played by wrong member of side in foursome   29-1/4

Played from beyond where original ball likely to be but not beyond where original ball found   27-2b/4

Played from point nearer hole than original ball because player erroneously thought original ball, which was visible, was out of bounds   27-2c/3

Played in absence of reasonable possibility original ball is lost or out of bounds   27-2a/3

Played in erroneous belief it is original ball   27-2b/7

Played solely in belief original ball might be in water hazard   27-2a/2

Player abandons original ball and walks forward to play provisional ball; original ball then found   27-2b/6

Player declares first ball from tee unplayable abandons provisional ball and claim he is lying three with third ball   28/2

Player discovers original ball in hole after searching five minutes and then continuing play with provisional ball   1-1/3

Possibility that original ball is in water hazard may not preclude play of provisional ball   27-2c/1

Serving as ball in play if original ball unplayable or in water hazard   27-2/1

Struck by original ball   19-5/5

Time permitted for search for original ball and provisional ball   27/4

Used as second ball when not determinable whether original ball is out of bounds   3-3/1

When provisional ball holed becomes ball in play   27-2b/2

Who plays provisional ball in foursome   29-1/3

Wrong ball played in belief it is provisional ball   15/7

PUTTING GREEN

Ball lifted because player feared ball might
    move   16-1b/1
Ball mark -
    Ball mark partially on and partially off
        putting green is on line of play   16-1c/1.5
    In position to assist opponent   16-1c/2
    Repairing a second time   16-1c/1
    Spike mark on line of putt repaired during
        repair of ball mark   16-1a/16
Ball overhanging hole -
    Casting shadow on ball   16-2/3
    Falls into hole after being addressed   18-2b/10
    Falls into hole after being lifted, cleaned and
        replaced   16-2/0.5
    Falls into hole after concession of next stroke   2-4/2
    Falls into hole after player waits 40 seconds   16-2/1
    Knocked away by opponent before player
        determines status   16-2/2
    Knocked away in disgust   18-2a/23
    Player jumps close to hole to cause ball to
        drop   1-2/4
Ball putted from wrong place lifted and putted
    from right place   20-7b/2
Ball replaced at wrong place and holed   20-7b/1
Ball replaced but ball-marker not removed;
    ball then moves   20-4/1
Casual water — See "CASUAL WATER:
Putting green"
Conceding opponent's next stroke -
    Agreement to concede short putts   1-3/2
    Ball falls into hole after concession of next
        stroke   2-4/2
    Ball resting against flagstick; putt conceded
        and ball removed before player can
        remove flagstick   17-4/2
    Concession of stroke refused by player and
        withdrawn by opponent; player then putts
        and misses   2-4/7
    In four-ball match player with putt for
        half picks up at suggestion of opponent
        because of misunderstanding; whether
        suggestion of opponent constitutes
        concession   30/5
    Opponent's ball knocked away by player
        after concession moves player's ball   18-2a/18
    Player concedes opponent's next stroke and
        knocks his ball away along own line of
        putt   16-1d/2
    Player concedes opponent's next stroke and
        plays before opponent has opportunity to
        lift ball   2-4/8
    Player concedes opponent's next stroke and
        rolls or knocks ball to opponent   16-1d/1
    Player concedes opponent's next stroke and
        then knocks opponent's ball into hole   2-4/1

PUTTING GREEN (Continued)

Conceding opponent's next stroke (Continued)

Player lifts ball in mistaken belief that next
stroke conceded — 2-4/3

Putting out after concession of stroke — 2-4/6

Whether lifting opponent's ball-marker is
concession of next stroke — 2-4/5

Whether picking up opponent's ball is
concession of next stroke — 2-4/4

Double green; status of half of green serving
hole not being played — 25-3/1

Flagstick attendant removes flagstick and
holds it upright behind hole; end of flagstick
touches green — 17-1/4.5

Flagstick stuck into green some distance from
hole by practical joker — 1-4/3

Hole — See "HOLE"

Hole plug — See "HOLE PLUG"

Line of putt -

Altered purposely by opponent or
fellow-competitor by stepping on it — 1-2/1

Ball lifted on putting green placed ahead
of ball-marker and then moved back to
original position — 16-1a/17

Brushing aside or mopping up casual water
on line of putt — 16-1a/1

Caddie casts shadow to indicate line of putt — 8-2b/1

Competitor sanctions repair of spike damage
on his line of putt by fellow-competitor — 13-2/36

Damaged accidentally by fellow-competitor's
caddie — 16-1a/14

Mushroom growing on line of putt — 16-1a/15

Old hole plug sunk or raised on line of putt — 16-1c/3

Placing ball-marker on line of putt — 20-1/19

Player and opponent or fellow-competitor
agree to repair spike marks on one
another's line of putt — 1-3/3

Player putting first when partner's ball
farther from hole stands on partner's or
opponent's line of putt — 30-3c/1

Player touches putting green in pointing
out line for putting for partner and
incidentally touches own line of putt — 30/2.5

Player walks on line of putt — 16-1a/12

Player who has holed out touches partner's
line of putt — 1-2/3.5

Removing dew from line of putt — 16-1a/3

Shielding line of putt from wind — 1-2/2

Spike mark on line of putt pressed down
when player repairs old hole plug — 16-1a/16.5

Spike mark on line of putt repaired during
repair of ball mark — 16-1a/16

Stepped on accidentally by opponent or
fellow-competitor — 16-1a/13

PUTTING GREEN (Continued)

Line of putt (Continued)

  Trademark aimed along line of putt when
    ball replaced   20-3a/2

  Whether touching inside of hole constitutes
    touching line of putt   16-1a/5

  Worm partially underground on line of putt   23/8

Local Rule — See "LOCAL RULE: Putting
green"

Loose impediments — See "LOOSE
IMPEDIMENTS: Putting green"

Marking position of ball — See "BALL:
Marking position when lifting"

Mud on ball touches putting green but ball
  itself does not touch green   16/1

Oscillating ball pressed into surface of putting
  green   18-2a/6

Position of caddie or partner -

  Caddie deliberately positioned off putting
    green on extension of line of putt behind
    ball   16-1f/1

  Caddie inadvertently positioned on
    extension of line of putt behind ball   16-1f/2

Rotating ball without marking position   18-2a/33

Spike mark damage repaired around hole   16-1c/4

Standing astride or on line of putt - Meaning
  of "line of putt"   16-1e/1

Testing surface -

  Caddie roughens surface of putting green
    but player does not benefit   16-1d/6

  Competitor's caddie tests putting green
    surfaces before stroke play round   7-1b/5

  Testing for wetness surface of putting green
    behind ball   16-1d/4

  Whether Rule prohibiting testing surface is
    breached if -

    Player concedes opponent's next stroke
      and knocks his ball away along own
      line of putt   16-1d/2

    Player concedes opponent's next stroke
      and rolls or knocks ball to opponent   16-1d/1

    Player returns ball to spot from which it
      was lifted by rolling it with putter   16-1d/3

    Player rubs ball on putting green for
      cleaning purposes   16-1d/5

Wrong putting green -

  When half of double green serving hole not
    being played constitutes   25-3/1

  Local Rule prohibiting dropping on apron
    when ball on wrong putting green   33-8/33

RAKE

Ball in bunker moves closer to hole when rake
  removed and ball will not remain at rest
  when replaced; all other parts of bunker are
  nearer hole   20-3d/2

RAKE (Continued)

Handle stuck into bunker before stroke	13-4/22
Placed in hazard before stroke	13-4/20
Thrown into bunker before stroke	13-4/21
Whether rakes should be placed in or outside bunker	Misc./2

REFEREE

Authority to declare ground under repair	34-2/1
Authorizes player to infringe a Rule	34-2/2
Disagreement with referee's decision	34-2/4
Flagstick attended by referee	17-1/3
Imposition of penalty by referee after any player in match has played from next tee	2-5/12
Procedure in determining ball farther from hole	10-1b/1
Reverses ruling made at last hole of match after players leave putting green	34-2/5
Warning player about to infringe Rule	34-2/3

ROAD OR PATH

Local Rule — See "LOCAL RULE: Road or path"	
Nearest point of relief from cart path is in casual water; nearest point of relief from casual water is back on cart path	1-4/8
Public road defined as out of bounds divides course; status of ball crossing road	27/20
Status of gravel used to surface road	23/14
What constitutes artificially-surfaced road or path	24/9

ROUGH

Dropping from rough to fairway in obtaining relief from obstruction	24-2b/8
Local Rule treating rough as lateral water hazard	33-8/35

RULE(S)

Agreement to waive — See "AGREEMENT TO WAIVE RULES"	
Incorrect information on	9/1
Refusal to comply with -	
Competitor not given opportunity to lift ball assisting fellow-competitor	3-4/1
Request to lift ball that might assist partner not honored	30-3f/11
Whether serious breach of Rules occurs if -	
Ball believed to be lost in bunker; competitor drops another ball in bunker and plays it; original ball then found outside bunker	20-7b/3
Ball deliberately deflected or stopped on putting green by fellow-competitor	19-1/5
Ball dropped in area where original ball lost; ball then played	27-1/3

RULE(S) (Continued)

Whether serious breach of Rules occurs if
(Continued)

Ball dropped outside bunker under option
of unplayable ball Rule requiring drop in
bunker — 28/10

Ball knocked out of bunker by fellow-
competitor's stroke at own ball not
replaced — 18-4/2

Ball played from spot where original ball
deflected out of bounds by maintenance
vehicle — 20-7/1

Opponent or fellow-competitor attending
flagstick for player fails to remove it — 17-3/2

Player plays second shot, declares ball
unplayable and returns to tee — 28/6

Player proceeding under lateral water
hazard Rule drops ball nearer hole than is
permissible — 26-1/21

Water hazard treated as lateral water hazard — 26-1/11

SAND — See also "HAZARD"

Ball covered by sand in bunker removed from
buried lie during search — 12-1/2

Lie through the green improved when sand
behind ball removed by backswing — 13-2/9

Player's lie affected by sand from partner's,
opponent's or fellow-competitor's stroke
from bunker — 13-2/8.5

Removing sand or loose soil from dropping
area — 13-2/11

Searching with clubhead for ball covered by
sand in bunker — 12-1/1

**SCORES AND SCORE CARDS — See also
"MARKER"**

Making competitors responsible for adding
scores — 33-1/7

Minus or zero net score — 2-1/2

Record score — Misc./1

Recording scores -

Competitor in four-ball stroke play records
score for hole not completed — 31-7a/1

Competitor's scores recorded on fellow-
competitor's card and vice versa — 6-6d/4

Gross score of partner with better net score
omitted from card — 31-4/1

Hole scores for first nine holes recorded in
boxes for second nine and vice versa — 6-6d/3

Hole scores recorded in wrong boxes; marker
corrects error by altering hole numbers on
card — 6-6a/3

In a four-ball Stableford competition on
handicap basis side's scores transposed at
a hole to side's advantage — 32-2a/2

SCORES AND SCORE CARDS (Continued)

Recording scores (Continued)

Lower gross score attributed to wrong partner	31-7a/2
No score recorded for one hole but total correct	6-6d/1
Requirement that alteration on score card be initialled	6-6a/6

Returning card -

Duplicate card returned when original lost	6-6a/7
Score card not returned promptly due to Committee failure to advise competitors where to return cards	6-6b/4

Score cards in sudden-death play-off	33-5/1

Signing card -

Competitor and marker sign score card in wrong places	6-6b/1
Competitor fails to sign first-round card; error discovered on completion of last round	6-6b/3
Competitor records initials in space reserved for signature	6-6b/2
Competitor's failure to countersign card blamed on lack of time provided by Committee	33-7/3
Competitor's failure to countersign card discovered after competition closed	34-1b/2
Marker not appointed by Committee signs cards	6-6b/5
Signing of score card in foursome stroke play	29/6

Winner's score not posted due to Committee error	34-1b/6

Wrong score -

Competitor correctly advised by fellow-competitor that he had incurred a penalty disagrees with fellow-competitor and fails to include penalty in his score; Committee advised of incident after competition had closed	34-1b/1.5
Competitor unaware of penalty returns wrong score; whether waiving or modifying disqualification penalty justified	33-7/4.5
Corrected by competitor after marker leaves area in which card returned	6-6b/7
Marker attests wrong score knowingly -	
Competitor aware score wrong	1-3/6
Competitor unaware score wrong	6-6a/5
Modifying penalty for returning wrong score	33-7/4
Omission of penalty stroke when score returned	34-1b/1
Omission of penalty strokes when score returned is due to incorrect ruling	34-3/1

SCORES AND SCORE CARDS (Continued)
Wrong score (Continued)
Player who has advanced in match is disqualified for wrong score in qualifying round — 34-1b/8
Spectators allege competitor's score incorrect — 6-6d/5
Total score recorded by competitor incorrect — 6-6d/2
Wrong score in qualifying round discovered during match play — 34-1b/7

SEARCHING FOR BALL — See "LOST BALL"

SNAKE
Ball at rest near rattlesnake — 1-4/10
Status of snake — 18/4

SPIKE MARK
Competitor sanctions repair of spike damage on his line of putt by fellow-competitor — 13-2/36
Opponent or fellow-competitor creates or eliminates spike marks on player's line of putt — 1-2/1
Player and opponent or fellow-competitor agree to repair spike marks on one another's line of putt — 1-3/3
Repair of spike mark damage around hole — 16-1c/4
Spike mark on line of putt repaired during repair of ball mark — 16-1a/16

SPORTSMANSHIP
Local Rule for breach of sportsmanship code — US/33-8/101

STABLEFORD COMPETITION
Breach of Rule by both partners at same hole in four-ball Stableford — 32-2b/1
Competing simultaneously in Stableford competition and stroke play competition — 32-1/1
Determination of honor in handicap Stableford competition — 32-1/3
In four-ball Stableford competition on handicap basis side's scores transposed at a hole but not to side's advantage — 32-2a/1
In a four-ball Stableford competition on handicap basis side's scores transposed at a hole to side's advantage — 32-2a/2
Omitting holes in Stableford competition — 32-1/2

STAKES
Defining out of bounds -
Ball lifted and dropped away from boundary stake under obstruction Rule — 18-2a/3
Boundary altered by unauthorized removal of boundary stake — 33-2a/19
Boundary stakes having no significance in play of hole being played — 24/5
Displaced boundary stake — 33-2a/20

STAKES (Continued)
  Defining out of bounds (Continued)
    Identifying   33-2a/18
    Player removes boundary post on line of
      play but replaces it before playing   13-2/25
    Removal of boundary stake interfering with
      swing   13-2/17
  Defining water hazard -
    Ball within natural margin of water hazard
      but outside stakes defining margin   26/2
    Hole of removed stake; status   25/18
    Local Rule providing relief from immovable
      water hazard stake for ball lying in water
      hazard   33-8/15
    Where to place stakes   33-2a/4
  Local Rule deeming all stakes on course to be
    immovable obstructions   33-8/16
  Stake supporting tree broken in attempt to
    remove it   13-2/16

STANCE
  Ball moves after player grounds club but
    before stance completed   18-2b/4
  Ball moving after stance taken but before
    address   18-2b/1
  Building -
    Player builds stance but corrects error before
      playing stroke   13-3/5
    Whether stance has been built if -
      Player knocks down side of bunker to get
        level stance   13-3/3
      Player plays stroke while kneeling on
        towel   13-3/2
      Player stands on mat on teeing ground   13-3/1
  Explanation of "fairly taking his stance"   13-2/1
  In hazard — See "HAZARD: Stance"

STARTING — See "TIME OF STARTING"

STEPS
  Wooden or earthen steps; status   24/12

STIPULATED ROUND
  Competitors play two holes not included in
    stipulated round   3/2
  Hole omitted in match by mistake   2-3/2
  Hole omitted in match purposely   2-3/3
  Holes played out of sequence in match   2-3/4
  Number of holes reduced after play has
    commenced   33-1/2
  Responsibility for knowing   11-5/2
  Starting players from 1st and 10th tees   33-1/3

STONE
  Ball moved by stone dislodged by partner's or
    opponent's stroke   18-1/8

STONE (Continued)

Ball outside bunker; stone in bunker on line of play pressed down or removed   13-2/31

Broken away from retaining wall in water hazard; status   24/6

Improving line of play by removing stone from wall   13-2/32

Large stone removable only with much effort   23-1/2

Serving as part of drain in bunker; status   24/7

Touching solidly embedded stone in hazard with club during backswing   13-4/6

STRIKING THE BALL

In anger player strikes ball played by player in following group   1-4/4

Whether ball fairly struck at if -

   Ball lying against fence moved by striking other side of fence   14-1/5

   Ball struck with billiard-type motion   14-1/2

   Ball struck with half an inch backswing   14-1/4

   Ball struck with wrong end of putter   14-1/3

   More than one club used to make stroke   14-1/7

   Player holds club with left hand and moves ball by striking shaft with other hand   14-1/6

   Stroke played with back of clubhead   14-1/1

Whether ball struck more than once if - Ball falls on clubface after stroke and sticks to mud thereon   14-4/1

   Ball strikes pipeline and on rebound is deflected by face of club   14-4/2

STROKE— See also "STRIKING THE BALL"

Ball adhering to face of club after stroke   1-4/2

Ball falls on club face after stroke and sticks to mud thereon   14-4/1

Bird's nest interferes   1-4/9

Caddie shields player from sun during stroke   14-2/3

Player aligns partner's club before stroke   14-2/1

Player holds umbrella over own head when playing stroke   14-2/2

Player plays stroke at part of abandoned ball which had broken into pieces   15/3

Stroke at own ball dislodges concealed ball   15/2

Stroke misses ball which is then accidentally knocked off tee after being addressed   11-3/1

Stroke misses wrong ball   15/1

Stroke played with ball lying out of bounds   15/6

Whether stroke taken if -

   Ball knocked from lip of hole in disgust   18-2a/23

   Ball moved accidentally by backward movement of club after stroke misses   18-2a/22

   Ball moved accidentally by practice swing -

     Prior to tee shot   18-2a/19

     When ball in play   18-2a/20

   Ball popped up is swung at in disgust   14/6

STROKE (Continued)
  Whether stroke taken if (Continued)
    Club breaks during backswing; swing
      completed   14/2
    Club breaks during downswing; swing
      completed but misses ball; clubhead falls
      and moves ball   14/5
    Club breaks during downswing; swing
      stopped short of ball; clubhead falls and
      moves ball   14/4
    Club stopped on downswing by agency
      other than player   14/1
    Clubhead separates from shaft on
      downswing   14/3
    In foursome, player misses ball accidentally
      when making stroke   29-1/6
    Intent to strike ball ceases during
      downswing; club not stopped but path of
      clubhead altered to avoid striking ball   14/1.5
    Player misses ball purposely in foursome so
      partner would play ball over water   29-1/7
    Player strikes at tree branch to move ball
      lodged higher in branch   14/7

STROKE PLAY —See also "BOGEY
  COMPETITIONS, FOUR-BALL STROKE
  PLAY, FOURSOMES and STABLEFORD
  COMPETITIONS"
  Competitor disqualified from handicap event
    claims gross prize   33-1/13
  Competitor plays with two players engaged in
    match   33-1/5
  Competitors play two holes not included in
    stipulated round   3/2
  Disqualification in play-off   3/1
  Doubt as to procedure -
    Ball dropped and played under water
      hazard Rule; original ball then found in
      hazard and holed out as second ball   26-1/5
    Ball dropped in wrong place and played;
      Rule 3-3 then invoked and second ball
      dropped in right place; both balls played
      out   3-3/3
    Ball dropped in wrong place but not played;
      Rule 3-3 then invoked and second ball
      dropped in right place; both balls played
      out   3-3/4
    Competitor picks up second ball   3-3/8
    Competitor plays original ball after doubtful
      situation has arisen and then invokes Rule
      3-3   3-3/6
    Competitor plays second ball without
      announcing intention to invoke Rule 3-3
      and fails to report facts to Committee   3-3/6.5
    Competitor plays three balls when doubtful
      of rights   3-3/10

STROKE PLAY (Continued)

Doubt as to procedure (Continued)

Guidelines for determining which ball counts when player proceeds under Rule 3-3.   3-3/0.5

Original ball strikes second ball or vice versa   3-3/7

Procedure if both original and second balls dropped in wrong place and played   3-3/5.5

Provisional ball used as second ball when not determinable whether original ball is out of bounds   3-3/1

Second ball played despite adverse ruling   3-3/2

Whether score with second ball counts if ball dropped in wrong place and played   3-3/5

Wrong ball played in belief it is second ball   15/7

Failure to hole out -

Ball blown into hole by competitor not replaced and holed out   3-2/2

Ball played from putting green deflected into hole by moving outside agency; stroke not replayed   19-1/3

Competitor in error does not hole out; error corrected before playing from next tee   3-2/3

Competitor picks up second ball   3-3/8

Fellow-competitor's ball knocked from lip of hole by competitor not replaced   3-2/1

Modifying penalty for not holing out   33-7/2

Player who putts with one hand and catches ball in hole with other hand does not place ball on lip of hole and hole out   1-2/5

Guidelines on whether to cancel round   33-2d/1

Holes relocated and/or tee-markers moved during round   33-2b/1

How to settle tie   33-6/2

Number of holes of competition reduced during competition   33-1/2

One player in match competes concurrently in stroke play competition   33-1/6

Play-off — See "PLAY-OFF"

Scoring — See "SCORES AND SCORE CARDS"

SUSPENSION OF PLAY

Asking advice when play suspended   8-1/20

Ball moved by wind or casual water while play suspended   18-1/11

Ball visible from tee disappears or is moved while play suspended   18-1/2

Competitors playing hole when play suspended discontinue play immediately but then complete hole before Committee orders resumption of play   6-8b/1

Completion of hole by one competitor in group after play suspended during play of hole   6-8b/3

Local Rule for suspension of play due to dangerous situation   US/33-8/102

SUSPENSION OF PLAY (Continued)

Options if play suspended after one competitor in group has played from tee — 6-8b/2

Play suspended by Committee; competitor does not resume play at time ordered by Committee — 6-8b/6

Player claiming danger from lightning refuses to resume play when resumption ordered by Committee — 6-8b/5

Player unable to resume suspended match at scheduled time — 6-8b/4

Playing characteristics of club changed while play suspended; error discovered before play resumed — 4-2/2

Replacement of club broken on practice ground while play suspended — 4-4a/6.5

Whether play should be suspended if hole surrounded by casual water — 33-2d/2

Whether play should be suspended if casual water covers teeing ground — 25-1b/4

TEEING GROUND

Ball falling off tee when stroke just touches it is picked up and re-teed — 18-2a/2

Ball moved accidentally by practice swing — 18-2a/19

Ball played out of turn from tee in stroke play abandoned and another ball played in proper order — 10-2c/1

Both player and partner drive at same tee in foursome play — 29-1/9

Breaking branch interfering with backswing on teeing ground — 13-2/14

Breaking off grass behind ball on teeing ground — 13-2/3

Casual water covering teeing ground — 25-1b/4

Changing partners in foursome match after driving from first tee — 29/1

Lifting ball in play but still within teeing ground — 11-3/2

Map of putting green indicating hole position displayed at tee — 33/6

Mixed foursome in which different tees used by men and women; tee shot out of bounds — 29/2

Original ball found within five minutes after another ball teed — 27-1/1

Original ball out of bounds; ball played under stroke-and-distance procedure falls off tee at address — 11-3/3

Player who misses tee shot presses down irregularities before next stroke — 13-2/2

Player who misses tee shot tees ball lower before playing next stroke — 18-2a/1

Players agree not to tee off in prescribed order to save time — 1-3/1

Playing from wrong -see "WRONG TEEING GROUND"

TEEING GROUND (Continued)

Playing outside -
Ball played from outside teeing ground goes
out of bounds   11-4b/6

Ball played from outside teeing ground in
foursome match   29-1/1

Competitor plays from outside teeing
ground in foursome stroke play; partner
replays stroke   29-1/2

Dispute as to whether competitor played
from outside teeing ground   34-3/4

Standing on mat on teeing ground   13-3/1

Starting players from 1st and 10th tees   33-1/3

Stroke misses ball; ball then accidentally
knocked off tee   11-3/1

Tee decreed to be in bounds for tee shot and
out of bounds thereafter   33-2a/13

Teed ball missed then hit out of bounds   20-5/1

Tee-markers -
Competitors determine spot from which to
play from tee when both tee-markers are
missing   11-4b/3

Competitors estimate area of teeing ground
when one tee-marker missing   11-4b/2

Holes relocated and/or tee-markers moved
during stroke play round   33-2b/1

Player alters teeing ground by relocating
tee-marker   11-2/2

Status after first stroke   11-2/1

THREE-BALL MATCH

Player concedes hole after which one opponent
plays wrong ball   2-4/10

Player plays out of turn from tee; one opponent
requests replay and other does not   30-2/1

TIES

Determining winner and positions in stroke
play play-off   33-6/3

Groupings for stroke play play-off   33-3/4

How to settle tie in handicap match   33-6/1

How to settle tie in stroke play   33-6/2

Players decide method of settling tie when
Committee fails to do so   33-6/4

TIME OF STARTING

All competitors must be present   6-3a/2

Competitor refuses to start because of weather
conditions; round subsequently cancelled   33-2d/3

Competitors determining own groupings and
starting times   33-3/3

Player not present at time of starting; course
closed at the time   33-3/2

Player unable to resume suspended match at
scheduled time   6-8b/4

TIME OF STARTING (Continued)
Postponement of final match due to injury of player — 6-3a/1
Status of starting time fixed by players — 33-3/1

TOWEL
Blows onto and moves ball — 18-2a/17
Loose impediments removed from line of putt with towel — 16-1a/8
Playing stroke while kneeling on towel — 13-3/2
Removing towel covering another player's clubs to determine club used — 8-1/11

TREE
Ball dislodged from tree -
By outside agency — 18-1/9
By striking at tree branch to move ball lodged higher in branch — 14/7
Circumstances in which player not penalized — 18-2a/27
Circumstances in which player penalized — 18-2a/28
Replacement of ball not possible — 18-2a/29
When player climbs tree to play stroke — 18-2a/26
Ball in fork of tree moves in relation to ground but not in relation to fork — 18/3
Ball in tree identified but not retrieved — 27/14
Ball in tree visible but not identifiable — 27/15
Ball lost in tree in ground under repair — 25/10
Ball unplayable in tree and player opts to drop within two club-lengths — 28/11
Branch broken on backswing and swing discontinued — 13-2/14.5
Breaking branch interfering with backswing on teeing ground — 13-2/14
Caddie holds back branch to prevent it from deflecting dropped ball — 20-2a/5
Dropped ball strikes tree branch then ground; whether re-drop required — 20-2c/1.3
Local Rule — See " LOCAL RULE: Trees"
Shaking water from tree branch interfering with backswing — 13-2/23
Stake supporting tree broken in attempt to remove it — 13-2/16
Status of -
Fallen tree — 23/7
Fallen tree attached to stump lying in fairway — 25/9
Fallen tree in process of being removed — 25/7
Moss in tree — 13-2/37
Tree basins — 33-2/10.5
Tree in bunker — 13/2
Tree stump — 25/8

UMBRELLA
Employment of umbrella carrier in addition to caddie — 6-4/5
Holding over own head when playing stroke — 14-2/2

UMBRELLA (Continued)
Placing in hazard before stroke — 13-4/20

UNDUE DELAY
Whether the Rule prohibiting undue delay is breached if -
Player ascertains whereabouts of opponent's ball before playing — 9-2/16
Player requests another player to lift her ball in absence of reasonable possibility that ball might interfere or assist — 22/3
Player returns to tee to retrieve forgotten club — 6-7/1
Player searches for lost ball after putting another ball into play — 27/9
Player searches ten minutes for lost ball — 6-7/2
Removal of large loose impediment delays play — 23-1/2
Second ball played despite adverse ruling — 3-3/2

UNPLAYABLE BALL — See "BALL: Unplayable"

WALL
Improving line of play by removing stone from wall — 13-2/32
Local Rule deeming ball in bounds until beyond boundary wall — 33-2a/16

WATER HAZARD — See also "HAZARD"
Ball apparently in water hazard found outside hazard after another ball played under stroke-and-distance procedure — 26/7
Ball assumed to be in water hazard found outside hazard after another ball played under stroke-and-distance procedure — 26/6
Ball declared unplayable in water hazard is dropped in hazard and played — 20-7/2
Ball dropped and played under water hazard Rule; original ball then found in hazard and holed out as second ball — 26-1/5
Ball lost in either water hazard or casual water overflowing hazard — 1-4/7
Ball moved into bounds by flow of water in water hazard — 26-1/8
Ball moved out of bounds by flow of water in water hazard — 26-1/7
Ball moving in water after address played while moving — 14-6/1
Ball played back into water hazard from putting green side of hazard — 26-1/6
Ball played under water hazard Rule; original ball then found outside hazard — 26-1/3
Ball played under water hazard Rule without reasonable evidence original ball in hazard; original ball then found in hazard — 26-1/4

WATER HAZARD (Continued)

Caddie lifts ball without player's authority 26-1/9

Casual water mistaken for water hazard; original ball played under water hazard Rule 25-1b/12

Casual water mistaken for water hazard; substituted ball played under water hazard Rule 25-1b/13

Changing relief option when re-dropping required 20-2c/5

Deeming body of water as both water hazard and lateral water hazard 33-2a/7

Explanation of options under Rules 26-2a and -2b 26-2/1

Hazard marked as water hazard where ball last crosses margin and as lateral hazard where ball comes to rest 26-1/12

Lateral -

  Clarification of "opposite margin" in Rule 26-1c(ii) 26-1/14

  Dropped ball rolling out of prescribed dropping area 20-2c/1

  Example of serious breach of lateral water hazard Rule 26-1/21

  Impossible to drop not nearer hole than point where ball last crossed margin 26-1/18

  Local Rule treating rough as lateral water hazard 33-8/35

  Opposite side of lateral water hazard defined as water hazard 26-1/13

  Order of play when two balls are lost in lateral water hazard 10/3

  Order of play when two balls lie in lateral water hazard and both players take relief 10/2

  Permissible dropping area so narrow player has difficulty dropping within it 26-1/19

  Point where ball last crossed margin determined and ball dropped and played; point then proves to be wrong point 26-1/17

  Point where ball last crossed margin determined and ball dropped; point then proves to be wrong point 26-1/16

  Procedures for relief 26-1/15

  Whether river forming part of course boundary should be defined as lateral water hazard 33-2a/11

Local Rule - see "LOCAL RULE: Water Hazard"

Man-made reservoir; status 26/4

Meaning of "reasonable evidence" in Rule 26-1 26-1/1

Overflow from water hazard; status 25/2

Placing ball on bank of water hazard instead of dropping to prevent ball rolling into water 26-1/10

Player proceeding under water hazard Rule drops ball in another hazard 26-1/2

WATER HAZARD (Continued)

Player substitutes another ball on putting green because original ball thrown to caddie for cleaning came to rest in lake — 15-1/6

Player who told opponent he would proceed under water hazard Rule changes mind after opponent plays — 9-2/13

Players inadvertently exchange balls recovered from water hazard — 15-1/4

Possibility that original ball in water hazard may not preclude play of provisional ball — 27-2c/1

Provisional ball played solely in belief original ball might be in water hazard — 27-2a/2

Provisional ball serving as ball in play if original ball in water hazard — 27-2/1

Stakes or lines defining margin — See "STAKES: Defining water hazard"

Stone broken away from retaining wall in water hazard — 24/6

Treated as lateral water hazard — 26-1/11

Treating ocean and beach as through the green — 33-2a/8

Under repair — 33-2a/5

Unidentifiable ball played in water hazard and lost — 26/5

When ball deemed to touch water hazard — 26/1

When water hazard is automatically lateral hazard — 26/3

WIND

Ball at rest moved by blowing tumbleweed — 18-1/6

Ball in plastic bag moves when bag blown to new position by wind — 18-1/7

Ball moved by wind replaced — 18-2a/7

Ball moved by wind while play suspended — 18-1/11

Ball replaced and at rest is thereafter moved by wind — 18-1/12

Moves ball-marker off green — 20-1/10

Shielding line of putt from wind — 1-2/2

Towel dropped by player is blown onto and moves ball — 18-2a/17

WORM

Status of worm partially underground — 23/8

WRONG BALL

Ball in bunker deemed unplayable, dropped in bunker and played; ball then discovered to be wrong ball — 15/14

Ball moved accidentally by player in playing wrong ball — 18-2a/21

Ball moved by wrong ball played by opponent — 18-5/1

Balls inadvertently exchanged by competitors at unknown place — 15-1/2

Competitor plays wrong ball and loses it; wrong ball may have been fellow-competitor's ball — 15-3/1

WRONG BALL (Continued)

Competitor's ball played by fellow-competitor; competitor substitutes another ball at wrong place, plays it and then abandons it and plays out original ball from right place — 20-7b/5

Competitor's ball played by fellow-competitor in bunker not replaced — 18-4/1

Declared unplayable and played under stroke-and-distance procedure; original ball then found — 28/14

Declared unplayable, dropped within two club-lengths and played before error discovered — 28/15

Dropped under unplayable ball Rule but not played — 15/13

Found out of bounds and played under stroke-and-distance procedure; original ball then found in bounds — 15/12

Hit out of bounds; another ball played under Rule 27-1; original ball then found nearby — 15/11

Hole at which wrong ball played unknown — 15-1/3

Order of play in foursome stroke play when wrong ball played — 29-1/8

Play of two different wrong balls between strokes with ball in play — 15-3/2

Play of wrong ball not rectified; error discovered after competition closed — 34-1b/3

Play of wrong ball not rectified on advice of Committee member — 33-7/5

Played in belief it is provisional or second ball — 15/7

Player concedes hole after which it is discovered opponent's last stroke was played with a wrong ball from a hazard — 2-4/9.5

Player concedes hole after which it is discovered that opponent had played wrong ball — 2-4/9

Player concedes hole after which opponent plays wrong ball — 2-4/10

Player discovers own ball in hole after playing wrong ball — 1-1/4

Player discovers own ball in hole after playing wrong ball; opponent claims hole and claim not disputed — 2-5/5

Player plays partner's ball — 30-3d/1

Player plays partner's ball; error discovered after opponents have played next strokes — 30-3d/3.5

Player unable to find his ball because another player played it — 27/6

Player wins hole with own ball after playing wrong ball; opponent lodges belated claim — 2-5/4

Player wins hole with wrong ball and partner picks up; error discovered at next hole — 30-3d/2

Player wins hole with wrong ball; error discovered at next hole — 9-2/8

WRONG BALL (Continued)

Players on opposite sides exchange balls during play of hole and their partners pick up; error discovered at next hole — 30-3d/3

Status as wrong ball of -

Ball changed during play of hole to aid identification — 15/6.5

Ball dropped and played under ground under repair Rule in absence of reasonable evidence original ball lost in ground under repair — 25-1c/2

Ball found after search exceeding five minutes which is then played — 27/8

Ball lifted, set aside and played from where set aside — 15/4

Ball played by player in following group hit by player in anger — 1-4/4

Ball played from out of bounds — 15/6

Ball played under Rule for ball lost in ground under repair after another ball played under stroke-and-distance procedure — 15/8

Ball played under water hazard Rule if original ball then found outside hazard — 26-1/3

Ball played under water hazard Rule without reasonable evidence original ball in hazard if original ball then found in hazard — 26-1/4

Ball substituted for lost original ball when player treats original ball as moved by outside agency in absence of reasonable evidence that ball moved by outside agency — 27-1/2.5

Ball thrown into bounds by outside agency and played — 15/9, 15/10

Balls inadvertently exchanged by players between holes — 15-1/1

Competitor's ball played from where set aside by fellow-competitor who lifted it — 15-3/3

Concealed ball dislodged by player's stroke at own ball — 15/2

Concealed ball dislodged by practice swing — 7-2/7

Original ball found and played after another ball put into play — 15/5

Original ball played after provisional ball played from point nearer hole than original ball likely to be — 27-2b/5

Part of abandoned ball which had broken into pieces — 15/3

Provisional ball played from point nearer hole than original ball because player erroneously thought original ball, which was visible, was out of bounds — 27-2c/3

Second ball played in match play — 3-3/9

WRONG BALL (Continued)
  Status as wrong ball of (Continued)
    Substituted ball played under water hazard
      Rule when original ball was in casual
      water 25-1b/13
    Stroke misses wrong ball 15/1
    Time permitted for search for lost ball after
      wrong ball played 27/2

WRONG INFORMATION
  After play of hole; when penalty applicable 9-2/15
  Causes opponent to lift his ball-marker 9-2/5
  Causes opponent with chance for half to pick
    up ball 9-2/6
  Competitor in sudden-death play-off gives
    wrong information 9-2/17
  Discovered after match conceded by opponent
    but before result announced 9-2/10
  Discovered several holes later 9-2/9
  Given after play of last hole; claim made after
    result of match announced 2-5/11
  Given as result of failure to report penalty -
    By player out of contention in four-ball
      match 30-3f/4
    Opponent lodges belated claim even though
      he was aware of act which resulted in
      penalty 2-4/15, 2-5/4
    Player wins hole with wrong ball and
      partner picks up; error discovered at next
      hole 30-3d/2
    Player wins hole with wrong ball; error
      discovered at next hole and opponent
      lodges claim 9-2/8
    Player wins match; breach of 14-club rule
      discovered before result announced 2-5/5.5
    Player's ball resting against flagstick lifted
      before being holed; others in four-ball
      match pick up mistakenly believing player
      won hole 30-3f/3
    Players on opposite sides exchange balls
      during play of hole and their partners
      pick up; error discovered at next hole 30-3d/3
  Given by caddie or partner 9-2/2
  Given by player; corrected before opponent
    plays next stroke but after opponent has
    conceded player's putt 9-2/7
  Giving voluntarily on strokes taken 9-2/3
  What constitutes wrong information 9-2/12
  Whether incorrect information on Rules is
    wrong information 9/1
  Whether wrong information given if -
    In foursome side drives for three holes
      in wrong order and does not inform
      opponents about penalty 29-2/2

WRONG INFORMATION (Continued)
Whether wrong information given if
(Continued)
Player concluding he played wrong ball
when opponent misread number on
player's ball concedes hole 9-2/11
Player plays partner's ball; error discovered
after opponents have played next strokes 30-3d/3.5
Player who told opponent he would proceed
under water hazard Rule changes mind
after opponent plays 9-2/13
Winner of match due to wrong information by
opponent makes no claim and loses in extra
holes 2-5/7

**WRONG PLACE — See "PLAYING FROM
WRONG PLACE"**

**WRONG PUTTING GREEN — See "PUTTING
GREEN: Wrong putting green"**

WRONG TEEING GROUND
Ball played from teeing ground of hole to be
played later in round lifted; ball replaced at
spot from which lifted and played out when
that hole subsequently reached 11-5/5
Ball played from wrong teeing ground in
stroke play; error corrected 11-5/4
Ball played out of bounds from wrong teeing
ground not recalled 11-5/3
Explanation of "next teeing ground" when
competitors have played from wrong teeing
ground 11-5/1
Use of wrong teeing ground attributable to
Committee failure to indicate hole numbers
on teeing grounds 11-5/2

THE RULES OF GOLF

Section I
ETIQUETTE

Courtesy on the Course

Safety

Prior to playing a stroke or making a practice swing, the player should ensure that no one is standing close by or in a position to be hit by the club, the ball or any stones, pebbles, twigs or the like which may be moved by the stroke or swing.

Consideration for Other Players

The player who has the honor should be allowed to play before his opponent or fellow-competitor tees his ball.

No one should move, talk or stand close to or directly behind the ball or the hole when a player is addressing the ball or making a stroke.

In the interest of all, players should play without delay.

No player should play until the players in front are out of range.

Players searching for a ball should signal the players behind them to pass as soon as it becomes apparent that the ball will not easily be found. They should not search for five minutes before doing so. They should not continue play until the players following them have passed and are out of range.

When the play of a hole has been completed, players should immediately leave the putting green.

Priority on the Course

In the absence of special rules, two-ball matches should have precedence over and be entitled to pass any three- or four-ball match, which should invite them through.

A single player has no standing and should give way to a match of any kind.

Any match playing a whole round is entitled to pass a match playing a shorter round.

If a match fails to keep its place on the course and loses more than one clear hole on the players in front, it should invite the match following to pass.

Care of the Course

Holes in Bunkers

Before leaving a bunker, a player should carefully fill up and smooth over all holes and footprints made by him.

Replace Divots; Repair Ball-Marks and Damage by Spikes

Through the green, a player should ensure that any turf cut or displaced by him is replaced at once and pressed down and that any damage to the putting green made by a ball is carefully repaired. Damage to the putting green caused by golf shoe spikes should be repaired *on completion of the hole*.

Damage to Greens — Flagsticks, Bags, etc.

Players should ensure that, when putting down bags or the flagstick, no damage is done to the putting green and that neither they nor their caddies damage the hole by standing close to it, in handling the flagstick or in removing the ball from the hole. The flagstick should be properly replaced in the hole before the players leave the putting green. Players should not damage the putting green by leaning on their putters, particularly when removing the ball from the hole.

Golf Carts

Local notices regulating the movement of golf carts should be strictly observed.

Damage Through Practice Swings

In taking practice swings, players should avoid causing damage to the course, particularly the tees, by removing divots.

Section II
DEFINITIONS

Addressing the Ball

A player has "addressed the ball" when he has taken his <u>stance</u> and has also grounded his club, except that in a <u>hazard</u> a player has addressed the ball when he has taken his stance.

Advice

"Advice" is any counsel or suggestion which could influence a player in determining his play, the choice of a club or the method of making a <u>stroke</u>.

Information on the Rules or on matters of public information, such as the position of hazards or the flagstick on the putting green, is not advice.

Ball Deemed to Move

See "Move or Moved."

Ball Holed

See "Holed."

Ball Lost

See "Lost Ball."

Ball in Play

A ball is "in play" as soon as the player has made a <u>stroke</u> on the <u>teeing ground</u>. It remains in play until holed out, except when it is <u>lost</u>, <u>out of bounds</u> or lifted, or another ball has been substituted under an applicable Rule, whether or not such Rule permits substitution; a ball so substituted becomes the ball in play.

Bunker

A "bunker" is a <u>hazard</u> consisting of a prepared area of ground, often a hollow, from which turf or soil has been removed and replaced with sand or the like. Grass-covered ground bordering or within a bunker is not part of the bunker. The margin of a bunker extends vertically downwards, but not upwards.

Caddie

A "caddie" is one who carries or handles a player's clubs during play and otherwise assists him in accordance with the Rules.

When one caddie is employed by more than one player, he is always deemed to be the caddie of the player whose ball is involved, and <u>equipment</u> carried by him is deemed to be that player's equipment, except when the caddie acts upon specific directions of another player, in which case he is considered to be that other player's caddie.

Casual Water

"Casual water" is any temporary accumulation of water on the <u>course</u> which is visible before or after the player takes his <u>stance</u> and is not in a <u>water hazard</u>. Snow and natural ice, other than frost, are either casual water or <u>loose</u> <u>impediments,</u> at the option of the player. Manufactured ice is an <u>obstruction.</u> Dew and frost are not casual water.

Committee

The "Committee" is the committee in charge of the competition or, if the matter does not arise in a competition, the committee in charge of the <u>course</u>.

Competitor

A "competitor" is a player in a stroke competition. A "fellow-competitor" is any person with whom the competitor plays. Neither is <u>partner</u> of the other.

In stroke play foursome and four-ball competitions, where the context so admits, the word "competitor" or "fellow-competitor" includes his partner.

Course

The "course" is the whole area within which play is permitted. See Rule 33-2.

Equipment

"Equipment" is anything used, worn or carried by or for the player except any ball he has played at the hole being played and any small object, such as a coin or a tee, when used to mark the position of a ball or the extent of an area in which a ball is to be dropped. Equipment includes a golf cart, whether or not motorized. If such a cart is shared by two or more players, the cart and everything in it are deemed to be the equipment of the player whose ball is involved except that, when the cart is being moved by one of the players sharing it, the cart and everything in it are deemed to be that player's equipment.

Note: A ball played at the hole being played is equipment when it has been lifted and not put back into play.

Fellow-Competitor
See "Competitor."

Flagstick
The "flagstick" is a movable straight indicator, with or without bunting or other material attached, centered in the hole to show its position. It shall be circular in cross-section.

Forecaddie
A "forecaddie" is one who is employed by the Committee to indicate to players the position of balls during play. He is an <u>outside agency</u>.

Ground Under Repair
"Ground under repair" is any portion of the <u>course</u> so marked by order of the Committee or so declared by its authorized representative. It includes material piled for removal and a hole made by a greenkeeper, even if not so marked. Stakes and lines defining ground under repair are in such ground. The margin of ground under repair extends vertically downwards, but not upwards.

Note 1: Grass cuttings and other material left on the course which have been abandoned and are not intended to be removed are not ground under repair unless so marked.

Note 2: The Committee may make a Local Rule prohibiting play from ground under repair.

Hazards
A "hazard" is any <u>bunker</u> or <u>water hazard</u>.

Hole
The "hole" shall be $4\frac{1}{4}$ inches (108mm) in diameter and at least 4 inches (100mm) deep. If a lining is used, it shall be sunk at least 1 inch (25mm) below the <u>putting green</u> surface unless the nature of the soil makes it impracticable to do so; its outer diameter shall not exceed $4\frac{1}{4}$ inches (108mm).

Holed
A ball is "holed" when it is at rest within the circumference of the hole and all of it is below the level of the lip of the hole.

Honor

The side entitled to play first from the <u>teeing ground</u> is said to have the "honor."

Lateral Water Hazard

A "lateral water hazard" is a <u>water hazard</u> or that part of a water hazard so situated that it is not possible or is deemed by the Committee to be impracticable to drop a ball behind the water hazard in accordance with Rule 26-1b.

That part of a water hazard to be played as a lateral water hazard should be distinctively marked.

Note: Lateral water hazards should be defined by red stakes or lines.

Line of Play

The "line of play" is the direction which the player wishes his ball to take after a stroke, plus a reasonable distance on either side of the intended direction. The line of play extends vertically upwards from the ground, but does not extend beyond the hole.

Line of Putt

The "line of putt" is the line which the player wishes his ball to take after a stroke on the putting green. Except with respect to Rule 16-1e, the line of putt includes a reasonable distance on either side of the intended line. The line of putt does not extend beyond the hole.

Loose Impediments

"Loose impediments" are natural objects such as stones, leaves, twigs, branches and the like, dung, worms and insects and casts or heaps made by them, provided they are not fixed or growing, are not solidly embedded and do not adhere to the ball.

Sand and loose soil are loose impediments on the <u>putting green</u>, but not elsewhere.

Snow and natural ice, other than frost, are either <u>casual water</u> or loose impediments, at the option of the player. Manufactured ice is an <u>obstruction</u>.

Dew and frost are not loose impediments.

Lost Ball

A ball is "lost" if:

a. It is not found or identified as his by the player

within five minutes after the player's side or his or their caddies have begun to search for it; or

b. The player has put another ball into play under the Rules, even though he may not have searched for the original ball; or

c. The player has played any stroke with a <u>provisional ball</u> from the place where the original ball is likely to be or from a point nearer the hole than that place, whereupon the provisional ball becomes the <u>ball in play</u>.

Time spent in playing a <u>wrong ball</u> is not counted in the five-minute period allowed for search.

Marker

A "marker" is one who is appointed by the Committee to record a <u>competitor's</u> score in stroke play. He may be a <u>fellow-competitor</u>. He is not a referee.

Matches

See "Sides and Matches."

Move or Moved

A ball is deemed to have "moved" if it leaves its position and comes to rest in any other place.

Observer

An "observer" is one who is appointed by the Committee to assist a <u>referee</u> to decide questions of fact and to report to him any breach of a Rule. An observer should not attend the flagstick, stand at or mark the position of the hole, or lift the ball or mark its position.

Obstructions

An "obstruction" is anything artificial, including the artificial surfaces and sides of roads and paths and manufactured ice, except:

a. Objects defining <u>out of bounds</u>, such as walls, fences, stakes and railings;

b. Any part of an immovable artificial object which is out of bounds; and

c. Any construction declared by the Committee to be an integral part of the course.

Out of Bounds

"Out of bounds" is ground on which play is prohibited.

When out of bounds is defined by reference to stakes or a fence or as being beyond stakes or a fence, the out of bounds line is determined by the nearest inside points of the stakes or fence posts at ground level excluding angled supports.

When out of bounds is defined by a line on the ground, the line itself is out of bounds.

The out of bounds line extends vertically upwards and downwards.

A ball is out of bounds when all of it lies out of bounds.

A player may stand out of bounds to play a ball lying within bounds.

Outside Agency

An "outside agency" is any agency not part of the match or, in stroke play, not part of the competitor's side, and includes a referee, a marker, an observer or a forecaddie. Neither wind nor water is an outside agency.

Partner

A "partner" is a player associated with another player on the same side.

In a threesome, foursome, best-ball or four-ball match, where the context so admits, the word "player" includes his partner or partners.

Penalty Stroke

A "penalty stroke" is one added to the score of a player or <u>side</u> under certain Rules. In a threesome or foursome, penalty strokes do not affect the order of play.

Provisional Ball

A "provisional ball" is a ball played under Rule 27-2 for a ball which may be <u>lost</u> outside a <u>water hazard</u> or may be <u>out of bounds</u>.

Putting Green

The "putting green" is all ground of the hole being played which is specially prepared for putting or otherwise defined as such by the Committee. A ball is on the putting green when any part of it touches the putting green.

Referee

A "referee" is one who is appointed by the Committee to accompany players to decide questions of fact and apply the Rules of Golf. He shall act on any breach of a Rule which he observes or is reported to him.

A referee should not attend the flagstick, stand at or mark the position of the hole, or lift the ball or mark its position.

Rub of the Green

A "rub of the green" occurs when a ball in motion is accidentally deflected or stopped by any <u>outside agency</u> (see Rule 19-1).

Rule

The term "Rule" includes Local Rules made by the Committee under Rule 33-8a.

Sides and Matches

Side: A player, or two or more players who are <u>partners</u>.

Single: A match in which one plays against another.

Threesome: A match in which one plays against two, and each side plays one ball.

Foursome: A match in which two play against two, and each side plays one ball.

Three-Ball: A match play competition in which three play against one another, each playing his own ball. Each player is playing two distinct matches.

Best-Ball: A match in which one plays against the better ball of two or the best ball of three players.

Four-Ball: A match in which two play their better ball against the better ball of two other players.

Stance

Taking the "stance" consists in a player placing his feet in position for and preparatory to making a <u>stroke</u>.

Stipulated Round

The "stipulated round" consists of playing the holes of the course in their correct sequence unless otherwise authorized by the Committee. The number of holes in a stipulated round is 18 unless a smaller number is authorized by the Committee. As to extension of stipulated round in match play, see Rule 2-3.

Stroke

A "stroke" is the forward movement of the club

made with the intention of fairly striking at and moving the ball, but if a player checks his downswing voluntarily before the clubhead reaches the ball he is deemed not to have made a stroke.

Teeing Ground

The "teeing ground" is the starting place for the hole to be played. It is a rectangular area two club-lengths in depth, the front and the sides of which are defined by the outside limits of two tee-markers. A ball is outside the teeing ground when all of it lies outside the teeing ground.

Through the Green

"Through the green" is the whole area of the course except:

a. The teeing ground and putting green of the hole being played; and

b. All hazards on the course.

Water Hazard

A "water hazard" is any sea, lake, pond, river, ditch, surface drainage ditch or other open water course (whether or not containing water) and anything of a similar nature.

All ground or water within the margin of a water hazard is part of the water hazard. The margin of a water hazard extends vertically upwards and downwards. Stakes and lines defining the margins of water hazards are in the hazards.

Note: Water hazards (other than lateral water hazards) should be defined by yellow stakes or lines.

Wrong Ball

A "wrong ball" is any ball other than:

a. The ball in play,

b. A provisional ball or

c. In stroke play, a second ball played under Rule 3-3 or Rule 20-7b.

Note: Ball in play includes a ball substituted for the ball in play when the player is proceeding under an applicable Rule which does not permit substitution.

Section III
THE RULES OF PLAY

THE GAME

Rule 1. The Game

1-1 General
The Game of Golf consists in playing a ball from the <u>teeing ground</u> into the hole by a <u>stroke</u> or successive strokes in accordance with the Rules.

1-2 Exerting Influence on Ball
No player or caddie shall take any action to influence the position or the movement of a ball except in accordance with the Rules.

> PENALTY FOR BREACH OF RULE 1-2:
> *Match play --- Loss of hole;*
> *Stroke play --- Two strokes.*

Note: In the case of a serious breach of Rule 1-2, the Committee may impose a penalty of disqualification.

1-3 Agreement to Waive Rules
Players shall not agree to exclude the operation of any Rule or to waive any penalty incurred.

> PENALTY FOR BREACH OF RULE 1-3:
> *Match play --- Disqualification*
> *of both sides; Stroke play ---*
> *Disqualification of competitors concerned.*

(Agreeing to play out of turn in stroke play — See Rule 10-2c.)

1-4 Points Not Covered by Rules
If any point in dispute is not covered by the Rules, the decision shall be made in accordance with equity.

1-1/1 Two Balls in Play Simultaneously at Different Holes

Q. Players on the 8th hole wish to play their approach shots to the 8th green, tee off at the 9th hole and then putt out on the 8th green. This is to avoid having to walk back up a hill to the 9th tee and to save time. Is it permissible?

A. No. Such procedure would be contrary to Rule 1-1 and the Definition of "Stipulated Round."

1-1/2 Player Unaware He Has Holed Out Puts Another Ball into Play

Q. A player, unable to find his ball, puts another ball into play. He then discovers that his original ball is in the hole. What is the ruling?

A. The score with the original ball counts. The play of the hole was completed when the player holed that ball.

1-1/3 Player Discovers Original Ball in Hole After Searching Five Minutes and Then Continuing Play with Provisional Ball

Q. At a par-3 hole, a player, believing his original ball may be lost, plays a provisional ball. He searches five minutes for the original ball and then plays the provisional ball onto the green. At that point, the original ball is found in the hole. What is the ruling?

A. The player's score is 1. The play of the hole was completed when the player holed the original ball (Rule 1-1).

1-1/4 Player Discovers Own Ball Is in Hole After Playing Wrong Ball

Q. A player played to a blind green and putted what he thought was his ball. He then discovered that his own ball was in the hole and that the ball he had putted was a wrong ball. What is the ruling?

A. Since the play of the hole was completed when the original ball was holed (Rule 1-1), the player was not in breach of Rule 15 for subsequently playing a wrong ball.

Player Discovers Own Ball in Hole After Playing Wrong Ball; Opponent Claims Hole and Claim Not Disputed — See 2-5/5.

Player with Lost Ball Concedes Hole; Ball Then Found in Hole — See 2-4/11.

1-2/1 Line of Putt Altered Purposely by Opponent or Fellow-Competitor by Stepping on It

Q. An opponent or a fellow-competitor purposely steps on the player's line of putt with the intention either of improving the line (*e.g.*, by pressing down a raised tuft of grass) or of damaging it (*e.g.*, by making spike marks). What is the ruling?

A. In either case, the opponent or the fellow-competitor was in breach of Rule 1-2. The penalty is loss of hole in match play or two strokes in stroke play, unless the Committee decides to impose a penalty of disqualification — See Note under Rule 1-2.

Competitor Sanctions Repair of Spike Damage on His Line of Putt by Fellow-Competitor — See 13-2/36.

Line of Putt Stepped on Accidentally by Opponent or Fellow-Competitor — See 16-1a/13.

Loose Impediments Brushed Along Line of Putt Rather Than to Side — See 16-1a/10.

Ball Lifted on Putting Green Placed Ahead of Ball-Marker and Then Moved Back to Original Position — See 16-1a/17.

Ball Mark in Position to Assist Opponent Repaired by Player — See 16-1c/2.

Placing Object Marking Position of Ball in Front of Ball — See 20-1/19.

1-2/2 Shielding Line of Putt from Wind

Q. May a player lay his golf bag parallel to the line of putt to shield the line from the wind?

A. No. Such procedure would be a breach of Rule 1-2.

1-2/3 Flagstick Lying on Putting Green Removed by Player to Prevent Another Player's Ball from Striking It

Q. B removes the flagstick, places it on the putting green behind the hole and putts. A, believing that B's ball will strike the flagstick, picks up the flagstick, allowing B's ball to roll beyond where the flagstick had been placed. What is the ruling?

A. In match play, A loses the hole for removing an obstruction which might influence the movement of the ball while the player's ball was in motion — Rule 1-2 or 24-1.

In stroke play, A incurs a penalty of two strokes — Rule 1-2 or 24-1.

B incurs no penalty.

Adjustment of Flagstick; Player's Rights — See 17/4.

Opponent or Fellow-Competitor Attending Flagstick for Player Deliberately Fails to Remove It; Player's Ball Strikes Flagstick — See 17-3/2.

Ball Deliberately Deflected or Stopped on Putting Green by Fellow-Competitor — See 19-1/5.

Removal of Loose Impediments Affecting Player's Play — See 23-1/10.

1-2/3.5 Player Repairs Hole After Holing Out But Before Opponent, Fellow-Competitor or Partner Holes Out

Q. After holing out, a player observes that the edge of the hole is ragged. He pats the ragged edge with his hand and smooth it. Does the player incur a penalty under Rule 1-2 if his opponent, fellow-competitor or partner has not holed out?

A. If the player smoothed the edge of the hole as a courtesy to following players, which seems likely, there is no penalty under Rule 1-2. However, he incurs a penalty under Rule 1-2 if he smoothed the edge of the hole for the express purpose of influencing the movement of the opponent's, fellow-competitor's or partner's ball.

Since the player had holed out, he is not subject to penalty under Rule 16-1a.

If a four-ball competition was involved and the player's partner had not completed the hole, the partner is subject to penalty under Rule 16-1a — See Definition of "Partner."

1-2/4 Player Jumps Close to Hole to Cause Ball to Drop

Q. A ball overhangs the lip of the hole. The player jumps close to the hole in the hope of jarring the earth and causing the ball to fall into the hole, which it does. Is this permissible?

A. No.

If the ball was still moving when the player jumped, the player took action to influence the movement of the ball in breach of Rule 1-2. In match play, he lost the hole. In stroke play, he incurred a penalty of two strokes, and the ball was holed.

If the ball was at rest when the player jumped, it should be assumed that the player caused the ball to move, and he incurred a penalty of one stroke in both match and stroke play under Rule 18-2a and was required to replace the ball.

If it is not possible to determine whether the ball was still moving, it should be presumed to be moving unless it was deemed to be at rest under Rule 16-2.

1-2/4.5 Player Leaves Putt Short and Instinctively Throws Putter at Ball

Q. A player putts and the ball comes to rest just short of the hole. The player then instinctively throws his putter toward the ball, but misses. Should the player incur a penalty for a breach of Rule 1-2 which prohibits taking action to influence the position of a ball?

A. No. See Decision 14/6 which deals with a similar case.

If the putter had moved the ball, the player would have incurred a penalty stroke under Rule 18-2a, and would be required to replace the ball.

1-2/5 Player Putts with One Hand and Catches Ball in Hole with Other Hand

Q. A player whose ball is on the lip of the hole putts with one hand and catches the ball with his other hand after the ball is below the level of the lip of the hole. What is the ruling?

A. The player purposely stopped his moving ball.

In match play, he lost the hole — Rule 1-2.

In stroke play, he incurred a penalty of two strokes and was required to place his ball on the lip of the hole and hole out — Rule 1-2. If he did not do so, he was disqualified under Rule 3-2 for failing to hole out.

In order for a ball to be holed (see Definition of "Holed"), it must be at rest within the circumference of the hole.

Ball Popped Up Swung at in Disgust — See 14/6.

Ball Overhanging Hole Knocked Away by Opponent Before Player Determines Status — See 16-2/2.

Casting Shadow on Ball Overhanging Hole — See 16-2/3.

1-2/6 Player Removes Loose Impediment Affecting Opponent's Lie in Hazard

Q. As a gesture of sportsmanship, a player removes a loose impediment in a hazard, thus improving the lie of his opponent's ball in the hazard. The player's ball was not in the hazard. What is the ruling?

A. Under Rule 1-2, the player incurs a penalty of loss of hole.

Caddie Holds Back Tree Branch to Prevent Branch from Deflecting Dropped Ball — See 20-2a/5.

Caddie Stops Dropped Ball Before It Comes to Rest; When Penalty Incurred — See 20-2c/4.

1-3/1 Players Agree Not to Tee Off in Prescribed Order to Save Time

Q. In match play, a player wins a hole. On his way to the next tee, the player returns to retrieve a club left at the last green and suggests that the opponent play first to save time. The opponent does so. Are the players in breach of Rule 1-3?

A. Yes, because they agreed to exclude the operation of Rule 10-1a. However, in these particular circumstances, the Committee would be justified in waiving the disqualification penalty under Rule 33-7. If the players subsequently agreed to exclude the operation of Rule 10-1a, they should be disqualified.

Competitors in Stroke Play Agree to Play Out of Turn But Not for Purpose of Giving One of Them an Advantage — See 10-2c/2.

1-3/2 Agreement to Concede Short Putts

Q. In a match, the two players agree in advance to concede all putts within a specified length. Is this contrary to Rule 1-3?

A. Yes. The players agreed to exclude the operation of Rule 1-1 and should be disqualified under Rule 1-3. Under Rule 2-4, the only stroke which may be conceded is the "next stroke" and it cannot be conceded in advance.

1-3/3 Player and Opponent or Fellow-Competitor Agree to Repair Spike Marks on One Another's Line of Putt

Q. A player and his opponent or fellow-competitor agree that they will repair spike marks on one another's line of putt. Is this a breach of Rule 1-3?

A. Yes. Both would be subject to disqualification for agreeing to waive Rule 16-1a (Touching Line of Putt).

1-3/4 Failure of Players to Apply Known Penalty

Q. In a match, a player discovers at the 2nd hole that he has 15 clubs in his bag contrary to Rule 4-4a, but his opponent refuses to apply the penalty. The extra club is declared out of play and the match continues. The Committee disqualifies both players. Is this correct?

A. Yes. Since the players agreed to waive the penalty, they should be disqualified under Rule 1-3.

1-3/5 Players Unaware Penalty Incurred

Q. In a match, A incurred a penalty stroke under Rule 12-2 for lifting his ball for identification without announcing his intention to B, his opponent. A did not penalize himself and B did not make a claim because neither A nor B was aware a penalty had been incurred. Should the Committee disqualify A and B under Rule 1-3 for agreeing to waive a penalty?

A. No. Since the players were not aware a penalty had been incurred, there could have been no agreement between them to waive the penalty.

Players Unable to Resolve Rules Problem Agree to Consider Hole Halved — See 2-1/1.

Disregarding Breach of Rules by Opponent — See 2-5/1.

1-3/6 Marker Attests Wrong Score Knowingly and Competitor Aware Score Wrong

Q. In stroke play, B failed to hole out at a hole. A few holes later he realized he had erred. A, B's marker and fellow-competitor, was aware both that B had infringed the Rules and that B knew this, but nevertheless he signed B's card. B was disqualified under Rule 3-2 (Failure to Hole Out). Should A, who knowingly overlooked the breach, be penalized?

A. A should have been disqualified for a breach of Rule 1-3.

Marker Attests Wrong Score Knowingly But Competitor Unaware Score Wrong — See 6-6a/5.

Competior Seeks Help from Fellow-Competitor to Avoid Penalty — See 33-7/7.

1-3/7 Agreement That Side Losing After 18 Holes of 36-Hole Match Will Concede Match

Q. Prior to a 36-hole match, the players agree that they will play only 18 holes and whoever is behind at that point will concede the match. Is this permissible?

A. No. Both players should be disqualified under Rule 1-3 for agreeing to exclude the operation of a condition of the competition (Rule 33-1).

Wrong Form of Play Used in Match Play Event — See 6-1/1.

Match Decided by Wrong Form of Play by Agreement — See 33-1/4.

1-3/8 Time Limit on Applying Penalty for Agreeing to Waive Rules in Match Play

Q. In a first-round match, A and B agreed to waive a Rule in breach of Rule 1-3. A won the match and three days later the Committee became aware of the breach. Should A be disqualified?

A. Yes. The time limit imposed by Rule 2-5 is not applicable in this case.

Player Who Has Reached Third Round of Match Play Disqualified for Agreeing to Waive Rules in First-Round Match — See 33/2.

Two Holes Purposely Omitted in Match — See 2-3/3.

Handicap Stroke Given at Incorrect Hole in Error — See 6-2a/2.

Discontinued Match Replayed Instead of Being Resumed from Where Play Stopped — See 2-3/5.

Competitor Requests That Ball in Position to Assist Him Should Not Be Lifted — See 22/6.

Competitor Refuses to Lift Ball Assisting Play — See 22/7.

1-4/1 Player Distracted by Ball Dropped by Another Player Mis-Hits Ball

Q. As A was making his backswing, B accidentally

dropped a ball, which rolled within six inches of A's ball. The appearance of the dropped ball startled A, causing him to top his shot. In equity, should A be permitted to replay his stroke?

A. No. Distractions are a common occurrence which players must accept.

1-4/2 Ball Adhering to Face of Club After Stroke

Q. A player plays a stroke from wet sand or soil and the ball adheres to the face of the club. What is the ruling?

A. In equity (Rule 1-4), the ball should be dropped, without penalty, as near as possible to the spot where the club was when the ball stuck to it. But see also Decision 14-4/1.

1-4/3 Flagstick Stuck into Green Some Distance from Hole by Practical Joker

Q. A practical joker removes the flagstick from the hole and sticks it into the putting green some distance from the hole. The players approaching the green are unaware of this action and they play towards the flagstick and not the hole. Do the players have the option to replay?

A. No. In equity (Rule 1-4), the players must accept the resultant advantage or disadvantage.

Player Lifts Ball in Mistaken Belief That Next Stroke Conceded — See 2-4/3.

Putting Out After Concession of Stroke Assists Partner — See 2-4/6.

Player Concedes Opponent's Next Stroke and Plays Before Opponent Has Opportunity to Lift Ball — See 2-4/8.

Ball-Marker Moved by Opponent's Caddie Accidentally — See 20-1/7.

Player Plays Away from Hole to Assist Partner — See 30-3f/6.

1-4/4 In Anger Player Strikes Ball Played by Player in Following Group

Q. A is nearly struck by a ball played by a player in the following group. In anger, A hits the ball back towards the group. Has A played a practice stroke or a wrong ball?

A. No. However, in equity (Rule 1-4), A should incur the general penalty of loss of hole in match play or two strokes in stroke play.

1-4/5 Removal of Obstruction in Hazard Would Move Loose Impediment

Q. In a hazard, a player's ball lies against a movable obstruction. A loose impediment lies on top of the obstruction in such a position that the player cannot remove the obstruction without also moving the loose impediment. Under Rule 24, the player is entitled to remove the movable obstruction, but under Rule 23 is not entitled to move the loose impediment. What is the procedure?

A. The player may remove the obstruction as authorized by Rule 24-1. If the loose impediment is incidentally moved in the process, in equity (Rule 1-4) the player incurs no penalty and he must place the loose impediment as nearly as possible at the spot where it originally lay.

1-4/6 Two Balls Lie Together in Hazard and Neither Is Identifiable

Q. Two balls lie together in a hazard. Both balls are playable. The ball nearer the hole would interfere with a stroke at the other ball, and vice versa. It appears likely that one of the balls is the player's ball. However, neither ball is identifiable because the markings on both balls are obscured by mud. What is the proper procedure if the other ball is (a) probably the ball of an opponent or a fellow-competitor or (b) an abandoned ball?

A. The Rules of Golf do not contemplate such a situation. In equity (Rule 1-4), the player may lift the ball farther from the hole following the procedure prescribed in Rule 12-2, and clean it to the extent necessary for identification.

In situation (a), if the lifted ball is a ball in play, it must be replaced. Before playing, the owner of the ball which had been lifted would be entitled to have the other ball lifted by its prospective owner under Rule 22.

In situation (b), if the lifted ball is an abandoned ball, the player may discard it and play the other ball.

Ball in Bunker Moves Closer to Hole When Obstruction Removed and Ball Will Not Remain at Rest When Replaced; All Other Parts of Bunker Are Nearer Hole — See 20-3d/2.

Loose Impediment Affecting Lie Moved When Ball Lifted — See 23-1/7.

Loose Impediment Affecting Lie Removed While Ball Lifted — See 23-1/8.

Opponent or Fellow-Competitor Removes Obstruction Affecting Player's Play — See 24/16.

1-4/7 Ball Lost in Either Water Hazard or Casual Water Overflowing Hazard

Q. A ball is lost. It is either in a water hazard or in casual water overflowing the hazard. What is the proper procedure?

A. In equity (Rule 1-4), the player must proceed under the water hazard Rule.

1-4/8 Nearest Point of Relief from Cart Path Is in Casual Water; Nearest Point of Relief from Casual Water Is Back on Cart Path

Q. A player's ball lies on a paved cart path and he takes relief under Rule 24-2b (i). The nearest point of relief is in a large puddle of casual water which adjoins the cart path. He drops the ball in the casual water in accordance with Rule 24-2b(i). He then discovers that the nearest point of relief from the casual water under Rule 25-1b(i) would be back on the cart path. What are the player's options?

A. In addition to his available options under the Rules, in equity (Rule 1-4) the player may obtain relief without penalty as follows: The point on the course nearest to where the ball originally lay on the cart path shall be determined which (a) is not nearer the hole, (b) avoids interference by both the cart path and the casual water and (c) is not in a hazard or on a putting green. The player shall lift the ball and drop it within one club-length of the point thus determined on ground which fulfills (a), (b) and (c) above.

If the dropped ball rolls into a position where there is interference by either the cart path or the casual water, Rule 20-2c applies.

1-4/9   Bird's Nest Interfering with Stroke

Q. A player's ball came to rest in a bird's nest or so close to the nest that he could not play a stroke without damaging it. Is he entitled to relief without penalty?

A. Yes. In equity (Rule 1-4), the player may, without penalty, drop the ball at the nearest spot not nearer the hole which would allow him to make his stroke without damaging the nest. If the ball lies in a hazard, it must be dropped in the hazard.

Lie or Line of Play Affected by Pitch-Mark Made by Partner's, Opponent's or Fellow-Competitor's Ball — See 13-2/8.

Player's Lie Affected by Sand from Partner's, Opponent's or Fellow-Competitor's Stroke from Bunker — See 13-2/8.5.

Extension of Line of Play Affected When Opponent or Fellow-Competitor Creates Footprints in Bunker — See 13-2/29.5.

Partner's, Opponent's or Fellow-Competitor's Divot Comes to Rest Near Player's Ball in Bunker — See 13-4/18.

Lie in Bunker Altered by Another Player Taking His Stance — See 20-3b/2.

Lie Altered by Removal of Gallery- Control Stake — See 20-3b/3.

Lie of Ball Altered by Tractor — See 20-3b/4.

1-4/10 Dangerous Situation; Rattlesnake or Bees Interfere with Play

Q. A player's ball comes to rest in a situation dangerous to the player, *e.g.*, near a live rattlesnake or a bees' nest. Must the player either play the ball as it lies or declare it unplayable and take relief under Rule 28?

A. No. It is not reasonable to expect the player to play from such a dangerous situation nor fair to require the player to suffer a penalty under Rule 28.

In equity (Rule 1-4), the player should be permitted, without penalty, to drop a ball in the nearest spot not nearer the hole which is not dangerous.

If the ball lay in a hazard, it should be dropped, if possible, in the same hazard and, if not, in a similar nearby hazard, but in either case not nearer the hole. If it is not possible for the player so to drop the ball in a hazard, he should drop it, under penalty of one stroke, outside the hazard, keeping the point where the original ball lay between the hole and the spot on which the ball is dropped.

Danger from Fire-Ants — See 33-8/22.

Player Lifts Opponent's Ball-Marker — See 2-4/5.

Procedure if Both Original and Second Balls Dropped in Wrong Place and Played — See 3-3/5.5.

Playing Characteristics of Club Changed While Play Suspended; Error Discovered Before Play Resumed — See 4-2/2.

Player's Team Mate in Gallery Hits Ball to Green to Show Player Whether Green Will Hold — See 8-1/23.

Advice Given by Team Coach or Captain — See 8-1/24.

Determination of Honor at Hole Following Disputed Hole — See 10-1a/2.

Competitors Estimate Area of Teeing Ground When One Tee-Marker Missing — See 11-4b/2.

Divots Replaced and Pressed Down in Area in Which Ball Is to Be Dropped — See 13-2/4.5.

Ball Thrown into Bounds by Outside Agency and Played; Neither Player Nor Caddie Aware of Action of Outside Agency — See 15/10.

Hole at Which Wrong Ball Played Unknown — See 15-1/3.

Opponent or Fellow-Competitor Attending Flagstick for

Player Fails to Remove It; Player's Ball Strikes Flagstick — See 17-3/2.

Ball Stolen by Outside Agency from Unknown Spot — See 18-1/5.

Ball Lodged in Tree Knocked Down by Outside Agency — See 18-1/9.

Ball Dislodged from Tree; Replacement of Ball Not Possible — See 18-2a/29.

Ball Deliberately Deflected or Stopped on Putting Green by Spectator — See 19-1/4.

Ball Deliberately Deflected or Stopped Through the Green by Spectator — See 19-1/4.1.

Ball Deliberately Deflected or Stopped on Putting Green by Fellow-Competitor — See 19-1/5.

Ball Deflected by Player's Golf Cart Being Pulled by Opponent or Fellow-Competitor Without Player's Knowledge — See 19-2/6.

Ball Moved in Measuring to Determine If Re-Drop Required — See 20-2c/6.

Lifting Ball to Determine Whether It Lies in Burrowing Animal Hole — See 25/21.

Ball Dropped from Casual Water in Bunker at Point of Maximum Relief Rolls Elsewhere — See 25-1b/6.

Dropped Ball Embeds; Procedure If Ball Again Embeds When Re-Dropped — See 25-2/2.5.

Lifting Ball to Determine Whether It Is Embedded — See 25-2/7.

Provisional Ball Not Distinguishable from Original Ball — See 27/11.

Gate in Boundary Fence — See 27/18.

Caddie Shared by Opponents' Side in Four-Ball Match Moves Player's Ball — See 30/2.

Player Who Has Reached Third Round of Match Play Disqualified for Agreeing to Waive Rules in First-Round Match — See 33/2.

Player Who Has Advanced in Match Play Is Disqualified for Wrong Score in Qualifying Round — See 34-1b/8.

Rule 2. Match Play

2-1. Winner of Hole; Reckoning of Holes

In match play the game is played by holes. Except as otherwise provided in the Rules, a hole is won by the side which holes its ball in the fewer strokes. In a handicap match the lower net score wins the hole.

The reckoning of holes is kept by the terms: so many "holes up" or "all square," and so many "to play."

A side is "dormie" when it is as many holes up as there are holes remaining to be played.

2-2. Halved Hole

A hole is halved if each side holes out in the same number of strokes.

When a player has holed out and his opponent has been left with a stroke for the half, if the player thereafter incurs a penalty, the hole is halved.

2-3. Winner of Match

A match (which consists of a <u>stipulated round</u>, unless otherwise decreed by the Committee) is won by the side which is leading by a number of holes greater than the number of holes remaining to be played.

The Committee may, for the purpose of settling a tie, extend the stipulated round to as many holes as are required for a match to be won.

2

2-4. Concession of Next Stroke, Hole or Match

When the opponent's ball is at rest or is deemed to be at rest under Rule 16-2, the player may concede the opponent to have holed out with his next stroke and the ball may be removed by either side with a club or otherwise.

A player may concede a hole or a match at any time prior to the conclusion of the hole or the match.

Concession of a stroke, hole or match may not be declined or withdrawn.

2-5. Claims

In match play, if a doubt or dispute arises between the players and no duly authorized representative of the Committee is available within a reasonable time, the players shall continue the match without delay. Any claim, if it is to be considered by the Committee, must be made before any player in the match plays from the next teeing ground or, in the case of the last hole of the match, before all players in the match leave the putting green.

No later claim shall be considered unless it is based on facts previously unknown to the player making the claim and the player making the claim had been given wrong information (Rules 6-2a and 9) by an opponent. In any case, no later claim shall be considered after the result of the match has been officially announced, unless the Committee is satisfied that the opponent knew he was giving wrong information.

2-6. General Penalty

The penalty for a breach of a Rule in match play is loss of hole except when otherwise provided.

2/1 Players in Singles Match Accompanied by Third Party

Q. Prior to a singles match between A and B, A stated to B that a third player, C, would be playing with them. B played the match under protest and lost. What ruling should the Committee give?

A. A single is a match in which one plays against another. Since B made a timely claim, the Committee should have awarded the match to B. If B had not protested, *i.e.*, had agreed that C accompany the match, the result of the match would stand as played.

Wrong Form of Play Used in Match Play Event — See 6-1/1.

Match Decided by Wrong Form of Play by Agreement — See 33-1/4.

2-1/1 Players Unable to Resolve Rules Problem Agree to Consider Hole Halved

Q. In a match, A putted to within three inches of the hole and then knocked his ball away. B, the opponent, objected. He stated that he wanted A's ball left by the hole. A and B were uncertain how to resolve the matter, so they agreed to consider the hole halved. Should A and B be disqualified under Rule 1-3?

A. No. There was no agreement to waive the Rules. Rather, the players were ignorant of the Rules.

Hole Not Completed by Either Player — See 2-5/3.

2-1/2 Minus or Zero Net Score

Q. In a handicap match, a player entitled to two handicap strokes at a par-3 hole scores a 2 or a hole-in-one. What would be his net score in each case?

A. The player's net score would be zero (0) if he scored a 2 or minus 1(-1) if he had a hole-in-one.

Determination of Honor in Handicap Match — See 10-1a/1.

2

2-2/1 Player Putting for Half Is Given Advice by Opponent

The following is an example of the application of the second paragraph of Rule 2-2:

> In a match, A has holed out. As B, A's opponent, is preparing to putt for a half, A gives B advice as to his line of putt. A would normally lose the hole for a breach of Rule 8-1, but Rule 2-2 becomes operative in these circumstances and the hole is halved.

Player Reporting Wrong Score Causes Opponent with Chance for Half to Pick Up — See 9-2/6.

Player Incorrectly Believing He Has Won a Hole Lifts Opponent's Ball-Marker; Opponent Had Putt for Half — See 2-4/5.

2-3/1 Players Under Impression Match Is Over Later Realize It Was All Square

Q. In a match , A and B left the 18th green under the impression that A had won. They later realized that in fact the match was all square. The matter was referred to the Committee. What is the ruling?

A. Since there was no indication that wrong information had been given, the match stands as played, with A the winner.

Players Mistakenly Believing Match Is All Square After 18 Holes Play Extra Hole Without Claim Being Made — See 2-5/6.

Rightful Winner of Match Makes No Claim and Agrees to Play Extra Holes — See 2-5/7.

Match Play Finalists Both Disqualified — See 33/3.

True State of Match Not Determinable — See 34-3/5.

2-3/2 Hole Inadvertently Omitted in Match; Error Discovered After Match Concluded

Q. The players in a match inadvertently omitted playing a hole. The error was discovered after the match had been played to a conclusion. What is the ruling?

A. The result should stand.

2-3/3 Two Holes Purposely Omitted in Match

Q. The players in a match agreed to omit two holes, *i.e.*, agreed to settle the match over 16 holes. Is this permitted?

A. No. The players should be disqualified under Rule 1-3 for excluding the operation of Rule 2-3 by failing to play the stipulated round.

2-3/4 Three Holes Played Out of Sequence in Match

Q. In an 18-hole match, the players by mistake play three holes out of sequence. The error is discovered before the match concludes. What is the ruling?

A. The holes played out of sequence should be disregarded and the match resumed at the proper hole. However, if such procedure would delay the competition, both players should be disqualified unless one of them concedes the match to the other.

2-3/5 Replaying Match When Play Discontinued Instead of Resuming from Where Play Stopped

Q. A match which was all square after 16 holes was discontinued by agreement due to darkness. The match should have been resumed at the 17th hole. However, the players, thinking it was in accordance with the Rules, replayed the match starting at the 1st tee. The result was posted. At that point the Committee became aware of the improper procedure, What is the ruling?

A. The result of the match as replayed should stand. The players were not subject to disqualification under Rule 1-3 because they were unaware that their procedure was contrary to the Rules.

2-4/1 Player Concedes Opponent's Next Stroke and Then Knocks Opponent's Ball into Hole

Q. A player conceded his opponent's next stroke and then, in attempting to knock the opponent's ball back to him, he inadvertently knocked the ball into the hole. The opponent, who had played three strokes prior to the concession, claimed a 3 for the hole. Was the claim valid?

A. No. The player conceded the opponent a 4 for the hole and, at that point, the opponent had completed the hole. It is irrelevant that the player subsequently knocked the opponent's ball into the hole, whether he did so inadvertently or otherwise.

Opponent's Ball Knocked Away by Player After Concession Moves Player's Ball — See 18-2a/18.

2-4/2 Ball Falls into Hole After Concession of Next Stroke

Q. A player's ball overhung the edge of the hole. After elapse of the time allowed in Rule 16-2, the opponent conceded the player's next stroke for a 5, after which the player's ball fell into the hole. What was the player's score for the hole?

A. The player's score was 5. It is immaterial that the player's ball fell into the hole after the opponent had conceded the player's next stroke. If the opponent had not conceded the next stroke, the player's score would also be 5 because in those circumstances the player would be deemed to have holed out with his last stroke and he would incur a penalty stroke — Rule 16-2.

Ball Overhanging Hole Knocked Away by Opponent Before Player Determines Status — See 16-2/2.

2-4/3 Player Lifts Ball in Mistaken Belief That Next Stroke Conceded

Q. In a match between A and B, B made a statement which A interpreted to mean that his (A's) next stroke was conceded. Accordingly, A lifted his ball. B then said that he had not conceded A's next stroke. What is the ruling?

A. If B's statement could reasonably have led A to think his next stroke had been conceded, in equity (Rule 1-4) A should replace his ball as near as possible to where it lay, without penalty.

Otherwise, A would incur a penalty stroke for lifting his ball without marking its position — Rule 20-1 — and he must replace his ball as near as possible to where it lay.

In Four-Ball Match Player with Putt for Half Picks Up in Error at Suggestion of Opponent Based on Misunderstanding — See 30/5.

2-4/4 Whether Picking Up Opponent's Ball Is Concession of Next Stroke

Q. In match play, A holes a putt and, thinking he has won the match, picks up B's ball. B then advises A that he (B) had a putt to win the hole. Did A concede B's next stroke when he picked up B's ball?

A. No. A incurred a penalty stroke under Rule 18-3b; B must replace his ball and now has two putts to win the hole.

2-4/5 Whether Lifting Opponent's Ball-Marker Is Concession of Next Stroke

Q. In a match, A, believing he has won a hole, picks up the coin marking the position of his opponent B's ball. In fact B had a putt to halve the hole. Should the picking up of B's ball-marker be considered a concession of B's next stroke?

A. No. In equity (Rule 1-4), A should be penalized one stroke. Therefore, under the second paragraph of Rule 2-2 the hole is automatically halved.

2-4/6 Putting Out After Concession of Stroke

Rule 2-4 does not cover the question of whether a player may putt out after his next stroke has been

conceded. A player incurs no penalty for holing out
in such circumstances. However, if the act would be of
assistance to a partner in a four-ball or best-ball match,
the partner is, in equity (Rule 1-4), disqualified for the
hole.

Agreement to Concede Short Putts — See 1-3/2.

2-4/7 Concession of Stroke Refused by Player and Withdrawn by Opponent; Player Then Putts and Misses

Q. In a match between A and B, A putts and his
ball comes to rest near the hole. B concedes A's next
stroke. A says: "No. I haven't holed out yet." B says:
"OK. Go ahead and putt." A putts and misses. In such
circumstances, is the concession invalidated?

A. No. When B conceded A's next stroke, A had completed the hole. Concession of a stroke may not be
declined or withdrawn — see Rule 2-4.

2-4/8 Player Concedes Opponent's Next Stroke and Plays Before Opponent Has Opportunity to Lift Ball

Q. In a match between A and B, A chips and his ball
comes to rest about one foot from the hole. B concedes
A's next stroke. A states that he wishes to lift his ball.
However, B proceeds to play his next stroke before A
has an opportunity to lift his ball and B's ball strikes
A's ball. What is the ruling?

A. B deprived A of his right to lift his ball after his
next stroke was conceded. In equity (Rule 1-4), B lost
the hole, whether or not his ball struck A's ball.

**Ball Resting Against Flagstick; Putt Conceded and Ball
Removed Before Player Can Remove Flagstick** — See 17-
4/2.

2-4/9 Player Concedes Hole After Which It Is Discovered Opponent Had Played Wrong Ball

Q. In a match between A and B, A has played two
strokes and the ball with which he played his second

stroke out of the rough is on the green. B, having played five, concedes the hole to A. A then discovers that he has played a wrong ball to the green. What is the ruling?

A. Since A did not play the wrong ball from a hazard, he lost the hole (Rule 15-2) before B conceded it to him. Therefore, B's concession was irrelevant.

2-4/9.5 Player Concedes Hole After Which It Is Discovered Opponent's Last Stroke Was Played with a Wrong Ball from a Hazard

Q. In a match between A and B, B has played four strokes and his ball lies three feet from the hole. A, who has played two strokes, plays a stroke out of a bunker to the edge of the hole. B concedes the hole.

A and B pick their balls up, whereupon A discovers that he has played a wrong ball from the bunker, but has incurred no penalty for doing so (Rule 15-2, second paragraph).

What is the ruling?

A. The concession stands — see Rule 2-4.

2-4/10 Player Concedes Hole After Which Opponent Plays Wrong Ball

Q. In a three-ball match, A loses his ball and concedes the hole to B and C. Subsequently, B plays a wrong ball. Is A's concession to B binding?

A. Yes.

Player Concluding He Played Wrong Ball When Opponent Misread Number on Player's Ball Concedes Hole — See 9-2/11.

2-4/11 Player with Lost Ball Concedes Hole; Ball Then Found in Hole

Q. In a match, A played his second shot towards the green but he could not find his ball. He conceded the hole to B, whose second shot was on the green.

2

The following players then found A's ball in the hole. What is the ruling?

A. Since a player may not concede a hole after conclusion of the hole — Rule 2-4 — A holed out in two strokes and won the hole if he made a claim before B played from the next teeing ground (Rule 2-5). If A did not do so, he lost the hole.

2-4/12 Player Concedes Hole on Basis of Invalid Claim

Q. In a match between A and B, A putts out of turn. B incorrectly claims that A loses the hole for putting out of turn. A protests but concedes the hole. Later, A, having consulted the Rule book, lodges an official protest with the Committee. How should the Committee rule?

A. Although B's claim was invalid — see Rule 10-1c -A lost the hole when he conceded it — Rule 2-4.

Handicap Stroke Claimed After Hole Conceded — See 6-2a/4.

2-4/13 Implied Concession of Hole Withdrawn

Q. A, unable to find his ball after a two-minute search, suggests to B, his opponent, that they move on to the next hole. A's ball is then found. A withdraws his suggestion to move on to the next hole and play is resumed. Before A plays his ball, B plays a stroke with a wrong ball. What is the ruling?

A. A's suggestion amounted to a concession of the hole and B won the hole. Concession of a hole may not be withdrawn — Rule 2-4. B's actions after A's concession could not deprive him of a hole already won.

2-4/14 Player Concedes Match Due to Misconception as to Opponent's Score at Last Hole

Q. In a match, A and B were all square playing the

last hole. A had a short putt for a 4. B holed a putt for a 4. A, mistakenly believing that B had holed out in three strokes, shook hands with B, conceded the match and lifted his ball. At that point B told A that he (B) had scored a 4. What is the ruling?

A. A conceded the match. Even if A had not conceded the match, he lost it when he lifted his ball without marking its position and thereby incurred a penalty stroke under Rule 20-1.

2-4/15 Player Concedes Match After Winning It When Opponent Lodges Invalid Claim Regarding Strokes Taken

Q. In a match, A and B were all square playing the last hole. A incurred a penalty without knowing it, and accordingly did not advise B of the penalty. B was aware of what had happened but did not realize it was a breach of the Rules either.

A won the hole and the match, and the result was posted.

Subsequently, a spectator informed B that A had incurred a penalty at the 18th hole. B then claimed the hole and the match, and A conceded the match to B.

Who was the rightful winner?

A. A won the match because a match can only be conceded prior to its conclusion (Rule 2-4).

A gave wrong information when he did not advise B that he had incurred a penalty and would have lost the hole had a timely claim been made — Rule 9-2. However, a belated claim by B was not valid for two reasons:

(1) it was not based on facts previously unknown to B, and

(2) the claim was made after the result of the match was announced — see Rule 2-5.

Agreement That Side Losing After 18 Holes of 36-Hole Match Will Concede Match — See 1-3/7.

2

Conceding Match to Avoid Disqualification — See 2-3/4 and 33-1/6.

2-4/16 Valid Timely Claim Made After Concession of Match

Q. In a match, A and B are playing the last hole. B is 1 up. A holes out for a 4. B putts from a wrong place and holes the putt for a 4. A congratulates B and concedes the match. Before leaving the putting green, A asks B if he (B) had putted from a wrong place. B acknowledges that he did so. A claims that B loses the hole under Rule 20-7a. Is the claim valid?

A. Yes. Concession of a match is not binding if subsequently a valid claim is timely made. A's valid claim was made within the time limit in Rule 2-5.

Player Omits Penalty Stroke When Advising Opponent as to Score for Hole; Error Discovered After Match Conceded by Opponent — See 9-2/10.

2-4/17 Player in Erroneous Belief Match Is Over Shakes Opponent's Hand and Picks Up Opponent's Ball

Q. In match play, A holes a putt and, thinking he has won the match, shakes hands with B and picks up B's ball. The referee advises B that he had a putt to win the hole and keep the match alive. Has B conceded the match by his acquiescence in A's action of shaking hands and picking up B's ball?

A. No. B was entitled to replace his ball and hole out. Since A incurred a one-stroke penalty under Rule 18-3b, B now had two putts to win the hole.

Player's Conscious Failure to Correct Opponent's Misunderstanding of State of Match Results in Opponent Conceding Match When in Fact Player Is Dormie — See 9-2/12.

2-4/18 Defaulting Player Plays Informal Match with Opponent and Wins

Q. B concedes a match to A. A and B then play an informal match and B wins it, 5 and 4. Should the

Committee post A as the winner by default or B as the winner by 5 and 4?

A. A should be posted as the winner by default.

2-4/19 Winner of Match Wishes to Default to Beaten Opponent

Q. In match play, A defeats B and then concedes the match to B because he (A) cannot continue in the competition. Is this permissible?

A. No. A won the match. A beaten player may not be reinstated in such circumstances. A should be posted as the winner and, since A cannot continue, A's opponent in the next round would win by default.

Under Rule 2-4, a side may concede a match at any time prior to conclusion of the match, but not thereafter.

2-4/20 Player Unable to Meet Match Play Schedule Defaults; Schedule Then Changed and Player Requests Reinstatement

Q. The final matches in a competition were to be played on a Saturday. A was to play B in one match. On Thursday, A defaulted to B, saying that he would be out of town on Saturday.

On Saturday, the course was unplayable and the matches were postponed until the following Saturday.

On Monday, A requested that he be reinstated. Should the Committee reinstate A?

A. No. A conceded the match as provided for in Rule 2-4. In the circumstances concession is irrevocable.

2-5/1 Player's Obligation re Lodging Claim

In match play, a player may disregard a breach of the Rules by his opponent, provided there is no agreement between the players. There is a difference between overlooking an opponent's breach and agreement with the opponent to waive a penalty. Rule 1-3 prohibits the latter.

2

2-5/2 Procedure for a Valid Claim

For a claim to be valid, the claimant must indicate the facts he believes give rise to the claim and must also indicate that he wants the Rules of Golf applied. He must do both within the time required by Rule 2-5. For example, Rule 16-1e prohibits putting from a stance astride an extension of the line of putt behind the ball. In a match between A and B, if A putts from a stance astride an extension of the line and B states "that is not allowed, you are penalized" or "I'm making a claim because of that stroke," the Committee should uphold the claim.

Statements by B such as "I'm not sure that's allowed" or "I don't think you can do that" do not by themselves constitute a valid claim because each statement does not contain both a reference to the facts giving rise to the claim and a desire to have the Rules of Golf applied.

Time Limit on Applying Penalty for Agreeing to Waive Rules in Match Play— See 1-3/8.

2-5/3 Player Lifts Ball Before Holing Out; Opponent Then Picks Up His Ball Claiming Player Loses Hole

Q. In match play, A's ball was resting against the flagstick but it was not holed. A, believing he had holed out, lifted his ball without first marking its position. In doing so, A incurred a penalty stroke under Rule 20-1. Since A was not aware that he had incurred a penalty, he did not inform B. B then played his next stroke and picked up, claiming that A's lifting of his ball entailed a penalty of loss of hole. A and B agreed to continue the match and refer B's claim to the Committee later. How should the Committee have ruled?

A. When A failed to inform B before B played his next stroke that he (A) had incurred a penalty, A lost the hole under Rule 9-2 for this failure. However, B made no claim under Rule 9-2. Accordingly, it should have been ruled that, since neither A nor B completed the hole, the hole was halved.

2-5/4 Player Wins Hole with Own Ball After Playing Wrong Ball; Opponent Lodges Belated Claim

Q. In a match, A and B are all square playing the last hole. A plays a wrong ball in the rough and discovers the error before his next stroke. A and B go back to look for A's ball without any question being raised as to whether A had incurred a penalty. A's ball is found. A plays out the hole with his original ball and wins the hole and the match.

Several days later B claims the last hole and the match by virtue of the fact that A played a wrong ball.

Is the claim valid?

A. No. A gave wrong information when he did not advise B that he (A) had incurred a penalty — Rule 9-2. However, a belated claim by B was not valid for two reasons:

(1) it was not based on facts previously unknown to B, and

(2) the claim was made after the result of the match was announced — See Rule 2-5.

Player Wins Hole with Wrong Ball; Error Discovered at Next Hole; Opponent Claims Previous Hole — See 9-2/8.

Player Wins Hole with Wrong Ball and Partner Picks Up; Error Discovered at Next Hole; Opponents Claim Hole — See 30-3d/2.

2-5/5 Invalid Claim Not Disputed

Q. In a match, A played a wrong ball to a green and then found his own ball in the hole. His own ball had been holed in three strokes, which was fewer strokes than B had taken. However, B claimed the hole on the ground that A had played a wrong ball. A did not dispute the claim. A lost the match.

Later, A learned that, because he had completed the hole when his own ball was holed and before play of a wrong ball, the play of the wrong ball was irrelevant and he was the rightful winner of the hole in question.

A then lodged a claim with the Committee. Was the claim valid?

A. No. Since A did not dispute B's invalid claim before B played from the next teeing ground, B's claim stands and B won the hole in question — Rule 2-5.

Player Concedes Hole on Basis of Invalid Claim — See 2-4/12.

Player Concedes Match After Winning It When Opponent Lodges Invalid Claim Regarding Strokes Taken — See 2-4/15.

2-5/5.5 Breach of 14-Club Rule Discovered After Match Concluded But Before Result Officially Announced

Q. On completion of the 14th hole in a match between A and B, A wins by 5 and 4. The players continue the round. After the 16th hole, it is discovered by the players that A has 15 clubs in his bag.

Before the result of the match has been officially announced, B reports the facts to the Committee and asks for a ruling. Is the claim valid?

A. Yes. Although the players had left the putting green of the last hole of the match, B's claim is based on facts previously unknown to him and he is deemed to have been given wrong information by A (Rule 9-2). The players must return to the 15th hole and resume the match. A is penalized under Rule 4-4a and is three up with four holes to play.

2-5/6 Players Mistakenly Believe Match Is All Square After 18 Holes and Play Extra Hole Without Claim Being Made

Q. In a match between A and B, A is 1 up after the prescribed 18 holes. However, both A and B believe the match is all square. So they play extra holes and B wins at the 20th hole. The error is then discovered. What is the ruling?

A. Since A did not make a claim before either player played from the tee at the 19th hole, the match must be considered all square at that point. Thus, B was the winner.

Players Under Impression Match Is Over Later Realize It Was All Square — See 2-3/1.

2-5/7 Rightful Winner of Match Makes No Claim and Agrees to Play Extra Holes

Q. In a match, A and B are all square going to the 18th hole. On completion of the 18th hole, B states that he has scored 7; A states that he (A) has scored 6. A and B go into the clubhouse under the impression that A has won the match. At that point B tells A that, on reflection, he (B) believes A scored 7 at the 18th hole. On recounting, A acknowledges that he had a 7.

By agreement, A and B resume the match; A wins it at the 20th hole and the result is posted.

That night, B discovers that, because A gave wrong information after completion of the 18th hole, under Rule 9-2 he (B) was rightfully the winner of the 18th hole and the match. B reports the matter to the Committee and claims the match. What is the ruling?

A. The match stands as played, with A the winner.

B's claim was not made within the time limit in Rule 2-5. B's claim would have been valid if he had refused to play extra holes or had played the extra holes under protest.

2-5/8 Status of Valid Claim If Players Accept Wrong Ruling from Someone Not on Committee and Continue Match

Q. In an 18-hole match between A and B, A's ball strikes the flagstick which was attended by B. A and B believe that a loss-of-hole penalty is incurred but they are in doubt as to which one of them incurs the penalty. Accordingly, before teeing off at the next hole, they agree to refer the matter to the Committee later.

At the conclusion of 18 holes, A and B agree that if B incurred a loss-of-hole penalty at the hole in question, the match is all square; if A incurred it, B has won the match by two holes. A and B seek a ruling from X, who is not on the Committee. X incorrectly advises A and B that B incurred the penalty and that the match is therefore all square.

A and B accept X's ruling, play extra holes and A wins.

Subsequently, the incident was brought to the attention of the Committee. What should the Committee do?

A. When A and B accepted X's incorrect ruling, they, in effect, settled the doubt themselves and, after A and B began playing extra holes, the Committee was no longer entitled to consider a claim. The match stands as played, with A the winner.

Valid Timely Claim Made After Concession of Match — See 2-4/16.

2-5/9 Player Agreeing with Opponent That Hole Was Halved Later Realizes He Has Won Hole; Player Then Makes Claim

Q. In a match between A and B, at the 16th hole A scored 6 and B scored 5. When leaving the putting green, B commented to A: "A half?" and A replied: "Yes."

A won the match at the 20th hole and the result was posted. Later, B realized that he had won the 16th hole and, if the mistake had not been made, he would have won the match 1 up.

A admitted that he had made a mistake. B reported the matter to the Committee and claimed the match. Is the claim valid?

A. No. The match stands as played, with A the winner. After the result of the match was posted, the claim by B could have been considered only if A had knowingly given wrong information as to the number of strokes he (A) had taken at the 16th hole — see Rule 2-5.

2-5/10 Player Accepting Erroneous Claim Disputes It After Result Announced

Q. In a match, A was in breach of a Rule. Although the penalty for a breach of the Rule in question was only one stroke, B, his opponent, claimed that A lost the hole. A did not dispute the claim. B won the match and the result was posted. Three days later, A protested to the Committee that B had misinformed him with respect to the Rules. What is the ruling?

A. The match stands as played. Under Rule 2-5, no claim may be considered after the result of a match has been announced unless the opponent knowingly gave wrong information. Incorrect information on the Rules is not wrong information. It is up to each player to know the Rules.

2-5/11 Wrong Information Given After Play of Last Hole; Claim Made After Result Announced

Q. In a match, A and B came to the last hole all square. After completion of the hole, A stated that he had scored 9 and B stated that he (B) has scored 8, making B the winner, 1 up. The result was recorded by the Committee.

A few minutes later, a spectator told A that B had scored 9 at the last hole. B reviewed the hole and acknowledged that he had made a mistake and that his actual score was 9. What is the ruling?

A. The match stands as played, with B the winner. Under Rule 2-5 no claim may be considered after the result of a match is announced unless wrong information has been given knowingly.

2-5/12 Imposition of Penalty by Referee After Any Player in Match Has Played from Next Tee

Q. In match play, may a referee penalize a player for a breach of a Rule at a hole if he does not become aware of the breach until someone in the match has played from the next teeing ground?

2

A. Yes, unless the facts giving rise to the penalty were known to the opponent.

2-5/13 Extra Stroke Taken by Mistake in Handicap Match; Status of Late Claim

Q. Prior to the start of a handicap match, the two players correctly advised one another as to the handicaps to which they were entitled. However, during the match, A, by mistake, took a stroke to which he was not entitled at a certain hole. The error was discovered several holes later. Could B, the opponent, then claim the hole in question?

A. No. A late claim would not be valid unless it was based on facts previously unknown to B and B had been given wrong information by A. In this case A did not give B wrong information as to the number of strokes to which he was entitled during the round, and it was B's responsibility to know the holes at which handicap strokes were to be given (see Note under Rule 6-2). The hole in question stands as played.

2-5/14 Opponent Disputes Player's Claim That Ball Is Unfit for Play

Q. In a match, A considers his ball unfit for play. A's opponent, B, disagrees. There is no referee or Committee member available for a ruling. In spite of B's disagreement, may A substitute another ball?

A. Yes. However, if B then makes a claim (Rule 2-5) and the Committee, after examination of the original ball, upholds B's claim, A would lose the hole. Otherwise, the result of the hole would stand as played.

A must ensure that the condition of the ball he considered unfit for play is preserved until the Committee examines it. Otherwise, the Committee should uphold B's claim.

Player with Lost Ball Concedes Hole; Ball Then Found in Hole and Player Claims Hole — See 2-4/11.

Second Ball Played in Match Play; No Claim Made — See 3-3/9.

Wrong Handicap Used in Match by Mistake; Error Discovered After Result Officially Announced; Status of Claim by Opponent — See 6-2a/5.

Match Discontinued by Agreement Due to Rain; One Player Subsequently Wishes to Resume; Opponent Refuses on Ground Course Unplayable and Makes Claim — See 6-8a/6.

Player Omits Penalty Stroke When Advising Opponent as to Score for Hole; Error Discovered After Match Conceded by Opponent; Opponent Lodges Claim — See 9-2/10.

Doubt Whether Ball Moved by Outside Agency; Opponent Lodges Claim — See 18-1/4.

In Foursome Side Drives for Three Holes in Wrong Order and Then Claim Is Made — See 29-2/2.

3

Rule 3. Stroke Play

3-1. Winner

The competitor who plays the <u>stipulated round</u> or rounds in the fewest strokes is the winner.

3-2. Failure to Hole Out

If a competitor fails to hole out at any hole and does not correct his mistake before he plays a <u>stroke</u> from the next <u>teeing ground</u> or, in the case of the last hole of the round, before he leaves the <u>putting green</u>, *he shall be disqualified*.

3-3. Doubt as to Procedure

a. PROCEDURE

In stroke play only, when during play of a hole a competitor is doubtful of his rights or procedure, he may, without penalty, play a second ball. After the situation which caused the doubt has arisen, the competitor should, before taking further action, announce to his marker or a fellow-competitor his decision to invoke this Rule and the ball with which he will score if the Rules permit.

The competitor shall report the facts to the <u>Committee</u> before returning his score card unless he scores the same with both balls; if he fails to do so, *he shall be disqualified*.

3

b. DETERMINATION OF SCORE FOR HOLE

If the Rules allow the procedure selected in advance by the competitor, the score with the ball selected shall be his score for the hole.

If the competitor fails to announce in advance his decision to invoke this Rule or his selection, the score with the original ball or, if the original ball is not one of the balls being played, the first ball put into play shall count if the Rules allow the procedure adopted for such ball.

Note: A second ball played under Rule 3-3 is not a provisional ball under Rule 27-2.

3-4. Refusal to Comply with a Rule

If a competitor refuses to comply with a Rule affecting the rights of another competitor, he shall be disqualified.

3-5. General Penalty

The penalty for a breach of a Rule in stroke play is two strokes except when otherwise provided.

3/1 Disqualification in Play-Off

Q. A competitor in a stroke play play-off incurs a penalty of disqualification. Does the disqualification apply to the play-off only or to the entire competition?

A. The disqualification applies only to the play-off.

3/2 Competitors Play Two Holes Not Included in Stipulated Round

Q. In stroke play, the stipulated round was 16 holes, *i.e.*, the 13th and 14th holes were omitted. After play of the 12th hole, one group elected to play the 13th and 14th holes without counting their scores for those holes. They then completed the round. What is the ruling?

3

A. The stipulated round consists of playing the holes of the course in the sequence prescribed by the Committee — see Definition of "Stipulated Round." These competitors were in breach of the conditions of the competition and the Committee should in this case impose a penalty of disqualification under Rule 33-7.

3-2/1 Fellow-Competitor's Ball Knocked from Lip of Hole by Competitor Not Replaced

Q. In stroke play, a competitor concedes his fellow-competitor a short putt and knocks the ball away. The fellow-competitor lifts his ball, does not replace it as required by Rule 18-4 and plays from the next tee. What is the ruling?

A. The fellow-competitor is disqualified — Rule 3-2.

Ball Played from Putting Green Deflected into Hole by Moving Outside Agency; Stroke Not Replayed — See 19-1/3.

3-2/2 Ball Blown into Hole by Competitor Not Replaced and Holed Out

Q. In stroke play, a competitor's ball stopped on the lip of the hole and on impulse he blew the ball into the hole. He did not replace the ball, as required by Rule 18-2a, and hole out. He played from the next tee. Is the competitor disqualified under Rule 3-2 for failing to hole out?

A. Yes.

Player Who Putts with One Hand and Catches Ball in Hole with Other Hand Does Not Place Ball on Lip of Hole and Hole Out — See 1-2/5.

3-2/3 Competitor in Error Does Not Hole Out; Error Corrected Before Playing from Next Tee

Q. In four-ball stroke play, A holed out in 4. B, A's partner, who was lying 3 and had marked and lifted his ball, forgot he had a handicap stroke. He did not

3

replace his ball and hole out or pick up his ball-marker. On the way to the next teeing ground, B remembered his stroke, returned to the green, replaced his ball where it previously lay and holed out for a net 3. Was this in order?

A. Yes, since B had not played from the next teeing ground (Rule 3-2).

Competitor Picks Up Second Ball — See 3-3/8.

Modifying Penalty for Not Holing Out — See 33-7/2.

3-3/0.5 Guidelines for Determining Which Ball Counts When Player Proceeds Under Rule 3-3

The purpose of Rule 3-3 is to allow a competitor to avoid a penalty when he is in doubt as to the proper procedure. The following are guidelines for determining the ball with which the competitor scores in various situations:

(1) If both balls are played in accordance with the Rules, the ball selected shall count if the competitor announces in advance his decision to invoke this Rule and announces in advance the ball with which he wishes to score. If the competitor does not announce or select in advance, the score with the original ball counts if played in accordance with the Rules. Otherwise the score with the second ball counts if played in accordance with the Rules.

(2) If the procedure with the ball selected in advance is not in accordance with the Rules, the other ball must count (see Decision 3-3/5).

(3) If neither ball is played in accordance with the Rules, the following applies:

(a) In a case where the competitor plays both balls from a wrong place but is not guilty of a serious breach with either ball, the score with the original ball counts, with an additional penalty under the applicable Rule (see Rule 20-7b).

(b) In a case where the competitor is guilty of a serious breach with one ball and not guilty of a

3

serious breach with the other ball, the score with the other ball counts, with an additional penalty under the applicable Rule (see Rule 20-7b and Decision 3-3/5.5).

(c) In a case where the competitor is guilty of a serious breach with both balls, the competitor shall be disqualified.

(4) If the original ball is played and then Rule 3-3 is invoked, the score with the original ball must count, even if the Rules do not allow the procedure adopted for that ball, *i.e.*, Rule 3-3 is not applicable in such circumstances.

3-3/1 Provisional Ball Used as Second Ball When Not Determinable Whether Original Ball Is Out of Bounds

Q. In stroke play, a player is in doubt as to whether his drive may be out of bounds. He plays a provisional ball under Rule 27-2. He finds the original ball and cannot determine whether it is out of bounds or not. The player wishes to consider the provisional ball as his second ball under Rule 3-3 and complete the play of the hole with both balls. Is this permissible?

A. Yes. In invoking Rule 3-3 after playing a provisional ball, the player must treat the provisional ball as a second ball. Although the Note to Rule 3-3 provides:"A second ball played under Rule 3-3 is not a provisional ball under Rule 27-2," the reverse is not true in the present case.

3-3/2 Second Ball Played Despite Adverse Ruling

Q. In stroke play, a competitor believes he is entitled to relief under a Rule, but a member of the Committee disagrees. In spite of the ruling by the Committee member, the competitor invokes Rule 3-3 and opts to score with the second ball. He plays his original ball as it lies and the second ball under the Rule he believes is applicable.

3

May a competitor invoke Rule 3-3 in such circumstances?

A. The answer depends upon whether or not the Committee has given authority to make final decisions to its individual members.

If the Committee member concerned has not been given authority to make final decisions, the competitor is entitled to invoke Rule 3-3.

If, on the other hand, the Committee member has been given authority to make final decisions, he may, despite his own view that the competitor is not entitled to relief, permit the competitor to invoke Rule 3-3. However, if the Committee member exercises his authority and gives the competitor a final decision that he is not entitled to the relief he claims, there is then no justification for the competitor invoking Rule 3-3, and he will incur a penalty of two strokes for undue delay (Rule 6-7) if he, nevertheless, goes ahead and invokes Rule 3-3. The score with his original ball, including this two-stroke penalty, must count.

3-3/3 Ball Dropped in Wrong Place and Played; Rule 3-3 Then Invoked and Second Ball Dropped in Right Place; Both Balls Played Out

Q. In stroke play, a competitor's ball comes to rest through the green on a paved path. He lifts the ball, drops it off the path at a point almost two club-lengths from the nearest point of relief (*i.e.*, he drops in a wrong place) and plays it. The competitor's marker advises the competitor that he (the marker) believes the ball must be dropped within one club-length of the nearest point of relief. The competitor, in doubt, invokes Rule 3-3, drops a second ball within one club-length of the nearest point of relief and otherwise in accordance with Rule 24-2b(i) and opts to score with the second ball. The competitor holes out with both balls. What is the ruling?

A. Rule 20-7b states in part: "If a competitor plays a stroke with his original ball which has been dropped or placed in a wrong place, he shall incur the penalty

3

prescribed by the applicable Rule and play out the hole with the ball." Thus, the competitor's score with the original ball, with a penalty of two strokes added, must count.

Rule 20-7b does not permit the second ball to count. However, the competitor incurs no penalty for having played the second ball.

3-3/4   Ball Dropped in Wrong Place But Not Played; Rule 3-3 Then Invoked and Second Ball Dropped in Right Place; Both Balls Played Out

Q. With reference to Decision 3-3/3, what would have been the ruling if the marker had advised the competitor of his possible error before the ball dropped in a wrong place was played and the competitor had invoked Rule 3-3 at that point?

A. Rule 20-7b would not have applied because Rule 3-3 was invoked before the ball dropped in a wrong place was played.

The score with the second ball would have counted and no penalty would have been incurred.

The competitor, had he not been in doubt, could have lifted the ball dropped in the wrong place, without penalty — Rule 20-6.

3-3/5   Whether Score with Second Ball Counts If Ball Dropped in Wrong Place and Played

Q. In stroke play, a competitor's ball came to rest on an artificially-surfaced road which had not been declared an integral part of the course. The competitor, not sure whether the road was an obstruction or an integral part of the course, invoked Rule 3-3 and announced that he wished his score with the second ball to count. He played his original ball as it lay and dropped and played a second ball under Rule 24-2b(i). He met all the requirements of that Rule, except that he dropped the second ball almost two club-lengths from the nearest point of relief, instead of

3

within one club-length. Does the score with the second ball count?

A. No. Rule 3-3b states in part: "If the Rules allow the procedure selected in advance by the competitor, the score with the ball selected shall be his score for the hole." In this case, the procedure selected in advance (*i.e.*, dropping the second ball almost two club-lengths from the nearest point of relief) is not allowed under the Rules. Accordingly, the score with the original ball counts.

3-3/5.5 Procedure If Both Original and Second Balls Dropped in Wrong Place and Played

Q. A competitor's ball crosses a water hazard in front of a putting green and then rolls back into the hazard. The competitor incorrectly believes that he is entitled to drop the ball on the green side of the hazard within two club-lengths of the point where the ball crossed the hazard margin when it rolled back into the hazard. A fellow-competitor incorrectly advises the competitor that he must drop the ball on the line of flight of his previous shot.

The competitor invokes Rule 3-3. He drops the original ball on the green side of the hazard and elects to score with that ball. He then drops a second ball on the line of flight of his previous shot. He holes out with both balls and then plays from the next tee.

Under Rule 3-3b and Decision 3-3/5, it would appear that the score with neither ball can count since both balls were dropped at a wrong place and played, and thus the Rules do not allow the procedure adopted for either ball. How should the Committee rule when the competitor reports the facts?

A. Rule 3-3 does not contemplate such a case. Therefore, the ruling must be made in accordance with equity (Rule 1-4).

In dropping the original ball on the green side of the hazard, the competitor was guilty of a serious breach of Rule 26-1. If the competitor was not guilty of a serious breach with respect to the second ball, the

3

score with that ball counts, with an additional two-stroke penalty added for breach of Rule 26-1. See also Rule 20-7b.

In a case where the competitor has played both balls from a wrong place but is not guilty of a serious breach with either ball, the score with the original ball counts, with a two-stroke penalty added.

In a case where the competitor is guilty of a serious breach with both balls, the competitor is disqualified.

3-3/6 Competitor Plays Original Ball After Doubtful Situation Has Arisen and Then Invokes Rule 3-3

Q. In stroke play, a competitor's ball lies in a water hazard. A movable stake defining the margin of the hazard interferes with the area of his intended swing. He plays his next stroke, avoiding the stake. It then occurs to him that he may have been entitled to remove the stake. The competitor informs his marker that he is invoking Rule 3-3 and elects to score with a second ball. He removes the stake and drops a second ball at the spot from which his original ball was played. He holes out with both balls. What is the ruling?

A. The situation which caused the doubt arose when the competitor's ball lay in the water hazard and the stake interfered with his swing. Since the competitor took further action, *i.e.,* played the original ball, after the situation which caused the doubt had arisen, the score with the original ball must count — see last paragraph of Rule 3-3b.

However, the competitor incurs no penalty for having played the second ball.

3-3/6.5 Competitor Plays Second Ball Without Announcing Intention to Invoke Rule 3-3 and Fails to Report Facts to Committee

Q. In stroke play, a competitor's ball came to rest on an artificially-surfaced road which had not been declared an integral part of the course. Without announcing his decision to invoke Rule 3-3 or the ball

3

with which he would score if the Rules permitted, the competitor dropped and played a second ball in accordance with Rule 24-2b. The competitor then played the original ball as it lay and completed play of the hole with both balls, scoring 4 with the original ball and 5 with the dropped ball.

The competitor returned his score card to the Committee with a score of 4 on the hole in question and failed to report the facts to the Committee.

What is the ruling?

A. Although the competitor did not announce his decision to invoke Rule 3-3, it is clear from the facts that he intended to invoke such Rule. As the competitor did not score the same with both balls and failed to report the facts to the Committee before returning his score card, he is disqualified under Rule 3-3a. (New)

3-3/7 Original Ball Strikes Second Ball or Vice Versa

Q. A competitor invokes Rule 3-3 and plays a second ball. Subsequently, the competitor makes a stroke at one ball and it strikes and moves the other ball. What is the ruling?

A. If both balls lay on the putting green prior to the stroke, the competitor incurs a penalty of two strokes if the score with the striking ball ultimately becomes the competitor's score for the hole — Rule 19-5. Otherwise, there is no penalty.

The striking ball must be played as it lies — Rule 19-5.

The moved ball must be replaced — Rule 18-5.

3-3/8 Competitor Picks Up Second Ball

Q. In stroke play, a competitor, uncertain whether the road his ball lies on is an obstruction or not, invokes Rule 3-3. He plays his original ball as it lies on the road and a second ball under Rule 24-2b(i), telling his marker he wishes his score with the second ball to count if the Rules permit. Having hit his original ball onto the green and the second ball into a bunker, the competitor picks up the second ball, holes out with the original ball and plays from the next tee. At this point the matter is referred to the Committee, which establishes that the road on which the competitor's ball lay was an obstruction. What is the ruling?

A. Since the road on which the competitor's ball lay was an obstruction and therefore Rule 24-2b(i) allowed the procedure selected by the competitor, the score with the second (or selected) ball would have counted if it had been holed out. However, since the competitor did not hole out with that ball, he is disqualified — Rule 3-2.

If, on the other hand, the road had not been an obstruction, there would have been no penalty. In that case, since the Rules would not have allowed the selected procedure, a score with the second ball would not have counted, and the competitor's score with his original ball would have been his score for the hole. There is no penalty for picking up a ball played under Rule 3-3 if that ball cannot count.

3-3/9 Second Ball Played in Match Play

Q. In a match between A and B, A was unsure of his rights at a hole. Neither A nor B was aware that Rule 3-3 applies only in stroke play, so A played a second ball and holed out with both balls. At the end of the round, the matter was referred to the Committee. What is the ruling?

A. A second ball played in match play is a wrong ball — See Definition of "Wrong Ball." Accordingly, A would have lost the hole had B claimed it under Rule 2-5 before either player had played from the next tee. However, B made no claim. Therefore, the score with A's original ball counts.

3-3/10 Competitor Plays Three Balls When Doubtful of Rights

Q. Are there any circumstances under which a competitor in stroke play, who is doubtful of his rights or procedure, may play a third ball under Rule 3-3?

3

A. No. If a competitor so proceeds, the score with the original ball or, if the original ball is not one of the balls being played, the first ball put into play shall count. If the Rules do not allow the procedure adopted for the original ball or the first ball put into play, the competitor incurs the penalty prescribed for the improper procedure.

Local Rule Allowing Play of Second Ball in Match Play — See 33-8/3.

Wrong Ball Played in Belief It Is Second Ball — See 15/7.

Ball Dropped and Played Under Water Hazard Rule; Original Ball Then Found in Hazard and Holed Out as Second Ball — See 26-1/5.

3-4/1 Competitor Not Given Opportunity to Lift Ball Assisting Fellow-Competitor

Q. In stroke play, A's ball lies near the hole in a position to assist B, whose ball lies off the green. A states his intention to lift his ball under Rule 22. However, B says that he does not want A's ball lifted. B plays before A has an opportunity to lift, and B's ball strikes A's ball. Should B be penalized?

A. B is disqualified under Rule 3-4.

4

CLUBS AND THE BALL

The United States Golf Association and the Royal and Ancient Golf Club of St. Andrews reserve the right to change the Rules and make and change the interpretations relating to clubs, balls and other implements at any time.

Rule 4. Clubs

If there may be any reasonable basis for doubt as to whether a club which is to be manufactured conforms with Rule 4 and Appendix II, the manufacturer should submit a sample to the United States Golf Association for a ruling, such sample to become its property for reference purposes. If a manufacturer fails to do so, he assumes the risk of a ruling that the club does not conform with the Rules of Golf.

A player in doubt as to the conformity of a club should consult the United States Golf Association.

4-1. Form and Make of Clubs

A club is an implement designed to be used for striking the ball.

A putter is a club designed primarily for use on the putting green.

The player's clubs shall conform with the provisions of this Rule and with the specifications and interpretations set forth in Appendix II.

a. GENERAL

The club shall be composed of a shaft and a head. All parts of the club shall be fixed so that the club is one unit. The club shall not be designed to be adjustable except for weight.

The club shall not be substantially different from the traditional and customary form and make.

(See also Appendix II.)

b. SHAFT

The shaft shall be generally straight, with the same bending and twisting properties in any direction, and shall be attached to the clubhead at the heel either directly or through a single plain neck or socket. A putter shaft may be attached to any point in the head.

c. GRIP

The grip consists of that part of the shaft designed to be held by the player and any material added to it for the purpose of obtaining a firm hold. The grip shall be substantially straight and plain in form and shall not be molded for any part of the hands.

d. CLUBHEAD

The distance from the heel to the toe of the clubhead shall be greater than the distance from the face to the back. The clubhead shall be generally plain in shape.

The clubhead shall have only one face designed for striking the ball, except that a putter may have two such faces if their characteristics are the same, they are opposite each other and the loft of each is the same and does not exceed 10 degrees.

e. CLUB FACE

The face shall not have any degree of concavity and, in relation to the ball, shall be hard and rigid. It shall be generally smooth except for such markings as are permitted by Appendix II.

f. WEAR

A club which conforms with Rule 4-1 when new is deemed to conform after wear through normal use. Any part of a club which has been purposely altered is regarded as new and must conform, in the altered state, with the Rules.

4

g. DAMAGE

If a player's club ceases to conform with Rule 4-1 because of damage sustained in the normal course of play, the player may:

(i) use the club in its damaged state, but only for the remainder of the <u>stipulated round</u> during which such damage was sustained; or

(ii) without unduly delaying play, repair it.

A club which ceases to conform because of damage sustained other than in the normal course of play shall not subsequently be used during the round.

(Damage changing playing characteristics of club — see Rule 4-2.)

(Damage rendering club unfit for play — see Rule 4-4a.)

4-2. Playing Characteristics Changed

During a <u>stipulated round</u>, the playing characteristics of a club shall not be purposely changed by adjustment or by any other means.

If the playing characteristics of a player's club are changed during a round because of damage sustained in the normal course of play, the player may:

(i) use the club in its altered state; or

(ii) without unduly delaying play, repair it.

If the playing characteristics of a player's club are changed because of damage sustained other than in the normal course of play, the club shall not subsequently be used during the round.

Damage to a club which occurred prior to a round may be repaired during the round, provided the playing characteristics are not changed and play is not unduly delayed.

4-3. Foreign Material

No foreign material shall be applied to the club face for the purpose of influencing the movement of the ball.

PENALTY FOR BREACH
OF RULE 4-1, -2 or -3:
Disqualification.

4-4. Maximum of Fourteen Clubs

a. SELECTION AND REPLACEMENT OF CLUBS

The player shall start a <u>stipulated round</u> with not more than fourteen clubs. He is limited to the clubs thus selected for that round except that, without unduly delaying play, he may:

> (i) if he started with fewer than fourteen, add as many as will bring his total to that number; and

> (ii) replace, with any club, a club which becomes unfit for play in the normal course of play.

The addition or replacement of a club or clubs may not be made by borrowing any club selected for play by any other person playing on the course.

b. PARTNERS MAY SHARE CLUBS

Partners may share clubs, provided that the total number of clubs carried by the partners so sharing does not exceed fourteen.

PENALTY FOR BREACH OF RULE 4-4a
or b, REGARDLESS OF NUMBER
OF EXCESS CLUBS CARRIED:

Match play --- At the conclusion of the hole at which the breach is discovered, the state of the match shall be adjusted by deducting one hole for each hole at which a breach occurred. Maximum deduction per round: two holes.

Stroke play --- Two strokes for each hole at which any breach occurred; maximum penalty per round: four strokes.

Bogey and par competitions --- Penalties as in match play.

Stableford competitions --- See Note to Rule 32-1b.

4

c. EXCESS CLUB DECLARED OUT OF PLAY

Any club carried or used in breach of this Rule shall be declared out of play by the player immediately upon discovery that a breach has occurred and thereafter shall not be used by the player during the round.

PENALTY FOR BREACH OF RULE 4-4c:
Disqualification.

4-1/1 Non-Conforming Club Carried But Not Used

Q. If a player unwittingly carries a non-conforming club but does not use it, would the Committee be justified, under Rule 33-7, in waiving or modifying the disqualification penalty?

A. No.

4-1/2 Material in Head of Metal Wood Club Broken Away from Shell

Q. A piece of material in the head of a metal wood club, which conformed with the Rules when manufactured, has broken away from the shell due to use, and it rattles around in the head. Rule 4-1a states in part: "All parts of the club shall be fixed so that the club is one unit." Is this metal wood club now non-conforming because of the loose piece of material?

A. No, because Rule 4-1f states in part: "A club which conforms with Rule 4-1 when new is deemed to conform after wear through normal use." The piece of material in the metal wood club in question broke loose from the shell due to wear through normal use.

Attachment to Grip or Shaft of Club of Player with Artificial Arm — See 14-3/15.

4-2/1 Material Applied to Top of Clubhead to Reduce Glare

4

Q. During a round, may a player put a bandaid or a strip of tape on the top of a clubhead to reduce glare?

A. Yes. This would not change the playing characteristics of the club.

Caddie Shields Player from Sun During Stroke — See 14-2/3.

Competitor Changes Weight of Club During Round; Breach Discovered After Competition Closed — See 34-1b/4.

4-2/1.5 Modifying Penalty for Holing Short Putt with Club Whose Playing Characteristics Changed Other Than in Normal Course of Play

Q. A player leaves a putt about an inch short of the hole. In disgust, he hits his shoe with the head of his putter. The impact bends the neck of the putter, changing its playing characteristics. The player then holes the one-inch putt with the putter.

Rule 4-2 states in part: "If the playing characteristics of a player's club are changed because of damage sustained other than in the normal course of play, the club shall not subsequently be used during the round." The penalty for breach of Rule 4-2 is disqualification. Would the Committee be justified in waiving or modifying the disqualification penalty in these circumstances, provided the player does not subsequently use the altered putter during the round?

A. No.

4-2/2 Playing Characteristics of Club Changed While Play Suspended; Error Discovered Before Play Resumed

Q. While play is suspended, a player changes the lie of four of his clubs. Before play is resumed, he becomes aware that Rule 4-2 prohibits changing the playing characteristics of a club during a round. If the original lie of the four clubs is restored, or if the player discards them before play is resumed, can he avoid the disqualification penalty prescribed by Rule 4-2?

A. Rule 4-2 is intended to ensure that, apart from damage sustained in the normal course of play, the playing characteristics of the clubs with which the player starts the stipulated round shall not be altered until he has finished it. Accordingly, although the stipulated round has been suspended and the player did not technically change the playing characteristics during the round, in equity (Rule 1-4):

(1) the player incurs no penalty if he discards the clubs in question before play is resumed and, assuming he started the round with 14 clubs, finishes the round with the remaining ten clubs, or

(2) if the player resumes play carrying the four clubs, whether or not he has attempted to restore the original playing characteristics, he should be disqualified, in view of the purpose of Rule 4-2. If the lie of a club has been changed, it would be impossible exactly to restore the original lie.

4-3/1 Applying Chalk to Club Face

Q. During a round, may a player apply chalk to the face of an iron club in order to obtain more backspin?

A. No.

4-3/2 Applying Saliva to Face of Club

Q. A player spat on the face of his club and did not wipe the saliva off before playing his next stroke. Is this permissible?

A. If the purpose of doing this was to influence the movement of the ball, the player was in breach of Rule 4-3 as saliva is "foreign material."

4-4a/1 Changing Clubs Because of Wet Grips

Q. May a player change clubs during a round if the grips become wet?

4

A. No. A club is "unfit for play" if it is structurally damaged, but not if the grip becomes slippery.

4-4a/2 Replacing Club When Grip Becomes Loose During Round

Q. The grip of a player's club becomes loose during a round. Is the club considered "unfit for play," in which case the player would be entitled to replace it under Rule 4-4a?

A. Yes.

4-4a/3 Club Broken While Used as Cane

Q. A player uses his putter as a cane while climbing a hill and the shaft breaks. May he replace the putter during the round?

A. Yes. A club broken accidentally in such circumstances is considered to have become "unfit for play in the normal course of play."

4-4a/4 Player Starting with 13 Clubs Breaks Putter in Anger and Replaces It

Q. A player who started a round with 13 clubs broke his putter in anger, *i.e.*, other than in the normal course of play, during the first nine holes. He bought another putter in the pro shop after the first nine holes and used it for the remainder of the round. Rule 4-4a(ii) permits replacing a club only if it becomes unfit for play in the normal course of play. Was the player subject to penalty?

A. No. Since he started with 13 clubs, he was entitled to add another club under Rule 4-4a(i).

4-4a/5 Club Broken Due to Habit of Hitting Head of Club on Ground

Q. Rule 4-4a states that a club may be replaced if it becomes damaged in the "normal course of play." A player has a habit of hitting the head of his putter

on the ground as he walks to the next tee, especially
after missing a putt. On one occasion, after missing
a short putt, the player hit the head of his putter on
the ground so hard that the putter broke. The player
said that he often taps the putter on the ground, and
that it was not done in anger or with the intention of
breaking the club. Should he be allowed to replace the
club?

A. No. If, in similar circumstances, a player subjects a
club to a strain which may result in its breaking, the
club should not be considered to have been damaged
in "the normal course of play."

4-4a/6 Replacement of Club Lost During Round

Q. A player who started a round with 14 clubs lost
his putter. May he replace it during the round?

A. No. A lost club is not one which has become "unfit
for play in the normal course of play."

4-4a/6.5 Replacement of Club Broken on Practice Ground While Play Suspended

Q. Play has been suspended by the Committee. Prior
to resuming play, a player is practicing on the practice
ground. While hitting a ball, the shaft of his sand
wedge breaks. In such circumstances, is the club considered to have become "unfit for play in the normal
course of play," in which case the player would be
entitled to replace the broken club under Rule 4-4a(ii)?

A. Yes.

4-4a/7 When Club Is Considered Added

Q. A player finds on the first green that he has no
putter and is carrying only 13 clubs. He continues play
but sends his caddie back to the clubhouse. The caddie
fetches one of two putters which he finds and gives it
to the player. May the player then tell the caddie to
take it back and fetch the other one instead?

A. Yes, provided he did not play a stroke with any club when the first putter was in his possession.

4

4-4a/8 Changing Clubs Between Rounds in 36-Hole Match

Q. In a 36-hole match, may a player who started with 14 clubs change putters after play of the first 18 holes and before the start of the second 18 holes?

A. Yes. Rule 4-4a prohibits such procedure only during a stipulated round. A 36-hole match comprises two stipulated rounds of 18 holes each — See Definition of "Stipulated Round."

4-4a/9 Replacing Club for Stroke Play Play-Off

Q. In stroke play, a competitor broke a club in anger, finished the round with 13 clubs and then learned that he would be involved in a sudden-death play-off. May the competitor replace his broken club for the play-off?

A. The play-off constituted a new round — see Definition of "Stipulated Round." The competitor was therefore entitled to replace his broken club.

4-4a/10 Competitor Withdraws During Round and Puts His Clubs in Fellow-Competitor's Bag

Q. In stroke play, B withdrew during a round, put his clubs in A's bag, making the total number of clubs in the bag exceed 14, and carried A's bag for the remainder of the round. Should A be penalized under Rule 4-4a?

A. No, provided he did not use any of B's clubs.

4-4a/11 Partners' Clubs Carried in One Bag

Q. In a foursome competition, is it permissible for partners to put both sets of clubs in one golf bag, provided each player uses only his own clubs?

A. Yes, provided each player's clubs are clearly identifiable.

4

4-4a/12 Fellow-Competitor's Club Put in Competitor's Bag by Mistake During Round Used Unintentionally by Competitor

Q. In stroke play, A and B both started with 14 clubs. They were using iron clubs of the same model. At one hole, B's caddie inadvertently put one of B's clubs into A's bag. At a subsequent hole, A played a stroke with B's club by mistake. What is the ruling?

A. Rule 4-4a states: "The player shall start a stipulated round with not more than 14 clubs. He is limited to the clubs thus selected . . ." A complied with the first sentence and therefore incurred no penalty for carrying B's club. However, when A played a stroke with B's club, he did not comply with the second sentence and was subject to penalty under Rule 4-4a.

4-4a/13 Excess Club Put in Player's Golf Bag After Player Has Counted His Clubs at 1st Tee; Error Discovered After Player Has Started Round

Q. A arrives at the 1st tee, counts his clubs and confirms that he is carrying fourteen. He then removes his driver from his golf bag, leaves the bag beside the tee and checks in with the starter. At this point, X, a player in another match or group, by mistake puts his putter in A's golf bag, which was identical to X's bag. A then drives from the 1st tee. During play of the 1st hole, A discovers that X's club has been put in his (A's) golf bag. Does A incur a penalty for starting the round with more than 14 clubs?

A. Yes.

4-4a/14 Carrying Weighted Training Club

Q. May a player carry a weighted training club in addition to the 14 clubs selected for the round?

A. No, but a weighted training club may be selected as one of 14 clubs carried by a player, provided it conforms with Rule 4-1. Rule 4 does not regulate the weight of the golf club.

4

4-4a/15   Retrieving Another Player's Lost Club

Q. A player carrying 14 clubs found another player's club on the course. He picked up the lost club, put it in his bag but did not use it, and handed it in at the pro shop when the round was completed. Was the player in breach of Rule 4-4a for carrying 15 clubs?

A. No.

4-4a/16   Clarification of Match Play Penalty

Q. Please confirm that the following is a correct interpretation of Rule 4-4a in a match between A and B:

1. After the 1st hole, it is discovered that B has more than 14 clubs:
   a. If B won the hole — the match is all square.
   b. If the hole was halved — A is 1 up.
   c. If A won the hole — A is 2 up.
2. After the 2nd hole, it is discovered that B has more than 14 clubs:
   a. If B won both holes — the match is all square.
   b. If B was 1 up — A is 1 up.
   c. If the match was all square — A is 2 up.
   d. If A was 1 up — A is 3 up.
   e. If A was 2 up — A is 4 up.
3. Later in the match, but before the players leave the last green, it is discovered that B has more than 14 clubs:
   a. If B was more than 2 up — 2 "ups" are deducted.
   b. If B was 2 up — the match is all square.
   c. If B was 1 up — A is 1 up.
   d. If the match was all square — A is 2 up.
   e. If A was 1 up — A is 3 up.
   f. If A was 2 up — A is 4 up.
   g. If A was more than 2 up — 2 "ups" are added to his "ups."

A. As the loss of hole penalty for a breach of Rule 4-4a is not applied to a specific hole, but to the state of the match at the conclusion of the hole at which the breach is discovered, your interpretation is correct.

4

Breach of 14–Club Rule Discovered After Match Concluded But Before Result Announced — See 2-5/5.5.

4-4a/17 Breach of 14-Club Rule in Stroke Play Discovered at 8th Hole; Where Penalty Strokes Applied

Q. In stroke play, A discovers during play of the 8th hole that he has 15 clubs in his bag and thus has incurred a penalty of four strokes under Rule 4-4a. How should the four-stroke penalty be applied?

A. A must add penalties of two strokes to his scores for the 1st and 2nd holes.

In four-ball stroke play, both A and his partner would add penalties of two strokes to their scores for the 1st and 2nd holes — see Rule 31-3.

4-4a/18 Excess Club Discovered Before Player Plays from 2nd Tee But After Opponent or Fellow-Competitor Has Played

Q. A player starts a round with 15 clubs. He discovers his error at the 2nd tee after his opponent or a fellow-competitor has played but before he has played. Does the player incur the maximum penalty of (a) deduction of two holes in match play or (b) four strokes in stroke play?

A. No. Since the player has not started play of the 2nd hole, he incurs a penalty of (a) deduction of one hole in match play or (b) two strokes in stroke play.

4-4a/19 Competitor Who Misplaces Putter Borrows Fellow-Competitor's Putter

Q. In stroke play, A, who had mistakenly left his putter at the previous green, borrows a putter from B, a fellow-competitor, and uses it. At the next tee, the Committee is advised of the situation. What is the ruling?

A. A was not entitled to borrow a club selected for play by any other person on the course– Rule 4-4a. A incurs a penalty of two strokes for a breach of Rule 4-4a and must immediately declare B's putter out of play as prescribed in Rule 4-4c. If A recovers his own putter, he may use it.

B may have his putter returned to him and use it for the remainder of the round.

4-4b/1 Borrowing Partner's Putter

Q. Neither A nor B, who were partners in a four-ball match, had 14 clubs, but between them they had more than 14 clubs. Several times during the round A borrowed B's putter. Is this permissible?

A. No. A and B should have had two holes deducted. The penalty would be applied to the state of the match at the conclusion of the hole at which it became known that a breach had occurred.

Using Partner's, Opponent's or Fellow-Competitor's Club for Measuring Purposes — See 20/1.

[4-4b/2 Reserved]

4-4c/1 Excess Club Declared Out of Play Before Round and Placed on Floor of Golf Cart

Q. Before the start of a round, a player discovers that there are 15 clubs in his golf bag. He declares one of the clubs out of play, removes it from his bag, places it on the floor of his golf cart and begins the round. Is the player subject to penalty?

A. Yes, for starting the round with more than 14 clubs. Rule 4-4c has to do with declaring an excess club out of play on discovery of a breach after a round has started. There is nothing in the Rules to permit carrying, during a round, an excess club declared out of play before the round.

5

Rule 5. The Ball

5-1. General

The ball the player uses shall conform to specifications set forth in Appendix III on maximum weight, minimum size, spherical symmetry, initial velocity and overall distance when tested under specified conditions.

5-2. Foreign Material

No foreign material shall be applied to a ball for the purpose of changing its playing characteristics.

PENALTY FOR BREACH
OF RULE 5-1 or 5-2:
Disqualification.

5-3. Ball Unfit for Play

A ball is unfit for play if it is visibly cut, cracked or out of shape. A ball is not unfit for play solely because mud or other materials adhere to it, its surface is scratched or scraped or its paint is damaged or discolored.

If a player has reason to believe his ball has become unfit for play during the play of the hole being played, he may during the play of such hole lift his ball without penalty to determine whether it is unfit.

Before lifting the ball, the player must announce his intention to his opponent in match play or his marker or a fellow-competitor in stroke play and mark the position of the ball.

He may then lift and examine the ball without cleaning it and must give his opponent, marker or fellow-competitor an opportunity to examine the ball.

If he fails to comply with this procedure, *he shall incur a penalty of one stroke.*

If it is determined that the ball has become unfit for play during play of the hole being played, the player may substitute another ball, placing it on the spot where the original ball lay. Otherwise, the original ball shall be replaced.

If a ball breaks into pieces as a result of a stroke, the stroke shall be cancelled and the player shall play a ball without penalty as nearly as possible at the spot from which the original ball was played (see Rule 20-5).

PENALTY FOR BREACH OF RULE 5-3:
> *Match play --- Loss of hole;*
> *Stroke play --- Two strokes.*

*If a player incurs the general penalty for breach of Rule 5-3, no additional penalty under the Rule shall be applied.

Note: If the opponent, marker or fellow-competitor wishes to dispute a claim of unfitness, he must do so before the player plays another ball.

(Cleaning ball lifted from putting green or under any other Rule — see Rule 21.)

5-1/1 Use of Ball Not Conforming with Prescribed Specifications

Q. If a player unwittingly plays one stroke with a ball which does not meet the prescribed specifications, would the Committee be justified, under Rule 33-7, in waiving or modifying the disqualification penalty?

A. No.

5-1/2 Condition Requiring Use of Ball on List of Conforming Golf Balls; Penalty for Breach

Q. If it is a condition of a competition that players must use a brand of ball on the current List of Conforming Golf Balls, may the Committee provide that the penalty for breach of the condition is loss of hole in match play or two strokes in stroke play for each hole at which a breach occurs rather than disqualification?

A. Yes.

5-1/3 Condition Requiring Use of Ball on List of Conforming Golf Balls; Ball Not on List Played as Provisional Ball

Q. It is a condition of the competition that players must use a brand of ball on the current List of Conforming Golf Balls. A player, believing his ball may be lost or out of bounds, plays a provisional ball. He subsequently finds his original ball and then discovers that the ball he played as his provisional ball was not on the List. What is the ruling?

A. The player incurs no penalty as the provisional ball was never the ball in play.

5-3/1 Ball Internally Damaged

Q. A player hit his tee shot and expressed the view that the ball behaved erratically in flight. Before his next shot he examined the ball but he could find no external damage and the ball was not out of shape. He commented that the ball must have been damaged internally by his last stroke and claimed the right to substitute another ball under Rule 5-3. Was the player entitled to invoke Rule 5-3?

A. No.

5-3/2 Ball Declared Unfit for Play Played at Later Hole

Q. A player damaged his ball at a certain hole, declared it unfit for play and substituted another ball.

At a subsequent hole he played the damaged ball. What is the ruling?

A. There is no penalty. However, the player may not again declare the ball (in the same condition) unfit for play.

5-3/3 Ball Not Unfit for Play Deemed Unfit

Q. In stroke play, a competitor, after announcing his intention of doing so, lifted his ball to check for damage, showed it to his marker and claimed that it was unfit for play. The marker disputed this claim, but the competitor insisted on substituting and playing another ball. Before completion of the hole, however, a Committee member was consulted and ruled that the ball taken out of play by the competitor was not, after all, unfit for play. What is the ruling?

A. The competitor should be penalized two strokes for a breach of Rule 5-3 or 15-1 and must hole out with the substituted ball.

In similar circumstances in match play, the player would lose the hole for a breach of Rule 5-3 or 15-1.

5-3/3.5 Player Lifts Ball on Putting Green, Throws Ball into Lake and Then Announces That Ball Is Unfit for Play

Q. A player mis-hits his approach shot but the ball comes to rest on the putting green. The player marks the position of his ball, inspects it and throws it into an adjacent lake from which it cannot be retrieved.

The player then announces to his opponent, marker or fellow-competitor that the ball was unfit for play and that he is substituting another ball. The player did not, as required by Rule 5-3, announce his intention in advance to his opponent in match play or his marker or a fellow-competitor in stroke play and give his opponent, marker or fellow-competitor an opportunity to examine the ball.

What is the ruling?

A. The player was entitled under Rule 16-1b to lift his ball without announcing his intentions. However, when he threw the ball into the lake, he deprived his opponent, marker or fellow-competitor of the opportunity to examine the ball and dispute the claim of unfitness, and he made it impossible to replace the original ball should such a dispute be resolved against him. Accordingly, he incurs a penalty of loss of hole in match play or two strokes in stroke play for a breach of Rule 5-3 or 15-1, but he may substitute another ball to complete the hole.

5-3/4 Ball Breaks into Pieces as a Result of Striking Paved Cart Path

Q. A player plays a stroke and the ball strikes a paved cart path. As a result of the impact with the cart path, the ball breaks into pieces. Should the ball be considered to have broken into pieces "as a result of a stroke," in which case the player must replay the stroke without penalty under the last paragraph of Rule 5-3?

A. Yes.

5-3/5 Ball Embedded in Hazard Lifted to Determine Whether Unfit for Play

Q. Under Rule 5-3, a ball in a hazard may be lifted to determine whether it is unfit for play. If a ball embedded in a bunker is lifted to determine whether it is unfit for play and the lie is altered in the lifting process, Rule 20-3b seems to make it clear that the original lie must be recreated and the ball must be placed in that lie. However, if the ball is embedded in a water hazard and the lie is altered in the lifting process, it would appear that, under Rule 20-3b, the ball must be placed in the nearest lie most similar to that which it originally occupied, not more than one club-length from the original lie. Is this correct?

A. No. Rule 5-3 states: "If it is determined that the ball has become unfit for play during play of the hole being played, the player may substitute another ball, placing it on the spot where the original ball

lay. Otherwise, the original ball shall be replaced."
Therefore, if a ball is embedded in a bunker or in a
water hazard and Rule 5-3 is invoked, the original
ball or a substituted ball must be embedded in the
original lie to the extent that the original ball was
embedded before Rule 5-3 was invoked. Rule 20-3b
does not apply in such cases.

5

5-3/6 Ball Thought to Be Unfit for Play Lifted Under Another Rule and Cleaned; Ball Then Determined to Be Unfit for Play

Q. A player believes that his ball may have become
unfit for play as a result of his previous stroke, but he
is unable to determine whether the ball is unfit due
to a large piece of mud adhering to it. He lifts his ball
to take relief from an area of ground under repair.
He then cleans the ball as permitted under Rule 25-
1b and determines that the ball is unfit for play. Is
the player subject to penalty under Rule 5-3 which
prohibits cleaning the ball?

A. No. The player is entitled to clean the ball as provided in Rule 25-1b.

Opponent Disputes Player's Claim That Ball Unfit for Play
— See 2-5/14.

6

PLAYER'S RESPONSIBILITIES

Rule 6. The Player

Definition

A "marker" is one who is appointed by the Committee to record a <u>competitor's</u> score in stroke play. He may be a <u>fellow-competitor</u>. He is not a <u>referee</u>.

6-1. Conditions of Competition

The player is responsible for knowing the conditions under which the competition is to be played (Rule 33-1).

6-2. Handicap

  a. MATCH PLAY

Before starting a match in a handicap competition, the players should determine from one another their respective handicaps. If a player begins the match having declared a higher handicap which would affect the number of strokes given or received, *he shall be disqualified*; otherwise, the player shall play off the declared handicap.

  b. STROKE PLAY

In any round of a handicap competition, the competitor shall ensure that his handicap is recorded on his score card before it is returned to the Committee. If no handicap is recorded on his score card before it is returned, or if the recorded handicap is higher than that to which he is entitled and this affects the number of strokes received, *he shall be disqualified* from that round of the handicap competition; otherwise, the score shall stand.

Note: It is the player's responsibility to know the holes at which handicap strokes are to be given or received.

6-3. Time of Starting and Groups

a. TIME OF STARTING
The player shall start at the time laid down by the Committee.

b. GROUPS
In stroke play, the competitor shall remain throughout the round in the group arranged by the Committee unless the Committee authorizes or ratifies a change.

PENALTY FOR BREACH OF RULE 6-3:
Disqualification.

(Best-ball and four-ball play — see Rules 30-3a and 31-2.)

Note: The Committee may provide in the conditions of a competition (Rule 33-1) that, if the player arrives at his starting point, ready to play, within five minutes after his starting time, in the absence of circumstances which warrant waiving the penalty of disqualification as provided in Rule 33-7, the penalty for failure to start on time is *loss of the first hole in match play or two strokes at the first hole in stroke play* instead of disqualification.

6-4. Caddie
The player may have only one <u>caddie</u> at any one time, *under penalty of disqualification.*

For any breach of a Rule by his caddie, the player incurs the applicable penalty.

6-5. Ball
The responsibility for playing the proper

ball rests with the player. Each player should put an identification mark on his ball.

6-6. Scoring in Stroke Play

a. RECORDING SCORES

After each hole the <u>marker</u> should check the score with the competitor and record it. On completion of the round the marker shall sign the card and hand it to the competitor. If more than one marker records the scores, each shall sign for the part for which he is responsible.

b. SIGNING AND RETURNING CARD

After completion of the round, the competitor should check his score for each hole and settle any doubtful points with the Committee. He shall ensure that the marker has signed the card, countersign the card himself and return it to the Committee as soon as possible.

PENALTY FOR BREACH OF RULE 6-6b:
Disqualification.

c. ALTERATION OF CARD

No alteration may be made on a card after the competitor has returned it to the Committee.

d. WRONG SCORE FOR HOLE

The competitor is responsible for the correctness of the score recorded for each hole. If he returns a score for any hole lower than actually taken, *he shall be disqualified.* If he returns a score for any hole higher than actually taken, the score as returned shall stand.

Note 1: The Committee is responsible for the addition of scores and application of the handicap recorded on the card — see Rule 33-5.

Note 2: In four-ball stroke play, see also Rule 31-4 and -7a.

6-7. Undue Delay

The player shall play without undue delay. Between completion of a hole and playing from the next teeing ground, the player shall not unduly delay play.

PENALTY FOR BREACH OF RULE 6-7:
> *Match play --- Loss of hole;*
> *Stroke play --- Two strokes.*

For repeated offense --- Disqualification.

If the player unduly delays play between holes, he is delaying the play of the next hole and the penalty applies to that hole.

6-8. Discontinuance of Play

a. WHEN PERMITTED

The player shall not discontinue play unless:
> (i) the Committee has suspended play;
> (ii) he believes there is danger from lightning;
> (iii) he is seeking a decision from the Committee on a doubtful or disputed point (see Rules 2-5 and 34-3); or
> (iv) there is some other good reason such as sudden illness.

Bad weather is not of itself a good reason for discontinuing play.

If the player discontinues play without specific permission from the Committee, he shall report to the Committee as soon as practicable. If he does so and the Committee considers his reason satisfactory, the player incurs no penalty. Otherwise, *the player shall be disqualified.*

Exception in match play: Players discontinuing match play by agreement are not subject to disqualification unless by so doing the competition is delayed.

Note: Leaving the course does not of itself constitute discontinuance of play.

b. PROCEDURE WHEN PLAY SUSPENDED BY COMMITTEE

When play is suspended by the Committee, if the players in a match or group are between

6

the play of two holes, they shall not resume play until the Committee has ordered a resumption of play. If they are in the process of playing a hole, they may continue provided they do so without delay. If they choose to continue, they shall discontinue either before or immediately after completing the hole, and shall not thereafter resume play until the Committee has ordered a resumption of play.

When play has been suspended by the Committee, the player shall resume play when the Committee has ordered a resumption of play.

> PENALTY FOR BREACH OF RULE 6-8b:
> *Disqualification.*

c. LIFTING BALL WHEN PLAY DISCONTINUED

When during the play of a hole a player discontinues play under Rule 6-8a, he may lift his ball. A ball may be cleaned when so lifted. If a ball has been so lifted, the player shall, when play is resumed, place a ball on the spot from which the original ball was lifted.

> PENALTY FOR BREACH OF RULE 6-8c:
> *Match play --- Loss of hole;*
> *Stroke play --- Two strokes.*

6-1/1 Wrong Form of Play Used in Match Play Event

Q. In a foursome match play competition, four players begin their match on a four-ball match play basis. The error is discovered after play of the 9th hole. What is the ruling?

A. It would be improper to decide any match by a form of play other than the prescribed form.

If the wrong form of play is used as a result of a Committee error, the match should be replayed. If the wrong form of play is used unintentionally by players, the match should be replayed; if, however, this would delay the competition, both sides should be disqualified unless one side concedes the match to the other — see Rules 2-4 and 6-1. If the wrong form of play is used intentionally by players, they should be disqualified — Rule 1-3.

Wrong Handicap Allowance Used in Match — See 6-2a/6.

Agreement to Waive Condition — See 1-3/7.

Responsibility for Knowing Stipulated Round — See 11-5/2.

6-2a/1 Failure to Determine Handicaps Prior to Start of Match

There is no penalty if players fail to determine one another's handicaps before starting a match. If this results in one of them not receiving a handicap stroke at a hole at which he is entitled to receive one, the hole stands as played.

6-2a/2 Handicap Stroke Given at Incorrect Hole in Error

Q. In a match between A and B, under the Handicap Stroke Table A was to receive a handicap stroke at the 9th hole. However, both A and B mistakenly believed that A should receive a handicap stroke at the 7th hole, and the match was played on this basis. Subsequently, the Committee became aware of the error. What should the Committee do?

A. The Committee should take no action. Since the players did not agree to deviate from the Handicap Stroke Table and did so by mistake, there was no breach of Rule 1-3. The match should stand as played. See Note under Rule 6-2.

6-2a/3 Handicap Stroke Wrongly Claimed at Hole; Error Discovered Before Hole Completed

Q. In match play, on the tee of a hole A states in error that he is to receive a handicap stroke at that hole. When A is preparing to putt, his opponent, B, recalls that A does not receive a handicap stroke. B so advises A and claims the hole on the ground that A gave wrong information. What is the ruling?

A. The hole should have been completed without a stroke being given to A, and with no penalty to either side. A did not give wrong information. It is up to each player to know the holes at which handicap strokes are to be given or received — see Note under Rule 6-2.

Extra Stroke Taken by Mistake in Handicap Match; Error Discovered Several Holes Later — See 2-5/13.

6-2a/4 Handicap Stroke Claimed After Hole Conceded

Q. In a handicap match, A holed out in 3. B, having a putt for a gross 4 and forgetting that he was entitled to a handicap stroke at the hole, conceded the hole to A. Before A or B played from the next teeing ground, B remembered that he had a handicap stroke at the last hole. What is the ruling?

A. A won the hole when B conceded it — Rule 2-4. It was B's responsibility to know the holes at which he received handicap strokes — see Note under Rule 6-2. Since B forgot about his handicap stroke, he must suffer the consequences.

6-2a/5 Wrong Handicap Used in Match by Mistake; Error Discovered After Result Officially Announced

Q. In a handicap match between A and B, A stated by mistake before the match began that his handicap was ten strokes, whereas in fact his handicap was nine strokes. The match was played on the basis that A's handicap was ten strokes. A won the match. The error was discovered after the result had been officially announced. What is the ruling?

A. The match stands as played. No claim by B could be considered unless A had known he was giving

wrong information about his handicap — See Rules
2-5 and 6-2a.

Wrong Handicap Used Due to Committee Misinformation
— See 33-1/12.

6

6-2a/6   Wrong Handicap Allowance Used in Match

Q. In a handicap match play competition, the conditions provided that, where handicaps were different,
an allowance of 3/4 of the difference would be used.
In one match, however, the players, unaware of this
condition, used the full difference, and the higher
handicapped player won. How should the Committee
rule?

A. The Committee should rule that the match stands
as played. The players failed to take note of the conditions of the competition (Rule 6-1) and have only
themselves to blame.

**Determination of Handicap Allowances in Four-Ball Match
If One Player Unable To Compete** — See 30-3a/3.

6-2b/1   Wrong Handicap Used in Stroke Play by Mistake; Error Discovered After Competition Closed

Q. In a stroke play competition, A believed that his
handicap was ten strokes, which he recorded on his
score card. In fact his handicap was nine strokes. He
won the event because of the error. The result of the
competition was announced and the error was then
discovered.

What is the ruling?

A. The competition should stand as played. Under
Rule 34-1b, a penalty under Rule 6-2b may not be
imposed after a handicap stroke play competition has
closed unless the competitor has knowingly played off
a handicap higher than that to which he was entitled.

6-2b/2 Wrong Handicap Knowingly Used in Stroke Play; Error Discovered After Competition Closed

Q. In late June, A submitted an entry form for a handicap stroke play competition to be held on July 10 and stated therein that his handicap was seven strokes, which was his correct handicap. On July 1, A's handicap was reduced to six strokes and he was aware of the reduction.

On July 10, he played in the stroke play competition and returned his score card with a handicap of seven strokes recorded thereon. Under the conditions for the event he should have recorded his up-to-date handicap of six strokes. After the competition was closed, it was discovered that A had played off seven, instead of six.

The Committee questioned A, and A stated that he had assumed he should play off the handicap recorded on his entry form. What should the Committee do?

A. A should not have assumed he should play off seven. Under 34-1b, he should be disqualified for knowingly playing off a handicap higher than that to which he was entitled.

6-2b/2.5 Competitor Records Incorrect Handicap for Partner in Foursome Stroke Play Competition; Error Discovered After Competition Closed

Q. A and B were partners in a foursome stroke play competition. At the conclusion of the round, A recorded on the score card that his handicap was eight strokes but, mistakenly and without B's knowledge, recorded B's handicap as ten strokes, whereas B knew that his handicap was nine. The mistake affected the number of strokes received by the side, but was not discovered until after the competition had closed. What is the ruling?

A. The side should be disqualified for returning a score card on which B's recorded handicap was higher than that to which he was entitled and this affected the number of strokes received (Rule 6-2b). Since B knew that his handicap was nine, the fact that the competition had closed makes no difference — see Rule 34-1b(ii).

6

6-2b/3 Competitor Wins Competition with Handicap Which Was Incorrect Due to Committee Error; Error Discovered Several Days Later

Q. The Committee erroneously posted a competitor's handicap as 17 when it should have been 16. The competitor won a stroke play event as a result of the error. May the Committee correct the error several days later and retract the prize?

A. Yes. There is no time limit on correcting such an error. Rule 34-1b is not applicable since it deals with penalties, not with Committee errors.

The competitor should not be disqualified but his net score should be increased by one stroke.

6-2b/4 Competitors in Foursome Competition Fail to Record Individual Handicaps on Score Card

Q. In a foursome stroke play competition, partners A and B correctly calculated their combined handicap allowance and recorded it on their score card, rather than their individual handicaps.

A and B were disqualified. Was the ruling correct?

A. Yes. In any round of a handicap stroke play competition, it is the responsibility of the competitor to ensure that his handicap is recorded on his score card before it is returned to the Committee (Rule 6-2b).

The word "competitor" includes his partner in a stroke play foursome competition — see Definition of "Competitor." Therefore, the individual handicaps of A and B should have been recorded on the score card. As only the combined handicap allowance was recorded, A and B were correctly disqualified.

6-3a/1 Postponement of Final Match Due to Injury of Player

If a player who reaches the final of a match play event suffers an injury and is unable to play at the time arranged, the Committee may, with the concurrence of the opponent, postpone the match for a reasonable period. This applies in all forms of match play.

Competitor Refuses to Start Because of Weather Conditions; Round Subsequently Canceled — See 33-2d/3.

Status of Starting Time Fixed by Players — See 33-3/1.

Player Not Present at Time of Starting; Course Closed at the Time — See 33-3/2.

6-3a/2 Time of Starting; All Competitors Must Be Present

Q. In a stroke play competition, A, B and C were drawn by the Committee to play together starting at 9:00 a.m. A and B were present at the appointed time. C arrived at 9:02 a.m. after A and B had played from the teeing ground, but just in time to play in the correct order.

What is the ruling?

A. C is disqualified for failure to start at the time laid down by the Committee (Rule 6-3a) unless circumstances warrant waiving the penalty under Rule 33-7.

All competitors in a group must be present and ready to play at the time laid down by the Committee, in this case 9:00 a.m. The order of play is not relevant.

If the Committee had adopted the Note to Rule 6-3 as a condition of the competition, the five-minute period would have started at the time laid down by the Committee. Therefore, in this case the time started at 9:00 a.m. and C would incur a penalty of two strokes, rather than be subject to disqualification. (New)

6-4/1 Meaning of "Specific Directions" in Definition of "Caddie"

Q. A and B are sharing a caddie. A asks the caddie to bring him a club. The caddie removes A's club from his bag, places both bags behind the green and walks towards A to give him his club. At that point B plays and his ball strikes one of the bags. What is the ruling?

A. B incurred a penalty under Rule 19-2 (Ball in Motion Deflected or Stopped by Player's Equipment).

The Definition of "Caddie" (second paragraph) provides that, when a caddie is shared by two players, the equipment he carries is deemed to belong to the player whose ball is involved in any incident (in this case, B).

The only exception to the above provision occurs when the shared caddie is acting upon the specific directions of another player. In this case, although A asked the caddie to bring him a club, he did not instruct the caddie, when complying with his request, to place the two bags in a particular position. In placing the bags where he did, therefore, the caddie was not acting on "specific directions" of A within the meaning of that term in the Definition of "Caddie." Before playing, B could have asked the caddie to move the bags if he thought his ball might strike them.

6-4/2 Who May Serve as Caddie

There is no restriction in the Rules of Golf as to whom a player may employ as his caddie. Restrictions may be imposed by a Committee, however, in the conditions of a competition.

6-4/2.5 Status of Individual Who Transports Player's Clubs on Motorized Golf Cart or Trolley

Q. During a round, a player's clubs are transported on a motorized golf cart or trolley by a friend who performs no other functions of a caddie. Is the friend considered to be the player's caddie?

A. Yes. By driving the cart or pulling the trolley, the friend is deemed to be carrying the player's clubs- see Definition of "Caddie."

Condition Banning Use of Caddies — See 33-1/10.

Condition Restricting Player in Choice of Caddie — See 33-1/11.

6-4/3 Player Whose Clubs Are Transported on Motorized Golf Cart Hires Individual to Perform All Other Functions of a Caddie

Q. A player whose clubs are transported on a motorized golf cart hires an individual to perform all the other duties of a caddie. Is this permissible, and is the individual considered to be a caddie?

A. The individual is considered to be a caddie.

This arrangement is permissible provided the player has not engaged someone else to drive the cart. In such a case, the cart driver, since he is transporting the player's clubs, is also a caddie. Rule 6-4 prohibits a player from having two caddies at any one time.

Thus, the arrangement is permissible (a) if the player and an opponent or a fellow-competitor are sharing the cart, even if the player walks and the opponent or fellow-competitor drives the cart, or (b) if the cart is not being shared with an opponent or a fellow-competitor and the player drives the cart.

6-4/4 Caddie Hires Boy to Carry All of Player's Clubs Except Putter

Q. A player's caddie hires a young boy to carry all of the player's clubs except his putter, which the caddie carries. The caddie assists the player in other ways, *i.e.*, attends the flagstick and gives advice. The young boy does not so assist. Is this permissible?

A. No. The player would be considered to have two caddies in contravention of Rule 6-4.

6-4/4.5 Another Caddie or Friend Carries Clubs While Player's Caddie Returns to Tee with Player's Glove

Q. A player walks from the putting green of the previous hole to the next tee with his driver while his caddie walks ahead with the clubs in order to save time. The caddie realizes he has his player's glove and gives the clubs to another player's caddie or friend to be carried while he takes the player his glove.

Did the player have two caddies in breach of Rule 6-4?

A. No. The casual act of someone assisting the player or his caddie in these circumstances does not constitute a breach of Rule 6-4. (New)

6-4/5 Umbrella Carrier Employed in Addition to Caddie

Q. May a player employ both a caddie and a second person to carry his umbrella and hold it over his head (except when a stroke is being made) to protect him from the sun or rain?

A. Yes. The second person would be an outside agency. However, the Committee may prohibit the employment of an umbrella carrier in the conditions of the competition.

6-4/6 Status of Carts Pulled by Double Caddie

Q. A and B are sharing a caddie who is pulling A's bag on one cart and B's on another. A plays a stroke and his ball strikes B's cart. With reference to the Definition of "Caddie," since B's cart was not being carried by the caddie, would it be considered B's equipment?

A. No. The cart is considered A's equipment in these circumstances. The word "carried" in the Definition should not be taken so literally as to exclude the pulling of a cart by a caddie.

6-4/7 Changing Caddies During Round

Q. May a player have more than one caddie during a round? If so, may each caddie give the player advice?

A. A player may have more than one caddie during a round, provided he has only one at a time. He is entitled to receive advice from whoever is his caddie at the time — see Definition of "Caddie."

6-4/8 Player in Competition Caddies for Another Player in Same Event

6

Q. Two players playing in the same competition at different times on the same day caddie for each other. Is this permissible?

A. Yes.

6-4/9 Competitor Withdraws During Round and Carries Fellow-Competitor's Clubs for Remainder of Round

Q. In stroke play, A, B's fellow-competitor and marker, withdrew during a round and ceased to play. He continued to mark B's card, and also carried B's clubs for the rest of the round. Is this permissible?

A. Yes. A became B's caddie as well as his marker when he started carrying B's clubs.

6-4/10 Acts Which Caddie May Perform

While the Rules do not expressly so state, the following are examples of acts which the caddie may perform for the player:

1. Search for the player's ball as provided in Rule 12-1.
2. Place the player's clubs in a hazard — Exception 1 under 13-4.
3. Repair old hole plugs and ball marks — Rules 16-1a (vi) and -1c.
4. Remove loose impediments on the line of putt or elsewhere — Rules 16-1a and 23-1.
5. Mark the position of a ball — Rule 20-1.
6. Clean the player's ball — Rule 21.
7. Remove movable obstructions — Rule 24-1.

Competitor's Caddie Practices on or Tests Putting Green Surfaces of the Course Before Stroke Play Round — See 7-1b/5.

Ball Thrown into Bounds by Outside Agency and Played; Caddie Aware of Action of Outside Agency — See 15/9.

Caddie Roughens Surface of Putting Green But Player Does Not Benefit — See 16-1d/6.

Caddie on Own Initiative Lifts Ball Considering It Unplayable — See 18-2a/15.

Caddie Lifts Ball in Water Hazard Without Player's Authority — See 26-1/9.

6-6a/1 Lone Competitor Appoints Own Marker

Q. In a stroke play competition, a lone competitor had no marker. No member of the Committee was present to appoint one. So the competitor played with two players playing a friendly game, and one of them served as his marker. Should the Committee accept the card?

A. Yes. Since the Committee failed to provide a marker, the Committee should give retrospective authority to the player who acted as the competitor's marker.

Retrospective Appointment of Marker by Committee — See 33-1/5.

6-6a/2 Competitor Plays Several Holes Without Marker

Q. A plays three holes by himself while his marker, B, rests. B then resumes play and marks A's scores for the holes he (A) played alone as well as his scores for the remainder of the holes. Should A's card be accepted?

A. No. A should have insisted on B accompanying him or have discontinued play and reported to the Committee. Since A was not accompanied by a marker for three holes, he did not have an acceptable score.

6-6a/3 Hole Scores Entered in Wrong Boxes; Marker Corrects Error by Altering Hole Numbers on Card

Q. In stroke play, a marker recorded some of the competitor's hole scores in the wrong boxes. He altered the hole numbers on the card to correct the error. Should the card be accepted?

A. Yes.

Hole Scores for First Nine Holes Recorded in Boxes for Second Nine and Vice Versa — See 6-6d/3.

6-6a/4 Marker Refuses to Sign Competitor's Card After Dispute Resolved in Favor of Competitor

Q. In stroke play, B, who was A's fellow-competitor and marker, refused to sign A's score card on the ground that A had played outside the teeing ground at the 15th hole. A claimed that he played from within the teeing ground.

The Committee decided in favor of A. Despite the Committee's decision, B continued to refuse to sign A's card. Should B be penalized?

A. No. A marker is not obliged to sign a card he believes to be incorrect, notwithstanding the determination of the Committee. However, the marker must report the facts and authenticate those scores which he considers correct.

The Committee should accept certification of A's score at the 15th hole by anyone who witnessed the play of the hole. If no witness is available, the Committee should accept A's score without certification.

6-6a/5 Marker Attests Wrong Score Knowingly But Competitor Unaware Score Wrong

Q. In stroke play, a competitor returned a wrong score because his score card did not include a penalty he had incurred. The competitor was unaware that he had incurred the penalty. The competitor's marker (a fellow-competitor) was aware of the penalty but nevertheless signed the card. The facts were discovered before the result of the competition was officially announced.

The competitor is, of course, disqualified — Rule 6-6d. Is the marker also subject to disqualification?

A. Yes. The Committee should disqualify the marker under Rule 33-7.

Marker Attests Wrong Score Knowingly and Competitor Aware Score Wrong — See 1-3/6.

6-6a/6 Requirement That Alteration on Score Card Be Initialled

Q. May a Committee require that alterations made on score cards be initialled?

A. No. Nothing is laid down in the Rules of Golf as to how alterations should be made on a score card.

6-6a/7 Duplicate Card Returned When Original Lost

Q. At the end of a round in stroke play, A discovered that he had lost B's card. A duplicate card was prepared, signed by both A and B and returned promptly. Should it be accepted?

A. Yes.

6-6b/1 Competitor and Marker Sign Score Card in Wrong Places

There is no penalty if a marker signs the competitor's score card in the space provided for the competitor's signature, and the competitor then signs in the space provided for the marker's signature.

6-6b/2 Competitor Records Initials in Space Reserved for Signature

Q. Instead of recording his usual signature on his score card, a competitor records his initials. Has the competitor met the requirements of Rule 6-6b?

A. Yes.

6-6b/3 Competitor Fails to Sign First-Round Card; Error Discovered on Completion of Last Round

Q. In a 36-hole stroke play event, it was discovered just before the results were announced that a competitor had omitted to sign his score card at the end of the first round. In all other respects the cards for both rounds were correct. Should he be disqualified?

A. Yes, because he was in breach of Rule 6-6b.

Signing of Score Card in Foursome Stroke Play — See 29/6.

Competitor's Failure to Countersign Card Blamed on Lack of Time Provided by Committee — See 33-7/3.

Competitor's Failure to Countersign Card Discovered After Competition Closed — See 34-1b/2.

6-6b/4 Score Cards Not Returned Promptly Due to Committee Failure to Advise Competitors Where to Return Cards

It is a duty of the Committee to inform competitors where and to whom to return their score cards. If the Committee fails to do so, and as a result some competitors delay in returning cards, a penalty of disqualification under Rule 6-6b or any other Rule would not be justified.

6-6b/5 Marker Not Appointed by Committee Signs Cards

Q. In stroke play, A and B were appointed by the Committee as markers for one another. During the round, C joined them as a spectator; from that point, C marked the cards of both A and B, signed them at the end of the round and returned them to A and B. A and B checked their respective cards, signed them and returned them to the Committee. Before the competition closed, the Committee became aware that A had not signed B's card and vice versa. What is the ruling?

A. Since C had not been appointed as a marker by the Committee and there were no exceptional circumstances, A and B should be disqualified under Rule 6-6b.

6-6b/6 Marker Disappears with Competitor's Score Card

Q. In a stroke play event, competitors were instructed to return their score cards at the scoreboard. Unbeknownst to a competitor, his marker leaves the course hastily at the end of the round and does not report to the scoreboard. He takes the competitor's score card with him. What should the Committee do?

A. The Committee should make every effort to reach the marker. If unsuccessful, the Committee should accept certification of the score by someone else who witnessed the round, perhaps the marker's caddie or the competitor's caddie. If no one other than the marker witnessed the round, the score should be accepted without attestation by a marker.

6-6b/7 Score Corrected by Competitor After Marker Leaves Area in Which Card Returned

Q. A marker signed a competitor's score card, gave it to the competitor and left the area. The competitor discovered an error in his score for the 14th hole; the marker had recorded a 5 when, in fact, the competitor had scored 4. Without consulting the Committee, the competitor corrected the card, signed it and handed it in to the Committee. Later, the Committee heard what had happened, interviewed the competitor and his marker and established that the competitor did, in fact, score 4 at the 14th hole. Was the competitor in breach of Rule 6-6b and thus disqualified?

A. Yes. When the competitor altered the score card, he invalidated the attestation of his score by the marker. Therefore, he effectively returned a score card which was not signed by the marker.

If the competitor had informed the Committee, before returning his card, that he was correcting the error, he would not have been subject to penalty.

6-6d/1 No Score Entered for One Hole But Total Correct

Q. In stroke play, A returned his score card. The Committee discovered that no score had been entered for the 17th hole; however, A's total score for the round as recorded on the card by A or his marker was correct. What is the ruling?

6

A. A should be disqualified for a breach of Rule 6-6d.

Gross Score of Partner with Better Net Score Omitted from Card — See 31-4/1.

6-6d/2 Total Score Recorded by Competitor Incorrect

Q. In stroke play, a competitor returns his score card to the Committee. The hole by hole scores are correct, but the competitor records a total score which is one stroke lower than his actual total score. Is the competitor subject to penalty?

A. No. The competitor is responsible only for the correctness of the score recorded for each hole — Rule 6-6d. The Committee is responsible for the addition of scores — Rule 33-5. If the competitor records a wrong total score, the Committee must correct the error, without penalty to the competitor.

6-6d/3 Hole Scores for First Nine Holes Recorded in Boxes for Second Nine and Vice Versa

Q. A competitor who started at the 10th hole returns a card with scores for the first nine holes recorded in the boxes for the second nine holes, and vice versa. Should he be disqualified since the scores for some holes were lower than actually taken?

A. Yes.

Hole Scores Entered in Wrong Boxes; Marker Corrects Error by Altering Hole Numbers on Card — See 6-6a/3.

6-6d/4 Competitor's Scores Recorded on Fellow-Competitor's Card and Vice Versa

Q. A and B are playing together in stroke play. A is B's marker and B is A's marker. The starter, by mistake, gives A his own card instead of B's, and vice versa. Or A and B are given each other's cards by the starter, and, by mistake, they exchange them. This results in A recording B's scores on his (A's) card and B recording A's scores on his (B's) card.

The error is discovered after the cards are returned. What is the ruling?

A. Assuming that at least one of the scores on A's card is lower than the score actually taken by A and at least one of the scores on B's card is lower than the score actually taken by B, both A and B are disqualified under Rule 6-6d.

If the error had been discovered before the cards were returned, no penalty would be incurred if A struck B's name from B's card and inserted his own, and vice versa.

6-6d/5 Spectators Allege Competitor's Score Incorrect

Q. All strokes played by A at the 18th hole were observed by spectators, but when the card was returned the recorded score for that hole was lower than that which the spectators alleged had been taken. What should the Committee do?

A. If any doubt arises as to the correctness of a card, the Committee should consult with the competitor and marker and also take into account the testimony of other witnesses.

If the evidence indicates that the recorded score for the 18th hole was lower than actually taken, the Committee should disqualify A — Rule 6-6d. Otherwise, no penalty should be applied.

Competitor in Four-Ball Stroke Play Records Score for Hole Not Completed — See 31-7a/1.

Competitor in Four-Ball Stroke Play Attributes Lower Gross Score to Wrong Partner — See 31-7a/2.

Modifying Penalty for Returning Wrong Score — See 33-7/4.

Competitor Unaware of Penalty Returns Wrong Score; Whether Waiving or Modifying Disqualification Penalty Justified — See 33-7/4.5.

Omission of Penalty Stroke When Score Returned — See 34-1b/1.

6

Omission of Penalty Strokes When Score Returned Is Due to Incorrect Ruling — See 34-3/1.

6-7/1 Player Returns to Tee to Retrieve Forgotten Club

Q. A player arrives at a green and discovers that he has left his putter at the tee. He returns to the tee to retrieve the putter. If this delays play, is the player subject to penalty?

A. Yes. Rule 6-7 (Undue Delay) and not Rule 6-8a (Discontinuance of Play) applies in this case.

6-7/2 Searching Ten Minutes for Lost Ball

Q. If a player searches for a lost ball for ten minutes, is he subject to penalty under Rule 6-7 for undue delay?

A. Yes.

Second Ball Played Despite Adverse Ruling — See 3-3/2.

Ascertaining Whereabouts of Opponent's Ball Before Playing — See 9-2/16.

Player Requests Another Player to Lift His Ball in Absence of Reasonable Possibility That Ball Might Interfere or Assist — See 22/3.

Removal of Large Loose Impediment Delays Play — See 23-1/2.

Player Searches for Lost Ball After Putting Another Ball into Play — See 27/9.

6-8a/1 Watching Television for 45 Minutes After Nine Holes

Q. In stroke play, a group went into the clubhouse after nine holes and watched the final round of a golf tournament on television for 45 minutes. Then the group resumed play. Should the members of the group be penalized under Rule 6-7 (Undue Delay) or Rule 6-8 (Discontinuance of Play)?

A. The competitors should be disqualified under Rule 6-8a.

6

6-8a/2 Taking Shelter While Waiting to Play

Q. In stroke play, a group preparing to start a hole is waiting for the group ahead to get out of range. May the group take shelter from the rain in a rain shelter close to the tee?

A. Yes, but the group must leave the shelter and resume play as soon as the group in front is out of range.

6-8a/3 Discontinuing Play Due to Physical Problem

Q. During a round, a player is incapacitated by heat exhaustion, a bee sting or because he has been struck by a golf ball. The player reports his problem to the Committee and requests the Committee to allow him some time to recuperate. Should the Committee comply with the request?

A. The matter is up to the Committee. Rule 6-8a(iv) permits a player to discontinue play because of sudden illness and the player incurs no penalty if he reports to the Committee as soon as practicable and the Committee considers his reason satisfactory. It would seem reasonable for a Committee to allow a player ten or 15 minutes to recuperate from such a physical problem but ordinarily allowing more time than that would be inadvisable.

6-8a/4 Discontinuing Play Due to Inoperable Motorized Cart

Q. In stroke play, two competitors are sharing a motorized golf cart. During the round the cart becomes inoperable. The competitors discontinue play and return to the clubhouse to obtain another cart. Should the competitors be penalized for discontinuing play?

6

A. If the competitors reported to the Committee as soon as practicable after discontinuing play (as required by Rule 6-8a), it is recommended that, since it may not always be reasonable to expect players to carry their own bags, the Committee may consider the reason for discontinuance satisfactory, in which case there would be no penalty provided the competitors resume play when directed to do so by the Committee.

6-8a/5 Match Discontinued by Agreement Due to Rain; One Player Subsequently Wishes to Resume; Opponent Refuses Although Course Playable

Q. In accordance with the Exception under Rule 6-8a, A and B discontinue a match due to rain. Subsequently, although the rain continues to fall, A wishes to resume play. B refuses because he does not want to play in the rain, not because he considers the course unplayable. What is the ruling?

A. B is disqualified — Rule 6-8a. The Exception to Rule 6-8a permits discontinuance of a match by mutual agreement. However, when A decided that he wanted to resume play, there was no longer an agreement and B was obliged to resume play.

6-8a/6 Match Discontinued by Agreement Due to Rain; One Player Subsequently Wishes to Resume; Opponent Refuses on Ground Course Unplayable

Q. In accordance with the Exception under Rule 6-8a, A and B discontinue a match due to rain. Subsequently, A wishes to resume play. B refuses on the ground that the course is unplayable. What is the ruling?

A. B is entitled to refer the dispute to a representative of the Committee if one is available within a reasonable time. If a Committee member is not available within a reasonable time, B is obliged to continue the match without delay — Rule 2-5. If B does not do so, he is disqualified under Rule 6-8a, which allows a player to discontinue play for a decision on a disputed point, but only within the limits prescribed in Rule 2-5.

However, before continuing the match B is entitled to make a claim that the course is unplayable — Rule 2-5. If B does so, (a) the match should be resumed at the spot at which it was discontinued if the Committee subsequently upholds B's claim, or (b) the match should stand as played if the Committee subsequently rejects B's claim.

Replaying Match When Play Discontinued Instead of Resuming from Where Play Stopped — See 2-3/5.

Player Returns to Tee to Retrieve Forgotten Club — See 6-7/1.

Discontinuing Play Because Hole-Liner Not Sunk Deep Enough — See 16/4.

Discontinuing Play Due to Raised or Sunken Hole Plug on Line of Putt — See 16-1c/3.

Competitor Discontinues Play Because of Weather Conditions; Round Subsequently Canceled — See 33-2d/3.

6-8b/1 Competitors Playing Hole When Play Suspended Discontinue Play Immediately But Then Complete Hole Before Committee Orders Resumption of Play

Q. In stroke play, a group was playing a hole when it was announced that play was suspended. The group discontinued play for 10 to 15 minutes and then decided to complete the hole, even though the Committee had not yet announced resumption of play. Is this permissible?

A. No. Competitors playing a hole when play is suspended may only continue play of that hole if they do so without delay — Rule 6-8b. The group in question was in breach of Rule 6-8b. The penalty is disqualification.

6-8b/2 Options If Play Suspended After One Competitor in Group Has Played from Tee

Q. In stroke play, A plays a stroke from the teeing ground and the competition is at that point suspended. May B, A's fellow-competitor, also play from the teeing ground, even though play has been suspended?

A. Yes. When A played from the teeing ground, play had commenced for that hole and thus A and B may continue play of the hole provided they do so without delay and then discontinue play either before or immediately after completing it.

6-8b/3 Completion of Hole by One Competitor in Group After Play Suspended During Play of Hole

Q. In stroke play, A plays a stroke from the teeing ground and play is at that point suspended. B, A's marker and fellow-competitor, decides not to play the hole until play is officially resumed. May A play alone and complete the hole?

A. Yes, provided B accompanies A until the hole is completed. Otherwise, A would have no marker for the hole and thus would not have an acceptable score for the round.

6-8b/4 Player Unable to Resume Suspended Match at Scheduled Time

Q. During a match play competition, the course becomes unplayable and play is suspended. The Committee announces that the suspended matches will be completed the next day. One player states that he is unable to play the next day. What is the ruling?

A. The player is disqualified under Rule 6-8b.

6-8b/5 Player Claiming Danger from Lightning Refuses to Resume Play When Resumption Ordered by Committee

Q. In a stroke play competition, the Committee, after having suspended play because of lightning, orders play to be resumed. Must a player resume play if he considers that there is still danger from lightning?

A. Rule 6-8a authorizes a player to discontinue play if he considers that there is danger from lightning. This is one of the rare occasions on which the player is virtually the final judge. The safety of players is paramount, especially as there is a common natural fear of lightning. Committees should not risk exposing players to danger.

However, if the Committee has used all reasonable means to ascertain the weather prospects and has concluded that no danger from lightning exists, it has the power to order resumption of play and to disqualify under Rule 6-8b any player who refuses to comply.

Local Rule for Suspension of Play due to Dangerous Situation — See US/33-8/102.

6-8b/6 Play Suspended by Committee; Competitor Does Not Resume Play at Time Ordered by Committee

Q. In stroke play, the Committee suspends play. Subsequently, the Committee advises all competitors that a siren will signify resumption of play at a specific time.

A competitor in one group resumed play about two minutes before the siren sounded, because he saw a group of competitors walking down an adjacent fairway. Should the competitor be disqualified under Rule 6-8b?

A. No. Due to the exceptional nature of resumption of play, such minor errors are inevitable, and a penalty of disqualification is too severe. Accordingly, if the Committee has ordered a resumption of play and a competitor is no more than five minutes late (or five minutes early) in resuming play, the Committee would be justified in modifying the disqualification penalty to two strokes or, if circumstances warrant, waiving it entirely under Rule 33-7.

In this case, modifying the penalty to two strokes would be appropriate.

6-8c/1 When Ball May Be Cleaned or Substituted After Play Has Been Discontinued

When play has been discontinued under Rule 6-8a, the player may lift and clean his ball or substitute another ball at any time before he addresses the ball or, if he does not address it, before he makes his next stroke at it on the resumption of play.

6

7

Rule 7. Practice

7-1. Before or Between Rounds

a. MATCH PLAY

On any day of a match play competition, a player may practice on the competition <u>course</u> before a round.

b. STROKE PLAY

On any day of a stroke competition or play-off, a competitor shall not practice on the competition <u>course</u> or test the surface of any putting green on the course before a round or play-off. When two or more rounds of a stroke competition are to be played over consecutive days, practice between those rounds on any competition course remaining to be played is prohibited.

Exception: Practice putting or chipping on or near the first <u>teeing ground</u> before starting a round or play-off is permitted.

PENALTY FOR BREACH OF RULE 7-1b:
Disqualification.

Note: The Committee may in the conditions of a competition (Rule 33-1) prohibit practice on the competition course on any day of a match play competition or permit practice on the competition course or part of the course (Rule 33-2c) on any day of or between rounds of a stroke competition.

7-2. During Round

A player shall not play a practice <u>stroke</u> either during the play of a hole or between the play of two holes except that, between the play of two holes, the player may practice putting or chipping on or near the <u>putting green</u> of the hole last played, any practice putting green or the <u>teeing ground</u> of the next hole to be played in the round, provided such practice stroke is not played from a hazard and does not unduly delay play (Rule 6-7).

Exception: When play has been suspended by the Committee, a player may, prior to resumption of play, practice (a) as provided in this Rule, (b) anywhere other than on the competition course and (c) as otherwise permitted by the Committee.

PENALTY FOR BREACH OF RULE 7-2:
Match play --- Loss of hole;
Stroke play --- Two strokes.

In the event of a breach between the play of two holes, the penalty applies to the next hole.

Note 1: A practice swing is not a practice <u>stroke</u> and may be taken at any place, provided the player does not breach the Rules.

Note 2: The Committee may prohibit practice on or near the <u>putting green</u> of the hole last played.

7-1b/1 One Practice Stroke Played on Course Before Stroke Play Round

Q. On the day of a stroke play competition, a competitor, before starting his round, played one practice stroke from a forward tee at the first hole into an out-of-bounds area. What is the ruling?

A. The competitor infringed Rule 7-1b and was subject to disqualification. However, the Committee would be justified, in the circumstances, in modifying the penalty to two strokes under Rule 33-7. If the competitor played more than one such stroke, modification of the disqualification penalty would not be appropriate.

7-1b/2 Waiving Penalty for Practice on Course

Q. A 36-hole stroke play competition was scheduled over consecutive days. After completing his first round, a competitor who was a member of the club at which the event was being held played several more holes and thus was subject to disqualification under Rule 7-1b.

Would the Committee be justified in waiving or modifying the penalty?

A. No.

7-1b/3 Competitor Who Practices on Competition Course After Qualifying Round Subsequently Is in Play-Off on Same Day

Q. After early completion of a stroke play qualifying round for a match play event, a competitor practiced on the competition course after the last group in the competition had teed off. After the conclusion of play, the competitor was tied for the last place in the match play event. Such a tie was to be decided by a sudden-death play-off which was scheduled to be played immediately. Was the competitor subject to disqualification from the play-off under Rule 7-1b? If so, would the Committee have been justified in waiving the penalty under Rule 33-7?

A. The competitor was subject to disqualification. Waiving the penalty is not recommended in such circumstances.

7-1b/4 Stroke Play Over 36 Holes on Two Courses; Player Completes First Round, Practices on Same Course and Is Later in Play-Off on That Course

Q. Stroke play to determine the qualifiers for match play was scheduled over 36 holes on consecutive days.

Eighteen holes were to be played on the East Course and 18 on the North Course. Any play-off was to be held on the East Course.

Several competitors who played their first qualifying round on the East Course wanted to play more golf. They knew that they would be in breach of Rule 7-1b if they played the North Course, so they played the East Course again.

After the second qualifying round, one of the competitors was tied for the last qualifier's place. Should he be disqualified from the play-off on the East Course under Rule 7-1b?

A. Yes.

7-1b/5 Competitor's Caddie Practices on or Tests Putting Green Surfaces of the Course Before Stroke Play Round

Q. In stroke play, a competitor's caddie practices on or tests the putting green surfaces of the course before the competitor tees off. In view of the second paragraph of Rule 6-4, is the competitor disqualified under Rule 7-1b?

A. No. A competitor is responsible for the actions of his caddie only during a round.

7-1b/6 Stroke Play Over 54 Holes on Consecutive Days; Second Round Canceled and Competitor Practices on Course Following Cancellation

Q. A 54-hole stroke play competition was scheduled to be played on consecutive days. The second round was canceled when the course became unplayable, and the competition was reduced to 36 holes. A competitor practiced on the course on the day of the second round after that round was canceled. Was the competitor subject to disqualification for a breach of Rule 7-1b?

A. Yes, because the competition was scheduled to be played over consecutive days. It is irrelevant that at the time the competitor practiced the competition was no longer to be played over consecutive days.

However, the Committee may in such circumstances permit practice on the course between rounds — see Note under Rule 7-1b.

7-1b/7 Competitor Practices Putting on 3rd Green After Finishing Hole During First Round of 36-Hole Stroke Play Competition

7

Q. A 36-hole stroke play competition was scheduled to be played on one day. During the first round a competitor, having holed out at the 3rd hole, plays a practice putt on the 3rd green. Is the competitor disqualified under Rule 7-1b for practicing on the course before his second round?

A. No. A competitor is entitled to do anything which the Rules permit him to do during a stipulated round. Rule 7-2 permits a player between the play of two holes to practice putting or chipping on or near the putting green of the hole last played, any practice putting green or the teeing ground of the next hole to be played in the round, provided such practice stroke is not played from a hazard and does not unduly delay play (Rule 6-7). (New)

Competitor Practices Putting on 18th Green Immediately After Finishing First Round of Stroke Play Competition Played Over Consecutive Days — See 7-2/8.

7-2/1 When Play of Hole Over

Q. In connection with Rule 7-2, which prohibits practice during play of a hole, when is play of a hole completed by a player?

A. *Singles match play* — When he has holed out, his next stroke has been conceded or he has conceded the hole.

Individual stroke play — When he has holed out.

Four-ball match play — When both he and his partner have holed out, their next strokes have been conceded or the side has conceded the hole.

Four-ball stroke play — When both he and his partner have holed out or picked up.

7-2/1.5 Completing Hole in Match Play After Result of Hole Decided

Q. In a match between A and B, A holes out for a 4. B has played four strokes and his ball lies in a bunker. Thus, the hole has been decided. If B plays from the bunker, would the stroke be considered a practice stroke? If so, a breach of Rule 7-2 would occur.

A. No. Strokes played in completing a hole the result of which has been decided are not practice strokes within the meaning of the term in Rule 7-2.

7-2/2 Putting on Fairway While Waiting to Play to Green

Q. While waiting to play to the putting green, a player dropped a ball on the fairway and struck it several times with his putter. When questioned, he stated that he was not practicing but was "killing time." What is the ruling?

A. The player was in breach of Rule 7-2.

In Anger Player Hits Ball Played by Player in Following Group — See 1-4/4.

7-2/3 Player Practices Putting Off Green While Waiting to Putt

Q. A player lifted his ball on the putting green and, while waiting for his opponent or a fellow-competitor to play, dropped his ball off the green and played a few practice putts. What is the penalty?

A. Under Rule 7-2 the player lost the hole in match play or incurred a penalty of two strokes in stroke play.

7-2/4 Hitting Plastic Ball Before Playing Ball in Play

Q. During play of a hole, a player plays a stroke with a plastic ball before playing his ball in play. Is he in breach of Rule 7-2?

A. Yes.

7

7-2/5 Hitting Practice Range Ball Back to Range

Q. During play of a hole, a player saw some balls from the adjoining practice range lying on the course and flicked one back to the range with his club. Is there a penalty under Rule 7-2?

A. In some circumstances the hitting of a practice range ball back towards the range during the play of a hole would be a breach of Rule 7-2, but the casual flicking of a range ball, apparently only for the purpose of tidying up the course, is not a breach.

7-2/5.5 Player Finds Ball and Hits It to Player Who Lost It

Q. As A was playing the 13th hole, X, who was playing the adjoining 14th, was searching for his ball on the 13th fairway. X could not find his ball and walked off down the 14th. A then found X's ball plugged in the 13th fairway and called to him. X requested that the ball be returned to him. As X was out of throwing range, A hit the ball to him with a short iron.

In doing so, should A be considered to have played a practice stroke in contravention of Rule 7-2?

A. No. Since A was acting out of courtesy, there is no penalty.

[7-2/6 Reserved]

7-2/7 Practice Swing Dislodges Concealed Ball

Q. A player makes a practice swing in the rough and dislodges a concealed ball. Is there any penalty?

A. No. Since the player had no intention of striking the concealed ball, his swing remained a practice swing and was not a stroke. Consequently, there is no question of his having played either a practice stroke (Rule 7-2) or a stroke with a wrong ball (Rule 15).

Ball Moved Accidentally by Practice Swing — See 18-2a/19 and 18-2a/20.

7-2/8   Competitor Practices Putting on 18th Green Immediately After Finishing First Round of Stroke Play Competition Played Over Consecutive Days

Q. In a 72-hole stroke play competition held over four consecutive days, a competitor, immediately after holing out at the 18th hole of the first round, plays a practice putt on the 18th green. Is the competitor disqualified under Rule 7-1b for practicing on the course between rounds?

A. No. Rule 7-2 permits practice putting or chipping on or near the putting green of the hole last played between the play of two holes. It follows that the same privilege applies immediately after completion of the last hole of the round, even though technically such practice would be between rounds, not during a round.

Rule 7-1b would apply if a competitor, after holing out at the 18th hole, left the course and later returned and played a practice putt on the 18th green.

Competitor Practices Putting on 3rd Green After Finishing Hole During First Round of 36-Hole Stroke Play Competition — See 7-1b/7.

Player in Foursome Match Practices Putts on Previous Green After Partner Has Driven from Next Tee — See 29/3.

Player Plays Practice Putt After He and Partner Have Holed Out But Before Opponents Hole Out — See 30/6.

Player After Picking Up Drops Ball Where Partner's Ball Lies and Plays Practice Stroke — See 30-3f/7.

In Four-Ball Player Disqualified for Next Hole Plays That Hole; Whether Strokes Played on That Hole Were Practice Strokes — See 30-3f/8.

Rule 8. Advice; Indicating Line of Play

8

Definitions

"Advice" is any counsel or suggestion which could influence a player in determining his play, the choice of a club or the method of making a <u>stroke</u>.

Information on the Rules or on matters of public information, such as the position of hazards or the flagstick on the putting green, is not advice.

The "line of play" is the direction which the player wishes his ball to take after a stroke, plus a reasonable distance on either side of the intended direction. The line of play extends vertically upwards from the ground, but does not extend beyond the hole.

8-1. Advice

A player shall not give advice to anyone in the competition except his partner. A player may ask for advice from only his partner or either of their caddies.

8-2. Indicating Line of Play

a. OTHER THAN ON PUTTING GREEN

Except on the <u>putting green</u>, a player may have the line of play indicated to him by anyone, but no one shall stand on or close to the line while the <u>stroke</u> is being played. Any mark placed during the play of a hole by the player or with his knowledge to indicate the line shall be removed before the stroke is played.

Exception: Flagstick attended or held up — see Rule 17-1.

b. ON THE PUTTING GREEN

When the player's ball is on the <u>putting green</u>, the player, his partner or either of their caddies may, before but not during the <u>stroke</u>, point out a line for putting, but in so doing the putting green shall not be touched. No mark shall be placed anywhere to indicate a line for putting.

> PENALTY FOR BREACH OF RULE:
> *Match play --- Loss of hole;*
> *Stroke play --- Two strokes.*

Note: In a team competition with or without concurrent individual competition, the Committee may in the conditions of the competition (Rule 33-1) permit each team to appoint one person, *e.g.*, team captain or coach, who may give <u>advice</u> (including pointing out a line for putting) to members of that team. Such person shall be identified to the Committee prior to the start of the competition.

8/1 Conditions of Team Competition Stipulate Who Is Authorized to Give Advice

Q. A condition of a team competition stipulates that only the Team Captain may give advice or that the person to be appointed by each team to give advice must be an amateur. Is this permitted.?

A. Yes. (New)

8-1/1 Seeking Information About Length of Hole

Q. A player asks his opponent or fellow-competitor the length of the hole about to be played. This information was not displayed on the teeing ground. Was the player in breach of Rule 8-1 which prohibits asking for advice?

A. No. Information as to the length of a hole is not advice within the meaning of the term in the Rules. This is factual information normally available to all players through score cards, tee signs, etc.

8

8-1/2 Inquiring as to Distance from Certain Object to Green

A player may ask anyone to inform him as to the distance from a permanent object, *e.g.*, tree, bunker, sprinkler head, etc., to the center of the putting green. Information as to the distance from a permanent object to a putting green is public information.

A player may ask only his partner or either of their caddies to inform him as to the distance from a non-permanent object, *e.g.*, his ball, to the putting green.

8-1/3 Asking If Distance Marker Accurate

Q. A player inquires of another player as to the accuracy of a 150-yard marker. Was the player in breach of Rule 8-1?

A. No.

[8-1/4 Reserved]

8-1/5 Seeking Information on Whereabouts of Another Player's Ball

Q. A player preparing to play to a putting green asks a spectator to advise him how far his opponent's or fellow-competitor's ball, which is on the green, lies from the flagstick. Was the player in breach of Rule 8-1?

A. No.

8-1/6 Asking Opponent or Fellow-Competitor What Club He Used at Previous Hole

Q. During play of the 6th hole, A asked B what club he had used for a shot at the 4th hole. Was A in breach of Rule 8-1?

A. No.

8

8-1/7 After Player Has Played to Green He Asks Opponent or Fellow-Competitor What Club He Used in Playing to Green

Q. A plays his second shot which lands on the green. B does likewise. A then asks B what club he used for his second shot. Was A in breach of Rule 8-1?

A. No.

8-1/8 Comment About Club Selection After Stroke

Q. After playing a stroke, a player says: "I should have used a 5-iron." Was the player in breach of Rule 8-1?

A. If the statement was made casually, there was no breach. If the statement was made to another player who had a shot to play from about the same position, there was a breach.

8-1/9 Misleading Statement About Club Selection

Q. A made a statement regarding his club selection which was purposely misleading and was obviously intended to be overheard by B, who had a similar shot. What is the ruling?

A. A was in breach of Rule 8-1 and lost the hole in match play or incurred a two-stroke penalty in stroke play.

8-1/10 Looking into Another Player's Bag to Determine Club Used

Q. A looks into B's bag to determine which club B used for his last stroke. Is this the equivalent of asking for advice?

A. No. Information obtained by observation is not advice. But see also Decision 8-1/11.

8

8-1/11 Removing Towel Covering Another Player's Clubs to Determine Club Used

Q. Decision 8-1/10 states that it is not a breach of Rule 8-1 for A to look into B's golf bag to determine which club B used for his last stroke. Suppose a towel was covering B's clubs and A removed the towel in order to determine which club B had used, would that be a breach of Rule 8-1?

A. Yes. A player is prohibited from obtaining such information through a physical act.

8-1/12 Double Caddie Informs One Employer About Club Used by Other

Q. When one caddie is employed by two players, A and B, who are not partners, is it permissible for A, who is about to play, to ask the caddie which club B used for a stroke from a nearby position?

A. Yes. A is entitled to seek from the caddie any information the caddie might possess.

8-1/13 Player Giving Opponent or Fellow-Competitor Instruction During Round

Q. During a round a player tells an opponent or a fellow-competitor that he is overswinging. Is this giving advice in breach of Rule 8-1?

A. Yes.

8-1/14 Competitor, After Finishing Hole, Demonstrates to Fellow-Competitor How to Play Shot

Q. In individual stroke play, A, who had holed out, demonstrated to B, whose ball was just off the green, how he should play his chip shot. What is the ruling?

A. B incurred no penalty as he did not seek advice. A incurred a penalty of two strokes for giving advice to B. The penalty would be applied to the hole being played.

8-1/15 Caddie Swings Club to Show Player How to Play Shot

Q. A player's caddie takes one of his clubs and swings it to show him how to play a certain shot. Is this permissible?

A. Yes, provided there is no undue delay. A player may always seek and accept advice from his caddie — Rule 8-1.

8-1/16 Suggesting to Competitor That He Declare His Ball Unplayable

Q. B's ball was lying badly. B was deliberating what action to take when A, his fellow-competitor, said: "You have no shot at all. If I were you, I would declare the ball unplayable." Was A giving advice, contrary to Rule 8-1?

A. Yes. A's suggestion could have influenced B "in determining his play." Thus, it constituted advice — see Definition of "Advice." It did not constitute "information on the Rules," which is not advice.

8-1/17 Request for Advice Made in Error to Opponent's Caddie Withdrawn Before Advice Given

Q. While surveying his putt, A sought advice from B's caddie, whom he mistook for his own caddie. A immediately realized his mistake and told B's caddie not to answer. The caddie said nothing. What is the ruling?

A. There should be no penalty.

8-1/18 Player Who Has Not Yet Played Seeks Advice from Player Who Has Finished Round

Q. May a player about to start his round seek advice as to clubs used at various holes from a player who has just finished?

A. Yes. Rule 8-1 applies only during the play of a round.

8-1/19 Advice Between Rounds in 36-Hole Match

Q. May a player seek advice, other than from his partner or caddie, after 18 holes in a 36-hole match?

A. Yes. Rule 8-1 applies only during a stipulated round. A 36-hole match consists of two 18-hole stipulated rounds — see Definition of "Stipulated Round."

8-1/20 Asking Advice When Play Suspended

Q. A is about to play the 6th hole, a par-3, when play is suspended by the Committee. Prior to the resumption of play, A asks X, who had already played the 6th, what club he used for his tee shot. Is A penalized under Rule 8-1?

A. No. The prohibition against giving or asking for advice applies only during a stipulated round. In this case, the stipulated round had been suspended.

8-1/21 Advice Given by Team Mate in Another Group in Stroke Play

Q. Individual and team competitions are being played concurrently in stroke play. A competitor is given advice by a team mate who is playing in another group. What is the ruling?

A. The team mate would be penalized two strokes.

8-1/22 Team Mates Playing as Fellow-Competitors Exchange Advice

Q. The format for a competition between two teams is as follows: Individual stroke play, with the winner being the team with the lowest aggregate score. Play is in groups of four, with two players from each team in each group.

In such an event, may two team members playing in the same group give each other advice?

A. No. The team mates are fellow-competitors and not partners in this type of event, which is not the same as four-ball stroke play (Rule 31, Preamble), and they would be penalized for each breach of Rule 8-1.

8-1/23 Player's Team Mate in Gallery Hits Ball to Green to Show Player Whether Green Will Hold

Q. In a team competition, A, a member of one team, is playing against B, a member of the opposing team. X, a team mate of A, is in the gallery. X drops a ball close to A's ball and hits it to the green to show A whether or not the green will hold. What is the ruling?

A. In equity (Rule 1-4), if A did nothing to stop X's irregular action, he should lose the hole in view of the purpose of Rule 8-1.

8-1/24 Advice Given by Team Coach or Captain

Q. A team competition is being played, and in the conditions the Committee has not authorized captains or coaches to give advice under the Note to Rule 8. A non-playing coach or captain gives advice during a round to one of the members of his team. What is the ruling?

A. There is no penalty. However, the player should take action to stop this irregular procedure. If he does not do so, he should, in equity (Rule 1-4), incur a penalty of two strokes in view of the purpose of Rule 8-1.

Conditions of Team Competition Stipulate Who is Authorized to Give Advice — See 8/1.

8-1/25 Advice Given on Request; Penalties in Various Forms of Play

In singles match play, if A asks for advice from B, it is irrelevant whether B gives advice because A lost the hole as soon as he asked.

In a four-ball match, A and B versus C and D, if A asks for advice from C and C gives advice, A and C are disqualified for the hole. The penalties do not apply to their partners — Rule 30-3f.

In stroke play, if A asks for advice from B, a fellow-competitor, A incurs a penalty of two strokes. If B gives advice, he also incurs a penalty of two strokes.

Absent Partner Gives Advice Before Joining Four-Ball Match — See 30-3a/2.

8-2a/1 Club Placed on Ground to Align Feet

Q. A player places a club on the ground parallel to the line of play to assist him in aligning his feet properly. Is this permissible?

A. Yes, provided the player removes the club before playing his stroke. Otherwise, a breach of Rule 8-2a would occur.

8-2a/2 Object Placed Beside or Behind Ball to Indicate Line of Play

Q. May a player place his pipe or a club beside his ball, or an object behind his ball, to indicate the line of play and leave the object there while playing a stroke?

A. No. Such action would be a breach of Rule 8-2a.

8-2b/1 Caddie Casts Shadow to Indicate Line of Putt

Q. A caddie cast his shadow on the putting green for the purpose of indicating to the player a line for putting. Is this permissible?

A. No. Such action is a breach of Rule 8-2b if the shadow remains in position while the stroke is being played.

8

[8-2b/2 Reserved]

8-2b/3 Caddie Touches Putting Green to Indicate Line of Play Before Player Chips from Off Green

Q. The caddie of a player who is preparing to play a chip shot from off the putting green touches the green with a club to indicate the line of play. What is the ruling?

A. There is no penalty. The prohibition against touching the putting green to indicate the line of play applies only if the player's ball lies on the putting green.

8-2b/4 Whether Team Captain Who Is Authorized to Give Advice May Be Required to Keep Off Putting Greens

Q. Under the Note to Rule 8, the Committee may provide in the conditions of a team competition that a team captain may give advice to members of his team, including pointing out a line of putting. May such a condition effectively prohibit pointing out a line for putting by requiring a captain or coach to keep off the putting greens?

A. Yes.

Ball-Marker in Position to Assist Another Player — See 20-1/11. **Trademark Aimed Along Line of Putt When Ball Replaced** — See 20-3a/2.

Player Touches Putting Green in Pointing Out Line for Putting for Partner and Incidentally Touches Own Line of Putt — See 30/2.5.

Rule 9. Information as to Strokes Taken

9

9-1. General
The number of strokes a player has taken shall include any penalty strokes incurred.

9-2. Match Play
A player who has incurred a penalty shall inform his opponent as soon as practicable, unless he is obviously proceeding under a Rule involving a penalty and this has been observed by his opponent. If he fails so to inform his opponent, he shall be deemed to have given wrong information, even if he was not aware that he had incurred a penalty.

An opponent is entitled to ascertain from the player, during the play of a hole, the number of strokes he has taken and, after play of a hole, the number of strokes taken on the hole just completed.

If during the play of a hole the player gives or is deemed to give wrong information as to the number of strokes taken, he shall incur no penalty if he corrects the mistake before his opponent has played his next stroke. If the player fails so to correct the wrong information, *he shall lose the hole.*

If after play of a hole the player gives or is deemed to give wrong information as to the number of strokes taken on the hole just completed and this affects the opponent's understanding of the result of the hole, he shall incur no penalty if he corrects his mistake before any player plays from the next <u>teeing ground</u> or, in the case of the last hole of the match, before all players leave the <u>putting green</u>. If the player fails so to correct the wrong information, *he shall lose the hole.*

9-3. Stroke Play

A competitor who has incurred a penalty should inform his marker as soon as practicable.

9

9/1 Incorrect Information on Rules

A player incurs no penalty for giving incorrect information on the Rules of Golf; this is not wrong information as that term is used in Rule 9. It is up to each player to know the Rules.

However, if it is established that a player has knowingly given incorrect information on the Rules, the Committee would be justified in imposing a penalty of disqualification under Rule 33-7.

[9-2/1 Reserved]

9-2/2 Wrong Information Given by Caddie or Partner

Q. If wrong information as to the number of strokes a player has taken is given to an opponent, not by the player himself, but by the player's partner or caddie, is the player liable to a penalty under Rule 9-2?

A. Yes.

9-2/3 Wrong Information on Strokes Taken Given Voluntarily

Q. In a match between A and B, A voluntarily told B during play of a hole that he had played three strokes, whereas in fact he had played four strokes. A did not correct the error before B played his next stroke. Was A subject to penalty under Rule 9-2?

A. Yes. When a player gives wrong information, it is irrelevant whether the error is contained in a response to a question from the player's opponent or in a voluntary statement by the player. It must be corrected before the opponent's next stroke is played.

9-2/4 Withholding Information on Strokes Taken Until Opponent's Turn to Play

Q. In a match between A and B, A asks B during play of a hole how many strokes he (B) has taken. B, whose turn it is to play, withholds the information until he has played his next stroke. Is B subject to penalty under Rule 9-2?

A. No, provided B gave the information before A played his next stroke.

9-2/5 Wrong Information Causes Opponent to Lift His Ball-Marker

Q. Rule 9-2 provides that, if during play of a hole a player gives wrong information to the opponent and does not correct the error before the opponent plays his next stroke, the player loses the hole. During play of a hole, a player gives wrong information to his opponent and the wrong information results in the opponent lifting the coin marking the position of his ball. Is the lifting of the coin by the opponent the equivalent of the opponent playing his next stroke?

A. Yes; the player loses the hole.

9-2/6 Player Reporting Wrong Score Causes Opponent with Chance for Half to Pick Up Ball

Q. In match play, A holed out and stated to B, his opponent, that he had scored a 4. B, having played four strokes, picked up assuming he had lost the hole. A then realized that he had scored a 5. He immediately told B. What is the ruling?

A. A gave wrong information as to the number of strokes taken and, under the principle of Rule 9-2, A would normally lose the hole. However, since A had holed out for no worse than a half, the hole was halved — see Rule 2-2.

Player Lifts Ball Before Holing Out; Opponent Then Picks Up His Ball and Claims Player Loses Hole — See 2-5/3.

In Four-Ball Match Player with Putt for Half Picks Up at Suggestion of Opponent Due to Misunderstanding — See 30/5.

Player's Ball Resting Against Flagstick Lifted Before Being Holed; Others in Four-Ball Match Pick Up Mistakenly Believing Player Won Hole — See 30-3f/3.

Wrong Information Given by Player Out of Contention in Four-Ball Match — See 30-3f/4.

9-2/7 Wrong Information Given by Player Corrected Before Opponent Plays Next Stroke But After Opponent Has Conceded Player's Putt

Q. In a match, A's ball was a few inches from the hole. B asked A, "How many will that be in the hole?" A answered, "6," whereupon B conceded A's next stroke, holed a putt for a 6 and assumed that he had halved the hole. B was then informed by A that he (A) had actually scored 5. The Committee ruled that A won the hole. Was this correct?

A. No. A gave wrong information as to his score during play of the hole and did not correct his mistake before B played his next stroke. Therefore, under Rule 9-2, A lost the hole.

However, the penalty would still have applied even if A had corrected his mistake after B had conceded A's next stroke and before B putted. The principle of Rule 9-2 applies if, after receiving wrong information, a player takes some action (*e.g.*, picks up or concedes the opponent's next stroke) which he might not have taken if wrong information had not been given.

In such a case, the answer does not turn on how close A's ball was to the hole or on the fact that B sank his putt and could not have done any better.

9-2/8 Player Wins Hole with Wrong Ball; Error Discovered at Next Hole; Opponent Claims Previous Hole

Q. In a match, A holed out in 3 at the 5th hole. His opponent, B, holed out in 4. After driving from the next tee, it was discovered that A had played a wrong ball at the 5th hole. B claimed the 5th hole. What is the ruling?

A. Since A failed to inform B promptly that he had incurred a penalty for playing a wrong ball, he is deemed to have given wrong information even though he was not aware that he had incurred a penalty (Rule 9-2). Thus, B's belated claim was valid (Rule 2-5) and the Committee should have ruled that B won the 5th hole.

Player Wins Hole with Own Ball After Playing Wrong Ball; Opponent Lodges Belated Claim — See 2-5/4.

Player Wins Hole with Wrong Ball and Partner Picks Up; Error Discovered at Next Hole — See 30-3d/2.

Players on Opposite Sides Exchange Balls During Play of Hole and Their Partners Pick Up; Error Discovered at Next Hole — See 30-3d/3.

Player Plays Partner's Ball; Error Discovered After Opponents Have Played Next Strokes — See 30-3d/3.5

9-2/9 Player Reports Wrong Score for Hole; Error Discovered Several Holes Later

Q. In match play, after completion of a hole, A inadvertently reports to B, his opponent, that he scored a 5, whereas in fact he scored a 6. This results in the hole being halved or won by A. A realizes his mistake several holes later. What is the ruling?

A. In either case, A loses the hole and the state of the match must be adjusted accordingly (Rule 9-2).

9-2/10 Player Omits Penalty Stroke When Advising Opponent as to Score for Hole; Error Discovered After Match Conceded by Opponent

Q. In a match, A and B were all square after 18 holes and were playing the 19th hole. A incurred a penalty stroke but was unaware of that fact. A holed out and told B that he had scored a 6. B played his sixth shot, missed the hole and conceded the match to A.

When returning to the clubhouse, A learned that he had incurred a penalty stroke and that his score had been 7, not 6. B claimed the match on the ground that A gave wrong information. What is the ruling?

A. B's claim was valid since the result had not been announced — see Rule 2-5. A lost the hole for giving wrong information, even though he may not have been aware that he had incurred a penalty — Rule 9-2.

Player Concedes Match After Winning It When Opponent Lodges Invalid Claim Regarding Strokes Taken — See 2-4/15.

Player Wins Match; Breach of 14-Club Rule Discovered Before Result Announced — See 2-5/5.5.

Winner of Match Due to Wrong Information by Opponent Makes No Claim and Loses in Extra Holes — See 2-5/7.

9-2/11 Player Concluding He Played Wrong Ball When Opponent Misread Number on Player's Ball Concedes Hole

Q. In a match, A and B are playing the same brand of ball (Brand X). The identification number on A's ball is "3" and A's name is imprinted on his ball. The identification number on B's ball is "5."

On completion of the 2nd hole, which A won, B picks up both balls and says, "Both 5's — which is yours?" A states that he was playing a "3" and therefore he must have played a wrong ball. A concedes the hole to B.

B wins the match and then discovers he has in his possession a Brand X ball with the identification number

"3" and A's name imprinted on it. A and B conclude that B misread the number at the 2nd hole. Did B give A wrong information?

A. No. Wrong information as the term is used in Rule 9 refers to the number of strokes taken.

A's concession of the 2nd hole must stand and the match must stand as played. It would have been advisable for A to inspect the two balls at the 2nd hole before conceding the hole.

9-2/12 Conscious Failure to Correct Opponent's Misunderstanding of State of Match; What Constitutes Wrong Information

Q. In a match, B is 1 up on A playing the 14th hole. A and B take 6's at the 14th hole, but B assuming A scored a 5, says: "We are now all square." A says nothing although he knows that both have scored 6 and he is still 1 down.

At the end of the 17th hole, B believing he is 2 down, concedes the match, although in fact he is only 1 down. Is A subject to penalty under Rule 9-2 for giving wrong information?

A. No. Rule 9-2 deals with giving wrong information as to the number of strokes taken at a hole and would include acquiescence by the player (whether oral or tacit) in a misstatement by his opponent of the number of strokes taken by the player. Wrong information does not include acquiescence by the player in a misstatement by his opponent of the result of a hole or the state of the match.

However, A's conscious failure to correct B's misunderstanding of the state of the match is so contrary to the spirit of the game that the Committee should disqualify A under Rule 33-7 and reinstate B.

9-2/13 Player Who Told Opponent He Would Proceed Under Water Hazard Rule Changes Mind After Opponent Plays

Q. In a match, B hit his tee shot short of a water hazard and A hit his into the hazard. Before B played his second shot he asked A what he was going to do. A said he was going to drop out and take a one-stroke penalty. B then played his second shot, after which A changed his mind and played his ball out of the hazard. Did A give wrong information, contrary to Rule 9-2?

A. No. A could have refused to answer B's question or replied that he would await B's play before deciding his own tactics. The fact that A did tell B what he planned to do does not preclude A from changing his mind.

9

9-2/14 Wrong Information Causes Opponent Mistakenly to Think He Has Putt for Half; Opponent Holes Putt and Then Error Discovered

Q. In a match between A and B, A's ball was a few inches from the hole. B conceded A's next stroke and then asked, "How many strokes did you take?" A answered, "6". B, lying 5, then holed a putt for a 6 and assumed that he had halved the hole. At that point, A told B that he (A) had actually scored 5. The Committee ruled that A won the hole. Was this correct?

A. Yes. The hole was over when A's putt was conceded and he had won the hole with a 5. Since A corrected the error before either player played from the next tee, no penalty was incurred — see Rule 9-2.

9-2/15 Wrong Information After Play of Hole; When Penalty Applicable

Q. Decision 9-2/14 implies that, if A had not corrected the error before playing from the next tee, he would have lost the hole under Rule 9-2. Is this correct? It would seem that A would not incur a penalty because he won the hole, and therefore the wrong information did not affect the result of the hole.

A. There is a penalty for giving wrong information after play of a hole which is not corrected before play from the next teeing ground unless the wrong information does not affect the opponent's understanding of the result of the hole just completed. Wrong information would not affect the opponent's understanding of the result of the hole in the following circumstances: A and B are playing a match. After play of a hole, A states that he scored 5 and B states that he (B) scored 7. After teeing off at the next hole, A states that he was incorrect in saying that he scored 5 and that, in fact, he scored 6 .

In Decision 9-2/14, the wrong information caused B to believe that the hole in question had been halved, when in fact B lost the hole. Accordingly, if A had not corrected the error before playing from the next tee, under Rule 9-2 the hole should have been awarded to B.

9

9-2/16 Ascertaining Whereabouts of Opponent's Ball Before Playing

Q. In a match, B's tee shot may be lost, out of bounds or in a water hazard. In view of the second paragraph of Rule 9-2, under which an opponent is entitled to ascertain from the player the number of strokes he has taken, may A go forward to determine the status of B's ball before he (A) plays from the tee?

A. No. A would be in breach of Rule 6-7 (Undue Delay) if he did so. A player may make such a determination only if it can be done without unduly delaying play.

9-2/17 Competitor in Sudden-Death Play-Off Gives Wrong Information

Q. In a stroke play sudden-death play-off, B has completed the hole in 5 strokes. A, who has a putt for a 5, inquires as to B's score for the hole, and B wrongly states that he (B) has holed out in 4 strokes. A picks up his ball without marking its position. B then corrects his mistake. What is the ruling?

A. B incurs no penalty. Rule 9 imposes no penalty for giving wrong information as to the number of strokes taken in stroke play.

A incurs a penalty of one stroke under Rule 20-1 for lifting his ball at rest without marking its position. Since this leaves A with a putt for a 6, he loses the play-off.

In Foursome Side Drives for Three Holes in Wrong Order and Then Claim Is Made — See 29-2/2.

9

ORDER OF PLAY

Rule 10. Order of Play

10

10-1. Match Play

a. TEEING GROUND

The side entitled to play first from the <u>teeing ground</u> is said to have the "honor."

The side which shall have the honor at the first teeing ground shall be determined by the order of the draw. In the absence of a draw, the honor should be decided by lot.

The side which wins a hole shall take the honor at the next teeing ground. If a hole has been halved, the side which had the honor at the previous teeing ground shall retain it.

b. OTHER THAN ON TEEING GROUND

When the balls are in play, the ball farther from the hole shall be played first. If the balls are equidistant from the hole, the ball to be played first should be decided by lot.

Exception: Rule 30-3c (best-ball and four-ball match play).

c. PLAYING OUT OF TURN

If a player plays when his opponent should have played, the opponent may immediately require the player to cancel the stroke so played and, in correct order, play a ball without penalty as nearly as possible at the spot from which the original ball was last played (see Rule 20-5).

10-2. Stroke Play

a. TEEING GROUND

The competitor entitled to play first from the <u>teeing ground</u> is said to have the "honor."

The competitor who shall have the honor at the first teeing ground shall be determined by the order of the draw. In the absence of a draw, the honor should be decided by lot.

The competitor with the lowest score at a hole shall take the honor at the next teeing ground. The competitor with the second lowest score shall play next and so on. If two or more competitors have the same score at a hole, they shall play from the next teeing ground in the same order as at the previous teeing ground.

b. OTHER THAN ON TEEING GROUND

When the balls are in play, the ball farthest from the hole shall be played first. If two or more balls are equidistant from the hole, the ball to be played first should be decided by lot.

Exceptions: Rules 22 (ball interfering with or assisting play) and 31-5 (four-ball stroke play).

c. PLAYING OUT OF TURN

If a competitor plays out of turn, no penalty is incurred and the ball shall be played as it lies. If, however, the Committee determines that competitors have agreed to play in an order other than that set forth in Clauses 2a and 2b of this Rule to give one of them an advantage, *they shall be disqualified.*

(Incorrect order of play in threesomes and foursomes stroke play — see Rule 29-3.)

10-3. Provisional Ball or Second Ball from Teeing Ground

If a player plays a <u>provisional ball</u> or a second ball from a <u>teeing ground</u>, he should do so after his opponent or fellow-competitor has played his first <u>stroke</u>. If a player plays a provisional ball or a second ball out of turn, Clauses 1c and 2c of this Rule shall apply.

10-4. Ball Moved in Measuring
If a ball is moved in measuring to determine which ball is farther from the hole, no penalty is incurred and the ball shall be replaced.

10/1 Order of Play When Two Balls Lie in Ground Under Repair and Both Players Take Relief

Q. A and B hit their balls into ground under repair. The balls are approximately 18 inches apart. A's ball is farther from the hole. Both players decide to take relief. Is the order of play for the next shot determined by the relative positions of the balls before relief is taken, or after?

A. The order of play is determined by the relative positions of the balls before relief is taken. A should play before B — see Rules 10-1b and -2b.

10/2 Order of Play When Two Balls Lie in Lateral Water Hazard and Both Players Take Relief

Q. A and B hit their balls into a lateral water hazard. The balls are approximately 18 inches apart. A's ball is farther from the hole but B's ball last crossed the hazard margin farther from the hole than A's ball. Both players decide to take relief from the hazard. What is the proper procedure?

A. Since A's ball lies farther from the hole, under Rule 10-1b or -2b A should play before B.

10/3 Order of Play When Two Balls Are Lost in Lateral Water Hazard

Q. A and B hit their balls into the same general area of a lateral water hazard. Both balls are lost in the hazard and therefore it is not known which ball is farther from the hole. However, B's ball last crossed the hazard margin farther from the hole than A's ball. What is the proper procedure?

A. The ball to be played first should be decided by lot, just as would be the case if the balls were equidistant from the hole — see Rules 10-1b and -2b.

10-1a/1 Determination of Honor in Handicap Match

Q. A and B are playing a match on a handicap basis. B has the honor at the 1st hole.

Both players score 5's at the 1st hole but A receives a handicap stroke and therefore has a net 4. Does A take the honor at the 2nd hole?

A. Yes. See Rules 2-1 and 10-1a.

10-1a/2 Determination of Honor at Hole Following Disputed Hole

Q. A dispute arises in a match between A and B, and A lodges a claim. A and B agree to continue the match and get a ruling later. Which player has the honor at the next hole?

A. In equity (Rule 1-4), the honor should be decided by lot, except that, if A's claim was to gain a half, B would retain the honor if he had it at the previous hole.

Players Agree Not to Tee Off in Prescribed Order to Save Time — See 1-3/1.

Determination of Honor in Four-Ball Match in Which Points Awarded for Both Better-Ball and Aggregate Scores — See 30/3.

10-1b/1 Procedure for Referee in Determining Ball Farther from Hole

Q. In a match, A's ball is on one side of the fairway and B's ball is on the other side. Both balls are about 100 yards from the hole. A plays and B questions whether A played out of turn. Is the referee obliged to pace off the distances to the hole to resolve the question?

A. No. In view of the distances involved, the referee would be justified in resolving the question by eye. If he could not do so, he would be justified in deciding by lot which player should have played first. If it was decided by lot that B should have played first, B would have the option of recalling A's stroke under Rule 10-1c.

Player Who Walks Off Green Under Mistaken Impression Partner Halved Hole Returns and Putts for Half — See 30/5.

Waiving Turn to Putt in Four-Ball Match — See 30-3c/2.

10-1c/1 Request for Player to Replay Stroke Withdrawn After Opponent Plays

Q. In a match between A and B, A played his tee shot out of turn. B requested A to abandon the ball and play in the correct order. However, after B played, he told A not to bother playing another ball. What is the ruling?

A. A was not obliged to comply with B's instruction to continue with the original ball. B incurred no penalty for giving the instruction.

Whether A continued with his original ball or played another ball in correct order as was his right, the result of the hole should stand as played.

10-1c/2 Player Requested to Lift Ball Due to Interference Plays Out of Turn Instead

Q. In match play, A's ball is on B's line of putt. B requests A to lift his ball under Rule 22. Instead of complying with the request, A putts out of turn. Does A lose the hole for a breach of Rule 22 or does Rule 10-1c apply, in which case there would be no penalty but B would have the right to require A to replay the stroke in correct order?

A. Rule 10-1c governs.

Player Smooth Irregularities in Bunker After Playing Out of Turn; Opponent Then Recalls Stroke and Player Must Drop Ball in Smoothed Area — See 13-4/39.

Player Wishing to Render Original Ball Lost Plays Provisional Ball Out of Turn — See 27-2b/1.

In Four-Ball Match Side Plays Out of Turn from Tee; Opponents Require One Member of Side to Replay But Not Other — See 30-1/1.

Player Plays Out of Turn from Tee in Three-Ball Match; One Opponent Requests Replay and Other Does Not — See 30-2/1.

10-2a/1 Determination of Honor in Handicap Stroke Play

Q. In a stroke play competition on a handicap basis, the handicap is deducted at the end of the round and not at individual holes. In such a competition, how is the honor determined?

A. According to gross scores.

Determination of Honor in Handicap Stableford Competition — See 32-1/3.

10-2b/1 Competitor Objects to Fellow-Competitor Putting Out of Turn

Q. In stroke play, A's ball is 40 feet from the hole and B's is 30 feet away. A putts and his ball comes to rest four feet from the hole. A prepares to hole out before B putts. B objects and claims that under the Rules (Rule 10-2b) he is entitled to putt before A.

Although putting out of turn in stroke play is generally condoned, should the Committee allow A to putt out of turn in these circumstances?

A. If A had lifted his ball when the objection was lodged, the Committee should rule that A is not entitled to putt out of turn, in view of Rule 10-2b.

If A had not lifted his ball at the time the objection was lodged, the answer depends on whether B would require A to lift his ball under Rule 22 (Ball Interfering with or Assisting Play) before he (B) putts. If so, the

Committee should rule that A is entitled to play out of turn, provided he does so without first lifting his ball, *i.e.*, Rule 22 permits a competitor in stroke play who is required to lift his ball because of interference to "play first rather than lift."

If B would not require A to lift his ball before he (B) putts, the Committee should rule that A is not entitled to putt out of turn.

Although condoning putting out of turn in stroke play may be questionable in view of the explicit language of Rule 10-2b, there is no penalty for doing so (Rule 10-2c), it is not in conflict with the intent of Rule 10-2b, and it may tend to speed play.

Accordingly, it is considered that the practice should not be discouraged.

10-2c/1 Ball Played Out of Turn from Tee Abandoned and Another Ball Played in Proper Order

Q. In stroke play, a competitor played out of turn from the teeing ground and, although he should have continued play with the ball played out of turn without penalty, he abandoned the ball and played another ball in proper order. What is the ruling?

A. When the competitor played another ball from the tee, the original ball was lost and the other ball was in play under penalty of stroke and distance — see Decision 27/17.

10-2c/2 Competitors in Stroke Play Agree to Play Out of Turn But Not for Purpose of Giving One of Them an Advantage

Q. In stroke play, A and B agree to play out of turn at the 10th hole to save time. There is no penalty under Rule 10-2c because they did not do so in order to give one of them an advantage. However, are they liable to disqualification under Rule 1-3 for agreeing to exclude the operation of Rule 10-2a or 10-2b as the case may be?

A. No. Rule 10-2c specifically governs and permits the procedure in stroke play. Accordingly, Rule 1-3 does not apply. As to match play, see Decision 1-3/1.

10

TEEING GROUND
Rule 11. Teeing Ground

11

Definition

The "teeing ground" is the starting place for the hole to be played. It is a rectangular area two club-lengths in depth, the front and the sides of which are defined by the outside limits of two tee-markers. A ball is outside the teeing ground when all of it lies outside the teeing ground.

11-1. Teeing

In teeing, the ball may be placed on the ground, on an irregularity of surface created by the player on the ground or on a tee, sand or other substance in order to raise it off the ground.

A player may stand outside the teeing ground to play a ball within it.

11-2. Tee-Markers

Before a player plays his first stroke with any ball from the teeing ground of the hole being played, the tee-markers are deemed to be fixed. In such circumstances, if the player moves or allows to be moved a tee-marker for the purpose of avoiding interference with his stance, the area of his intended swing or his line of play, *he shall incur the penalty for a breach of Rule 13-2.*

11-3. Ball Falling Off Tee

If a ball, when not in play, falls off a tee or is

knocked off a tee by the player in addressing it, it may be re-teed without penalty, but if a <u>stroke</u> is made at the ball in these circumstances, whether the ball is moving or not, the stroke counts but no penalty is incurred.

11-4. Playing from Outside Teeing Ground

a. MATCH PLAY

If a player, when starting a hole, plays a ball from outside the <u>teeing ground</u>, the opponent may immediately require the player to cancel the stroke so played and play a ball from within the teeing ground, without penalty.

b. STROKE PLAY

If a competitor, when starting a hole, plays a ball from outside the <u>teeing ground</u>, *he shall incur a penalty of two strokes* and shall then play a ball from within the teeing ground.

If the competitor plays a stroke from the next teeing ground without first correcting his mistake or, in the case of the last hole of the round, leaves the <u>putting green</u> without first declaring his intention to correct his mistake, *he shall be disqualified.*

Strokes played by a competitor from outside the teeing ground do not count in his score.

11-5. Playing from Wrong Teeing Ground
The provisions of Rule 11-4 apply.

11

Decisions relating to Rule 11-1:

Breaking Off Grass Behind Ball on Teeing Ground — See 13-2/3.

Breaking Branch Interfering with Backswing on Teeing Ground — See 13-2/14.

Player Who Misses Tee Shot Presses Down Irregularities Before Next Stroke — See 13-2/2.

Standing on Mat on Teeing Ground — See 13-3/1.

Player Who Misses Tee Shot Tees Ball Lower Before Playing Next Stroke — See 18-2a/1.

Teed Ball Missed Then Hit Out of Bounds — See 20-5/1.

Casual Water Covering Teeing Ground — See 25-1b/4.

Mixed Foursome in Which Different Tees Used by Men and Women; Tee Shot Out of Bounds — See 29/2.

11-2/1 Status of Tee-Markers After First Stroke

Q. Under Rule 11-2, tee-markers are deemed to be fixed when playing the first stroke from the teeing ground. Are tee-markers obstructions thereafter?

A. Yes.

11-2/2 Player Alters Teeing Ground by Relocating Tee-Marker

Q. Before or after playing from a teeing ground, a player relocated one tee-marker, or both of them, because in his view the tee-markers were too close together, too far back, aimed in the wrong direction, or for some similar reason. Is there any penalty if a player so alters a teeing ground?

A. Yes. The player should be disqualified under Rule 33-7 in either match play or stroke play. In four-ball play, the player's partner should also be disqualified.

Holes Relocated and/or Tee-Markers Moved During Stroke Play Round — See 33-2b/1.

11-3/1 Stroke Misses Ball; Ball Then Accidentally Knocked Off Tee

Q. A player teed his ball within the teeing ground. He made a stroke at the ball but missed it. He addressed the ball again and accidentally knocked it off the tee. What is the ruling?

A. When the player made a stroke at the ball, it was in play and Rule 11-3 no longer applied. When the ball in play moved after it was addressed, the player incurred a penalty stroke and was obliged to replace the ball-Rule 18-2b.

Ball Falling Off Tee When Stroke Just Touches It Is Picked Up and Re-Teed — See 18-2a/2.

11-3/2 Lifting Ball in Play But Still Within Teeing Ground

Q. A player played his first stroke from a teeing ground and barely moved the ball, which remained within the teeing ground. The player claimed that, since the ball was still within the teeing ground, he was entitled to re-tee it. Was the player correct?

A. No. When the player made a stroke, the ball was in play — see Definition of "Ball in Play." If a player moves his ball in play without authority, he incurs a penalty stroke under Rule 18-2a. There is no authority for moving a ball in play on a teeing ground.

11-3/3 Original Ball Out of Bounds; Ball Played Under Stroke-and-Distance Procedure Falls Off Tee at Address

Q. A player played his original ball out of bounds from the teeing ground. Under Rule 27-1, he teed up another ball. When addressing the ball, he touched it and it fell off the tee. What is the ruling?

A. There is no penalty, because a teed ball is not in play until a stroke has been made at it (see Definition of "Ball in Play'). The ball may be re-teed (Rule 11-3).

[11-4a/1   Reserved]

[11-4b/1   Reserved]

11-4b/2 Competitors Estimate Area of Teeing Ground When One Tee-Marker Missing

Q. In stroke play, competitors in a group, finding one tee-marker missing from a teeing ground, determine for themselves the area of the teeing ground based on the position of the remaining tee-marker and the shape of the tee. What is the ruling?

A. The correct procedure is to discontinue play until the Committee resolves the problem.

However, if the Committee is satisfied that the competitors did not gain an advantage by playing from the place they judged to be the teeing ground, it would be appropriate for the Committee, in equity (Rule 1-4), to accept their scores, without penalty. Otherwise, they incur the penalty prescribed in Rule 11-4b.

11-4b/3 Competitors Determine Spot from Which to Play from Tee When Both Tee-Markers Are Missing

Q. In stroke play, the competitors in a group, finding no tee-markers on a particular hole, determine for themselves the spot from which to begin play on the hole, and tee off. What is the ruling?

A. It would be appropriate for the Committee to accept without penalty the scores of the competitors in question if there was evidence as to where the tee-markers were intended to be and the competitors determined the teeing ground from such evidence and played from within such teeing ground. Sufficient evidence might include spots of paint established to show where the tee-markers were to be installed or, if the tee-markers were removed during a round, depressions or other marks on the ground indicating where the tee-markers had been located.

In the absence of such evidence, the competitors should be disqualified under Rule 11-4b unless, before playing from the next tee, they discontinue play, get the Committee to establish tee-markers and replay the hole from within the established teeing ground. Any competitor so replaying would incur a penalty of two strokes — Rule 11-4b.

[11-4b/4   Reserved]

[11-4b/4.5   Reserved]

[11-4b/5   Reserved]

11-4b/6 Ball Played from Outside Teeing Ground Goes Out of Bounds

Q. In stroke play, A played from outside the teeing ground and his ball came to rest out of bounds. He played another ball from within the teeing ground. Is he penalized stroke and distance under Rule 27-1, as well as two strokes under Rule 11-4b?

A. No. A is penalized only two strokes under Rule 11-4b. The ball played from outside the teeing ground was not in play. Therefore, the fact that it came to rest out of bounds was irrelevant and the stroke itself did not count.

11

Competitor Plays from Outside Teeing Ground in Foursome Stroke Play; Partner Replays Stroke — See 29-1/2.

11-5/1 Explanation of "Next Teeing Ground" When Competitors Have Played From Wrong Teeing Ground

Q. In stroke play, two competitors, have completed the 11th hole, played from the 15th tee, completed the hole and played from the 16th tee. Before playing their second shots they realized their mistake, returned to the 12th tee and completed the round. On reporting the incident the competitors were each penalized two strokes, as the Committee interpreted the "next teeing ground" referred to in Rule 11-4b to be that of the 12th hole. Was this correct?

A. No. When the competitors played from the 16th tee, they had played from the "next teeing ground" and could not correct their error. Therefore, they should have been disqualified.

11-5/2 Use of Wrong Teeing Ground Attributable to Committee Failure to Indicate Hole Numbers on Teeing Ground

Q. In a stroke play competition, the Committee failed to place a sign at each teeing ground indicating the hole number. As a result, a group which had just finished the 4th hole played from the teeing ground of the 12th hole, rather than the 5th hole. Should the members of the group be penalized under Rule 11-4b in the circumstance?

A. Yes

The Committee was remiss in not placing a sign at each teeing ground. However, each player is responsible for knowing the stipulated round, this being one of the conditions of the competition.

11-5/3 Ball Played Out of Bounds from Wrong Teeing Ground Not Recalled

Q. A played B in a match. A drove out of bounds from the wrong teeing ground. B did not recall the stroke. What is the ruling?

A. As A played from the wrong teeing ground and B did not require him to cancel the stroke and play a ball from within the correct teeing ground, A's ball is deemed to have been put into play.

Therefore, under Rule 27-1 A must drop a ball, under penalty of one stroke, as nearly as possible at the spot from which the original ball was played, *i.e.*, on the wrong teeing ground. He could not tee the ball because the original ball was not played from the teeing ground of the hole being played (Rule 20-5).

Ball Played from Outside Teeing Ground in Foursome Match — See 29-1/1.

11-5/4 Ball Played From Wrong Teeing Ground in Stroke Play; Error Corrected

Q. In stroke play, after finishing the 10th hole, A and B played from the teeing ground of the 15th hole instead of the 11th hole. They realized their error before completing the 15th hole, returned to the 11th tee and completed the round. What is the ruling?

A. A and B each incurred a penalty of two strokes under Rule 11-4b. They were correct in discontinuing play at the 15th hole and returning to the 11th hole. Strokes played at the 15th hole, when it was played out of order, did not count. (Formerly 11-4b/4)

11-5/5 Ball Played from Teeing Ground of Hole to Be Played Later in Round Lifted; Ball Replaced at Spot from Which Lifted and Played Out When That Hole Subsequently Reached

Q. In stroke play, after playing the 8th hole, A, by mistake, played from the teeing ground of the 18th hole, instead of the 9th hole. A marked the position of the ball, lifted it and played from the teeing ground of the 9th hole. He added a two-stroke penalty to his score for the 9th hole under Rule 11-4b for playing from the wrong teeing ground, *i.e.*, playing from the 18th tee. A played the holes from the 10th to the 17th. He then replaced his ball at the spot on the 18th hole from which he had lifted it, played out the hole and returned his score card. Did A proceed correctly?

A. No. A should have disregarded the original stroke played from the 18th tee and replayed from that tee after completion of the 17th hole. In failing to do so, A did not play the stipulated round — see Definition of "Stipulated Round" — and thus did not have an acceptable score.

PLAYING THE BALL

Rule 12. Searching for and Identifying Ball

12

Definitions

A "hazard" is any <u>bunker</u> or <u>water hazard</u>.

A "bunker" is a <u>hazard</u> consisting of a pre-pared area of ground, often a hollow, from which turf or soil has been removed and re-placed with sand or the like. Grass-covered ground bordering or within a bunker is not part of the bunker. The margin of a bunker extends vertically downwards, but not upwards.

A "water hazard" is any sea, lake, pond, river, ditch, surface drainage ditch or other open water course (whether or not containing water) and anything of a similar nature.

All ground or water within the margin of a water hazard is part of the water hazard. The margin of a water hazard extends vertically upwards and downwards. Stakes and lines defining the margins of water hazards are in the hazards.

12-1. Searching for Ball; Seeing Ball

In searching for his ball anywhere on the course, the player may touch or bend long grass, rushes, bushes, whins, heather or the like, but only to the extent necessary to find and identify it, provided that this does not improve the lie of the ball, the area of his intended swing or his line of play.

A player is not necessarily entitled to see his ball when playing a stroke.

In a <u>hazard</u>, if a ball is covered by <u>loose impediments</u> or sand, the player may remove by probing, raking or other means as much thereof as will enable him to see a part of the ball. If an excess is removed, no penalty is incurred and the ball shall be re-covered so that only a part of the ball is visible. If the ball is moved in such removal, no penalty is incurred; the ball shall be replaced and, if necessary, re-covered. As to removal of loose impediments outside a hazard, see Rule 23.

If a ball lying in <u>casual water</u>, <u>ground under repair</u> or a hole, cast or runway made by a burrowing animal, a reptile or a bird is accidentally moved during search, no penalty is incurred; the ball shall be replaced, unless the player elects to proceed under Rule 25-1b.

If a ball is believed to be lying in water in a <u>water</u> <u>hazard</u>, the player may probe for it with a club or otherwise. If the ball is moved in so doing, no penalty is incurred; the ball shall be replaced, unless the player elects to proceed under Rule 26-1.

PENALTY FOR BREACH OF RULE 12-1:
Match play --- Loss of hole;
Stroke play --- Two strokes.

12-2. Identifying Ball
The responsibility for playing the proper ball rests with the player. Each player should put an identification mark on his ball.

Except in a <u>hazard</u>, the player may, without penalty, lift a ball he believes to be his own for the purpose of identification and clean it to the extent necessary for identification. If the ball is the player's ball, he shall replace it. Before lifting the ball, the player must announce his intention to his opponent in match play or his marker or a fellow-competitor in stroke play and mark the position of the ball. He must then give his opponent, marker or fellow-competitor an opportunity to observe the lifting and replacement. If he lifts his ball without announcing his intention in advance, marking the position of the ball or giving his opponent, marker or fellow-competitor an opportunity to observe, or if he lifts his ball for identification in a hazard, or cleans it more than necessary for identification, *he shall incur a penalty of one stroke* and the ball shall be replaced.

If a player who is required to replace a ball fails to do so, *he shall incur the penalty* for a breach of Rule 20-3a, but no additional penalty under Rule 12-2 shall be applied.

12

12-1/1 Searching with Clubhead for Ball Covered by Sand in Bunker

Q. If a ball is covered by sand in a bunker, may a clubhead be used in searching?

A. Yes.

12-1/2 Ball Covered by Sand in Bunker Removed from Buried Lie During Search

Q. A ball buried in sand in a bunker is removed from the buried lie during search. The player replaces and re-covers it as required by Rule 12-1, third paragraph. May the player then remove as much sand as will enable him to see a part of the ball?

A. Yes.

12-1/3 Top of Ball in Hazard Covered by Leaves But Part of Ball Visible from Another Angle

Q. The top of a ball in a hazard is covered by leaves so that it is not visible when the player addresses it. However, a portion of the ball is visible from another angle. Is it permissible for the player to remove enough leaves to see the ball when addressing it?

A. No. A player is entitled to remove loose impediments covering a ball in a hazard only if the ball is not visible from any angle.

12-2/1 Identifying Ball by Brand and Number Only

Q. In the area in which his ball presumably came to rest, a player finds a ball of the same brand and identification number as the ball he is playing. The player assumes it is his ball, even though it does not carry an identification mark as suggested in Rule 12-2, and plays it. Should the player be considered to have played a wrong ball?

A. No, unless (1) there is reasonable evidence that, because of the ball's condition, it is not the player's ball or (2) subsequently it is established that another ball of the same brand and identification number was lying in the area at the time the player played and either ball, from a condition standpoint, could be the player's ball.

Player Unable to Distinguish His Ball from Another Ball — See 27/10.

Provisional Ball Not Distinguishable from Original Ball — See 27/11.

Identification of Ball Through Testimony of Spectator — See 27/12.

Refusal to Identify Ball — See 27/13.

12-2/2 Touching and Rotating Half-Buried Ball in Rough for Identification Purposes

Q. A ball is half buried in the rough. Having announced his intention in advance to his opponent, marker or fellow-competitor, the player, for the purpose of identifying the ball, touches the ball and rotates it. By so doing he identifies the ball as his ball. Is there a penalty?

A. Yes, for touching the ball other than as provided for in the Rules — Rule 18-2a. Under Rules 12-2 and 20-1, a ball may be lifted (or touched and rotated) for identification purposes after its position has been marked. If the player had marked the position of the ball before rotating it, there would have been no penalty, assuming the rotating did not result in the ball being cleaned beyond the extent necessary to identify it.

12-2/3 Touching and Rotating Half-Buried Ball in Hazard for Identification Purposes

Q. A ball is half buried in a water hazard and is not identifiable. Having announced his intention in advance to his opponent, marker or fellow-competitor, the player touches the ball and rotates it. By so doing he is able to identify the ball as his ball. Is such procedure permissible?

A. No. Neither Rule 12-2 nor any other Rule permits a player to touch his ball in a hazard for identification purposes. Accordingly, the player was in breach of Rule 18-2a for touching his ball purposely and incurred a penalty of one stroke.

Two Balls Lie Together in Hazard and Neither Is Identifiable — See 1-4/6.

Caddie on Own Initiative Lifts Ball for Identification — See 18-2a/14.

Ball Dislodged from Tree for Identification Purposes by Shaking Tree or Throwing Club — See 18-2a/27.

Position of Ball Lifted for Identification Not Marked, Intention to Lift Not Announced and Ball Cleaned Beyond Extent Necessary to Identify It — See 21/4.

Ball in Tree Identified But Not Retrieved — See 27/14.

Ball in Tree Visible But Not Identifiable — See 27/15.

Rule 13. Ball Played as It Lies; Lie, Area of Intended Swing and Line of Play; Stance

13

Definitions

A "hazard" is any <u>bunker</u> or <u>water hazard</u>.

A "bunker" is a <u>hazard</u> consisting of a prepared area of ground, often a hollow, from which turf or soil has been removed and replaced with sand or the like. Grass-covered ground bordering or within a bunker is not part of the bunker. The margin of a bunker extends vertically downwards, but not upwards.

A "water hazard" is any sea, lake, pond, river, ditch, surface drainage ditch or other open water course (whether or not containing water) and anything of a similar nature.

All ground or water within the margin of a water hazard is part of the water hazard. The margin of a water hazard extends vertically upwards and downwards. Stakes and lines defining the margins of water hazards are in the hazards.

The "line of play" is the direction which the player wishes his ball to take after a stroke, plus a reasonable distance on either side of the intended direction. The line of play extends vertically upwards from the ground, but does not extend beyond the hole.

13-1. Ball Played as It Lies

The ball shall be played as it lies, except as otherwise provided in the Rules.

(Ball at rest moved — see Rule 18.)

13-2. Improving Lie, Area of Intended Swing or Line of Play

Except as provided in the Rules, a player shall not improve or allow to be improved:

the position or lie of his ball,

the area of his intended swing,

his line of play or

a reasonable extension of that line beyond the hole or

the area in which he is to drop or place a ball by any of the following actions:

moving, bending or breaking anything growing or fixed (including immovable <u>obstructions</u> and objects defining <u>out of bounds</u>) or

removing or pressing down sand, loose soil, replaced divots, other cut turf placed in position or other irregularities of surface except as follows:

as may occur in fairly taking his <u>stance</u>,

in making a <u>stroke</u> or the backward movement of his club for a stroke,

on the <u>teeing ground</u> in creating or eliminating irregularities of surface, or

on the <u>putting green</u> in removing sand and loose soil as provided in Rule 16-1a or in repairing damage as provided in Rule 16-1c.

The club may be grounded only lightly and shall not be pressed on the ground.

Exception: Ball lying in or touching hazard — see Rule 13-4.

13-3. Building Stance

A player is entitled to place his feet firmly in taking his stance, but he shall not build a stance.

13

13-4. Ball Lying in or Touching Hazard

Except as provided in the Rules, before making a <u>stroke</u> at a ball which lies in or touches a hazard (whether a <u>bunker</u> or a <u>water hazard</u>), the player shall not:

　　a. Test the condition of the hazard or any similar hazard,

　　b. Touch the ground in the hazard or water in the water hazard with a club or otherwise, or

　　c. Touch or move a <u>loose impediment</u> lying in or touching the hazard.

Exceptions:

1. Provided nothing is done which constitutes testing the condition of the hazard or improves the lie of the ball, there is no penalty if the player (a) touches the ground in any hazard or water in a water hazard as a result of or to prevent falling, in removing an <u>obstruction</u>, in measuring or in retrieving or lifting a ball under any Rule or (b) places his clubs in a <u>hazard</u>.

2. The player after playing the stroke, or his <u>caddie</u> at any time without the authority of the player, may smooth sand or soil in the hazard, provided that, if the ball still lies in the hazard, nothing is done which improves the lie of the ball or assists the player in his subsequent play of the hole.

Note: At any time, including at address or in the backward movement for the stroke, the player may touch with a club or otherwise any obstruction, any construction declared by the Committee to be an integral part of the course or any grass, bush, tree or other growing thing.

PENALTY FOR BREACH OF RULE:
Match play --- Loss of hole;
Stroke play --- Two strokes.

(Searching for ball --- see Rule 12-1.)

13

13/1 Sand Spilling Over Margin of Bunker

Q. If sand spills over the margin of a bunker, is the sand part of the bunker?

A. No.

13/2 Status of Tree in Bunker

Q. Is a tree in a bunker part of the bunker?

A. No. Grass-covered ground within a bunker is not part of the bunker. The same principle applies to a tree. The margin of a bunker does not extend upwards.

13/3 Ball on Edge of Bunker Overhanging Sand

13

Q. Is a ball in a bunker if it lies on the edge of the bunker overhanging, but not touching, the sand?

A. No. The margin of a bunker, unlike that of a water hazard, does not extend vertically upwards.

13/4 Ball Completely Embedded in Lip of Bunker

Q. A player's ball is completely embedded in the vertical lip of a bunker. The lip is not grass-covered, so it is part of the bunker. Is the ball considered to be lying through the green? If so, the player would be entitled to drop the ball behind the bunker if he declares it unplayable.

A. No. An embedded ball is considered to be lying in the part of the course where it entered the ground.

13/5 Ball Lying on Obstruction in Bunker

Q. If a ball is lying on either a movable or an immovable obstruction in a bunker, is the ball considered to be in the bunker?

A. Yes. Although the margin of a bunker does not extend upwards, a ball lying on an obstruction in a bunker is in the bunker.

13-2/1 Explanation of "Fairly Taking His Stance"

Q. Rule 13-2 states that a player shall not improve the position or lie of his ball, the area of his intended swing or his line of play or a reasonable extension of that line beyond the hole by moving, bending or breaking anything growing or fixed. An exception permits a player to do so in "fairly taking his stance." What is the significance of "fairly"?

A. Without "fairly," the exception would permit improvement of position or lie, area of intended swing or line of play by anything which could be said to be taking a stance. For example, a player might be entitled to cut down grass, bushes and even trees which happened to interfere with a perfect stance. The use of "fairly" is intended to limit the player to what is reasonably necessary to take a stance without unduly improving his lie, area of intended swing or line of play. The player is not entitled to a normal stance or swing. He must accommodate to the situation in which the ball is found and take a stance as normal as the circumstances permit. What is fair must be determined in the light of all the circumstances.

Examples of actions which do constitute fairly taking a stance are:
— backing into a branch or young sapling if that is the only way to take a stance (see Definition of "Stance"), even if this causes the branch to move out of the way or the sapling to bend or break.
— bending a branch of a tree with the hands in order to get under the tree to play a ball.

Examples of actions which do not constitute fairly taking a stance are:
— deliberately moving, bending or breaking branches with the hands to get them out of the way of the backswing or stroke.
— standing on a branch to prevent it interfering with the backswing or stroke.
— hooking one branch on another or braiding two weeds for the same purpose.
— bending with a hand a branch obscuring the ball after the stance has been taken.

13

— bending an interfering branch with a leg in taking a stance when the stance could have been taken without bending the branch.

13-2/2 Player Who Misses Tee Shot Presses Down Irregularities Before Next Stroke

Q. In playing a tee shot A misses the ball. Before playing his next stroke, A presses down turf behind the ball. Is this permissible, since the ball is in play?

A. Yes. Rule 13-2 permits eliminating irregularities of surface on the teeing ground, whether or not the ball is in play.

13-2/3 Breaking Off Grass Behind Ball on Teeing Ground

Q. Under Rule 13-2, it is permissible to eliminate irregularities of surface on the teeing ground. Is it also permissible to break off or pull out grass growing behind a ball on the teeing ground?

A. Yes.

13-2/4 Greenkeeping Staff Member Rakes Bunker When Player's Ball Lies Therein

Q. If a member of the greenkeeping staff rakes a bunker when the player's ball lies therein and the raking improves the lie of the ball or the line of play, is the player penalized under Rule 13-2?

A. If the staff member raked the bunker on the instructions, or with the sanction, of the player, the player would incur a penalty. Otherwise, there would be no penalty.

13-2/4.5 Divots Replaced and Pressed Down in Area in Which Ball Is to Be Dropped

Q. A player plays a stroke. He replaces and presses down his divot and other divots nearby. He then discovers that his ball is lost or out of bounds. The player must now drop a ball as nearly as possible at the spot from which his previous stroke was played — Rule 27-1. In these circumstances, is the player in breach of Rule 13-2, which prohibits improving the area in which a ball is to be dropped by pressing down a replaced divot?

A. No. When the player pressed down the divots, he was unaware that he would be required to drop a ball in the area. Therefore, in equity (Rule 1-4) he is not penalized.

13-2/5 Replacing or Removing Undetached Divot

Q. A player's ball comes to rest in front of a divot which is folded over but not completely detached. The divot interferes with his backswing. May the player replace or remove the divot before playing?

A. No. A divot which is not completely detached is not a loose impediment. It is something fixed and therefore its removal or replacement would be a breach of Rule 13-2 as the lie and area of intended swing would be improved.

13-2/6 Replacing Divot in Divot Hole Behind Ball

Q. A player's ball comes to rest just in front of a divot hole. May the player replace the divot before playing his next stroke?

A. Yes. However, the pressing down of a replaced divot is specifically prohibited by Rule 13-2 if the act would improve the lie of the ball or the area of the player's intended swing. The careful player will play his shot first and then replace and press down the loose divot.

13-2/7 When Divot Replaced

Q. Under Rule 13-2 a player may not remove or press down a replaced divot. When is a divot considered replaced?

A. When substantially all of it, with the roots downwards, lies in a divot hole. The hole need not be the one from which the divot was extracted.

13-2/8 Player's Lie or Line of Play Affected by Pitch-Mark Made by Partner's, Opponent's or Fellow-Competitor's Ball

Q. A player's lie or line of play through the green is affected by a pitch-mark made by his partner's, his opponent's or a fellow-competitor's ball. Is the player entitled to relief?

A. If the pitch-mark was there before the player's ball came to rest, he is not entitled to relief without penalty.

If the pitch-mark was created after the player's ball came to rest, in equity (Rule 1-4) he may repair the pitch-mark. A player is entitled to the lie which his stroke gave him.

13-2/8.5 Player's Lie Affected by Sand from Partner's, Opponent's or Fellow-Competitor's Stroke from Bunker

Q. A's ball is on the apron between the green and a bunker. A's partner, opponent or fellow-competitor (B) plays from the bunker and deposits sand on and around A's ball. Is A entitled to any relief?

A. Yes. A is entitled to the lie and line of play he had when his ball came to rest. Accordingly, in equity (Rule 1-4) he is entitled to remove the sand deposited by B's stroke and lift his ball and clean it, without penalty.

13-2/9 Lie Through the Green Improved When Sand Behind Ball Removed by Backswing

Q. A player's ball lies in a sandy area through the green and there is a mound of sand a few inches behind his ball. The player makes his stroke and in the process he removes the mound of sand with the clubhead on his backswing, improving his lie. Is the player subject to penalty?

A. No, provided that he did not ground his club other than lightly and that he took a normal backswing.

13-2/10 Pitch-Mark in Dropping Area Repaired Before Ball Dropped

Q. Through the green, a player's ball was embedded in its own pitch-mark in a closely mown area. He lifted the ball under Rule 25-2 but, before dropping it, repaired the pitch-mark. Is such repair permissible?

A. No. The player was in breach of Rule 13-2 when he improved the area in which his ball was to be dropped by pressing down an irregularity of surface.

Dropped Ball Rolls into Pitch-Mark from Which Lifted —
See 25-2/3.

13

13-2/11 Removing Sand or Loose Soil from Dropping Area

Q. Through the green, may a player remove or brush away sand or loose soil from the area in which he is preparing to drop a ball?

A. No. Rule 13-2 prohibits improving the area in which a ball is to be dropped by removing sand or loose soil. Sand and loose soil are loose impediments only on the putting green.

Ball Played from Bunker Is Out of Bounds or Lost; Player Tests Condition of Bunker or Smooth Footprints Before Dropping Another Ball in Bunker — See 13-4/37.

[13-2/12 Reserved]

13-2/13 Bending Grass in Removal of Loose Impediments

Q. A player whose ball was in long grass rolled a stone away from the ball, pressing down some of the long grass in the process. Was he in breach of Rule 13-2?

A. Yes, if the pressing down of the grass improved the position or lie of his ball, the area of his intended swing or his line of play.

13-2/14 Breaking Branch Interfering with Backswing on Teeing Ground

Q. On the teeing ground, a player broke off a branch of a tree which was interfering with his swing. The player maintained that such action was not a breach of Rule 13-2 because his ball was not yet in play. Was the player correct?

13

A. No. The player was in breach of Rule 13-2 for improving the area of his intended swing. Although Rule 13-2 allows a player to eliminate irregularities of surface on the teeing ground, it does not allow him to break a branch interfering with his swing. The penalty would apply even if the player, before playing his next stroke, re-teed elsewhere on the teeing ground — see Decision 13-2/24.

13-2/14.5 Branch Broken on Backswing and Swing Discontinued

Q. A player's ball lies under a tree. The player fairly takes his stance and starts his backswing with the intention of making a stroke. Near the top of his backswing his club strikes a branch and breaks it. At that point he discontinues his swing.

Rule 13-2 states in part: " . . . a player shall not improve . . . the area of his intended swing . . . except . . . in making a stroke or the backward movement of his club for a stroke." Is the player exempt from penalty under this exception?

A. No, because the swing was discontinued the backward movement of the club was not in fact the backward movement for a stroke.

13-2/15 Area of Intended Swing Improved by Removing Immovable Obstruction

Q. A player's swing is interfered with by an immovable obstruction. The player and his caddie, with great effort, remove the obstruction. Is the player subject to penalty?

A. Yes, for a breach of Rule 13-2. An immovable obstruction is something fixed. Rule 13-2 prohibits a player from improving the area of his intended swing by moving anything fixed.

13-2/15.5 Position of Ball Worsened When Obstruction Removed; Player Replaces Obstruction

Q. A player's ball comes to rest near a tree. A branch of the tree is being held back by a rope installed for gallery control. The player removes the rope (movable obstruction). This releases the branch and worsens the position of the ball. The player then re-installs the rope which results in the branch being held back as before. Was the player in breach of Rule 13-2 when he re-installed the rope?

13

A. Yes.

If an outside agency had removed the rope without the player's authority or sanction, the player would be entitled to re-install the rope without penalty.

Grounding Club, Removing Leaves and Improving Area of Intended Swing in Water Hazard — See 13-4/28.

13-2/16 Stake Supporting Tree Broken in Attempt to Remove It

Q. A stake supporting a young tree interferes with a player's stroke. He tries to remove it, but it cannot readily be removed and it breaks. What is the ruling?

A. The player was in breach of Rule 13-2 for breaking the stake. However, as the stake was not readily removable, it was an immovable obstruction and relief could have been taken, without penalty, under Rule 24-2b.

13-2/17 Removal of Boundary Stake Interfering with Swing

Q. A player removes a stake defining out of bounds which interferes with his swing. Is this permissible?

A. No. Objects defining out of bounds are fixed. Improving the position of a ball by moving anything fixed is a breach of Rule 13-2.

Boundary Post on Line of Play Removed But Replaced Before Stroke — See 13-2/25.

13-2/18 Improving Position of Ball by Bending Boundary Fence

Q. Part of a boundary fence is bowed towards the course so that it is inside the out of bounds line formed by the fence posts. A player's ball comes to rest against this part of the fence. Decision 24/4 states that the player is not entitled to drop the ball away from the fence under Rule 24-2b. May the player push back the bowed section of the fence to obtain a measure of relief?

A. No. Such action would be a breach of Rule 13-2, which prohibits improving the lie or position of a ball or the area of the intended swing by bending anything fixed (including objects defining out of bounds).

Part of Boundary Fence Within Boundary Line — See 24/4.

Gate in Boundary Fence — See 27/18.

13-2/19 Improving Area of Intended Swing by Moving Growing or Fixed Object Situated Out of Bounds

Q. A young tree or a fixed artificial object situated out of bounds interferes with a player's swing. May the player move, bend or break the tree or fixed artificial object without penalty?

A. No. Such action would be a breach of Rule 13-2.

13-2/20 Part of Fence Off Course Leans Across Boundary and Interferes with Swing

Q. Part of a fence which is beyond white stakes defining out of bounds, and therefore not a boundary fence, leans onto the course and interferes with a player's swing. May the player push the fence back into an upright position or treat it as an obstruction?

A. Rule 13-2 prohibits improving the position of the ball by moving anything fixed, even if such thing is off the course. Therefore, the player may not push the fence back. However, that part of the fence leaning onto the course is an immovable obstruction and the player is entitled to relief under Rule 24-2b.

13-2/21 Area of Intended Swing Improved by Repairing Pitch-Mark Made by Ball on Previous Stroke

13

Q. A pitch-mark made by the ball as a result of the previous stroke interferes with a player's backswing. Before playing his next stroke, the player steps on the pitch-mark, improving the area of his intended swing. Is this permissible?

A. No. The player was in breach of Rule 13-2 which prohibits improving the area of the intended swing by pressing down irregularities of surface.

13-2/22 Knocking Down Leaves with Practice Swing

Q. A player's ball lies near a tree or bush. The player knocks down leaves with a practice swing. Is this a breach of Rule 13-2?

A. It depends on the circumstances. In some cases, the knocking down of a number of leaves would not improve the area of the intended swing, in which case there would be no breach of the Rules. In other cases, the knocking down of one large leaf might improve the area of the intended swing, in which case there would be a breach of Rule 13-2.

13-2/23 Shaking Water from Tree Branch Interfering with Backswing

Q. After heavy rain, a player plays a stroke that comes to rest under a tree. A branch of the tree interferes with the player's backswing. Before playing his next stroke, the player shakes the water off this branch in order to eliminate the possibility of dislodged water distracting him. Is this a breach of Rule 13-2?

A. Yes. In moving the branch, the player eliminated the distraction caused by the water and thereby improved the area of his intended swing.

13-2/24 Area of Originally Intended Swing Improved by Breaking Branch; Area of Swing Finally Used Not Affected by Branch

13

Q. A player, intending to play in a certain direction, took a practice backswing for a stroke in that direction and broke a branch impeding his backswing. The player then decided to play in a different direction. The area of his intended swing for a stroke in this new direction was not improved by the breaking of the branch. In such circumstances, would the player incur a penalty under Rule 13-2?

A. Yes. The player was in breach of Rule 13-2 as soon as he improved the area of the originally intended swing. The penalty is not avoided if he subsequently plays in another direction, even if the breaking of the branch had no effect on the area of the swing for a stroke in the new direction.

13-2/25 Player Removes Boundary Post on Line of Play But Replaces It Before Playing

Q. A player removes a post defining out of bounds on his line of play. He realizes he has made a mistake and replaces it before playing his next stroke. What is the ruling?

A. The player was in breach of Rule 13-2 the moment he moved the post and there was nothing he could do to avoid the penalty. The replacement of the post before the next stroke was irrelevant.

13-2/26 Natural Object Interfering with Swing Moved to Determine Whether It Is Loose

Q. A player cannot determine whether a long blade of grass, a twig, a tumbleweed or some similar natural object interfering with his swing through the green is loose or is attached to its roots. The player moves the object to the extent necessary to make a determination and discovers that the object is attached. If the movement of the natural object results in the area of the player's intended swing being improved, is the player subject to penalty under Rule 13-2?

A. No, provided he returns the natural object to its original position before playing his next stroke. A player is entitled to determine whether such a natural object which interferes with the area of his intended swing is loose provided that, if the object is found not to be loose, (1) it has not become detached and (2) it is returned to its original position before the next stroke.

13

[13-2/27 Reserved]

13-2/28 Smoothing Irregularities in Bunker Situated Between Ball and Hole

Q. There is a bunker between A's ball and the hole. Before playing, A smooth footprints and other irregularities in the bunker on his line of play. Was A in breach of Rule 13-2?

A. Yes, such action would improve the line of play, contrary to Rule 13-2.

13-2/29 Creating and Then Smoothing Footprints in Bunker on Line of Play

Q. There is a bunker between a player's ball and the hole. The player walks through the bunker to remove a rake on his line of play, to measure the distance to the hole or for any other reason. On his way back to his ball, he smooth the footprints he made, restoring the line to its original condition. Is such smoothing permissible?

A. No. If a player worsens his line of play, he is not entitled to restore the line to its original condition. If he does so, he has improved the line in breach of Rule 13-2 and incurs a penalty of loss of hole in match play or two strokes in stroke play.

13-2/29.5 Extension of Line of Play Affected When Opponent or Fellow-Competitor Creates Footprints in Bunker

Q. A's ball lies behind the green. The ball of his opponent or fellow-competitor (B) lies in a bunker in front of the green, which is on an extension of A's line of play.

It is A's turn to play but before he does so, B walks into the bunker to assess his next stroke, thereby creating footprints. A believes that his ball might come to rest in the bunker. Is A entitled to have the bunker restored to the condition which existed when A's ball came to rest?

A. Yes. In equity (Rule 1-4), A may have the bunker restored to its former condition because the footprints were created by B after A's ball came to rest. The bunker may be restored by anyone.

13-2/30 Testing Condition of Bunker Before Deciding Whether to Play Through It

Q. A player's ball lies behind a bunker. May he test the condition of the bunker to determine whether it is feasible to putt through it?

A. The Rules do not prohibit a player from testing the condition of a hazard except when his ball lies in or touches the hazard — see Rule 13-4. However, if such testing improved the line of play, the player would be in breach of Rule 13-2.

13-2/31 Ball Outside Bunker; Stone in Bunker on Line of Play Pressed Down or Removed

Q. A player's ball is lying behind a bunker and he decides to putt through the bunker. There is a small stone (loose impediment) in the bunker on his line of play. May he push the stone down into the sand or remove it?

A. Sand may not be pressed down if the act would improve the line of play — Rule 13-2. However, Rule 23-1 permits the removal of a loose impediment in a hazard when the ball is not lying in the hazard.

13-2/32 Improving Line of Play by Removing Stone from Wall

Q. A stone wall on the course (immovable obstruction) is on A's line of play. A removes a stone from the top of the wall. Is this permissible?

A. No. An immovable obstruction is fixed. In removing part of an immovable obstruction, A was in breach of Rule 13-2. The same ruling would apply if the wall had been declared an integral part of the course.

13

13-2/32.5 Improving Line of Play by Removing Part of Fence

Q. A fence which is not a boundary fence does not interfere with a player's swing but it is on his line of play. May the player remove a part of the fence, which is readily movable, in order to improve his line of play?

A. No. A fence is an immovable obstruction and thus is something fixed. If a player removes a part of something fixed and in so doing improves his line of play, he is in breach of Rule 13-2.

13-2/33 Outside Agency Removes Immovable Obstruction on Player's Line of Play

Q. A stake supporting a young tree has been deemed an immovable obstruction by the Committee. A player's ball comes to rest in such a position that the stake intervenes on his line of play but does not interfere with his swing or stance. At that point, an outside agency removes the stake. What is the ruling?

A. If the player allowed the outside agency to remove the stake, the player loses the hole in match play or incurs a penalty of two strokes in stroke play for a breach of Rule 13-2.

If the player did not know the stake had been removed, or if he knew it but was not in a position to prevent it, there is no penalty and the player may replace the stake, but he is not required to do so.

Relief from Obstruction Incidentally Gives Relief from Intervention on Line of Play — See 24-2b/7.

Window of Clubhouse Opened and Ball Played Through Window — See 24-2b/14.

Opening Barn Doors to Play Shot Through Barn — See 24-2b/15.

Improving Line of Play When Taking Relief from Abnormal Ground Condition — See 25-1b/3.

13-2/34 Mopping Up Casual Water on Line of Play

Q. A pool of casual water was on the putting green between the player's ball, which was lying short of the green, and the hole. The player's caddie mopped up the water. Was this permissible?

A. No. The player incurred a penalty of loss of hole in match play or two strokes in stroke play for a breach of Rule 13-2.

Brushing Aside or Mopping Up Casual Water on Line of Putt — See 16-1a/1.

Ball Mark Partially On and Partially Off Putting Green Is on Line of Play — See 16-1c/1.5.

13-2/35 Removal of Dew or Frost

The removal of dew or frost from the area behind or to the side of a player's ball is permitted. Such action is deemed not to improve the position or lie of the ball or the area of the player's intended swing.

The removal of dew or frost from the player's line of play is not permitted. Such action is deemed to improve the line of play and is a breach of Rule 13-2 or, on the putting green, Rule 16-1a, unless it occurs incidentally to some other action permitted under the Rules, *e.g.*, removing loose impediments, repairing ball marks on the putting green, etc. (Revised)

Removing Dew or Frost from Line of Putt — See 16-1a/3.

13-2/36 Competitor Sanctions Repair of Spike Damage on His Line of Putt by Fellow-Competitor

Q. If a fellow-competitor purposely improves the competitor's line of putt by repairing spike damage, the fellow-competitor is penalized under Rule 1-2. If the fellow-competitor's action is sanctioned, tacitly or otherwise, by the competitor, is the competitor also subject to penalty?

13

A. Yes, under Rule 13-2, for allowing his line of play to be improved.

Repair of Spike Mark Damage Around Hole — See 16-1c/4.

13-2/37 Status of Moss or Creepers in Tree

Q. May moss, or a creeper, in a tree be removed if its removal would improve the line of play?

A. No. Trees are the natural habitat of some mosses and creepers. Accordingly, such plants growing in a tree may not be moved — see Rule 13-2.

Moss or a creeper which has fallen to the ground, and is not growing there, is a loose impediment and may be removed, without penalty — see Rule 23-1.

13-3/1 Standing on Mat on Teeing Ground

Q. Is it permissible for a player to carry a mat and stand on it when playing from the teeing ground?

A. No. The player would be building a stance in breach of Rule 13-3.

13-3/2 Playing Stroke While Kneeling on Towel

Q. A player's ball was under a tree in such a position that he found it expedient to play his next stroke while on his knees. Because the ground was wet, the player placed a towel on the ground at the spot where his knees would be situated so that the knees of his trousers would not get wet. He then knelt on the towel and played his stroke. Was the player subject to penalty under Rule 13-3 for building a stance?

A. Yes.

13-3/3 Knocking Down Side of Bunker to Get Level Stance

Q. A player knocks down the side of a bunker with his foot in an effort to get his feet on the same level. Is this permissible?

A. No. Such action constitutes building a stance in breach of Rule 13-3.

[13-3/4 Reserved]

13-3/5 Player Builds Stance But Corrects Error Before Playing Stroke

Q. A player's ball is lodged in the branch of a tree just beyond his reach with a club. The player positions his motorized golf cart under the tree, stands on the cart and prepares to make a stroke at his ball. At that point, the player is advised that he is building a stance, contrary to Rule 13-3. If the player removes the cart and does not play a stroke while standing on it, does he nevertheless incur a penalty for a breach of Rule 13-3?

A. No. If a player builds a stance through use of an object such as a golf cart, stone or brick, he incurs no penalty if he removes the object before playing his next stroke.

However, if a player builds a stance through alteration of the ground on which he is taking his stance, it is impossible for him to restore the ground to its original state. Accordingly, a player who builds a stance in such manner incurs the penalty prescribed in Rule 13-3, whether or not he attempts to restore the ground to its original state before playing his next stroke.

13-4/1 Touching Sand in Bunker When Ball Lies Outside Bunker

Q. A ball lies just outside a bunker. The player takes his stance in the bunker. May the player ground his club on the sand in the bunker or touch the sand during his backswing?

A. Yes. Since the ball was not in or touching the bunker, Rule 13-4 does not apply. However, the player may ground his club only lightly — see Rule 13-2.

13

13-4/2 Leaning on Club in Bunker While Waiting to Play

Q. A, whose ball lies in a bunker, leans on a club in the bunker while waiting for B to play. What is the ruling?

A. A was in breach of Rule 13-4b for touching the ground in the hazard with his club before making a stroke.

13-4/3 Touching Ground in Hazard with Several Practice Swings

Q. In stroke play, a competitor in ignorance of the Rules took several practice swings in a hazard, touching the ground each time. What is the penalty?

A. Two strokes for a breach of Rule 13-4.

13-4/3.5 Player Uses Cane or Club to Enter or Leave Hazard When Ball Lies in Hazard

Q. A player, to prevent falling, uses a cane or club to enter a hazard to play his ball which lies in the hazard.

Is the player in breach of Rule 13-4b which prohibits touching ground in the hazard?

A. No, provided nothing is done which constitutes testing the condition of the hazard or improves the lie of the ball- see Exception 1 to Rule 13-4.

13-4/4 Touching Grass with Club in Practice Swing in Hazard

Q. A player takes a practice swing in a water hazard without grounding his club, but his club touches some long grass. Is there a penalty?

A. No, provided the player did not improve his lie or test the condition of the hazard.

When Club Grounded in Grass — See 18-2b/5.

13-4/5 Touching Mound Made by Burrowing Animal with Backswing in Bunker

Q. A player's ball and a mound made by a burrowing animal are in a bunker. The mound interferes with the player's backswing, but the player elects not to take relief under Rule 25-1b(ii). During his backswing, the player's club touches the mound. Is the player in breach of Rule 13-4?

A. Yes. Rule 13-4 prohibits touching the ground in a hazard before making a stroke, which is the forward movement of the club. In a hazard, a mound made by a burrowing animal is ground in the hazard.

13-4/6 Touching Solidly Embedded Stone in Hazard with Club During Backswing

Q. A player's ball lies in a hazard. In making his backswing for the stroke, the player's club touches a solidly embedded stone in the hazard. Is the stone considered "ground in the hazard"?

A. Yes.

[13-4/7 Reserved]

[13-4/8   Reserved]

[13-4/8.5   Reserved]

[13-4/9   Reserved]

[13-4/10   Reserved]

13-4/11   Smoothing Footprints Made in Search for Ball in Bunker Before Playing Stroke from Bunker

Q. A player searches for his ball in a bunker and in the process makes numerous footprints. He subsequently finds his ball. Before playing his stroke, may the player smooth the footprints?

A. No, such action would be a breach of Rule 13-4. However, there would be no breach if the player's caddie smoothed the footprints on his own initiative, provided that the smoothing did not improve the lie of the ball or assist the player in his subsequent play of the hole — see Exception 2 to Rule 13-4.

13-4/12   Ball Touched Accidentally with Club in Hazard But Not Moved

Q. A player, when addressing his ball which was lying in a bunker or was partially submerged in water in a water hazard, accidentally touches the ball with his club, but without moving it. Does this constitute touching the ground in a hazard or water in a water hazard in breach of Rule 13-4?

A. No.

13-4/13   Accidentally Moving Loose Impediment in Hazard

Q. A player accidentally moves a loose impediment in a hazard. Does the player incur a penalty?

A. No, provided the loose impediment was not moved in making the backswing and the lie of the ball or area of the intended swing was not improved.

13-4/14 Player Accidentally Kicks Pine Cone into Bunker and Picks It Up

Q. A player's ball went into a bunker. The player accidentally kicked a pine cone, and it rolled into the bunker. He picked up the pine cone which was not interfering with his stance or the area of his intended swing. Did he incur a penalty?

A. Yes. A pine cone is a loose impediment — see Definition of "Loose Impediments" — and may not be removed when both the impediment and the ball lie in a hazard (Rule 13-4c). By removing the pine cone from the bunker, the player incurred a penalty of loss of hole in match play or two strokes in stroke play for a breach of Rule 13-4c.

13-4/15 Ball in Hazard Moves When Loose Impediment Removed

Q. In stroke play, a competitor's ball in a hazard moves due to his removal of a loose impediment in the hazard. What is the ruling?

A. The competitor incurs a penalty of three strokes — two for moving a loose impediment in a hazard (Rule 13-4c) and one because the ball moved (Rule 18-2a). The ball must be replaced (Rule 18-2a).

13-4/16 Removal of Loose Impediment in Water Hazard Covering Wrong Ball

Q. A player plays his ball into a water hazard. He finds a ball in the hazard and removes a loose impediment partially covering it. He discovers that the ball is not his ball. He searches for his ball but does not find it. He proceeds under Rule 26-1. Is the player subject to penalty under Rule 13-4 for removing the loose impediment?

A. Yes.

Removal of Obstruction in Hazard Would Move Loose Impediment — See 1-4/5.

13-4/17 Loose Impediment Removed from Water Hazard; Player Then Decides Not to Play from Hazard

Q. A player whose ball was in a water hazard removed a loose impediment from the hazard. He then decided not to play from the hazard. He proceeded under Rule 26-1. Was the player absolved from the penalty incurred under Rule 13-4 for removing the loose impediment in view of the fact that he subsequently invoked Rule 26-1 and did not play his ball from the hazard?

A. No.

Player Removes Loose Impediment Affecting Opponent's Lie in Hazard — See 1-2/6.

Player Lifts Loose Impediment in Bunker When His Ball and Partner's Ball in Bunker — See 30-3f/1.

Competitor Lifts Loose Impediment in Bunker When His Ball and Partner's Ball in Bunker — See 31-8/1.

13-4/18 Partner's, Opponent's or Fellow-Competitor's Divot Comes to Rest Near Player's Ball in Bunker

Q. A player's partner, opponent or fellow-competitor plays a stroke from near a bunker and the divot comes to rest near the player's ball lying in the bunker. May the divot be removed?

A. A player is entitled to the lie which his stroke gave him. Accordingly, in equity (Rule 1-4) the divot may be removed without penalty.

The same would apply if the player's ball was lying in a water hazard.

13-4/18.5 Pine Cone Falls from Tree and Comes to Rest Behind Ball Lying in Bunker

Q. A pine cone falls from a tree and comes to rest behind a ball which is lying in a bunker. Under the principle in Decision 13-4/18, may the player remove the pine cone without penalty?

A. No. The principle in Decision 13-4/18 is applied only in cases in which the lie of a ball has been altered as a result of an act by another player or caddie, or by a spectator or other animate outside agency. In this case, the lie was altered through natural causes.

13-4/19 Player Preparing to Play from Bunker Requests Another Player Who Has Just Played from Bunker to Smooth His Footprints

Q. In a match between A and B, both balls lie in a bunker and B's ball is farther from the hole. B plays out of the bunker. A then asks B to rake the bunker in case A's ball rolls backwards into B's footprints if A fails to get out of the bunker. What is the ruling?

A. B was entitled to rake the bunker under Exception 2 to Rule 13-4. A incurs no penalty for having asked B to rake the bunker.

13-4/20 Umbrella or Rake Placed in Hazard Before Stroke

Q. May a player place an umbrella or a rake in a bunker before playing a stroke from the bunker?

A. Placing an umbrella or rake in a hazard is equivalent to placing clubs in the hazard — see Exception 1 to Rule 13-4. There is no penalty, providing nothing is done which may constitute testing the soil or improving the lie of the ball. But see Decision 13-4/22.

13-4/21 Rake Thrown into Bunker Before Stroke

Q. A player's ball lies in a bunker. He casually throws a rake into the bunker for use after his stroke. The rake does not move his ball or improve the lie of the ball. Does the player incur a penalty?

A. No. Placing a rake in a bunker is permissible. In this case, throwing the rake into the bunker was the equivalent of placing it.

If the rake had moved the ball, the player would incur a penalty of one stroke for causing his ball to move; and the ball would have to be replaced — Rule 18-2a.

13-4/22 Rake Handle Stuck in Bunker Before Stroke

Q. A takes a rake into a bunker so that he can smooth his footprints after playing from the bunker. He sticks the handle of the rake into the sand prior to playing his stroke. Is this permissible?

A. No. A was in breach of Rule 13-4 which prohibits testing the condition of a hazard when the ball lies in the hazard.

13-4/23 When Stance Taken in Bunker

13

Q. In a bunker, when is a player deemed to have taken his stance and thus to have addressed the ball?

A. Whether a stance has been taken is a question of fact to be determined in the light of the circumstances in each case. In a bunker, some "digging in" with the feet would normally precede the completion of the stance.

13-4/24 Stance in Bunker Taken Without Club

Q. A player whose ball was in a bunker entered it without a club, dug in with his feet and simulated a stroke. He then left the bunker, got a club, dug in again with his feet at the same place and made a stroke.

The Committee asked the player why he had gone through this exercise. He replied that he had wanted to get the "feel" of the shot he was about to make and that the purpose of the simulated stroke was to determine which club to use and what kind of stroke to make. He stated that he was not testing the condition of the hazard or building a stance when he dug his feet in for the simulated stroke.

How should the Committee have ruled?

A. The Committee should have ruled that no penalty was incurred.

Rule 13-3 states: "A player is entitled to place his feet firmly in taking his stance."

The Definition of "Stance" states: "Taking the 'stance' consists in a player placing his feet in position for and preparatory to making a stroke."

On the first occasion, the player was "placing his feet in position for and preparatory to making a stroke," even though he had no club in his hands. If it were ruled otherwise, a player would be in breach of Rule 13-4 if he selected a club for a bunker shot, took his stance with the club in hand and then decided to play the stroke with another club.

13

Ball Moves After Stance Taken in Hazard Without Club — See 18-2b/2.

13-4/25 Taking Firm Stance in Bunker Some Distance from Where Ball Lies in Bunker to Simulate Next Stroke

Q. While waiting to play a bunker shot, A went to another part of the bunker, took a firm stance and simulated his bunker shot without using a club. Was A in breach of Rule 13-4?

A. Yes. A tested the condition of the bunker in breach of Rule 13-4a.

13-4/26 Taking Stance in Bunker and Then Changing Clubs

Q. A player takes his stance in a bunker and firmly places his feet in the sand. He then leaves his position to change clubs and thereafter takes his stance a second time. Is the player considered to have tested the condition of the hazard, contrary to Rule 13-4?

A. No. Rule 13-3 allows a player to place his feet firmly in taking his stance in a bunker or elsewhere. There is nothing in the Rules to prohibit changing clubs or taking a stance twice in a bunker.

Ball Moves While Player in Process of Taking Stance in Bunker — See 18-2b/3.

13-4/27 Player in Bunker Takes Firm Stance and Then Smooth Footprints When He Decides to Play Different Type Shot

Q. A player places his feet firmly in the sand in a bunker, intending to play an explosion shot. He then changes his mind and decides to play a chip shot. He takes a different club and, before playing, smooth out his original footprints because he does not want his feet so firmly implanted for a chip shot. Is this permissible?

A. No. The player incurs a penalty under Rule 13-4a for testing the condition of the hazard. Rule 13-3 allows him to place his feet firmly in taking his stance. However, there is nothing in the Rules to permit the player to place his feet firmly and then smooth the footprints before the stroke, even if the smoothing is due to the player having changed his mind as to the type of stroke. If it were otherwise, the way would be open for a player to test the condition of a bunker with his feet beyond any testing incident to taking his stance.

13

13-4/28 Grounding Club, Removing Leaves and Improving Area of Intended Swing in Water Hazard

Q. In stroke play, a player whose ball lies in a water hazard takes several practice swings, touching the ground each time and removing leaves. He also bends a shrub, improving the area of his intended swing. What is the penalty?

A. Four strokes — two strokes for grounding his club and removing leaves (Rule 13-4) and two strokes for improving the area of his intended swing by bending a shrub (Rule 13-2).

13-4/29 Grounding Club Outside Water Hazard When Playing Stroke at Ball in Hazard

Q. A player's ball touches a line defining the margin of a water hazard. So the ball is in the hazard. In addressing the ball for his next stroke, may the player's club be grounded outside the hazard?

A. Yes.

13-4/30 Grounding Club on Bridge in Water Hazard

Q. A player's ball lies on a bridge over a water hazard within the margins of the hazard when extended upwards. May the player ground his club?

A. Yes. A bridge is an obstruction. In a hazard, the club may touch an obstruction at address or in the backward movement for the stroke — see Note under Rule 13-4. Touching the bridge prior to address is also permissible, since an obstruction in a water hazard is not "ground in the hazard."

This applies even if the bridge has been declared an integral part of the course.

13-4/31 Touching Sand in Bunker During Backswing

Q. A player playing a shot in a bunker accidentally touched the sand when making his backswing. What is the ruling?

A. The player was in breach of Rule 13-4b when he touched the ground in the bunker with his club before making the stroke — see Definition of "Stroke."

13-4/32 Club Touches Partially Embedded Pine Needle on Backswing in Bunker

Q. A player whose ball lies in a bunker touches a partially embedded pine needle with his club on his backswing. What is the ruling?

A. The player is in breach of Rule 13-4c. A partially embedded pine needle is not solidly embedded and is not considered to be fixed; therefore, it is a loose impediment (see Definition of "Loose Impediments").

13-4/33 Bunker Covered by Leaves; Player Touches Leaves During Backswing

Q. A player hits a ball into a bunker which is covered by leaves (loose impediments). The player removes as many leaves as will enable him to see a part of the ball in accordance with Rule 12-1. If the player then touches some of the leaves on his backswing, is he in breach of the Rules?

A. Yes. If the player touches leaves on his backswing, he is in breach of Rule 13-4c which prohibits a player from touching a loose impediment in a hazard before making a stroke in the hazard. A stroke does not begin until after the completion of the player's backswing — see Definition of "Stroke."

If fallen leaves in bunkers seasonally create an abnormal problem, the Committee may make a Local Rule declaring accumulations of leaves in bunkers to be ground under repair. Rule 25-1b(ii) would then apply.

13-4/34 Touching Bare Earth Wall of Bunker on Backswing

Q. In playing from a bunker, a player touches a bare earth wall of the bunker with his club on his backswing. What is the ruling?

A. The player touched the ground in the hazard in breach of Rule 13-4b. The Note to Rule 13-4 permits a player's club to touch an obstruction (such as an artificial wall) on his backswing. However, an earth wall of a bunker is not an artificial wall.

Local Rule for Bunker Faces Consisting of Stacked Turf — See 33-8/39.

13-4/35 Hitting Sand in Bunker with Club After Failing to Extricate Ball

Q. A played a stroke in a bunker and failed to get

the ball out. He then swung his club into the sand, but his action did not affect his new lie in the bunker. However, since A had to play another stroke in the bunker, was he in breach of Rule 13-4?

A. Yes. Neither of the Exceptions under Rule 13-4 applies to A's action.

Hitting Sand in Bunker with Club After Failing to Extricate Ball; Foursome Match — See 29/5.

Hitting Sand in Bunker with Club After Failing to Extricate Ball; Partner's Ball in Same Bunker — See 30-3f/2.

13-4/35.5 Ball Played from Bunker onto Grass Bank; Player Hits Sand with Club; Ball Then Rolls Back into Bunker

Q. A player plays from a bunker and the ball lands on the grass bank of the bunker. Before the ball comes to rest, the player swings his club into the sand, after which the ball rolls back into the bunker.

Rule 13-4b prohibits touching the ground in a hazard when the ball lies in the hazard. Does the player incur a penalty under this Rule even though the ball was outside the bunker when the club was swung into the sand?

A. No. However, if the club was still touching the sand when the ball rolled back into the bunker, a breach of Rule 13-4 occurred, and any doubt on this point should be resolved against the player.

13-4/36 Smoothing Irregularities in Bunker After Stroke But Before Ball Extricated

Q. A plays a stroke in a bunker but he hits too far behind the ball and fails to extricate it from the bunker. He smooth irregularities in the area where the stroke was played. Exception 2 to Rule 13-4 permits smoothing provided that the lie of the ball is not improved and the player is not assisted in his subsequent play of the hole. The smoothing does not improve the new lie of the ball. However, B claims that the smoothing assisted A in his subsequent play of the hole because it constituted testing the consistency of the sand. Is B right?

A. No. A was able to test the consistency of the sand during his first stroke in the bunker, and he would gain no additional information by smoothing the sand at the place where that stroke was played.

No claim by B that A's smoothing of the sand assisted him in his subsequent play of the hole would be valid unless, as a result of a subsequent stroke in the bunker, A's ball rolled back into the smoothed area.

13-4/37 Ball Played from Bunker Is Out of Bounds or Lost; Player Tests Condition of Bunker or Smooth Footprints Before Dropping Another Ball in Bunker

13

Q. A player plays from a bunker and his ball comes to rest out of bounds or is lost. He smooth his footprints in the bunker at the place where he must drop a ball under Rule 27-1 or, before dropping a ball under Rule 27-1, he takes a few practice swings touching the sand in the bunker. Is the player in breach of Rule 13-4?

A. No. The prohibitions in Rule 13-4 apply only when the player's ball lies in or touches the hazard.

Furthermore, Exception 2 under Rule 13-4 allows a player, after playing his ball out of a hazard, to smooth sand or soil in the hazard, without restriction. This right supersedes any conflicting provisions in other Rules, including Rule 13-2.

13-4/38 Sand Smoothed After Ball Played Out of Bunker; Ball Later Returns to Smoothed Area

Q. After playing his ball out of a greenside bunker, the player smooth his footprints. He then discovers that his ball is in another bunker on the other side of the green. He plays out of the second bunker and the ball comes to rest in the smoothed area of the first bunker. What is the ruling?

A. No penalty was incurred. The player did not smooth his footprints in the first bunker while his ball still lay in that bunker — see Exception 2 to Rule 13-4.

If, however, the player had failed to extricate his ball from the first bunker with his first stroke and had smoothed his footprints while his ball still lay in that bunker, he would have incurred a penalty if, as a result of a subsequent stroke in the bunker, his ball had rolled back into the smoothed area.

Greenkeeping Staff Member Rakes Bunker When Player's Ball Lies Therein — See 13-2/4.

Smoothing Irregularities in Bunker Situated Between Ball and Hole — See 13-2/28.

Extension of Line of Play Affected When Opponent or Fellow-Competitor Creates Footprints in Bunker — See 13-2/29.5.

Testing Condition of Bunker Before Deciding Whether to Play Through It — See 13-2/30.

Ball Outside Bunker; Stone in Bunker on Line of Play Pressed Down or Removed — See 13-2/31.

13-4/39 Player Smooth Irregularities in Bunker After Playing Out of Turn in Match Play; Opponent Then Recalls Stroke and Player Must Drop Ball in Smoothed Area

Q. In a match between A and B, A's ball lay in a bunker near the green and B's ball was on the green. B's ball was farther from the hole but A played first. B recalled the stroke under Rule 10-1c. In the meantime. A had raked his footprints. Did A incur a penalty?

A. If A's ball played out of turn came to rest outside the bunker, there was no breach of Rule 13-4b because A's ball was not lying in the bunker when he raked the footprints, *i.e.*, the prohibitions in Rule 13-4 apply only when the player's ball lies in or touches the hazard.

If A's ball still lay in the bunker, he was in breach of Rule 13-4 because it must be assumed that the smoothing assisted him in his subsequent play of the hole. Exception 2 to Rule 13-4 exempts the player from penalty for assisting himself in the subsequent play of a hole by smoothing footprints if the ball lies outside the hazard when the smoothing takes place, but not if the ball still lies in the hazard.

Ball Lying on Grass-Covered Ground in Bunker Declared Unplayable — See 28/9.

Ball Unplayable in Bunker Dropped Outside Bunker Under Option Requiring Drop in Bunker — See 28/10.

13

Rule 14. Striking the Ball

Definition

A "stroke" is the forward movement of the club made with the intention of fairly striking at and moving the ball, but if a player checks his downswing voluntarily before the clubhead reaches the ball he is deemed not to have made a stroke.

14-1. Ball to Be Fairly Struck At

The ball shall be fairly struck at with the head of the club and must not be pushed, scraped or spooned.

14-2. Assistance

In making a stroke, a player shall not accept physical assistance or protection from the elements.

> PENALTY FOR BREACH
> OF RULE 14-1 or -2:
> *Match play --- Loss of hole;*
> *Stroke play --- Two strokes.*

14-3. Artificial Devices and Unusual Equipment

If there may be any reasonable basis for doubt as to whether an item which is to be manufactured would, if used by a player during a round, cause the player to be in breach of Rule 14-3, the manufacturer should submit a sample to the United States Golf Association for a ruling, such sample to become its property for reference purposes. If a manufacturer fails to do so, he assumes the risk of an unfavorable ruling.

A player in doubt as to whether use of an item would constitute a breach of Rule 14-3 should consult the United States Golf Association.

Except as provided in the Rules, during a stipulated round the player shall not use any artificial device or unusual equipment:

> a. Which might assist him in making a stroke or in his play; or

> b. For the purpose of gauging or measuring distance or conditions which might affect his play; or

> c. Which might assist him in gripping the club, except that plain gloves may be worn, resin, tape or gauze may be applied to the grip (provided such application does not render the grip non-conforming under Rule 4-1c) and a towel or handkerchief may be wrapped around the grip.

PENALTY FOR BREACH OF RULE 14-3:
Disqualification.

14-4. Striking the Ball More than Once

If a player's club strikes the ball more than once in the course of a <u>stroke</u>, the player shall count the stroke and *add a penalty stroke*, making two strokes in all.

14-5. Playing Moving Ball

A player shall not play while his ball is moving.

Exceptions:

Ball falling off tee — Rule 11-3.

Striking the ball more than once — Rule 14-4.

Ball moving in water — Rule 14-6.

When the ball begins to move only after the player has begun the <u>stroke</u> or the backward movement of his club for the stroke, he shall incur no penalty under this Rule for playing a moving ball, but he is not exempt from any penalty incurred under the following Rules:

Ball at rest moved by player — Rule 18-2a.

Ball at rest moving after address — Rule 18-2b.

Ball at rest moving after loose impediment touched — Rule 18-2c.

14-6. Ball Moving in Water

When a ball is moving in water in a <u>water hazard</u>, the player may, without penalty, make a <u>stroke</u>, but he must not delay making his stroke in order to allow the wind or current to improve the position of the ball. A ball moving in water in a water hazard may be lifted if the player elects to invoke Rule 26.

PENALTY FOR BREACH
OF RULE 14-5 or -6:
Match play --- Loss of hole;
Stroke play --- Two strokes.

14

14/1 Club Stopped on Downswing by Agency Other Than Player

Q. If a player starts his downswing and his clubhead is deflected or stopped by an agency other than himself, *e.g.*, the branch of a tree, is he deemed to have made a stroke?

A. Yes.

14/1.5 Intent to Strike Ball Ceases During Downswing; Club Not Stopped But Path of Clubhead Altered to Avoid Striking Ball

Q. A player begins his downswing with the intention of striking the ball but decides during the downswing not to strike the ball. The player is unable to stop the club before it reaches the ball, but he is able to swing intentionally over the top of the ball. Is the player deemed to have made a stroke?

A. No. The player has checked his downswing voluntarily by altering the path of his downswing and missing the ball even though the swing carried the clubhead beyond the ball.

However, any doubt in such a case must be resolved against the player. If, for example, the clubhead struck the ball there would be insufficient evidence to support a claim that the player had not made a stroke.

14/2 Club Breaks During Backswing; Swing Completed

Q. The head of a player's club separated from the shaft during his backswing. The player completed the swing but missed the ball. Is the player deemed to have made a stroke?

A. No. A stroke is "the forward movement of the club..." A shaft by itself is not a club — see Rule 4-1a.

14/3 Clubhead Separates from Shaft on Downswing

Q. A player starts his downswing and the clubhead separates from the shaft. The player continues his swing but no contact is made with the ball. Did the player make a stroke?

A. Yes.

14/4 Club Breaks During Downswing; Swing Stopped Short of Ball; Clubhead Falls and Moves Ball

Q. The shaft of a player's club broke during his downswing. The player stopped his swing short of the ball, but the clubhead fell and moved the ball. What is the ruling?

A. The player did not make a stroke — see Definition of "Stroke."

If the ball was not in play, *i.e.*, the incident involved a tee shot, no penalty was incurred, and a ball must be played from the teeing ground.

If the ball was in play, the player would incur a one-stroke penalty under Rule 18-2a or -2b and the ball must be replaced.

14/5 Club Breaks During Downswing; Swing Completed But Misses Ball; Clubhead Falls and Moves Ball

Q. The shaft of a player's club broke during his downswing. The player continued his swing and missed the ball. However, the clubhead fell and moved the ball. What is the ruling?

A. The stroke counts but the player incurs no penalty. The ball must be played as it lies.

14

14/6 Ball Popped Up Swung at in Disgust

Q. A player's ball is lying against a root. He makes a stroke and the ball pops up into the air. In disgust, he swings at it on the way down, but misses. Was the swing in disgust a stroke?

A. No. Such an instinctive swing in anger is not a stroke. Nor should the player be considered to have taken action to influence the movement of the ball in breach of Rule 1-2. However, if the player had struck the ball accidentally while it was in motion, he would have incurred a penalty of loss of hole in match play or two strokes in stroke play — Rules 19-2a and -2b.

Ball Knocked from Lip of Hole in Disgust — See 18-2a/23.

14/7 Striking at Tree Branch to Move Ball Lodged Higher in Branch

Q. A player's ball is lodged in a tree branch beyond the reach of a club. The player swings at a lower part of the branch with a club for the purpose of dislodging the ball, and the ball falls to the ground. Has the player made a stroke?

A. No, because the player did not strike at the ball —
see Definition of "Stroke." The player incurred a one-
stroke penalty under Rule 18-2a (Ball at Rest Moved
by Player) and must replace the ball.

Since the spot where the ball lay is unreachable and
the ball therefore cannot be replaced, the player must
proceed under the unplayable ball Rule, incurring an
additional penalty stroke — see Decisions 18-1/9 and
18-2a/29.

Stroke at Own Ball Dislodges Concealed Ball — See 15/2.

**Ball Moved Accidentally by Practice Swing Prior to Tee
Shot** — See 18-2a/19.

**Ball Moved Accidentally by Practice Swing Through the
Green** — See 18-2a/20.

**Ball Moved Accidentally by Backward Movement of Club
After Stroke Misses** — See 18-2a/22.

**Player Misses Ball Purposely in Foursome So Partner
Would Play Ball Over Water** — See 29-1/7.

14-1/1 Playing Stroke with Back of Clubhead

Q. May a player play a left-handed stroke with the
back of the head of a right-handed club?

A. Yes. A player may play a stroke with any part of
the clubhead, provided the ball is fairly struck at (Rule
14-1) and the club conforms with Rule 4-1.

14-1/2 Striking Ball with Billiard-Type Motion

Q. A player holed a short putt by squatting behind
the ball (but not on an extension of the line of putt
behind the ball) and striking the ball with the bottom
of the clubhead, using a motion similar to that used
in playing a shot in billiards or shuffleboard. Was the
player in breach of Rule 14-1?

A. Yes. Such a manner of moving the ball constitutes
a push in golf.

14-1/3 Putting with Wrong End of Putter

Q. A player misses a short putt and hastily holes the

ball with the wrong (handle) end of his putter. What is the ruling?

A. The player incurs a penalty of loss of hole in match play or two strokes in stroke play for a breach of Rule 14-1, which requires that the ball be struck at with the head of the club. In stroke play, the stroke with the wrong end of the putter counts, and, since the ball was holed, the player had completed play of the hole.

14-1/4 Striking Ball with Half an Inch Backswing

Q. A player's ball lies close to an out of bounds fence, but there is room behind the ball to insert an iron club or a putter and leave a space of half an inch between the ball and the face of the club. If the player plays a stroke with such a limited backswing, is he in breach of Rule 14-1?

A. It is possible to strike a ball fairly with a half inch backswing. However, in most such cases the player would be pushing the ball, contrary to Rule 14-1. In the absence of strong evidence to the contrary, it should be ruled that the player has pushed the ball.

In order to strike the ball fairly, it must be swung at with the clubhead. If the ball is moved by any other method, it has been pushed, scraped or spooned.

If a ball is fairly struck at, there is only momentary contact between the clubhead and the ball or whatever intervenes between the clubhead and the ball.

14-1/5 Moving Ball Lying Against Fence by Striking Other Side of Fence

Q. A player's ball lies against a board at the base of an out of bounds fence. He swings a club from the out of bounds side of the fence against the board, *i.e.*, swings at the ball with the board intervening between the club and the ball. The stroke moves the board which causes the ball to move away from the fence. Is such a stroke permissible?

A. Yes. The player fairly struck at the ball even though other material intervened between the club and the

14

ball. The Definition of "Out of Bounds" allows a player to "stand out of bounds to play a ball lying within bounds."

14-1/6 Player Holds Club with Left Hand and Moves Ball by Striking Shaft with Other Hand

Q. A player addresses his ball lying in high grass on a steep bank. His ball does not move, but the player believes it will move if he takes a backswing. Accordingly, the player holds the club with his left hand and strikes the shaft of the club with his right hand, thereby moving the ball. Is this permissible?

A. No. The player pushed the ball, contrary to Rule, 14-1.

14-1/7 Using More Than One Club to Make Stroke

Q. A player, whose ball was lodged in a bush, swung at the ball with three clubs to minimize the chance of missing it. Is this permissible?

A. No. Rule 14-1 requires that the ball be struck at with the" head of the club;" the word "club" is in the singular. The player was in breach of this Rule when he swung at the ball with three clubs.

14-2/1 Player Aligns Partner's Club Before Stroke

Q. A player aligns his partner's putter and then moves away before his partner plays. Is this permissible?

A. Yes. Rule 14-2 (Assistance) does not apply prior to making a stroke.

14-2/2 Player Holds Umbrella Over Own Head When Playing Stroke

Q. A player playing in the rain holds an umbrella over his head with one hand while holing a very short putt, gripping the putter with the other hand. Is this permissible?

A. Yes. Rule 14-2 prohibits a player, while making a stroke, from accepting protection from the elements from someone other than himself. However, it does not prohibit him from protecting himself.

14-2/3 Caddie Shields Player from Sun During Stroke

Q. May a player's caddie purposely stand between the player and the setting sun so that the sun's glare is not in the player's face while he is playing a stroke?

A. No. Such procedure is a breach of Rule 14-2.

Material Applied to Top of Clubhead to Reduce Glare — See 4-2/1.

14

14-3/1 Distance Meter Attached to Golf Cart

Q. May a player attach a meter to his golf cart for the purpose of measuring the distances of shots?

A. No. Use of such a meter during a round would be a breach of Rule 14-3.

14-3/2 Pencil or Score Card Used to Assist in Gauging Distance

Q. It is possible to gauge distance to a putting green by holding a score card or pencil at arm's length and comparing it with the height of the flagstick. Is such a practice permissible?

A. Yes, provided the score card or pencil has not been specially marked. Use of anything specially marked to gauge distance is a breach of Rule 14-3.

14-3/3 Standard Spectacles and Field Glasses

Neither standard spectacles nor field glasses which have no range-finder attachments are artificial devices within the meaning of the term in Rule 14-3.

14-3/4 Use of Compass During Round

Q. A player uses a compass during a round to assist him in determining wind direction or the direction of the grain in the greens or for some other similar reason. Is the player in breach of Rule 14-3?

A. Yes.

14-3/5 Booklet Providing Distances to Hole from Various Points

Q. A booklet contains illustrations of the holes on a course, including isolated trees, bunkers, etc. Super-imposed on each illustration is a yardage scale in increments of ten yards. Thus, a player using such a booklet can determine how far his ball lies from a putting green or a tee. Is use of such a booklet during a round contrary to Rule 14-3?

A. No.

14-3/6 Holding Ball in Hand Against Grip When Putting

Q. A player putts with a golf ball held in his left hand against the grip. He claims the pressure transmitted to the grip through the ball assists him in putting. Is such use of a ball permissible?

A. No. A ball is an artificial device when used in such a manner.

14-3/7 Player with Injured Right Wrist Inserts Left Thumb Under Elastic Bandage on Right Wrist and Hand

Q. A player, who wore an elastic bandage around his right wrist and hand because of an injury, inserted his left thumb under the bandage where it crosses his right palm, and played a number of strokes with his left thumb so located. Is this permissible?

A. No. Because of the injury, the player was entitled to wear the elastic bandage. However, when he inserted his left thumb under the bandage, he was in breach of Rule 14-3.

14-3/8 Adhesive Tape

Q. May a player bind certain fingers together with adhesive tape or apply such tape to a golf glove?

A. The use of adhesive tape for any medical reason, *e.g.*, to reduce blisters or to eliminate the possibility of skin splits between the fingers, is not contrary to the Rules. However, if a player binds fingers together with tape solely to aid himself in gripping the club, he is in breach of Rule 14-3.

Applying tape to a golf glove to prevent the glove from slipping or to reduce wear is not a breach of Rule 14-3.

14

14-3/9 Player Putts with One Hand and Steadies Himself with Club Held in Other Hand

Q. A player, while putting with one hand, uses another club to lean on and steady himself. In the circumstances, is the club the player leans on an artificial device, contrary to Rule 14-3?

A. Yes.

Player Uses Cane or Club to Enter or Leave Hazard When Ball Lies in Hazard — See 13-4/3.5.

14-3/10 Device Which Emits Click If Swing Timed Properly

Q. There is a device on the market featuring a grip and weighted shaft which emits a click if the player makes a practice swing with it and the swing is correctly timed. Is use of such a device during a round a breach of Rule 14-3?

A. Yes.

14-3/11 Plumb-Line

Q. Is a plumb-line, *i.e.*, a weight suspended on a string, an artificial device within the meaning of the term in Rule 14-3?

A. Yes.

14-3/12 Club Used as Plumb-Line

Q. May a player use his putter as a plumb-line to assist him in determining the slope on a putting green?

A. Yes. Such a practice is not a breach of Rule 14-3.

14-3/13 Golf Ball Warmer or Hand Warmer

Q. Is the use of a golf ball warmer or hand warmer during a round a breach of Rule 14-3?

A. Use of a golf ball warmer is a breach of Rule 14-3.

Use of a hand warmer is permissible.

14-3/14 Electronic Instrument Used to Find Ball

Q. Transmitters have been embedded in a brand of golf ball. When used with a special radio receiver, a player may find such a ball readily because the transmitter emits a signal which grows louder as the receiver moves closer to the ball. Is the use of such a ball permissible?

A. Use of such a ball is not, of itself, contrary to the Rules. However, use of such a ball in conjunction with the receiver is a breach of Rule 14-3.

14-3/15 Artificial Limbs

An artificial leg or arm is not an artificial device within the meaning of the term in Rule 14-3, even if an artificial leg has been modified to aid a player in playing the game or an artificial arm has a fitting specially designed for gripping a golf club. However, if the Committee believes that an artificial limb so modified would give the player an undue advantage over other players, the Committee has authority to deem it to be an artificial device contrary to Rule 14-3.

Clubs used by a player with an artificial arm must conform with Rule 4-1 except that an attachment may be fitted to the grip or shaft to assist the player to hold the club. However, if the Committee believes that the use of a club modified in this way would give the player an undue advantage over other players, it should deem the attachment an artificial device contrary to Rule 14-3.

14-3/16 Use of Instructional Material

During a round it is a breach of Rule 14-3 to listen to audio tapes or view video tapes containing instructional or other information which might assist a player in his play, or use any electronic device containing such information.

14

14-4/1 Ball Falls on Club Face After Stroke and Sticks to Mud Thereon

Q. A player, playing a stroke at his ball on the bank of a bunker, hit the ball straight up. The ball came down and adhered to mud on the face of the club. Was the player in breach of Rule 14-4?

A. No. However, the player stopped his ball and was in breach of Rule 19-2.

In match play, the player loses the hole — Rule 19-2a.

In stroke play, the player incurs a penalty of two strokes and must drop the ball as near as possible to the spot where the ball adhered to the club — Rule 19-2b.

But see Decision 1-4/2.

14-4/2 Ball Strikes Pipeline and on Rebound Is Deflected by Face of Club

Q. A player's ball strikes a pipeline and on the rebound hits the face of his club. Is the player consid-

ered to have struck the ball more than once in breach
of Rule 14-4?

A. No. The player did not strike the ball more than
once. He struck it once and it rebounded and hit the
face of his club. Rule 19-2 applies.

14-5/1   Ball Moving During Backswing Struck While Moving

Q. A player's ball starts moving during his backswing
and he strikes the ball while it is still moving. What
is the ruling?

A. There is no penalty under Rule 14-5 because the
ball began to move after the player had begun his
backswing. However, if the player caused the ball
to move, had addressed it or had removed a loose
impediment within a club-length of it, he incurred a
penalty stroke — Rule 18-2a, b or c.

14-6/1   Ball Moving in Water Hazard After Address Played While Moving

Q. A ball was at rest in shallow, rapidly-running water in a water hazard. After the player addressed it,
the ball moved, presumably due to the current, and
while it was moving the player played it. What is the
ruling?

A. There is no penalty. Rule 14-6 supersedes Rule 18-
2b (Ball Moving After Address) in such a case.

Rule 15. Playing a Wrong Ball

Definition

A "wrong ball" is any ball other than:

a. The <u>ball in play</u>,
b. A <u>provisional ball</u> or
c. In stroke play, a second ball played under Rule 3-3 or Rule 20-7b.

Note: Ball in play includes a ball substituted for the ball in play when the player is proceeding under an applicable Rule which does not permit substitution.

15-1. General

A player must hole out with the ball played from the <u>teeing ground</u> unless a Rule permits him to substitute another ball. If a player substitutes another ball when proceeding under an applicable Rule which does not permit substitution, that ball is not a <u>wrong ball</u>; it becomes the <u>ball in play</u> and, if the error is not corrected as provided in Rule 20-6, *the player shall incur a penalty of loss of hole in match play or two strokes in stroke play.*

15-2. Match Play

If a player plays a stroke with a <u>wrong ball</u> except in a <u>hazard</u>, *he shall lose the hole.*

If a player plays any strokes in a hazard with a wrong ball, there is no penalty. Strokes played in a hazard with a wrong ball do not count in the player's score. If the wrong ball belongs to another player, its owner shall place a ball on the spot from which the wrong ball was first played.

If the player and opponent exchange balls during the play of a hole, the first to play the wrong ball other than from a hazard shall lose the hole; when this cannot be determined, the hole shall be played out with the balls exchanged.

15-3. Stroke Play

If a competitor plays a stroke or strokes with a <u>wrong ball</u>, *he shall incur a penalty of two strokes*, unless the only stroke or strokes played with such ball were played when it was lying in a hazard, in which case no penalty is incurred.

The competitor must correct his mistake by playing the correct ball. If he fails to correct his mistake before he plays a stroke from the next <u>teeing ground</u> or, in the case of the last hole of the round, fails to declare his intention to correct his mistake before leaving the <u>putting green</u>, *he shall be disqualified*.

Strokes played by a competitor with a wrong ball do not count in his score.

If the wrong ball belongs to another competitor, its owner shall place a ball on the spot from which the wrong ball was first played.

(Lie of ball to be placed or replaced altered — see Rule 20-3b.)

15

15/1 Stroke Misses Wrong Ball

Q. A player swings at and misses a wrong ball. What is the ruling?

A. Since the player made a stroke with a wrong ball, he lost the hole in match play (Rule 15-2) or incurred a two-stroke penalty in stroke play (Rule 15-3).

15/2 Player's Stroke at Own Ball Dislodges Concealed Ball

Q. A player plays a stroke with his own ball in the rough and also hits an old abandoned ball which was hidden beneath his ball. Since he struck the hidden ball, did he play a wrong ball?

A. No. The player played a stroke with his own ball, not with the hidden ball. Since he did not play a stroke with the hidden ball, Rule 15 is not applicable. The player must play his ball as it lies.

Practice Swing Dislodges Concealed Ball — See 7-2/7.

Ball Moved Accidentally by Player in Playing Wrong Ball — See 18-2a/21.

15/3 Player Plays Stroke at Part of Abandoned Ball Which Had Broken into Pieces

Q. A ball had broken into pieces and had been abandoned. Part of it was lying in heavy grass. A player mistook the part for his ball in play and played a stroke with it. The player asserts that part of a ball is not a ball and, therefore, that he has not played a wrong ball. Is the player correct?

A. No. Since the player made a stroke with a wrong ball, he lost the hole in match play (Rule 15-2) or incurred a two-stroke penalty in stroke play (Rule 15-3).

15/4 Player Lifts Ball, Sets It Aside and Plays It from Where Set Aside

Q. A player marks the position of his ball on the putting green, lifts the ball and sets it aside. By mistake, he putts the ball from the spot at which he set it aside. What is the ruling?

A. When a ball is lifted under Rule 20-1, it is out of play — see Definition of "Ball in Play." When the player played a stroke with his ball while it was out of play, he played a wrong ball (Rule 15).

In match play, the player lost the hole — Rule 15-2.

In stroke play, he incurred a penalty of two strokes and was required to correct the error before playing from the next tee; otherwise, he would be disqualified — Rule 15-3.

15/5 Original Ball Found and Played After Another Ball Put into Play

Q. A player unable to find his ball after a brief search plays another ball (Ball B) under Rule 27-1. His original ball is then found within five minutes after search for it began. The player lifted Ball B and continued to play with the original ball. Was this correct?

A. No. The original ball was lost when Ball B was put into play — see Definition of "Lost Ball." When the player lifted Ball B, he incurred a penalty stroke under Rule 18-2a. When he played a stroke with the original ball after it was out of play, he played a wrong ball — see Definitions of "Ball in Play" and "Wrong Ball" — and incurred a penalty of loss of hole in match play or an additional two strokes in stroke play — Rule 15. In stroke play, the player would be disqualified if, before playing from the next teeing ground, he did not replace Ball B and play out the hole with it — Rule 15-3.

Original Ball Played After Provisional Ball Played from Point Nearer Hole Than Original Ball Likely to Be — See 27-2b/5.

Ball Found After Search Exceeding Five Minutes Is Then Played — See 27/8.

Provisional Ball Played from Point Nearer Hole Than Original Ball Because Player Erroneously Thought Original Ball, Which Was Visible, Was Out of Bounds — See 27-2c/3.

15/6 Stroke Played with Ball Lying Out of Bounds

Q. A player plays a stroke at his ball which is lying out of bounds. What is the ruling?

A. A ball lying out of bounds is no longer in play and thus is a wrong ball — see Definitions of "Ball in Play" and "Wrong Ball." Accordingly, in match play,

the player loses the hole. In stroke play, he incurs a
two-stroke penalty and must proceed under Rule 27-1,
incurring the additional one-stroke penalty prescribed
in that Rule.

15/6.5 Ball Changed During Play of Hole to Aid Identification

Q. A and B realized after playing their tee shots on a
par-5 hole that they were playing balls with identical
markings. To avoid confusion, A lifted his ball before playing his second shot, substituted a ball with
different markings and played out the hole. Is this
permissible?

A. A was not proceeding under an applicable Rule,
so the substituted ball was a wrong ball — see Definitions of "Ball in Play" and "Wrong Ball".

In match play, A loses the hole — Rule 15-2.

In stroke play, A incurs a penalty of two strokes (Rule
15-3) and must correct the error before playing from
the next tee; otherwise he is disqualified.

Furthermore, in stroke play the player incurs an additional penalty of one stroke under Rule 18-2a for
lifting his ball without authority.

Second Ball Played in Match Play — See 3-3/9.

15/7 Wrong Ball Played in Belief It Is Provisional or Second Ball

Q. A player, thinking his original ball may be lost or
out of bounds, plays a provisional ball under Rule 27-
2a. Before reaching the place where his original ball
is likely to be, he plays a wrong ball, believing it is
his provisional ball. He then finds his original ball in
bounds and, correctly, abandons the provisional ball.
Does the player incur a penalty under Rule 15 for
playing a wrong ball, even though that wrong ball
was played in mistake for a provisional ball which
never became the ball in play?

A. Yes. Although a penalty incurred in play of a provisional ball is normally canceled if the provisional

ball has to be abandoned under Rule 27-2c (*e.g.,* a one-stroke penalty under Rule 18-2b if the provisional ball moves after being addressed), this does not apply when the penalty is for playing a wrong ball.

The same ruling would apply if a competitor played a wrong ball in the belief that it was a second ball played under Rule 3-3 (Doubt as to Procedure in Stroke Play).

15/8 Ball Played Under Rule for Ball Lost in Ground Under Repair After Another Ball Played Under Stroke-and-Distance Procedure

Q. A player's ball was lost in ground under repair. He played another ball under the lost ball Rule (Rule 27-1). The player then realized that he was entitled to relief without penalty under Rule 25-1c (Ball Lost in Ground Under Repair). So he abandoned the ball played under Rule 27-1, dropped a ball in accordance with Rule 25-1c and played out the hole. What is the ruling?

A. The ball played under Rule 27-1 was played under an applicable Rule and, therefore, was in play — see Definition of "Ball in Play." When the player played a ball under Rule 25-1c, he played a wrong ball and incurred the penalty prescribed in Rule 15.

Ball Dropped and Played Under Ground Under Repair Rule in Absence of Reasonable Evidence Original Ball Lost in Ground Under Repair — See 25-1c/2.

Ball Played Under Water Hazard Rule; Original Ball Then Found Outside Hazard — See 26-1/3.

Ball Played Under Water Hazard Rule Without Reasonable Evidence Original Ball in Hazard; Original Ball Then Found in Hazard — See 26-1/4.

Lost Ball Treated as Moved by Outside Agency in Absence of Reasonable Evidence to That Effect — See 27-1/2.5.

15/9 Ball Thrown into Bounds by Outside Agency and Played; Caddie Aware of Action of Outside Agency

Q. A's ball was found lying in bounds and A played a shot towards the green. Then a man appeared and said that A's ball had come to rest out of bounds in his garden. He said he had thrown it onto the course and had told A's caddie what he had done. The caddie had not reported this to A. What is the ruling?

A. Under Rule 6-4, A must assume responsibility for his caddie's failure to tell him what the man said.

A's ball was no longer the ball in play when it came to rest out of bounds. Therefore, it was a wrong ball — see Definitions of "Ball in Play" and "Wrong Ball." When A played a stroke with the wrong ball, he incurred the penalty prescribed in Rule 15 and, in stroke play, was obliged to proceed under Rule 27-1.

15/10 Ball Thrown into Bounds by Outside Agency and Played; Neither Player Nor His Caddie Aware of Action of Outside Agency

Q. Decision 15/9 states that, if an outside agency throws a player's ball back onto the course from out of bounds and advises the player's caddie to this effect, the player is penalized for playing a wrong ball if he plays the ball from its position in bounds. What would be the ruling if neither the player nor his caddie knew the player's ball had been thrown back onto the course?

A. In equity (Rule 1-4), there would be no penalty for playing a wrong ball (Rule 15). If the player discovers before playing from the next teeing ground that his original ball was out of bounds, he must go back and proceed under Rule 27-1. If the discovery is not made until later than this, the score with the wrong ball stands.

15/11 Wrong Ball Hit Out of Bounds; Another Ball Played Under Rule 27-1; Original Ball Then Found Nearby

Q. A player plays what he believes to be his ball and hits it out of bounds. He plays another ball under Rule 27-1 and then discovers that the ball he hit out of bounds was a wrong ball and that his original ball is lying in bounds. What is the ruling?

A. In match play, the player loses the hole for playing a wrong ball (Rule 15-2).

In stroke play, the ball the player hit out of bounds was a wrong ball, and the ball played under Rule 27-1 was a continuation of the play of that wrong ball.

The player incurred a penalty of two strokes under Rule 15-3 and he was obliged to hole out with his original ball.

15/12 Wrong Ball Found Out of Bounds Played Under Stroke-and-Distance Procedure; Original Ball Then Found in Bounds

Q. A player finds a ball out of bounds, thinks it is his original ball, plays it at the spot from which the original ball was played and then finds his original ball in bounds. What is the ruling?

A. The original ball is lost and the ball found out of bounds is in play under penalty of stroke and distance. See Decision 27/17.

15/13 Wrong Ball Dropped Under Unplayable Ball Rule But Not Played

Q. A player finds a ball he believes is his ball, declares it unplayable and drops it under Rule 28. He then discovers that the ball is not his, *i.e.*, it is a wrong ball. What is the ruling?

A. There is no penalty for lifting and dropping a wrong ball. A penalty is applicable only if a stroke is played with a wrong ball — Rule 15. The player would be entitled to resume search for his own ball.

Wrong Ball Declared Unplayable Played Under Stroke-and-Distance Procedure; Original Ball Then Found — See 28/14.

Wrong Ball Declared Unplayable, Dropped Within Two Club-Lengths and Played Before Error Discovered — See 28/15.

15/14 Ball in Bunker Deemed Unplayable, Dropped in Bunker and Played; Ball Then Discovered to Be Wrong Ball

Q. A player, believing that a ball lying very badly in a bunker is his ball, declares it unplayable, drops it in the bunker under Rule 28, plays it out and then discovers that he has played a wrong ball. Is he liable to penalty for playing a wrong ball since he had ample opportunity to examine the ball when he lifted it under Rule 28?

A. No. Rule 15 exempts a player from penalty for playing a wrong ball in a hazard, even in the circumstances described.

Player Discovers Own Ball in Hole After Playing Wrong Ball — See 1-1/4.

In Anger Player Hits Ball Played by Player in Following Group — See 1-4/4.

Player Wins Hole with Wrong Ball; Error Discovered at Next Hole — See 9-2/8.

15

Competitor's Ball Played by Fellow-Competitor in Bunker Not Replaced — See 18-4/1.

Ball Moved by Wrong Ball Played by Opponent — See 18-5/1.

Competitor's Ball Played by Fellow-Competitor; Competitor Substitutes Another Ball at Wrong Place, Plays It and Then Abandons It and Plays Out Original Ball from Right Place — See 20-7b/5.

Casual Water Mistaken for Water Hazard; Substituted Ball Played Under Water Hazard Rule — See 25-1b/13.

Time Permitted for Search for Lost Ball After Wrong Ball Played — See 27/2.

Order of Play in Foursome Stroke Play When Wrong Ball Played — See 29-1/8.

Player Plays Partner's Ball — See 30-3d/1.

Player Wins Hole with Wrong Ball and Partner Picks Up; Error Discovered at Next Hole — See 30-3d/2.

Players on Opposite Sides Exchange Balls During Play of Hole and Their Partners Pick Up; Error Discovered at Next Hole — See 30-3d/3.

Player Plays Partner's Ball; Error Discovered After Opponents Have Played Next Strokes — See 30-3d/3.5.

15-1/1 Balls Inadvertently Exchanged by Players Between Holes

Q. After completion of a hole, the balls of A and B were inadvertently exchanged and A played B's ball from the next teeing ground. Did A play a wrong ball?

A. No. A ball played from the teeing ground into the hole is not a wrong ball, even if it does not belong to the player — see Definitions of "Ball in Play" and "Wrong Ball."

15-1/2 Balls Inadvertently Exchanged by Competitors at Unknown Place

Q. In stroke play, it was discovered after play of a hole that A had holed out with B's ball and vice versa. Both A and B were certain that they had holed out at this hole with the balls they played from the teeing ground. Thus, it was concluded that they had exchanged balls during play of a previous hole or between two holes. What is the ruling?

A. If it cannot be established that the balls were exchanged during play of a hole, A and B should be given the benefit of the doubt and it should be assumed that the balls were inadvertently exchanged between play of two holes, in which case no penalty would be imposed.

15-1/2.5 Balls Inadvertently Exchanged by Players After One Ball Struck and Moved the Other

Q. A plays to the green and his ball strikes and moves B's ball which was lying on the green. Both balls come to rest on the green. B, acting under Rules 18-5 and 20-3c, lifts A's ball by mistake and places it as near as possible to where his (B's) ball lay before it was moved. B then holes out with A's ball after which A, by mistake, holes out with B's. What is the ruling?

A. Stroke play: A played a wrong ball. He incurs a penalty of two strokes, must retrieve his ball from B, replace it on the spot from which B had lifted it and hole out with it before playing from the next tee; otherwise A is disqualified (Rule 15-3).

B mistakenly substituted another ball when proceeding under an applicable Rule (Rules 18-5 and 20-3c) which does not permit substitution. Accordingly, as stated in Rule 15-1, B did not play a wrong ball but, as prescribed in Rule 15-1, since he did not correct the error as provided in Rule 20-6, he must add a penalty of two strokes to the score made in part with A's ball.

Match play: B lost the hole when he played A's ball. A's subsequent play of a wrong ball is irrelevant.

15-1/3 Hole at Which Wrong Ball Played Unknown

Q. A player discovers after the 6th hole that he is not playing the ball with which he started the round. He does not know when he first played the different ball. What is the ruling in:

(a) stroke play?
(b) match play when:
  (i) he has won every hole?
  (ii) he has lost every hole?
  (iii) he has won 4 holes, lost 1 hole and halved 1 hole?
  (iv) he has lost 4 holes, won 1 hole and halved 1 hole?

A. The Committee must determine whether the different ball is a wrong ball or not and give the player the benefit of any doubt — see Decision 15-1/2. Thus, if the different ball might have been put into play under a Rule or if the player might have put the different ball into play at the start of a hole, the Committee should rule in favor of the player and the player incurs no penalty in either match play or stroke play.

If, however, the conclusion is that a wrong ball has been played:

(a) in stroke play, the player is disqualified, unless the conclusion is that the wrong ball was played at the 6th hole and the player rectifies his mistake as prescribed in Rule 15-3.

15

(b) in match play, the Committee must determine on a balance of probabilities the hole at which the wrong ball was played and the player loses that hole, the state of the match being adjusted accordingly, if necessary. If it is impossible to determine the hole at which the wrong ball was played, in equity (Rule 1-4):

(i) the player loses one of the holes which he had won and becomes 4 up instead of 6 up.

(ii) the player remains 6 down.

(iii) the player becomes one hole worse off, *i.e.*, he becomes 2 up instead of 3 up.

(iv) as in (iii), *i.e.*, he becomes 4 down instead of 3 down.

15-1/4 Players Inadvertently Exchange Balls Recovered from Water Hazard

Q. A and B played into a water hazard at approximately the same spot. One caddie was authorized to retrieve both balls and he handed A's ball to B and B's ball to A. Each player dropped the ball handed to him behind the hazard under Rule 26-1b and played to the green. On reaching the green, they discovered the exchange of balls. Should they be penalized under Rule 15-1?

A. No. Rule 26-1b authorizes the player to drop "a ball." Accordingly, the substitution of another ball is permissible.

[15-1/5 Reserved]

15-1/6 Player Substitutes Another Ball on Putting Green Because Original Ball Thrown to Caddie for Cleaning Came to Rest in Lake

Q. A player, whose ball was on the putting green, marked the ball's position, lifted it and threw it to his caddie for cleaning. The caddie failed to catch the ball and it went into a lake and could not be retrieved. The player holed out with another ball. Was this correct?

15

A. No. Rule 16-1b, under which the ball was lifted, does not permit substitution of another ball. Accordingly, the player incurred a penalty of loss of hole in match play or two strokes in stroke play — Rule 15-1.

15-1/7 Player Mistakenly Substitutes Another Ball on Putting Green; Error Discovered Before Stroke Played

Q. A player marks the position of his ball on the putting green and lifts the ball. By mistake he places another ball on the spot from which his original ball was lifted. He discovers his error before playing his next stroke, places his original ball on the spot from which it was lifted and holes out with it. What is the ruling?

A. There is no penalty. The player corrected the error and did not play a stroke with the other ball. Therefore, a penalty under Rule 15-1 was not applicable. Further, the other ball effectively marked the position of his original ball. So a penalty under Rule 20-1 was not applicable.

Ball Mistakenly Substituted When Dropped; Correction of Error — See 20-6/3.

15-1/8 Competitor Mistakenly Substitutes Another Ball on Putting Green; Error Discovered After Stroke Played from Next Teeing Ground

Q. A competitor in stroke play lifted his ball on the putting green and by mistake replaced it with another ball. He holed out and drove off the next tee. What is the ruling?

A. The competitor incurs a penalty of two strokes — Rule 15-1.

15-1/9 Competitor Who Lifts His Ball and Fellow-Competitor's Ball Inadvertently Exchanges Balls When Replacing Them

Q. In stroke play, A's ball and B's ball are in the same area on the putting green. A marks the position of, and lifts, both balls with B's consent. When A replaces them, they are inadvertently exchanged and A putts out, from the right place, with B's ball and vice versa. What is the ruling?

A. Each player is penalized two strokes under Rule 15-1.

Because he authorized A to lift his ball, B cannot be exempted from penalty (Rule 20-1).

Ball Not Unfit for Play Deemed Unfit — See 5-3/3.

Competitor's Ball Lifted Without Authority by Fellow-Competitor's Caddie Who Subsequently Substitutes Another Ball Which Competitor Plays — See 20-1/5.

Decisions relating to Rule 15-2:

Player Concedes Hole After Which It Is Discovered That Opponent Had Played Wrong Ball — See 2-4/9.

Player Concedes Hole After Which Opponent Plays Wrong Ball — See 2-4/10.

Player Wins Hole with Own Ball After Playing Wrong Ball; Opponent Lodges Belated Claim — See 2-5/4.

Player Wins Hole with Wrong Ball; Error Discovered at Next Hole — See 9-2/8.

Ball Moved by Wrong Ball Played by Opponent — See 18-5/1.

15-3/1 Competitor Plays Wrong Ball and Loses It; Wrong Ball May Have Been Fellow-Competitor's Ball

Q. In stroke play, A and B drive into the same area in the rough. B finds a ball and hits it into the middle of a deep water hazard. A finds a ball which turns out to be B's ball. No other ball is found in the area, so presumably B played A's ball. B incurs a penalty of two strokes under Rule 15-3 and he must play his own ball. What is the proper procedure for A?

A. Since there was reasonable evidence that B played A's ball, A should place another ball at the spot from which B played the wrong ball, without penalty — Rule 15-3.

15-3/2 Play of Two Different Wrong Balls Between Strokes with Ball in Play

Q. In stroke play, a competitor plays a wrong ball to a putting green. He discovers his error and returns to the spot from which the wrong ball was played. He finds another ball and plays it to the green. He then discovers that he has played another wrong ball. Is the penalty two strokes or four strokes?

A. Two strokes for a breach of Rule 15-3. A penalty of four strokes for playing two wrong balls in succession before a stroke with the correct ball would not be justified.

15-3/3 Fellow-Competitor Lifts Competitor's Ball and Sets It Aside; Competitor Plays Ball from Where Set Aside

Q. In stroke play, B marked the position of A's ball on the putting green, lifted it and placed it nearby on the green. A failed to replace the ball. He putted it from where it lay and holed out. The error was then discovered. What is the ruling?

A. When a ball is lifted, it is out of play — see Definition of "Ball in Play." When A played a stroke with his ball which was out of play, he played a wrong ball.

If A knew that B had lifted his ball, he incurred a penalty of two strokes under Rule 15-3 and was required to replace his ball on the correct spot and play out the hole.

If A did not know that B had lifted his ball, A could not be penalized for playing a wrong ball. If he became aware of the mistake before playing from the next tee, he was required to replace his ball on the correct spot, without penalty, and complete the hole. If he learned of the mistake after playing from the next tee, the score with the wrong ball would stand and there would be no penalty.

Play of Wrong Ball Not Rectified; Error Discovered After Competition Closed — See 34-1b/3.

Play of Wrong Ball Not Rectified on Advice of Committee Member — See 33-7/5.

THE PUTTING GREEN
Rule 16. The Putting Green

Definitions

The "putting green" is all ground of the hole being played which is specially prepared for putting or otherwise defined as such by the Committee. A ball is on the putting green when any part of it touches the putting green.

The "line of putt" is the line which the player wishes his ball to take after a stroke on the putting green. Except with respect to Rule 16-1e, the line of putt includes a reasonable distance on either side of the intended line. The line of putt does not extend beyond the hole.

A ball is "holed" when it is at rest within the circumference of the hole and all of it is below the level of the lip of the hole.

16-1. General

a. TOUCHING LINE OF PUTT

The line of putt must not be touched except:

(i) the player may move sand and loose soil on the putting green and other <u>loose impediments</u> by picking them up or by brushing them aside with his hand or a club without pressing anything down;

(ii) in addressing the ball, the player may place the club in front of the ball without pressing anything down;

(iii) in measuring — Rule 10-4;

16

(iv) in lifting the ball — Rule 16-1b;

(v) in pressing down a ball-marker;

(vi) in repairing old hole plugs or ball marks on the putting green — Rule 16-1c; and

(vii) in removing movable <u>obstructions</u> — Rule 24-1.

(Indicating line for putting on putting green — see Rule 8-2b.)

b. LIFTING BALL

A ball on the <u>putting green</u> may be lifted and, if desired, cleaned. A ball so lifted shall be replaced on the spot from which it was lifted.

c. REPAIR OF HOLE PLUGS, BALL MARKS AND OTHER DAMAGE

The player may repair an old hole plug or damage to the <u>putting green</u> caused by the impact of a ball, whether or not the player's ball lies on the putting green. If the ball is moved in the process of such repair, it shall be replaced, without penalty. Any other damage to the putting green shall not be repaired if it might assist the player in his subsequent play of the hole.

d. TESTING SURFACE

During the play of a hole, a player shall not test the surface of the <u>putting green</u> by rolling a ball or roughening or scraping the surface.

e. STANDING ASTRIDE OR ON LINE OF PUTT

The player shall not make a <u>stroke</u> on the <u>putting green</u> from a stance astride, or with either foot touching, the line of putt or an extension of that line behind the ball.

f. POSITION OF CADDIE OR PARTNER

While making a <u>stroke</u> on the putting green, the player shall not allow his caddie, his partner or his partner's caddie to position himself on or close to an extension of the line of putt behind the ball.

g. PLAYING STROKE WHILE ANOTHER BALL IN MOTION

The player shall not play a stroke while another ball is in motion after a stroke from the putting green, except that, if a player does so, he incurs no penalty if it was his turn to play.

(Lifting ball interfering with or assisting play while another ball in motion — see Rule 22.)

PENALTY FOR BREACH OF RULE 16-1:
> *Match play --- Loss of hole;*
> *Stroke play --- Two strokes.*

16-2. Ball Overhanging Hole

When any part of the ball overhangs the lip of the hole, the player is allowed enough time to reach the hole without unreasonable delay and an additional ten seconds to determine whether the ball is at rest. If by then the ball has not fallen into the hole, it is deemed to be at rest. If the ball subsequently falls into the hole, the player is deemed to have holed out with his last stroke, and *he shall add a penalty stroke to his score* for the hole; otherwise there is no penalty under this Rule.

(Undue delay — see Rule 6-7.)

16

16/1 Mud on Ball Touches Putting Green But Ball Itself Does Not Touch Green

Q. A player's ball lies off the putting green, overhanging but not touching the green. A clump of mud adhering to the ball touches the green. Is the ball considered to be on the green?

A. No. However, if a ball lies on the green but does not actually touch the green because it is perched on mud, the ball is considered to be on the green.

Status of Half of Double Green Serving Hole Not Being Played — See 25-3/1.

16/2 Ball Embedded in Side of Hole; All of Ball Below Lip of Hole

Q. A player's ball embeds in the side of a hole. All of the ball is below the level of the lip of the hole. What is the ruling?

A. The ball should be considered holed even though all of the ball is not within the circumference of the hole as required by the Definition of "Holed."

16/3 Ball Embedded in Side of Hole; All of Ball Not Below Lip of Hole

Q. A player's ball embeds in the side of a hole. Part of the ball is above the level of the lip of the hole. What is the ruling?

A. The ball is not holed — see Definition of "Holed." The player may play the ball as it lies or lift the ball under Rule 16-1b, repair the damage under Rule 16-1c and place the ball on the lip of the hole.

16/4 Hole-Liner Not Sunk Deep Enough

Q. Players discover that a hole-liner is not sunk at least one inch below the putting green surface as prescribed in the Definition of "Hole." What should they do?

A. The players should call the matter to the attention of a Committee member if one is present. If feasible, the Committee member should attempt to have the fault corrected.

However, the players must not discontinue play in the meantime, because correction might not be possible and, if possible, might take considerable time.

16/5 Ball Strikes Edge of Hole-Liner and Bounces Out of Hole

Q. A player's ball struck the rim of a hole-liner, which had not been sunk deep enough, and bounced out of the hole. Should the ball be considered holed in such circumstances?

A. No. Under the Definition of "Holed," the ball must be at rest within the circumference of the hole.

16/5.5 Player Holes Short Putt and Allegedly Removes Ball from Hole Before It Is at Rest

Q. A player strikes a short putt into the hole and removes the ball from the hole. His opponent or a fellow-competitor claims he heard the ball bouncing in the bottom of the hole-liner at the time the player was removing the ball from the hole, and therefore the ball cannot be considered holed in view of the Definition of "Holed" which states: "A ball is holed when it is at rest within the circumference of the hole . . ." What is the ruling?

A. The ball is holed. The words "at rest" are in the Definition of "Holed" to make it clear that if a ball falls below the lip and thereafter bounces out, it is not holed.

16/6 Cutting Hole on Slope

Q. If a new hole is to be located in a part of a putting green having a gentle slope, should the hole be cut vertically or should it be cut at a slight angle to take the slope into consideration? If the hole is cut vertically, all points on the rim of the hole-liner will not be equidistant from the surface of the green.

A. The hole should be cut vertically, regardless of slope. It is not required that all points on the rim of the hole-liner be equidistant from the surface of the green, but they should be at least one inch below the surface — see Definition of "Hole."

16/7 Two Holes on Each Green of Nine-Hole Course

Q. 1. Is it permissible for a Committee to make two holes on each green of a nine-hole course, one (A) for use in play of the first nine holes and the other (B) for use in play of the second nine?

Q. 2. If so, what is the status of hole B on each green when hole A is in use, and vice versa?

A. 1. Yes.

A. 2. The hole not in use on each green is a hole made by a greenkeeper — see Definition of "Ground Under Repair" — and Rule 25-1 is applicable.

Player Putts with One Hand and Catches Ball in Hole with Other Hand — See 1-2/5.

Marking Position of Ball on Putting Green — See Decisions under Rule 20-1.

16-1a/1   Brushing Aside or Mopping Up Casual Water on Line of Putt

Q. May a player whose ball lies on a putting green brush aside casual water on his line of putt, or mop it up with a towel?

A. No. Such action would be a breach of Rule 16-1a (Touching Line of Putt).

Mopping Up Casual Water on Line of Play — See 13-2/34.

[16-1a/2   Reserved]

16-1a/3   Removing Dew of Frost from Line of Putt

Q. May a player brush dew or frost from his line of putt?

A. No. Rule 16-1a prohibits touching the line of putt except in removal of loose impediments, repair of ball marks, etc. Dew or frost is not a loose impediment — see Definition of "Loose Impediments." Accordingly, such action would be a breach of Rule 16-1a. (Revised)

Removal of Dew or Frost Other Than from Line of Putt — See 13-2/35.

16-1a/4   Scooping Casual Water from Hole

Q. A player scoops casual water from the hole with a paper cup. Is this permissible?

A. Yes, provided the line of putt, which includes the rim of the hole, is not touched.

16-1a/5 Touching Inside Edge of Hole

Q. Prior to putting, a player touched the inside of the hole. Should he be considered to have touched his line of putt in breach of Rule 16-1a?

A. Yes, unless the hole was materially damaged and the player was entitled to repair it. In this connection, see Decision 16-1a/6.

Player Repairs Hole After Holing Out But Before Opponent, Fellow-Competitor or Partner Holes Out — See 1-2/3.5.

16-1a/6 Damaged Hole; Procedure for Player

Q. Prior to putting, a player discovers that the hole has been damaged. What is the proper procedure?

A. If the damage is clearly identifiable as a ball mark, the player may repair it (Rule 16-1c).

If the damage is not clearly identifiable as a ball mark, then:

> (a) If the damage is such that the proper dimensions of the hole have not been changed materially, the player should continue play without repairing the hole. If he touches the hole in such circumstances, a breach of Rule 16-1a occurs.

> (b) If the proper dimensions of the hole have been changed materially, the player should request the Committee to have the hole repaired. If a Committee Member is not readily available, the player may repair the damage, without penalty.

If a player repairs a materially damaged hole when a Committee Member is readily available, he incurs a penalty for a breach of Rule 16-1a.

16-1a/7 Player Repairs Depression on Line of Putt Created When Partially Embedded Acorn Removed

Q. A player removed with his hand an embedded acorn on his line of putt. The acorn was not solidly embedded, so it was a loose impediment. The player then repaired the depression in which the acorn lay. Was the repair of the depression a breach of Rule 16-1a?

A. Yes.

16-1a/8 Loose Impediments Removed from Line of Putt with Cap or Towel

Q. A player removes loose impediments from his line of putt by brushing them aside with his cap or with a towel. Is this permissible?

A. No. Such action is a breach of Rule 16-1a, which permits the player to brush aside loose impediments on the line of putt only with his hand or a club.

16

Worm Partially Underground on Line of Putt — See 23/8.

16-1a/9 Brushing Loose Impediments Off Line of Putt with Palm of Hand

Q. A player, with about one dozen strokes with the whole palm of his hand, attempted to remove small leaves, which are difficult to remove by any method, from his line of putt. Is this permissible under Rule 16-1a?

A. The action described exceeded that authorized by Rule 16-1a and was a breach of the Rule.

16-1a/10 Loose Impediments Brushed Along Line of Putt Rather Than to Side

Q. In removing loose impediments from his line of putt by brushing with a putter, a player brushed along the line for about one foot before brushing the impediments to the side. Did the player infringe Rule 16-1?

A. Under Rule 16-1a a player is allowed to brush aside loose impediments on his line of putt. The casual movement of the putter along the line of putt would not be a breach of the Rules unless in the process the player did something to the putting green which might influence the movement of his ball when played (Rule 1-2).

16-1a/11   Raised Tuft of Grass on Line of Putt Brushed to Determine Whether It Is Loose

Q. A player cannot determine whether a raised tuft of grass on his line of putt is loose or is attached to its roots. The player brushes the raised tuft lightly with his hand and discovers that it is attached. The position of the raised tuft is altered slightly by the brushing, but it has not become detached. Is the player in breach of Rule 16-1a?

A. No, provided he restores the raised tuft to its original position before the next stroke.

A player is entitled to determine whether such a natural object on his line of putt is loose provided that, if the object is found not to be loose, (1) it has not become detached and (2) it is restored to its original position before the next stroke if its position is altered.

16-1a/12   Player Walks on Line of Putt

Q. A player walked on his line of putt. Did he incur a penalty for a breach of Rule 16-1a?

A. Yes, if he did so intentionally. No, if he did so accidentally and the act did not improve the line.

16-1a/13   Line of Putt Stepped on Accidentally by Opponent or Fellow-Competitor

Q. An opponent or a fellow-competitor accidentally steps on the player's line of putt. What is the ruling?

A. There is no penalty. Rule 1-2 is not applicable.

Line of Putt Altered Purposely by Opponent or Fellow-Competitor by Stepping on It — See 1-2/1.

16

16-1a/14 Line of Putt Damaged Accidentally by Fellow-Competitor's Caddie

Q. In a stroke play competition, a fellow-competitor holes a long putt for an eagle. His caddie jumps in the air in excitement and makes a deep footprint on the competitor's line of putt. Is the competitor entitled to any relief?

A. Yes. The competitor would be justified in requesting the Committee to grant relief. The Committee should repair the damage or, if it is not possible to do so promptly, declare the damaged area to be ground under repair, in which case relief would be obtainable under Rule 25-1b(iii).

The competitor would be in breach of Rule 16-1a if he repaired the damage himself.

16-1a/15 Mushroom Growing on Line of Putt

Q. A mushroom is growing on a player's line of putt. Is the player entitled to relief?

A. The player would be justified in discontinuing play and requesting the Committee to remove the mushroom. The Committee should comply.

If such an abnormal condition is a recurring problem on a course, the Committee should make a Local Rule to the effect that mushrooms on the putting green are to be treated as ground under repair.

16-1a/16 Spike Mark on Line of Putt Repaired During Repair of Ball Mark

Q. A player stepped on a ball mark in the act of repairing it and incidentally pressed down a spike mark on his line of putt. Did the player incur a penalty under Rule 16-1a?

A. Yes.

16-1a/16.5 Spike Mark on Line of Putt Pressed Down When Player Repairs Old Hole Plug

Q. An old hole plug is raised on the player's line of

16

putt. The player steps on the hole plug to make it level with the surface of the putting green. In so doing he presses down a spike mark within the hole plug. Was the player in breach of Rule 16-1a when he pressed down the spike mark?

A. No. Rule 16-1a permits touching the line of putt "in repairing old hole plugs."

If the spike mark had been near but not within the old hole plug, the ruling would be different. In these circumstances, the player would have been able to step on the hole plug without affecting the spike mark.

16-1a/17 Ball Lifted on Putting Green Placed Ahead of Ball-Marker and Then Moved Back to Original Position

Q. When replacing his ball on the putting green, a player has a habit of placing the ball ahead of his ball-marker and then rolling or sliding the ball to its original position. Is such a procedure permissible?

A. Such a procedure is not recommended but is not a breach of Rule 16-1a which permits touching the line of putt in lifting (or replacing) the ball. However, if in the process the player does something to the putting green which might influence the movement of the ball when played, *e.g.*, presses down a raised tuft of grass, he is in breach of Rule 1-2.

Shielding Line of Putt from Wind — See 1-2/2.

Player and Opponent or Fellow-Competitor Agree to Repair Spike Marks on One Another's Line of Putt — See 1-3/3.

Caddie Touches Putting Green to Indicate Line of Play Before Player Chips from Off Green — See 8-2b/3.

Competitor Sanctions Repair of Spike Damage on His Line of Putt by Fellow-Competitor — See 13-2/36.

Placing Ball-Marker on Line of Putt — See 20-1/19.

Player Touches Putting Green in Pointing Out Line for Putting for Partner and Incidentally Touches Own Line of Putt — See 30/2.5.

Player Putting First When Partner's Ball Farther from Hole Stands on Partner's or Opponent's Line of Putt — See 30-3c/1.

16

16-1b/1 Ball on Putting Green Lifted Because Player Feared Ball Might Move

Q. A player lifted his ball on the putting green under Rule 16-1b, cleaned it and replaced it. As the player approached the ball to play his next stroke, he feared the ball might move. So he lifted the ball again, replaced it and played. What is the ruling?

A. There is no penalty, provided the player marked the position of his ball both times. Rule 16-1b permits the lifting of a ball on the putting green for any reason.

Rotating Ball on Putting Green Without Marking Position — See 18-2a/33.

Ball Replaced on Putting Green But Ball-Marker Not Removed; Ball Then Moves — See 20-4/1.

Ball Replaced at Wrong Place on Putting Green and Holed — See 20-7b/1.

16-1c/1 Repair of Ball Mark a Second Time

Q. A ball mark has been repaired by a player. The ball mark is on the line of putt of a following player. May the following player further repair the ball mark?

A. Yes, provided it is still clearly identifiable as a ball mark.

16-1c/1.5 Ball Mark Partially on and Partially Off Putting Green Is on Line of Play

Q. If a player's ball lies just off the putting green and there is a ball mark on his line of play, he is entitled to repair the ball mark if it is on the green (Rule 16-1c), but not if it is off the green (Rule 13-2). What is the ruling if a ball mark on the line of play is partially on and partially off the green?

A. Since it is impracticable to allow the repair of only that part of the ball mark which is on the putting green, the player may repair the entire ball mark.

16-1c/2 Ball Mark in Position to Assist Opponent

Q. A and B are playing a match. At a par-3 hole, both are on the green with their tee shots. A's ball comes to rest four feet from the hole. B's ball is fifteen feet from the hole. Upon reaching the green, A prepares to repair his ball mark. B tells A not to do so until he (B) has putted because A's ball mark is so situated that B's ball might be deflected into the hole by it. A objects, stating that he wishes to repair his ball mark immediately. May A do so?

A. No. If A were to repair the ball mark, he would lose the hole under Rule 1-2. A has no right to repair a ball mark affecting B's play if B requests A not to repair it, unless the ball mark also physically affects A's play and it is A's turn to play.

16-1c/3 Old Hole Plug Sunk or Raised on Line of Putt

Q. A player's ball lies on the green. An old hole plug is sunk or raised on the player's line of putt. What relief is available to the player?

A. The player may attempt to raise or lower the plug to make it level with the surface of the putting green — Rule 16-1c. If this is impossible, he may discontinue play and request the Committee to raise or lower the plug. If the Committee cannot level the plug without unduly delaying play, the Committee should declare the plug to be ground under repair, in which case the player would be entitled to relief under Rule 25-1b(iii).

Whether Sunken Hole Plug Is "Hole Made by Greenkeeper" — See 25/17.

16-1c/4 Repair of Spike Mark Damage Around Hole

Q. A player's ball lies on or near the putting green. Before playing his next stroke, he taps down spike marks in the vicinity of the hole. Is this permissible?

A. No. Such action would be a breach of Rule 16-1c since repair of spike marks in the vicinity of the hole might assist the player in his subsequent play of the hole.

16-1d/1 Player Concedes Opponent's Next Stroke and Rolls or Knocks Ball to Opponent

Q. A player concedes his opponent's next stroke and either picks up the opponent's ball and rolls it to the opponent or knocks it back to him with a club. The player did so only for the purpose of returning the opponent's ball to him, not to test the surface of the putting green. Was the player in breach of Rule 16-1d (Testing Surface)?

A. No. Such casual action is not a breach of Rule 16-1d.

16-1d/2 Player Concedes Opponent's Next Stroke and Knocks His Ball Away Along Own Line of Putt

Q. A player concedes his opponent's next stroke and knocks his ball away on the same line on which he (the player) must subsequently putt. Is this a breach of Rule 16-1d?

A. It is a question of fact whether or not the player's action was for the purpose of testing the surface of the putting green. The manner and apparent purpose of the action would be the determining factors in each individual case.

16-1d/3 Player Returns Ball to Spot from Which It Was Lifted by Rolling It with Putter

Q. A player marks the position of his ball on the putting green, lifts the ball and sets it aside. When it is turn to putt,he rolls the ball with his putter back to the spot from which it was lifted. Was the player in breach of Rule 16-1d (Testing Surface)?

A. No, provided the action of rolling the ball was not for the purpose of testing the surface of the green. This method of replacing a ball is not recommended, but it is not a breach of the Rules.

16-1d/4 Testing for Wetness Surface of Putting Green Behind Ball

Q. A player placed the palm of his hand on the putting green behind his ball to determine if the green was wet. He did not roughen or scrape the surface. Was the player in breach of Rule 16-1d (Testing Surface)?

A. No. Rule 16-1d only prohibits rolling a ball or roughening or scraping the putting surface for testing purposes. Since the line of putt was not touched, Rule 16-1a also was not infringed.

16-1d/5 Rubbing Ball on Putting Green for Cleaning Purposes

Q. May a player clean his ball by rubbing it on the putting green?

A. Yes, provided the act is not for the purpose of testing the surface of the putting green. It is recommended that a ball be cleaned in other ways to eliminate any question as to the player's intentions.

16

16-1d/6 Caddie Roughens Surface of Putting Green But Player Does Not Benefit

Q. A caddie tests the surface of the green by roughening the grass. His employer tells him immediately that he is not allowed to do that under the Rules. The player receives no information from the caddie about the condition of the green. Is the player penalized under Rule 16-1d?

A. Yes. The reference to the player in Rule 16-1d includes his caddie. Thus, the Rule prohibits the caddie, as well as the player, from testing the surface of the putting green. Under Rule 6-4, the player incurs the applicable penalty for a breach of a Rule by his caddie.

16-1e/1 Meaning of "Line of Putt" in Context of "Standing Astride or on Line of Putt"

Q. With reference to the above sketch, the broken line is a direct line from the ball to the hole and the solid line is the line on which the player intends his ball to travel. Which line is "the line of putt" for purposes of application of Rule 16-1e (Standing Astride or on Line of Putt)? If the broken line is "the line of putt," the player will be in breach of Rule 16-1e. If the solid line is the "line of putt," he will not be in breach of the Rule.

A. The solid line is "the line of putt."

16

16-1f/1 Caddie Deliberately Positioned Off Putting Green on Extension of Line of Putt Behind Ball

Q. A player preparing to play a stroke on the putting green positions his caddie off the green on an extension of the line of putt behind the ball, so that the caddie may assist him in alignment while putting. Was the player in breach of Rule 16-1f?

A. Yes. Rule 16-1f applies when the ball lies on the green. The position of the caddie in terms of whether he is on or off the green is irrelevant.

16-1f/2 Caddie Inadvertently Positioned on Extension of Line of Putt Behind Ball

Q. A player's caddie inadvertently stood on an extension of the player's line of putt behind the ball when the player made a stroke on the putting green. The caddie was on the edge of the green watching another player drive from the next tee. Neither the player nor the caddie was aware that the caddie was so positioned. Was the player subject to penalty under Rule 16-1f?

A. No. The main purpose of Rule 16-1f is to prohibit a caddie from positioning himself behind the player while the player putts to advise the player on alignment or otherwise assist him. In this case, the caddie was not so positioned.

16-2/0.5 Ball Overhanging Hole Is Lifted, Cleaned and Replaced; Ball Then Falls into Hole.

Q. After an approach shot, a player's ball is overhanging the hole. The player walks up to the hole without unreasonable delay and notices that there is mud on the ball. The player marks the position of the ball and lifts it. He then cleans the ball and replaces it. The ball remains on the lip of the hole for about five seconds and then, as the player is preparing to tap it into the hole, the ball falls into the hole. What is the ruling?

A. Under Rule 16-2 , if a ball falls into the hole after it is deemed to be at rest, the player is deemed to have holed out with his last stroke and he shall add a penalty stroke to his score for the hole. In this case, when the player marked the position of the ball it must have been at rest. The ball must be considered to have been at rest when it was replaced; otherwise, it would have to be replaced again (Rule 20-3d).

Accordingly, the player is deemed to have holed out with his last stroke and must add a penalty stroke to his score for the hole.

16-2/1 Ball Overhanging Hole Falls into Hole After Player Waits 40 Seconds

Q. A player's ball overhangs the edge of the hole. The player walks up to the hole. He then waits about 40 seconds, after which the ball falls into the hole. Is the player subject to penalty?

A. Yes. The player incurs a penalty of one stroke–Rule 16-2.

16-2/2 Ball Overhanging Hole Knocked Away by Opponent Before Player Determines Status

Q. In a match between A and B, A putts and his ball apparently comes to rest, but is overhanging the hole. Within five seconds, B concedes A's next stroke and knocks his ball away. Was B entitled to knock A's ball away?

A. No. Under Rule 16-2, A is allowed a reasonable time to reach the hole and an additional ten seconds to determine whether his ball is at rest. Since B infringed A's rights, B was in breach of Rule 1-2 (Exerting Influence on Ball) and lost the hole, assuming that Rule 2-2 (Halved Hole) did not apply.

Player Jumps Close to Hole to Cause Ball Overhanging Hole to Drop — See 1-2/4.

Ball Blown into Hole by Competitor Not Replaced and Holed Out — See 3-2/2.

Ball Falls into Hole After Concession of Next Stroke — See 2-4/2.

Ball Overhanging Hole Falls into Hole After Being Addressed — See 18-2b/10.

16

16-2/3 Casting Shadow on Ball Overhanging Hole

Q. A player's ball came to rest overhanging the edge of the hole. The player walked up to the hole and cast his shadow on the ball, believing that this would cause the grass to wilt and his ball to fall into the hole. Was the player in breach of Rule 1-2 (Exerting Influence on Ball) when he cast his shadow on the ball?

A. No.

Rule 17. The Flagstick

17-1. Flagstick Attended, Removed or Held Up

Before and during the <u>stroke</u>, the player may have the flagstick attended, removed or held up to indicate the position of the hole. This may be done only on the authority of the player before he plays his stroke.

If, prior to the stroke, the flagstick is attended, removed or held up by anyone with the player's knowledge and no objection is made, the player shall be deemed to have authorized it. If anyone attends or holds up the flagstick or stands near the hole while a stroke is being played, he shall be deemed to be attending the flagstick until the ball comes to rest.

17-2. Unauthorized Attendance

a. MATCH PLAY

In match play, an opponent or his caddie shall not, without the authority or prior knowledge of the player, attend, remove or hold up the flagstick while the player is making a stroke or his ball is in motion.

b. STROKE PLAY

In stroke play, if a fellow-competitor or his caddie attends, removes or holds up the flagstick without the competitor's authority or prior knowledge while the competitor is making a stroke or his ball is in motion, *the fellow-competitor shall incur the penalty* for breach of this Rule. In such circumstances, if the competitor's ball strikes the flagstick, the person attending it or anything carried by him, the competitor incurs no penalty and the ball shall be played as it lies, except that, if the stroke was played from the putting green, the stroke shall be cancelled, the ball replaced and the stroke replayed.

PENALTY FOR BREACH
OF RULE 17-1 or -2:
Match play --- Loss of hole;
Stroke play --- Two strokes.

17-3. Ball Striking Flagstick or Attendant
The player's ball shall not strike:

a. The flagstick when attended, removed or held up by the player, his partner or either of their caddies, or by another person with the player's authority or prior knowledge; or

b. The player's caddie, his partner or his partner's caddie when attending the flagstick, or another person attending the flagstick with the player's authority or prior knowledge or anything carried by any such person; or

c. The flagstick in the hole, unattended, when the ball has been played from the putting green.

PENALTY FOR BREACH OF RULE 17-3:
Match play --- Loss of hole; Stroke play --- Two strokes, and the ball shall be played as it lies.

17-4. Ball Resting Against Flagstick
If the ball rests against the flagstick when it is in the hole, the player or another person authorized by him may move or remove the flagstick and if the ball falls into the hole, the player shall be deemed to have holed out with his last stroke; otherwise, the ball, if moved, shall be placed on the lip of the hole, without penalty.

17/1 Attachment to Flagstick to Indicate Position of Hole on Green

Q. A thin disc or sleeve is attached to the flagstick to indicate the distance of the hole from the front of the green. If the disc is placed near the bottom of the flagstick it means that the hole is at the front of the green; if it is placed near the top of the flagstick it means that the hole is at the back of the green. Is this permitted?

A. Yes, provided the attachment is circular in cross-section.

17/2 Different Colored Flags Used to Indicate Position of Hole on Green

Q. May a Committee use flagsticks with flags of two different colors, one color being used when the hole is at the front of the green and the other when the hole is at the back?

A. Yes.

17/3 Flagstick Tapered or of Varying Diameters

Q. May a flagstick be tapered or have a slender metal ferrule at the base?

A. Yes. The Definition does not prohibit sections of varying diameters. The Definition requires that the flagstick be circular in cross-section. This is to prohibit non-circular features in the lower part of the flagstick.

17/4 Adjustment of Flagstick; Player's Rights

Q. A player playing from off the green and wishing to leave the flagstick in the hole may find that the flagstick is leaning towards his ball (a disadvantage) or away from his ball (an advantage). What are the player's rights in such a situation?

A. The flagstick may be left as it is or centered in the hole, as contemplated by the Definition of "Flagstick."

The flagstick may not be adjusted to a more favorable position than centered. To do so would infringe Rule 1-2 (Exerting Influence on Ball).

An opponent or fellow-competitor who centers the flagstick incurs no penalty, but the player may have it restored to its original position. (Revised)

[17/5 Reserved]

17/6 Ball Lodged in Flag Attached to Flagstick

Q. A player's ball lodges in the flag attached to a flagstick. What is the procedure?

A flagstick is a movable obstruction and Rule 24-1 applies. The ball may be placed on the lip of the hole.

17/7 Hole-Liner Pulled Out by Flagstick Attendant and Ball Falls into Unlined Hole

Q. A flagstick attendant removes the flagstick and, in the process, pulls out the hole-liner. The player's ball rolls into the unlined hole. What is the ruling?

A. The player incurs no penalty and the ball is holed. A hole need not contain a lining — see Definition of "Hole."

17/8 Ball Strikes Hole-Liner Pulled Out with Flagstick

Q. A player played a stroke from the putting green. The ball struck the hole-liner, which had stuck to the bottom of the flagstick and had come out of the hole when the person attending the flagstick removed the flagstick. Is there any penalty?

A. No. A hole-liner is an outside agency. Accordingly, if the hole-liner was moving when the ball struck it, the stroke is canceled and the ball must be replaced — Rule 19-1b. If the hole-liner was not moving, the ball must be played as it lies — Rule 19-1. In case of doubt, the ball must be played as it lies.

17/9 Attendant Removes Flagstick Whereupon Knob Falls from Top of Flagstick and Deflects Ball

Q. After a player putts, the flagstick attendant removes the flagstick and a knob attached to the top of the flagstick falls off. The knob strikes the player's moving ball and deflects it. What is the ruling?

A. Once detached the knob was no longer a part of the flagstick. It was an outside agency. Therefore, the stroke is canceled and the ball must be replaced — Rule 19-1b.

Flagstick Lying on Putting Green Removed by Player to Prevent Another Player's Ball from Striking It — See 1-2/3.

Flagstick Stuck into Green Some Distance from Hole by Practical Joker — See 1-4/3.

Ball Moved by Flagstick Accidentally Dropped on Ball — See 18-2a/24.

17-1/1 Meaning of "Stands Near the Hole"

Q. Rule 17-1 states that, if anyone "stands near the hole," he is deemed to be attending the flagstick. Is such a person considered to be standing "near the hole" if he is close enough to touch the flagstick?

A. Yes.

17-1/2 Opponent or Fellow-Competitor Declines to Attend Flagstick

Q. Does a player have any redress if he requests his opponent or a fellow-competitor to attend the flagstick for him and the opponent or fellow-competitor declines?

A. No.

17-1/3 Flagstick Attended by Referee, Observer or Marker at Player's Request

Q. A player requests a referee, observer or marker to attend the flagstick and the referee, observer or marker does so. Is the player subject to penalty?

A. A referee or observer should not attend the flagstick — see Definitions of "Referee" and "Observer." However, a player incurs no penalty if he makes such a request and the referee or observer complies. A marker may attend the flagstick, even if he is not a fellow-competitor.

17-1/4 Flagstick Attendant Stands Behind Hole

Q. May a person attending the flagstick stand directly behind the hole, instead of to the side of it?

A. Yes. A flagstick attendant might have to stand behind the hole to avoid standing on the line of putt of another player.

17-1/4.5 Flagstick Attendant Removes Flagstick and Holds It Upright Behind Hole; End of Flagstick Touches Green

Q. A player preparing to putt asks his caddie to attend the flagstick. The caddie removes the flagstick from the hole and holds it upright two or three inches directly behind the hole, with the end of the flagstick touching the putting green. He attends the flagstick in this manner to eliminate the risk of the flagstick sticking in the hole. Is such a procedure a breach of the Rules?

A. No, but such a practice is not recommended because of the possibility of damage to the putting green.

17-1/5 Holding Flagstick with One Hand and Putting with Other Hand

Q. A player holds the flagstick with one hand and holes a short putt, gripping the putter with his other hand. Is this permissible?

A. Yes, provided the flagstick has been removed from the hole and the ball therefore does not strike it. If the ball were to strike the flagstick, a breach of Rule 17-3a would occur.

17-3/1 Holing Out Without Ball Touching Flagstick

Q. A player plays a stroke from the putting green without having the flagstick attended. The ball stops momentarily on the lip of the hole and then falls into the hole. The player claims that the ball fell into the hole without striking the flagstick and therefore he incurs no penalty under Rule 17-3. Is the claim valid?

A. No. A ball is not holed until it is at rest in the hole — See Definition of "Holed." If the flagstick is in the hole, it is impossible for a ball to come to rest in the hole without striking the flagstick.

17-3/2 Opponent or Fellow-Competitor Attending Flagstick for Player Fails to Remove It; Player's Ball Strikes Flagstick

Q. A requests B, his opponent or a fellow-competitor, to attend the flagstick, and B complies. A putts too firmly and B fails to remove the flagstick. A's ball strikes the flagstick. What is the ruling?

A. If B failed to remove the flagstick for the purpose of causing A to incur a penalty, B is disqualified in both match play and stroke play for a serious breach of Rule 1-2. In stroke play, in equity (Rule 1-4) A must replay the stroke without penalty.

If B's failure to remove the flagstick was for the purpose of preventing A's ball from going beyond the flagstick and not for the purpose of causing A to incur a penalty, in match play B lost the hole under Rule 1-2 when he failed to remove the flagstick before A's ball reached the hole. The fact that A's ball subsequently struck the flagstick (a breach of Rule 17-3a) is irrelevant since B had already lost the hole. In stroke play, B incurs a penalty of two strokes under Rule 1-2, and A incurs the same penalty under Rule 17-3a.

If B's failure to remove the flagstick was not deliberate, *e.g.*, the flagstick stuck in the socket or B was distracted and did not see A putt, A incurs a penalty of loss of hole in match play or two strokes in stroke play under Rule 17-3. B incurs no penalty.

17

17-3/3   Ball Strikes Flagstick Lying on Green

Q. Consider the following situations and give a ruling in each case:

(a) A player putts too strongly and his ball strikes the flagstick which has been removed by someone in his match or group and placed on the putting green behind the hole.

(b) A player plays his second shot to the green and the ball strikes the flagstick which had been blown down by the wind and was lying on the green.

(c) A player, not believing he can reach the green which is occupied by the preceding match or group, plays his second shot at a par-5 hole and the ball rolls onto the green and strikes the flagstick which has been removed from the hole and placed on the green by someone in the preceding match or group.

A. The following are the rulings:

(a) The player incurs a penalty under Rule 17-3a.

(b) and (c) No penalty is incurred. Rule 17-3a is not applicable in either case. It applies only when the flagstick has been removed with the player's authority or prior knowledge by someone in the player's match or group.

17

17-3/4   Flagstick Attended by Partner Without Express Authority of Player; Ball Strikes Flagstick or Partner

Q. In four-ball play, A is preparing to play from off the putting green. B, A's partner, attends the flagstick without A's knowledge or express authority. A plays and his ball strikes B or the flagstick. What is the ruling?

A. If the flagstick is attended by the player's caddie, his partner or his partner's caddie, *i.e.*, by a member of the player's side, it is deemed to be attended with the player's knowledge and authority. Accordingly, under Rule 17-3 A incurs a penalty of loss of hole in match play or two strokes in stroke play. In stroke play, A must play the ball as it lies. B incurs no penalty.

17-3/5 Flag Struck by Ball When Flagstick Attended

Q. While the flagstick was being attended, a player's ball struck the flag attached to the flagstick. Did the player incur a penalty under Rule 17-3a?

A. Yes. The flag is part of the flagstick.

17-3/6 Marking Position of Hole with Club

Q. The flagstick has been removed. A wants the position of the hole marked but he does not want to waste time retrieving the flagstick. So A asks B to place the grip end of his putter in the hole. Is this permissible?

A. Yes, but a putter used to mark the position of the hole must be treated as a flagstick for the purposes of applying the Rules.

Ball at Rest Kicked Away from Hole by Spectator Attending Flagstick — See 18-1/10.

Player Attending Flagstick for Opponent Struck by Ball of Opponent's Partner Who Played Out of Turn — See 30-3f/5.

17-4/1 Ball Resting Against Flagstick Lifted Before Being Holed

Q. A player's ball is resting against the flagstick, but it is not holed because all of it is not below the level of the lip of the hole. However, the player, believing the ball is holed, picks it up. What is the ruling?

A. The player incurs a penalty stroke under Rule 20-1 for lifting his ball without marking its position. The player must replace the ball against the flagstick and may then apply Rule 17-4.

Player's Ball Resting Against Flagstick Lifted Before Being Holed; Others in Four-Ball Match Pick Up Mistakenly Believing Player Won Hole — See 30-3f/3.

17

17-4/2 Ball Resting Against Flagstick; Putt Conceded and Ball Removed Before Player Can Remove Flagstick

Q. In a match, A plays a stroke from off the green and his ball comes to rest against the flagstick. B, A's opponent, concedes A's next stroke and removes A's ball. Despite B's concession, is A entitled to have the ball replaced to enable him to exercise his rights under Rule 17-4?

A. Yes. When A's ball was resting against the flagstick, Rule 17-4 applied and A was entitled to have the flagstick moved or removed to see whether the ball would fall into the hole. B had no right to remove the ball and concede the next stroke until A had an opportunity to proceed under Rule 17-4. By removing A's ball, B was in breach of Rule 18-3b and incurred a penalty stroke; A should then have replaced his ball against the flagstick and applied Rule 17-4.

17-4/3 Ball Resting Against Flagstick Moves Away from Hole When Flagstick Removed by Opponent or Fellow-Competitor

Q. A player's ball is resting against the flagstick. Without the player's authority, his opponent or a fellow-competitor removes the flagstick and the ball moves away from the hole. What is the ruling?

A. In match play, the opponent incurs a penalty stroke and the ball must be replaced against the flagstick — Rule 18-3b.

In stroke play, the ball must be replaced against the flagstick without penalty to anyone — Rule 18-4.

In either form of play, the player may then move or remove the flagstick as prescribed in Rule 17-4.

BALL MOVED, DEFLECTED OR STOPPED
Rule 18. Ball at Rest Moved

Definitions

A ball is deemed to have "moved" if it leaves its position and comes to rest in any other place.

An "outside agency" is any agency not part of the match or, in stroke play, not part of the competitor's side, and includes a referee, a marker, an observer or a forecaddie. Neither wind nor water is an outside agency.

"Equipment" is anything used, worn or carried by or for the player except any ball he has played at the hole being played and any small object, such as a coin or a tee, when used to mark the position of a ball or the extent of an area in which a ball is to be dropped. Equipment includes a golf cart, whether or not motorized. If such a cart is shared by two or more players, the cart and everything in it are deemed to be the equipment of the player whose ball is involved except that, when the cart is being moved by one of the players sharing it, the cart and everything in it are deemed to be that player's equipment.

Note: A ball played at the hole being played is equipment when it has been lifted and not put back into play.

A player has "addressed the ball" when he has taken his <u>stance</u> and has also grounded his

18

club, except that in a <u>hazard</u> a player has addressed the ball when he has taken his stance.

Taking the "stance" consists in a player placing his feet in position for and preparatory to making a <u>stroke</u>.

18-1. By Outside Agency

If a ball at rest is moved by an <u>outside agency</u>, the player shall incur no penalty and the ball shall be replaced before the player plays another <u>stroke</u>.

(Player's ball at rest moved by another ball — see Rule 18-5.)

18-2. By Player, Partner, Caddie or Equipment

a. GENERAL

When a player's ball is <u>in play</u>, if:

(i) the player, his partner or either of their caddies lifts or moves it, touches it purposely (except with a club in the act of addressing it) or causes it to move except as permitted by a Rule, or

(ii) equipment of the player or his partner causes the ball to move,

the player shall incur a penalty stroke. The ball shall be replaced unless the movement of the ball occurs after the player has begun his swing and he does not discontinue his swing.

Under the Rules no penalty is incurred if a player accidentally causes his ball to move in the following circumstances:

In measuring to determine which ball farther from hole — Rule 10-4

In searching for covered ball in hazard or for ball in <u>casual water, ground under repair</u>, etc. — Rule 12-1

In the process of repairing hole plug or ball mark — Rule 16-1c

In the process of removing <u>loose impediment</u> on <u>putting green</u> — Rule 18-2c

In the process of lifting ball under a Rule — Rule 20-1

18

In the process of placing or replacing ball under a Rule — Rule 20-3a

In complying with Rule 22 relating to lifting ball interfering with or assisting play

In removal of movable obstruction — Rule 24-1.

b. BALL MOVING AFTER ADDRESS

If a player's <u>ball in play moves</u> after he has <u>ad-dressed</u> it (other than as a result of a stroke), the player shall be deemed to have moved the ball and *shall incur a penalty stroke*. The player shall replace the ball unless the movement of the ball occurs after he has begun his swing and he does not discontinue his swing.

c. BALL MOVING AFTER LOOSE IMPEDI-MENT TOUCHED <u>Through the green</u>, if the ball <u>moves</u> after any <u>loose</u> <u>impediment</u> lying within a club-length of it has been touched by the player, his partner or either of their caddies and before the player has <u>addressed</u> it, the player shall be deemed to have moved the ball and *shall incur a penalty stroke*. The player shall replace the ball unless the movement of the ball occurs after he has begun his swing and he does not discontinue his swing.

On the <u>putting green</u>, if the ball or the ball-marker moves in the process of removing any loose impediment, the ball or the ball-marker shall be replaced. There is no penalty provided the movement of the ball or the ball-marker is directly attributable to the removal of the loose impediment. Otherwise, the player shall incur a penalty stroke under Rule 18-2a or 20-1.

18-3. By Opponent, Caddie or Equipment in Match Play

a. DURING SEARCH

If, during search for a player's ball, it is

18

moved by an opponent, his caddie or his <u>equipment</u>, no penalty is incurred and the player shall replace the ball.

b. OTHER THAN DURING SEARCH

If, other than during search for a ball, the ball is touched or moved by an opponent, his caddie or his <u>equipment</u>, except as otherwise provided in the Rules, *the opponent shall incur a penalty stroke.* The player shall replace the ball.

(Ball moved in measuring to determine which ball farther from the hole — see Rule 10-4.)

(Playing a wrong ball — see Rule 15-2.)

(Ball moved in complying with Rule 22 relating to lifting ball interfering with or assisting play.)

18-4. By Fellow-Competitor, Caddie or Equipment in Stroke Play

If a competitor's ball is moved by a fellow-competitor, his caddie or his <u>equipment</u>, no penalty is incurred. The competitor shall replace his ball.

(Playing a wrong ball — see Rule 15-3.)

18-5. By Another Ball

If a ball in play and at rest is moved by another ball in motion after a stroke, the moved ball shall be replaced.

*PENALTY FOR BREACH OF RULE:
Match play --- Loss of hole;
Stroke play --- Two strokes.

*If a player who is required to replace a ball fails to do so, he shall incur the general penalty for breach of Rule 18 but no additional penalty under Rule 18 shall be applied.

Note 1: If a ball to be replaced under this Rule is not immediately recoverable, another ball may be substituted.

Note 2: If it is impossible to determine the spot on which a ball is to be placed, see Rule 20-3c.

18/1 Ball Moves Vertically Downwards

Q. A ball lying in long grass slips vertically downwards. Or a ball is accidentally stepped on and pressed down, say a quarter of an inch, in the grass or into the ground. In each case, has the ball moved?

A. Yes, unless the ball returns to its original position. The direction of movement is immaterial.

18/2 Ball Oscillates During Address

Q. In addressing the ball, a player accidentally causes the ball to oscillate, but it returns to its original position. Has the ball "moved"?

A. No.

18/3 Ball in Fork of Tree Moves in Relation to Ground But Not in Relation to Fork

Q. A ball rests in the fork of a branch of a tree. The player climbs the tree to play his next stroke. The branch bends under his weight. Although the ball has moved relative to the ground, it has not moved relative to the fork. Is the ball deemed to have moved?

18

A. The ball is deemed not to have moved since it did not move in relation to the fork of the tree in which it was lodged.

18/4 When Snake Is Outside Agency

Q. Is a snake an outside agency or a loose impediment?

A. A live snake is an outside agency. A dead snake is a loose impediment.

18/5 Placing Clubhead on Ground in Front of Ball When Addressing

Q. A player takes his stance and places his clubhead on the ground in front of the ball without pressing anything down. Before the player grounds the club behind the ball, the ball moves. Has the player "addressed the ball" so that he is subject to penalty under Rule 18-2b?

A. Yes.

When Club Grounded in Grass — See 18-2b/5.

18/6 When Player Who Putts "Side-Saddle" Has Addressed Ball

Q. A player who putts "side-saddle" usually stands directly behind the ball, places the clubhead on the ground behind the ball and aligns the clubhead. The player then moves to the side so as not to infringe Rule 16-1e and makes his stroke. When is the player deemed to have addressed the ball?

A. The player has addressed the ball when he moves to the side. The player has not placed his feet in position for a stroke, and therefore has not taken his stance, until he has moved to the side, and a ball is not addressed until a player has taken his stance.

18/7 Explanation of "Any Ball He Has Played"

Q. The Definition of "Equipment" excludes "any ball he (the player) has played at the hole being played." What does this mean?

A. The phrase means any ball the player has played at the hole being played except during any period when it has been lifted and has not been put back into play. Accordingly, the ball in play, a provisional ball, a second ball played under Rule 3-3 or Rule 20-7b and a ball being used for practice are not equipment.

Player Lifts His Ball on Putting Green and Sets It Aside; Opponent's or Fellow-Competitor's Ball Played from Green Subsequently Strikes Player's Ball — See 19-5/1.

18/7.5 Player's Ball Moved by Ball Accidentally Dropped by Opponent or Fellow-Competitor

Q. A lifts his ball on the putting green. He then accidentally drops the ball and it strikes and moves B's ball, which is in play and at rest. What is the ruling?

A. A ball which has been lifted and not put back into play is equipment — see the Note under Definition of "Equipment."

In match play, A incurs a penalty stroke and B must replace his ball — Rule 18-3b.

In stroke play, there is no penalty and B must replace his ball — Rule 18-4.

Rule 19-5 (Ball in Motion Deflected or Stopped by Another Ball) does not apply because A's ball was not "in motion after a stroke." (Revised)

18/8 Ball Moved by Golf Cart Shared by Two Players

Under the Definition of "Equipment," equipment includes a golf cart, whether or not motorized. If two players share a golf cart, the cart and everything in it are deemed to be the equipment of the player whose ball is involved; except that, when the cart is being moved by one of the players, the cart and everything in it are deemed to be that player's equipment.

Thus, for example, in a singles match, if A and B are sharing a cart and the cart moves A's ball which was at rest, A would be penalized one stroke if he was driving or pulling the cart (Rule 18-2a). B would be penalized one stroke if he was driving or pulling the cart (Rule 18-3b), unless the incident occurred during search (Rule 18-3a).

18

18/9 Whether Glove Used as Indicating Mark Is Equipment

Q. A player entitled to drop a ball marks with his glove the spot on which the ball is to be dropped or the outer limit of the area within which the ball is to be dropped. The dropped ball then strikes the glove.

If the glove is a "small object," it is not equipment of the player, and the ball would not be re-dropped. Otherwise, the glove is equipment and the ball must be re-dropped under Rule 20-2a.

What is the status of the glove?

A. A glove is not a "small object" within the meaning of that term in the Definition of "Equipment." Therefore, it is equipment and the ball must be re-dropped.

18/10 Ball Falls into Bunker When Person Walks Nearby

Q. A ball at rest on the edge of a bunker falls into the bunker when X (a spectator, the player, an opponent or a fellow-competitor) walks nearby. Should the ball be replaced in accordance with Rules 18-1 to -4 or must the ball be played as it lies in the bunker?

A. The answer depends on whether X in any way caused the ball to move. If it is determined that X did not in any way cause the ball to move, there is no penalty and the ball must be played as it lies.

If it is determined that X caused the ball to move, it must be replaced. If X is the player, the player incurs a penalty stroke under Rule 18-2a; if X is an opponent, the opponent incurs a penalty stroke under Rule 18-3b. In all other cases, there is no penalty.

Whether X caused the ball to move is a question of fact to be determined in the light of all the circumstances. Relevant circumstances might include the distance between X and the ball and the nature of the ground. In the absence of evidence that X caused the ball to move, it should be concluded that the ball's movement was a coincidence.

18/11 Meaning of "Immediately Recoverable"

Q. With reference to Note 1 under Rule 18, when is a ball to be replaced deemed not to be "immediately recoverable"?

A. When it cannot be retrieved within a few seconds.

18-1/1 Treating Ball as Moved by Outside Agency Rather Than Lost

To treat a ball which cannot be found as moved by an outside agency rather than lost (Rule 27), there must be reasonable evidence to that effect. All available testimony should be considered. In the absence of such evidence, the ball must be treated as lost.

Lost Ball Treated as Moved by Outside Agency in Absence of Reasonable Evidence to That Effect — See 27-1/2.5.

18-1/2   Ball Visible from Tee Disappears or Is Moved While Play Suspended

Q. A player's tee shot came to rest and was visible from the tee by all players in the match or group. At that point play was suspended. The player took cover and did not lift the ball. When play was resumed, the player's ball was missing or was found some distance from where it was seen to come to rest. What is the procedure?

A. It must be assumed that the ball was moved by an outside agency. Therefore, the player should replace his ball (or place a ball if his own is not immediately recoverable) at the spot from which his ball was moved, without penalty (Rule 18-1). If this spot is not determinable, Rule 20-3c would apply.

18-1/3   Player Unaware Ball Moved by Outside Agency Does Not Replace Ball

18

Q. In stroke play, a player's ball was moved by an outside agency. Neither the player nor his caddie was aware that his ball had been moved, so the player did not replace the ball. He completed the hole, teed off at the next hole and then learned that his ball had been moved at the previous hole. What is the ruling?

A. It would be inequitable to impose a penalty for failure to replace a ball moved by an outside agency as required by Rule 18-1 if neither the player nor his caddie knew the ball had been moved. Accordingly, the score made with the moved ball would stand.

18-1/4   Spectator Says Ball Was Moved by Outside Agency But Player Not Sure

Q. A spectator tells a player that his ball has been moved by an outside agency. Neither the player nor his caddie was aware the ball had been moved. Is the player obliged to take the spectator's word and replace the ball on the spot from which the spectator said it was moved?

A. No. In stroke play, if it is impractical to get a decision from the Committee, the player should, under Rule 3-3, hole out both with the original ball and a second ball played from the spot from which the original ball is alleged to have been moved, and request the Committee to decide the matter at the end of the round. In reaching a decision, the Committee should interrogate the spectator, if possible.

In match play, if there is no referee or representative of the Committee available within a reasonable time, the player and his opponent should, if possible, agree on the place from which the player should play his next stroke. If agreement cannot be reached, the player must proceed as he thinks best, and if the opponent does not agree with the action taken, he should lodge a claim under Rule 2-5 so that the Committee may make a decision under Rule 34-3.

18-1/5 Ball Stolen by Outside Agency from Unknown Spot

18

Q. At a par-3 hole, part of the green and the adjoining area cannot be seen from the tee. In this unseen area are a bunker, fairway and a dry water hazard. A player plays towards this obscured area and cannot tell where the ball comes to rest. When the players are near the green, they see a boy running away with a ball in his hand. The boy throws the ball back and the player identifies it as his ball.

The player is unable to determine from where to play his next stroke under Rule 18-1. He does not know whether the ball was on the green, on the fairway or in one of the hazards.

How should he proceed?

A. As it was impossible to know where the ball should have been replaced under Rule 18-1, the player should, in equity (Rule 1-4), drop the ball in an area which was neither the most, nor the least, favorable of the various areas where it was equally possible that the ball originally lay.

18-1/6 Ball at Rest Moved by Blowing Tumbleweed

Q. A tumbleweed blowing across the course strikes a ball at rest and knocks it into the hole. What is the procedure?

A. In the circumstances, a tumbleweed is an outside agency. Rule 18-1 applies and the ball must be replaced without penalty.

18-1/7 Ball in Plastic Bag Moves When Bag Blown to New Position by Wind

Q. A player's ball comes to rest in a plastic bag that is lying on the ground. Before the player can invoke Rule 24-1b, a gust of wind blows the bag and the ball to a new position. In proceeding under Rule 24-1b, should the player drop the ball directly under the place where it originally lay in the bag or where it now lies in the bag?

A. Wind is not an outside agency. However, if an object being moved by the wind moves a ball, the object is an outside agency in the circumstances — see Decision 18-1/6.

In this case, the bag, not the wind, caused the ball to move. Accordingly, under Rules 18-1 and 24-1b, the player must drop the ball directly under the place where it originally lay in the bag.

18-1/8 Ball Moved by Stone Dislodged by Partner's or Opponent's Stroke

Q. In match play, a player played a stroke and dislodged a large stone. The stone struck his partner's or an opponent's ball which was lying about four yards ahead and moved it. What is the ruling?

A. The stone was an outside agency and Rule 18-1 applies. The partner or opponent must replace his ball.

18

In the circumstances, the player should not be held to have moved the ball. Accordingly, Rules 18-2a(i) and 18-3b are not applicable and no penalty is incurred.

18-1/9 Ball Lodged in Tree Knocked Down by Outside Agency

Q. A player's ball is lodged in a tree about eight feet off the ground. A spectator knocks the ball down from the tree. In complying with Rule 18-1, it is impossible to replace the ball in the prescribed manner in the tree because the spot where it lay in the tree is unknown or unreachable. What is the ruling?

A. Rules 20-3c and -3d cover cases in which the spot where a ball is to be placed or replaced is not determinable or a ball fails to remain on the spot on which it is placed. However, these Rules do not contemplate a case such as this one. Thus, in equity (Rule 1-4), if the position of the ball in the tree was such that the player could have made a stroke at it, the ball must be placed in the tree as near as possible to the spot from which it was moved, without penalty. Otherwise, the player must proceed under the unplayable ball Rule.

18

18-1/10 Ball at Rest Kicked Away from Hole by Spectator Attending Flagstick

Q. In stroke play, a competitor asked a spectator to attend the flagstick. The competitor putted and his ball stopped one inch short of the hole. The spectator then kicked the ball away. What is the ruling?

A. There was no infringement of Rule 17-3b because the competitor's ball had come to rest short of the hole. The spectator was not the competitor's caddie and so he was an outside agency. Under Rule 18-1 the competitor was required to replace his ball and hole out without penalty.

18-1/11 Ball Moved by Wind or Casual Water While Play Suspended

Q. While play is suspended, wind or casual water moves a ball. Since wind or water is not an outside agency and therefore Rule 18-1 does not apply, must the ball be played from its new position?

A. No. The ball must be replaced. If the spot is not determinable, see Rule 20-3c. Rule 33-2d states in part: "When play has been temporarily suspended, it shall be resumed from where it was discontinued." This overrides other provisions in the Rules under which the result would be different.

Ball-Marker Moved Off Green by Wind or Casual Water — See 20-1/10.

18-1/12 Ball Replaced and at Rest Is Thereafter Moved by Wind

Q. A player replaces his ball on the putting green and the ball is at rest. Before the player addresses the ball, a sudden gust of wind blows the ball farther from the hole. The player plays the ball from its new position. Is that correct?

A. Yes. Wind is not an outside agency — see Definition of "Outside Agency." Accordingly, Rule 18-1 does not apply.

18

18-2a/1 Player Who Misses Tee Shot Tees Ball Lower Before Playing Next Stroke

Q. A player playing from the teeing ground misses the ball completely. He pushes his tee farther into the ground and plays. Is there a penalty?

A. Yes. As the ball was in play after the player had made a stroke at it, he incurred a penalty of one stroke under Rule 18-2a when he teed the ball lower, and a penalty of loss of hole in match play or a total penalty of two strokes in stroke play because the ball was not subsequently replaced — see penalty statement under Rule 18.

Lifting Ball in Play But Still Within Teeing Ground — See 11-3/2.

18-2a/2 Ball Falling Off Tee When Stroke Just Touches It Is Picked Up and Re-Teed

Q. When starting a hole, a player, in making his first stroke, just touched the ball and it fell off the tee. He picked up the ball, re-teed it and played out the hole. What is the ruling?

A. When the player made a stroke the ball was in play. When he then lifted the ball, he was in breach of Rule 18-2a and incurred a penalty stroke. When he failed to replace the ball on the spot where it came to rest after being knocked off the tee, he incurred a penalty of loss of hole in match play or a total of two strokes in stroke play — see penalty statement under Rule 18.

Ball Putted from Wrong Place Lifted and Putted from Right Place — See 20-7b/2.

18-2a/3 Ball Lifted and Dropped Away from Boundary Stake Under Obstruction Rule

Q. A player's swing is interfered with by a stake defining out of bounds. The player mistakenly considers the stake an obstruction and he lifts his ball and drops it in the manner prescribed in Rule 24-2b. What is the ruling?

A. The player incurs a penalty of one stroke under Rule 18-2a and he must replace his ball before playing his next stroke. Otherwise, he loses the hole in match play or he incurs a total penalty of two strokes in stroke play — see penalty statement under Rule 18.

18-2a/4 Ball Lifted and Dropped Away from Movable Obstruction

Q. A player's ball comes to rest against a movable obstruction. The player lifts the ball and drops it away from the obstruction instead of removing the obstruction as provided in Rule 24-1. What is the ruling?

A. The player incurs a penalty of one stroke under Rule 18-2a and he must replace his ball before playing his next stroke. Otherwise, he loses the hole in match play or he incurs a total penalty of two strokes in stroke play — see penalty statement under Rule 18.

[18-2a/5   Reserved]

18-2a/6   Oscillating Ball Pressed into Surface of Putting Green

Q. A ball lying on the putting green was oscillating due to wind. The player firmly pressed the ball into the surface of the green and the ball stopped oscillating. The player then holed out. Was the player in breach of the Rules?

A. Yes. The player incurred a penalty stroke under Rule 18-2a when he moved his ball by pressing on it. Since the original lie of the ball was altered when the ball was firmly pressed down, the player was obliged to proceed under Rule 20-3b. Since he did not do so, he lost the hole in match play and incurred a total penalty of two strokes in stroke play — see penalty statement under Rule 18.

18-2a/7   Ball Moved by Wind Replaced

Q. In stroke play, a competitor's ball was moved by wind. Since wind is not an outside agency (see Definition of "Outside Agency"), he should have played it from where it came to rest, but he replaced it. What is the ruling?

A. The competitor incurred one penalty stroke under Rule 18-2a, and, before playing his next stroke, he should have replaced the ball on the spot where it came to rest after being moved by the wind. If he did not do so, he incurred a total penalty of two strokes — see penalty statement under Rule 18.

18-2a/8   Ball Played from Ground Under Repair Picked Up and Relief Taken Under Ground Under Repair Rule

Q. A player, unaware that his ball was in ground under repair, played the ball as it lay. The player then learned that his ball had been in ground under repair, picked up the ball played from the ground under repair, dropped it in accordance with Rule 25-1b and played out the hole. What is the ruling?

A. When the player played from the ground under repair, which is permissible, relief under Rule 25-1b was no longer available and the ball was in play where it lay.

When the player picked up his ball in play, he incurred a penalty stroke — Rule 18-2a. Since he did not replace the ball, he incurred a penalty of loss of hole in match play or a total penalty of two strokes in stroke play — see penalty statement under Rule 18.

Provisional Ball Lifted in Erroneous Belief Original Ball Is in Bounds — See 27-2b/8.

Provisional Ball Lifted Subsequently Becomes Ball in Play — See 27-2b/9.

18-2a/9 Ball Lifted Without Authority Dropped Instead of Being Replaced

Q. A player lifted his ball without being entitled to under the Rules and incurred a penalty stroke under Rule 18-2a. He then learned of his error, dropped the ball at the spot from which it was lifted instead of replacing it as required by Rule 18-2a, and played it. What is the ruling?

18

A. The player incurred a penalty of loss of hole in match play or a total of two strokes in stroke play — see penalty statement under Rule 18.

18-2a/10 Dropped Ball Lifted and Re-Dropped When It Should Have Been Played as It Lay; Ball Then Lifted Again and Placed

Q. In stroke play, a competitor whose ball was in a lateral water hazard elected to take relief under Rule 26-1c(i). When a ball was dropped, it rolled towards the hole but came to rest not more than two club-lengths from where it first struck the ground and not nearer the hole than the point where the original ball last crossed the margin of the water hazard.

Incorrectly believing that Rule 20-2c applied, the competitor lifted the ball and re-dropped it, whereupon the ball rolled towards the hole as before. The competitor again lifted the ball, placed it where it first struck the ground when re-dropped and played his next stroke. Is the competitor penalized two strokes or four strokes?

A. Two strokes. The ball when first dropped was in play — see Rule 20-4. The competitor was in breach of Rule 18-2a when he lifted it. Because the competitor failed to replace his ball at the spot at which it came to rest when first dropped, he incurred a total penalty of two strokes — see penalty statement under Rule 18. There are a number of Decisions under which a competitor who infringes the same Rule several times prior to a stroke is penalized for only one infringement, *e.g.*, Decisions 15-3/2 and 19-2/7.

18-2a/11 Ball Wrongly Thought to Be Out of Bounds Lifted; Competitor Proceeds Under Rule 27-1

Q. In stroke play, a competitor hit his tee shot into the practice area. He thought the ball was out of bounds. He lifted the ball and proceeded under Rule 27-1. After again playing from the tee, he discovered that the practice area was not out of bounds. What is the ruling?

A. The competitor was subject to a total penalty of two strokes for lifting his ball in play and failing to replace it — see Rule 18-2a and penalty statement under Rule 18.

18

18-2a/12 Player Entitled to Relief from Condition Lifts Ball; Player Then Replaces Ball and Plays It from Original Position

Q. A player elects to take relief from an immovable obstruction or abnormal ground condition and lifts his ball. He then realizes that the only area in which he may drop under the Rules is such that his ball, when dropped, will almost certainly be unplayable. He replaces his ball and plays it from its original position. What is the ruling?

A. The player was entitled to lift the ball to take relief under Rule 24 or 25. However, by subsequently deciding not to take relief, his right to lift the ball was negated and he incurred a penalty stroke under Rule 18-2a for having lifted his ball in play.

18-2a/13 Ball Lifted Without Authority and Cleaned

Q. A player's ball comes to rest on the apron of a green. Mistakenly believing that the ball is on the green, the player marks, lifts and cleans it. The player incurs a penalty stroke under Rule 18-2a for lifting the ball without authority under the Rules. Does the player incur an additional penalty stroke under Rule 21 for cleaning the ball?

A. No. Rule 21 states that a ball may be cleaned when lifted except when it has been lifted in accordance with Rule 5-3, 12-2 or 22.

Player Lifts Ball Without Authority Due to Misunderstanding Committee Member's Instructions — See 34-3/3.5.

18-2a/14 Caddie on Own Initiative Lifts Ball for Identification

Q. During search for A's ball, A's caddie found a ball and lifted it for identification without the authority of A and without A's announcing in advance his intention to do so. The ball was identified as A's. What is the ruling?

A. Since the ball was lifted other than in accordance with the Rules, Rule 18-2a applies and A incurs a penalty of one stroke. Rule 18-2a overrides Rule 12-2 in the circumstances. Accordingly, an additional penalty of one stroke under Rule 12-2 for failing to announce the intention to lift the ball for identification purposes is not applicable.

Caddie Lifts Ball in Water Hazard Without Player's Authority — See 26-1/9.

18-2a/15 Caddie on Own Initiative Lifts Ball Considering It Unplayable

Q. A player's caddie, considering the player's ball to be in an unplayable lie, lifted the ball before the player had an opportunity to inspect the lie. What is the ruling?

A. A player's caddie may not declare the player's ball to be unplayable — Rule 28. The player incurred a penalty of one stroke under Rule 18-2a when the caddie lifted the ball. The player was obliged to replace the ball and then decide whether or not to invoke the unplayable ball Rule.

18-2a/16 Competitor's Ball Picked Up by Fellow-Competitor at Competitor's Request

Q. A competitor, mistakenly thinking his ball in play in the rough was a wrong ball, asked his fellow-competitor to pick up the ball. The fellow-competitor did so and then the error was discovered. Is the competitor subject to penalty under Rule 18-2a or exempt from penalty by virtue of Rule 18-4?

A. Because the lifting of the ball by the fellow-competitor was at the request of the competitor, it would not be correct to exonerate the competitor under Rule 18-4.

The competitor incurred a one-stroke penalty under Rule 18-2a and he was required to replace his ball.

18

18-2a/17 Towel Dropped by Player Is Blown onto and Moves Ball

Q. A player dropped a towel on the ground. The wind blew the towel onto the player's ball and moved it. What is the ruling?

A. As the player's equipment caused the ball to move, the player incurred a penalty stroke and must replace the ball — Rule 18-2a.

Ball Blown into Hole by Competitor Not Replaced and Holed Out — See 3-2/2.

18-2a/18 Opponent's Ball Knocked Away by Player After Concession Moves Player's Ball

Q. In singles match play, A concedes B's next stroke

and knocks B's ball away. B's ball in motion moves A's ball. What is the ruling?

A. As A caused his own ball to move, he incurred a penalty of one stroke under Rule 18-2a, and he must replace his ball.

18-2a/19 Ball Moved Accidentally by Practice Swing Prior to Tee Shot

Q. Before playing from the teeing ground, a player took a practice swing, in the course of which he accidentally struck and moved the teed ball with his club. Did the player play a stroke or incur a penalty?

A. The player did not make a stroke — see Definition of "Stroke." Since the ball was not in play — see Definition of "Ball in Play" — he incurred no penalty under Rule 18-2a. The player must put a ball into play from the teeing ground.

18-2a/20 Ball in Play Moved Accidentally by Practice Swing

18

Q. A player makes a practice swing and accidentally moves his ball in play with his club. Has he made a stroke?

A. No. He had no intention of moving the ball — see Definition of "Stroke."

However, he incurs a penalty stroke under Rule 18-2a for moving his ball in play, and the ball must be replaced.

Player Instinctively Throws Putter at Ball and Moves It — See 1-2/4.5.

Club Breaks During Downswing; Swing Stopped But Clubhead Falls and Moves Ball — See 14/4.

Ball Moved by Putter Dropped by Player Approaching Ball to Lift It — See 20-1/14.

Ball Moved by Ball-Marker Dropped Accidentally by Player — See 20-1/15.

Ball Moved in Removing Ball-Marker After Replacing Ball — See 20-3a/1.

Ball Accidentally Kicked by Player Asked to Lift It Due to Interference — See 22/4.

18-2a/21   Ball Moved Accidentally by Player in Playing Wrong Ball

Q. In a bunker, A plays a wrong ball. In doing so, he accidentally moves a nearby ball which turns out to be his ball. Does A incur a penalty?

A. Yes. A could have had the nearby ball lifted under Rule 22. As it is, A incurs a penalty of one stroke for moving his ball and must replace the ball on the spot from which it was moved. If the lie has been altered, it should be recreated as required by Rule 20-3b.

A does not, however, incur a penalty for playing a wrong ball in a hazard — see Rule 15.

Ball Moved by Stone Dislodged by Partner's Stroke — See 18-1/8.

Caddie Shared by Members of Opposite Sides in Four-Ball Match Moves Ball — See 30/1.

Player's Ball Moved by Partner in Playing His Own Ball — See 30-3f/9.

18

18-2a/21.3   Ball Moved Accidentally and Original Lie Altered; Player Places Ball in Wrong Place and Plays

Q. A player accidentally steps on his ball in the rough and pushes it into the ground, incurring a penalty stroke under Rule 18-2a. Instead of placing the ball in the nearest most similar lie within one club-length of the original lie as required by Rule 20-3b, the player places the ball almost two club-lengths away from the original lie and plays his next stroke.

In match play, it is clear that the player incurs the general penalty for a breach of Rule 18 or 20-3b, and loses the hole.

In stroke play, does the player incur an additional penalty of two strokes for a breach of Rule 20-3b or a total penalty of two strokes under Rule 18?

A. In stroke play, the player incurs a total penalty of two strokes under Rule 18.

Rule 18 requires replacement of a ball moved accidentally. If some other Rule — in this case Rule 20-3b — requires a moved ball to be placed somewhere else, the player is considered to be in breach of Rule 18 if he places the ball other than as prescribed by the other Rule.

18-2a/21.5 Ball Moved Accidentally; Spot Where Ball Originally Lay Not Determinable; Player Places Ball Instead of Dropping It

Q. A player accidentally moves his ball in the rough, incurring a penalty stroke under Rule 18-2a. The spot where the ball originally lay is not determinable. Instead of dropping the ball as near as possible to the spot where it originally lay as required by Rule 20-3c, the player places the ball as near as possible to that spot.

In match play, it is clear that the player incurs the general penalty for a breach of Rule 18 or 20-3c, and loses the hole.

In stroke play, does the player incur an additional penalty of two strokes for a breach of Rule 20-3c or a total penalty of two strokes under Rule 18?

A. In stroke play, the player incurs a total penalty of two strokes under Rule 18 — see Decision 18-2a/21.3.

18-2a/22 Ball Moved Accidentally by Backward Movement of Club After Stroke Misses; Ball Comes to Rest Out of Bounds

Q. A player misses a shot completely and, in swinging his club back, he accidentally knocks his ball backwards. Was the backward swing a stroke? If the ball comes to rest out of bounds, how does the player proceed?

A. The backward swing was not a stroke. A stroke is the forward movement of the club made with the intention of fairly striking at, and moving, the ball — see Definition of "Stroke."

In addition to counting the missed stroke, the player incurs a penalty stroke for moving his ball with the backward swing (Rule 18-2a), and the ball must be replaced. The fact that the ball lay out of bounds is irrelevant.

18-2a/23 Ball Knocked from Lip of Hole in Disgust

Q. In stroke play, a competitor's ball stops on the lip of the hole. In disgust the competitor knocks his ball off the green with the back of his putter. What is the ruling?

A. The competitor must replace the ball under penalty of one stroke — Rule 18-2a. The competitor is not considered to have made a stroke.

Player Jumps Close to Hole to Cause Ball to Drop and Ball Drops — See 1-2/4.

Ball Stopped by Player's Foot Moves When Foot Removed — See 19-2/1.

Ball Moves Prior to Address and Is Accidentally Stopped by Player's Club; Player Removes Club and Ball Rolls Away — See 19-2/1.5.

18

18-2a/24 Ball Moved by Flagstick Accidentally Dropped on Ball

Q. A player accidentally dropped the flagstick on his ball and moved it. The player replaced the ball. What is the ruling?

A. The player incurred a penalty of one stroke under Rule 18-2a, unless he was exempt from penalty under a specific Rule, *e.g.*, Rule 10-4 (Ball Moved in Measuring).

Rake Thrown into Bunker Before Stroke Moves Ball — See 13-4/21.

Ball Moved in Measuring to Determine If Re-Drop Required — See 20-2c/6.

[18-2a/25   Reserved]

18-2a/26   Ball Dislodged from Tree When Player Climbs Tree to Play Stroke

Q. As a player is climbing a tree to play a ball lodged in the tree, the ball falls to the ground. Does the player incur a penalty?

A. Yes, one stroke under Rule 18-2a, and the ball must be replaced.

18-2a/27   Ball Dislodged from Tree; Circumstances in Which Player Not Penalized

Q. A player whose ball is lodged high in a tree wishes to dislodge it by shaking the tree or throwing a club so that he can identify it and proceed under the unplayable ball Rule. Is this permissible?

A. Yes. The player should state his intention before taking such action to avoid any question being raised as to whether a penalty would be incurred under Rule 18-2a.

18-2a/28   Ball Dislodged from Tree; Circumstances in Which Player Penalized

Q. A player could not find his ball. Believing the ball might be lodged in a tree, he shook the tree and his ball fell to the ground. He played the ball from where it came to rest. What is the ruling?

A. The player incurred one penalty stroke under Rule 18-2a for moving his ball. He should have replaced the ball. Since he did not do so, in match play he lost the hole and in stroke play he incurred a total penalty of two strokes — see penalty statement under Rule 18.

18-2a/29   Ball Dislodged from Tree; Replacement of Ball Not Possible

Q. A player, believing his ball is lodged in a tree, shakes the tree in order to dislodge it. His ball falls to the ground. According to Decision 18-2a/28, the player incurs a penalty of one stroke under Rule 18-2a and must replace his ball. Suppose, however, that the player cannot replace his ball either:

(1) because the spot where it lay in the tree is not determinable, or

(2) because the ball fails to remain on the correct spot when replaced, or

(3) because the player cannot reach the spot where the ball lay.

How should the player proceed in each of these three circumstances?

A. Rule 20-3c and -3d would normally cover circumstances (1) and (2), but these Rules do not contemplate a situation such as the one described. Accordingly, in equity (Rule 1-4), in the first two circumstances the ball must be placed in the tree as near as possible to the spot from which it was moved, and in the third circumstance the player must proceed under the unplayable ball Rule, incurring an additional penalty stroke.

Striking at Tree Branch to Move Ball Lodged Higher in Branch — See 14/7.

18

18-2a/30 Ball Moves After Player Takes Several Practice Swings Near Ball and Touches Grass Behind Ball

Q. A player took several practice swings about one foot from his ball which was lying in light rough, and his club came in contact with the ground. He then took his stance, touched grass behind the ball with the clubhead but did not ground the club. At that point the ball moved.

The player claimed that no penalty was incurred because he had not touched a loose impediment within one club-length of the ball or addressed the ball. However, the Committee judged that the practice swings and the touching of the grass behind the ball caused the ball to move, and therefore the player incurred a penalty stroke under Rule 18-2a. Was the Committee correct?

A. It is a question of fact whether the player caused his ball to move and thus incurred a penalty under Rule 18-2a. Because of the practice swings and touching of the grass, the weight of evidence is against the player and therefore the Committee's decision was correct.

18-2a/31 Ball Touched Accidentally in Removing Loose Impediments

Q. In removing loose impediments from the vicinity of his ball lying through the green, the player accidentally touches the ball with his hand but does not move it. Is there any penalty?

A. No. Under Rule 18-2a there is only a penalty if the player, his partner or either of their caddies purposely touches the player's ball; it may be touched accidentally provided it does not move.

Ball Moved Accidentally by Foot During Removal of Loose Impediment on Putting Green — See 18-2c/1.

Holding Ball in Place While Removing Obstruction — See 24-1/4.

18-2a/32 Ball Touched with Fir Cone or Stick to Prevent Movement When Loose Impediments Removed

Q. A player placed a fir cone or stick against his ball to prevent the ball from moving when he moved some loose impediments. Is this permissible?

A. No. The player purposely touched his ball in play, contrary to Rule 18-2a, and incurred a penalty of one stroke.

Touching and Rotating Half-Buried Ball in Rough for Identification Purposes — See 12-2/2.

Touching and Rotating Half-Buried Ball in Hazard for Identification Purposes — See 12-2/3.

18-2a/33 Rotating Ball on Putting Green Without Marking Position

Q. A player rotates his ball on the putting green to line up the trademark with the hole. He did not lift the ball, mark its position or change its position. Is there a penalty?

A. Yes, one stroke for touching the ball other than as provided for in the Rules — Rule 18-2a. Under Rules 16-1b and 20-1, a ball on the putting green may be lifted (or touched and rotated) after its position has been marked. If the player had marked the position of the ball before rotating it, there would have been no penalty.

18-2b/1 Ball Moves After Stance Taken But Before Address

Q. Outside a hazard, the player took his stance but did not ground his club. The ball moved. What is the ruling?

A. As the player had not addressed the ball, he did not incur a penalty under Rule 18-2b (see Definition of "Addressing the Ball").

If, however, the player caused the ball to move, he was subject to penalty and the ball should have been replaced – Rule 18-2a.

18

18-2b/2 Ball Moves After Stance Taken in Hazard Without Club

Q. A player enters a hazard without a club and positions his feet for the purpose of determining how he wishes to play the shot. Has he taken his stance (and thus addressed the ball) so that, if the ball thereafter moves, he is subject to penalty under Rule 18-2b?

A. Yes. See Decision 13-4/24.

18-2b/3 Ball Moves While Player in Process of Taking Stance in Bunker

Q. In a bunker, a player's ball moved when he was in the process of, but had not completed, taking his stance. What is the ruling?

A. Since the ball moved before the player had addressed it (see Definition of "Addressing the Ball"), the player incurred no penalty under Rule 18-2b.

If, however, the player's approach to the ball or the act of taking his stance caused the ball to move, the player incurred a penalty stroke under Rule 18-2a and the ball must be replaced.

When Stance Taken in Bunker — See 13-4/23.

Ball Moving in Water Hazard After Address — See 14-6/1.

18-2b/4 Ball Moves After Player Grounds Club But Before Stance Completed

Q. A player's routine prior to playing a stroke is as follows: He first grounds the club directly behind the ball with his feet together. Then he gradually widens his feet to shoulder width. At that point, he makes the stroke.

If the ball moves after he grounds the club but before he widens his stance to shoulder width, does he incur a penalty stroke under Rule 18-2b (Ball Moving After Address)?

A. No. A player has not addressed the ball until he completes taking his stance, *i.e.*, his feet are essentially in the position in which he normally places them when making a stroke.

However, if the ball moved after the club was placed in position but before the player had completed taking his stance, he incurs a penalty stroke under Rule 18-2a for having caused the ball to move and must replace the ball, unless there is strong evidence that wind or some other agency caused the ball to move.

18-2b/5 When Club Grounded in Grass

Q. When is a club considered grounded in long grass?

A. When the grass is compressed to the point where it will support the weight of the club.

18-2b/6 Ball Perched on Heather Moves When Club Rested on Heather

Q. A's ball is perched on a tuft of heather. He takes his stance and rests his club on the heather behind the ball. The ball moves. What is the ruling?

A. Resting the club on heather or grass behind the ball constitutes grounding it. Accordingly, A had addressed the ball and Rule 18-2b applies. A incurs a penalty stroke and must replace his ball.

18-2b/7 Ball Moves After Player Addresses It and Then Steps Away

Q. A player takes his stance and grounds his club. Realizing that the ball is precariously balanced and may move, he steps away from the ball and starts again. This time he does not ground his club, but before he strikes the ball, it moves. What is the ruling?

A. The player incurs a penalty stroke under Rule 18-2b, and the ball must be replaced.

18-2b/8 Player Addresses Ball, Steps Away, Lifts Ball and Replaces It; Ball Then Moves

Q. On the putting green, a player addressed the ball. He stepped away from the ball, marked its position and lifted it. He then replaced the ball and, before he addressed it, the ball moved. Since the ball was lifted and out of play after it was addressed, was the player subject to penalty under Rule 18-2b when it moved after it was put back into play?

A. No. The ball must be played as it lies. Once the ball has been lifted the presumption inherent in the Rule that the act of addressing the ball caused the ball to move is no longer valid.

After Ball Addressed on Putting Green Ball Moved in Removal of Loose Impediment — See 18-2c/2.

Ball Dropped in Improper Manner Moves When Addressed; Player Then Lifts Ball and Drops It in Proper Manner — See 20-2a/4.

18-2b/9 Ball Moves After Address and Comes to Rest Out of Bounds

Q. A player's ball is lying on a slope. When he addresses the ball it moves and comes to rest out of bounds. What is the ruling?

A. If a ball moves after the player addresses it, he incurs a one-stroke penalty and the ball must be replaced — Rule 18-2b.

18-2b/10 Ball Falls into Hole After Being Addressed

Q. A player's ball is on the lip of the hole. He addresses the ball and it falls into the hole. What is the ruling?

A. If the ball was overhanging the hole and the time limit in Rule 16-2 had expired, the player incurs a penalty stroke under Rule 16-2 and he is deemed to have holed out with his last stroke. If the ball was not overhanging the hole or if the time limit had not expired, the player incurs a penalty stroke and the ball must be replaced — Rule 18-2b.

18

18-2b/11 Ball Moved by Another Ball After Being Addressed

Q. After a player has addressed his ball, a ball played from elsewhere strikes and moves the player's ball. Does Rule 18-5 supersede Rule 18-2b?

A. Yes. The player's ball must be replaced, without penalty.

18-2b/12 Ball Moves After Address and Is Stopped by Player's Club

Q. After a player addresses his ball, the ball moves backwards. Before the player can remove his club, the ball is stopped by the clubhead. What is the ruling?

A. The player incurs a penalty stroke under Rule 18-2b and the ball must be replaced. Rule 19-2 does not apply in these circumstances.

Stroke Misses Ball Which Is Then Accidentally Knocked Off Tee After Being Addressed — See 11-3/1.

Ball Addressed; Club Breaks on Downswing; Swing Stopped But Clubhead Falls and Moves Ball — See 14/4.

Provisional Ball Moves After Being Addressed — See 15/7.

Ball in Rough Moves Downward When Addressed; Ball Will Not Remain at Rest When Replaced — See 20-3d/3.

Order of Play in Foursome Match If Player Accidentally Moves Ball After Address — See 29-1/5.

18-2c/1 Ball Moved Accidentally by Foot During Removal of Loose Impediment on Putting Green

Q. A player in the process of removing a loose impediment on the putting green accidentally moved his ball with his foot. What is the ruling?

A. The player incurs a penalty stroke under Rule 18-2a, and the ball must be replaced.

Rule 18-2c provides that the player incurs no penalty if, on the putting green, his ball moves in the process of removing a loose impediment. However, this Rule applies only where the moving of a ball is directly attributable to removal of a loose impediment. In this case, removal of the loose impediment did not cause the ball to move.

18

18-2c/2 After Ball Addressed on Putting Green Ball Moved in Removal of Loose Impediment

Q. After a player addresses his ball on the putting green, an insect alights on the ball. The player bends over without moving his feet and, in attempting to brush the insect off the ball, moves the ball several inches. Is the player subject to a penalty stroke under Rule 18-2b?

A. No. An insect is a loose impediment — see Definition of "Loose Impediments" and Decision 23-1/5.

Under Rule 18-2c, a player incurs no penalty if a ball

on the putting green moves while he is in the process of removing a loose impediment.

Rule 18-2c supersedes Rule 18-2b in this case.

Ball in Hazard Moves When Loose Impediment Removed — See 13-4/15.

Loose Impediments Affecting Lie Removed While Ball Lifted — See 23-1/8.

18-2c/3 Loose Impediments Within One Club-Length Removed; Ball Lifted and Replaced; Ball Moves Before Address

Q. A player removed loose impediments within a few inches of his ball lying through the green, lifted the ball because it interfered with the opponent's play and, after the opponent played, replaced his ball. Before the player addressed the ball, it moved. Since the ball was lifted and out of play after the loose impediments were removed, is the player penalized under Rule 18-2c?

A. No. The ball must be played as it lies. Once the ball has been lifted, the presumption inherent in the Rule that the removal of the loose impediments caused the ball to move is no longer valid.

Competitor Seeks Help in Removal of Loose Impediment to Avoid Penalty — See 33-7/7.

18-3b/1 Ball Moved Accidentally by Opponent in Playing His Own Ball

Q. In singles match play, A's ball is lying close to B's. It is B's turn to play. Although B has the right under Rule 22 to require A to mark and lift his ball, he fails to do so. In making a stroke at his ball, B causes A's ball to move. What is the procedure?

A. B incurs a penalty of one stroke under Rule 18-3b for moving A's ball and A must replace his ball. If A's lie has been altered, Rule 20-3b applies.

Ball Moved by Stone Dislodged by Opponent's Stroke — See 18-1/8.

18

18-3b/2 Opponent's Stroke Disturbs Bushes Causing Player's Ball to Move

Q. In playing a stroke, an opponent disturbed some bushes, causing the player's ball to move. What is the ruling?

A. The opponent incurs a penalty stroke (Rule 18-3b) and the player must replace his ball.

18-3b/3 Ball Accidentally Stepped on by Opponent's Caddie

Q. The opponent's caddie accidentally stepped on the player's ball. What is the ruling?

A. The opponent incurs a one-stroke penalty (Rule 18-3b) unless the caddie was searching for the ball, in which case there would be no penalty — Rule 18-3a.

18-3b/4 Opponent's Caddie Lifts Player's Ball After Player Claims Another Ball

Q. In a match, the player finds a ball and claims it as his. The opponent's caddie then finds another ball and lifts it. It is subsequently discovered that the ball the opponent's caddie lifted was the player's ball. Should the opponent incur a penalty under Rule 18-3b?

A. No. Rule 18-3b does not contemplate an opponent moving a player's ball in such circumstances. The player must replace his ball, without penalty to anyone.

18

18-3b/5 Opponent's Caddie Lifts Player's Ball Which May or May Not Have Been Out of Bounds

Q. An opponent's caddie lifted the player's ball and informed the player that the ball was out of bounds. The player claimed that his ball might have been in bounds. What is the ruling?

A. If the Committee establishes that the ball was in bounds, the opponent incurs a penalty stroke under Rule 18-3b and the player must replace his ball.

If the ball was out of bounds, the opponent incurs no penalty.

If the position of the ball cannot be established, the benefit of the doubt should be given to the player.

Player Mistakenly Believing She Has Won Match Picks Up Opponent's Ball — See 2-4/4 and 2-4/17.

Ball Resting Against Flagstick; Putt Conceded and Ball Removed Before Player Can Remove Flagstick — See 17-4/2.

Ball Resting Against Flagstick Moves Away from Hole When Opponent Removes Flagstick — See 17-4/3.

Player's Ball Lifted by Opponent Without Authority — See 20-1/2.

Player's Ball Lifted by Opponent Without Authority; Player Lifts Ball-Marker, Claims Hole and Opponent Disputes Claim — See 20-1/3.

Caddie Shared by Members of Opposite Sides in Four-Ball Match Moves Ball — See 30/1.

Caddie Shared by Opponents' Side in Four-Ball Match Moves Player's Ball — See 30/2.

Player's Ball Lifted by Opponent Without Authority in Four-Ball Match — See 30-3f/10.

18

18-4/1 Competitor's Ball Played by Fellow-Competitor in Bunker Not Replaced

Q. In stroke play, A's ball in a bunker was played by his fellow-competitor, B. B failed to get the ball out of the bunker and then discovered he had played a wrong ball. A played his ball from the spot to which B had played it and then learned that he should have replaced his ball. What is the ruling?

A. Rule 18-4 required A to replace his ball. A incurred a penalty of two strokes for a breach of Rule 18-4 when he played a stroke with his ball from the spot to which it had been played by B.

B incurred no penalty. There is no penalty for playing a stroke with a wrong ball in a hazard.

18-4/2 Competitor's Ball Knocked Out of Bunker by Fellow-Competitor's Stroke at Own Ball

Q. In stroke play, B, in playing a stroke at his ball in a bunker, accidentally hits A's ball which was also in the bunker. Both balls come to rest outside the bunker. A plays his ball from the spot to which it has been moved by B's stroke. What is the ruling?

A. A was required to replace his ball in the bunker — Rule 18-4. A's breach of Rule 18-4 was a serious one and he should have been disqualified under Rule 20-7b unless the serious breach was rectified as prescribed in that Rule. B incurred no penalty — Rule 18-4.

Fellow-Competitor's Ball Knocked from Lip of Hole by Competitor Not Replaced — See 3-2/1.

18-4/3 Fellow-Competitor Lifts Competitor's Ball Conceding Next Stroke in Stroke Play Play-Off

Q. In a stroke play play-off, B picks up A's ball, conceding A a 4. B then holed a putt for a 3 to win the play-off. Is B subject to penalty for conceding a putt in stroke play?

A. B incurs no penalty — Rule 18-4. If B had not holed in 3 to win the play-off, A would have been obliged to replace his ball and hole out (Rule 18-4).

Ball Resting Against Flagstick Moves Away from Hole When Flagstick Removed by Fellow-Competitor — See 17-4/3.

Competitor's Ball Picked Up by Fellow-Competitor at Competitor's Request — See 18-2a/16.

Competitor's Ball Lifted Without Authority by Fellow-Competitor — See 20-1/4.

18-5/1 Ball Moved by Wrong Ball Played by Opponent

Q. In match play, an opponent plays a wrong ball from a bunker and the wrong ball knocks the player's ball into the hole. What is the ruling?

A. No penalty is incurred and the player must replace his ball — Rule 18-5.

Opponent's Ball Knocked Away by Player After Concession Moves Player's Ball — See 18-2a/18.

Ball Moved by Another Ball After Being Addressed — See 18-2b/11.

Competitor's Ball Played from Putting Green Moves Ball on Green Belonging to Competitor Playing in Another Group — See 19-5/2.

18-5/2 Original Ball Struck by Provisional Ball

Q. A player's provisional ball played from the tee strikes and moves his original ball. What is the ruling?

A. There is no penalty. The original ball must be replaced — Rule 18-5.

Original Ball Strikes Second Ball or Vice Versa — See 3-3/7.

Provisional Ball Struck by Original Ball — See 19-5/5.

18

Rule 19. Ball in Motion Deflected or Stopped

Definitions

An "outside agency" is any agency not part of the match or, in stroke play, not part of the competitor's side, and includes a referee, a marker, an observer or a forecaddie. Neither wind nor water is an outside agency.

"Equipment" is anything used, worn or carried by or for the player except any ball he has played at the hole being played and any small object, such as a coin or a tee, when used to mark the position of a ball or the extent of an area in which a ball is to be dropped. Equipment includes a golf cart, whether or not motorized. If such a cart is shared by two or more players, the cart and everything in it are deemed to be the equipment of the player whose ball is involved except that, when the cart is being moved by one of the players sharing it, the cart and everything in it are deemed to be that player's equipment.

Note: A ball played at the hole being played is equipment when it has been lifted and not put back into play.

19-1. By Outside Agency

If a ball in motion is accidentally deflected or stopped by any <u>outside agency</u>, it is a <u>rub of the green</u>, no penalty is incurred and the ball shall be played as it lies except:

a. If a ball in motion after a stroke other than on the <u>putting green</u> comes to rest in or on any moving or animate outside agency, the player shall, <u>through the green</u> or in a <u>hazard</u>, drop the ball, or on the putting green place the ball, as near as possible to the spot where the outside agency was when the ball came to rest in or on it, and

b. If a ball in motion after a stroke on the putting green is deflected or stopped by, or comes to rest in or on, any moving or animate outside agency except a worm or an insect, the stroke shall be cancelled, the ball replaced and the stroke replayed.

If the ball is not immediately recoverable, another ball may be substituted.

(Player's ball deflected or stopped by another ball — see Rule 19-5.)

Note: If the referee or the Committee determines that a player's ball has been purposely deflected or stopped by an <u>outside agency</u>, Rule 1-4 applies to the player. If the outside agency is a fellow-competitor or his caddie, Rule 1-2 applies to the fellow-competitor.

19-2. By Player, Partner, Caddie or Equipment

a. MATCH PLAY

If a player's ball is accidentally deflected or stopped by himself, his partner or either of their caddies or <u>equipment</u>, *he shall lose the hole.*

b. STROKE PLAY

If a competitor's ball is accidentally deflected or stopped by himself, his partner or either of their caddies or <u>equipment</u>, *the competitor shall incur a penalty of two strokes.* The ball shall be played as it lies, except when it comes to rest in or on the competitor's, his partner's or either of their caddies' clothes or equipment, in which case the competitor shall <u>through the green</u> or in a <u>hazard</u> drop the ball, or on the <u>putting green</u> place the ball, as near as possible to where the article was when the ball came to rest in or on it.

Exception: Dropped ball — see Rule 20-2a.

(Ball purposely deflected or stopped by player, partner or caddie — see Rule 1-2.)

19-3. By Opponent, Caddie or Equipment in Match Play

If a player's ball is accidentally deflected or stopped by an opponent, his caddie or his <u>equipment</u>, no penalty is incurred. The player may play the ball as it lies or, before another <u>stroke</u> is played by either side, cancel the stroke and play a ball without penalty as nearly as possible at the spot from which the original ball was last played (see Rule 20-5). If the ball has come to rest in or on the opponent's or his caddie's clothes or equipment, the player may <u>through the green</u> or in a <u>hazard</u> drop the ball, or on the putting green place the ball, as near as possible to where the article was when the ball came to rest in or on it.

Exception: Ball striking person attending flagstick — see Rule 17-3b.

(Ball purposely deflected or stopped by opponent or caddie — see Rule 1-2.)

19-4. By Fellow-Competitor, Caddie or Equipment in Stroke Play

See Rule 19-1 regarding ball deflected by outside agency.

19-5. By Another Ball

If a player's ball in motion after a stroke is deflected or stopped by a ball at rest, the player shall play his ball as it lies. In stroke play, if both balls lay on the <u>putting green</u> prior to the stroke, *the player incurs a penalty of two strokes*. Otherwise, no penalty is incurred.

If a player's ball in motion after a stroke is deflected or stopped by another ball in motion, the player shall play his ball as it lies. There is no penalty unless the player was in breach

19

of Rule 16-1g, in which case *he shall incur the penalty for breach of that Rule.*

Exception: Ball in motion after a stroke on the putting green deflected or stopped by moving or animate outside agency — see Rule 19-1b.

PENALTY FOR BREACH OF RULE:
Match play --- Loss of hole;
Stroke play --- Two strokes.

19/1 Ball Deflected or Stopped by Golf Cart Shared by Two Players

Under the Definition of "Equipment," equipment includes a golf cart, whether or not motorized. If two players share a golf cart, the cart and everything in it are deemed to be the equipment of the player whose ball is involved; except that, when the cart is being moved by one of the players, the cart and everything in it are deemed to be that player's equipment.

Thus, for example, in a singles match, if A and B are sharing a cart and A's ball in motion is deflected or stopped by the cart, A loses the hole (Rule 19-2a) unless the cart is being driven or pulled by B when the incident occurs. If B is driving or pulling the cart, there is no penalty, and A would have the option of playing his ball as it lies or replaying the stroke (Rule 19-3).

19-1/1 Ball Deflected by Direction Post

Q. A ball is deflected by a direction post. What is the ruling?

A. It is a rub of the green and the ball must be played as it lies, without penalty.

19-1/2 Player's Ball Deflected by Stroke of Player in Another Group

Q. A hit his ball over onto another fairway where,

before it came to rest, it was struck by X in the course of striking his own ball. X's ball went 20 yards. A's ball could not be found. What is the ruling?

A. Each player was an outside agency in relation to the other.

Under Rule 19-1, A would have been obliged to play his ball as it lay, without penalty, if it had been found. Since it was not found, A must proceed under Rule 27-1, incurring a penalty of stroke and distance.

X must play his ball as it lies, without penalty.

Ball Played from Spot Where Original Ball Deflected Out of Bounds by Maintenance Vehicle — See 20-7/1.

19-1/3 Ball Played from Putting Green Deflected into Hole by Moving Outside Agency; Stroke Not Replayed

Q. In stroke play, a competitor putts and his ball is deflected into the hole by a moving outside agency other than a worm or an insect. The competitor did not replay the stroke as required by Rule 19-1b and played from the next tee. What is the ruling?

A. The competitor is disqualified under Rule 3-2 for failing to hole out.

19

19-1/4 Ball Deliberately Deflected or Stopped on Putting Green by Spectator

Q. A player plays a stroke on the putting green and, while the ball is still in motion, a spectator deliberately deflects or stops it. What is the ruling?

A. The Committee must act in equity — see Note under Rule 19-1. The stroke should be canceled and the ball should be replaced, without penalty.

19-1/4.1 Ball Deliberately Deflected or Stopped Through the Green by Spectator

Q. A player overshoots a green. A spectator (X) who is standing behind the green deliberately deflects or stops the ball. According to the Note under Rule 19-1, equity (Rule 1-4) applies. What is the equitable procedure in this case?

A. In a case where the ball might have come to rest where X was situated if he had not deliberately deflected or stopped it, the player should be required to drop the ball at the spot where X was situated. For example, if another spectator (Y) had been behind X, the ball might have struck Y, if X had avoided it, and come to rest where X was situated.

If there is no question that the ball would have come to rest somewhere else if X had not deflected or stopped it, the Committee must make a judgment as to where the ball would have come to rest, giving the player the benefit of any doubt. For example, if no person or object had been behind X and without any doubt the ball would have come to rest either in a lateral water hazard behind the green or in the rough just short of the hazard, the Committee should require the player to drop the ball in the rough just short of the hazard.

19-1/5 Ball Deliberately Deflected or Stopped on Putting Green by Fellow-Competitor

Q. At the last hole of a stroke play event, A has a putt to beat B by one stroke. A putts and B, seeing that A's ball might go into the hole, deliberately deflects it. What is the ruling?

A. In equity (Rule 1-4), A should replay his stroke, without penalty — see Note under Rule 19-1. B should be disqualified for a serious breach of Rule 1-2 (Exerting Influence on Ball).

19-1/6 Ball Picked Up or Deflected by Dog on Putting Green After Stroke from Off Green

Q. A ball played from off the green was about a foot from the hole and still in motion when it was moved by a dog to a spot about ten feet from the hole. The ball was either deflected by the dog or the dog picked it up, ran with it and dropped it. What is the ruling?

A. If the ball was deflected, it would be played as it lay, without penalty, from the spot to which it was moved by the dog — Rule 19-1.

If the dog picked up the ball, the player should have placed the ball, without penalty, as near as possible to the spot where the original ball was when the dog picked it up — Rule 19-1a.

19-1/7 Ball Picked Up or Deflected by Dog on Putting Green After Stroke on Green

Q. A player plays a stroke on the putting green and, while the ball is still in motion, it is picked up and carried away, or is deflected, by a dog. What is the ruling?

A. In either case, the stroke is canceled and the ball must be replaced — Rule 19-1b.

[19-1/8 Reserved]

[19-1/9 Reserved]

19-1/10 Ball in Motion After Stroke on Putting Green Deflected by Ball Played at Another Hole

Q. A player plays a stroke on a putting green. While the ball is in motion, a ball played at another hole strikes the player's ball and knocks it into a bunker. What is the ruling?

A. Since the player's ball was deflected by a moving outside agency, the player's stroke is canceled and he must replace his ball — Rule 19-1b. Rule 19-5, second paragraph, does not apply — see Exception under that Rule.

Ball Strikes Hole-Liner Pulled Out with Flagstick — See 17/8.

Attendant Removes Flagstick Whereupon Knob Falls from Top of Flagstick and Deflects Ball — See 17/9.

19-2/1 Ball Stopped by Player's Foot Moves When Foot Removed

Q. A player making a stroke on the bank of a bunker hits the ball to the top of the bank. The ball then rolls back down the bank and comes to rest against the player's foot. The player removes his foot and the ball rolls into his footprint. What is the ruling?

A. In match play, the player loses the hole (Rule 19-2a).

In stroke play, the player incurs a penalty of two strokes (Rule 19-2b) and must replace the ball on the spot at which it came to rest against his foot. A further penalty under Rule 18-2a (Ball at Rest Moved by Player) would not be appropriate in the circumstances.

19-2/1.5 Ball Moves Prior to Address and Is Accidentally Stopped by Player's Club; Player Removes Club and Ball Rolls Away

Q. A player's ball lies on a steep slope through the green. The player takes his stance but, fearing the ball might move, does not ground his club and so has not addressed the ball. The ball rolls backwards and is stopped accidentally by the player's club. The player then removes his club and the ball rolls farther down the slope. Is the player subject to penalty under Rule 19-2?

A. Yes, and in stroke play the ball must be replaced on the spot at which it was stopped. A further penalty under Rule 18-2a (Ball at Rest Moved by Player) would not be appropriate in the circumstances.

Ball Moves After Address and Is Stopped by Player's Club — See 18-2b/12.

19-2/2 Player's Ball Strikes Own Caddie and Comes to Rest Out of Bounds

Q. A player's ball accidentally strikes his caddie, who is standing in bounds, and the ball comes to rest out of bounds. What is the ruling?

A. In match play, the player loses the hole — Rule 19-2a.

In stroke play, the player incurs a penalty of two strokes (Rule 19-2b) and, since the ball lies out of bounds, he must proceed under Rule 27-1, incurring another penalty stroke.

19-2/3 Player's Ball Strikes Own Caddie Standing Out of Bounds and Comes to Rest on Course

Q. A player's ball accidentally strikes his caddie standing out of bounds and comes to rest in bounds. What is the ruling?

A. In match play, the player loses the hole — Rule 19-2a.

In stroke play, the player incurs a penalty of two strokes and, since the ball came to rest in bounds, it is in play -Rule 19-2b.

19-2/4 Player's Ball Strikes Own Caddie Standing Out of Bounds and Comes to Rest Out of Bounds

19

Q. A player's ball accidentally strikes his caddie standing out of bounds and comes to rest out of bounds. What is the ruling?

A. In match play, the player loses the hole — Rule 19-2a.

In stroke play, the player incurs a penalty of two strokes (Rule 19-2b) and, since the ball lies out of bounds, he must proceed under Rule 27-1, incurring another penalty stroke.

Ball Falls on Club Face After Stroke and Sticks to Mud Thereon — See 14-4/1.

Ball Strikes Pipeline and on Rebound Is Deflected by Face of Club — See 14-4/2.

Caddie Stops Dropped Ball Before It Comes to Rest; When Penalty Incurred — See 20-2c/4.

19-2/5 Ball Deflected or Stopped by Clubs Belonging to Different Side But Carried in Same Bag

Q. A had his bag of clubs on a golf cart. B had only a few clubs which A carried for him in his bag. B played a stroke which was deflected by the clubs. What is the ruling?

A. Under the principle in the Definition of "Caddie," the clubs should be deemed B's equipment.

In match play, B lost the hole — Rule 19-2a.

In stroke play, B incurred a penalty of two strokes and must play his ball as it lies — Rule 19-2b.

19-2/6 Ball Deflected or Stopped by Player's Golf Cart Being Pulled by Opponent or Fellow-Competitor

Q. A player's ball strikes his own golf cart while it is being pulled by an opponent or a fellow-competitor. What is the ruling?

A. Since the player is not sharing the cart with any other player, it remains his equipment even when it is being pulled by an opponent or a fellow-competitor.

If the player was aware that his cart was being pulled by an opponent or a fellow-competitor, in match play the player loses the hole — Rule 19-2a. In stroke play, he incurs a penalty of two strokes and must play the ball as it lies — Rule 19-2b.

But if he was not aware, in equity (Rule 1-4) no penalty is incurred, and the ball must be played as it lies.

19-2/7 Ball Strikes Competitor's Golf Bag and Then His Caddie

Q. In stroke play, a competitor's ball strikes his golf bag lying on the ground and then bounces off it and hits his caddie. Is the penalty two strokes or four strokes?

A. Two strokes — Rule 19-2b.

Ball Popped Up Swung at in Disgust and Hit — See 14/6.

19-3/1 Ball Accidentally Strikes Opponent Standing Out of Bounds and Comes to Rest Out of Bounds

Q. In match play, a player's ball accidentally strikes his opponent, who is standing out of bounds. The ball comes to rest out of bounds. What is the ruling?

A. There is no penalty and the player is entitled to replay the stroke — Rule 19-3.

Tee Marking Position of Player's Ball Deflects Opponent's Ball — See 20-1/17.

19-3/2 Dropped Ball Accidentally Deflected by Opponent or His Caddie

Q. In match play, a player drops his ball under a Rule and the ball is accidentally deflected by the opponent or his caddie. What is the ruling?

A. The player has the option of playing his ball as it lies or re-dropping it — Rule 19-3.

19-5/1 Player Lifts His Ball on Putting Green and Sets It Aside; Opponent's or Fellow-Competitor's Ball Played from Green Subsequently Strikes Player's Ball

19

Q. B lifts his ball on the putting green and sets it aside elsewhere on the green. A then putts and his ball is deflected or stopped by B's ball. What is the ruling?

A. In match play, A must play his ball as it lies, without penalty — Rule 19-5.

In stroke play, A incurs a penalty of two strokes and he must play his ball as it lies — Rule 19-5.

In either form of play, B must replace his ball on the spot from which it was lifted — Rule 20-3a.

Although the Note under Definition of "Equipment" states that the ball which has been lifted and not put

back into play is equipment, Rule 19-5, which specifically applies when a ball in motion after a stroke is
deflected by a ball at rest, overrides Rules 19-3 and -4
in this case. (Revised)

Explanation of "Any Ball He Has Played" — See 18/7.

19-5/1.5 After Player Putts Opponent or Fellow-Competitor Drops His Ball; Player's Ball Strikes Opponent's or Fellow-Competitor's Ball After It Is at Rest

Q. A plays a stroke on the putting green. B, A's opponent or fellow-competitor, then accidentally drops
his ball, which he had lifted. A's ball strikes B's ball
after B's ball has come to rest. What is the ruling?

A. In match play, A must play his ball as it lies —
Rule 19-5, first paragraph. Neither A nor B incurs a
penalty.

In stroke play, A must play his ball as it lies — Rule
19-5, first paragraph. A incurs no penalty because B's
ball did not lie on the putting green prior to A's stroke.
B also incurs no penalty.

In either form of play, B must replace his ball on the
spot from which it was lifted — Rule 20-3a.

Although the Note under Definition of "Equipment"
states that a ball which has been lifted and not put
back into play is equipment, Rule 19-5, which specifically applies when a ball in motion after a stroke is
deflected by a ball at rest, overrides Rules 19-3 and -4
in this case. (Revised)

Explanation of "Any Ball He Has Played" — See 18/7.

19-5/1.7 Ball Dropped on Putting Green by Opponent or Fellow-Competitor Falls on Player's Moving Ball

Q. A plays a stroke on the putting green. B, A's opponent or a fellow-competitor, accidentally drops his
ball, which he had lifted, and it falls on A's ball which
is still in motion. What is the ruling?

A. In match play, A must play his ball as it lies — Rule 19-5, second paragraph. Neither A nor B incurs a penalty.

In stroke play, B's ball was an outside agency. Since A's ball was deflected by a moving outside agency, A must replay his stroke without penalty under Rule 19-1b — see Exception under Rule 19-5. B incurs no penalty.

In either form of play, B must replace his ball on the spot from which it was lifted — Rule 20-3a.

Although the Note under Definition of "Equipment" states that a ball which has been lifted and not put back into play is equipment, Rule 19-5, which specifically applies when a ball in motion after a stroke is deflected by a ball at rest, overrides Rules 19-3 and -4 in this case. (Revised)

Explanation of "Any Ball He Has Played" — See 18/7.

19-5/2 Competitor's Ball Played from Putting Green Strikes Ball on Green Belonging to Competitor Playing in Another Group

Q. In stroke play, C and D are playing together. A and B are playing immediately behind C and D. C's ball lies on the putting green and, since D is searching for his ball, C and D invite A and B to play through. Subsequently, A putts and his ball strikes C's ball. What is the ruling?

A. A incurs a penalty of two strokes and must play his ball as it lies — Rule 19-5. C must replace his ball without penalty — Rule 18-5.

19-5/3 Competitor's Ball Played on Putting Green Deflected by Balls of Two Fellow-Competitors

Q. In stroke play, a competitor plays a stroke on the putting green. His ball strikes a fellow-competitor's ball and is deflected. Before the competitor's ball comes to rest it strikes another fellow-competitor's ball. Under Rule 19-5, is the competitor penalized two strokes or four strokes?

A. Two strokes.

19-5/4 Competitor's Ball Played from Putting Green Touches But Does Not Move Ball of Fellow-Competitor Lying on Green

Q. In stroke play, A putts and his ball comes to rest touching B's ball. B's ball did not move nor did B's ball prevent A's ball from rolling any farther. What is the ruling?

A. Since A's ball was not deflected or stopped by B's ball, A incurs no penalty under Rule 19-5 or any other Rule. However, if there is any doubt as to whether B's ball moved or prevented A's ball from rolling any farther, it should be resolved against A.

19-5/5 Provisional Ball Struck by Original Ball

Q. A player's original ball strikes and moves his provisional ball. What is the ruling?

A. There is no penalty except that, in stroke play, if both balls lay on the putting green prior to the stroke, the player incurs a penalty of two strokes. The original ball must be played as it lies.

Original Ball Strikes Second Ball or Vice Versa — See 3-3/7.

Competitor Not Given Opportunity to Lift Ball Assisting Fellow-Competitor; Fellow-Competitor's Ball Strikes Competitor's Ball — See 3-4/1.

Explanation of "Any Ball He Has Played" — See 18/7.

Player's Ball Moved by Ball Accidentally Dropped by Opponent or Fellow-Competitor — See 18/7.5.

Provisional Ball Strikes Original Ball — See 18-5/2.

RELIEF SITUATIONS AND PROCEDURE

Rule 20. Lifting, Dropping and Placing; Playing from Wrong Place

20-1. Lifting

A ball to be lifted under the Rules may be lifted by the player, his partner or another person authorized by the player. In any such case, the player shall be responsible for any breach of the Rules.

The position of the ball shall be marked before it is lifted under a Rule which requires it to be replaced. If it is not marked, *the player shall incur a penalty of one stroke* and the ball shall be replaced. If it is not replaced, *the player shall incur the general penalty* for breach of this Rule but no additional penalty under Rule 20-1 shall be applied.

If a ball or the ball-marker is accidentally moved in the process of lifting the ball under a Rule or marking its position, the ball or the ball-marker shall be replaced. There is no penalty provided the movement of the ball or the ball-marker is directly attributable to the specific act of marking the position of or lifting the ball. Otherwise, the player shall incur a penalty stroke under this Rule or Rule 18-2a.

Exception: If a player incurs a penalty for

20

failing to act in accordance with Rule 5-3 or 12-2, no additional penalty under Rule 20-1 shall be applied.

Note: The position of a ball to be lifted should be marked by placing a ball-marker, a small coin or other similar object immediately behind the ball. If the ball-marker interferes with the play, <u>stance</u> or <u>stroke</u> of another player, it should be placed one or more clubhead-lengths to one side.

20-2. Dropping and Re-dropping

a. BY WHOM AND HOW A ball to be dropped under the Rules shall be dropped by the player himself. He shall stand erect, hold the ball at shoulder height and arm's length and drop it. If a ball is dropped by any other person or in any other manner and the error is not corrected as provided in Rule 20-6, *the player shall incur a penalty stroke.*

If the ball touches the player, his partner, either of their caddies or their equipment before or after it strikes a part of the course, the ball shall be re-dropped, without penalty. There is no limit to the number of times a ball shall be re-dropped in such circumstances.

(Taking action to influence position or movement of ball — see Rule 1-2.)

20

b. WHERE TO DROP

When a ball is to be dropped as near as possible to a specific spot, it shall be dropped not nearer the hole than the specific spot which, if it is not precisely known to the player, shall be estimated.

A ball when dropped must first strike a part of the course where the applicable Rule requires it to be dropped. If it is not so dropped, Rules 20-6 and -7 apply.

c. WHEN TO RE-DROP

A dropped ball shall be re-dropped without penalty if it:

(i) rolls into a <u>hazard</u>;

(ii) rolls out of a hazard;

(iii) rolls onto a <u>putting green</u>;

(iv) rolls <u>out of bounds</u>;

(v) rolls to a position where there is interference by the condition from which relief was taken under Rule 24-2 (immovable obstruction) or Rule 25-1 (abnormal ground condition);

(vi) rolls and comes to rest more than two club-lengths from where it first struck a part of the course; or

(vii) rolls and comes to rest nearer the hole than its original position or estimated position (see Rule 20-2b) unless otherwise permitted by the Rules. If the ball when re-dropped rolls into any position listed above, it shall be placed as near as possible to the spot where it first struck a part of the course when re-dropped.

If a ball to be re-dropped or placed under this Rule is not immediately recoverable, another ball may be substituted.

20-3. Placing and Replacing

a. BY WHOM AND WHERE

A ball to be placed under the Rules shall be placed by the player or his partner. If a ball is to be replaced, the player, his partner or the person who lifted or moved it shall place it on the spot from which it was lifted or moved. In any such case, the player shall be responsible for any breach of the Rules.

If a ball or the ball-marker is accidentally moved in the process of placing or replacing the ball, the ball or the ball-marker shall be replaced. There is no penalty provided the movement of the ball or the ball-marker is directly attributable to the specific act of placing or replacing the ball or removing the ball-marker. Otherwise, the player shall incur a penalty stroke under Rule 18-2a or 20-1.

20

b. LIE OF BALL TO BE PLACED OR RE-PLACED ALTERED

If the original lie of a ball to be placed or replaced has been altered:

(i) except in a <u>hazard</u>, the ball shall be placed in the nearest lie most similar to the original lie which is not more than one club-length from the original lie, not nearer the hole and not in a hazard;

(ii) in a <u>water hazard</u>, the ball shall be placed in accordance with Clause (i) above, except that the ball must be placed in the water hazard;

(iii) in a <u>bunker</u>, the original lie shall be recreated as nearly as possible and the ball shall be placed in that lie.

c. SPOT NOT DETERMINABLE

If it is impossible to determine the spot where the ball
is to be placed or replaced:

(i) <u>through the green</u>, the ball shall be dropped as near as possible to the place where it lay but not in a <u>hazard</u>;

(ii) in a hazard, the ball shall be dropped in the hazard as near as possible to the place where it lay;

(iii) on the <u>putting green</u>, the ball shall be placed as near as possible to the place where it lay but not in a hazard.

d. BALL FAILS TO REMAIN ON SPOT

If a ball when placed fails to remain on the spot on which it was placed, it shall be re-placed without penalty. If it still fails to remain on that spot:

(i) except in a <u>hazard</u>, it shall be placed at the nearest spot not nearer the hole or in a hazard where it can be placed at rest;

(ii) in a hazard, it shall be placed in the hazard at the nearest spot not nearer the hole where it can be placed at rest.

PENALTY FOR BREACH
OF RULE 20-1, -2 or -3:
Match play --- Loss of hole;
Stroke play --- Two strokes.

20-4. When Ball Dropped or Placed Is in Play

If the player's <u>ball in play</u> has been lifted, it is again in play when dropped or placed.

A substituted ball becomes the ball in play if it is dropped or placed under an applicable Rule, whether or not such Rule permits substitution. A ball substituted under an inapplicable Rule is a <u>wrong ball</u>.

20-5. Playing Next Stroke from Where Previous Stroke Played

When, under the Rules, a player elects or is required to play his next <u>stroke</u> from where a previous stroke was played, he shall proceed as follows: If the stroke is to be played from the teeing ground, the ball to be played shall be played from anywhere within the <u>teeing ground</u> and may be teed; if the stroke is to be played from <u>through the green</u> or a <u>hazard</u>, it shall be dropped; if the stroke is to be played on the putting green, it shall be placed.

PENALTY FOR BREACH OF RULE 20-5:
Match play --- Loss of hole;
Stroke play --- Two strokes.

20

20-6. Lifting Ball Wrongly Dropped or Placed

A ball dropped or placed in a wrong place or otherwise not in accordance with the Rules but not played may be lifted, without penalty, and the player shall then proceed correctly.

20-7. Playing from Wrong Place

For a ball played from outside the teeing ground or from a wrong teeing ground — see Rule 11-4 and -5.

a. MATCH PLAY

If a player plays a stroke with a ball which has been dropped or placed in a wrong place, *he shall lose the hole.*

b. STROKE PLAY

If a competitor plays a stroke with (i) his original ball which has been dropped or placed in a wrong place, (ii) a substituted ball which has been dropped or placed under an applicable Rule but in a wrong place or (iii) his ball in play when it has been moved and not replaced in a case where the Rules require replacement, *he shall,* provided a serious breach has not occurred, *incur the penalty prescribed by the applicable Rule* and play out the hole with the ball.

If, after playing from a wrong place, a competitor becomes aware of that fact and believes that a serious breach may be involved, he may, provided he has not played a stroke from the next teeing ground or, in the case of the last hole of the round, left the putting green, declare that he will play out the hole with a second ball dropped or placed in accordance with the Rules. The competitor shall report the facts to the Committee before returning his score card; if he fails to do so, *he shall be disqualified.* The Committee shall determine whether a serious breach of the Rule occurred. If so, the score with the second ball shall count and *the competitor shall add two penalty strokes to his score with that ball.*

If a serious breach has occurred and the competitor has failed to correct it as prescribed above, *he shall be disqualified.*

Note: If a competitor plays a second ball, penalty strokes incurred by playing the ball ruled not to count and strokes subsequently taken with that ball shall be disregarded.

20/1 Club to Be Used in Measuring Club-Length

Q. A player, taking relief under a Rule, uses his driver to measure the one club-length or two club-lengths prescribed in the relevant Rule. He drops a ball correctly and the ball rolls less than two driver-lengths, but more than two putter-lengths, from where the ball first struck the ground when dropped.

Under Rule 20-2c, a dropped ball must be re-dropped if it rolls more than two club-lengths. If the ball comes to rest in a poor lie, may the player opt to use his putter to measure the distance his ball has rolled, in which case he would re-drop under Rule 20-2c and escape the poor lie?

A. No. A player may use any club in measuring, including a club belonging to a partner, an opponent or a fellow-competitor, but he must continue to use that club for all measuring required in the given situation.

20-1/0.5 Whether Player Himself Must Lift Ball

Q. Rule 20-1 states: "A ball to be lifted under the Rules may be lifted by the player, his partner or another person authorized by the player." On the other hand, other rules, *e.g.*, Rules 24-2b (i) and 25-1b (i), state that the player shall lift the ball. Does Rule 20-1 override other Rules which imply that the player himself must lift the ball?

A. Yes.

20

20-1/1 Ball Lifted from Putting Green in Mistaken Belief It Is Wrong Ball

Q. A player, mistakenly believing the ball he has played onto a putting green is a wrong ball, picks the ball up without marking its position. He then discovers that the ball is his ball in play. What is the ruling?

A. The player incurs a penalty stroke and he must replace his ball (Rule 20-1).

20-1/2 Player's Ball Lifted by Opponent Without Authority

Q. In a match between A and B, B, without A's authority, marked the position of, and lifted, A's ball on the putting green. Is B subject to penalty?

A. Yes. Under Rule 20-1, a player's ball may be lifted by his opponent only with the authority of the player. Since B was not entitled to lift A's ball, B incurred a penalty stroke — Rule 18-3b.

Player's Ball Lifted Without Authority by Opponent in Four-Ball Match — See 30-3f/10.

Player Lifts Ball in Mistaken Belief That Next Stroke Conceded — See 2-4/3.

Player Concedes Match Due to Misconception as to Opponent's Score at Last Hole and Picks Up Ball — See 2-4/14.

Player Lifts Ball, Sets It Aside and Plays It from Where Set Aside — See 15/4.

Ball Resting Against Flagstick Lifted Before Being Holed — See 17-4/1.

Player's Ball Resting Against Flagstick Lifted Before Being Holed; Others in Four-Ball Match Pick Up Mistakenly Believing Player Won Hole — See 30-3f/3.

Ball Putted from Wrong Place Lifted and Putted from Right Place — See 20-7b/2.

Caddie Lifts Ball in Water Hazard Without Player's Authority — See 26-1/9.

20

20-1/3 Ball Marked and Lifted by Opponent Without Player's Authority; Player Lifts Ball-Marker, Claims Hole and Opponent Disputes Claim

Q. In a match, B marks the position of A's ball and lifts it without A's authority. B holes out. A picks up the ball-marker with which B had marked the position of his (A's) ball and claims the hole. B disputes the claim. What is the ruling?

A. B incurs a penalty stroke — Rule 18-3b — for lifting A's ball without authority. A incurs a penalty stroke for lifting the ball-marker (Rule 20-1). A must replace his ball and hole out; otherwise, A loses the hole.

20-1/4 Competitor's Ball Lifted Without Authority by Fellow-Competitor

Q. In stroke play, a fellow-competitor lifts a competitor's ball on the putting green without the authority of the competitor. Such action is contrary to Rule 20-1. What is the ruling?

A. There is no penalty, but the competitor must replace the ball — Rule 18-4.

Competitor Who Lifts His Ball and Fellow-Competitor's Ball Inadvertently Exchanges Balls When Replacing Them — See 15-1/9.

Fellow-Competitor Lifts Competitor's Ball and Sets It Aside; Competitor Plays Ball from Where Set Aside — See 15-3/3.

20-1/5 Competitor's Ball Lifted Without Authority by Fellow-Competitor's Caddie Who Subsequently Substitutes Another Ball Which Competitor Plays

Q. A competitor's ball lying on the putting green is lifted by a fellow-competitor's caddie without the authority of the competitor. Subsequently, the fellow-competitor's caddie by mistake substitutes another ball and the competitor plays it. The error is then discovered. What is the ruling?

A. When a competitor authorizes another person to lift his ball, the competitor is responsible for any breach of the Rules (Rule 20-1). The converse is generally true, *i.e.*, the competitor is not responsible for a breach of a Rule caused by the unauthorized lifting of his ball. Thus, in this case, the competitor should not be penalized under Rule 15-1. The competitor should hole out with the substituted ball, without penalty.

20

Player Mistakenly Substitutes Another Ball on Putting Green; Error Discovered Before Stroke Played — See 15-1/7.

20-1/5.5 Ball-Marker Moved Accidentally by Player

Q. A player marked the position of his ball on the putting green and lifted the ball. When it was the player's turn to play, he could not find his ball-marker. Subsequently, he found the ball-marker stuck to the sole of his shoe. He concluded that he had accidentally stepped on it while assisting his partner in lining up a putt. What is the ruling?

A. The player incurs a penalty stroke under Rule 20-1 which requires that the position of a ball be marked before it is lifted, and contemplates that the ball-marker will remain in position until the ball is replaced. The player must place the ball as near as possible to its original position but not nearer the hole — Rule 20-3c.

Under the last paragraph of Rule 20-1, a player is exempt from penalty if his ball-marker is accidentally moved in the process of lifting the ball or marking its position. In this case the ball-marker was not moved during such process.

20-1/6 Ball-Marker Moved Accidentally by Player in Process of Marking Position of Ball

Q. A player marked the position of his ball with a coin, lifted the ball and pressed down the coin with the sole of his putter. He walked to the edge of the green and then noticed that the coin had stuck to the sole of the putter. What is the ruling?

A. The last paragraph of Rule 20-1 states: "If a ball or a ball-marker is accidentally moved in the process of lifting the ball under a Rule or marking its position, no penalty is incurred and the ball or the ball-marker shall be replaced."

Accordingly, no penalty is incurred and the ball or the ball-marker must be replaced. If the spot where the ball or the ball-marker lay is not known, it must be placed as near as possible to where it lay but not nearer the hole — Rule 20-3c.

20-1/7 Ball-Marker Moved by Opponent's Caddie Accidentally

Q. A player's caddie accidentally kicked his opponent's ball-marker closer to the hole. What is the ruling?

A. In equity (Rule 1-4), the ball-marker should have been replaced as near as possible to the spot where it lay and the player should incur a penalty of one stroke.

Whether Lifting Opponent's Ball-Marker Is Concession of Next Stroke — See 2-4/5.

20-1/8 Ball-Marker Lifted by Player Who Mistakenly Believes He Has Won Hole

Q. A player, mistakenly believing he has won a hole, picks up his ball-marker. What is the ruling?

A. The player incurs a one-stroke penalty — Rule 20-1 — and must replace his ball.

Wrong Information Causes Opponent to Lift His Ball-Marker — See 9-2/5.

Player Who Walks Off Green Under Mistaken Impression Partner Halved Hole Returns and Putts for Half — See 30/4.

20-1/9 Ball-Marker Lifted by Outside Agency

Q. A marked the position of his ball on the putting green while a following match or group was playing through. After the following match or group had played through, A could not find his ball-marker. It apparently had been lifted by one of the players playing through. What is the ruling?

A. Under Rule 20-3c, A must place his ball as near as possible to where it lay on the green.

20-1/10 Ball-Marker Moved Off Green by Wind or Casual Water

Q. While play is suspended due to a rainstorm, a player's ball-marker, which was made of a lightweight material, is moved off a putting green by wind or casual water. What is the procedure?

A. Under Rule 20-3c, the player must place his ball as near as possible to where it lay on the green.

The fact that the player used a light-weight ball-marker does not affect the result — see Decision 20-1/18.

Ball Moved by Wind or Casual Water While Play Suspended — See 18-1/11.

20-1/11   Ball-Marker in Position to Assist Another Player

Q. A player marks the position of his ball on the putting green and the ball-marker is so located that it might be of assistance to the opponent or a fellow-competitor in lining up his putt. Accordingly, the player prepares to move his ball-marker one or two clubhead-lengths to the side, but the opponent or fellow-competitor says he wants the ball-marker left where it is. What is the ruling?

A. The player is entitled to move his ball-marker to the side. The opponent or fellow-competitor may not insist on its being left where it is in view of the purposes of Rules 8-2b and 22a.

20-1/12   Marking Position of Ball with Toe of Club

Q. A player, prior to lifting his ball under a Rule, marked the position of the ball by placing the toe of a club at the side of, or behind, the ball. Is this permissible?

A. Yes.

[20-1/13   Reserved]

20-1/14   Ball Moved by Putter Dropped by Player Approaching Ball to Lift It

Q. A player, approaching his ball on the putting green to lift it, dropped his putter on his ball and moved it. Is it correct that there is no penalty in view of Rule 20-1 under which a player incurs no penalty if he

20

accidentally moves his ball in the process of lifting it?

A. No. The player incurred a penalty stroke under Rule 18-2a because the movement of the ball was not directly attributable to the specific act of marking the position of or lifting the ball.

20-1/15 Ball Moved by Ball-Marker Dropped Accidentally by Player

Q. A player preparing to lift his ball on the putting green reaches into his pocket to obtain a coin with which to mark the ball's position. He pulls out a coin which falls to the ground and strikes and moves his ball. In view of the third paragraph of Rule 20-1, is the player exempt from the penalty prescribed in Rule 18-2a?

A. No. A player is exempt from penalty under the third paragraph of Rule 20-1 only if, in the specific act of placing a coin behind a ball to mark its position, his hand, the coin or the placement of the coin causes the ball to move.

Position of Ball Marked Before Obstruction Removed; Ball Moves When Ball-Marker Removed — See 24-1/5.

20

20-1/16 Marking Position of Ball by Scratching Line on Putting Green

Q. Is it permissible to mark the position of a ball on the putting green by scratching a line on the green with a tee?

A. Yes, provided the surface of the putting green is not tested (Rule 16-1d) and the scratched line does not indicate a line for putting (Rule 8-2b). However, this practice is not recommended due to the possibility of damage to the putting surface. Rather, the position of a ball should be marked by placing a ball-marker, a small coin or other similar object immediately behind the ball — see Note under Rule 20-1.

20-1/17 Tee Marking Position of Player's Ball Deflects Opponent's Ball

Q. In a match, B used a wooden tee to mark the position of his ball. A's ball was deflected by the tee. What is the ruling?

A. The tee was not B's equipment — see Definition of "Equipment." There is no penalty. A must play his ball as it lies.

A should have requested B to move the tee one or more clubhead-lengths to the side or to mark the position of his ball with a ball-marker, a small coin or other similar object — see Note under Rule 20-1.

20-1/18 Position of Ball Marked with Daisy

Q. A player plucked a daisy and marked the position of his ball with it. Is this permissible?

A. Yes. However, it is inadvisable to mark the position of a ball with something, such as a daisy, that might be blown away.

Rotating Ball on Putting Green Without Marking Position — See 18-2a/33.

20-1/19 Placing Object Marking Position of Ball Other Than Behind Ball

20

Q. When marking the position of a ball, must the ball-marker be placed behind the ball, or may it also be placed to the side of or in front of the ball?

A. There is no restriction. However, if a player positions his ball-marker in front of the ball on the putting green and in the process does something to the green which might influence the movement of the ball when played, *e.g.*, presses down a raised tuft of grass, he is in breach of Rule 1-2.

Placing a ball-marker in front of the ball is not recommended but it is not a breach of Rule 16-1a because this Rule permits touching the line of putt in lifting a ball, and marking the position of the ball is part of the lifting process.

20-1/20 Player Places Ball-Marker Approximately Two Inches Behind Ball

Q. A player consistently places his ball-marker approximately two inches behind the ball on the green. He says that he does so to ensure that he does not accidentally move the ball. Does such a procedure comply with the Rules?

A. No. A player who places a ball-marker two inches behind his ball cannot be considered to have marked the position of the ball with sufficient accuracy. Accordingly, each time he does so, the player incurs a penalty of one stroke, as provided in Rule 20-1, and must place the ball as near as possible to the spot from which it was lifted — Rule 20-3c.

The player's action was unnecessary because Rule 20-1 states that no penalty is incurred if a ball is accidentally moved in the process of marking or lifting it under a Rule.

20-1/21 Position of Ball Not Marked But Player Able to Replace Ball Because of Adjacent Blemish

Q. There is a distinct blemish immediately behind a ball lying on a putting green. The player claims he may lift his ball without marking its position because the blemish effectively marks the position. Is the player correct?

A. No. Under Rule 20-1, the position of a ball must be marked before the ball is lifted. Using a blemish as a ball-marker is not acceptable.

Position of Ball Lifted for Identification Not Marked, Intention to Lift Not Announced and Ball Cleaned Beyond Extent Necessary to Identify It — See 21/4.

20-1/22 Knocking Ball Aside After Marking Position Instead of Lifting

Q. A player, whose ball is on the putting green, marks the position of his ball and knocks the ball aside with his putter instead of lifting it. What is the ruling?

20

A. Knocking the ball aside was the equivalent of lifting it under Rule 20-1. There would be no penalty unless the act was for the purpose of testing the putting surface (Rule 16-1d) or playing a practice stroke (Rule 7-2).

20-2a/1 Penalty When Ball Dropped in Other Than Prescribed Manner

Q. If a ball is dropped in a manner other than that prescribed in Rule 20-2a and the error is not corrected, it is stated in that Rule that the penalty is one stroke. However, the general penalty for a breach of Rule 20-2 is loss of hole in match play or two strokes in stroke play. Which penalty applies?

A. The one-stroke penalty specifically prescribed in Rule 20-2a applies.

20-2a/2 Spinning Ball When Dropping

Q. A player puts spin on a ball purposely when dropping it. What is the ruling?

A. The player incurs a penalty of one stroke under Rule 20-2a for dropping the ball in an improper manner, unless he corrects his mistake as permitted by Rule 20-6.

20

Dropped Ball Accidentally Deflected by Opponent or His Caddie — See 19-3/2.

20-2a/3 Ball Dropped in Improper Manner and in Wrong Place

Q. A player obtaining relief from ground under repair dropped a ball in a manner not conforming with Rule 20-2a and in a wrong place. What is the ruling?

A. If the player corrected the errors before playing his next stroke, there was no penalty — Rule 20-6.

If the player failed to correct the errors before playing his next stroke:

(a) In match play, he lost the hole for playing from a wrong place — Rule 20-7a.

(b) In stroke play, he incurred a penalty of three strokes — one stroke for dropping in an improper manner (Rule 20-2a) and two strokes for a breach of Rule 25-1b (see Rule 20-7b).

20-2a/4 Ball Dropped in Improper Manner Moves When Addressed; Player Then Lifts Ball and Drops It in Proper Manner

Q. A player drops his ball other than in the manner prescribed in Rule 20-2a. He addresses the ball and the ball moves. He then is advised that he dropped his ball improperly. So, as permitted by Rule 20-6, he lifts the ball, drops it properly and plays. According to Rule 20-6, the player incurs no penalty for the improper drop. Does he incur a penalty stroke under Rule 18-2b because the ball moved after it was addressed, even though the ball was subsequently lifted and re-dropped?

A. Yes. The ball was in play when it was first dropped, even though it was dropped in an improper manner (Rule 20-4). When it moved after being addressed, the penalty prescribed in Rule 18-2b was applicable.

Pitch-Mark in Dropping Area Repaired Before Ball Dropped — See 13-2/10.

Removing Sand or Loose Soil from Dropping Area — See 13-2/11.

Removal of Loose Impediments from Area in Which Ball to Be Dropped — See 23-1/6.

20

Who Drops Ball in Foursome Competition — See 29/4.

20-2a/5 Caddie Holds Back Tree Branch to Prevent Branch from Deflecting Dropped Ball

Q. May a player have his caddie hold back a tree branch that is waist high and situated at the spot at which the player wishes to drop his ball under a Rule?

If the branch is not held back, the dropped ball might lodge in the branch or, in any case, the branch will be likely to deflect the dropped ball.

A. No. Such an act would be exerting influence on the position or movement of the ball, contrary to Rule 1-2.

Dropped Ball Strikes Tree Branch Then Ground; Whether Re-Drop Required —- See 20-2c/1.3.

20-2b/1 Dropped Ball Never Strikes Ground

Q. A player drops a ball where the applicable Rule requires. It lodges in a bush without striking the ground. What is the ruling?

A. The ball is in play. It struck a part of the course where required by the applicable Rule and did not roll into a position requiring it to be re-dropped under Rule 20-2c.

20-2c/0.5 Ball Dropped from Ground Under Repair Area Rolls to Position Where Area Interferes with Stance; Whether Re-Drop Required

Q. A player's ball lies in ground under repair through the green. The player elects to take relief and drops the ball in accordance with Rule 25-1b(i). The ball remains outside the ground under repair area but it rolls to a position where the player would have to stand in the area to play his stroke. Must the player re-drop the ball?

A. Yes. The ball has rolled "to a position where there is interference by the condition from which relief was taken" — see Rule 20-2c(v).

The same applies if a player is taking relief from an immovable obstruction.

20-2c/1 Dropped Ball Rolling Out of Prescribed Dropping Area

Q. A player taking relief under the Rules sometimes appears to obtain more relief than he is entitled to because the relevant Rule allows him some latitude within which to drop and the dropped ball then rolls some distance from the place where it was dropped. When a Rule prescribes an area within which a ball must be dropped, *e.g.*, within one or two club-lengths of a particular point, should it be re-dropped if it rolls outside the area so prescribed?

A. No, not necessarily. Provided the ball has been correctly dropped (Rule 20-2a) and does not roll into any of the positions listed in Rule 20-2c, it is in play and must not be re-dropped. In particular, under Rule 20-2c(vi), the ball may roll up to two club-lengths from the point where it first struck a part of the course when dropped, and this may result in its coming to rest an appreciable distance farther from the condition from which relief is being taken. For example:

(a) a ball dropped within two club-lengths of the margin of a lateral water hazard may come to rest almost four club-lengths from the hazard margin without the player being required to re-drop it under Rule 20-2c; and

(b) a ball dropped away from an immovable obstruction within one club-length of the nearest point of relief may come to rest almost three club-lengths from the nearest point of relief without the player being required to re-drop it under Rule 20-2c.

20-2c/1.3 Dropped Ball Strikes Tree Branch Then Ground; Whether Re-Drop Required

20

Q. A player drops a ball within the area prescribed by the applicable Rule. It bounces off a tree branch and as a result strikes the ground outside that area. What is the ruling?

A. The ball struck a part of the course (the branch) where the applicable Rule requires (Rule 20-2b). Therefore, provided it does not roll into any of the positions listed in Rule 20-2c, it is in play and must not be re-dropped. In measuring the two club lengths to determine if a re-drop is required under Rule 20-2c(vi), the point on the ground immediately below the spot where the ball first struck a part of the course (the branch) shall be used for measuring purposes.

20-2c/1.5 Ball Rolls Towards Hole When Dropped at Spot from Which Previous Stroke Played

Q. A player is required or elects to play his next stroke at the spot from which his previous stroke was played. He is able to identify that specific spot by reference to the divot hole which his previous stroke made. He drops a ball immediately behind that divot hole. The ball rolls nearer the hole than the spot from which the previous stroke was played, but not more than two club-lengths from where it first struck the ground. What is the ruling?

A. Rule 20-2c(vii) requires a ball to be re-dropped if it "rolls and comes to rest nearer the hole than its original position or estimated position unless otherwise permitted by the Rules." The original position is the spot from which the previous stroke was played. Since the dropped ball rolled nearer the hole than that spot, it must be re-dropped.

However, in many such cases the player cannot determine exactly the spot from which his previous stroke was played. In those cases, the player has satisfied the requirements of the Rule if he uses his best endeavors to estimate the spot. The estimated spot is treated as the specific spot (see Rule 20-2b) and the ball must be re-dropped if it rolls nearer the hole than the estimated spot.

The same principle applies if the spot where a ball is to be placed is not determinable and the player is required, under Rule 20-3c, to drop the ball as near as possible to the spot where it lay.

20-2c/2 Ball Dropped Third Time When Placement Required After Second Drop

Q. A player dropped his ball twice under a Rule and each time the ball rolled nearer the hole. He then dropped the ball a third time instead of placing it as required by Rule 20-2c. What is the ruling?

A. Before playing a stroke, the player may lift the ball and place it as prescribed in Rule 20-2c, without penalty Rule 20-6. If he fails to do so and plays the ball, he incurs a penalty of loss of hole in match play or two strokes in stroke play for a breach of Rule 20-2c.

20-2c/3 Placing Ball Instead of Dropping When Obvious Dropped Ball Will Roll into Hazard, Etc.

Q. A player is required to drop a ball. However, it is obvious that the ball when dropped will roll into a hazard, more than two club-lengths, etc., in which case it must be re-dropped and then placed under Rule 20-2c. In such a case, is it permissible to waive the dropping requirement and allow the player initially to place the ball?

A. No. Dropping and then re-dropping are necessary to resolve any doubt as to whether the ball will roll into a hazard, etc., and to establish the spot at which the ball must be placed, if necessary.

20-2c/4 Caddie Stops Dropped Ball Before It Comes to Rest; When Penalty Incurred

There is no penalty if a player's caddie deliberately stops a ball dropped by the player after the ball has rolled to a position from which the player would be required to re-drop it under Rule 20-2c, provided it is reasonable to assume that the ball would not return to a position at which Rule 20-2c would be inapplicable. However, if a player's caddie acts prematurely and stops a dropped ball before it has reached such a position, the player incurs a penalty of loss of hole in match play or two strokes in stroke play under Rule 1-2 — see reference to Rule 1-2 under Rule 20-2a — and must drop the ball as near as possible to the spot where it was when the caddie stopped it.

20

20-2c/5 Changing Relief Option When Re-Dropping Required

Q. A player declares his ball unplayable. Of the three options available under Rule 28, he elects Rule 28b and drops the ball within two club-lengths of the spot where it lay. The ball rolls and comes to rest nearer the hole than its original position, so the player is required by Rule 20-2c to re-drop. May the player now proceed under a different option, *e.g.*, Rule 28c?

A. No. If the player did so, he would be in breach of Rule 20-2c. The same principles would apply when proceeding under Rule 26-1.

20-2c/6 Ball Moved in Measuring to Determine If Re-Drop Required

Q. A player drops his ball in accordance with the Rules. The ball rolls and the player is uncertain whether it has come to rest more than two club-lengths from where it first struck a part of the course. The player measures to determine whether he must re-drop under Rule 20-2c(vi) and in doing so accidentally causes the ball to move. What is the ruling if (a) the ball had rolled more than two club-lengths or (b) the ball had not rolled more than two club-lengths?

A. In equity (Rule 1-4) and by analogy with Rule 10-4, no penalty is incurred in either case. If the ball had rolled more than two club-lengths, it must be re-dropped. If the ball had not rolled more than two club-lengths, it must be replaced.

Changing Relief Option After Ball Dropped in a Wrong Place — See 20-6/2.

After Relief Taken from Obstruction for Stroke Towards Green, Obstruction Interferes with Stance for Necessary Sideways Stroke — See 24-2b/9.5.

Ball Dropped from Casual Water in Bunker at Point of Maximum Relief Rolls Elsewhere — See 25-1b/6.

Permissible Dropping Area So Narrow Player Has Difficulty Dropping Within It — See 26-1/19.

20-3a/0.5 Whether Player Himself Must Place or Replace Ball

Q. Rule 20-3a states: "A ball to be placed under the Rules shall be placed by the player or his partner. If a ball is to be replaced, the player, his partner or the person who lifted or moved it shall place it on the spot from which it was lifted or moved." On the other hand, other Rules, *e.g.*, Rules 15-2 and -3 and 18-2b and -2c state that the player shall place or replace the ball. Does Rule 20-3a override other Rules which imply that the player himself must place or replace the ball?

A. Yes.

20-3a/1 Ball Moved in Removing Ball-Marker After Replacing Ball

Q. A player replaces his ball under a Rule and, in the act of removing the object marking its position, accidentally moves the ball. What is the ruling?

A. Removal of the ball-marker is part of the replacement process. Accordingly, under Rule 20-3a, no penalty is incurred, and the ball must be replaced.

20-3a/2 Trademark Aimed Along Line of Putt When Ball Replaced

Q. When a player is replacing his ball, is it permissible for him to position the ball so that the trademark is aimed along the line of putt to indicate the line of play?

A. Yes.

Player Returns Ball to Spot from Which Lifted by Rolling It with Putter — See 16-1d/3.

Ball Replaced at Wrong Place on Putting Green and Holed — See 20-7b/1.

Removal of Loose Impediments from Spot on Which Ball to Be Placed — See 23-1/6.5.

Placing Ball on Bank of Water Hazard Instead of Dropping to Prevent Ball Rolling into Water — See 26-1/10.

Penalty for Repeatedly Replacing Ball Nearer Hole on Green — See 33-7/6.

20-3b/1 Lie of Lifted Ball in Bunker Altered by Another Player's Stroke

Q. The balls of A and B are in the same heel mark in a bunker. B's ball is farther from the hole. A lifts his ball under Rule 22, and B plays and obliterates the heel mark. What should A do?

A. Under Rule 20-3b, A is required to recreate his original lie as nearly as possible, including the heel mark, and place his ball in that lie.

20-3b/2 Lie in Bunker Altered by Another Player Taking His Stance

Q. In playing from a bunker, B, in taking his stance, pushed up a mound of sand behind A's ball, which had not been lifted. What is the ruling?

A. In equity (Rule 1-4), and by analogy to Rule 20-3b, A's original lie should be recreated as nearly as possible by removing the mound of sand.

20-3b/3 Lie Altered by Removal of Gallery-Control Stake

Q. A ball comes to rest adjacent to a gallery-control stake. A marshal removes the stake and in so doing raises the turf in front of the ball. What is the ruling?

A. In this case the original lie could easily be restored. Accordingly, in equity (Rule 1-4), the raised turf should be pressed down so that the original lie is recreated as nearly as possible.

20

Lie or Line of Play Affected by Pitch-Mark Made by Partner's, Opponent's or Fellow-Competitor's Ball — See 13-2/8.

Player's Lie Affected by Sand from Partner's, Opponent's or Fellow-Competitor's Stroke from Bunker — See 13-2/8.5.

20-3b/4 Lie of Ball Altered by Tractor

Q. A ball lies on a fairway. A tractor crosses the fairway and creates a ridge close to the ball which makes the ball virtually unplayable. Is the player entitled to relief?

A. Yes. In this case the original lie could not easily be restored. Accordingly, in equity (Rule 1-4), and under the principle of Rule 20-3b, the player should place his ball, without penalty, in the nearest lie most similar to that which it originally occupied, but not more than one club-length from the original lie, not nearer the hole and not in a hazard.

20-3b/5 Lie of Ball to Be Replaced Altered and Spot Where Ball Originally Lay Not Determinable

Q. In stroke play, B plays A's ball and in the process removes a divot. The original lie of A's ball has been altered and it is impossible to determine the spot where A's ball originally lay. Should A proceed under Rule 20-3b or Rule 20-3c?

A. Since the lie of A's ball was altered, Rule 20-3b applies.

Lie of Ball Embedded in Hazard Altered When Ball Lifted to Determine Whether Unfit for Play — See 5-3/5.

Lie Altered When Player Presses Oscillating Ball into Surface of Putting Green — See 18-2a/6.

Ball Moved Accidentally and Original Lie Altered; Player Places Ball in Wrong Place and Plays — See 18-2a/21.**3.**

Decisions relating to Rule 20-3c:

20

Ball Lodged in Tree Knocked Down from Unknown Place by Outside Agency — See 18-1/9.

Ball Moved Accidentally; Spot Where Ball Originally Lay Not Determinable; Player Places Ball Instead of Dropping It — See 18-2a/21.**5.**

Ball Dislodged from Tree by Player; Spot Where Ball Lay Not Determinable — See 18-2a/29.

Ball-Marker Moved Accidentally by Player — See 20-1/5.**5**

Ball-Marker Moved Accidentally by Player in Process of Marking Position of Ball — See 20-1/6.

Ball-Marker Lifted by Outside Agency — See 20-1/9.

Ball-Marker Moved Off Green by Wind or Casual Water — See 20-1/10.

Lie of Ball to Be Replaced Altered and Spot Where Ball Originally Lay Not Determinable — See 20-3b/5.

20-3d/1 Placed Ball Rolls into Hole

Q. A replaces his ball on the putting green. As he is about to address the ball, it rolls into the hole. Should the ball be replaced or is A deemed to have holed out with his previous stroke?

A. The answer depends on whether the ball, when replaced, remained at rest for a few seconds before it started rolling. If it did, A is deemed to have holed out with his previous stroke. If not, A is required to replace the ball — Rule 20-3d.

Ball Overhanging Hole Is Lifted, Cleaned and Replaced; Ball Then Falls into Hole — See 16-2/0.5.

Ball Dislodged from Tree by Player; Ball Fails to Remain on Correct Spot When Replaced — See 18-2a/29.

20-3d/2 Ball in Bunker Moves Closer to Hole When Obstruction Removed and Ball Will Not Remain at Rest When Replaced; All Other Parts of Bunker Are Nearer Hole

Q. A ball came to rest against a movable obstruction, a rake, in a bunker. When the rake was moved the ball rolled nearer the hole. According to Rule 24-1, the ball had to be replaced. Due to the slope and the fact that the sand was firm, the ball, when replaced, rolled closer to the hole.

20

Under Rule 20-3d, if a ball will not remain on the spot where it originally lay, it must be placed at the nearest spot not nearer the hole where it can be placed at rest. The spot where the ball originally lay was farther from the hole than any other part of the bunker. Thus, there was nowhere to place the ball at rest in the bunker which was not nearer the hole. What is the proper procedure if:

1. The only way the ball would remain at rest at the spot where it lay would be to press it lightly into the sand?
2. The sand is so hard that it is impossible to replace the ball?

A. There is nothing in the Rules of Golf permitting a player to press his ball lightly into the sand or ground to make it remain at rest. Accordingly, in either case, since the player could not place the ball in conformity with the Rules, he should, in equity (Rule 1-4), have dropped the ball, under penalty of one stroke, outside the bunker, keeping the point where the ball lay directly between the hole and the spot on which the ball is dropped.

Whether Rakes Should be Placed in or Outside Bunkers — See Misc./2.

20-3d/3 Ball In Rough Moves Downward When Addressed; Ball Will Not Remain at Rest When Replaced

Q. A player's ball is sitting up in the rough about three inches above the ground. He addresses the ball. It moves downward about two inches and comes to rest at Point X. The player attempts to replace the ball as required by Rule 18-2b, but the ball falls downward to Point X. Under Rule 20-3d, he again attempts to replace the ball, with the same result. The player must now place the ball at the nearest spot not nearer the hole where it can be placed at rest — Rule 20-3d.

If the nearest spot where the ball will remain at rest is Point X, must the player place the ball there, even though that point is vertically below the original lie?

A. Yes.

20

20-4/1 Ball Replaced on Putting Green But Ball-Marker Not Removed; Ball Then Moves

Q. A player replaces his ball on the putting green but does not remove his ball-marker. Subsequently the wind moves his ball to a new position. What is the ruling?

A. Under Rule 20-4, a ball is in play when it is replaced, whether or not the object used to mark its position has been removed. Consequently the ball must be played from the new position — see Decision 18-1/12.

Original Ball Found Within Five-Minute Search Period After Another Ball Dropped — See 27-1/2.

Ball Dropped Under Unplayable Ball Rule Comes to Rest in Original Position or Another Position at Which Ball Is Unplayable — See 28/3.

20-5/1 Teed Ball Missed Then Hit Out of Bounds

Q. A player plays a stroke from a teeing ground and misses the ball. He plays a second stroke and hits the ball out of bounds. In proceeding under Rule 27-1, may he tee a ball anywhere within the teeing ground or must he drop a ball where the original ball was teed?

A. The player may tee a ball anywhere within the teeing ground.

20-6/1 Ball Dropped When Required to Be Placed or Placed When Required to Be Dropped; Correction of Error

Q. A player dropped a ball when he should have placed it or placed it when he should have dropped it. Before playing a stroke, may the player lift the ball, without penalty, under Rule 20-6 and proceed correctly?

A. Yes.

20

Ball Dropped Third Time When Placement Required After Second Drop; Correction of Error — See 20-2c/2.

20-6/2 Changing Relief Option After Ball Dropped in a Wrong Place

Q. A player declares his ball unplayable and elects to take relief under Rule 28c. He drops the ball in a wrong place and is advised of this fact. He then lifts his ball under Rule 20-6 and states that he wishes to proceed under Rule 28b. Is the player entitled to proceed under Rule 28b?

A. Yes. Decision 20-2c/5 suggests a different conclusion. However, in that case Rule 20-2c is invoked and that Rule implies that a ball to be re-dropped must be re-dropped under the option originally invoked.

20-6/3 Ball Mistakenly Substituted When Dropped; Correction of Error

Q. A player's ball lies on a paved cart path. In taking relief from the obstruction, he mistakenly drops a ball other than the original ball. He discovers his error before playing his next stroke. How should he proceed?

A. Since the player is not entitled to substitute a ball when proceeding under Rule 24-2b, the player must lift the substituted ball, without penalty, and drop the original ball in accordance with the Rules. (New)

20-7/1 Ball Played from Spot Where Original Ball Deflected Out of Bounds by Maintenance Vehicle

Q. A player's tee shot travels about 175 yards and, while still in motion, is deflected out of bounds by a golf course maintenance vehicle. The player, claiming the vehicle should not have been there, dropped a ball near the spot where the maintenance vehicle deflected the original ball, completed play of the hole and stated that he had incurred no penalty. Was the player correct?

A. No. A maintenance vehicle is an outside agency. The original ball would have been played as it lay, without penalty, if it had been in bounds — Rule 19-1. Since the ball was out of bounds, the player was obliged to proceed under Rule 27-1, incurring a penalty of stroke and distance.

20

The player, in dropping a ball near where the original ball was deflected and playing it, played from a wrong place.

In match play, he incurred a penalty of loss of hole -Rule 20-7a. In stroke play, he incurred a penalty of two strokes — Rule 27-1 — and, since the breach was a serious one, he was subject to disqualification unless he corrected the error, as provided in the second paragraph of Rule 20-7b, before playing from the next teeing ground.

Ball Moved Accidentally and Original Lie Altered; Player Places Ball in Wrong Place and Plays — See 18-2a/21.3.

Casual Water Mistaken for Water Hazard; Original Ball Played Under Water Hazard Rule — See 25-1b/12.

Player Plays Second Shot, Declares Ball Unplayable and Returns to Tee — See 28/6.

Player Plays from a Wrong Place on Basis of Incorrect Ruling — See 34-3/3.

20-7/2 Ball Declared Unplayable in Water Hazard Is Dropped in Hazard and Played

Q. A player declares his ball unplayable in a water hazard and drops the ball in the water hazard, thinking that Rule 28b or c is applicable, and plays it. He then realizes that it is not permissible to declare a ball unplayable in a water hazard. What is the ruling?

A. The player played the ball from a wrong place, *i.e.*, a place not permitted by Rule 26-1, the water hazard relief Rule.

In match play, the player loses the hole (Rule 20-7a).

In stroke play, if a serious breach of the water hazard Rule was not involved, the player, in addition to incurring the penalty stroke provided for in Rule 26-1, incurs a two-stroke penalty for playing from a wrong place and must play out the hole with the ball played out of the water hazard — see first paragraph of Rule 20-7b and Rule 26-1.

If a serious breach of the water hazard Rule was involved, the player must, before playing from the next teeing ground, play a ball in accordance with Rule 26-1 and add two penalty strokes to the score with that ball; otherwise the player is disqualified — see second and third paragraphs of Rule 20-7b.

20-7b/1 Ball Replaced at Wrong Place on Putting Green and Holed

Q. In stroke play, a competitor in replacing his ball on the putting green inadvertently put the ball in a wrong place nearby and holed out. The error was then discovered and the competitor put his ball in the right place and holed out. What is the ruling?

A. The score with the ball played from the wrong place counts and the competitor must add two penalty strokes to that score (Rule 16-1b or 20-3a and Rule 20-7b).

The competitor incurs no penalty for having putted from the right place after holing out from a wrong place.

20-7b/2 Ball Putted from Wrong Place Lifted and Putted from Right Place

Q. In stroke play, A mistakenly replaced his ball in front of B's ball-marker (which was near A's ball-marker) and putted. The ball came to rest about one foot from the hole. The error was then discovered and A lifted his ball without marking its position, placed it in front of his own ball-marker and finished the hole. What is the ruling?

A. When A replaced his ball in front of B's ball-marker and putted, he played from a wrong place and incurred a penalty of two strokes; the ball was in play — Rule 20-7b.

When A then lifted his ball from where it lay about one foot from the hole without marking its position and did not replace it, he incurred the general penalty (two strokes) for a breach of Rule 20-1 — see second paragraph of Rule 20-1.

Thus, A incurred a total penalty of four strokes.

20-7b/3 Ball Believed to Be Lost in Bunker; Competitor Drops Another Ball in Bunker and Plays It; Original Ball Then Found Outside Bunker

Q. In stroke play, A played a long shot to the green and the ball appeared to have come to rest in a bunker beside the green. The ball was not found in the bunker. A dropped a ball in the bunker and played it onto the green. A then discovered his original ball behind the green. What is the ruling?

A. A's original ball became a lost ball when he dropped another ball in the bunker under Rule 27-1, and the dropped ball was in play.

Since the place where the ball was dropped was well in advance of the spot from which the original ball was last played, A was guilty of a serious breach of the relevant Rule (Rule 27-1) in failing to go back to that spot, and he should have been disqualified unless he rectified the breach as prescribed in Rule 20-7b.

Ball Knocked Out of Bunker by Fellow-Competitor's Stroke at Own Ball Not Replaced — See 18-4/2.

Ball Dropped Outside Bunker Under Option of Unplayable Ball Rule Requiring Drop in Bunker — See 28/10.

[20-7b/4   Reserved]

20-7b/5   Competitor's Ball Played by Fellow-Competitor; Competitor Substitutes Another Ball at Wrong Place, Plays It and Then Abandons It and Plays Out Original Ball from Right Place

Q. In stroke play, A, B and C hit their tee shots into the same area. After B and C have played their second shots, A discovers that the remaining ball is not his and assumes that his ball has been played by B. Since his (A's) original ball is not immediately recoverable, A substitutes another ball as permitted by Note 1 under Rule 18, places it on the spot from which B played his second shot and plays it to the green. There it is discovered that it was C, not B, who wrongly played A's ball and that A has therefore played the substituted ball from a wrong place. A accepts a two-stroke penalty under the relevant Rule (Rule 18-1), but he then abandons the substituted ball, thinking he must correct his error. A picks up his original ball, goes back to the spot where C played his second shot, plays it from there and holes out with it. A then drives from the next tee. Did A proceed correctly?

A. No. A's procedure was correct up to the point when he abandoned the substituted ball. Instead of abandoning the substituted ball, A should have

20

played out the hole with it in accordance with Rule 20-7b, adding to his score the two-stroke penalty he had correctly accepted under Rule 18-1. The substituted ball, albeit played from the wrong place, was now A's ball in play, and his original ball was out of play. When A went back and played his original ball from the right place (*i.e.,* from where C had wrongly played it), he was therefore playing a wrong ball and, since he did not correct the error before playing from the next tee, he was disqualified under Rule 15-3.

Guidelines for Which Ball Counts When Player Proceeds Under Rule 3-3 — See 3-3/0.5.

Ball Dropped in Wrong Place and Played; Rule 3-3 Then Invoked and Second Ball Dropped in Right Place; Both Balls Played Out — See 3-3/3.

Ball Dropped in Wrong Place But Not Played; Rule 3-3 Then Invoked and Second Ball Dropped in Right Place; Both Balls Played Out — See 3-3/4.

Whether Score with Second Ball Counts If Ball Dropped in Wrong Place and Played — See 3-3/5.

Procedure If Both Original and Second Balls Dropped in Wrong Place and Played — See 3-3/5.5.

Ball Dropped in Improper Manner and in Wrong Place — See 20-2a/3.

Water Hazard Treated as Lateral Water Hazard — See 26-1/11.

Point Where Ball Last Crossed Margin of Lateral Water Hazard Determined and Ball Dropped and Played; Point Then Proves to Be Wrong Point — See 26-1/17.

Example of Serious Breach of Lateral Water Hazard Rule — See 26-1/21.

Ball Dropped in Area Where Original Ball Lost; Ball Then Played — See 27-1/3.

20

Rule 21. Cleaning Ball

A ball on the putting green may be cleaned when lifted under Rule 16-1b. Elsewhere, a ball may be cleaned when lifted except when it has been lifted:

a. To determine if it is unfit for play (Rule 5-3);

b. For identification (Rule 12-2), in which case it may be cleaned only to the extent necessary for identification; or

c. Because it is interfering with or assisting play (Rule 22).

If a player cleans his ball during play of a hole except as provided in this Rule, he shall incur a penalty of one stroke and the ball, if lifted, shall be replaced.

If a player who is required to replace a ball fails to do so, he shall incur the penalty for breach of Rule 20-3a, but no additional penalty under Rule 21 shall be applied.

Exception: If a player incurs a penalty for failing to act in accordance with Rule 5-3, 12-2 or 22, no additional penalty under Rule 21 shall be applied.

21

21/1 Removing Lime from Ball

Q. Lime has been used to mark lines on the ground for gallery-control purposes. A ball lands on such a line and some lime adheres to the ball. May the player remove the lime?

A. No, unless the ball is in a position from which it may be lifted under the Rules and cleaned under Rule 21.

21/2 Removing Grass Adhering to Ball

Q. Through the green, is it permissible to remove cut grass adhering to a ball?

A. No. Such action is prohibited by Rule 21. Anything adhering to a ball is not a loose impediment — see Definition of "Loose Impediments."

Removal of Insect on Ball — See 23-1/5.

21/3 Whether Ball Cleaned Through Act of Caddie Throwing It to Player

Q. A caddie, with authority of the player, lifts the player's ball because it interferes with the play of another player and throws the ball to the player, who catches it. It is not permissible to clean a ball lifted because of interference. Does the act of throwing and catching the ball constitute cleaning it?

A. Whether or not a ball is cleaned is a question of fact. The action described could result in a ball being cleaned. Any doubt should be resolved against the player.

21/4 Position of Ball Lifted for Identification Not Marked, Intention to Lift Not Announced and Ball Cleaned Beyond Extent Necessary to Identify It

Q. A player lifted his ball for identification purposes without announcing his intention to his opponent, marker or a fellow-competitor. Thus, he was in breach of Rule 12-2. He also failed to mark the position of the ball before he lifted it in breach of Rule 20-1 and cleaned the ball more than was necessary for it to be identified, a breach of Rule 21. The penalty for breach of each of these Rules is one stroke. Does the player incur a penalty of three strokes?

A. No. The player incurs a penalty of one stroke for failing to act in accordance with Rule 12-2. An additional penalty under Rule 20-1 or Rule 21 is not justified- see Rule 12-2 and Exception under Rule 21.

Ball in Ground Under Repair Thought to be Unfit for Play Lifted and Cleaned —– See 5-3/6.

When Ball May Be Cleaned or Substituted After Play Has Been Discontinued — See 6-8c/1.

Ball Lifted Without Authority and Cleaned — See 18-2a/13.

21

Rule 22. Ball Interfering with or Assisting Play

Any player may:

a. Lift his ball if he considers that the ball might assist any other player or

b. Have any other ball lifted if he considers that the ball might interfere with his play or assist the play of any other player,

but this may not be done while another ball is in motion. In stroke play, a player required to lift his ball may play first rather than lift. A ball lifted under this Rule shall be replaced.

If a ball is accidentally moved in complying with this Rule, no penalty is incurred and the ball shall be replaced.

PENALTY FOR BREACH OF RULE:
> *Match play --- Loss of hole;*
> *Stroke play --- Two strokes.*

Note: Except on the putting green, the ball may not be cleaned when lifted under this Rule — see Rule 21.

22

22/1 Mental Interference by Another Ball

Q. In order for A to be entitled to have B's ball lifted because of interference, does B's ball have to be on or near A's line of play and thus in a position to interfere physically with A's ball? Or may A also have B's ball lifted if it is off his line of play but catches his eye and thus constitutes mental interference?

A. A player may, under Rule 22, have another ball lifted if the ball interferes either physically or mentally with his play.

22/2 Player Claims That Another Ball Lying 30 Yards Away Interferes with His Play

Q. B's ball is three feet from the green on a direct line to the hole with A's ball which is 30 yards from the green. May A require B to lift his ball, on the ground that the ball interferes with his play?

A. Yes.

22/3 Player Requests Another Player to Lift His Ball in Absence of Reasonable Possibility Ball Might Interfere or Assist

Q. A's ball is on the putting green. B's ball is 100 yards from the green. B requests A to lift his ball under Rule 22 as it might interfere with his (B's) play. This happens several times during the round. Is such procedure permissible?

A. Rule 22 is intended to cover situations where there is a reasonable possibility that one ball might assist or interfere with another ball. If the Rule is being abused, as in this case, the Committee would be justified in penalizing B for undue delay — Rule 6-7.

22

22/4 Ball Accidentally Kicked by Player Asked to Lift It Due to Interference

Q. A requests B to lift his (B's) ball because it interferes with A's play. As B is walking up to his ball to lift it, he accidentally kicks it. What is the ruling?

A. No penalty is incurred and B must replace his ball — See last paragraph of Rule 22.

22/5 Assisting Ball Lifted by Opponent Replaced on Request; Player's Ball Then Strikes Opponent's Ball and Opponent Lodges Claim

Q. In a match between A and B, A's ball is near the hole in a position to serve as a backstop for B's ball. A lifts his ball to clean it. B requests A to replace his ball before he (B) putts. A protests but B insists that, under the Rules, A must replace his ball immediately. A replaces his ball but disputes B's right to require him to do so and claims the hole. B putts and his ball strikes A's ball and stops very close to the hole. A replaces his ball and holes out for a 4. B then holes out for a 4. The match continues and the claim is later referred to the Committee. How should the Committee rule?

A. The hole stands as played. The Rules do not require A to replace his ball, but B was not in breach of the Rules by asking A to replace it — see Rule 22.

22/6 Competitor Requests That Ball in Position to Assist Him Should Not Be Lifted

Q. In stroke play, B's ball lies just off the putting green. A's ball lies near the hole in a position to serve as a backstop for B's ball. B requests A not to lift his ball. Is such a request proper?

A. No. If a competitor and a fellow-competitor were to agree to exclude the operation of Rule 22, both should be disqualified under Rule 1-3.

22

Competitor Not Given Opportunity to Lift Ball Assisting Fellow-Competitor — See 3-4/1.

Ball-Marker in Position to Assist Another Player — See 20-1/11.

Request to Lift Ball That Might Assist Partner Not Honored — See 30-3f/11.

Player Requested to Lift Ball Due to Interference Plays Out of Turn Instead — See 10-1c/2.

22/7 Ball Assisting Fellow-Competitor on Putting Green; Procedure for Committee Member If Competitor Does Not Lift Ball

Q. In stroke play, a competitor's ball is in a position to assist the play of a fellow-competitor and the competitor is in a position to lift the ball under Rule 22 without delaying the fellow-competitor's play. However, the competitor does not take any action to invoke the Rule. Would a Committee member be justified in intervening and requesting the competitor to invoke the Rule to protect himself and the rest of the field?

A. Yes. If the competitor were to object, there would be strong evidence of an agreement to exclude the operation of Rule 22 in contravention of Rule 1-3. The Committee member would be justified in so advising the competitors involved and warning that any further such evidence might result in disqualification of both under Rule 1-3.

Two Balls Lie Together in Hazard and Neither Is Identifiable — See 1-4/6.

Interfering Ball in Bunker Lifted; Lie Altered by Another Player's Stroke — See 20-3b/1.

Abandoned Ball Interferes with Play — See 24-1/2.

22

Rule 23. Loose Impediments

Definition

"Loose impediments" are natural objects such as stones, leaves, twigs, branches and the like, dung, worms and insects and casts or heaps made by them, provided they are not fixed or growing, are not solidly embedded and do not adhere to the ball.

Sand and loose soil are loose impediments on the <u>putting green</u> but not elsewhere.

Snow and natural ice, other than frost, are either <u>casual water</u> or loose impediments, at the option of the player. Manufactured ice is an <u>obstruction</u>.

Dew and frost are not loose impediments.

23-1. Relief

Except when both the <u>loose impediment</u> and the ball lie in or touch a <u>hazard</u>, any loose impediment may be removed without penalty. If the ball moves, see Rule 18-2c.

When a ball is in motion, a loose impediment which might influence the movement of the ball shall not be removed.

> PENALTY FOR BREACH OF RULE:
> *Match play --- Loss of hole;*
> *Stroke play --- Two strokes.*

(Searching for ball in hazard — see Rule 12-1.)

(Touching line of putt — see Rule 16-1a.)

23

23/1 When Loose Impediment Transformed into Obstruction

Loose impediments may be transformed into obstructions through processes of construction or manufacturing. For example, a log (loose impediment) which has been split and had legs attached has been changed by construction into a bench (obstruction); or a piece of coal (loose impediment) is an obstruction when manufactured into a charcoal briquet.

23/2 Meaning of "Solidly Embedded" in Definition of "Loose Impediments"

Q. The Definition of "Loose Impediments" states that a stone is a loose impediment if it is not "solidly embedded." When is a stone solidly embedded?

A. If a stone is partially embedded and may be picked up with ease, it is a loose impediment. When there is doubt as to whether a stone is solidly embedded or not, it should not be removed.

23/3 Half-Eaten Pear

Q. A half-eaten pear lies directly in front of a ball in a bunker and there is no pear tree in the vicinity of the bunker. In the circumstances, is the pear an obstruction rather than a loose impediment, in which case the player could remove it without penalty?

A. No. A pear is a natural object. When detached from a tree it is a loose impediment. The fact that a pear has been half-eaten and there is no pear tree in the vicinity does not alter the status of the pear.

23/4 Fruit Skins

Q. Is a banana skin or other fruit skin a loose impediment?

A. Yes.

23/5 Ant Hill

Q. Is an ant hill a loose impediment?

A. Yes. A player is entitled to remove an ant hill under Rule 23-1.

23/6 Dead Land Crab

Q. A ball lodges against a dead land crab in a bunker. May the crab be removed without penalty?

A. No. A dead land crab is a natural object and thus a loose impediment and not an obstruction. Removal of the crab would be a breach of Rule 13-4.

Dead Snake — See 18/4.

23/7 Fallen Tree

Q. Is a fallen tree a loose impediment?

A. If it is still attached to the stump, no; if it is not attached to the stump, yes.

23/8 Worm Partially Underground

Q. Is a worm, when half on top of the surface of the ground and half below, a loose impediment which may be removed? Or is it fixed or solidly embedded and therefore not a loose impediment?

A. A worm which is half underground is not "fixed or growing" or "solidly embedded" within the meaning of those terms in the Definition of "Loose Impediments." Accordingly, such a worm may be removed under Rule 16-1a(i) or Rule 23.

23

23/9 Embedded Acorn

Q. Is an embedded acorn a loose impediment?

A. Not if the acorn is solidly embedded — see Definition of "Loose Impediments."

Club Touches Partially Embedded Pine Needle on Backswing in Bunker — See 13-4/32.

Player Repairs Depression on Line of Putt Created When Partially Embedded Acorn Removed — See 16-1a/7.

23/10 Ball Embedded in Fruit

Q. A ball is embedded in an orange lying under an orange tree. What is the ruling?

A. The player must play the ball as it lies or declare it unplayable. Since the orange was adhering to the ball, it was not a loose impediment.

Grass Adhering to Ball — See 21/2.

23/11 Loose Soil Remaining When Molehill Swept Flat

Q. Decision 25/23 states that a molehill, when swept flat, loses its status as such and relief under Rule 25 is no longer available. Is the loose soil remaining a loose impediment?

A. No, unless it is on the putting green — see Definition of "Loose Impediments."

23/12 Aeration Plugs

Q. Are plugs of compacted soil produced through aeration of fairways loose impediments?

A. Yes. Loose soil is not a loose impediment. However, such plugs, since they consist of compacted soil, are loose impediments.

23/13 Clod of Earth

Q. Is a loose clod of earth a loose impediment?

A. Yes. Loose soil is not a loose impediment except on the putting green. However, a clod of earth is not loose soil.

23/14 Gravel Used to Surface Road

Q. A player hits his ball onto a gravel-covered road. Even though he is entitled to relief from this obstruction, he prefers to play the ball from the road. May he remove gravel that might interfere with his stroke?

A. Yes. Gravel is a loose impediment and a player may remove loose impediments under Rule 23-1. This right is not canceled by the fact that, when a road is covered with gravel, it becomes an artificially-surfaced road and thus an obstruction.

Status of Moss or Creepers in Tree — See 13-2/37.

Grass Cuttings — See 25/11.

23-1/1 Means by Which Loose Impediments May Be Removed

Q. Worm casts are loose impediments. By what means may such casts be removed?

A. Except on the line of putt, loose impediments may be removed by any means.

On the line of putt, the player is restricted to removing loose impediments by picking them up or by brushing them aside with his hand or a club without pressing anything down.

23-1/2 Large Stone Removable Only with Much Effort

Q. A player's ball lies in the rough directly behind a loose stone the size of a watermelon. The stone can be removed only with much effort. Is it a loose impediment which may be removed?

A. Yes. Stones of any size (not solidly embedded) are loose impediments and may be removed, provided removal does not unduly delay play (Rule 6-7).

23

23-1/3 Assistance in Removing Large Loose Impediment

Q. May spectators, caddies, fellow-competitors, etc., assist a player in removing a large loose impediment?

A. Yes.

23-1/4 Breaking Off Part of Large Loose Impediment

Q. If part of a large branch which has fallen from a tree (and thus is a loose impediment) interferes with a player's swing, may the player break off the interfering part rather than move the whole branch?

A. Yes.

Bending Grass in Removal of Loose Impediment — See 13-2/13.

Determining Whether Natural Object Interfering with Area of Intended Swing Is Loose Impediment — See 13-2/26.

23-1/5 Removal of Insect on Ball

Q. A live insect is stationary or crawling on a player's ball which is lying through the green. May the player remove the insect with his fingers or blow the insect off the ball?

A. Yes, in both cases, under Rule 23-1. A live insect is not considered to be adhering to the ball and therefore is a loose impediment — see Definition of "Loose Impediments."

23-1/6 Removal of Loose Impediments from Area in Which Ball to Be Dropped

Q. Through the green, is it permissible for a player to remove loose impediments from the area in which he is preparing to drop his ball?

A. Yes.

23-1/6.5 Removal of Loose Impediments from Spot on Which Ball to Be Placed

Q. A player taking relief under a Rule drops his ball and it rolls more than two club-lengths. He re-drops under Rule 20-2c, with the same result. He must now place the ball as near as possible to the spot where it first struck the ground when re-dropped — Rule 20-2c. Before he places the ball, may he remove loose impediments on or around the spot on which the ball is to be placed?

A. Yes.

23-1/7 Loose Impediment Affecting Lie Moved When Ball Lifted

Q. A loose impediment affecting a player's lie is moved when the player lifts his ball under a Rule which requires him to replace the ball. In equity (Rule 1-4), should the player be required to replace the loose impediment?

A. Yes.

23-1/8 Loose Impediments Affecting Lie Removed While Ball Lifted

Q. A player's ball lies in an area through the green where there are a number of loose impediments, including a tree branch against which the ball has come to rest. It appears likely that the ball will move if the player moves the tree branch. The player wishes to lift the ball under Rule 5-3 (Ball Unfit for Play) or Rule 12-2 (Identifying Ball), or he is requested to lift it under Rule 22 (Ball Interfering with or Assisting Play). He lifts the ball but, before replacing it, he removes the loose impediments in the area, including the tree branch against which the ball was resting. Is this permissible?

A. No. Under Rule 18-2c, through the green a player incurs a penalty if his ball moves after a loose impediment within one club-length of it has been touched. It would circumvent Rule 18-2c if, before a ball is replaced, it was permissible to remove loose impediments which affected the player's lie before the ball was lifted. In equity (Rule 1-4), the player should be penalized one stroke.

In such circumstances, if a player wishes to remove loose impediments affecting his lie, he should do so either before lifting the ball or after replacing it. If his ball then moves, under Rule 18-2c the player incurs a penalty stroke and must replace the ball.

23

Removing Sand or Loose Soil from Dropping Area — See 13-2/11.

Loose Impediments Within One Club-Length Removed; Ball Lifted and Replaced; Ball Moves Before Address — See 18-2c/3.

23-1/9 Removal of Loose Impediment Lying Out of Bounds

Q. A loose impediment lying out of bounds interferes with a player's stance. May the player remove the impediment?

A. Yes.

Player Removes Loose Impediments Affecting Opponent's Lie in Hazard — See 1-2/6.

Removal of Obstruction in Hazard Would Move Loose Impediment — See 1-4/5.

Replacing or Removing Undetached Divot — See 13-2/5.

Ball Outside Bunker; Stone in Bunker on Line of Play Pressed Down or Removed — See 13-2/31.

Accidentally Moving Loose Impediment in Hazard — See 13-4/13.

Player Accidentally Kicks Pine Cone into Bunker and Picks It Up — See 13-4/14.

Ball in Hazard Moves When Loose Impediment Removed — See 13-4/15.

Removal of Loose Impediment in Water Hazard Covering Wrong Ball — See 13-4/16.

Loose Impediment Removed from Water Hazard; Player Then Decides Not to Play from Hazard — See 13-4/17.

Ball Touched Accidentally in Removing Loose Impediment — See 18-2a/31.

Ball Touched with Fir Cone or Stick to Prevent Movement When Loose Impediment Removed — See 18-2a/32.

Pine Needles Piled for Removal Interfere with Line of Play After Ball Dropped Away — See 25-1b/17.

Player Lifts Loose Impediment in Bunker When His Ball and Partner's Ball in Bunker — See 30-3f/1.

Competitor Lifts Loose Impediment in Bunker When His Ball and Partner's Ball in Bunker — See 31-8/1.

23

23-1/10 Removal of Loose Impediments Affecting Player's Play

Q. A player with a downhill putt picks up loose impediments between his ball and the hole but leaves some behind the hole. The opponent or fellow-competitor wants to remove the impediments behind the hole as they may serve as a backstop, but the player objects. May the opponent or fellow-competitor remove the loose impediments behind the hole?

A. No. When it is the player's turn to play, his opponent or a fellow-competitor has no right to remove loose impediments affecting the player's play if the player requests the opponent or fellow-competitor not to do so. If the opponent or fellow-competitor ignores the request, he is in breach of Rule 1-2.

In the absence of a request not to remove loose impediments affecting the player's play, an opponent or fellow-competitor who does so incurs no penalty.

In either instance, if the player replaces the loose impediments he is in breach of Rule 1-2.

Removal of Dew or Frost from Line of Putt — See 16-1a/3.

Loose Impediments Removed from Line of Putt with Cap or Towel — See 16-1a/8.

Brushing Loose Impediments Off Line of Putt with Palm of Hand — See 16-1a/9.

Loose Impediments Brushed Along Line of Putt Rather Than to Side — See 16-1a/10.

Determining Whether Natural Object on Line of Putt Is Loose Impediment — See 16-1a/11.

Ball Moved Accidentally by Foot During Removal of Loose Impediment on Putting Green — See 18-2c/1.

23

Competitor Seeks Help in Removal of Loose Impediment to Avoid Penalty — See 33-7/7.

Rule 24. Obstructions

Definition

An "obstruction" is anything artificial, including the artificial surfaces and sides of roads and paths and manufactured ice, except:

a. Objects defining <u>out of bounds</u>, such as walls, fences, stakes and railings;

b. Any part of an immovable artificial object which is out of bounds; and

c. Any construction declared by the Committee to be an integral part of the course.

24-1. Movable Obstruction

A player may obtain relief from a movable <u>ob- struction</u> as follows:

a. If the ball does not lie in or on the obstruction, the obstruction may be removed. If the ball moves, it shall be replaced, and there is no penalty provided that the movement of the ball is directly attributable to the removal of the obstruction. Otherwise, Rule 18-2a applies.

b. If the ball lies in or on the obstruction, the ball may be lifted, without penalty, and the obstruction removed. The ball shall <u>through the green</u> or in a <u>hazard</u> be dropped, or on the <u>putting green</u> be placed, as near as possible to the spot directly under the place where the ball lay in or on the obstruction, but not nearer the hole.

The ball may be cleaned when lifted under Rule 24-1.

24

When a ball is in motion, an obstruction which might influence the movement of the ball, other than an attended flagstick or equipment of the players, shall not be removed.

24-2. Immovable Obstruction

a. INTERFERENCE

Interference by an immovable <u>obstruction</u> occurs when a ball lies in or on the obstruction, or so close to the obstruction that the obstruction interferes with the player's <u>stance</u> or the area of his intended swing. If the player's ball lies on the <u>putting green</u>, interference also occurs if an immovable obstruction on the putting green intervenes on his line of putt. Otherwise, intervention on the line of play is not, of itself, interference under this Rule.

b. RELIEF

Except when the ball lies in or touches a water hazard or a <u>lateral water hazard</u>, a player may obtain relief from interference by an immovable <u>obstruction</u>, without penalty, as follows:

(i) *Through the Green*: If the ball lies <u>through the green</u>, the point on the <u>course</u> nearest to where the ball lies shall be determined (without crossing over, through or under the obstruction) which (a) is not nearer the hole, (b) avoids interference (as defined) and (c) is not in a <u>hazard</u> or on a <u>putting green</u>. The player shall lift the ball and drop it within one club-length of the point thus determined on ground which fulfils (a), (b) and (c) above.

Note: The prohibition against crossing over, through or under the <u>obstruction</u> does not apply to the artificial surfaces and sides of roads and paths or when the ball lies in or on the obstruction.

(ii) *In a Bunker*: If the ball lies in or touches a <u>bunker</u>, the player shall lift and

24

drop the ball in accordance with Clause (i) above, except that the ball must be dropped in the bunker.

(iii) *On the Putting Green*: If the ball lies on the <u>putting green</u>, the player shall lift the ball and place it in the nearest position to where it lay which affords relief from interference, but not nearer the hole nor in a hazard.

The ball may be cleaned when lifted under Rule 24-2b.

(Ball rolling to a position where there is interference by the condition from which relief was taken — see Rule 20-2c(v).)

Exception: A player may not obtain relief under Rule 24-2b if (a) it is clearly unreasonable for him to play a stroke because of interference by anything other than an immovable obstruction or (b) interference by an immovable obstruction would occur only through use of an unnecessarily abnormal stance, swing or direction of play.

Note: If a ball lies in or touches a <u>water hazard</u> (including a <u>lateral water hazard</u>), the player is not entitled to relief without penalty from interference by an immovable obstruction. The player shall play the ball as it lies or proceed under Rule 26-1.

c. BALL LOST

Except in a water hazard or a lateral water hazard, if there is reasonable evidence that a ball is lost in an immovable obstruction, the player may, without penalty, substitute another ball and follow the procedure prescribed in Rule 24-2b. For the purpose of applying this Rule, the ball shall be deemed to lie at the spot where it entered the obstruction. If the ball is lost in an underground drain pipe or culvert the entrance to which is in a hazard, a ball must be dropped in that hazard or the player may proceed under Rule 26-1, if applicable.

24

PENALTY FOR BREACH OF RULE:
Match play --- Loss of hole;
Stroke play --- Two strokes.

24/1 Stile Attached to Boundary Fence

Q. Is a stile attached to a boundary fence an obstruction?

A. Yes, unless the Committee declares it to be an integral part of the course under Rule 33-2a(iv).

Exposed Water Pipe Adjacent and Parallel to Boundary Fence — See 33-2a/1.

24/2 Angled Supports or Guy Wires Supporting Boundary Fence

Q. Angled supports or guy wires support a boundary fence or a protective net above such a fence. If the angled supports or guy wires extend onto the course, are they obstructions?

A. Any part of such an angled support or guy wire which is in bounds is an obstruction.

24/3 Concrete Bases of Boundary Fence Posts

Q. Posts of a boundary fence have been set in concrete bases 14 inches in diameter. Are the parts of the bases within the boundary of the course obstructions?

A. No. Such a base is part of the fence and thus no part of it is an obstruction — see Definition of "Obstructions." If such bases are at or below ground level, the boundary line is the inside points of the fence posts at ground level. If they are above ground level, the Committee should clarify the location of the boundary line.

24

24/4 Part of Boundary Fence Within Boundary Line

Q. Part of a boundary fence is bowed towards the course so that it is inside the boundary line formed by the fence posts. A player's ball comes to rest against this part of the fence. Is the player entitled to relief under Rule 24-2b?

A. No. A fence defining out of bounds is not an obstruction even if part of it is inside the boundary line formed by the fence posts — see Definitions of "Obstructions" and "Out of Bounds."

Improving Position of Ball by Bending Boundary Fence — See 13-2/18.

Gate in Boundary Fence — See 27/18.

Displaced Boundary Stake — See 33-2a/20.

24/5 Boundary Stakes Having No Significance in Play of Hole Being Played

Q. White stakes installed between the 7th and 8th holes define out of bounds during play of the 7th hole, but they have no significance during play of the 8th hole. Are such stakes obstructions during play of the 8th hole?

A. No. However, it is recommended that, by Local Rule, the stakes be deemed immovable obstructions during play of the 8th hole.

Removal of Boundary Stake Interfering with Swing — See 13-2/17.

24/6 Stone Broken Away from Retaining Wall in Water Hazard

Q. A player's ball in a water hazard is in a playable lie but it is directly behind a stone which has broken away from a retaining wall in the hazard. The wall is an immovable obstruction from which the player is not entitled to relief without penalty. Is the stone which has broken away a movable obstruction, in which case the player may remove it before playing a stroke?

A. Yes.

24/7 Stone Serving as Part of Drain in Bunker

Q. A large stone has been placed at the entrance to a drain in a bunker to prevent sand from washing into the drain. What is the status of such a stone?

A. The stone is an immovable obstruction since it serves as part of the drain which is itself an immovable obstruction. The status of such a stone should be clarified by the Committee.

24/8 Parked Car

Q. A player's ball lies under a parked car. What is the procedure?

A. If the car is readily movable, it should be treated as a movable obstruction and moved — see Rule 24-1.

If the car is not readily movable, it should be treated as an immovable obstruction and the player is entitled to relief as provided in Rule 24-2b.

24/9 Artificially-Surfaced Road or Path

Q. An artificially-surfaced road or path is an obstruction. What constitutes artificial surfacing?

A. A road or path to which any foreign material, *e.g.*, concrete, tar, gravel, wood chips, etc., has been applied is artificially surfaced and thus an obstruction.

24

Gravel Used to Surface Road — See 23/14.

24/10 Paved Area

Q. Is a paved area, such as a paved car park or parking lot, an obstruction?

A. Yes. A paved area has the same status as an artificially-surfaced road.

24/11   Wooden Planks

Q. Is wood which has been manufactured into planks an obstruction?

A. Yes.

Ball Lying on Obstruction in Bunker — See 13/5.

When Loose Impediment Transformed into Obstruction — See 23/1.

Half-Eaten Pear — See 23/3.

Tree Basins — See 33-2a/10.**5**.

24/12   Wooden or Earthen Steps

Wooden steps which have been constructed on a steep bank are obstructions — see Decision 23/1.

Steps which have been cut into a steep bank but which have not been covered with any artificial material such as wooden planks are not obstructions.

[24/13   Reserved]

24/14   Turf Raised by Underground Pipe

Q. A water pipe is partly underground and partly above ground. In some areas where the pipe is underground it has raised the turf. Is such turf, which has been raised by an obstruction, considered part of the obstruction?

A. No.

[24/15   Reserved]

24/16   Opponent or Fellow-Competitor Removes Obstruction Affecting Player's Play

Q. An opponent or a fellow-competitor removes either a movable or an immovable obstruction which affects the player's play. What is the ruling?

24

A. If the obstruction was movable, in equity (Rule 1-4) the opponent loses the hole, or the fellow-competitor incurs a two-stroke penalty, if the player had asked him not to remove it; otherwise, there is no penalty.

If the obstruction was immovable, the opponent loses the hole, or the fellow-competitor incurs a two-stroke penalty.

24-1/1 Movable Obstruction Defined

Q. When is an obstruction considered to be movable?

A. An obstruction is movable if it may be moved without unreasonable effort, without unduly delaying play in contravention of Rule 6-7 and without damaging course property, unless it has been declared to be immovable by the Committee.

When Tee-Markers Are Obstructions — See 11-2/1.

Direction Posts — See 33/4.

24-1/2 Abandoned Ball

Q. A player's ball comes to rest against an abandoned ball. What is the procedure?

A. An abandoned ball is a movable obstruction. The player may remove it under Rule 24-1.

Rule 22, which deals specifically with one ball interfering with another, does not apply. It applies only if a ball in play interferes with another ball in play.

24

24-1/3 Movable Artificial Object Lying Out of Bounds

Q. A movable artificial object lying out of bounds interferes with a player's stance. May the player remove it?

A. Yes. Rule 24-1 applies.

24-1/4 Holding Ball in Place While Removing Obstruction

Q. During removal of a movable obstruction, may a player hold his ball to prevent it from moving?

A. No. Such procedure would be a breach of Rule 18-2a. There is no penalty if a ball moves during removal of a movable obstruction provided the movement of the ball is directly attributable to the removal of the obstruction.

24-1/5 Position of Ball Marked Before Obstruction Removed; Ball Moves When Ball-Marker Removed

Q. A player's ball lies against a movable obstruction. Before removing the obstruction, the player marks the position of his ball so that he will be able to replace the ball precisely if the ball moves when the obstruction is removed. The player removes the obstruction and the ball does not move. However, the ball moves when the ball-marker is removed. What is the ruling?

A. The ball-marker is itself a movable obstruction. Accordingly, under Rule 24-1, the player incurs no penalty and he must replace the ball.

Flagstick Lying on Putting Green Removed by Player to Prevent Another Player's Ball from Striking It — See 1-2/3.

Removal of Obstruction in Hazard Would Move Loose Impediment — See 1-4/5.

Position of Ball Worsened When Obstruction Removed; Player Replaces Obstruction — See 13-2/15.5.

Ball in Plastic Bag Moves When Bag Blown to New Position by Wind — See 18-1/7.

Ball Lifted and Dropped Away from Movable Obstruction — See 18-2a/4.

Ball in Bunker Moves Closer to Hole When Obstruction Removed and Ball Will Not Remain at Rest When Replaced; All Other Parts of Bunker Are Nearer Hole — See 20-3d/2.

24

[24-2/1 Reserved]

[24-2/2 Reserved]

24-2a/1 Mental Interference by Obstruction

Q. A player's ball lies several inches to the side of a sprinkler head. The sprinkler head does not physically interfere with the player's stance or the area of his intended swing. However, the sprinkler head bothers the player mentally. Is the player entitled to relief under Rule 24-2b?

A. No. See Rule 24-2a.

24-2a/2 Meaning of "Area of His Intended Swing"

Q. I am having trouble with the words "area of his intended swing" in Rule 24-2a. In the following diagram, the line X-Y represents a protective screen 25 feet high.

Consider a ball at point B, approximately two feet from the screen. One theory is that the player's "intended swing" can only be at the flagstick, in which case there would be interference and relief would be granted under Rule 24-2b(i).

Another theory is that the owner of the ball at point B could not play towards the flagstick even after maximum relief and that he must, therefore, elect to play towards point X or point Y. If he were a right-handed player and he chose point Y, he would get no relief because there would be no interference. If he chose point X, the screen would interfere with his stance and swing and so he would determine the nearest point at which there would be no interference with a swing

24

towards point X and drop within one club-length of that point.

Consider a ball nearly touching the screen at point A. If the player must take relief for a stroke towards the flagstick, the nearest point avoiding interference would be point A3. If the player could take relief for a stroke towards point Y, however, the nearest point avoiding interference would be only a foot or so from the screen at point A1 and it would be proper for the player to measure through the obstruction and drop at point A2, because point A2 is within one club-length of point A1 and there would be no interference with stance or swing at point A2.

What would the owners of the balls at points A and B be entitled to do?

A. A player is entitled to relief from an immovable obstruction if the ball lies in or on the obstruction or the obstruction interferes with his stance or the area of his intended swing in the direction in which he would have played if the immovable obstruction had not been there. The area of his intended swing would normally be towards the hole. However, the direction of his intended swing must not be clearly unreasonable — see Exception under Rule 24-2b. On these bases, the nearest point of relief for the owner of the ball at point A, which must be determined without crossing over, through or under the screen, would be point A3 and for the ball at point B the nearest point would be point B1.

If the player at point A elected to play in the direction of Y and such direction of play was not clearly unreasonable in the absence of the screen, the nearest point of relief would be point A1 and the player would be entitled to drop at point A2. (Formerly 24-2/2)

24

[24-2b/1   Reserved]

[24-2b/2   Reserved]

24-2b/3　Clarification of "Point on the Course Nearest to Where the Ball Lies"

Q. Please clarify the term "point on the course nearest to where the ball lies" in Rule 24-2b(i).

A. When the position of a ball is such that there is interference by an immovable obstruction, there is a specific point on the course (not nearer the hole, nor on a putting green nor in a hazard) nearest to which the ball originally lay at which, if the ball were so positioned, interference would cease to exist.

That point is "the point on the course nearest to where the ball lies." If the ball does not lie in or on an obstruction, and an artificially-surfaced road or path is not involved, the point in question is the nearest one avoiding interference which can be reached without crossing over, through or under the obstruction.

In determining the nearest point where interference would cease to exist, the club with which the player would expect to play the next stroke must be used. In measuring the one club-length from the nearest point, the player may use any club. The prohibition against crossing over, through or under an obstruction does not apply when measuring from the nearest point the one club-length within which the player must drop the ball. (Formerly 24-2/3)

Diagrams Illustrating "Point on the Course Nearest to Where the Ball Lies" — See 25-1b/2.

24-2b/3.5　Player Unable Physically to Determine "Nearest Point"

Q. In proceeding under Rule 24-2b(i) or 25-1b(i), "the point on the course nearest to where the ball lies "is, according to Decisions 24-2b/3 and 25-1b/1, determined with the club with which the player would expect to play the next stroke. What is the procedure if a player is unable physically to determine the nearest point because that point is within the trunk of a tree or a large bush?

A. The nearest point within the tree or bush must be estimated and the player must drop the ball within one club-length of the estimated point. (Formerly 24-2/3.5)

24-2b/4 Club Used to Determine "Nearest Point" Not Used for Next Stroke

Q. The first sentence of the last paragraph of Decision 24-2b/3 states: "In determining the nearest point where interference would cease to exist, the club with which the player would expect to play the next stroke must be used." If the subsequent lie of the ball were such that it was expedient for the player to play his next stroke with some other club, may the player use the other club?

A. Yes. (Formerly 24-2/4)

24-2b/4.5 Ball Found in Immovable Obstruction But Not Immediately Recoverable

Q. If a player's ball is found in an immovable obstruction, but is not immediately recoverable, may he substitute another ball and take relief, without penalty, under Rule 24-2b?

A. Yes.

Meaning of Immediately Recoverable — See 18/11.

Player Entitled to Relief from Obstruction Lifts Ball; Player Mistakenly Substitutes Ball When Dropped; Correction of Error — See 20-6/3.

24-2b/5 Clarification of Relief Procedure from Obstruction in Bunker

Q. Rule 24-2b(ii), which gives relief from an immovable obstruction in a bunker, provides that the player must proceed in accordance with Rule 24-2b(i), except that the ball must be dropped in the bunker. Rule 24-2b(i), on the other hand, requires that the ball be dropped on ground which is not in a hazard. Would you please explain this apparent conflict?

A. Under Rule 24-2b(ii), it is intended that the player follow the procedure in Rule 24-2b(i), with the last

24

clause of Rule 24-2b(ii) superseding Clause (c) of Rule 24-2b(i). Thus, if a ball lies in a bunker, there is interference by an immovable obstruction and the player elects to take relief, the following is the proper procedure:

The point nearest to where the ball lies shall be determined (without crossing over, through or under the obstruction) which (a) is not nearer the hole, (b) avoids interference (as defined) and (c) is within the hazard. The player shall lift the ball and drop it within one club-length of the point thus determined on ground which fulfills (a), (b) and (c) above. (Formerly 24-2/5)

24-2b/6 Relief from Immovable Obstruction Incidentally Results in Relief from Boundary Fence

Q. A player's ball is in such a position that a boundary fence and an immovable obstruction near the fence both interfere with the area of the player's intended swing. If the player takes relief from the obstruction under Rule 24-2b, he will incidentally get relief from the fence. Is the player entitled to invoke Rule 24-2b in such circumstances?

A. Yes. (Formerly 24-2/6)

24-2b/7 Relief from Obstruction Interfering with Swing Incidentally Gives Relief from Intervention on Line of Play

Q. A player's ball lies behind an immovable obstruction. The obstruction interferes with the player's swing and also intervenes on his line of play. In obtaining relief from interference with his swing, must the player drop the ball in such a position that intervention on the line of play is maintained?

A. No. Since the obstruction interferes with the player's swing, the player is entitled to relief under Rule 24-2b. If, in proceeding under this Rule, the player could drop the ball in a place which would also avoid intervention on his line of play, he is entitled to do so. (Formerly 24-2/7)

24-2b/8 Dropping from Rough to Fairway in Obtaining Relief from Obstruction

Q. A player whose ball lies in the rough close to the fairway is entitled to relief from an immovable obstruction. In obtaining relief under Rule 24-2b(i), may the player drop the ball on the fairway?

A. Yes. There is no distinction in the Rules between fairway and rough; both are covered by the term "through the green." (Formerly 24-2/8)

24-2b/9 After Relief from Obstruction Second Obstruction Interferes

Q. A player obtaining relief from an immovable obstruction drops his ball in such a position that another immovable obstruction interferes with his swing. What is the procedure?

A. The player is entitled to relief from the second obstruction as provided in Rule 24-2b. (Formerly 24-2/9)

24-2b/9.5 After Relief Taken from Obstruction for Stroke Towards Green, Obstruction Interferes with Stance for Necessary Sideways Stroke

Q. With regard to the illustration above, Point X is the original position of the ball and Point A is the nearest point of relief from the obstruction (cart path). The player drops his ball within one club-length of Point A (within the shaded area) and it comes to rest on the cart path at Point B. He re-drops as required by Rule 20-2c, again dropping within one club-length of Point A and the ball comes to rest at Point C.

24

At Point C there is no interference by the cart path for a stroke towards the green. However, the player cannot play towards the green from Point C because of intervention by the tree. His only reasonable stroke is sideways to the fairway, and his stance for such a stroke would be on the cart path. Is the player now required to place the ball as near as possible to the spot where it first struck the ground when re-dropped under the penultimate paragraph of Rule 20-2c?

A. No. The player is not entitled to place the ball because at Point C there is no interference by the cart path for a stroke towards the green, the intended direction of play when relief was taken. However, as a result of the tree, the player has a new situation. He is entitled to take relief under Rule 24-2b(i) for the sideways stroke since this is not an unnecessarily abnormal direction of play — see Exception under Rule 24-2b — and his nearest point of relief would be Point D. After the ball is dropped within one club-length of Point D (within the shaded area) and it comes to rest at Point E, the player may play in any direction he wishes. (Formerly 24-2/9.5)

Nearest Point of Relief from Cart Path Is in Casual Water; Nearest Point of Relief from Casual Water Is Back on Cart Path — See 1-4/8.

Ball Lying on Immovable Obstruction Is Dropped Away; Ball Rolls to Position Where Player Would Have to Stand on Obstruction; Whether Re-Drop Required — See 20-2c/0.5.

24-2b/10 Obstruction in Ground Under Repair Interferes with Player's Swing

Q. An immovable obstruction situated within an area defined as ground under repair interferes with the area of the player's intended swing. May the player take relief from the obstruction under Rule 24-2b, drop his ball in the ground under repair and then have the option of playing the ball as it lies or proceeding under Rule 25-1b which provides relief from ground under repair?

A. Yes. (Formerly 24-2/10)

Player Entitled to Relief from Obstruction Lifts Ball; Player Then Replaces Ball and Plays It from Original Position — See 18-2a/12.

24-2b/11   Ball Lying on Elevated Obstruction

Q. A ball comes to rest on a bridge over a deep hollow. What is the ruling?

A. Under Rule 24-2b, the player may drop the ball within one club-length of the point on the ground in the hollow directly beneath where the ball lay on the bridge, *i.e.,* vertical distance is disregarded. (Formerly 24-2/11)

24-2b/12   Ball in Drainpipe Under Course; Entrance to Drainpipe Is Out of Bounds

Q. A ball enters an underground drainpipe the entrance to which is out of bounds. The ball is found in the drainpipe under an area which is through the green. What is the ruling?

A. Under Rule 24-2b(i), the player is entitled to drop the ball, without penalty, within one club-length of the spot on the ground immediately above its resting place in the drainpipe, but not nearer the hole and not in a hazard or on a putting green. A boundary line extends vertically upwards and downwards — see Definition of "Out of Bounds."

If the player cannot find or identify the ball, he must proceed under Rule 27-1 because the entrance to the drainpipe is out of bounds (see Rule 24-2c).

Ball Lost in Underground Drainpipe — See 24-2c/1.

24

24-2b/13   Ball Bounces Across Obstruction After Drop

Q. A player taking relief from a water pipe on the ground drops his ball correctly under Rule 24-2b but the ball bounces over the pipe and comes to rest on the other side in a position where there is no interference by the pipe. The player is not required to re-drop under Rule 20-2c. What is the ruling?

A. The ball must be played as it lies. Rule 24-2b does not permit or require the player to re-drop. The prohibition against crossing over, through or under the obstruction in determining the nearest point does not have any relevance to what the ball does after it strikes the ground. (Formerly 24-2/13)

Crossing Over Obstruction in Obtaining Relief from Ground Under Repair — See 25-1b/14.

24-2b/14 Window of Clubhouse Opened and Ball Played Through Window

Q. A competitor hit a ball into a clubhouse which was not out of bounds and had not been declared an integral part of the course. In order to play it out, he opened a window, claiming that it was a movable (or partially movable) obstruction. Was this permissible?

A. Yes. The clubhouse was an immovable obstruction. However, any part of it designed to be movable, such as a window or door, may be moved to any position if this can be done without undue delay.

The same principle would apply if the clubhouse had been declared an integral part of the course. (Formerly 24-2/14)

Improving Line of Play by Removing Stone from Wall — See 13-2/32.

Improving Line of Play by Removing Part of Fence — See 13-2/32.5.

Outside Agency Removes Immovable Obstruction on Player's Line of Play — See 13-2/33.

24

24-2b/15 Opening Barn Doors to Play Shot Through Barn

Q. May a player open the doors of a barn to enable him to play a shot through the barn?

A. Yes. A barn is an immovable obstruction, but the doors are movable and may be opened. See also Decision 24-2b/14. (Formerly 24-2/15)

24-2b/15.3 Status of Movable Part of Drainage Hose

Q. In a water hazard, a player's swing is interfered with by a drainage hose. One end of the hose is immovable, *i.e.*, it is anchored in the ground. However, that part of the hose interfering with the player's swing can readily be moved to one side or the other. Is the player entitled to move the hose to the side so that is does not interfere with his swing?

A. Yes, since the part of the hose interfering with player's swing is designed to be movable. (Formerly 24-2/15.3)

Area of Intended Swing Improved by Removing Immovable Obstruction — See 13-2/15.

Stake Supporting Tree Broken in Attempt to Remove It — See 13-2/16.

24-2b/16 Obstruction Interferes But Ball Unplayable Due to Some Other Condition

Q. A player's ball lies between two exposed tree roots. The ball is clearly unplayable due to the roots. An immovable obstruction is so located that it would interfere with the player's backswing if the player could play the ball. The player claims he is entitled to relief, without penalty, under Rule 24-2b(i). Is the player correct?

A. No. See Exception under Rule 24-2b. The player must invoke Rule 28. (Formerly 24-2/16)

24-2b/17 Obstruction Interferes with Abnormal Stroke; Abnormal Stroke Reasonable in Circumstances

24

Q. A right-handed player's ball is so close to a boundary fence on the left of a hole that the player, in order to play towards the hole, must play left-handed. In playing a left-handed stroke, the player's backswing would be interfered with by an immovable obstruction. Is the player entitled to relief from the obstruction?

A. The player is entitled to relief since employment of an abnormal (left-handed) stroke is necessary in the circumstances — see Exception under Rule 24-2b.

The proper procedure is for the player to take relief for a left-handed stroke in accordance with Rule 24-2b(i).

The player may then use a normal right-handed swing for his next stroke. If the obstruction interferes with the swing or stance for the right-handed stroke, the player may take relief for the right-handed stroke in accordance with Rule 24-2b(i). (Formerly 24-2/17)

24-2b/18 Obstruction Interferes with Abnormal Stroke; Abnormal Stroke Not Reasonable in Circumstances

Q. A right-handed player's ball is in a poor lie. A nearby immovable obstruction would not interfere with a normal right-handed swing but it would interfere with a left-handed swing. The player says he wishes to play his next stroke left-handed and, since the obstruction would interfere with such a stroke, he is entitled to proceed under Rule 24-2b. May the player invoke Rule 24-2b?

A. No. If the only reason for the player to use a left-handed stroke is to escape a poor lie, use of an abnormal (left-handed) stroke is not justifiable and the player is not entitled to invoke Rule 24-2b — see Exception under Rule 24-2b. (Formerly 24-2/18)

24-2b/19 Stroke at Ball Not Reasonable Due to Interference by Immovable Obstruction and Casual Water

Q. A player's ball lies against an immovable obstruction in casual water. It is clearly unreasonable for him to play a stroke because of interference by either of them. The Exceptions to Rule 24-2b and Rule 25-1b appear to preclude free relief from either because of interference by the other. Is this correct?

A. No. The player may take relief without penalty under either Rule 24-2b or Rule 25-1b. The purpose of the Exception to each of these Rules is to prevent the player from fortuitously obtaining free relief when it is clearly unreasonable for him to play a stroke because of interference by something from which free relief is not available. (Formerly 24-2/19)

24-2b/20 Interference by Line on Ground Consisting of Lime

Q. A ball comes to rest on a line on the ground consisting of lime which has been drawn for gallery-control purposes. Is the player entitled to relief under Rule 24-2b?

A. No. Such a line is not an obstruction. (Formerly 24-2/20)

24-2b/21 Interference by Immovable Artificial Object Situated Out of Bounds

Q. An immovable artificial object situated out of bounds interferes with a player's swing. May the player obtain relief as provided in Rule 24-2b?

A. No. Immovable artificial objects off the course are not obstructions (see Definition of "Obstructions"); therefore, the Rules provide no relief without penalty. (Formerly 24-2/21)

Part of Fence Off Course Leans Across Boundary and Interferes with Swing — See 13-2/20.

24-2c/1 Ball Lost in Underground Drainpipe

Q. A player's ball goes into an underground drainpipe, but he cannot reach or identify it. What is the ruling?

A. An underground drainpipe or culvert is an obstruction. If there is reasonable evidence that the ball is lost in the immovable obstruction, the player may invoke Rule 24-2c by dropping a ball in accordance with Rule 24-2b(i). For the purpose of applying this Rule, the ball shall be deemed to lie at the spot where it entered the obstruction.

24

If the entrance to the underground drainpipe or culvert is in a hazard, Rule 24-2c applies and the ball must be dropped in that hazard or the player may proceed under Rule 26-1, if applicable.

If the entrance to the underground drainpipe or culvert is out of bounds, the player must proceed under Rule 27-1.

24

Rule 25. Abnormal Ground Conditions and Wrong Putting Green

Definitions

"Casual water" is any temporary accumulation of water on the <u>course</u> which is visible before or after the player takes his <u>stance</u> and is not in a <u>water hazard</u>. Snow and natural ice, other than frost, are casual water or <u>loose impediments</u>, at the option of the player. Manufactured ice is an <u>obstruction</u>. Dew and frost are not casual water.

"Ground under repair" is any portion of the <u>course</u> so marked by order of the Committee or so declared by its authorized representative. It includes material piled for removal and a hole made by a greenkeeper, even if not so marked. Stakes and lines defining ground under repair are in such ground. The margin of ground under repair extends vertically downwards, but not upwards.

Note 1: Grass cuttings and other material left on the course which have been abandoned and are not intended to be removed are not ground under repair unless so marked.

Note 2: The Committee may make a Local Rule prohibiting play from ground under repair.

25

25-1. Casual Water, Ground Under Repair and Certain Damage to Course

a. INTERFERENCE

Interference by <u>casual water</u>, <u>ground under repair</u> or a hole, cast or runway made by a burrowing animal, a reptile or a bird occurs when a ball lies in or touches any of these conditions or when such a condition on the course interferes with the player's <u>stance</u> or the area of his intended swing.

If the player's ball lies on the <u>putting green</u>, interference also occurs if such condition on the putting green intervenes on his line of putt.

If interference exists, the player may either play the ball as it lies (unless prohibited by Local Rule) or take relief as provided in Clause b.

b. RELIEF

If the player elects to take relief, he shall proceed as follows:

(i) *Through the Green*: If the ball lies <u>through the green</u>, the point on the <u>course</u> nearest to where the ball lies shall be determined which (a) is not nearer the hole, (b) avoids interference by the condition, and (c) is not in a <u>hazard</u> or on a <u>putting green</u>. The player shall lift the ball and drop it without penalty within one club-length of the point thus determined on ground which fulfils (a), (b) and (c) above.

(ii) *In a Hazard*: If the ball lies in or touches a <u>hazard</u>, the player shall lift and drop the ball either:

(a) Without penalty, in the hazard, as near as possible to the spot where the ball lay, but not nearer the hole, on ground which affords maximum available relief from the condition;

or

(b) *Under penalty of one stroke*, outside the hazard, keeping the point where the

25

ball lay directly between the hole and the spot on which the ball is dropped.

Exception: If a ball lies in or touches a water hazard (including a <u>lateral water hazard</u>), the player is not entitled to relief without penalty from a hole, cast or runway made by a burrowing animal, a reptile or a bird. The player shall play the ball as it lies or proceed under Rule 26-1.

(iii) *On the Putting Green*: If the ball lies on the <u>putting green</u>, the player shall lift the ball and place it without penalty in the nearest position to where it lay which affords maximum available relief from the condition, but not nearer the hole nor in a <u>hazard</u>. The ball may be cleaned when lifted under Rule 25-1b.

(Ball rolling to a position where there is interference by the condition from which relief was taken — see Rule 20-2c(v).)

Exception: A player may not obtain relief under Rule 25-1b if (a) it is clearly unreasonable for him to play a stroke because of interference by anything other than a condition covered by Rule 25-1a or (b) interference by such a condition would occur only through use of an unnecessarily abnormal stance, swing or direction of play.

c. BALL LOST UNDER CONDITION COVERED BY RULE 25-1

It is a question of fact whether a ball lost after having been struck toward a condition covered by Rule 25-1 is lost under such condition. In order to treat the ball as lost under such condition, there must be reasonable evidence to that effect. In the absence of such evidence, the ball must be treated as a lost ball and Rule 27 applies.

(i) *Outside a Hazard* — If a ball is lost outside a <u>hazard</u> under a condition covered by Rule 25-1, the player may take relief as follows: the point on the <u>course</u> nearest to where the ball last crossed the margin of

25

the area shall be determined which (a) is not nearer the hole than where the ball last crossed the margin, (b) avoids interference by the condition and (c) is not in a hazard or on a <u>putting green</u>. He shall drop a ball without penalty within one club-length of the point thus determined on ground which fulfils (a), (b) and (c) above.

(ii) *In a Hazard* — If a ball is lost in a <u>hazard</u> under a condition covered by Rule 25-1, the player may drop a ball either:

(a) Without penalty, in the hazard, as near as possible to the point at which the original ball last crossed the margin of the area, but not nearer the hole, on ground which affords maximum available relief from the condition

or

(b) *Under penalty of one stroke*, outside the hazard, keeping the point at which the original ball last crossed the margin of the hazard directly between the hole and the spot on which the ball is dropped.

Exception: If a ball lies in a <u>water hazard</u> (including a <u>lateral water hazard</u>), the player is not entitled to relief without penalty for a ball lost in a hole, cast or runway made by a burrowing animal, a reptile or a bird. The player shall proceed under Rule 26-1.

25-2. Embedded Ball

A ball embedded in its own pitch-mark in the ground in any closely mown area <u>through the green</u> may be lifted, cleaned and dropped, without penalty, as near as possible to the spot where it lay but not nearer the hole. "Closely mown area" means any area of the <u>course</u>, including paths through the rough, cut to fairway height or less.

25-3. Wrong Putting Green

A player must not play a ball which lies on a <u>putting green</u> other than that of the hole being played. The ball must be lifted and the player must proceed as follows: The point on the <u>course</u> nearest to where the ball lies shall be determined which (a) is not nearer the hole and (b) is not in a <u>hazard</u> or on a putting green. The player shall lift the ball and drop it without penalty within one club-length of the point thus determined on ground which fulfils (a) and (b) above. The ball may be cleaned when so lifted.

Note: Unless otherwise prescribed by the Committee, the term "a putting green other than that of the hole being played" includes a practice putting green or pitching green on the course.

PENALTY FOR BREACH OF RULE:
Match play --- Loss of hole;
Stroke play --- Two strokes.

25/1 Soft, Mushy Earth

Q. Is soft, mushy earth casual water?

A. No. Soft, mushy earth is not casual water unless water is visible on the surface before or after the player takes his stance — see Definition of "Casual Water."

25/2 Overflow from Water Hazard

Q. If a pond (water hazard) has overflowed, is the overflow casual water?

A. Yes. Any overflow of water from a water hazard which is outside the margin of the hazard is casual water.

Ball Lost in Either Water Hazard or Casual Water Overflowing Hazard — See 1-4/7.

25

25/3 Pitch-Mark Filled with Casual Water

Q. A player's ball plugged deeply in short rough. No casual water was visible on the surface, but the pitch-mark in which the ball came to rest filled with water. Was the player's ball in casual water?

A. Yes.

25/4 Water Visible as Result of Undue Effort with Feet

Q. In a wet area, casual water is not visible before or after the player takes his normal stance. However, by pressing down hard with one foot, the player causes water to appear around the sole of his shoe. Is the player entitled to relief under Rule 25-1b?

A. No. Water visible through undue effort with the feet is not casual water — see Definition of "Casual Water."

25/5 Casual Water on Putting Green Visible When Player Walks Beside Line of Putt But Not Visible Elsewhere

Q. A player's ball lies on a putting green. Casual water is not visible on the green. However, when the player walks beside his line of putt, casual water is visible around the player's feet. Is the player entitled to relief?

A. Not unless there is casual water visible around the player's feet when he takes his stance — see Definition of "Casual Water."

25 [25/6 Reserved]

Mopping Up Casual Water on Line of Play — See 13-2/34.

Brushing Aside or Mopping Up Casual Water on Line of Putt — See 16-1a/1.

Ball Moved by Wind or Casual Water While Play Suspended — See 18-1/11.

Ball-Marker Moved Off Green by Wind or Casual Water — See 20-1/10.

Removal of Casual Water on Putting Green by Committee — See 33/1.

25/7   Fallen Tree in Process of Being Removed

Q. A greenkeeper is in the process of sawing up a fallen tree and stacking the wood. What is the status of such a tree?

A. The tree in its entirety is ground under repair as it constitutes "material piled for removal" — see Definition of "Ground Under Repair."

25/8   Tree Stump

Q. Do the Rules provide relief without penalty from a tree stump?

A. No, not unless it has been marked as ground under repair or it is in the process of being unearthed or cut up for removal, in which case it is "material piled for removal" and thus automatically ground under repair — see Definition of "Ground Under Repair."

A tree stump which the Committee intends to remove, but which is not in the process of being removed, is not automatically ground under repair.

25/9   Fallen Tree Attached to Stump

Q. A tree has fallen onto a fairway due to a windstorm and is still attached to the stump. Does it constitute ground under repair?

A. No. However, a player could request relief from the Committee and the Committee would be justified in declaring the area covered by the tree to be ground under repair.

25

Damage to Line of Putt Caused by Fellow-Competitor's Caddie — See 16-1a/14.

Declaring Area as Ground Under Repair During Competition Round — See 33-2a/2.

Extensive Damage Due to Heavy Rain and Traffic — See 33-2a/3.

Referee's Authority to Declare Ground Under Repair —
See 34-2/1.

25/10 Ball Lost in Tree in Ground Under Repair

Q. A ball is lost in a tree growing in an area marked
as ground under repair. Is the player entitled to relief
without penalty under Rule 25-1c?

A. No. Such a ball is not lost in ground under repair,
because the margin of ground under repair does not
extend upwards. The player must proceed under Rule
27-1.

25/11 Grass Cuttings

Grass cuttings are only ground under repair if they
have been piled for removal — see Note 1 under
Definition of "Ground Under Repair." If cuttings piled
for removal interfere with a player's stance or swing,
the player is entitled to relief under Rule 25-1b.

Grass cuttings are loose impediments (see Definition
of "Loose Impediments"), whether or not they are
piled for removal, and may be removed by the player
— Rule 23-1.

25/12 Cracks in Earth

Q. Are cracks in the earth which occur in hot and dry
conditions ground under repair? Do the Rules of Golf
provide relief?

A. No. However, a player whose ball is in a large
crack would be justified in requesting the Committee
to declare the crack to be ground under repair, and
the Committee would be justified in doing so.

25/13 Bunker Totally Under Repair

If an entire bunker is being renovated, it does not lose
its status as a hazard. However, it is recommended
that the Committee should, during the renovation period, define the bunker as ground under repair and

25

classify it as through the green. If such a bunker has been defined as ground under repair but has not been classified as through the green, the player may, under Rule 25-1b(ii):

(a) drop the ball without penalty in the bunker as near as possible to the spot where the ball lay, but not nearer the hole, on ground which affords maximum available relief, *i.e.* , ground which is most nearly normal, or

(b) drop the ball under penalty of one stroke behind the bunker, keeping the point where the ball lay between the hole and the spot on which the ball is dropped.

Water Hazard Under Repair — See 33-2a/5.

25/14 Explanation of "Hole Made by Greenkeeper" in Definition of "Ground Under Repair"

Q. What constitutes a "hole made by greenkeeper"?

A. A "hole made by a greenkeeper" is usually ground temporarily dug up in connection with course maintenance, such a hole made in removing turf or a tree stump, laying pipelines, etc.

25/15 Aeration Holes

Q. Is an aeration hole a hole made by a greenkeeper within the meaning of that term in the Definition of "Ground Under Repair"?

A. No.

Local Rule for Aeration Holes — See 33-8/32.

25/16 Rut Made by Tractor

25

Q. Is a rut made by a tractor considered a hole made by a greenkeeper and thus ground under repair? If not, should the Committee declare such a rut to be ground under repair?

A. Such a rut is not a hole made by a greenkeeper. The Committee would be justified in declaring a deep rut to be ground under repair, but not a shallow indentation made by greenkeeping equipment.

25/17 Sunken Hole Plug

Q. Is an old hole plug which has sunk below the level of the surface of the putting green a hole made by a greenkeeper and therefore ground under repair?

A. No. Rule 16-1c applies.

Hole on Putting Green Not in Use — See 16/7.

25/18 Hole of Removed Stake Defining Water Hazard

Q. A stake defining the margin of a water hazard is removed. Is the hole in which the stake was previously located a "hole made by a greenkeeper" and thus ground under repair?

A. Yes, but such a hole is in the water hazard — see Definition of "Water Hazard" — and Rule 25-1b(ii) applies.

25/19 Burrowing Animal

Q. What is a burrowing animal? Dogs dig holes. Is a dog a burrowing animal?

A. A burrow is a hole or tunnel in the ground made by certain animals, such as rabbits, moles, ground hogs and gophers, for shelter and habitation. Thus, a burrowing animal is an animal that makes a hole in which it may live. Since a dog does not dig holes for habitation or shelter, a hole made by a dog is not a burrowing animal hole.

25

25/20 Holes Made by Non-Burrowing Animals

Q. According to Decision 25/19, a hole dug by a dog is not a burrowing animal hole. Thus the Rules provide no relief. Would a Committee be justified in marking such a hole as ground under repair?

A. Yes.

25/21 Lifting Ball to Determine Whether It Lies in Burrowing Animal Hole

Q. May a player whose ball lies in a depression, other than in a water hazard, lift his ball to determine if it is in a hole made by a burrowing animal?

A. In equity (Rule 1-4), the player may lift the ball, without penalty, provided he announces his intention in advance to his opponent in match play or his marker or a fellow-competitor in stroke play and gives his opponent, marker or fellow-competitor an opportunity to observe the lifting. If the ball is in a burrowing animal hole, he is entitled to relief under Rule 25-1b. Otherwise, the ball must be replaced and the opponent, marker or fellow-competitor given an opportunity to observe the replacement. A ball so lifted may not be cleaned unless it is found to be lying in a burrowing animal hole and the player elects to take relief under Rule 25.

Ball Found in Burrowing Animal Hole After Five-Minute Search — See 27/7.

25/22 Salamander

Q. Is a salamander mound a cast or runway made by a burrowing animal?

A. Yes. A salamander is considered a burrowing animal and relief is available under Rule 25-1b, unless the ball lies in a water hazard.

Crawfish Mound — See 25-1b/18.

25

25/23 Molehills

Q. Molehills are casts made by a burrowing animal. If the greenkeeping staff have swept them flat, but the surface is still irregular, do molehills cease to be classified as casts made by a burrowing animal?

A. If it is established that mounds of soil are casts (or remains of casts) made by moles, relief is permissible under Rule 25-1b. However, when such a mound has been swept flat, it becomes an irregularity of surface and there is no relief without penalty.

25-1/1 Ball in Casual Water Difficult to Retrieve

Q. There is reasonable evidence that a player's ball came to rest in a large puddle of casual water. A ball is visible in the casual water, but the player cannot retrieve it or identify it as his ball without unreasonable effort.

The player abandons the ball and proceeds under Rule 25-1c, which provides relief for a ball lost in casual water. Was the player justified in doing so?

A. Yes. A player is not obliged to use unreasonable effort to retrieve a ball in casual water, for identification purposes.

However, if it would not take unreasonable effort to retrieve a ball in casual water, the player must retrieve it. If it turns out to be the player's ball and he elects to take relief, he must proceed under Rule 25-1b(i); otherwise, he must proceed under Rule 25-1c(i).

25-1a/1 Ball Outside Ground Under Repair Area But High Grass Within Area Interferes with Swing

Q. The margins of ground under repair do not extend vertically upwards. If the ball lies outside ground under repair and high grass within the ground under repair interferes with a player's swing, but there is no interference with the stance, does the player get relief?

25

A. The answer depends on the circumstances.

Rule 25-1a provides that interference by ground under repair occurs when the condition interferes with the area of the player's intended swing. If the long grass was a part of, or the result of, the condition which caused the Committee to declare the area to be ground under repair, *e.g.*, a soggy area which was too soft to mow, relief should be granted. Otherwise, long grass should be treated like branches of a tree or a bush in ground under repair, and relief should be denied.

25-1a/2 Casual Water on Putting Green Intervenes Between Ball Off Green and Hole

Q. A player's ball lies just off the putting green and casual water on the green intervenes between the ball and the hole. Is the player entitled to relief?

A. No. See also Decision 13-2/34.

Casual Water on Putting Green; Whether Player Entitled to Relief for Intervention if Ball is on Green and Nearest Point of Relief is off Green — See 25-1b/10.5.

25-1b/1 Clarification of "Point on the Course Nearest to Where the Ball Lies"

Q. Please clarify the term "point on the course nearest to where the ball lies" in Rule 25-1b(i).

A. When the position of a ball is such that there is interference by casual water, ground under repair, etc., there is a specific point on the course (not nearer the hole, nor on a putting green nor in a hazard) nearest to which the ball originally lay at which, if the ball were so positioned, interference would cease to exist. That point is "the point on the course nearest to where the ball lies."

In determining the nearest point where interference would cease to exist, the club with which the player would expect to play the next stroke must be used. In measuring the one club-length from the nearest point, the player may use any club.

Player Unable Physically to Determine "Nearest Point" — See 24-2b/3.5.

25

25-1b/2 Diagrams Illustrating "Point on the Course Nearest to Where the Ball Lies"

The following diagrams which illustrate the term "point on the course nearest to where the ball lies" in Rule 25-1b(i) in the case of both a right-handed and a left-handed player, should be considered in conjunction with Decision 25-1b/1.

The "point nearest" must be strictly interpreted. A player is not permitted to choose on which side of the ground under repair or casual water he will drop the ball, unless there are two equidistant "points nearest." Even if one side of the ground under repair or casual water is fairway and the other is bushes, if the "point nearest" is in the bushes then the player, if taking relief, must drop the ball within one club-length of that point, even though he may have to drop the ball in a virtually unplayable lie.

The same procedure applies under Rule 24-2b dealing with immovable obstructions. In this connection see Decision 24-2b/3.

B1 = position of ball in ground under repair, etc.

P1 = "point nearest"

P1-A-A = shaded area within which ball to be dropped, radius of one club-length from P1, measured with any club

B2 = position of ball in ground under repair

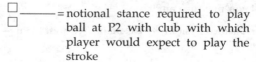 = notional stance required to play ball at P2 with club with which player would expect to play the stroke

P2 = "point nearest"

P2-C-C = shaded area within which ball to be dropped, radius of one club-length from P2, measured with any club

B1 and B2 are the positions of the ball in ground under repair, etc.

P1 is the "point nearest" B1

P2 is the "point nearest" B2

Shaded area P1-A-A = dropping area for ball at B1

Shaded area P2-C-C = dropping area for ball at B2

□
□ ——— = player's notional stance to play
            ball at P1

25-1b/3 Improving Line of Play When Taking Relief from Abnormal Ground Condition

Q. In certain circumstances, in complying with Rule 25-1b, it is possible for a player incidentally to improve his line of play, *e.g.*, avoid playing over a bunker or a tree. Is this permissible?

A. Yes. If a player's ball is in one of the conditions covered by Rule 25 and if, in taking relief in accordance with the procedure laid down in Rule 25-1b, his line of play is improved, this is his good fortune.

Player Entitled to Relief from Abnormal Ground Condition Lifts Ball; Player Then Replaces Ball and Plays It from Original Position — See 18-2a/12.

25

25-1b/4 Casual Water Covering Teeing Ground

Q. What is the procedure if, after part of the field in a competition has played a particular hole, the teeing ground of that hole becomes completely covered with casual water?

A. Rule 25-1b does not give relief. In such a case, the matter should be brought to the attention of the Committee.

In match play, the Committee may relocate the teeing ground.

In stroke play, if the conditions are such that removal of the casual water might be possible, the Committee should suspend play and attempt to remove the casual water. If the removal of the casual water is impossible, the Committee may (1) suspend play until the teeing ground is playable or cancel the round — Rule 33-2d - or (2) relocate the teeing ground if this could be done without giving any competitor an undue advantage or disadvantage.

Hole Surrounded by Casual Water — See 33-2d/2.

25-1b/5 Explanation of "Maximum Available Relief" from Casual Water in Bunker

Q. In a bunker completely covered by casual water, is the place providing "maximum available relief" the spot which will provide the most relief for both lie and stance or just lie?

A. The term applies to both lie and stance. The spot providing "maximum available relief" might be such that the ball will be in shallower water than the player's feet after he takes his stance, or vice versa.

25-1b/6 Ball Dropped from Casual Water in Bunker at Point of Maximum Relief Rolls Elsewhere

Q. A player whose ball lies in a bunker completely covered by casual water drops his ball under Rule 25-1b(ii) at a spot where there is 1/4 inch of casual water. This spot is the nearest spot providing maximum available relief. The ball rolls into a spot where there is about 1/2 inch of casual water. What is the ruling?

A. In equity (Rule 1-4), and under the principle of Rule 20-2c(v), the player may re-drop and, if the ball so rolls again, place the ball where it first struck a part of the course when re-dropped.

25-1b/7 Ball to Be Dropped in Bunker Dropped Outside Bunker and Rolls into Bunker

Q. A player's ball lies in casual water in a bunker. The player elects to proceed under the first option of Rule 25-1b(ii) and determines that the nearest spot in the hazard and not nearer the hole which offers maximum available relief (Spot A) is at the back of the bunker. The player does not drop his ball in the bunker at Spot A because he fears it will plug in the sand. Rather, he drops the ball behind Spot A on a slope outside the bunker. The ball rolls down the slope and comes to rest at Spot A. Is the player subject to penalty?

A. Yes, unless he lifts the ball and proceeds correctly, as provided in Rule 20-6. Under the first option of Rule 25-1b(ii), the player is required to drop the ball in the hazard. If the player, although proceeding under the first option, drops the ball outside the hazard and plays it, he is in breach of Rule 25 and the penalty is loss of hole in match play or two strokes in stroke play.

25-1b/8 Player's Options When Bunker Completely Covered by Casual Water

Q. If a player's ball lies in a bunker completely covered by casual water, what are his options?

A. The player may play the ball as it lies or:
(1) drop the ball in the bunker without penalty at the nearest place, not nearer the hole, where the depth of the casual water is least — first option of Rule 25-1b(ii); or
(2) drop the ball behind the bunker under penalty of one stroke — second option of Rule 25-1b(ii); or
(3) declare the ball unplayable and proceed in accordance with Rule 28.

25

25-1b/9 Player Who Invokes First Option of Rule 25-1b(ii) Then Wishes to Invoke Second Option

Q. A player's ball is in a bunker completely covered by casual water. Under the first option of Rule 25-1b(ii), he drops his ball on ground in the bunker affording maximum available relief. He then decides he would have been better off to invoke the second option and drop behind the bunker. May he then invoke the second option?

A. No. Rule 25-1b(ii) permits the player to proceed under either Option 1 or Option 2. He is not entitled to invoke Option 1 and then, if he does not like the result, invoke Option 2.

25-1b/10 Casual Water on Putting Green; Nearest Relief Is Off Green

Q. A player whose ball is on a putting green is entitled to relief from casual water. However, the nearest position affording maximum available relief which is not nearer the hole or in a hazard is off the green in the rough. If the player opts to take relief, must he place the ball in the rough?

A. Yes. See Rule 25-1b(iii).

25-1b/10.5 Casual Water on Putting Green; Whether Player Entitled to Relief for Intervention If Ball Is On Green and Nearest Point of Relief If Off Green

Q. In Illustration X, a player's ball lies at Point 1 in casual water on the putting green. In Illustration Y, a player's ball lies at Point 1 on the putting green with casual water intervening on his line of putt.

Under Rule 25-1b(iii), the player is not entitled to place the ball at Point 4, which is on the green, because Point 4 is farther from Point 1 than either Point 2 or Point 3, both of which are off the green. It would seem that Point 2 may be the correct point because there is no relief if a ball lies off the green and casual water on the green intervenes on the line of play. In taking relief, must the player place the ball at Point 2 or Point 3?

A. Since, in both illustrations, the ball lies on the putting green, the player is entitled to relief with respect to the lie of the ball and intervention on his line. Accordingly, in either case the player must place the ball at Point 3, the nearest point which affords maximum available relief with respect to both situations.

25-1b/11 Ball in Casual Water Within Ground Under Repair

Q. A ball lies in casual water within an area defined as ground under repair. May a player take relief from the casual water under Rule 25-1b, drop the ball in the ground under repair, and then either play the ball as it lies or take relief from the ground under repair under Rule 25-1b?

A. Yes.

Nearest Point of Relief from Cart Path Is in Casual Water; Nearest Point of Relief from Casual Water Is Back on Cart Path — See 1-4/8.

25

25-1b/12 Casual Water Mistaken for Water Hazard; Original Ball Played Under Water Hazard Rule

Q. A player whose ball is in casual water mistakes the casual water for a water hazard. He retrieves his original ball, drops it 10 yards behind the casual water in accordance with the water hazard Rule and plays it. His error is then discovered. What is the ruling?

A. The player did not follow the procedure prescribed in Rule 25-1b(i) for dropping a ball from casual water; he dropped the ball in a wrong place. In match play, he loses the hole — Rule 20-7a. In stroke play, he incurs a penalty of two strokes — Rules 25-1b(i) and 20-7b.

25-1b/13 Casual Water Mistaken for Water Hazard; Substituted Ball Played Under Water Hazard Rule

Q. A player whose ball is in casual water mistakes the casual water for a water hazard. The player does not retrieve his original ball. Rather, he drops another ball 10 yards behind the casual water in accordance with the water hazard Rule and plays it. His error is then discovered. What is the ruling?

A. The ball dropped under the water hazard Rule (Rule 26-1) was not substituted under an applicable Rule; therefore it was a wrong ball — see Definitions of "Ball in Play" and "Wrong Ball."

In match play, the player loses the hole — Rule 15-2.

In stroke play, the player incurs a penalty of two strokes — Rule 15-3 — and he is required to proceed under Rule 25-1b(i) — see Decision 25-1/1.

25-1b/14 Crossing Over Obstruction In Obtaining Relief from Ground Under Repair

25

Q. An exposed pipeline (obstruction) abuts an area of ground under repair. A player's ball is in the ground under repair. The player wishes to measure over the pipeline in proceeding under Rule 25-1b. May the player do so?

A. Yes. There is nothing in the Rules prohibiting measuring over an obstruction in obtaining relief from ground under repair.

25-1b/14.5 Ball Declared Unplayable Dropped in Ground Under Repair from Which Play Prohibited; Ball Then Dropped Under Ground Under Repair Rule

Q. A player declared his ball unplayable. In proceeding under Rule 28b or c, the player dropped his ball in an area of ground under repair from which play was prohibited by Local Rule. He then took the mandatory relief under Rule 25-1b. Is this procedure permitted?

A. Yes.

Ball in Ground Under Repair Thought to be Unfit for Play Lifted and Cleaned — See 5-3/6.

Obstruction in Ground Under Repair Interferes with Player's Swing — See 24-2b/10.

Ball Embedded in Ground Under Repair in Closely Mown Area — See 25-2/4.

25-1b/15 Measuring Across Ground Under Repair in Obtaining Relief

Q. A player obtaining relief from a narrow strip of ground under repair through the green determines the point (Point A) nearest to where the ball lies which is not nearer the hole, avoids interference and is not in a hazard or on a putting green. Point A is on the right-hand side of the ground under repair. Within one club-length of Point A is a point (Point B) on the left side of the ground under repair which meets the requirements of Rule 25-1b(i). May the player drop his ball at Point B?

A. Yes. There is nothing in Rule 25-1b prohibiting measuring the one club-length across ground under repair in obtaining relief.

Ball Dropped from Ground Under Repair Area Rolls to Position Where Area Interferes with Stance; Whether Re-Drop Required — See 20-2c/0.5.

25

25-1b/16 Ball Equidistant from Two Points Which Meet Requirements of Ground Under Repair Rule

Q. Through the green, the player's ball lies in ground

under repair and he opts for relief under Rule 25-1b(i). There is no single "point nearest to where the ball lies" which is not nearer the hole, avoids interference, etc. Rather, there are two such points equidistant from the spot where the ball lies. May the player drop within one club-length of either point?

A. Yes.

After Declaring Ball Unplayable and Lifting It, Player Discovers That Ball Was in Ground Under Repair — See 28/13.

25-1b/17 Pine Needles Piled for Removal Interfere with Line of Play After Ball Dropped Away

Q. A player whose ball lies in pine needles piled for removal drops away under Rule 25-1b. The ball comes to rest in such a position that the pile of pine needles intervenes on his line of play. May the player remove the pine needles from his line of play?

A. Yes. Pine needles piled for removal are loose impediments or ground under repair. Initially, the player was entitled to remove the pine needles under Rule 23-1 (Loose Impediments) or drop away, as he did, under Rule 25-1b.

After the player dropped away a new situation existed and he was no longer entitled to invoke Rule 25-1b. However, he was not prohibited from removing the pine needles under Rule 23-1.

Ball Played from Ground Under Repair Picked Up and Relief Taken Under Ground Under Repair Rule — See 18-2a/8.

25-1b/18 Crawfish Mound Interferes with Stance or Swing

Q. When a crawfish digs a hole, it creates a sizable mound of mud. If such a mound interferes with a player's stance or swing, does he get relief under Rule 25-1b?

A. Yes, provided the player's ball does not lie in a water hazard — see Exception under Rule 25-1. A crawfish is a burrowing animal.

25

Touching Mound Made by Burrowing Animal with Backswing in Bunker — See 13-4/5.

25-1b/19 Ball Lies on Mound Made by Burrowing Animal; Unreasonable to Play Stroke Due to Bush

Q. A ball lies under a bush. It is unreasonable for the player to play a stroke because of the bush. However, the ball lies on a mound made by a burrowing animal. Is the player entitled to relief without penalty under Rule 25-1b because his ball lies on a mound made by a burrowing animal?

A. No — see Exception under Rule 25-1b.

Stroke at Ball Not Reasonable Due to Interference by Immovable Obstruction and Casual Water — See 24-2b/19.

25-1b/20 Stance Interfered With by Burrowing Animal Hole; Unreasonable to Play Stroke Because of Other Condition

Q. A player's ball is in an indentation at the base of a tree in such a position that it is clearly unreasonable for him to play a stroke. The player claims relief without penalty under Rule 25-1 because his stance for a stroke at the ball in the indentation would be on a burrowing animal hole. Is the player entitled to relief without penalty under Rule 25-1b?

A. No — see Exception under Rule 25-1b.

25-1b/21 Cast of Burrowing Animal Interferes with Stroke Towards Green; Tree Prevents Such Stroke

Q. A player's ball is behind a tree. A cast behind the ball made by a burrowing animal would interfere with the backswing for a stroke towards the green but not with a sideways stroke, which is the only reasonable stroke. May the player say he intends to play towards the green into the tree, take relief without penalty under Rule 25-1b and, after dropping out from behind the tree, play towards the green?

25

A. No — see Exception under Rule 25-1b.

25-1b/22 Cast of Burrowing Animal Interferes with Sideways Stroke; When Relief Granted

Q. A ball is behind a tree so that a sideways stroke is the only reasonable stroke for the player. However, a cast made by a burrowing animal interferes with the backswing for a sideways stroke. Is the player entitled to relief under Rule 25-1b?

A. Yes, and if relief gets the player out from behind the tree, he is entitled to play towards the green.

25-1b/23 Ball Enters Burrowing Animal Hole Out of Bounds and Comes to Rest in Bounds

Q. The entrance to a burrowing animal hole is out of bounds, but most of the burrow is in bounds under the course. A ball enters the hole from out of bounds and comes to rest in bounds under ground classified as through the green. What is the procedure?

A. Under Rule 25-1b, the player may drop the ball, without penalty, within one club-length of the point on the ground directly above its position in the burrow. In such cases, vertical distance is disregarded in applying the Rules.

25-1b/24 Ball Enters Burrowing Animal Hole in Bounds and Comes to Rest Out of Bounds

Q. A player's ball entered a rabbit hole, the mouth of which was in bounds but only about a foot from a boundary fence. The rabbit hole sloped steeply down below the fence, so that the ball came to rest beyond the boundary line. What is the ruling?

A. Whether or not a ball is out of bounds depends on where it lies in relation to the boundary of the course and this must be measured vertically upwards or downwards — see Definition of "Out of Bounds."

In the case cited, the ball was lying out of bounds and Rule 27-1 applied. Relief could not be obtained under Rule 25-1, *i.e.*, from a hole made by a burrowing animal.

25-1b/25 Ball Enters Burrowing Animal Hole in Bunker and Comes to Rest Underneath Putting Green

Q. A ball enters a burrowing animal hole in a green-side bunker and comes to rest beneath the putting green. As the ball is not in the bunker or on the putting green, is relief taken in accordance with Rule 25-1b(i), *i.e.*, through the green?

A. Yes.

25-1c/1 Meaning of "Reasonable Evidence" in Rule 25-1c

Q. An area of casual water preceded by high rough is in a hollow not visible from the tee. A ball driven into this area is lost. The ball may be lost in the casual water or it may be lost in the high rough. Is there reasonable evidence that the ball is lost in the casual water?

A. No. In such circumstances, there is not reasonable evidence that the ball is lost in casual water. The player must proceed under Rule 27-1.

25-1c/2 Ball Dropped and Played Under Ground Under Repair Rule in Absence of Reasonable Evidence Original Ball Lost in Ground Under Repair

Q. A player, after a search of less than one minute, considers that his ball is lost in ground under repair, although there is not reasonable evidence to that effect. He drops a ball under Rule 25-1c and plays it. His original ball is then found beyond the ground under repair area. What is the ruling?

A. The ball dropped under Rule 25-1c was not substituted under an applicable Rule; thus, it was a wrong ball — see Definitions of "Ball in Play" and "Wrong Ball."

25

In match play, the player lost the hole — Rule 15-2.

In stroke play, the player incurred a penalty of two strokes, and he must hole out with his original ball, which remained in play — Rule 15-3.

Ball Played Under Rule for Ball Lost in Ground Under Repair After Another Ball Played Under Stroke-and-Distance Procedure — See 15/8.

25-1c/3 Ball Played in Ground Under Repair Area Lost in Same Area

Q. A player plays a stroke at his ball which is lying in a large area of ground under repair. The player advances the ball but not far enough to get it out of the ground under repair. The ball cannot be found. What is the ruling?

A. The player may drop a ball outside the ground under repair area, without penalty, as provided in Rule 25-1c.

Alternatively, the player may, under penalty of one stroke, drop a ball in the ground under repair as nearly as possible at the spot from which his original ball was last played — Rule 27-1 (Ball Lost).

25-2/1 Ball Bounces Out of Its Pitch-Mark and Spins Back into It

Q. A player's ball lands in soft ground in a closely mown area through the green, bounces out of its pitch-mark and then spins back into the pitch-mark. Is the player entitled to relief under Rule 25-2?

A. Yes. If a ball spins back into its pitch-mark, it is embedded in the pitch-mark.

25-2/2 Dropped Ball Embeds

Q. A player takes relief under an applicable Rule and drops a ball on a fairway. The ball embeds on impact. Is the player entitled to relief under Rule 25-2?

A. Yes.

25-2/2.5 Dropped Ball Embeds; Procedure If Ball Again Embeds When Re-Dropped

Q. According to Decision 25-2/2, if a ball dropped on a fairway embeds on impact, the player is entitled to relief under Rule 25-2. What is the proper procedure if a ball embeds each time it is dropped?

A. If a ball embeds when dropped and embeds again when re-dropped, the player may,in equity (Rule 1-4), place the ball as near as possible to the spot where it embedded when re-dropped, but not nearer the hole.

If the player drops the ball more than twice, the ball embeds each time and he then becomes aware that he was entitled to place the ball after the second drop, he may place the ball as near as possible to the spot where it embedded on the second drop.

25-2/3 Dropped Ball Rolls into Pitch-Mark from Which Lifted

Q. A ball dropped under Rule 25-2 rolls back into the pitch-mark from which it was lifted. Is the player entitled to re-drop?

A. Yes. If a ball rolls back into its pitch-mark, it is embedded in the pitch-mark.

Pitch-Mark in Dropping Area Repaired Before Ball Dropped — See 13-2/10.

25-2/4 Ball Embedded in Ground Under Repair in Closely Mown Area

25

Q. A player's ball is embedded in ground under repair in a closely mown area through the green. May the player drop the ball within the ground under repair under Rule 25-2 (Embedded Ball) and then elect whether to play the ball as it lies or take relief from the ground under repair under Rule 25-1b?

A. Yes.

25-2/5 Ball Embedded in Grass Bank or Face of Bunker

Q. Are grass banks or faces of bunkers considered to be "closely mown areas" under Rule 25-2 (Embedded Ball) and may relief be taken from them under that Rule?

A. No, not unless they are cut to fairway height or less.

25-2/6 Ball on Steep Bank Driven Straight into Ground

Q. A player's ball lies on a steep bank in the fairway. He plays a stroke and drives the ball straight into the bank, *i.e.*, the ball is never airborne. Is the player entitled to relief without penalty under Rule 25-2?

A. No. Under Rule 25-2, relief is provided if a ball is embedded in its own pitch-mark. The word "pitch-mark" implies that the ball has become airborne.

25-2/7 Lifting Ball to Determine Whether It Is Embedded

Q. A player's ball lies on a fairway and he believes the ball may be embedded in its own pitch-mark. Is the player entitled to lift the ball to determine whether it is embedded?

A. In equity (Rule 1-4), the player may lift the ball, without penalty, provided he announces his intention in advance to his opponent in match play or his marker or a fellow-competitor in stroke play and gives his opponent, marker or fellow-competitor an opportunity to observe the lifting. If the ball is embedded in the ground, he is entitled to relief under Rule 25-2. Otherwise, the ball must be replaced and the opponent, marker or fellow-competitor given an opportunity to observe the replacement. A ball so lifted may not be cleaned unless it is found to be embedded in the ground and the player elects to take relief under Rule 25-2.

Ball Completely Embedded in Lip of Bunker — See 13/4.

25-3/1 Status of Half of Double Green Serving Hole Not Being Played

Q. One half of a U-shaped putting green serves as the 11th green and the other half serves as the 17th green. In play of the 17th hole, if a ball comes to rest on the part of the green serving the 11th hole, does Rule 25-3 (Wrong Putting Green) apply?

A. No, not unless the Committee divides the green by use of stakes or a line and declares one part to be the green of the 11th hole and the other part to be the green of the 17th hole. The Definition of "Putting Green" gives a Committee this right.

25

Rule 26. Water Hazards (Including Lateral Water Hazards)

Definitions

A "water hazard" is any sea, lake, pond, river, ditch, surface drainage ditch or other open water course (whether or not containing water) and anything of a similar nature.

All ground or water within the margin of a water hazard is part of the water hazard. The margin of a water hazard extends vertically upwards and downwards. Stakes and lines defining the margins of water hazards are in the hazards.

Note: Water hazards (other than <u>lateral water hazards</u>) should be defined by yellow stakes or lines.

A "lateral water hazard" is a <u>water hazard</u> or that part of a water hazard so situated that it is not possible or is deemed by the Committee to be impracticable to drop a ball behind the water hazard in accordance with Rule 26-1b.

That part of a water hazard to be played as a lateral water hazard should be distinctively marked.

Note: Lateral water hazards should be defined by red stakes or lines.

26-1. Ball in Water Hazard

It is a question of fact whether a ball lost after having been struck toward a <u>water hazard</u>

26

is lost inside or outside the hazard. In order to treat the ball as lost in the hazard, there must be reasonable evidence that the ball lodged in it. In the absence of such evidence, the ball must be treated as a lost ball and Rule 27 applies.

If a ball lies in, touches or is lost in a water hazard (whether the ball lies in water or not), *the player may under penalty of one stroke*:

a. Play a ball as nearly as possible at the spot from which the original ball was last played (see Rule 20-5);

or

b. Drop a ball behind the water hazard, keeping the point at which the original ball last crossed the margin of the water hazard directly between the hole and the spot on which the ball is dropped, with no limit to how far behind the water hazard the ball may be dropped.

or

c. *As additional options available only if the ball lies in, touches or is lost in a lateral water hazard*, drop a ball outside the water hazard within two club-lengths of (i) the point where the original ball last crossed the margin of the water hazard or (ii) a point on the opposite margin of the water hazard equidistant from the hole. The ball must be dropped and come to rest not nearer the hole than the point where the original ball last crossed the margin of the water hazard.

The ball may be cleaned when lifted under this Rule.

(Ball moving in water in a water hazard — see Rule 14-6.)

26-2. Ball Played Within Water Hazard

a. BALL COMES TO REST IN HAZARD

If a ball played from within a water hazard comes to rest in the hazard after the stroke, the player may:

26

(i) proceed under Rule 26-1; or

(ii) *under penalty of one stroke*, play a ball as nearly as possible at the spot from which the last stroke from outside the hazard was played (see Rule 20-5).

If the player proceeds under Rule 26-1a, he may elect not to play the dropped ball. If he so elects, he may:

a. Proceed under Rule 26-1b, adding the additional penalty of one stroke prescribed by that Rule;

or

b. Proceed under Rule 26-1c, if applicable, adding the additional penalty of one stroke prescribed by that Rule;

or

c. Add an additional penalty of one stroke and play a ball as nearly as possible at the spot from which the last stroke from outside the hazard was played (see Rule 20-5).

b. BALL LOST OR UNPLAYABLE OUTSIDE HAZARD OR OUT OF BOUNDS

If a ball played from within a water hazard is lost or declared unplayable outside the hazard or is out of bounds, the player, after taking a *penalty of one stroke* under Rule 27-1 or 28a, may:

(i) play a ball as nearly as possible at the spot in the hazard from which the original ball was last played (see Rule 20-5); or

(ii) proceed under Rule 26-1b, or if applicable Rule 26-1c, *adding the additional penalty of one stroke* prescribed by the Rule and using as the reference point the point where the original ball last crossed the margin of the hazard before it came to rest in the hazard; or

(iii) *add an additional penalty of one stroke* and play a ball as nearly as possible at

26

the spot from which the last stroke from outside the hazard was played (see Rule 20-5).

Note 1: When proceeding under Rule 26-2b, the player is not required to drop a ball under Rule 27-1 or 28a. If he does drop a ball, he is not required to play it. He may alternatively proceed under Clause (ii) or (iii).

Note 2: If a ball played from within a water hazard is declared unplayable outside the hazard, nothing in Rule 26-2b precludes the player from proceeding under Rule 28b or c.

PENALTY FOR BREACH OF RULE:
Match play --- Loss of hole;
Stroke play --- Two strokes.

26/1 When Ball Deemed to Touch Water Hazard

Q. Rule 26-1 applies to a ball that "lies in, touches or is lost in a water hazard." Does a ball touch a water hazard when some part of the ball breaks the plane that extends vertically upwards from the margin of the hazard, even though the ball does not touch the ground or grass inside the hazard?

A. Yes, since the Definition of "Water Hazard" provides that "the margin of a water hazard extends vertically upwards."

26/2 Ball Within Natural Margin of Water Hazard But Outside Stakes Defining Margin

Q. Stakes defining the margin of a water hazard were improperly installed. As a result, an area which clearly was part of the water hazard was outside the stakes and, thus, technically was outside the hazard. A player's ball came to rest in water in this area. The player claimed that, in view of the alignment of the stakes, his ball was in casual water through the green. Was the claim valid?

A. No. The Committee erred in not properly defining the margin of the hazard as required by Rule 33-2a, but a player is not entitled to take advantage of such an error. Since it was clear that the place where the player's ball lay was within the natural boundaries of the water hazard, the claim should not be upheld.

26/3 When Water Hazard Is Automatically Lateral Hazard

Q. A ditch (water hazard) on the left of a hole is in bounds, but the left-hand margin is out of bounds. Accordingly, it is impossible to drop behind the water hazard as required by Rule 26-1b. Is a player restricted to playing the ball as it lies or proceeding under Rule 26-1a?

A. No. Such a ditch is a lateral water hazard, whether or not the Committee has declared it to be so — see Definition of "Lateral Water Hazard." Accordingly, a player would also be entitled to proceed under Rule 26-1c(i).

26/4 Man-Made Reservoir

Q. Is a man-made reservoir considered a water hazard?

A. Yes.

26/5 Unidentifiable Ball Played in Water Hazard and Lost

Q. A player's ball came to rest in a water hazard. He found a ball in the hazard but could not identify it. He played the ball into deep water within the hazard and the ball was lost. May the player assume that the ball he played in the hazard was not his ball, in which case the stroke played in the hazard would not count?

A. No. There was not reasonable evidence that the ball played was other than the player's ball. Lacking

26

such evidence, he must count the stroke. The burden of proof is on the player.

26/6 Ball Assumed to Be in Water Hazard Found Outside Hazard After Another Ball Played Under Stroke-and-Distance Procedure

Q. A player assumes his original ball to be in a water hazard, although there was not reasonable evidence to that effect. Using the option in Rule 26-1a, he plays another ball at the spot from which the original ball was played. He then finds his original ball outside the hazard. What is the ruling?

A. The original ball is lost and the other ball is in play under penalty of stroke and distance — see Decision 27/17.

26/7 Ball Apparently in Water Hazard Found Outside Hazard After Another Ball Played Under Stroke-and-Distance Procedure

Q. A player's ball appears to have come to rest in a water hazard. Without comment, the player plays another ball at the spot from which the original ball was played and then finds his original ball outside the hazard. What is the ruling?

A. The original ball is lost and the other ball is in play under penalty of stroke and distance — see Decision 27/17.

Removal of Obstruction in Hazard Would Move Loose Impediment — See 1-4/5.

Player Who Told Opponent He Would Proceed Under Water Hazard Rule Changes Mind After Opponent Plays — See 9-2/13.

Stone Broken Away from Retaining Wall in Water Hazard — See 24/6.

Overflow from Water Hazard — See 25/2.

Hole of Removed Stake Defining Water Hazard — See 25/18.

Where to Place Lines or Stakes Defining Margin of Water Hazard — See 33-2a/4.

Water Hazard Under Repair — See 33-2a/5.

Pond Is Water Hazard from Men's Tee and Lateral Water Hazard from Women's Tee — See 33-2a/6.

Deeming Body of Water as Both Water Hazard and Lateral Water Hazard — See 33-2a/7.

Treating Ocean and Beach as Through the Green — See 33-2a/8.

How to Mark Island Green — See 33-2a/10.

26-1/1 Meaning of "Reasonable Evidence" in Rule 26-1

The term "reasonable evidence" in Rule 26-1 is purposely and necessarily broad so as to permit sensible judgments to be reached on the basis of all the relevant circumstances of particular cases. As applied in this context, a player may not deem his ball lost in a water hazard simply because he thinks the ball may be in the hazard. The evidence must be preponderantly in favor of its being in the hazard. Otherwise, the ball must be considered lost outside the hazard and the player must proceed under Rule 27-1. Physical conditions in the area have a great deal to do with it. For example, if a water hazard is surrounded by a fairway on which a ball could hardly be lost, the existence of reasonable evidence that the ball is in the hazard would be more likely than if there was deep rough in the area. Observing a ball splash in a water hazard would not necessarily provide reasonable evidence as splashing balls sometimes skip out of hazards. It would depend on all the circumstances.

Changing Relief Option When Re-Dropping Required — See 20-2c/5.

26-1/2 Player Proceeding Under Water Hazard Rule Drops Ball in Another Hazard

26

Q. A player's ball lies in a water hazard. In applying Rule 26-1b, the player drops a ball in a bunker or another water hazard. Is this permissible?

A. Yes.

26-1/3 Ball Played Under Water Hazard Rule; Original Ball Then Found Outside Hazard

Q. A player believed his original ball came to rest in a water hazard. He searched for about a minute but did not find his ball. So he dropped another ball behind the hazard under Rule 26-1 and played it. He then found his original ball outside the hazard within five minutes of having begun search for it. What is the ruling?

A. If there was reasonable evidence that the original ball was in the water hazard, the player was entitled to invoke Rule 26-1 and, when he dropped a ball under that Rule, that ball was in play and the original ball had to be abandoned.

If there was not reasonable evidence that the original ball was in the water hazard, the ball dropped under Rule 26-1 was not dropped under an applicable Rule and therefore was not the ball in play — see Definition of "Ball in Play." Accordingly, it was a wrong ball — see Definition of "Wrong Ball" — and the player lost the hole in match play or incurred a two-stroke penalty in stroke play — Rule 15. In stroke play, the player would be obliged to continue play with the original ball, which remained in play.

26-1/4 Ball Played Under Water Hazard Rule Without Reasonable Evidence Original Ball in Hazard; Original Ball Then Found in Hazard

Q. A player's ball carried over a water hazard into some trees. It could not be determined whether the ball bounced back into the hazard or came to rest in the trees. Therefore, there was not reasonable evidence that the ball was in the hazard.

26

The player did not search for his original ball. He assumed that it was in the hazard, dropped a ball behind the hazard at a spot which conformed with Rule 26-1b and played that ball onto the green. As he was walking to the green, he found his original ball in the hazard. What is the ruling?

A. The first paragraph of Rule 26-1 states in part: "In order to treat the ball as lost in the hazard, there must be reasonable evidence that the ball lodged in it. In the absence of such evidence, the ball must be treated as a lost ball and Rule 27 applies." Since the player treated the ball as lost in the hazard at a time when there was not reasonable evidence to that effect, the ball dropped and played under the water hazard Rule was a wrong ball — see last paragraph of Decision 26-1/3. The fact that the original ball was subsequently found in the hazard is irrelevant.

In match play, the player lost the hole — Rule 15-2.

In stroke play, the player incurred a penalty of two strokes and he was obliged to continue play with the original ball, which remained the ball in play — Rule 15-3.

26-1/5 Ball Dropped and Played Under Water Hazard Rule; Original Ball Then Found in Hazard and Holed Out as Second Ball

Q. In stroke play, a competitor, unable to find his ball in a water hazard, drops another ball behind the hazard under Rule 26-1b and plays it. He then finds his original ball in the hazard. Not being sure of his rights, he plays out both balls under Rule 3-3, opting to score with the original ball. What is the ruling?

A. When the competitor dropped the ball behind the hazard, that ball became the ball in play — see Definition of "Ball in Play." The score with that ball was the competitor's score for the hole. The score with the original ball could not count because that ball was no longer the ball in play. However, the competitor incurs no penalty for playing out with the original ball.

26-1/6 Ball Played Back into Water Hazard from Putting Green Side of Hazard

Q. A player plays his second shot over a water hazard into a bunker behind the green. He skulls his third shot and the ball comes to rest in the water hazard. The ball is not playable. What are the player's options?

A. The player may, under penalty of one stroke:

26

(a) drop a ball behind the water hazard, keeping the point at which the original ball last crossed the hazard margin between the hole and the spot on which the ball is dropped — Rule 26-1b. This procedure would probably make it necessary for the player to return to the tee side of the hazard and play over the hazard again; or

(b) drop a ball in the bunker at the spot where his second shot came to rest — Rule 26-1a.

26-1/7 Ball Moved Out of Bounds by Flow of Water in Water Hazard

Q. The flow of water in a water hazard carries a ball out of bounds. May the player invoke Rule 26-1?

A. No. Since the ball lies out of bounds, the player must proceed under Rule 27-1. Water is not an outside agency — see Definition of "Outside Agency" — and thus the ball would not be replaced under Rule 18-1.

In a situation where it is likely that a ball will be carried out of bounds by the flow of water in a water hazard, it is suggested that a screen be installed to prevent such an occurrence.

26-1/8 Ball Moved into Bounds by Flow of Water in Water Hazard

Q. A ball lands in a river out of bounds and the flow of water carries the ball into bounds. That part of the river which is in bounds is defined as a water hazard. May the player invoke Rule 26-1?

A. Yes, since the ball lies within the boundaries of the course. The ball should be considered to have last crossed the hazard margin at the boundary line. If it is not possible to drop behind the hazard under Rule 26-1b, which seems likely, the player is entitled to proceed under Rule 26-1c — see Decision 26/3. If that is not possible, the player must proceed under Rule 26-1a, incurring a stroke-and-distance penalty, or play the ball as it lies in the river.

26

26-1/9 Caddie Lifts Ball in Water Hazard Without Player's Authority

Q. A player's ball lying in a water hazard is lifted by the player's caddie without the player's authority. What is the ruling?

A. The player incurred a one-stroke penalty when his caddie lifted his ball — Rule 18-2a. The player may either replace the ball as required by Rule 18-2a or proceed under Rule 26-1 and incur an additional one-stroke penalty under that Rule.

26-1/10 Placing Ball on Bank of Water Hazard Instead of Dropping to Prevent Ball Rolling into Water

Q. A player's ball lies in a playable position on the bank of a water hazard. The player hits the ball out of bounds. If he proceeds under Rule 27-1 and drops a ball on the bank as nearly as possible at the spot from which the original ball was played, the ball will be likely to roll into deep water. May he place the ball in such circumstances, rather than drop it?

A. No. However, the player is not obliged to drop a ball within the hazard in accordance with Rule 27-1. He may take the penalty stroke provided in Rule 27-1 and then, under an additional penalty of one stroke, put a ball into play outside the hazard in accordance with either Rule 26-2b(ii) or 26-2b(iii).

Ball Lost in Either Water Hazard or Casual Water Overflowing Hazard — See 1-4/7.

Players Inadvertently Exchange Balls Recovered from Water Hazard — See 15-1/4.

Ball Declared Unplayable in Water Hazard Is Dropped in Hazard and Played — See 20-7/2.

Casual Water Mistaken for Water Hazard; Original Ball Played Under Water Hazard Rule — See 25-1b/12.

Casual Water Mistaken for Water Hazard; Substituted Ball Played Under Water Hazard Rule — See 25-1b/13.

26

26-1/11 Water Hazard Treated as Lateral Water Hazard

Q. In stroke play, a competitor played a stroke over a water hazard and the ball spun back into the hazard. The competitor, in error, treated the hazard as a lateral water hazard and dropped the ball under Rule 26-1c(i) within two club-lengths of where it crossed the hazard margin when it spun back into the hazard. He played the ball onto the green and then his procedure was questioned. What is the ruling?

A. The competitor was guilty of a serious breach of Rule 26-1. He must, under penalty of two strokes, rectify the error as provided in Rule 20-7b, second paragraph, or be disqualified.

26-1/12 Hazard Marked as Water Hazard Where Ball Last Crosses Margin and as Lateral Hazard Where Ball Comes to Rest

Q. A body of water is defined in part as a water hazard and in part as a lateral water hazard. A ball last crosses the hazard margin at a spot where it is marked as a water hazard but it comes to rest in that part of the hazard marked as a lateral water hazard. In addition to playing the ball as it lies, what are the player's options?

A. Since the ball never crossed a margin of the hazard where it is defined as a lateral water hazard, the options in Rule 26-1c are not available. Thus, the player is limited to the options in Rules 26-1a and -1b.

26-1/13 Opposite Side of Lateral Water Hazard Defined as Water Hazard

26

Q. A player hit a ball into a lateral water hazard. The player wanted to drop within two club-lengths of a point on the opposite margin of the hazard equidistant from the hole, as permitted under Rule 26-1c. However, the opposite margin was marked as a water hazard. Was the player entitled to drop a ball within two club-lengths of the point in question on the opposite margin?

A. Yes. In such a case, relief is determined according to the status of the hazard at the point where the ball last crossed the hazard margin.

26-1/14 Clarification of "Opposite Margin" in Rule 26-1c(ii)

Q. Please clarify the words "opposite margin" in Rule 26-1c. With regard to the above illustration, "XI" indicates where a ball in the hazard last crossed the hazard margin. May the player drop a ball within two club-lengths of "Y1"? And, may a player whose ball last crossed the hazard margin at "X2" drop a ball within two club-lengths of "Y2," and so on?

A. With respect to "X1," "Y1" is "a point on the opposite margin of the water hazard equidistant from the hole." Accordingly, the player would be entitled to drop a ball within two club-lengths of "Y1."

The same applies in the cases of "X3" — "Y3" and "X4" — "Y4," but not in the case of "X2" — "Y2." A "point on the opposite margin" is a point across the hazard from "the point where the original ball last crossed the margin of the hazard." "Y2" is not across the hazard from "X2" because an imaginary straight line from "X2" to "Y2" crosses land outside the hazard.

26

26-1/15 Procedures for Relief from Lateral Water Hazard

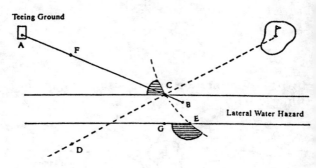

In the above illustration, a player has played a ball from the teeing ground (Point A) into the lateral water hazard at Point B. It last crossed the margin of the hazard at Point C. He may play the ball as it lies or, under penalty of one stroke:

(a) play another ball from the teeing ground — Rule 26-1a;

(b) drop a ball anywhere on the far side of the hazard on the dotted line from the hole through Point C, *e.g.*, Point D — Rule 26-1b;

(c) drop a ball in the shaded area on the near side of the hazard which is all ground within two club-lengths of Point C, but not nearer the hole than Point C — Rule 26-1c(i); or

(d) drop a ball in the shaded area on the far side of the hazard which is all ground within two club-lengths of Point E, but not nearer the hole than Point E — Rule 26-1c(ii).

26

The player may not drop a ball on the so-called "line-of-flight" at Point F or anywhere else on the line the ball followed from A to B, except in the shaded area on the near side. Nor may he drop a ball within two club-lengths of Point G, the point on the far side of the hazard directly opposite Point C.

26-1/16 Point Where Ball Last Crossed Margin of Lateral Water Hazard Determined and Ball Dropped; Point Then Proves to Be Wrong Point

Q. In stroke play, A's ball goes into a lateral water hazard and is not found. A uses his best judgment in determining the point where the ball last crossed the hazard margin. B, A's marker and a fellow-competitor, agrees with that judgment and A drops a ball in accordance with Rule 26-1c, using the agreed point on the margin as the reference point. Before A plays his next stroke, C, another fellow-competitor, says that A's ball last crossed the hazard margin 20 yards beyond the point judged by A to be the point where the ball last crossed. A's ball is then found where C said it would be. What is the ruling?

A. Since he dropped his ball in a wrong place, A should, under Rule 20-6, lift the dropped ball and drop it in a right place, without penalty. A is precluded from lifting the ball dropped in a wrong place and playing the original ball from the hazard. The original ball was lost when another ball was put into play under Rule 26-1 — see Definition of "Lost Ball."

26-1/17 Point Where Ball Last Crossed Margin of Lateral Water Hazard Determined and Ball Dropped and Played; Point Then Proves to Be Wrong Point

Q. In the circumstances described in Decision 26-1/16, what is the ruling if A, having dropped a ball in a wrong place, plays it before his error is discovered?

A. A must continue play with the ball played from a wrong place, without penalty. Applying a penalty under Rule 26-1 for playing from a wrong place (see Rule 20-7b) is not appropriate. Otherwise, a competitor would risk incurring a penalty every time he makes an honest judgment as to the point where his ball last crosses a water hazard margin and that judgment subsequently proves incorrect.

26

26-1/18   Impossible to Drop Not Nearer Hole Than Point Where Ball Last Crossed Margin of Lateral Water Hazard

Q. When a ball last crosses the margin of a lateral water hazard at the side of a putting green, it is sometimes impossible to drop a ball within two club-lengths of the point where the ball last crossed the hazard margin without dropping nearer the hole than that point. What is the procedure in such a case?

A. It is usually possible to drop a ball on the near side of a lateral water hazard and conform with Rule 26-1c(i) by dropping the ball close to the hazard margin. Where this is impossible, the player must proceed under one of the other options provided in Rule 26-1.

Part of Lateral Water Hazard Where Impossible to Drop Not Nearer Hole; Procedure for Committee — See 33-2a/9.

26-1/19   Permissible Dropping Area Under Lateral Water Hazard Rule So Narrow Player Has Difficulty Dropping Within It

When a ball comes to rest in a lateral water hazard and relief is taken under Rule 26-1c, the ball must be dropped (1) outside the hazard and (2) not nearer the hole than the point where the ball last crossed the margin of the hazard (Point X). When the lateral water hazard is behind or to the side of the putting green, the permissible dropping area may be very narrow. If the ball, when dropped, first strikes a part of the course in the hazard or nearer the hole than Point X, the drop does not count for the purpose of determining when the ball must be placed under Rule 20-2c. The player must lift the ball and continue to drop it until the ball first strikes a part of the course within the permissible dropping area. Only if the ball has been dropped in the permissible dropping area twice and, each time, either rolls into the hazard or nearer the hole than Point X may it be placed as permitted by Rule 20-2c. If a ball is placed otherwise than as described, and is played, a breach of Rule 26-1c occurs.

Stakes and lines defining the margins of water hazards should be placed along the natural limits of the hazard. However, minor deviation to alleviate the

26

dropping area problem would be appropriate. Alternatively, a Ball Drop (or Dropping Zone) should be established.

26-1/20 Allowing Drop Opposite Spot Where Ball Comes to Rest in Lateral Water Hazard

Q. A lateral water hazard is so situated that it is difficult to determine where a ball lying in the hazard last crossed the hazard margin. Would it be permissible to make a Local Rule to the effect that a player whose ball lies in this hazard may drop a ball, under penalty of one stroke, within two club-lengths of the point on the hazard margin opposite where the original ball came to rest in the hazard, instead of within two club-lengths of where the original ball last crossed the hazard margin, *i.e.*, the Local Rule would modify Rule 26-1c?

A. No. Such modification of Rule 26-1c is not authorized. Moreover, the suggested Local Rule would be inoperable if the player's ball was lost in the hazard.

26-1/21 Example of Serious Breach of Lateral Water Hazard Rule

Q. In stroke play, A and B drive into a lateral water hazard. They determine where their original balls last crossed the hazard margin and elect to proceed under Rule 26-1c, taking a penalty of one stroke. A drops a ball slightly closer to the hole than the spot where his ball last crossed the hazard margin; B drops a ball 50 yards closer to the hole. A and B play their next strokes. What is the ruling?

A. A incurs an additional penalty of two strokes for a breach of Rule 26-1c and must play out the hole with the ball dropped in a wrong place and played — see Rule 20-7b, first paragraph.

26

B is guilty of a serious breach of Rule 26-1c. He incurs an additional penalty of two strokes and, before playing from the next teeing ground, he must drop another ball in accordance with Rule 26-1c and play out the hole; otherwise B is disqualified — see Rule 20-7b, third paragraph.

26-2/1 Explanation of Options Under Rules 26-2a and -2b

Regarding the above illustration, A and B play from the tee. A's ball comes to rest in the water hazard at Point A. B's ball comes to rest at Point B. Both A and B elect to play from the hazard. A fails to get out of the hazard. He plays to Point X, and his ball is not playable. B plays to Point Y, which is out of bounds.

Under penalty of one stroke, A may:

    (a) drop a ball at Point A and play again from there, playing 4 (Rule 26-2a(i)); or

    (b) drop a ball anywhere on dotted line E-E and play from there, playing 4 (Rule 26-2a(i)); or

    (c) play another ball from the tee, playing 4 (Rule 26-2a(ii)).

If A drops a ball at Point A and the ball comes to rest at a spot from which he judges he cannot play, he may, adding an additional penalty of one stroke, either drop a ball anywhere on the dotted line E-E or play another ball from the tee, playing 5.

B, after taking the penalty stroke prescribed in Rule 27-1, may drop a ball at Point B and play again from there, playing 4 (Rule 26-2b(i)).

Alternatively, B, after taking the penalty stroke prescribed in Rule 27-1, may drop a ball at Point B and elect not to play that ball or elect not to drop a ball at Point B. In either case, he shall then:

    (a) under an additional penalty of one stroke, drop a ball anywhere on dotted line F-F and play from there, playing 5 (Rule 26-2b(ii)); or

(b) under an additional penalty of one stroke, play another ball from the tee, playing 5 (Rule 26-2b(iii)).

Rule 27. Ball Lost or Out of Bounds; Provisional Ball

If the original ball is lost in an immovable obstruction (Rule 24-2) or under a condition covered by Rule 25-1 (casual water, ground under repair and certain damage to the course), the player may proceed under the applicable Rule. If the original ball is lost in a water hazard, the player shall proceed under Rule 26.

Such Rules may not be used unless there is reasonable evidence that the ball is lost in an immovable obstruction, under a condition covered by Rule 25-1 or in a water hazard.

Definitions

A ball is "lost" if:

a. It is not found or identified as his by the player within five minutes after the player's side or his or their caddies have begun to search for it; or

b. The player has put another ball into play under the Rules, even though he may not have searched for the original ball; or

c. The player has played any stroke with a <u>provisional</u> ball from the place where the original ball is likely to be or from a point nearer the hole than that place, whereupon the provisional ball becomes the <u>ball in play</u>.

Time spent in playing a <u>wrong ball</u> is not counted in the five-minute period allowed for search.

27

"Out of bounds" is ground on which play is prohibited.

When out of bounds is defined by reference to stakes or a fence, or as being beyond stakes or a fence, the out of bounds line is determined by the nearest inside points of the stakes or fence posts at ground level excluding angled supports.

When out of bounds is defined by a line on the ground, the line itself is out of bounds.

The out of bounds line extends vertically upwards and downwards.

A ball is out of bounds when all of it lies out of bounds.

A player may stand out of bounds to play a ball lying within bounds.

A "provisional ball" is a ball played under Rule 27-2 for a ball which may be <u>lost</u> outside a <u>water hazard</u> or may be <u>out of bounds</u>.

27-1. Ball Lost or Out of Bounds

If a ball is <u>lost</u> outside a <u>water hazard</u> or is out of bounds, the player shall play a ball, *under penalty of one stroke*, as nearly as possible at the spot from which the original ball was last played (see Rule 20-5).

PENALTY FOR BREACH OF RULE 27-1:
Match play --- Loss of hole;
Stroke play --- Two strokes.

27-2. Provisional Ball

a. PROCEDURE

If a ball may be <u>lost</u> outside a <u>water hazard</u> or may be <u>out of bounds</u>, to save time the player may play another ball provisionally as nearly as possible at the spot from which the original ball was played (see Rule 20-5). The player shall inform his opponent in match play or his marker or a fellow-competitor in stroke play that he intends to play a <u>provisional ball</u>, and he shall play it before he or his partner goes forward to search for the original ball. If he fails to do so and plays another ball, such

27

ball is not a provisional ball and becomes the <u>ball in play</u> *under penalty of stroke and distance* (Rule 27-1); the original ball is deemed to be lost.

b. WHEN PROVISIONAL BALL BECOMES BALL IN PLAY

The player may play a provisional ball until he reaches the place where the original ball is likely to be. If he plays a stroke with the provisional ball from the place where the original ball is likely to be or from a point nearer the hole than that place, the original ball is deemed to be <u>lost</u> and the provisional ball becomes the ball in play *under penalty of stroke and distance* (Rule 27-1).

If the original ball is lost outside a water hazard or is out of bounds, the provisional ball becomes the ball in play, *under penalty of stroke and distance* (Rule 27-1).

c. WHEN PROVISIONAL BALL TO BE ABANDONED

If the original ball is neither lost outside a water hazard nor out of bounds, the player shall abandon the provisional ball and continue play with the original ball. If he fails to do so, any further strokes played with the provisional ball shall constitute playing a <u>wrong ball</u> and the provisions of Rule 15 shall apply.

Note: If the original ball lies in a water hazard, the player shall play the ball as it lies or proceed under Rule 26. If it is lost in a water hazard or unplayable, the player shall proceed under Rule 26 or 28, whichever is applicable.

27

27/1 Player Directs Caddie Not to Search for His Ball Until Others Can Assist

Q. A hits a long drive into heavy rough. B hits a short drive into heavy rough. A's caddie starts walking towards the area where A's ball may be to search for A's ball. Everyone else, including A, walks towards the area where B's ball may be to look for B's ball. A directs his caddie also to look for B's ball and delay search for his (A's) ball until everyone else can assist. Is such procedure permitted?

A. Yes.

27/2 Time Permitted for Search for Lost Ball After Wrong Ball Played

Q. In stroke play, a competitor searches for his ball for three minutes, finds a ball, plays it and then discovers he has played a wrong ball. He returns to the area from which the wrong ball was played and resumes search for his ball. How much time is he allowed for further search — two minutes or five minutes?

A. Two minutes — see Definition of "Lost Ball."

27/3 Time Permitted for Search When Lost Ball Found and Then Lost Again

Q. A player finds his ball in high rough after a two-minute search, leaves the area to get a club and, when he returns, is unable to find the ball. Is he allowed three minutes or five minutes to find his ball?

A. Three minutes.

27/4 Time Permitted for Search for Original Ball and Provisional Ball

Q. Is a player allowed five minutes to search for his original ball and five more minutes to search for his provisional ball, or just a total of five minutes?

27

A. If the two balls are so close together that, in effect, both balls would be searched for simultaneously, a total of five minutes for search is allowed. Otherwise, the player is allowed to search five minutes for each ball.

27/5 Player Searching for Ball Mistakes His Ball for Opponent's

Q. In a match, A begins to search for his ball, finds a ball which he believes to be his opponent's ball and resumes his search. Five minutes elapse without his finding and identifying his ball. Thereafter it is discovered that the ball which he found and believed to be his opponent's was in fact his ball. What is the ruling?

A. Since A did not identify a ball as his ball within five minutes after search for it began, A's ball was lost — see Definition of "Lost Ball."

27/6 Player Unable to Find His Ball Because Another Player Played It

Q. A and B hit their tee shots into the same general area. A found a ball and played it. B went forward to look for his ball and could not find it. After a few minutes, B started back to the tee to put another ball into play. On the way, he found A's ball and knew then that A had played his (B's) ball in error. What is the ruling?

A. In match play, A lost the hole (Rule 15-2).

In stroke play, A incurred a penalty of two strokes for playing a wrong ball and must then play his own ball (Rule 15-3). A's ball was not lost even if A and B had been searching for more than five minutes because A had not "begun to search for it (his ball)"; the searching had been for B's ball — see Definition of "Lost Ball."

On the other hand, B began to search for his ball as soon as he went forward to look for it. If less than five minutes had elapsed before B found A's ball, B should have placed a ball on the spot from which A had wrongly played his (B's) ball and continued play, without penalty — see last paragraph of Rule 15-3. However, if five minutes had expired, B's original ball was lost and he was obliged to put another ball into play under penalty of stroke and distance (Rule 27-1).

27

27/7 Ball Found in Burrowing Animal Hole After Five-Minute Search

Q. A player's tee shot comes to rest in an area containing heavy rough and a large burrowing animal hole. After a search of five minutes, the referee advises the player that there is not reasonable evidence that the ball is lost in the burrowing animal hole. He instructs the player to return to the tee and put another ball into play under Rule 27-1. As the player is returning to the tee, his ball is found in the burrowing animal hole by spectators. Would the referee be within his rights in recalling the player and permitting him to proceed under Rule 25-1 on the ground that a decision by the referee on "reasonable evidence," if subsequently proved wrong in fact, should in equity be reversed?

A. No. When five minutes elapsed and there was not reasonable evidence that the ball was lost in the burrowing animal hole, the ball was lost and Rule 27-1 was applicable.

Ball Lost in Underground Drainpipe — See 24-2c/1.

27/8 Ball Found After Search Exceeding Five Minutes Is Then Played

Q. A player searches for his ball for five minutes and does not find it. He continues to search, finds the ball and plays it. What is the ruling?

A. The ball was lost and therefore out of play when the five-minute period allowed for search expired — see Definitions of "Ball in Play" and "Lost Ball." When the player played a stroke with a ball out of play, he played a wrong ball — see Definition of "Wrong Ball" — and incurred a penalty of loss of hole in match play or two strokes in stroke play — Rules 15-2 and -3. In stroke play, he was disqualified if he did not correct the error by proceeding under Rule 27-1 before playing from the next tee — Rule 15-3.

27

27/9 Player Searches for Lost Ball After Putting Another Ball into Play

Q. According to Rule 27, if a player hits his tee shot into the woods and tees up and plays another ball without announcing it as a provisional ball, the second ball becomes the ball in play and the original ball is lost. In such a case, is the player precluded from searching for his original ball?

A. No. But the player may not play the ball if he finds it and must not unduly delay play.

27/10 Player Unable to Distinguish His Ball from Another Ball

Q. A and B hit their tee shots into the same area. Both balls were found but, because A and B were playing identical balls and neither had put an identification mark on his ball, they could not determine which ball was A's and which was B's. What is the ruling?

A. Since neither player could identify a ball as his ball, both balls were lost — see Definition of "Lost Ball."

This incident underlines the advisability of the player putting an identification mark on his ball — see Rules 6-5 and 12-2, Preamble.

27/11 Provisional Ball Not Distinguishable from Original Ball

A player entitled to play a provisional ball from the tee plays it into the same area as his original ball. The balls have identical markings and the player cannot distinguish between them. Following are various situations and the solutions, which are based on equity (Rule 1-4), when the above circumstances exist:

Situation 1: One ball is found in a water hazard and the other ball is not found.

Solution 1: The ball which was found must be presumed to be the provisional ball.

Situation 2: Both balls are found in a water hazard.

Solution 2: The player must return to the tee and play another ball; he would be playing 3.

Situation 3: One ball is found in a water hazard and one ball is found in the rough.

27

Solution 3: The player must return to the tee and play another ball; he would be playing 3.

Situation 4: One ball is found in bounds and the other ball is lost or found out of bounds.

Solution 4: The ball in bounds must be presumed to be the provisional ball.

Situation 5: Both balls are found in bounds and (1) both balls are playable, (2) one ball is playable and the other unplayable or (3) both balls are unplayable.

Solution 5: One could argue that both balls are lost. It would be inequitable to require the player to return to the tee, playing 5, when the player has found both balls but does not know which is the original and which the provisional. Accordingly, the player must select one of the balls, treat it as his provisional and abandon the other.

27/12 Identification of Ball Through Testimony of Spectator

Q. A's ball and B's ball came to rest close together. Neither A nor B could identify one of the balls as his ball because they were using balls with identical markings. A spectator who saw both shots land was able to state which ball belonged to A and which one belonged to B. May his testimony be accepted, or should both balls be deemed lost because they could not be identified by A and B?

A. If the Committee determined that, based on information given by the spectator, A and B were able to identify their balls, the balls should not be deemed lost. Otherwise, they would have to proceed under Rule 27-1.

27

27/13 Refusal to Identify Ball

Q. A player purposely refuses to identify a ball as his. What can the opponent or a fellow-competitor do in such a case?

A. An opponent or fellow-competitor has the right to be satisfied about the identification of a player's ball.

If a player has dishonestly not identified his ball, the opponent or fellow-competitor may refer the dispute to the Committee — Rule 34-3. In such a case, the Committee would be justified in imposing a penalty of disqualification under Rule 33-7.

Identifying Ball by Brand and Number Only — See 12-2/1.

27/14 Ball in Tree Identified But Not Retrieved

Q. A player's ball is lodged high in a tree. He identifies it with the aid of binoculars but is unable to retrieve it. Is the ball lost, in which case the player must invoke Rule 27-1?

A. No. Since the ball was identified, it was not lost — see Definition of "Lost Ball." The player may invoke the unplayable ball Rule (Rule 28).

27/15 Ball in Tree Visible But Not Identifiable

Q. A player is certain that his ball is lodged high in a tree. He can see a ball in the tree, but he cannot identify it as his ball. Is the player's ball lost, in which case he must proceed under Rule 27-1?

A. Yes.

27/16 Ball Declared Lost Is Found Before Another Ball Put into Play

Q. A player searched for his ball for two minutes, declared it lost and started back to play another ball at the spot from which the original ball was played. Before he put another ball into play, his original ball was found within the five-minute period allowed for search. What is the ruling?

A. A player cannot render a ball lost by a declaration — See Definition of "Lost Ball." The original ball remained in play — see Definition of "Ball in Play."

27

Searching Ten Minutes for Lost Ball — See 6-7/2.

27/17 Status of Original Ball If Another Ball Played Under Stroke-and-Distance Procedure

In general, if a player after playing a stroke plays another ball under a stroke-and-distance procedure, the original ball is lost and the other ball is the ball in play under penalty of stroke and distance.

Such a position is supported by:

(a) the Definition of "Ball in Play," which provides that another ball becomes the ball in play if it has been substituted under any applicable Rule;

(b) the Definition of "Lost Ball," which provides that a ball is lost if the player has put another ball into play under the Rules, *i.e.*, played another ball under a stroke-and-distance procedure; and

(c) Rule 27-2a, which provides: "The player shall inform his opponent in match play or his marker or a fellow-competitor in stroke play that he intends to play a provisional ball, and he shall play it before he or his partner goes forward to search for the original ball. If he fails to do so and plays another ball, such ball is not a provisional ball and becomes the ball in play under penalty of stroke and distance (Rule 27-1); the original ball is deemed to be lost."

Original Ball Found and Played After Another Ball Put into Play — See 15/5.

27/18 Gate in Boundary Fence

Q. A gate in a boundary fence swings onto the course. Sometimes the gate is open and sometimes it is closed. If the gate is open, may a player close it if it interferes with his swing?

A. A gate in a boundary fence, when closed, is part of the boundary fence, is not an obstruction (see Definition of "Obstructions") and may not be moved.

A gate in a boundary fence, if open, is not covered by the Rules. In equity (Rule 1-4), a player who finds a gate in a boundary fence open may leave it as he finds it or close it, but he must not move it to any other position.

Removal of Boundary Stake Interfering with Swing — See 13-2/17.

Improving Position of Ball by Bending Boundary Fence — See 13-2/18.

Improving Area of Intended Swing by Moving Growing or Fixed Object Situated Out of Bounds — See 13-2/19.

Part of Fence Off Course Leans Across Boundary and Interferes with Swing — See 13-2/20.

Player Removes Boundary Post on Line of Play But Replaces It Before Playing — See 13-2/25.

Stroke Played with Ball Lying Out of Bounds — See 15/6.

Ball Lifted and Dropped Away from Boundary Stake Under Obstruction Rule — See 18-2a/3.

27/19 When Ball Inside Boundary Fence Is Out of Bounds

Q. In view of the Definition of "Out of Bounds," is it correct to say that, if the posts of a boundary fence are on the golf course side of the fence, the diameter of the posts is greater than the diameter of a golf ball and the fence is straight, a ball lying against the inside of the fence would be out of bounds?

A. Yes.

Stile Attached to Boundary Fence — See 24/1.

Angled Supports or Guy Wires Supporting Boundary Fence — See 24/2.

Concrete Bases of Boundary Fence Posts — See 24/3.

Part of Boundary Fence Within Boundary Line — See 24/4.

Ball Moved Out of Bounds by Flow of Water in Water Hazard — See 26-1/7.

27

Ball Moved into Bounds by Flow of Water in Water Hazard — See 26-1/8.

Exposed Water Pipe Adjacent and Parallel to Boundary Fence — See 33-2a/1.

27/20   Public Road Defined as Out of Bounds Divides Course; Status of Ball Crossing Road

Q. A public road defined as out of bounds divides a course. A ball crosses the road and comes to rest on the part of the course on the other side of the road. Is the ball out of bounds?

A. No. Since the ball lies on the course, it is in bounds unless a Local Rule provides otherwise. However, because it is unfair that a ball on the road is out of bounds and a ball beyond it is in bounds, it is suggested that the following Local Rule should be adopted:

> "A ball which crosses a public road defined as out of bounds and comes to rest beyond that road is out of bounds, even though it may lie on another part of the course."

Boundary Stakes Having No Significance in Play of Hole Being Played — See 24/5.

Tee Decreed to Be in Bounds for Tee Shot and Out of Bounds Thereafter — See 33-2a/13.

Internal Out of Bounds Applying to Stroke from Teeing Ground Only — See 33-2a/14.

Establishing Boundary Line Inside Fence on Property Line — See 33-2a/15.

Deeming Ball in Bounds Until Beyond Boundary Wall — See 33-2a/16.

Identifying Stakes Defining Out of Bounds — See 33-2a/18.

Boundary Altered by Unauthorized Removal of Boundary Stake — See 33-2a/19.

Displaced Boundary Stake — See 33-2a/20.

27-1/1   Original Ball Found Within Five-Minute Search Period After Another Ball Teed

Q. A player plays from the teeing ground, searches briefly for his ball and then goes back and tees another ball. Before he plays the teed ball, and within the five-minute search period, the original ball is found. May the player abandon the teed ball and play the original ball?

A. Yes. The teed ball was not in play since the player had not yet made a stroke at it — see Definition of "Ball in Play."

27-1/2 Original Ball Found Within Five-Minute Search Period After Another Ball Dropped

Q. A player plays his second shot, searches for his ball briefly and then goes back and drops another ball under Rule 27-1. Before he plays the dropped ball, and within the five-minute search period, the original ball is found. May the player abandon the dropped ball and play the original ball?

A. No. The dropped ball was in play (Rule 20-4) and the original ball was lost.

27-1/2.5 Lost Ball Treated as Moved by Outside Agency in Absence of Reasonable Evidence to That Effect

Q. A player who is unable to find his ball treats it as moved by an outside agency, rather than lost, although there is no reasonable evidence to that effect. Accordingly, he drops a ball where he thinks his original ball came to rest (Rule 18-1) and plays it, rather than taking a stroke-and-distance penalty for relief for a lost ball (Rule 27-1). What is the ruling?

A. The ball dropped under Rule 18-1 was not substituted under an applicable Rule; thus it was a wrong ball — see Definitions of "Ball in Play" and "Wrong Ball."

In match play, the player loses the hole — Rule 15-2.

In stroke play, the player incurs a penalty of two strokes (Rule 15-3) and must proceed under the applicable Rule (Rule 27-1), incurring the additional one-stroke penalty prescribed in that Rule.

27

Original Ball Found and Played After Another Ball Put into Play — See 15/5.

Ball Believed to Be Lost in Bunker; Competitor Drops Another Ball in Bunker and Plays It; Original Ball Then Found Outside Bunker — See 20-7b/3.

Ball Lost in Tree in Ground Under Repair — See 25/10.

27-1/3 Ball Dropped in Area Where Original Ball Lost; Ball Then Played

Q. A player, unable to find his ball, drops another ball in the area where his original ball was lost and plays that ball. What is the ruling?

A. In match play, the player loses the hole — Rule 20-7a.

In stroke play, he incurs a two- stroke penalty under Rule 27-1 and, since the breach of that Rule was a serious one, he must rectify it; otherwise, he is disqualified — Rule 20-7b.

Ball Played from Outside Teeing Ground Goes Out of Bounds — See 11-4b/6.

Stroke Played with Ball Lying Out of Bounds — See 15/6.

Ball Thrown into Bounds by Outside Agency and Played; Caddie Aware of Action of Outside Agency — See 15/9.

Ball Thrown into Bounds by Outside Agency and Played; Neither Player Nor His Caddie Aware of Action of Outside Agency — See 15/10.

Ball Wrongly Thought to Be Out of Bounds Lifted; Competitor Proceeds Under Rule 27-1 — See 18-2a/11.

Ball Moved Accidentally by Backward Movement of Club After Stroke Misses; Ball Comes to Rest Out of Bounds — See 18-2a/22.

Ball Moves After Address and Comes to Rest Out of Bounds — See 18-2b/9.

Opponent's Caddie Lifts Player's Ball Which May or May Not Have Been Out of Bounds — See 18-3b/5.

Player's Ball Strikes Own Caddie and Comes to Rest Out of Bounds — See 19-2/2.

Player's Ball Strikes Own Caddie Standing Out of Bounds and Comes to Rest on Course — See 19-2/3.

Player's Ball Strikes Own Caddie Standing Out of Bounds and Comes to Rest Out of Bounds — See 19-2/4.

27

Ball Strikes Opponent Standing Out of Bounds and Comes to Rest Out of Bounds — See 19-3/1.

Teed Ball Missed Then Hit Out of Bounds — See 20-5/1.

Ball Played from Spot Where Original Ball Deflected Out of Bounds by Maintenance Vehicle — See 20-7/1.

Ball Enters Burrowing Animal Hole Out of Bounds and Comes to Rest in Bounds — See 25-1b/23.

Ball Enters Burrowing Animal Hole in Bounds and Comes to Rest Out of Bounds — See 25-1b/24.

Ball Played in Ground Under Repair Area Lost in Same Area — See 25-1c/3.

Tee Shot Out of Bounds in Mixed Foursome in Which Different Tees Used by Men and Women — See 29/2.

27-2/1 Provisional Ball Serving as Ball in Play If Original Ball Unplayable or in Water Hazard

Q. May a player announce that a second ball he is going to play is both (a) a provisional ball in case the original ball is lost outside a water hazard or out of bounds and (b) the ball in play in case the original ball is unplayable or in a water hazard?

A. No.

27-2/2 Member of Committee Finds Player's Original Ball; Player Prefers to Continue with Provisional Ball

Q. Is a member of the Committee or a forecaddie obliged to inform a player that his original ball has been found, even if it is clear that the player does not plan to search for it because he would prefer to continue play with the provisional ball he has played?

A. Yes.

Provisional Ball Used as Second Ball When Not Determinable Whether Original Ball Is Out of Bounds — See 3-3/1.

Condition Requiring Use of Ball on List of Conforming Golf Balls; Ball Not on List Played as Provisional Ball — See 5-1/3.

Wrong Ball Played in Belief It Is Provisional Ball — See 15/7.

27

Provisional Ball Moves After Being Addressed — See 15/7.

Original Ball Struck by Provisional Ball — See 18-5/2.

Provisional Ball Struck by Original Ball — See 19-5/5.

Who Plays Provisional Ball in Foursome — See 29-1/3.

Provisional Ball Played by Wrong Member of Side in Foursome — See 29-1/4.

27-2a/1 Announcement of Provisional Ball

Q. A player shanked a ball and there was a good chance that the ball came to rest out of bounds. The player then dropped another ball and played it. It was clear that the player intended the dropped ball to be a provisional ball, but he did not inform his opponent, marker or a fellow-competitor that he playing a provisional ball. In such a situation, can a player's actions constitute announcement that he is playing a provisional ball?

A. No. Rule 27-2a specifically provides that the player must inform his opponent, marker or a fellow-competitor that he intends to play a provisional ball.

27-2a/2 Provisional Ball Played Solely in Belief Original Ball Might Be in Water Hazard

Q. A player's tee shot might be in a water hazard, but clearly it is not lost outside a water hazard or out of bounds. The player announces that, since his ball might be in the hazard, he is going to play a provisional ball and he does so. Rule 27-2a seems to prohibit a provisional ball in the circumstances. What is the ruling?

A. The player did not play a provisional ball which, according to the Definition of "Provisional Ball," is a ball played under Rule 27-2 for a ball which may be lost outside a water hazard or may be out of bounds. The second ball from the tee was in play since it was not a provisional ball.

27

27-2a/3 Play of Provisional Ball in Absence of Reasonable Possibility Original Ball Is Lost or Out of Bounds

Q. In the absence of reasonable possibility that a ball is lost outside a water hazard or is out of bounds, may the player play a provisional ball?

A. No. If a player plays a ball under such circumstances, the ball is not a provisional ball but the ball in play — see Decision 27-2a/2.

27-2a/4 Play of a Second Provisional Ball

Q. If a player properly plays a provisional ball and believes that it may be out of bounds, may he play a second provisional ball before going forward to look for the original ball and the first provisional ball?

A. Yes. The second provisional ball bears to the first provisional ball the same relationship as the first provisional ball bears to the original ball.

27-2b/1 Continuation of Play with Provisional Ball Without Searching for Original Ball

Q. At a par-3 hole, a player hits his tee shot into dense woods. He then hits a provisional ball which comes to rest near the hole. In view of the position of the provisional ball, the player does not wish to find his original ball. He does not search for it and walks directly towards his provisional ball to continue play with it. His opponent (or fellow-competitor) believes it would be beneficial to him if the original ball were found. May the opponent (or fellow-competitor) search for five minutes for the player's ball?

A. Yes, provided that in the meantime the player does not play a stroke with the provisional ball, it being nearer the hole than the place where the original ball is likely to be. The player is entitled to play such a stroke. If he does, the original ball is then lost under Rule 27-2b and further search for it would serve no purpose. In match play, if the player so proceeds and his provisional ball is closer to the hole than his opponent's ball, his opponent may recall the stroke —

27

Rule 10-1c. However, recalling the stroke would not change the status of the original ball, which was lost when the provisional ball was played out of turn. See also Decision 27-2c/2.

27-2b/2 When Provisional Ball Holed Becomes Ball in Play

Q. At a short hole, A's tee shot may be out of bounds or lost, so he plays a provisional ball, which he holes. A does not wish to look for his original ball. B, A's opponent or a fellow-competitor, goes to look for the original ball. When does the provisional ball become the ball in play?

A. The provisional ball becomes the ball in play as soon as A picks it out of the hole, provided his original ball has not already been found in bounds within five minutes of B starting to search for it.

27-2b/3 Original Ball Is Beyond Provisional Ball; Player Searches Briefly for Original Ball, Plays Provisional Ball and Then Finds Original Ball

Q. A player's provisional ball comes to rest short of where the original ball is likely to be. After a two-minute search for the original ball, the player goes back, plays a second stroke with the provisional ball and then his original ball is found within the five-minute time limit. What is the ruling?

A. The player must continue play with the original ball. Play of a provisional ball does not render the original ball lost until it has been played from the place where the original ball is likely to be or from a point nearer the hole than that place — Rule 27-2b.

27 ## 27-2b/4 Provisional Ball Played from Beyond Where Original Ball Likely to Be But Not Beyond Where Original Ball Found

Q. A player, believing his tee shot might be lost or in a road defined as out of bounds, played a provisional ball. He searched for his original ball but did not find it. He went forward and played his provisional ball. Then he went further forward and found his original ball in bounds. The original ball must have bounced down the road and then come back into bounds, because it was found much farther from the tee than anticipated. Was the original ball still the ball in play?

A. No. The player played a stroke with the provisional ball from a point nearer the hole than the place where the original ball was likely to be. When he did so, the provisional ball became the ball in play and the original ball was lost — Rule 27-2b.

The place where the original ball in fact lay was irrelevant.

27-2b/5 Original Ball Played After Provisional Ball Played from Point Nearer Hole Than Original Ball Is Likely to Be

Q. A player, unable to find his original ball, goes forward and plays a second stroke with his provisional ball from a point nearer the hole than the place where the original ball is likely to be. His original ball is then found and he plays it. What is the ruling?

A. When the player played his second stroke with the provisional ball, the original ball was out of play and the provisional ball was in play — Rule 27-2b. In playing a stroke with a ball out of play (the original ball), the player played a wrong ball — see Definition of "Wrong Ball" -and was subject to penalty as prescribed in Rule 15.

27-2b/6 Player Abandons Original Ball and Walks Forward to Play Provisional Ball; Original Ball Then Found

Q. A player, having searched for a minute for his original ball, abandoned it and walked forward to continue play with his provisional ball. Before he played the provisional ball, some spectators found the original ball before the five-minute search period expired. What is the ruling?

27

A. The original ball remained the ball in play since it was found within five minutes after search for it had begun and the player had not played a stroke with the provisional ball from the place where the original ball was likely to be or from a point nearer the hole than that place — Rule 27-2b.

Player Discovers Original Ball in Hole After Searching Five Minutes and Then Continuing Play with Provisional Ball — See 1-1/3.

27-2b/7 Provisional Ball Played in Erroneous Belief It Is Original Ball

Q. A player, believing his original ball may be out of bounds, plays a provisional ball which comes to rest in the same area. He finds a ball which he believes is his original ball, plays it and then discovers that the ball he played was his provisional ball. What is the ruling?

A. If a player reaches the place where his original ball is likely to be and plays another stroke with a provisional ball, the provisional ball is in play and the original ball is lost — Rule 27-2b.

27-2b/8 Provisional Ball Lifted in Erroneous Belief Original Ball Is in Bounds

Q. A player, believing his original ball might be out of bounds, played a provisional ball which came to rest short of where the original ball came to rest. He walked forward, saw his original ball and, believing the original ball to be in bounds, picked up the provisional ball. He then discovered that the original ball was out of bounds. What is the ruling?

A. Since the original ball was out of bounds, the provisional ball was in play — Rule 27-2b. When the player lifted the ball in play (provisional ball) without authority under the Rules, he incurred a penalty stroke and was required to replace it — Rule 18-2a.

27

27-2b/9 Provisional Ball Lifted Subsequently Becomes Ball in Play

Q. In stroke play, a competitor, believing his original ball might be lost, plays a provisional ball. He finds a ball he believes is his original ball, plays a stroke at it, picks up his provisional ball and then discovers that the ball he played was not his original ball, but rather a wrong ball. He resumes search for his original ball but cannot find it. What is the ruling?

A. The competitor lifted a ball which was to become the ball in play, *i.e.*, the provisional ball — see Rule 27-2b. Accordingly, the competitor incurred a stroke-and-distance penalty under Rule 27-1 as a result of losing his original ball, a two-stroke penalty under Rule 15-3 for playing a wrong ball and a one-stroke penalty under Rule 18-2a for picking up his provisional ball. He was required to replace and play out the provisional ball.

27-2c/1 Possibility That Original Ball Is in Water Hazard May Not Preclude Play of Provisional Ball

Q. Is it true that, if a player's original ball may have come to rest in a water hazard, the player is precluded from playing a provisional ball?

A. No. Even though the original ball may be in a water hazard, the player is entitled to play a provisional ball if the original ball might also be lost outside the water hazard or out of bounds. In such a case, if the original ball is found in the water hazard, the provisional ball must be abandoned — Rule 27-2c.

27-2c/2 Original Ball Found; Player Wishes to Ignore It and Continue Play with Provisional Ball

Q. At a par-3 hole, a player hits his tee shot into a heavy thicket and, since his ball may be lost, he hits a provisional ball, which comes to rest near the hole. In the circumstances, it is advantageous to the player not to find his original ball, in which case the provisional ball would become the ball in play. Accordingly, the

27

player does not search for the original ball; he walks directly towards his provisional ball. While the player is on his way to his provisional ball, his original ball is found by a member of the Committee, a forecaddie, his opponent or a fellow-competitor. The player is advised that his original ball has been found. May the player ignore the original ball and continue play with the provisional ball?

A. No. The player must inspect the ball which has been found and, if it is the player's original ball, he must continue play with it (or proceed under the unplayable ball Rule). The provisional ball must be abandoned — Rule 27-2c. See also Decision 27-2b/1.

27-2c/3 Provisional Ball Played from Point Nearer Hole Than Original Ball Because Player Erroneously Thought Original Ball, Which Was Visible, Was Out of Bounds

Q. A player's ball came to rest 20 yards over a green and beyond a white stake which the player's caddie said was a boundary stake. The player played a provisional ball which came to rest short of the green, but closer to the hole than his original ball. The player played the provisional ball onto the green. At that point, he walked behind the green towards his original ball, which had been visible all along, and discovered that the white stake was not a boundary stake and that his original ball was in bounds. What is the ruling?

A. The player should have determined the status of his original ball before playing a second stroke with the provisional ball and, since the original ball was not out of bounds, he should have abandoned the provisional ball. When he failed to do so, the second stroke with the provisional ball was a stroke with a wrong ball — Rule 27-2c.

In match play, the player lost the hole (Rule 15-2).

In stroke play, he incurred a two-stroke penalty (Rule 15-3) and was required to hole out with the original ball.

27

27-2c/4 Original Ball and Provisional Ball Found Out of Bounds

Q. A player finds both his original ball and his provisional ball out of bounds. The balls were played from the tee. When the player returns to the tee and plays another ball, has he taken 3 strokes or 5?

A. The player will have taken 5 strokes when he plays the third ball from the tee. A stroke played with a provisional ball and any penalty related to it are not disregarded unless the provisional ball is abandoned as provided in Rule 27-2c.

27

Rule 28. Ball Unplayable

The player may declare his ball unplayable at any place on the course except when the ball lies in or touches a <u>water hazard</u>. The player is the sole judge as to whether his ball is unplayable.

If the player deems his ball to be unplayable, he shall, *under penalty of one stroke*:

a. Play a ball as nearly as possible at the spot from which the original ball was last played (see Rule 20-5);

or

b. Drop a ball within two club-lengths of the spot where the ball lay, but not nearer the hole;

or

c. Drop a ball behind the point where the ball lay, keeping that point directly between the hole and the spot on which the ball is dropped, with no limit to how far behind that point the ball may be dropped.

If the unplayable ball lies in a <u>bunker</u>, the player may proceed under Clause a, b or c. If he elects to proceed under Clause b or c, a ball must be dropped in the bunker.

The ball may be cleaned when lifted under this Rule.

PENALTY FOR BREACH OF RULE:
Match play --- Loss of hole;
Stroke play --- Two strokes.

28

28/1 When Necessary to Find and Identify Ball Declared Unplayable

Q. A player hits his tee shot into a deep canyon. The player immediately declares the ball unplayable and plays another ball from the tee under the stroke-and-distance option of Rule 28. May a player declare unplayable a ball which has not been found?

A. Yes. A player may proceed under the stroke-and-distance option (Rule 28a) without finding his ball.

However, since Rules 28b and c require reference to where the ball lay, the player must find and identify his ball in order to proceed under either of these options.

28/2 Player Declares First Ball from Tee Unplayable, Abandons Provisional Ball and Claims He Is Lying Three with Third Ball

Q. A player hit his tee shot deep into the woods on the right. The player then hit a provisional ball into the same woods. The player did not search for either ball.

The player declared his first ball unplayable, said he was abandoning his provisional ball and hit a third ball from the tee. The player maintained that his third ball was in play and that he was lying 3. He based his argument on Rule 28, which states that the player is the sole judge as to whether his ball is unplayable, and on Decision 28/1, which says in effect that a player may proceed under the stroke-and-distance option of the unplayable ball Rule without finding his ball. The Committee ruled that the player's stroke with the third ball was his fifth stroke, but the wording of Decision 28/1 leaves a little doubt. Did the Committee rule correctly?

A. Yes. The player may not declare the first ball from the tee unplayable, disregard the provisional ball and put another ball into play under a stroke-and-distance penalty because, having played the provisional ball, he must find the original ball before he can declare it unplayable. Unless the original ball was found, the

28

provisional ball would automatically become the ball in play.

This case differs from Decision 28/1. No provisional ball was played in that case.

28/3 Ball Dropped Under Unplayable Ball Rule Comes to Rest in Original Position or Another Position at Which Ball Is Unplayable

Q. A player declared his ball unplayable and, under Rule 28b, dropped his ball within two club-lengths of the spot where it lay. The ball came to rest in the original position or another position at which the ball was unplayable. What is the ruling?

A. The ball was in play when it was dropped — Rule 20-4. Thus, if the ball came to rest in the original position, the player must again invoke the unplayable ball Rule, incurring an additional penalty stroke, unless he decides to play the ball as it lies. The same applies if the ball came to rest in another position at which it was unplayable, assuming that the ball did not roll into a position covered by Rule 20-2c, in which case re-dropping without penalty would be required.

28/4 Ball Declared Unplayable Through the Green Dropped in Hazard

Q. A player's ball lies through the green. The player declares the ball unplayable. In proceeding under Rule 28b or c, the player drops a ball in a hazard. Is this permissible?

A. Yes.

Ball Declared Unplayable Dropped in Ground Under Repair from Which Play Prohibited; Ball Then Dropped Under Ground Under Repair Rule — See 25-1b/14.5.

Ball Declared Unplayable in Water Hazard Is Dropped in Hazard and Played — See 20-7/2.

28/5 Regression Under Unplayable Ball Rule

28

Q. A player plays a stroke from Point A to Point B. Point B is in an area from which it is very difficult to extricate a ball. The player considers declaring the ball unplayable but this would result in a stroke-and-distance penalty (Rule 28a). Dropping behind under Rule 28c is impossible due to a boundary fence and dropping within two club-lengths under Rule 28b is not feasible because it would require a considerable number of such drops to escape the area. The player plays from Point B and moves the ball a few feet to Point C, where the ball is clearly unplayable. Under Rule 28a, may the player:

(a) declare the ball unplayable at Point C and drop a ball under penalty of one stroke at Point B, and then

(b) declare the ball unplayable at Point B and drop a ball, under an additional penalty of one stroke, at Point A?

A. No. Under Rule 28a, the player would be entitled to drop a ball only at the place from which he played his last stroke (Point B).

In the circumstances, the player's only alternative is to invoke Rule 28b a sufficient number of times (starting at Point C and dropping the ball sideways within two club-lengths each time) to get the ball into a playable position.

28/6 Player Plays Second Shot, Declares Ball Unplayable and Returns to Tee

Q. With regard to Decision 28/5, if Point A is the teeing ground and Point B is the spot from which the second shot was played, what is the penalty if the player, having declared his ball unplayable at Point C, returns to the tee and plays out the hole from there?

A. The player was entitled to drop and play a ball at Point B under Rule 28a, but not Point A. When he played a ball from Point A, he played from a wrong place.

In match play, the player incurs a penalty of loss of hole for a breach of Rule 28 — see also Rule 20-7a.

28

In stroke play, a serious breach of Rule 28 is involved. Accordingly, the player is disqualified unless the serious breach is corrected as provided in Rule 20-7b.

Except in the special circumstances covered by Rule 26-2, the Rules do not allow a player to regress beyond the spot from which his last stroke was played, in this case Point B. Such action generally constitutes a serious breach, as in this case.

28/7 Player Misses Ball and Declares It Unplayable

Q. A player's tee shot comes to rest in tree roots. He makes a stroke, fails to move the ball and then declares the ball unplayable. May the player return to the tee, playing 4, under Rule 28a?

A. No. Rule 28a permits the player to play "a ball . . . at the spot from which the original ball was last played." The original ball was last played from the tree roots, not the tee.

28/8 Ball Declared Unplayable; Place from Which Previous Stroke Played Is Nearer Hole

Q. A player's ball strikes a rock and bounces farther away from the hole than the spot from which the stroke was played. The player declares the ball unplayable. May the player invoke the stroke-and-distance option of Rule 28 in the circumstances?

A. Yes.

28/9 Ball Lying on Grass-Covered Ground Within Bunker Declared Unplayable

Q. A player's ball is lying on grass-covered ground within a bunker. The player declares the ball unplayable and elects to drop it under Rule 28c. Must he drop it in the bunker?

A. No. Grass-covered ground within a bunker is not part of the bunker. Accordingly, the player may drop the ball behind the bunker.

28

28/10   Ball Dropped Outside Bunker Under Option Requiring Drop in Bunker

Q. In stroke play, a competitor declares his ball un-playable in a bunker and, purporting to proceed un-der Rule 28b or c, drops a ball outside the bunker, whereas both such provisions require that a ball be dropped in the bunker. What is the penalty?

A. Generally, the penalty should be disqualification for a serious breach of Rule 28, unless rectified under Rule 20-7b. However, if the position of the ball after it is dropped out of the bunker is not substantially different from what it would have been if the competi-tor had invoked the stroke-and-distance option under Rule 28a, the penalty would be two strokes for breach of Rule 28.

28/11   Ball Unplayable in Tree and Player Opts to Drop Within Two Club-Lengths

Q. A player's ball is eight feet off the ground, lodged in a tree. The player declares the ball unplayable. May the player proceed under option b of Rule 28 which permits him to drop a ball within two club-lengths of where his ball lay unplayable?

A. Yes. The player would be entitled to drop a ball within two club-lengths of the point on the ground immediately below the place where the ball lay in the tree. In some instances this may allow the player to drop a ball on a putting green.

Ball Unplayable in Tree Dislodged by Shaking Tree or Throwing Club — See 18-2a/27.

Ball in Tree Identified But Not Retrieved Declared Un-playable — See 27/14.

28/12   Ball Unplayable at Base of Cliff and Player Wishes to Drop Within Two Club-Lengths of Point Above Ball

28

Q. Under Decision 28/11, if a ball in a tree is declared unplayable, the player may, under Rule 28b, drop a ball within two club-lengths of the spot on the ground directly beneath where the ball lies.

Suppose a player declares unplayable a ball lying at the base of a cliff and wishes to proceed under Rule 28b. May the player drop a ball within two club-lengths of a point directly above where the ball lies in order to get himself onto the top of the cliff?

A. No.

In Decision 28/11, the player was permitted to ignore vertical distance in taking relief under Rule 28b only because his ball was off the ground. In this case, the ball at the base of the cliff is on the ground.

28/13 After Declaring Ball Unplayable and Lifting It, Player Discovers Ball Was in Ground Under Repair

Q. A player lifts his ball after declaring it unplayable and then discovers that the ball was lying in ground under repair. Do the declaration and the lifting of the ball commit the player to proceeding under Rule 28?

A. No. Provided the player has not put a ball into play under Rule 28, he is not precluded by that Rule from taking relief, without penalty, under the ground under repair Rule (Rule 25).

In match play, however, the player would be in breach of Rule 9-2 (Information as to Strokes Taken) if he declared his ball unplayable and then, after his opponent had played his next stroke, he proceeded under the ground under repair Rule.

28/14 Wrong Ball Declared Unplayable Played Under Stroke-and-Distance Procedure; Original Ball Then Found

Q. A player finds a stray ball, which he mistakenly thinks is his, in a bad lie. He declares it unplayable and decides to adopt the procedure in Rule 28a. After going back, he plays the stray ball under penalty of stroke and distance at the spot from which his original ball was played. He then finds his original ball in a playable position. What is the ruling?

28

A. The original ball is lost and the stray ball played under penalty of stroke and distance is in play — see Decision 27/17.

The ruling would have been different if the player had decided to proceed under either Rule 28b or 28c — see Decision 28/15.

28/15 Wrong Ball Declared Unplayable, Dropped Within Two Club-Lengths and Played Before Error Discovered

Q. A player finds a stray ball, which he mistakenly thinks is his, in a bad lie. He declares it unplayable and decides to adopt the procedure in Rule 28b. He drops the stray ball within two-club-lengths of the spot where it lay and plays it. He then finds his original ball in a playable position.

In Decision 28/14 the basic situation is exactly the same, but in that case the player elected to proceed under Rule 28a and it was ruled that the stray ball played under penalty of stroke and distance was in play.

What is the ruling in this case?

A. The procedures in Rules 28b and 28c cannot be applied except with reference to the position of the player's ball in play, and this must first be found and identified — see Decision 28/1. In the present case, the stray ball dropped and played by the player was neither his original ball nor a ball substituted under an applicable Rule; it was therefore a wrong ball — see Definitions of "Ball in Play" and "Wrong Ball." The player incurred a penalty of loss of hole in match play or two strokes in stroke play — Rule 15. In stroke play, he must continue play with his original ball.

The ruling in Decision 28/14 was different because, when a player plays a ball under the stroke-and-distance procedure, the location of his original ball is irrelevant and it need not even have been found and identified.

28

Wrong Ball Dropped Under Unplayable Ball Rule But Not Played — See 15/13.

Caddie on Own Initiative Lifts Ball Considering It Unplayable — See 18-2a/15.

Changing Relief Option When Re-Dropping Required — See 20-2c/5.

Changing Relief Option After Ball Dropped in a Wrong Place — See 20-6/2.

28

OTHER FORMS OF PLAY

Rule 29. Threesomes and Foursomes

Definitions

Threesome: A match in which one plays against two, and each side plays one ball.

Foursome: A match in which two play against two, and each side plays one ball.

29-1. General

In a threesome or a foursome, during any stipulated round the partners shall play alternately from the teeing grounds and alternately during the play of each hole. Penalty strokes do not affect the order of play.

29-2. Match Play

If a player plays when his partner should have played, *his side shall lose the hole.*

29-3. Stroke Play

If the partners play a stroke or strokes in incorrect order, such stroke or strokes shall be cancelled and *the side shall incur a penalty of two strokes.* The side shall correct the error by playing a ball in correct order as nearly as possible at the spot from which it first played in incorrect order (see Rule 20-5). If the side plays a stroke from the next teeing ground without first correcting the error or, in the case of the last hole of the round, leaves the putting green without declaring its intention to correct the error, *the side shall be disqualified.*

29

29/1 Changing Partners After Driving from First Tee

Q. A and B are to play C and D in a foursome match in which the conditions of the competition permit substitutions. D is absent at the time the match is to start. Accordingly, E is substituted for D. C plays the first stroke for side C-E. At that point, D arrives. May D be reinstated in the match since E has not played a stroke?

A. No. Once any player in a foursome match has played from the first tee, the composition of neither side may be changed.

29/2 Mixed Foursome in Which Different Tees Used by Men and Women; Tee Shot Out of Bounds

Q. In a mixed foursome in which the men play from the men's tees and the women play from the women's tees, a man hits a tee shot out of bounds. Does his partner play the next stroke from the men's tee or the women's tee?

A. The partner must play from the men's tee.

29/3 Player in Foursome Match Practices Putts on Previous Green After Partner Has Driven from Next Tee

Q. A and B are partners in a foursome match. A was practicing putts on the 11th green after B drove off the 12th tee. Was A playing practice strokes during the play of a hole?

A. Yes. A and B lost the 12th hole for a breach of Rule 7-2.

29/4 Dropping Ball in Foursome Competition

Q. Rule 20-2a provides that "the player himself" must drop a ball. Under the Definition of "Partner," it is stated that, in the case of threesomes and foursomes, the term "player" includes his partner where the context so admits. When a side in a foursome is required to drop a ball, may either member of the side drop it?

A. No. In view of the requirement of Rule 20-2a that the player himself shall drop the ball, the member of the side whose turn it is to play next must drop the ball.

29/5 Hitting Sand in Bunker with Club After Failing to Extricate Ball; Foursome Match

Q. In a foursome match, A and B are partners. A plays a bunker shot, fails to get the ball out and takes a swing with his club into the sand. This action does not improve the position of the ball in the bunker.

Rule 13-4 provides that, when a ball lies in a hazard, the *player* "shall not touch the ground in the hazard . . . with a club." When A took the swing, it was B's turn to play the next stroke for side A-B. So, presumably, B was the "player" insofar as the Rules were concerned. Accordingly, it would appear A-B would incur no penalty under Rule 13-4 as a result of A's swing. Is this correct?

A. No. In a foursome, the word "player" includes his partner — see Definition of "Partner." A-B incur a penalty of loss of hole for a breach of Rule 13-4 — see Decision 13-4/35.

29/6 Signing of Score Card in Foursome Stroke Play

Q. Rule 31-4 dealing with scoring in four-ball stroke play states: "Only one of the partners need be responsible for complying with Rule 6-6b." What is the ruling in this regard in foursome stroke play?

A. Although Rule 29 is silent on the matter, in foursome stroke play only one of the partners need be responsible for complying with Rule 6-6b.

Competitor Records Incorrect Handicap for Partner in Foursome Stroke Play Competition; Error Discovered After Competition Closed — See 6-2b/2.5.

29

Competitors in Foursome Competition Fail to Record Individual Handicaps on Score Card — See 6-2b/4.

29-1/1 Ball Played from Outside Teeing Ground in Foursome Match

Q. A and B are playing C and D in a foursome match. A plays from outside the teeing ground and Side A-B is required by C and D to replay the stroke. Should A or B replay it?

A. A must replay the stroke. The original stroke does not count.

29-1/2 Competitor Plays from Outside Teeing Ground in Foursome Stroke Play; Partner Replays Stroke

Q. In foursome stroke play A plays in correct order but from outside the teeing ground. B, his partner, then plays from within the teeing ground, whereas A should have done so. What is the ruling?

A. The side is penalized two strokes for playing from outside the teeing ground (Rule 11-4) and two strokes for playing in incorrect order (Rule 29-3). A must now play another ball from within the teeing ground. Otherwise, the side is disqualified.

29-1/3 Who Plays Provisional Ball in Foursome

Q. A and B are partners in a foursome. A drives and there is doubt whether the ball is out of bounds. They decide to play a provisional ball. Who plays it?

A. The provisional ball is played by B.

29-1/4 Provisional Ball Played by Wrong Member of Side in Foursome

Q. A and B were partners in a foursome competition. A drove from the tee and, since the ball might be lost, A-B elected to play a provisional ball. A played the provisional ball, whereas, under Rule 29, B should have played it. What is the ruling?

A. If the original ball was found in bounds and thus the provisional ball did not become the ball in play, there was no penalty.

If the original ball was lost and the provisional ball became the ball in play, A-B lost the hole in match play (Rule 29-2) or incurred a penalty of two strokes in stroke play (Rule 29-3). In stroke play, the provisional ball would have to be abandoned and B would have to play from the tee — Rule 29-3.

29-1/5 Order of Play If Player Accidentally Moves Ball After Address

Q. In a foursome match, a player accidentally moves the ball after addressing it and incurs a penalty of one stroke under Rule 18-2b. The ball is replaced. Does the player or his partner play the next stroke?

A. The player must play the next stroke. Penalty strokes do not affect the order of play (Rule 29-1).

29-1/6 Player Misses Ball Accidentally When Making Stroke

Q. In a foursome event, A and B are partners. A attempts to strike the ball and misses. Whose turn is it to play?

A. An accidental miss is a stroke — see Definition of "Stroke." It is B's turn to play.

29-1/7 Player Misses Ball Purposely So Partner Would Play Ball Over Water

Q. A and B, partners in a foursome competition, were faced with a difficult shot over a pond. A, a poor player, swung but purposely missed the ball. B, an expert player, then played the ball to the green. Is this permissible?

29

A. No. Since A had no intention of moving the ball, he did not play a stroke — see Definition of "Stroke" — and it remained his turn to play.

When B played instead of A, A and B incurred a penalty of loss of hole in match play or two strokes in stroke play — Rules 29-2 and -3. In stroke play, A must play a ball at the spot from which B played. If A did not do so before the side played from the next teeing ground, A and B were disqualified — Rule 29-3.

29-1/8 Order of Play in Foursome Stroke Play When Wrong Ball Played

Q. In foursome stroke play, A played a wrong ball. Who plays the next shot, A or his partner, B?

A. A must play the next stroke. In a foursome competition, penalty strokes do not affect the order of play — see Rule 29-1. The side A-B incurs a penalty of two strokes — Rule 15-3.

29-1/9 Both Player and Partner Drive at Same Tee in Foursome Play

Q. A and B are partners in foursome play. At the 5th hole, forgetting that they were playing a foursome, A and then B drive. What is the correct procedure:
  (a) if it was A's turn to drive?
  (b) if it was B's turn to drive?

A. In either case A and B are in breach of Rule 29-1 because they both played from the teeing ground instead of playing alternately. A and B incur a penalty of loss of hole in match play or two strokes in stroke play. In stroke play, the side must complete the hole with the ball driven by the player whose turn it was to play and abandon the other ball.

29-2/1 Wrong Partners Drive for Both Sides in Foursome Match

Q. A and B are playing C and D in a foursome match. A and C drive off at a hole at which B and D should have driven. The error is then discovered. What is the ruling?

A. The side which drove first loses the hole under Rule 29-2.

29-2/2 Side Drives for Three Holes in Wrong Order and Then Claim Is Made

Q. In a foursome match, A and B are playing C and D. A drives at the 9th hole and again, in error, at the 10th hole. B drives at the 11th and A drives at the 12th. The error is then discovered. C and D claim the 10th, 11th and 12th holes, and the matter is referred to the Committee. What is the ruling?

A. A and B lose the 12th hole under Rule 29-2.

C and D's claim of the 10th and 11th holes could have been considered only if C and D had been given wrong information by A and B and the claim had been based on facts previously unknown to C and D. A and B are deemed to have given wrong information to C and D — see first paragraph of Rule 9-2. However, C and D must have seen A and B play out of order on all three holes. Therefore, the claim was not based on facts previously unknown to C and D.

Rule 30. Three-Ball, Best-Ball and Four-Ball Match Play

Definitions

Three-Ball: A match play competition in which three play against one another, each playing his own ball. Each player is playing two distinct matches.

Best-Ball: A match in which one plays against the better ball of two or the best ball of three players.

Four-Ball: A match in which two play their better ball against the better ball of two other players.

30-1. Rules of Golf Apply

The Rules of Golf, so far as they are not at variance with the following special Rules, shall apply to three-ball, best-ball and four-ball matches.

30-2. Three-Ball Match Play

a. BALL AT REST MOVED BY AN OPPONENT

Except as otherwise provided in the Rules, if the player's ball is touched or moved by an opponent, his <u>caddie</u> or <u>equipment</u> other than during search, Rule 18-3b applies. *That opponent shall incur a penalty stroke in his match with the player*, but not in his match with the other opponent.

30

b. BALL DEFLECTED OR STOPPED BY AN OPPONENT ACCIDENTALLY

If a player's ball is accidentally deflected or stopped by an opponent, his <u>caddie</u> or <u>equipment</u>, no penalty shall be incurred. In his match with that opponent the player may play the ball as it lies or, before another stroke is played by either side, he may cancel the stroke and play a ball without penalty as nearly as possible at the spot from which the original ball was last played (see Rule 20-5). In his match with the other opponent, the ball shall be played as it lies.

Exception: Ball striking person attending flagstick — see Rule 17-3b.

(Ball purposely deflected or stopped by opponent — see Rule 1-2.)

30-3. Best-Ball and Four-Ball Match Play

a. REPRESENTATION OF SIDE

A side may be represented by one partner for all or any part of a match; all partners need not be present. An absent partner may join a match between holes, but not during play of a hole.

b. MAXIMUM OF FOURTEEN CLUBS

The side shall be penalized for a breach of Rule 4-4 by any partner.

c. ORDER OF PLAY

Balls belonging to the same side may be played in the order the side considers best.

d. WRONG BALL

If a player plays a stroke with a <u>wrong ball</u> except in a <u>hazard</u>, *he shall be disqualified for that hole*, but his partner incurs no penalty even if the wrong ball belongs to him. If the wrong ball belongs to another player, its owner shall place a ball on the spot from which the wrong ball was first played.

e. DISQUALIFICATION OF SIDE

(i) *A side shall be disqualified* for a breach of any of the following by any partner:

Rule 1-3 — Agreement to Waive Rules.

Rule 4-1, -2 or -3 — Clubs.

Rule 5-1 or -2 — The Ball.

Rule 6-2a — Handicap (playing off higher handicap).

Rule 6-4 — Caddie.

Rule 6-7 — Undue Delay (repeated offense).

Rule 14-3 — Artificial Devices and Unusual Equipment.

(ii) *A side shall be disqualified* for a breach of any of the following by all partners:

Rule 6-3 — Time of Starting and Groups.

Rule 6-8 — Discontinuance of Play.

f. EFFECT OF OTHER PENALTIES

If a player's breach of a Rule assists his partner's play or adversely affects an opponent's play, *the partner incurs the applicable penalty in addition to any penalty incurred by the player.*

In all other cases where a player incurs a penalty for breach of a Rule, the penalty shall not apply to his partner. Where the penalty is stated to be loss of hole, the effect shall be to disqualify the player for that hole.

g. ANOTHER FORM OF MATCH PLAYED CONCURRENTLY

In a best-ball or four-ball match when another form of match is played concurrently, the above special Rules shall apply.

30/1 Caddie Shared by Members of Opposite Sides in Four-Ball Match Moves Ball

Q. A caddie shared by A and C, who were on opposite sides in a four-ball match, moves A's ball. What is the ruling?

30

A. If the caddie was not acting upon directions of C, A is penalized one stroke — see Definition of "Caddie" and Rule 18-2a.

If the caddie was acting upon directions of C, C is penalized one stroke under Rule 18-3b.

30/2 Caddie Shared by Opponents' Side in Four-Ball Match Moves Player's Ball

Q. A and B are playing C and D in a four-ball match. A caddie shared by C and D accidentally moves A's ball. Who is penalized?

A. Rule 18-3b provides that, if a player's ball is moved by an opponent's caddie, that opponent incurs a penalty stroke. However, when opponents share a caddie, there is no fair way of assigning the penalty to one member of the side. Accordingly, in equity (Rule 1-4), both C and D incur a penalty stroke.

A must replace his ball — Rule 18-3b.

30/2.5 Player Touches Putting Green in Pointing Out Line for Putting for Partner and Incidentally Touches Own Line of Putt

Q. In a four-ball match, A and B are partners and their balls lie on the putting green. A touches the green in pointing out a line for putting for B. Incidentally, the spot which A touches is on his (A's) line of putt.

B is disqualified for the hole under Rule 8-2b. Is A disqualified for the hole under Rule 16-1a?

A. No.

Player Who Has Holed Out Touches Partner's Line of Putt — See 1-2/3.5.

30/3 Determination of Honor in Four-Ball Match in Which Points Awarded for Both Better-Ball and Aggregate Scores

Q. In a four-ball match, one point is awarded for the better-ball score at each hole and one point is awarded for the aggregate score at each hole. How is the honor determined?

A. The Rules of Golf do not cover such a match — see Definition of "Sides and Matches." It is recommended that the honor be determined by the better-ball score only.

30/4 Player Who Walks Off Green Under Mistaken Impression Partner Halved Hole Returns and Putts for Half

Q. A and B are playing C and D in a four-ball match. At one hole C and D hole out and their better-ball score is 4. A, who had marked the position of his ball and lifted it, has a putt for a 4 but he mistakenly thinks B has scored a 4. Accordingly, A walks off the green, leaving his ball-marker on the green. B immediately advises A that he (B) scored a 5. So A returns to the green, replaces his ball and holes out for a 4.

C and D claim the hole on the ground that A cannot come back and putt after walking off the green, thinking his partner had halved the hole. Are C and D correct?

A. No. Since A had not waived his turn to putt and there was no undue delay, A was entitled to proceed as he did. If, however, A had not left his ball-marker on the green, and therefore the position of his ball was no longer marked, he would have incurred a penalty stroke under Rule 20-1 and would no longer have had a putt for the half.

30/5 In Four-Ball Match Player with Putt for Half Picks Up in Error at Suggestion of Opponent Based on Misunderstanding

Q. A and B are playing C and D in a four-ball match. A has holed out in 4, the better ball for his side. When C holes out, A remarks: "Nice 4, C. D, you may pick your ball up." C does not correct A by stating he had a 5 and allows his partner D to pick his ball up although D still has a putt for a half.

30

Upon leaving the putting green, it occurs to C that he has allowed D to pick up when D had an opportunity to halve the hole. In the circumstances, could A's remark be construed as a concession of D's putt?

A. No. A's suggestion that D might pick up D's ball was based on A's mistaken impression that C had scored a 4 and that therefore D's putt could have no bearing on the result.

C should have corrected A's mistaken impression before D picked up his ball. Since C failed to do so and D did not finish the hole, C's score of 5 for the hole was C-D's better-ball score. Thus, C and D lost the hole.

30/6 Player Plays Practice Putt After He and Partner Have Holed Out But Before Opponents Hole Out

Q. In a four-ball match, A plays a practice putt after he and his partner have holed out but before the opponents have holed out. Was A in breach of Rule 7-2?

A. No. Rule 7-2 prohibits practicing during play of a hole. A did not practice during play of the hole because he and his partner had completed it. However, A was guilty of a breach of etiquette.

Flagstick Attended by Partner Without Express Authority of Player; Ball Strikes Flagstick or Partner — See 17-3/4.

30-1/1 Side Plays Out of Turn from Tee; Opponents Require One Member of Side to Replay But Not Other

Q. A and B are playing C and D in a four-ball match. At one hole A and B drive out of turn. C and D require that A abandon his ball and replay in correct order and that B continue with his original ball. A and B maintain that if A is required to drive again then B must also do so. What is the ruling?

A. Rule 10-1c states in part: "... the opponent may immediately require the player to abandon the ball

30

so played..." In this context, "immediately" means before anyone else plays.

Accordingly, if A and B played in that order, C and D could not require A to replay his stroke after B had played, but they could require B to replay. If A and B played in the order B-A, A could be required to replay, but not B.

30-2/1 Player Plays Out of Turn from Tee in Three-Ball Match; One Opponent Requests Replay and Other Does Not

Following are the rulings in a three-ball match if A, B and C are scheduled to play in that order from the tee, B inadvertently drives first and A and C disagree on whether B should be required to replay the stroke under Rule 10-1c:

(a) If A wants B to replay the stroke but C does not, B must complete the hole with two balls. He must replay the stroke in his match with A, and continue with his original ball in his match with C.

(b) If C wants B to replay the stroke but A does not, B must continue with his original ball in both matches. B did not play out of turn with respect to C. Accordingly, C has no right to require B to replay the stroke.

If A, B and C are scheduled to play in that order from the tee, C inadvertently drives first and A and B disagree on whether C should be required to replay, C must complete the hole with two balls. He must replay his stroke in his match with the opponent who requires him to replay and continue with his original ball in his match with the other opponent.

30-3a/1 Absent Partner Joins Match During Play of Hole

Q. Rule 30-3a states in part: "An absent partner may join a match between holes, but not during play of a hole." If A and B are to play C and D in a four-ball match and A is absent when the match begins, what is the ruling if A joins the match during play of a hole?

30

A. A incurs the general penalty prescribed in Rule 2-6 and thus is disqualified for the hole. If any of A's strokes assisted B's play, B also is disqualified for the hole -Rule 30-3f.

30-3a/2   Absent Partner Gives Advice Before Joining Match

Q. A and B are to play C and D in a four-ball match. A is absent when the match begins. A arrives just after B, C and D have teed off at the 3rd hole. According to Decision 30-3a/1, A is prohibited from joining the match until the 4th hole. Is it permissible for A to give B advice during the play of the 3rd hole?

A. Yes.

30-3a/3   Determination of Handicap Allowances in Four-Ball Match If One Player Unable to Compete

Q. In a four-ball handicap match, the player with the lowest handicap is unable to play. Should the absent player be disregarded in determining the handicap allowances?

A. No. Under Rule 30-3a, a side may be represented by one partner for all or any part of the match. In determining handicap allowances, the handicaps of the three players should be reduced by the handicap of the absent player.

If a wrong handicap is declared for the absent player, Rule 6-2a applies. (New)

30-3c/1   Player Putting First When Partner Farther from Hole Stands on Partner's or Opponent's Line of Putt

Q. A and B are partners in a four-ball match. A's ball is closer to the hole than any other ball and it is B's turn to play. A-B decide that A shall putt before B — Rule 30-3c. However, in doing so A would be standing on B's line of putt or the line of putt of an opponent. What is the ruling?

30

A. A would be entitled to putt first even if he would be standing on B's line. Rule 30-3c takes precedence over Rule 16-1a which prohibits touching the line of putt.

A would also be entitled to putt first if he would be standing on an opponent's line of putt. However, it would be a sporting gesture by A-B if they relinquished A's right to putt first in these circumstances.

30-3c/2 Waiving Turn to Putt in Four-Ball Match

Q. In a four-ball match, A and B are playing C and D. All four balls are on the green in three strokes. The balls of A and C are about ten feet from the hole; B's ball is two feet away and D's is three feet away. C picks up his ball. A leaves his ball on the green, but tells B and D to "battle it out." D putts first and holes; B then putts and misses. May A then putt for a half?

A. No. A and B abandoned A's right to complete the hole by allowing D to putt before A and B when it was A-B's turn to play. Under Rule 30-3c, A-B could have opted for B to putt before A. However, if B had done so and missed, it would then have been A's turn to play.

The answer is different if B's ball is three feet away, D's is two feet away and B putts and misses. In these circumstances, A may putt, provided he does so before D putts.

30-3d/1 Player Plays Partner's Ball

Q. A and B are partners in a four-ball match. By mistake, A putts B's ball and A is disqualified for the hole under Rule 30-3d for playing a wrong ball. B replaces his ball as required by Rule 30-3d and holes his putt. The opponents then claim that B also is disqualified for the hole under Rule 30-3f because A's act of putting B's ball assisted B in determining how much his putt would break, etc. Is the claim valid?

A. No. Rule 30-3d specifically provides that B incurs no penalty. Rule 30-3f is not applicable.

30

30-3d/2 Player Wins Hole with Wrong Ball and Partner Picks Up; Error Discovered at Next Hole

Q. In a four-ball match, Side A-B holed out for a 4. C, a member of Side C-D, then holed a putt for a 3 and his partner, D, picked up what he thought was his ball. After playing from the next tee, it was discovered that C had putted out at the previous hole with D's ball. Side A-B claimed the hole. What is the ruling?

A. C gave wrong information to Side A-B when he did not promptly advise Side A-B that he had incurred a penalty for playing a wrong ball — see Rule 9-2. Accordingly, a belated claim by Side A-B was valid — Rule 2-5.

It should have been ruled that C was disqualified for the hole — Rule 9-2 or Rule 30-3d — and, since D did not complete the hole, Side A-B won the hole.

30-3d/3 Players on Opposite Sides Exchange Balls During Play of Hole and Their Partners Pick Up; Error Discovered at Next Hole

Q. A and B were playing C and D in a four-ball match. At the 2nd hole, by mistake A played C's ball and then C played A's. C holed out with A's ball, scoring 5. A holed out C's ball, scoring 4. B and D picked up. Thus, A and B "won" the hole. The error was discovered during play of the 3rd hole, and Side C-D lodged a claim. What is the ruling?

A. A and C were disqualified for the 2nd hole for playing wrong balls. They should have informed their opponents as soon as practicable, which in this case was as soon as they had the opportunity to discover that they had done so, *i.e.*, when they reached the balls wrongly played to play them again. Because they failed to do so, they gave wrong information (Rule 9-2) and, under Rule 2-5, a belated claim that A (and C as well) was disqualified for the 2nd hole for a breach of Rule 30-3d should be upheld.

It could be argued that B and D's play of the 2nd hole was adversely affected (in that they picked up) and that accordingly Rule 30-3f applies. However, Rule

30-3d specifically provides that the "partner incurs no penalty." This applies even if play of the wrong ball would have assisted the partner — See Decision 30-3d/1 — and by implication it applies in the related case of an adverse effect on an opponent's play.

Furthermore, applying Rule 30-3f for the breaches of Rule 9-2 would not have been proper because those breaches were the direct result of the penalties incurred under Rule 30-3d.

Accordingly, if B picked up before D, Side C-D won the hole. If D picked up before B, Side A-B won the hole. If the order in which B and D picked up was not determinable, the Committee should have ruled that the 2nd hole was halved.

30-3d/3.5 Player Plays Partner's Ball; Error Discovered After Opponents Have Played Next Strokes

Q. A and B are playing C and D in a four-ball match. At the 2nd hole, after the tee shots A mistakenly plays B's ball and fails to inform C and D that he has done so before either of them plays his second stroke. The error is then discovered and C and D claim the hole. What is the ruling?

A. A is disqualified for the hole because he played a wrong ball (Rule 30-3d). B incurs no penalty for A having played his ball (Decision 30-3d/1).

A was not in breach of Rule 9-2 for failing to inform C and D before they played their second strokes that he had incurred a penalty under Rule 30-3d. Even if A had been in breach of Rule 9-2 and this had adversely affected the play of C or D, B would not be subject to penalty under Rule 30-3f. In this connection, see Decision 30-3d/3.

30-3f/1 Player Lifts Loose Impediment in Bunker When His Ball and Partner's Ball in Bunker

Q. A and B are partners in a four-ball match. A's ball and B's ball are in the same bunker. A lifts a loose

30

impediment lying in the bunker. A is disqualified for the hole for a breach of Rule 13-4. Does B incur a penalty?

A. If A's infringement assisted B's play, B also is disqualified for the hole — Rule 30-3f. Otherwise, B incurs no penalty.

30-3f/2 Hitting Sand in Bunker with Club After Failing to Extricate Ball; Partner's Ball in Same Bunker

Q. In a four-ball match A and B were partners. A played a stroke in a bunker and failed to get the ball out of the bunker. He then swung his club into the sand in the bunker, but this action did not affect his new lie in the bunker:

    (a) What is the ruling if B's ball lay in the same bunker when A swung his club into the sand?

    (b) What is the ruling if B's ball lay elsewhere?

A. In either case, A is disqualified for the hole (Rule 13-4 and Decision 13-4/35). The penalty does not apply to B unless A's action assisted B's play or adversely affected an opponent's play (Rule 30-3f).

30-3f/3 Player's Ball Resting Against Flagstick Lifted Before Being Holed; Others in Match Pick Up Mistakenly Believing Player Won Hole

Q. In a four-ball match, A's ball rested against the flagstick but it was not holed in terms of the Definition of "Holed." Instead of proceeding under Rule 17-4, A picked up the ball without marking its position. The other three players, believing that A had won the hole, picked up. Before anyone played from the next tee, a spectator pointed out that A's ball had not been holed. The players immediately asked the Committee for a ruling. What would be the correct ruling?

A. A incurred a penalty stroke under Rule 20-1 when he lifted his ball without marking its position. Since A did not inform the opponents about the penalty before they picked up, A was disqualified for the hole for giving wrong information — Rule 9-2. Since A's infringement adversely affected the opponents, *i.e.*, caused them to pick up, A's partner was also disqualified for the hole -Rule 30-3f. Thus, the opponents won the hole.

30-3f/4 Wrong Information Given by Player Out of Contention in Four-Ball Match

Q. A and B are playing C and D in a four-ball match, and the situation is as follows:

A's ball is on the green; he lies 3.

B's ball is in a bunker; he lies 5 and it is his turn to play.

C's ball is on the green; he lies 4.

D has picked up.

After B addresses his ball in the bunker, the ball moves and B incurs a penalty stroke under Rule 18-2b. B does not inform anyone that he has incurred a penalty stroke. B then replaces his ball and plays onto the green.

A then holes out for a 5 and C does likewise.

B is disqualified for the hole under Rule 9-2 for failing to inform C or D, before C played his next stroke, that he (B) had incurred a penalty stroke. Is A also disqualified for the hole under Rule 30-3f on the ground that B's failure to inform C or D of his (B's) penalty stroke adversely affected C's play?

A. No. B was clearly out of contention, and the result of the hole was dependent upon A and C alone. Accordingly, B's failure to inform C or D about the penalty could not have adversely affected C's play.

30-3f/5 Player Attending Flagstick for Opponent Struck by Ball of Opponent's Partner Who Played Out of Turn

Q. A and B are playing C and D in a four-ball match. It is B's turn to play and C is attending the flagstick at B's request. A, whose ball is in a deep bunker in such position that he cannot see C, plays out of turn and his ball strikes C. What is the ruling?

30

A. B authorized C to attend the flagstick which is the equivalent of A having authorized attendance of the flagstick. See Definition of "Partner," which provides that in a four-ball match, where the context so admits, the word "player" includes his partner.

Accordingly, A is disqualified for the hole (Rule 17-3b), but the penalty does not apply to B (Rule 30-3f).

30-3f/6   Player Plays Away from Hole to Assist Partner

Q. In a four-ball competition, a player purposely putts away from the hole to a position slightly farther from the hole than the spot where his partner's ball lies and on the same line to the hole as his partner's ball. The player then putts towards the hole, and the roll of his ball is helpful to his partner in determining how much his putt will break, etc. Is such procedure contrary to the Rules?

A. Such procedure is contrary to the spirit of the game. In match play, in equity (Rule 1-4), the player should be disqualified for the hole and, since his action assisted his partner's play, the partner should incur the same penalty — Rule 30-3f.

In stroke play, the player should incur a penalty of two strokes and, under Rule 31-8, the partner should incur the same penalty.

Putting Out After Concession of Stroke; Act Assists Partner — See 2-4/6.

Advice Given on Request of Opponent in Four-Ball Match — See 8-1/25.

Player Plays Partner's Ball; Act Assists Partner — See 30-3d/1.

30-3f/7   Player After Picking Up Drops Ball Where Partner's Ball Lies and Plays Practice Stroke

Q. In four-ball play, A and B are partners. A hits his tee shot out of bounds and decides not to complete play of the hole. B was undecided on club selection for his second shot, so A drops a ball near B's ball and hits a shot towards the green. What penalties were incurred?

A. Since the side, *i.e.*, both A and B, had not completed the play of the hole, A was practicing during play of the hole and thus was in breach of Rule 7-2.

Since it must be assumed that the breach assisted B, he would also be penalized — Rules 30-3f and 31-8.

30-3f/8 Player Disqualified for Next Hole Plays That Hole

Q. In a four-ball match, A practices chip shots to the 18th green between play of the 9th and 10th holes. Thus, A is disqualified for the 10th hole under Rule 7-2. If A plays the 10th hole, is B, A's partner, also subject to disqualification for the 10th hole if A's play of the hole assists B's, *e.g.*, with regard to club selection?

A. Since A was disqualified for the 10th hole, the strokes played by him on that hole were practice strokes. Therefore, A was in breach of Rule 7-2 each time he played a stroke on the 10th and, if B was assisted by any such stroke, B incurred the applicable penalty.

Absent Partner Joins Match During Play of Hole — See 30-3a/1.

30-3f/9 Player's Ball Moved by Partner in Playing His Own Ball

Q. In four-ball match play, A and B are partners. In playing his own ball, B accidentally strikes A's ball with his club and causes it to move. What is the procedure?

A. A incurs a penalty stroke under Rule 18-2a and must replace his ball. Assuming the infringement did not assist B, B incurs no penalty — Rule 30-3f.

30-3f/10 Player's Ball Lifted Without Authority by Opponent in Four-Ball Match

Q. In a four-ball match, an opponent lifted a player's ball on the putting green after marking its position.

30

He did this without the authority of the player. Is the opponent subject to penalty?

A. Yes. Rule 20-1 prohibits such action. Accordingly, the opponent incurs a penalty stroke under Rule 18-3b, but the penalty does not apply to his partner — see Rule 30-3f. The player must replace his ball.

30-3f/11 Request to Lift Ball That Might Assist Partner Not Honored

Q. A and B are playing C and D in a four-ball match. B's ball is near the hole in a position to serve as a backstop for A's ball. C requests B to lift his ball. B does not comply. A putts and his ball strikes B's ball. What is the ruling?

A. B is disqualified for the hole for failing to comply with Rule 22. Since the infringement assisted A, he is also disqualified for the hole — Rule 30-3f.

Rule 31. Four-Ball Stroke Play

In four-ball stroke play two competitors play as partners, each playing his own ball. The lower score of the partners is the score for the hole. If one partner fails to complete the play of a hole, there is no penalty.

31-1. Rules of Golf Apply

The Rules of Golf, so far as they are not at variance with the following special Rules, shall apply to four-ball stroke play.

31-2. Representation of Side

A side may be represented by either partner for all or any part of a <u>stipulated round</u>; both partners need not be present. An absent competitor may join his partner between holes, but not during play of a hole.

31-3. Maximum of Fourteen Clubs

The side shall be penalized for a breach of Rule 4-4 by either partner.

31-4. Scoring

The marker is required to record for each hole only the gross score of whichever partner's score is to count. The gross scores to count must be individually identifiable; otherwise *the side shall be disqualified.* Only one of the partners need be responsible for complying with Rule 6-6b.

(Wrong score — see Rule 31-7a.)

31-5. Order of Play

Balls belonging to the same side may be played in the order the side considers best.

31-6. Wrong Ball

If a competitor plays a stroke with a <u>wrong ball</u> except in a <u>hazard</u>, *he shall add two penalty strokes to his score for the hole* and shall then play the correct ball. His partner incurs no penalty even if the wrong ball belongs to him.

If the wrong ball belongs to another competitor, its owner shall place a ball on the spot from which the wrong ball was first played.

31-7. Disqualification Penalties

a. BREACH BY ONE PARTNER
A side shall be disqualified from the competition for a breach of any of the following by either partner:

Rule 1-3 — Agreement to Waive Rules.

Rule 3-4 — Refusal to Comply with Rule.

Rule 4-1, -2 or -3 — Clubs.

Rule 5-1 or -2 — The Ball.

Rule 6-2b — Handicap (playing off higher handicap; failure to record handicap).

Rule 6-4 — Caddie.

Rule 6-6b — Signing and Returning Card.

Rule 6-6d — Wrong Score for Hole, *i.e.*, when the recorded score of the partner whose score is to count is lower than actually taken. If the recorded score of the partner whose score is to count is higher than actually taken, it must stand as returned.

Rule 6-7 — Undue Delay (repeated offense).

Rule 7-1 — Practice Before or Between Rounds.

Rule 14-3 — Artificial Devices and Unusual Equipment.

Rule 31-4 — Gross Scores to Count Not Individually Identifiable.

b. BREACH BY BOTH PARTNERS
A side shall be disqualified:
  (i) for a breach by both partners of Rule
6-3 (Time of Starting and Groups) or Rule
6-8 (Discontinuance of Play), or
  (ii) if, at the same hole, each partner is in
breach of a Rule the penalty for which is
disqualification from the competition or for
a hole.

c. FOR THE HOLE ONLY
  In all other cases where a breach of a Rule
would entail disqualification, *the competitor
shall be disqualified only for the hole at which the
breach occurred.*

31-8. Effect of Other Penalties
  If a competitor's breach of a Rule assists his
partner's play, *the partner incurs the applicable
penalty in addition to any penalty incurred by the
competitor.*
  In all other cases where a competitor incurs
a penalty for breach of a Rule, the penalty shall
not apply to his partner.

Decisions relating to Rule 31:

**Competitor Who Has Holed Out Touches Partner's Line of
Putt** — See 1-2/3.**5.**

**Flagstick Attended by Partner Without Express Authority
of Competitor; Ball Strikes Flagstick or Partner** — See 17-
3/4.

Decision relating to Rule 31-3:

**Breach of 14-Club Rule in Stroke Play Discovered at 8th
Hole; Where Penalty Strokes Applied** — See 4-4a/17.

31-4/1 Gross Score of Partner with Better Net
Score Omitted from Card

Q. In four-ball stroke play on handicap, partners A
and B both holed out in 4 at the 8th hole; partner A

did not receive a handicap stroke at the hole, but partner B did. The marker, who was a fellow-competitor, recorded a gross score of 4 for A, who did not receive a stroke, and no gross score for B. However, the marker also recorded a net 3 in the better-ball column.

On completion of the round, the card, in all other respects correct, was signed and returned to the Committee. Both the marker and the partners were interviewed, and it was established that in fact both partners had gross scores of 4 at the 8th hole. What is the ruling?

A. Under Rules 6-6b and 31-4, it was the responsibility of one of the partners to check the side's better-ball gross score for each hole before countersigning the card.

When checking the card, the partner concerned should have noticed that there was no gross score recorded for B at the 8th hole and should have corrected this mistake. As he did not do so, A's gross 4 was the side's score for the hole. It is the responsibility of the Committee — and not the competitor — to record the better-ball net score for each hole.

31-7a/1 Competitor Records Score for Hole Not Completed

Q. A and B are partners in four-ball stroke play. At the 10th hole, A picks up and B holes out in 5 strokes. The marker records a score of 6 for A and a score of 5 for B. The card is returned with these scores recorded. Is any penalty incurred because A-B returned a card containing a score for A at a hole which A did not complete?

A. No. Rule 31-7a provides that disqualification of a side under Rule 6-6d applies only when the recorded score of the partner whose score is to count is lower than actually taken. The score recorded for A was not A-B's lower score for the 10th hole. Accordingly, no penalty is applicable.

Side's Scores Transposed at a Hole in Handicap Competition But Not to Side's Advantage — See 32-2a/1.

31-7a/2 Lower Gross Score Attributed to Wrong Partner

Q. A and B were partners in four-ball stroke play. At the 11th hole, A picked up and B holed out in 4 strokes. The marker inadvertently recorded a score of 4 for A. The card was returned. What is the ruling?

A. It was A's recorded score of 4 which was the side's gross score to count. As this was lower than the score actually taken by A, the side is disqualified under Rule 31-7a. (New)

Side's Scores Transposed at a Hole in Handicap Competition to Side's Advantage — See 32-2a/2.

31-8/1 Competitor Lifts Loose Impediment in Bunker When His Ball and Partner's Ball Are in Bunker

Q. A and B are partners in a four-ball stroke play competition. A's ball and B's ball are in the same bunker. A lifts a loose impediment lying in the bunker. A is penalized two strokes for a breach of Rule 13-4. Does B incur a penalty?

A. If A's infringement assisted B's play, B also is penalized two strokes — Rule 31-8. Otherwise, B incurs no penalty.

Competitor Plays Away from Hole to Assist Partner — See 30-3f/6.

Competitor After Picking Up Drops Ball Where Partner's Ball Lies and Plays Practice Stroke — See 30-3f/7.

Rule 32. Bogey, Par and Stableford Competitions

32-1. Conditions
Bogey, par and Stableford competitions are forms of stroke competition in which play is against a fixed score at each hole. The Rules for stroke play, so far as they are not at variance with the following special Rules, apply.

a. BOGEY AND PAR COMPETITIONS
The reckoning for bogey and par competitions is made as in match play. Any hole for which a competitor makes no return shall be regarded as a loss. The winner is the competitor who is most successful in the aggregate of holes.

The marker is responsible for marking only the gross number of strokes for each hole where the competitor makes a net score equal to or less than the fixed score.

Note: Maximum of 14 clubs — Penalties as in match play — see Rule 4-4.

b. STABLEFORD COMPETITIONS
The reckoning in Stableford competitions is made by points awarded in relation to a fixed score at each hole as follows:

Hole Played In	Points
More than one over fixed score or no score returned	0
One over fixed score	1
Fixed score	2

One under fixed score	. . . .	3
Two under fixed score	. . . .	4
Three under fixed score	. . .	5
Four under fixed score	. . . .	6

The winner is the competitor who scores the highest number of points.

The marker shall be responsible for marking only the gross number of strokes at each hole where the competitor's net score earns one or more points.

Note: Maximum of 14 clubs (Rule 4-4) — Penalties applied as follows: From total points scored for the round, deduction of two points for each hole at which any breach occurred; maximum deduction per round: four points.

32-2. Disqualification Penalties

a. FROM THE COMPETITION

A competitor shall be disqualified from the competition for a breach of any of the following:

Rule 1-3 — Agreement to Waive Rules.

Rule 3-4 — Refusal to Comply with Rule.

Rule 4-1, -2 or -3 — Clubs.

Rule 5-1 or -2 — The Ball.

Rule 6-2b — Handicap (playing off higher handicap; failure to record handicap).

Rule 6-3 — Time of Starting and Groups.

Rule 6-4 — Caddie.

Rule 6-6b — Signing and Returning Card.

Rule 6-6d — Wrong Score for Hole, except that no penalty shall be incurred when a breach of this Rule does not affect the result of the hole.

Rule 6-7 — Undue Delay (repeated offense).

Rule 6-8 — Discontinuance of Play.

Rule 7-1 — Practice Before or Between Rounds.

Rule 14-3 — Artificial Devices and Unusual Equipment.

> b. FOR A HOLE
> In all other cases where a breach of a Rule would entail disqualification, *the competitor shall be disqualified only for the hole at which the breach occurred.*

32-1/1 Competing Simultaneously in Bogey or Stableford Competition and Stroke Play Competition

Q. Is it permissible for a player to compete simultaneously in a bogey or Stableford competition and a stroke play competition?

A. Yes, since bogey and Stableford competitions are forms of stroke play competition.

32-1/2 Omitting Holes in Bogey or Stableford Competition

Q. In a bogey or Stableford competition, may a player omit two holes of the round and return a score for 16 holes?

A. Yes. Under Rule 32-1a, any hole for which a competitor makes no return in a bogey competition is regarded as a loss. Under Rule 32-1b, if no score is returned on a hole in a Stableford competition, the competitor scores no points for that hole.

32-1/3 Determination of Honor in Handicap Stableford Competition

Q. In a Stableford competition the reckoning is made as in match play and strokes are taken according to the handicap stroke table. If B has the honor at a hole, and A and B have the same gross score at that hole but A receives a handicap stroke, who has the honor at the next hole?

A. A has the honor because of a better net score.

32

32-2a/1 Four-Ball Stableford Competition on Handicap Basis; Side's Scores Transposed at a Hole But Not to Side's Advantage

Q. A and B were partners in a four-ball Stableford competition on a handicap basis. At a hole where A, but not B, received a handicap stroke, A scored a 4 (net 3) and B scored a 5. The marker inadvertently transposed the scores, recording a 5 (net 4) for A and a 4 for B. The card was returned with these scores recorded. What is the ruling?

A. There is no penalty. Although B's recorded score of 4 was lower than actually taken by him, since it was not lower than the recorded score of net 4 for A (which was higher than actually taken by A), there was no breach of Rule 31-7a. Nor was there a breach of Rule 32-2a, since the error did not affect the result of the hole.

The same ruling would apply in a four-ball bogey or par competition on a handicap basis. (Revised)

32-2a/2 Four-Ball Stableford Competition on Handicap Basis; Side's Scores Transposed at a Hole to Side's Advantage

Q. A and B were partners in a four-ball Stableford competition on a handicap basis. At a hole, A scored 4 (net 3) and B scored 5 (net 4). The marker inadvertently transposed the scores, recording a 5 (net 4) for A and a 4 (net 3) for B. The card was returned with these scores recorded. What is the ruling?

A. B's recorded score of 4 (net 3) was the lower recorded score. As this was lower than the score actually taken by B and was also lower than A's recorded score of 5 (net 4), the result of the hole was affected and the side is disqualified under Rule 32-3a for a breach of Rule 31-7a.

The same ruling would apply in a four-ball bogey or par competition on a handicap basis. (New)

32-2b/1 Breach of Rule by Both Partners at Same Hole in Four-Ball Stableford

Q. A and B are partners in a four-ball Stableford competition. During the play of a hole, A and B find they have exchanged balls at the previous hole. What is the ruling?

A. A and B are not disqualified from the competition but only for the hole at which they exchanged balls, for which they score no points.

ADMINISTRATION

Rule 33. The Committee

33-1. Conditions; Waiving Rule

The Committee shall lay down the conditions under which a competition is to be played.

The Committee has no power to waive a Rule of Golf.

Certain special rules governing stroke play are so substantially different from those governing match play that combining the two forms of play is not practicable and is not permitted. The results of matches played and the scores returned in these circumstances shall not be accepted.

In stroke play the Committee may limit a referee's duties.

33-2. The Course

a. DEFINING BOUNDS AND MARGINS

The Committee shall define accurately:

(i) the <u>course</u> and <u>out of bounds</u>,

(ii) the margins of <u>water hazards</u> and <u>lateral water hazards</u>,

(iii) <u>ground under repair</u>, and

(iv) <u>obstructions</u> and integral parts of the course.

b. NEW HOLES

New holes should be made on the day on

33

which a stroke competition begins and at such other times as the Committee considers necessary, provided all competitors in a single round play with each hole cut in the same position.

Exception: When it is impossible for a damaged hole to be repaired so that it conforms with the Definition, the Committee may make a new hole in a nearby similar position.

c. PRACTICE GROUND

Where there is no practice ground available outside the area of a competition <u>course</u>, the Committee should lay down the area on which players may practice on any day of a competition, if it is practicable to do so. On any day of a stroke competition, the Committee should not normally permit practice on or to a putting green or from a hazard of the competition course.

d. COURSE UNPLAYABLE

If the Committee or its authorized representative considers that for any reason the course is not in a playable condition or that there are circumstances which render the proper playing of the game impossible, it may, in match play or stroke play, order a temporary suspension of play or, in stroke play, declare play null and void and cancel all scores for the round in question. When play has been temporarily suspended, it shall be resumed from where it was discontinued, even though resumption occurs on a subsequent day. When a round is cancelled, all penalties incurred in that round are cancelled.

(Procedure in discontinuing play — see Rule 6-8.)

33-3. Times of Starting and Groups

The Committee shall lay down the times of starting and, in stroke play, arrange the groups in which competitors shall play.

33

When a match play competition is played over an extended period, the Committee shall lay down the limit of time within which each round shall be completed. When players are allowed to arrange the date of their match within these limits, the Committee should announce that the match must be played at a stated time on the last day of the period unless the players agree to a prior date.

33-4. Handicap Stroke Table
The Committee shall publish a table indicating the order of holes at which handicap strokes are to be given or received.

33-5. Score Card
In stroke play, the Committee shall issue for each competitor a score card containing the date and the competitor's name or, in foursome or four-ball stroke play, the competitors' names.

In stroke play, the Committee is responsible for the addition of scores and application of the handicap recorded on the card.

In four-ball stroke play, the Committee is responsible for recording the better-ball score for each hole and in the process applying the handicaps recorded on the card, and adding the better-ball scores.

In bogey, par and Stableford competitions, the Committee is responsible for applying the handicap recorded on the card and determining the result of each hole and the overall result or points total.

33-6. Decision of Ties
The Committee shall announce the manner, day and time for the decision of a halved match or of a tie, whether played on level terms or under handicap.

A halved match shall not be decided by stroke play. A tie in stroke play shall not be decided by a match.

33

33-7. Disqualification Penalty; Committee Discretion

A penalty of disqualification may in exceptional individual cases be waived, modified or imposed if the Committee considers such action warranted.

Any penalty less than disqualification shall not be waived or modified.

33-8. Local Rules

a. POLICY

The Committee may make and publish Local Rules for abnormal conditions if they are consistent with the policy of the Governing Authority for the country concerned as set forth in Appendix I to these Rules.

b. WAIVING PENALTY

A penalty imposed by a Rule of Golf shall not be waived by a Local Rule.

33/1 Removal of Casual Water on Putting Green by Committee

Q. If casual water accumulates on a putting green during a round, would it be appropriate for the Committee to remove the casual water by mopping it up with a towel or by other means?

A. Yes, and the Committee may also enlist the help of players to do so.

Casual Water Covering Teeing Ground — See 25-1b/4.

Dividing Double Green — See 25-3/1.

33/2 Player Who Has Reached Third Round of Match Play Disqualified for Agreeing to Waive Rules in First-Round Match

Q. Decision 1-3/8 provides that there is no time limit on applying the disqualification penalty under Rule 1-3 for agreeing to waive a Rule. If A, who agreed with his opponent to waive a Rule in a first-round match, has advanced to the third round before the Committee becomes aware of the breach of Rule 1-3, what should the Committee do?

A. The Committee must rule in accordance with equity (Rule 1-4). For guidelines, see Decision 34-1b/8.

33/3 Match Play Finalists Both Disqualified

If both finalists in a match play competition are disqualified, the event must conclude without a winner.

33/4 Direction Posts

If direction posts may interfere with the line of play, they should, where practicable, be installed so as to be movable.

33/5 Distance Markers

Q. May a Committee install markers on a hole to indicate distances to the green?

A. Yes.

33/6 Map of Putting Green Indicating Hole Position Displayed at Tee

Q. At the teeing ground of each hole, a Committee has displayed a map of the putting green. The position of the hole on the green is indicated on each map. Is this proper?

A. Yes. Displaying such maps is not contrary to the Rules.

33/7 Whether Player Disqualified in Match Play Event Entitled to Prize Won Prior to Disqualification

Q. If a player in a match play event is disqualified, should he be entitled to any prize he had previously won in the event?

A. Yes.

33

Indicating Hole Numbers on Teeing Grounds — See 11-5/2.

Artificial Limbs — See 14-3/15.

Ball Assisting Fellow-Competitor on Putting Green; Procedure for Committee Member If Competitor Does Not Lift Ball — See 22/7.

Preventing Ball from Being Carried Out of Bounds by Flow of Water in Water Hazard — See 26-1/7.

Player's Ball Found by Committee Member; Player Prefers to Continue with Provisional Ball — See 27-2/2.

33-1/1 Altering Conditions After Competition Starts

Q. A condition of a stroke play competition provided that scores must be returned by 7:30 P.M. At 5:00 P.M., a member of the Committee extended the deadline to accommodate four late-arriving competitors. Is such action proper?

A. No. Once a competition has started, the conditions should be altered only in very exceptional circumstances. In this case, no such circumstances existed.

Players Exclude Operation of Condition — See 1-3/7.

33-1/2 Number of Holes of Stroke Play Competition Reduced During the Competition

Q. A 72-hole stroke play competition is scheduled over four consecutive days. Eighteen holes are to be played each day. On the third day, all competitors finish the first nine holes but a number of competitors are still playing the second nine holes. At that point, the course becomes unplayable due to heavy rain and play is suspended. The rain continues and it is impossible to resume play that day. What are the Committee's options?

A. Under Rules 33-1 and 33-2d, the Committee has the following choices:

(a) resume play the next day and finish the third round, and then play the last 18 holes that day or on a subsequent day,

(b) cancel the third round, replay it on a subsequent day and then play the last 18 holes that day or on a subsequent day,

(c) reduce to three the number of rounds of the competition and finish the suspended third round on a subsequent day, or cancel the third round and replay it on a subsequent day, or

(d) cancel the third and fourth rounds and declare the leader after 36 holes to be the winner.

The third and fourth choices are undesirable. It is preferable not to reduce the number of rounds of a competition when the competition is in progress.

The Committee does not have the authority to reduce the number of holes of a stipulated round once play has commenced in that round.

33-1/3 Starting Players from 1st and 10th Tees

Q. May the Committee start play in a competition from both the 1st and the 10th tees?

A. Yes. See Definition of "Stipulated Round," which says that the holes are to be played in correct sequence unless otherwise authorized by the Committee.

33-1/4 Match Decided by Wrong Form of Play by Agreement of Players

Q. The four participants in a first-round match thought the competition was a foursome competition, whereas it was in fact a four-ball competition. They played the first hole on a foursome basis and then learned of their error. Rather than go back and begin again on a four-ball basis, they agreed (1) to continue playing a foursome and (2) that in the four-ball competition the side losing the foursome match would default to the winning side.

The matter came to the Committee's attention after the side receiving the default reached the semi-finals of the four-ball event. What should the Committee do?

A. The side should be disqualified under Rule 1-3 for agreeing to decide a match other than as prescribed

33

in the conditions, and the Committee should decide how the competition should be concluded.

Wrong Form of Play Used in Match Play Event — See 6-1/1.

33-1/5 Competitor in Stroke Play Event Plays with Two Players Engaged in Match

Q. A competitor in a stroke play competition had no other competitor with whom to play. So he joined two players engaged in a match and one of those players served as his marker. Is such procedure considered combining stroke play and match play, contrary to Rule 33-1?

A. No. The competitor was playing stroke play only and the other two players were playing match play only. The Committee should retrospectively appoint the player concerned as the competitor's marker — see Definition of "Marker."

33-1/6 One Player in Match Competes Concurrently in Stroke Play Competition

Q. A and B played a match. A concurrently competed in a stroke play competition. What should the Committee do?

A. Under Rule 33-1, both the result of the match and the score returned by A in the stroke play event were unacceptable.

If the match was to be played on any day in a prescribed period, A and B must replay the match within the prescribed period. If it was too late for A and B to replay the match within the period, A and B are disqualified, unless one concedes the match to the other — see Rule 2-4.

It would not be proper to allow A to replay the round in the stroke play competition. A had already competed in that competition, and his score was unacceptable.

Competing Simultaneously in Bogey or Stableford Competition and Stroke Play Competition — See 32-1/1.

33-1/7 Making Competitors Responsible for Adding Scores

Q. May the Committee make it a condition of a competition that competitors are responsible for the addition of scores?

A. No. Such a condition would modify Rule 33-5.

Requirement That Alteration on Score Card Be Initialled — See 6-6a/6.

33-1/8 Use of Golf Carts in Competition

Q. May a player use a golf cart during a competition?

A. Yes, unless such equipment is prohibited in the conditions of the competition (Rule 33-1).

33-1/9 Breach of Condition Prohibiting Golf Carts

Q. A condition of a competition prohibits the use of golf carts. If a player infringes this condition, what is the penalty?

A. If no penalty is stated, the general penalty applies at each hole where the cart is used, *i.e.*, loss of hole in match play (Rule 2-6) or two strokes in stroke play (Rule 3-5).

Who May Serve as Caddie — See 6-4/2.

33-1/10 Banning Caddies

Q. May a Committee, as a condition of a competition, ban the use of caddies?

A. Yes. However, since the Rules make specific provision for the employment of a caddie by a player, such a condition is not recommended.

33-1/11 Restriction on Caddies

Q. May a Committee, in the conditions of a competition, restrict a player in his choice of a caddie? For

33

example, may a Committee for a junior competition prohibit a player from employing a parent as a caddie?

A. Yes.

Prohibiting Employment of Umbrella Carrier — See 6-4/5.

33-1/12 Wrong Handicap Used Due to Committee Misinformation

Q. The players in a four-ball match were unsure as to the handicaps to which they were entitled under the conditions of the competition. They consulted a member of the Committee who wrongly advised them as to the condition regarding handicaps. This resulted in Player A receiving one less handicap stroke than he was entitled to receive. Player A's side lost the match, 4 and 3. The Committee representative's error was then discovered. What should the Committee do?

A. The Committee should resolve the matter in whatever manner it considers most equitable. The Committee could let the result stand or require a replay of the match.

All players except Player A received the correct number of handicap strokes and Player A received only one less stroke than he should have received. In view of this fact and the rather one-sided result, it is recommended that the fairest solution would be to let the result stand.

33-1/13 Competitor Disqualified from Handicap Event Claims Gross Prize

Q. In a stroke play event, a competitor played off a higher handicap than that to which he was entitled. Although the event was primarily a handicap one, there was also a gross prize, and the competitor concerned had the lowest gross score.

The competitor was disqualified from the handicap competition under Rule 6-2b, but he claimed the gross prize. Should he receive the gross prize?

A. Yes.

Condition Requiring Use of Ball on List of Conforming Golf Balls; Penalty for Breach — See 5-1/2.

33

33-2a/1 Exposed Water Pipe Adjacent and Parallel to Boundary Fence Causes Problems; Suggested Procedure

Q. An exposed water pipe (obstruction) which is parallel to, and about six inches inside, a boundary fence is causing problems.

If a ball lies between the fence and the water pipe, the player in proceeding under Rule 24-2b(i) must drop the ball many yards away because in determining the "point nearest" the player may not cross over the obstruction.

Further, if a ball lies on the golf course side of the water pipe and near the boundary fence, the prohibition against free relief from the fence is effectively negated because in most cases the player would be entitled to drop away from the fence by taking free relief from the water pipe under Rule 24-2b. Is there a solution to this dilemma?

A. It is suggested that the water pipe be declared an integral part of the course and thus not an obstruction — See Definition of "Obstructions" — in which case the player would have to play the ball as it lies or declare it unplayable.

Stone Serving as Part of Drain in Bunker — See 24/7.

33-2a/2 Declaring Area as Ground Under Repair During Competition Round

Q. A's ball is in a poor lie in a washed-out area which warrants being marked as ground under repair but is not so marked. He declares the ball unplayable and proceeds under Rule 28, incurring a one-stroke penalty.

Subsequently, in the same competition round, B's ball is in the same area. B requests the Committee to declare the area ground under repair. Would the Committee be justified in declaring the area ground under repair in such circumstances?

33

A. Yes; this applies in either match or stroke play. However, it is preferable that all areas which warrant marking as ground under repair should be so marked before the start of a competition.

33-2a/3 Extensive Damage Due to Heavy Rain and Traffic

When heavy rains have resulted in many areas of unusual damage to the course (such as deep ruts caused by vehicles or footprints by spectators) and it is not feasible to define them with stakes or lines, a notice to players along the following lines is suggested:

> "Ground under repair may include areas of unusual damage, including areas where spectators or other traffic have combined with wet conditions to affect materially the ground surface, but only when so declared by a Committee member."

Without such notice, Committee members have authority to declare unusual damage to be ground under repair, if so authorized. However, a notice has the advantage of advising all players that relief from unusual damage might be given.

Line of Putt Damaged by Fellow-Competitor's Caddie — See 16-1a/14.

Old Hole Plug Sunk or Raised on Line of Putt — See 16-1c/3.

Fallen Tree Attached to Stump — See 25/9.

Cracks in Earth — See 25/12.

Rut Made by Tractor — See 25/16.

Holes Made by Non-Burrowing Animals — See 25/20.

33-2a/4 Where to Place Lines or Stakes Defining Margin of Water Hazard

Lines and stakes defining the margins of a water hazard should be placed as nearly as possible along the natural limits of the hazard, *i.e.*, where the ground breaks down to form the depression containing the water. See also Decision 26-1/19.

Ball Within Natural Margin of Water Hazard But Outside Stakes Defining Margin — See 26/2.

33-2a/5   Water Hazard Under Repair

Q. Should areas under repair in a water hazard be defined as ground under repair?

A. Because it is usual for a ball in a water hazard to be unplayable, areas under repair should not normally be defined as ground under repair.

Bunker Totally Under Repair — See 25/13.

33-2a/6   Pond Is Water Hazard from Men's Tee and Lateral from Women's Tee

Q. A pond on a par-3 hole meets the Definition of a lateral water hazard in play from the women's tee but not from the men's tee. How should the Committee handle this situation?

A. The pond should be defined as a water hazard with yellow stakes or a yellow line and there should be a Local Rule to the effect that the hazard is a lateral water hazard in play from the women's tee.

33-2a/7   Deeming Body of Water as Both Water Hazard and Lateral Water Hazard

A given part of body of water must not be defined as both a water hazard and a lateral water hazard in play of a particular hole, except in the circumstances described in Decision 33-2a/6.

A given part of a body of water may be defined as a water hazard in play of one hole and a lateral water hazard in play of another hole.

A given part of a body of water may be defined as a water hazard and another part of the same body of water as a lateral water hazard.

33-2a/8 Treating Ocean and Beach as Through the Green

There is no authority in the Rules for a Committee to treat the ocean and adjoining beach and rocks as through the green. Such treatment results in a more severe penalty in many instances than is the case if the ocean, beach and rocks are properly defined as a water hazard or lateral water hazard.

Permissible Dropping Area Under Lateral Water Hazard Rule So Narrow Player Has Difficulty Dropping Within It — See 26-1/19.

33-2a/9 Part of Lateral Water Hazard Where Impossible to Drop Not Nearer Hole

If part of a lateral water hazard at the side of a putting green is so configured that it may be impossible to drop a ball within two club-lengths of the point where the ball last crossed the hazard margin without dropping nearer the hole than that point, the following is suggested: (1) the part of the hazard where the situation exists should be distinctively marked; (2) one or two Ball Drops (or Dropping Zones) should be established; and (3) a Local Rule should state that, if a ball in the lateral water hazard last crossed the margin of the hazard in the marked area, the player may, under penalty of one stroke, drop a ball in the Ball Drop or, if two Ball Drops are established, in the nearer of the two Ball Drops.

33-2a/10 How to Mark Island Green

Q. A putting green is situated on an island in a lake. The water between the tee and the green is defined as a water hazard. The water on each side is marked as a lateral water hazard. How should the water behind the island be marked?

A. The Committee would be justified in marking the water behind the island as a lateral water hazard.

Alternatively, the Committee might consider defining the entire lake as a water hazard, establishing a Ball Drop (or Dropping Zone) and adopting a Local Rule giving a player whose ball lies in the hazard the option of dropping a ball in the Ball Drop, under penalty of one stroke.

33-2a/10.5   Status of Tree Basins

Q. What is the status under the Rules of tree wells or tree basins?

A. There is no relief under the Rules from tree basins which are not made of artificial materials.

If a tree basin has an artificial wall, the wall is an obstruction unless the Committee deems it to be an integral part of the course under Rule 33-2a.

33-2a/11   River Forming Part of Course Boundary

Q. When a river forms part of the boundary of a course, should it be defined as a lateral water hazard or as out of bounds?

A. It is up to the Committee to decide (Rule 33-2a).

33-2a/12   Internal Boundary Between Holes

Q. It is proposed to install boundary stakes between two holes as a safety measure. It would prevent players playing a dog-leg hole from driving onto the fairway of another hole in order to cut the "dog-leg." Is it permissible to establish such a boundary?

A. Yes. For the recommended status of such boundary stakes, see Decision 24/5.

33-2a/13   Tee Decreed to Be in Bounds for Tee Shot and Out of Bounds Thereafter

Q. A Committee has decreed that ground surrounding a certain teeing ground is in bounds for tee shots and out of bound thereafter. Is this permissible?

A. No. In play of a particular hole, an area cannot be both in bounds and out of bounds.

33-2a/14   Internal Out of Bounds Applying to Stroke from Teeing Ground Only

A Committee may make a Local Rule under Rule 33-2a declaring part of an adjoining hole to be out of bounds when playing a particular hole, but it is not permissible for a Committee to make a Local Rule placing an area of the course out of bounds to a stroke played from the teeing ground only.

33-2a/15   Establishing Boundary Line Inside Fence on Property Line

Q. Along a fence on our property line, *i.e.*, the fence is a boundary fence, there are flower beds. To save time and protect the flowers, it is proposed to move the boundary line inward several feet by establishing white stakes along the inside edge of the flower bed. Is this permitted by the Rules?

A. Yes.

Stile Attached to Boundary Fence — See 24/1.

Concrete Bases of Boundary Fence Posts — See 24/3.

33-2a/16   Deeming Ball in Bounds Until Beyond Boundary Wall

Q. Because a boundary wall is in disrepair and the inside face is irregular, the Committee has declared by Local Rule that a ball is not out of bounds until it is beyond the wall. Is this permissible or must the inside face of the wall serve as the boundary line?

A. Such procedure is permissible. There is nothing in the Rules stating that, in the case of a boundary wall, the inside face of the wall serves as the boundary line.

[33-2a/17   Reserved]

33-2a/18   Identifying Stakes Defining Out of Bounds

Q. Should the words "Out of Bounds" or the letters "OB" be imprinted on white stakes defining out of bounds?

A. White stakes defining out of bounds should be so marked to clarify their status, or the following should be printed on score cards: "Out of Bounds — Defined by inside points, at ground level, of white stakes."

33-2a/19 Boundary Altered by Unauthorized Removal of Boundary Stake

In stroke play, a boundary line has been altered through unauthorized removal of a boundary stake, and therefore there is an area (Area X) which is in bounds if the removed stake is disregarded and out of bounds if the removed stake is replaced.

Q1. A's ball comes to rest in Area X. A is aware that the boundary has been altered. He asks the Committee for a ruling. What is the ruling?

A1. The Committee should replace the removed stake, *i.e.*, restore the original boundary line and require A to proceed under Rule 27-1, unless the Committee knows that one or more preceding competitors had, in ignorance of the fact that a stake has been removed, played from Area X. In that case, the Committee should allow the altered boundary line to stand for the remainder of the competition, and A would play his ball as it lay.

Q2. What would be the ruling if the Committee determined that one or more competitors had, in ignorance of the fact that a stake was missing, played from Area X and one or more other competitors had treated Area X as out of bounds and proceeded under Rule 27-1?

A2. If the inconsistent treatment of Area X could significantly affect the result of the competition, the round should be canceled and replayed. Otherwise, the round should stand.

33-2a/20 Displaced Boundary Stake

Q. A boundary stake has fallen down, or has been removed without authority of the Committee. The stake is lying several feet from the hole in which it had been situated. It is obvious that the stake had been displaced.

A player's ball comes to rest in bounds near the hole in which the boundary stake had been situated. The ball is in such a position that, if the boundary stake were reinstalled, it would interfere with the player's swing.

Is the player required to replace the stake before playing his next stroke?

A. No. If a boundary fence or stake is leaning towards the course and as a result interferes with a player's swing, the player is not allowed to straighten the fence or the stake — see Decision 13-2/18. It follows that, if a boundary fence or stake is leaning away from the course, the player is not allowed to straighten it.

A displaced boundary stake is a movable obstruction. Therefore, the player may replace it but he is not required to do so.

33-2b/1 Holes Relocated and/or Tee-Markers Moved During Stroke Play Round

Q. During a round in a stroke play competition, one or more holes were relocated and/or tee-markers moved. What is the proper procedure?

A. If this was authorized by the Committee, the round should be declared null and void. In stroke play, the Committee is prohibited from relocating a hole except as provided in the Exception to Rule 33-2b and from moving tee-markers except in circumstances such as those in Decision 25-1b/4.

If this was done without the authority or sanction of the Committee, generally the round should be declared null and void. However, if the course has not been altered significantly and no competitor has been given an undue advantage or disadvantage, the Committee would be justified in letting the round stand.

33-2d/1 Guidelines on Whether to Cancel Round

Q. In stroke play, in what circumstances should a Committee cancel a round?

33

A. There is no hard-and-fast rule. The proper action depends on the circumstances in each case and must be left to the judgment of the Committee.

Generally, a round should be canceled only in a case where it would be grossly unfair not to cancel it. For example, if some competitors begin a round under extremely adverse weather conditions, conditions subsequently worsen and further play that day is impossible, it would be unfair to the competitors who started not to cancel the round.

Number of Holes of Stroke Play Competition Reduced During the Competition — See 33-1/2.

33-2d/2 Hole Surrounded by Casual Water

If all the area around the hole contains casual water, in stroke play the course should be considered unplayable and the Committee should suspend play under Rule 33-2d. In match play, the Committee should relocate the hole.

Casual Water Covering Teeing Ground — See 25-1b/4.

33-2d/3 Competitor Refuses to Start or Picks Up Because of Weather Conditions; Round Subsequently Canceled

Q. In stroke play, A refuses to start at the time arranged by the Committee because of inclement weather, and B picks up during the round for the same reason. Subsequently, the course becomes unplayable and the Committee cancels the round and reschedules it for the next day. Are A and B entitled to play the next day?

A. Yes. When a round is canceled all penalties incurred in the round are canceled — see Rule 33-2d.

Player Unable to Resume Suspended Match at Scheduled Time — See 6-8b/4.

33-2d/4 Match Begun in Ignorance That Course Closed

Q. Two players began a match at 10 A.M. After the

33

players had played two holes, a member of the Committee arrived and advised them that the course had been closed since 9 A.M., but no notice to this effect had been posted at the 1st tee. Should the match be replayed entirely or resumed at the 3rd hole?

A. The match should be replayed entirely. Play on the course while it was closed should be considered null and void.

Replacement of Club Broken on Practice Ground While Play Suspended — See 4-4a/6.5.

Ball Moved by Wind or Casual Water While Play Suspended — See 18-1/11.

33-3/1 Status of Starting Time Fixed by Players

Q. It was a condition of a match play competition that each match must be played on the day and at the time published unless the players agreed to a prior date and time. A and B agreed to play their match at a specified time on a prior date. However, B arrived late. Was B subject to disqualification under Rule 6-3a?

A. Yes. The starting time agreed by A and B had the same status as a starting time fixed by the Committee.

33-3/2 Player Not Present at Time of Starting;Course Closed at the Time

Q. A and B were scheduled to play a match at 9:00 A.M., at which time the course was closed due to weather conditions. A was present at the appointed time. B, assuming the course would be closed, was not present. B arrived at noon, at which time the course was still closed. A claimed the match because B was not present at 9:00 A.M. Was the claim valid?

A. No. As the course was closed, and it was impossible for A and B to start at the appointed time or within a reasonable time thereafter, a new starting time for the match should be arranged.

33-3/3 Competitors Determining Own Groupings and Starting Times

Q. May a Committee permit competitors in a stroke play competition to determine their own groupings and starting times?

A. Yes. Rule 33-3 does not prohibit such an arrangement.

Postponement of Final Match Due to Injury of Player — See 6-3a/1.

All Competitors Must Be Present at Time of Starting — See 6-3a/2.

33-3/4 Groupings for Stroke Play Play-Off

Q. Is there any Rule limiting the number of competitors in a group in a stroke play play-off? For example, if 11 competitors are in a play-off, should they be separated into a group of five and a group of six? Or should they be separated into two groups of four and one group of three?

A. There is no Rule. The matter is up to the Committee. However, it is suggested that normally there should be no more than five competitors in any group.

33-4/1 Alteration of Handicap Stroke Table

Q. As provided in the Definition of a "Stipulated Round," the Committee has authorized certain matches to begin at the 6th hole. The higher-handicapped player in such matches is disadvantaged because, under the Handicap Stroke Table, the first handicap stroke is allocated to the 5th hole and, thus, it is not used if a match is concluded in less than 18 holes. Would it be permissible to alter the Handicap Stroke Table for such matches?

A. Yes.

Handicap Stroke Given at Incorrect Hole in Error — See 6-2a/2.

Stroke Allowance When Settling Tie in Handicap Match — See 33-6/1.

33-5/1 Score Cards in Sudden-Death Play-Off

Q. Must competitors involved in a sudden-death play-off in stroke play return score cards to the Committee?

A. Yes, but only if the Committee has issued a score card for each competitor in accordance with Rule 33-5. Otherwise, the competitors should not be penalized if they fail to return score cards.

33-5/2 Wrong Handicap Applied by Committee Results in Player Not Receiving Prize

Q. In a stroke play competition, A returns a card showing the handicap to which he is entitled and the Committee applies the wrong handicap or miscalculates the correct net score. This results in another competitor receiving prize to which A was entitled. The error is discovered after the competition has closed. What is the ruling?

A. The Committee should correct its error by retrieving the prize and awarding it to A. There is no time limit for correcting such an error. Rule 34-1b is not applicable since it deals with penalties and not with Committee errors.

33-5/3 Misapplication of Handicap Affects Match Play Draw

Q. Misapplication of a player's handicap by the Committee on a score card for the qualifying round of a match play event results in an incorrect draw. The error is discovered during the first round of match play. What should the Committee do?

A. The Committee should deal with the matter in the fairest way possible. The Committee should consider amending the draw and canceling the matches affected by the amendment if this is practicable.

Total Score Recorded by Competitor Incorrect — See 6-6d/2.

Competitors Made Responsible for Adding Scores — See 33-1/7.

33

33-6/1 How to Settle Tie in Handicap Match

Q. How should a tie in a handicap match be settled?

A. The matter is up to the Committee, which should announce the procedure in advance — Rule 33-6.

It is recommended that a handicap match which ends all square should be played off hole by hole until one side wins a hole. The play-off should start at the hole where the match began. Handicap strokes should be allowed as in the prescribed round.

33-6/2 How to Settle Tie in Stroke Play

Q. In a stroke play competition, how should a tie be settled?

A. It is up to the Committee, except that a tie shall not be decided by a match. The Committee should announce the procedure in advance.

(1) In the event of a tie in a scratch stroke play competition, an 18-hole play-off is recommended. If that is not feasible, a sudden-death play-off is recommended.

(2) In handicap stroke play, a play-off over 18 holes with handicaps is recommended. If a shorter play-off is necessary, the percentage of 18 holes to be played should be applied to the players' handicaps to determine their play-off handicaps. It is advisable to arrange for a percentage of holes that will result in whole numbers in handicaps.

(3) In either a scratch or handicap stroke play competition, if a play-off of any type is not feasible, matching cards is recommended. The method of matching cards should be announced in advance. An acceptable method of matching cards is to determine the winner on the basis of the best score for the last nine holes. If the tying players have the same score for the last nine, determine the winner on the basis of the last six holes, last three holes and finally the 18th hole. If such a method is used in

33

a handicap stroke play competition, one-half, one-third, one-sixth, etc., of the handicaps should be deducted.

(4) If the conditions of the competition provide that ties shall be decided over the last nine, last six, last three and last hole, they should also provide what will happen if this procedure does not produce a winner.

33-6/3 Determining Winner and Positions in Stroke Play Play-Off

If there is a stroke play play-off between two competitors and one of them is disqualified or concedes defeat, it is not necessary for the other to complete the play-off hole or holes to be declared the winner.

If there is a play-off involving more than two competitors and not all of them complete the play-off hole or holes, the order in which the competitors are disqualified or decide to withdraw shall determine their positions in the play-off.

33-6/4 Players Decide Method of Settling Tie When Committee Fails to Do So

Q. A and B, in a club match play event in which the Committee had not prescribed how a halved match would be decided, finished their stipulated round all square. A suggested that the tie be decided by an 18-hole play-off. B reluctantly agreed. A won the play-off. B protested to the Committee. He argued that the match should have been settled by a sudden-death play-off, since that is the customary manner of deciding a tie in club events. What should the Committee do?

A. Since the Committee did not prescribe the method of settling the tie, it was appropriate for the players to determine the method. Since the players agreed to an 18-hole play-off, the match should stand as played.

Groupings for Stroke Play Play-Off — See 33-3/4.

33-7/1 Authority to Waive or Modify Disqualification Penalty

Only the Committee as a whole has authority to waive or modify a penalty of disqualification under Rule 33-7. A referee or an individual member of the Committee may not take such action.

33-7/2 Modifying Penalty for Not Holing Out in Stroke Play

Q. In stroke play, a competitor missed a short putt at the 16th hole, knocked his ball off the green, picked it up and teed off at the next hole without having holed out at the 16th.

After the competitor returned his score card, a fellow-competitor brought the matter to the attention of the Committee. The competitor admitted the error and expressed the view that his fellow-competitors were unsportsmanlike in not calling the error to his attention when the incident occurred.

In such circumstances, would the Committee be justified in modifying to two strokes the disqualification penalty provided in Rule 3-2?

A. No. Rule 33-7 should never be invoked in the case of disqualification for failing to hole out in stroke play. The competitor in such a case has not played the course.

Failure of the fellow-competitors to advise the competitor of his error is not a good reason for modifying the penalty. It is the responsibility of the competitor to know the Rules.

Waiving or Modifying Penalty for Carrying Non-Conforming Club — See 4-1/1.

Modifying Penalty for Holing Short Putt with Club Whose Playing Characteristics Changed Other Than in Normal Course of Play — See 4-2/1.5.

Waiving or Modifying Penalty for Use of Non-Conforming Ball — See 5-1/1.

When Play Suspended by Committee, Modifying or Waiving Penalty for Resuming Play Other Than at Time Ordered by Committee — See 6-8b/6.

33-7/3 Competitor's Failure to Countersign Card Blamed on Lack of Time Provided by Committee

Q. In a 36-hole stroke play competition played in one day over two courses, a competitor returned his first-round score card to the Committee but he failed to countersign it. After the second round the Committee informed him that he was disqualified. The competitor blamed the Committee for the error. He said the Committee, in attempting to get him to leave promptly for the course on which the second round was being played, caused him to return his first-round card hurriedly and that he had been given insufficient time to check and countersign the card. The competitor requested the Committee to waive the penalty under Rule 33-7. Would the Committee be justified in doing so?

A. No. If the competitor did not feel he was given sufficient time to check and sign his first-round card, he should have protested before he returned the card.

33-7/4 Modifying Penalty for Returning Wrong Score

Q. A marker inadvertently recorded a 4 for a competitor on a hole at which the competitor's score was actually 5. The competitor failed to check his score for each hole and therefore did not discover the error. The competitor returned his card to the Committee.

Later, the competitor discovered the error while observing the scoreboard. He immediately reported the error to the Committee. Would it be appropriate in such circumstances to invoke Rule 33-7 and waive or modify the disqualification penalty prescribed in Rule 6-6d?

A. No. A penalty of disqualification may be waived or modified only in exceptional circumstances. Under Rule 6-6d, the competitor is responsible for the correctness of the score recorded for each hole.

33-7/4.5 Competitor Unaware of Penalty Returns Wrong Score; Whether Waiving or Modifying Disqualification Penalty Justified

Q. A competitor returns his score card and the score for one hole is lower than actually taken due to failure to include a penalty of two strokes which he did not know he had incurred. The error is discovered before the competition has closed.

Would the Committee be justified, under Rule 33-7, in waiving or modifying the penalty of disqualification prescribed in Rule 6-6d?

A. No. It is the responsibility of the competitor to know the Rules and their interpretations as contained in "Decisions on the Rules of Golf."

Players Agree Not to Tee Off in Prescribed Order to Save Time; Whether Waiving Penalty of Disqualification Justified — See 1-3/1.

Imposing Disqualification Penalty When Marker Attests Wrong Score Knowingly — See 6-6a/5.

Modifying Penalty for One Practice Stroke on Course Before Stroke Play Round — See 7-1b/1.

Waiving Penalty for Practice on Course — See 7-1b/2.

Waiving Penalty for Competitor Who Practices on Course After Qualifying Round and Is Subsequently in Play-Off on Same Day — See 7-1b/3.

Imposing Disqualification Penalty for Failing to Correct Opponent's Misunderstanding of State of Match — See 9-2/12.

33-7/5 Play of Wrong Ball Not Rectified on Advice of Committee Member

Q. In stroke play, a competitor played a wrong ball at the 14th hole. He discovered the error after holing out. Before teeing off at the 15th, he asked a member of the Committee as to the procedure. The Committee member told the competitor to proceed and consult the Committee when the round was completed, instead of telling him to rectify the error as prescribed in Rule 15-3.

Should the player be disqualified as prescribed in Rule 15-3?

A. No. In the circumstances, the competitor should incur a penalty of two strokes for a breach of Rule 15-3, but the disqualification penalty which he also incurred under that Rule should be waived by the Committee under Rule 33-7.

33-7/6 Competitor Repeatedly Replaces Ball Nearer Hole on Green

Q. On completion of a round in stroke play, a competitor's marker reports that the competitor, after lifting his ball on the putting green, repeatedly placed it nearer the hole than the spot from which it was lifted. The Committee, after gathering all available evidence, concludes that the marker's report is correct. What should the Committee do?

A. The competitor should be disqualified under Rule 33-7.

Imposing Disqualification Penalty for Playing Two Holes Not Included in Stipulated Round — See 3/2.

Imposing Disqualification Penalty for Knowingly Giving Incorrect Information on Rules — See 9/1.

Imposing Disqualification Penalty for Altering Teeing Ground — See 11-2/2.

Imposing Disqualification Penalty for Refusing to Identify Ball — See 27/13.

33-7/7 Competitor Seeks Help from Fellow-Competitor to Avoid Penalty

Q. A competitor's ball is lying through the green. He asks a fellow-competitor to remove a loose impediment lying near the ball because he knows that, if his ball moves after a loose impediment within a club-length is moved by an outside agency, the competitor incurs no penalty. The fellow-competitor removes the loose impediment. What is the ruling?

A. Irrespective of whether or not the ball moves as a result of removing the loose impediment, the action of the competitor is so contrary to the spirit of the game that the Committee should disqualify him under Rule 33-7.

The fellow-competitor incurs no penalty for removing the loose impediment unless the Committee is satisfied that he was aware of the competitor's intention to circumvent a Rule. In that instance, he should also be disqualified under Rule 33-7.

33-8/1 Local Rule for Temporary Putting Green Waives Requirement to Hole Out

Q. A course has been going through a period of renovation necessitating the use of temporary putting greens from time to time.

A Local Rule states that a player whose ball lies on a temporary green may either pick up his ball, counting two putts, or putt out.

Is such a Local Rule authorized?

A. No. Rule 1-1 provides: "The Game of Golf consists in playing a ball from the teeing ground into the hole by a stroke or successive strokes in accordance with the Rules." Any Local Rule under which a player would not be required to play the ball into the hole waives this basic Rule and is not authorized.

33-8/2 Local Rule Allows Drop on Green Side of Water Hazard When Ball Fails to Clear Hazard

Q. At two holes a player must hit the ball about 100 yards in order to carry over water hazards. A Local Rule has been adopted to assist golfers who cannot drive over the hazards. The Local Rule states:

> "If a player's first two tee shots do not carry the water hazard, he may drop his ball on the Ball Drop across the hazard, under penalty of two strokes."

Is such a Local Rule authorized?

A. No. Such a Local Rule is contrary to Rule 1-1 which says the game "consists in playing a ball from the teeing ground into the hole by a stroke or successive strokes in accordance with the Rules."

33-8/3 Local Rule Allowing Play of Second Ball in Match Play

Q. May a Committee make a Local Rule allowing play of a second ball in match play when a player is in doubt as to his rights?

A. No. Rule 3-3 specifically restricts the play of a second ball to stroke play.

33-8/4 Local Rule for Events in Which Motorized Golf Carts Permitted

Q. A competition involving stroke play qualifying followed by match play is to be held. Motorized golf carts will be permitted. Play will be in couples. There are enough carts available to provide each couple with a cart. No caddies will be available. Should a Local Rule clarifying the status of the carts be made?

A. It is suggested that the following Local Rule be adopted:

> "A motorized cart is part of the player's equipment:
> (1) When one cart is shared by two players, the cart and any person or thing in it is deemed to be the equipment of the player whose ball is involved, except that, when the cart is being moved by one of the players, the cart and its contents are deemed to be the equipment of that player.
> (2) A player or players using a cart may appoint someone to drive the cart, in which case the driver is considered to be the caddie of the player or players.
> (3) Use of a cart by anyone other than the player or players using it or the appointed driver is prohibited. Any player allowing unauthorized use of his cart is subject to penalty as follows at each hole at which a breach occurs: Match play — Loss of hole; Stroke play — Two strokes."

If some caddies are available, it is suggested that they be assigned in an equitable way and that the above suggested Local Rule be adopted with Item (2) amended to read as follows:

> "A player or players using a cart may appoint someone to drive the cart if no caddie is available,

in which case the driver is considered to be the caddie of the player or players."

33-8/5 Local Rule Permitting Competitors to Discontinue Play by Agreement in Bad Weather

Q. May the Committee for a stroke play event make a Local Rule permitting competitors to discontinue play by agreement among themselves in bad weather?

A. No. Such a Local Rule would modify Rule 6-8a.

Local Rule for Suspension of Play due to Dangerous Situation — See US/33-8/102.

33-8/6 Local Rule Prohibits Practice During Round on Putting Green of Hole Last Played; Competitor Practices on Last Green After Holing Out

Q. In a 72-hole stroke play competition, a Local Rule stated: "A competitor during a round shall not play any practice stroke on or near the putting green of any hole he has played in the round."

At the 72nd hole, a competitor missed a short putt, holed out and then retried his putt. What is the ruling?

A. The competitor had completed his round when he holed out — see Decision 7-2/1. Accordingly he incurred no penalty.

33-8/7 Local Rule Requiring Player to Play Out of Turn on Putting Green

Q. A proposed Local Rule would require that, on the putting green, a player must play continuously until he has holed out. Would such a Local Rule be acceptable?

A. No. Such a Local Rule would modify Rules 10-1b and -2b, which require that the ball farther from the hole shall be played first.

33

33-8/8 Local Rule Providing Relief from Tree Roots

Q. May a Committee make a Local Rule providing relief without penalty if a player's stroke is interfered with by exposed tree roots?

A. No. A Local Rule is authorized only if an abnormal condition exists. The existence of exposed tree roots is not abnormal.

33-8/9 Local Rule Providing Relief from Damage to Bunkers Caused by Children

Q. At our course some holes are accessible to the general public, and children play in the bunkers leaving footprints, holes and sand castles.

May the Committee make a Local Rule allowing a player, without penalty, either to drop his ball outside a bunker damaged by children or to lift his ball from such damage, smooth out the sand and replace the ball?

A. No. This would be a modification of Rule 13-4.

33-8/10 Local Rule Prohibiting Removal of Flagstick

Q. May a Committee make a Local Rule for wintertime play prohibiting removal of the flagstick? The purpose would be to reduce traffic around the hole in the winter when the putting greens are very soft.

A. No. Such a Local Rule would modify the Rules of Golf.

33-8/11 Local Rule Waiving Penalty for Ball Striking Unattended Flagstick

Q. Is it permissible for a Committee to make a Local Rule for winter play waiving the penalty incurred under Rule 17-3c (Ball Striking Flagstick When Unattended) in order to reduce the damage caused to the area around the hole and to speed up play?

A. No.

33

33-8/12 Local Rule for Ball Deflected by Sprinkler Head

Q. May a Committee make a Local Rule allowing a player to replay a stroke, without penalty, if his ball has been deflected by a sprinkler head?

A. No. A sprinkler head is an outside agency (see Definition of "Outside Agency"). The deflection of a ball by it is a rub of the green and the ball must be played as it lies — see Rule 19-1.

33-8/13 Local Rule for Ball Deflected by Power Line

Q. An overhead power line at our 8th hole is so situated that a perfectly played shot can be deflected. Would it be proper for the Committee to make a Local Rule allowing a player whose ball is deflected by this power line to replay the stroke, without penalty, if he wishes?

A. No. However, a Local Rule requiring a player to replay the stroke would be acceptable. The following text is suggested:

> "If a ball strikes the power line at the 8th hole, the player must disregard that stroke, abandon the ball and play another ball as nearly as possible at the spot from which the original ball was played in accordance with Rule 20-5 (Playing Next Stroke from Where Previous Stroke Played)."

33-8/14 Local Rule Deeming Interior Boundary Fence to Be an Obstruction

Q. There is a practice range in the middle of our course. The range is surrounded by a fence which defines the range as out of bounds. Would a Local Rule be authorized under which this particular boundary fence, since it is within the course, is treated as an obstruction?

A. No, such a Local Rule is not authorized. An interior boundary fence is not an abnormal condition.

33-8/15 Local Rule Providing Relief from Interference by Immovable Water Hazard Stake for Ball Lying in Water Hazard

Q. If the stakes defining the margins of water hazards are immovable, may the Committee make a Local Rule providing relief without penalty if a player's ball lies in a water hazard and such a stake interferes with his swing or stance?

A. No. Such stakes are immovable obstructions (see Note to Rule 24).

33-8/16 Local Rule Deeming All Stakes on Course to Be Immovable Obstructions

Q. It is proposed to adopt a Local Rule providing that all stakes on the course, *i.e.*, stakes defining the margins of water hazards, ground under repair, etc., are deemed to be immovable obstructions. The Local Rule would not, of course, apply to boundary stakes since they are not on the course. Is such a Local Rule permissible?

A. Yes.

33-8/17 Local Rule Providing Line-of-Sight Relief from Irrigation-Control Boxes

Q. Irrigation-control boxes, which are about two feet wide and four feet high, have been installed near a number of fairways. Would it be appropriate for a Committee to adopt a Local Rule under which relief would be provided from such boxes when they intervene on the line of play, *i.e.*, line-of-sight relief?

A. No. Providing line-of-sight relief from permanent immovable obstructions is not authorized, except in very unusual circumstances. It is not unusual for irrigation-control boxes to be located near fairways.

33-8/18 Local Rule Providing Line-of-Sight Relief from Protective Fence Near Line of Play

If a wire fence is erected to protect players on the tee of one hole from errant shots played at another hole, and it is relatively close to the line of play of the other hole, it would be permissible to make a Local Rule allowing a player whose ball is in such a position that the fence intervenes on his line of play to drop the ball, without penalty, not nearer the hole in a specified Ball Drop (or Dropping Zone).

33-8/19 Local Rule Permitting Relief on Specified Side of Paved Path

Q. A paved path is parallel to the left side of the 12th hole. If a ball is on the path and the nearest point of relief under Rule 24-2b is on the left side of the path, the player effectively gets no relief as there is a very sharp incline on the left of the path that goes down 30 feet. Would it be appropriate to make a Local Rule giving relief in all cases on the fairway side of this path?

A. No. Rule 33-8 states: "The Committee shall make and publish Local Rules for abnormal conditions." It is not abnormal for areas adjacent to paved paths to have dense underbrush, trees, sharp slopes, etc., thereby providing no practical relief.

Furthermore, it would not be appropriate to establish Ball Drops (or Dropping Zones) on the fairway side of the path to alleviate the problem.

33-8/20 Local Rule Providing Relief from Unsurfaced Road for Tee Shot Only

Q. A road which is not artificially-surfaced crosses a fairway 225 yards from the tee. May the Committee adopt a Local Rule granting relief of the type afforded by Rule 24-2b(i) or Rule 25-1b(i) for tee shots, but not subsequent shots, coming to rest on the road?

A. No. The Committee has authority to provide relief from interference by the road but does not have authority so to limit its application.

[33-8/21   Reserved]

33-8/22 Local Rule Treating Ant Hills as Ground Under Repair

Q. An ant hill is a loose impediment and may be removed, but there is no other relief without penalty. Some ant hills are conical in shape and hard, and removal is not possible, but relief under Rule 25-1b is not available since an ant is not a burrowing animal. If such ant hills interfere with the proper playing of the game, would a Local Rule providing relief be authorized?

A. Yes. A Local Rule stating that such ant hills are to be treated as ground under repair would be justified.

Such a Local Rule is also justified on courses where fire-ants exist. A fire-ants' mound or hill is removable, but its removal will cause the fire-ants to swarm out of the ground. When this occurs, anyone in the vicinity is in danger of being bitten by the ants, and the bite of a fire-ant can cause serious illness.

If a Local Rule giving relief from fire-ants has not been adopted and a ball is so close to a fire-ants' mound that the player is in danger, the player is, in equity, entitled to relief as prescribed in Decision 1-4/10.

33-8/23 Local Rule Denying Relief from Ground Under Repair During Play of Particular Hole

Q. An area of ground under repair is situated on the fairway of the 2nd hole, which is parallel to the 1st hole. Is it permissible to make a Local Rule prohibiting relief from this ground under repair during the play of the 1st hole?

A. No.

33-8/24 Local Rule Permitting Relief from Edging Grooves Around Putting Green

Q. Edging grooves, which are about three inches deep and one-quarter to one-half inch wide, are cut at the perimeters of the putting greens to control the creeping of bermuda grass onto the greens. If a ball comes to rest on such a groove, it is impossible to putt the ball with any degree of accuracy. Would a Local Rule providing relief be authorized?

A. Yes. It would be proper to make a Local Rule giving relief if a ball lies on such a groove, but not solely because a groove might affect the player's stance. The Local Rule should read as follows:

> "If a ball lies on an edging groove around a putting green, the player may, without penalty, lift the ball, clean it and place it out of the groove in the nearest position to where it lay, whether on or off the putting green, which is not nearer the hole."

Local Rule for Mushrooms on Line of Putt — See 16-1a/15.

33-8/25 Local Rule for Ground Under Repair Adjacent to Artificially-Surfaced Cart Path

Q. When ground under repair is adjacent to an artificially- surfaced cart path (an obstruction), sometimes a player, after obtaining relief from one condition, is interfered with by the other condition. Thus, another drop under another Rule results. This is cumbersome and could lead to complications. Would it be proper to eliminate the problem by means of a Local Rule under which ground under repair adjacent to an artificially-surfaced cart path would have the same status as the cart path?

A. Yes. If white lines are used to define ground under repair, a Local Rule is suggested as follows:

> "White-lined areas tying into artificially-surfaced roads or paths are declared to have the same status as the roads or paths, *i.e.*, they are obstructions, not ground under repair. Relief, without penalty, is provided under Rule 24-2b(i)."

33-8/26 Local Rule Altering Ground Under Repair Relief Procedure

Q. It is planned to define an area containing young trees as ground under repair. Would it be permissible

33

to make a Local Rule requiring that, if a player elects to take relief from this area, he must drop the ball behind the area, keeping the trees between himself and the hole?

A. No. However, if it is not feasible to proceed in conformity with the ground under repair Rule, establishment of special areas on which balls may be dropped is authorized.

33-8/27 Local Rule Providing Relief Without Penalty from Flooded Bunker

Q. May a Committee make a Local Rule allowing a player to drop out of any bunker filled with casual water, without penalty, notwithstanding Rule 25-1b(ii)?

A. No. Such a Local Rule is not acceptable as it waives a penalty imposed by a Rule of Golf, contrary to Rule 33-8b.

33-8/28 Local Rule Permitting Re-Dropping or Placing When Dropped Ball Embeds in Bunker

Q. Our bunkers frequently have casual water in them. The texture of the sand in the bunkers is such that a ball dropped under Rule 25-1b(ii)(a) embeds itself in the wet sand to the depth of the ball or deeper.

Would it be proper to make a Local Rule permitting a ball that embeds in a bunker after being dropped from casual water in the bunker to be re-dropped or placed?

A. No. It is not abnormal for a ball dropped in a bunker to embed itself in the sand.

33-8/29 Local Rule Requiring Player to Take Relief Under Penalty from Tree Nursery or Plantation

Q. May a Committee make a Local Rule requiring that a ball lying in a tree nursery or plantation be dropped outside it under penalty of one stroke?

33

A. No. If the Committee wishes to prohibit play in such an area, it may declare it to be ground under repair from which relief without penalty is mandatory. However, a Local Rule imposing a penalty of one stroke is not permitted.

33-8/30   Local Rule for Protection of Young Trees

If the Committee wishes to prevent damage to young trees, the following Local Rule is recommended:

> "Protection of young trees identified by _____ — If such a tree interferes with a player's stance or the area of his intended swing, the ball must be lifted, without penalty, and dropped in accordance with the procedure prescribed in Rule 24-2b(i) (Immovable Obstruction). The ball may be cleaned when so lifted."

33-8/31   Local Rule Providing Relief from Accumulations of Leaves Through the Green

The Committee may make a temporary Local Rule declaring accumulations of leaves through the green at certain holes to be ground under repair (see Definition of "Ground Under Repair") and Rule 25-1 will apply.

The Local Rule should be restricted to the hole(s) at which trouble with leaves occurs and it should be withdrawn as soon as conditions permit. Particular attention is drawn to the opening paragraph of Rule 25-1c; unless there is reasonable evidence that a ball which cannot be found is lost in the leaves, it must be treated as lost elsewhere and Rule 27 applies.

For fallen leaves in a bunker — See Decision 13-4/33.

33-8/32   Local Rule for Aeration Holes

Q. Decision 25/15 states that an aeration hole is not a hole made by a greenkeeper. May the Committee make a Local Rule giving relief for a ball which comes to rest in such a hole?

A. Yes. The following Local Rule is recommended:

> "If a ball comes to rest in an aeration hole, the player may, without penalty, lift the ball and clean it. Through the green, the player shall drop the ball as near as possible to where it lay, but not nearer the hole. On the putting green, the player shall place the ball at the nearest spot not nearer the hole which avoids such situation."

33-8/33 Local Rule Prohibiting Dropping on Apron When Ball on Wrong Putting Green

Q. Balls from the 13th tee frequently come to rest on the 15th green, and the point of nearest relief under Rule 25-3 is the closely mown apron of the green. Much damage is being caused to this apron. May the Committee make a Local Rule requiring that a ball be dropped not only clear of the putting surface but also clear of the apron of this green?

A. Yes. The following wording for a Local Rule is suggested:

> "For the purpose of Rule 25-3, the putting green of the 15th hole includes the apron surrounding the green."

33-8/34 Local Rule Establishes Ball Drop or Dropping Zone; Procedure for Dropping

Q. When it is not feasible to proceed in conformity with Rule 26-1, it is permissible to establish a special area -a Ball Drop or Dropping Zone. A special area — Ball Drop — has been established at a certain hole and the following Local Rule has been made:

> "Ball in water hazard last crossing margin of hazard between green stakes: A ball may be dropped in the area marked 'Ball Drop,' under penalty of one stroke."

The Ball Drop has been defined with a white line. Under the Local Rule:

(a) Is the white line considered to be within the Ball Drop?

(b) Does the player have to stand within the Ball Drop when dropping the ball?

(c) Does the dropped ball first have to strike the ground within the Ball Drop?

(d) Does the dropped ball have to come to rest within the Ball Drop?

(e) If the dropped ball rolls into a hazard, onto a putting green, out of bounds or more than two club-lengths from where it first struck the ground, does Rule 20-2c apply?

A. (a) Yes. By analogy to the Definitions of "Ground Under Repair" and "Water Hazard," a line defining a Ball Drop is within the Ball Drop.

(b) No.

(c) Yes.

(d) No.

(e) Yes.

33-8/35 Local Rule Treating Rough as a Lateral Water Hazard

Q. The areas immediately adjacent to the fairways consist of large embedded boulders, thick desert brush and prickly cactus. A player whose ball comes to rest in such areas has no opportunity to play a stroke. Would it be proper to make a Local Rule under which such areas would be treated as lateral water hazards?

A. No. There are many courses where the areas adjacent to the fairways are of such a nature that a ball therein is almost always lost or unplayable. Thus, such a situation is not abnormal.

33-8/36 Local Rule Giving Free Relief for Ball in Water Hazard

Q. A drainage ditch crosses our 15th hole 190 yards from the tee. The Committee has marked that portion of the ditch within the limits of the fairway and a

33

Local Rule allows a player relief, without penalty, if his tee shot lies in the ditch within the fairway limits.

Is this a proper Local Rule?

A. No. A drainage ditch is a water hazard — see Definition of "Water Hazard." Under Rule 26-1, the penalty for relief from a water hazard is one stroke. Rule 33-8b prohibits waiving this penalty by Local Rule.

33-8/37 Local Rule Allowing Drop in Water Hazard Behind Point Where Ball Lies Unplayable in Hazard

Q. A water hazard varies from 100 yards to 250 yards in width, and there is little or no water in it. In most cases a ball in the hazard can be played. However, it sometimes happens that a ball fails by a few yards to carry the hazard and ends up unplayable in water.

Under Rule 26-1, the player must either drop behind the hazard or at the spot from which his previous stroke was played. In either case, the relief point is up to 250 yards away. In such circumstances, may the Committee make a Local Rule permitting a player to drop a ball in the hazard under penalty of one stroke, as well as out of the hazard?

A. No.

Local Rule Allowing Drop Opposite Spot Where Ball Comes to Rest in Lateral Water Hazard — See 26-1/20.

Local Rule When Pond is Water Hazard from Men's Tee and Lateral from Women's Tee — See 33-2a/6.

Local Rule for Part of Lateral Water Hazard Where Impossible to Drop Not Nearer Hole — See 33-2a/9.

Local Rule for Island Green — See 33-2a/10.

33-8/38 Local Rule Deeming Out of Bounds Ball Which Crosses Boundary But Comes to Rest on Course

Q. Is it permissible to make a Local Rule that a ball is out of bounds if it crosses a boundary, even if it recrosses the boundary and comes to rest on the same

33

part of the course? The purpose of the Local Rule would be to prevent players from cutting across a "dog-leg."

A. No. A ball is out of bounds only when all of it lies out of bounds — see Definition of "Out of Bounds."

The Local Rule suggested in Decision 27/20 deals with a different situation, *i.e.*, one in which a ball crosses an out of bounds area and comes to rest on a different part of the course.

Local Rule for Boundary Stakes Having No Significance in Play of Hole Being Played — See 24/5.

Local Rule for Public Road Dividing Course Which Is Defined as Out of Bounds — See 27/20.

Local Rule Deeming Ball in Bounds Until Beyond Boundary Wall — See 33-2a/16.

33-8/39 Local Rule for Bunker Faces Consisting of Stacked Turf

Q. May a Committee make a Local Rule stating that the face of a bunker which consists of stacked turf is neither (a) part of the bunker nor (b) a "closely mown area" (Rule 25-2)?

A. Yes.

Rule 34. Disputes and Decisions

34-1. Claims and Penalties

a. MATCH PLAY

In match play if a claim is lodged with the Committee under Rule 2-5, a decision should be given as soon as possible so that the state of the match may, if necessary, be adjusted.

If a claim is not made within the time limit provided by Rule 2-5, it shall not be considered unless it is based on facts previously unknown to the player making the claim and the player making the claim had been given wrong information (Rules 6-2a and 9) by an opponent. In any case, no later claim shall be considered after the result of the match has been officially announced, unless the Committee is satisfied that the opponent knew he was giving wrong information.

b. STROKE PLAY

In stroke play no penalty shall be rescinded, modified or imposed after the competition has closed, except that *a penalty of disqualification shall be imposed* at any time after the competition has closed if a competitor:

(i) returned a score for any hole lower than actually taken (Rule 6-6d) for any reason other than failure to include a penalty which he did not know he had incurred; or

(ii) returned a score card on which he had recorded a handicap which he knew

34

was higher than that to which he was entitled, and this affected the number of strokes received (Rule 6-2b); or

(iii) was in breach of Rule 1-3.

A competition is deemed to have closed when the result has been officially announced or, in stroke play qualifying followed by match play, when the player has teed off in his first match.

34-2. Referee's Decision

If a referee has been appointed by the Committee, his decision shall be final.

34-3. Committee's Decision

In the absence of a referee, any dispute or doubtful point on the Rules shall be referred to the Committee, whose decision shall be final.

If the Committee cannot come to a decision, it shall refer the dispute or doubtful point to the Rules of Golf Committee of the United States Golf Association, whose decision shall be final.

If the dispute or doubtful point has not been referred to the Rules of Golf Committee, the player or players

have the right to refer an agreed statement through the Secretary of the Club to the Rules of Golf Committee for an opinion as to the correctness of the decision given. The reply will be sent to the Secretary of the Club or Clubs concerned.

If play is conducted other than in accordance with the Rules of Golf, the Rules of Golf Committee will not give a decision on any question.

34-1b/1 Omission of Penalty Stroke When Score Returned

Q. In stroke play, a competitor returned an incorrect score for a hole due to failure to include a penalty stroke. After the competition closed the error was discovered. Does Rule 34-1b allow imposition of a disqualification penalty for a breach of Rule 6-6d?

A. As stated in Rule 34-1b, the Committee should impose a penalty of disqualification if the competitor knew he had incurred the penalty but intentionally or unintentionally failed to add the penalty to his score, but not if the competitor did not know he had incurred the penalty.

Omission of Penalty Strokes When Score Returned Is Due to Incorrect Ruling — See 34-3/1.

34-1b/1.5 Competitor Correctly Advised by Fellow-Competitor That He Had Incurred a Penalty Disagrees with Fellow-Competitor and Fails to Include Penalty in His Score; Committee Advised of Incident After Competition Had Closed

Q. In stroke play, A, in ignorance of the Rules and with the concurrence of B, his marker, removed a stone from a water hazard when his ball lay in the hazard. Subsequently, A was advised by C, a fellow-competitor, that he (A) was in breach of Rule 13-4. A disagreed, failed to settle the doubtful point with the Committee at the end of the round and returned his score card without including a two-stroke penalty for a breach of Rule 13-4.

After the competition had closed, C advised the Committee of the incident. Should A be disqualified?

A. Yes. Rule 34-1b says in effect that a competitor shall be disqualified after the competition has closed if he had returned a score which did not include a penalty he knew he had incurred. As C pointed out to A that he had proceeded incorrectly and A took no action to check whether he had incurred a penalty before returning his card, the Committee should decide that A knew that he had incurred a penalty.

34-1b/2 Competitor's Failure to Countersign Card Discovered After Competition Closed

Q. Shortly after a stroke play competition had closed,

34

it was found that the card of the winner had not been countersigned. Should the Committee take any action?

A. No. As the competition had closed when the breach of Rule was discovered, no penalty can be applied and the result of the competition must stand.

34-1b/3 Play of Wrong Ball in Stroke Play Not Rectified; Error Discovered After Competition Closed

Q. In stroke play, A played a wrong ball at the 5th hole but he did not realize it until he had holed out at that hole. Before teeing off at the 6th hole, A and B, who was A's marker, concluded that A had incurred a two-stroke penalty. Accordingly, B added two penalty strokes to A's score for the 5th hole and A and B teed off at the 6th hole without A having rectified his mistake as required under Rule 15-3. A was not aware that he should have rectified the error.

Before returning his card, A advised the Committee of the incident. The Committee confirmed that the penalty was two strokes but did not ask A whether the error had been rectified.

A won the competition. Several days later the runner-up claimed that A should be disqualified under Rule 15-3. What is the ruling?

A. The competition stands as played, with A the winner. Under Rule 34-1b, a penalty of disqualification may not be imposed after a competition is closed if the competitor did not know he had incurred the penalty.

34-1b/4 Competitor Changes Weight of Club During Round; Breach Discovered After Competition Closed

Q. It was reported a few days after conclusion of a stroke play event that the winner had changed the weight of his putter twice during play. Should he be penalized?

A. The Committee must decide whether the competitor knew he was in breach of the Rules in changing the weight of his putter during the course of the round (Rule 4-2). If he knew, the Committee should disqualify him. Otherwise, as provided in Rule 34-1b, no penalty shall be imposed.

34-1b/5 Disqualification Penalty Wrongly Applied to Winner of Event; Error Discovered After Two Other Competitors Play Off for First Place

Q. In the final round of a stroke play competition, the Committee disqualified A for recording on his score card a total score which was one stroke less than his actual score. A's hole by hole scores were correct. The Committee was in error. A would have won the event if he had not been disqualified.

As a result of A's disqualification, B and C play off for first place and B wins the play-off. Before the result of the competition is announced, the Committee discovers that A should not have been penalized.

Should the Committee rectify its error?

A. Yes. The penalty applied to A should be rescinded and A should be declared the winner — see Rule 34-1b.

34-1b/6 Winner's Score Not Posted Due to Committee Error

Q. In a stroke play event, the winner's prize is awarded to B. The next day A advises the Committee that he had returned a lower score than B. A check reveals that A is correct and that, in error, the Committee had failed to post A's score. What should be done?

A. Rule 34-1b does not apply to Committee errors of this kind. The prize should be retrieved from B and given to A, the rightful winner.

Wrong Handicap Used Due to Error by Committee; Error Discovered Several Days Later — See 6-2b/3.

Wrong Handicap Applied by Committee Results in Player Not Receiving Prize — See 33-5/2.

34

34-1b/7 Wrong Score in Qualifying Round Discovered During Match Play

Q. On completion of the stroke play qualifying round for a match play competition, a player unintentionally failed to include in his score for a hole a penalty he knew he had incurred. After the player had advanced in the match play phase, the error was discovered. What should be done?

A. The player should be disqualified. Under Rule 34-1b, the penalty for a breach of Rule 6-6d was applicable after the qualifying competition was closed.

Wrong Handicap Used in Stroke Play by Mistake; Error Discovered After Competition Closed — See 6-2b/1.

Wrong Handicap Knowingly Used in Stroke Play; Error Discovered After Competition Closed — See 6-2b/2.

Competitor Records Incorrect Handicap for Partner in Foursome Stroke Play Competition; Error Discovered After Competition Closed — See 6-2b/2.5.

34-1b/8 Player Who Has Advanced in Match Play Is Disqualified for Wrong Score in Qualifying Round

Q. The Committee discovers that by mistake A, who has advanced to the fourth round of a match play competition returned a score lower than actually taken in the qualifying round. A was disqualified. What is the proper procedure with regard to the players beaten by A?

A. The Committee must determine further procedure in equity (Rule 1-4). The choices are:
   (a) cancel the competition;
   (b) consider the disqualification penalty applicable only from the time of its discovery, thus giving A's next opponent a default;
   (c) reinstate the player last eliminated by A; or
   (d) require all players eliminated by A to play off for his position.

34-2/1 Referee's Authority to Declare Ground Under Repair

Q. Does the referee of a match have authority to declare an area ground under repair during the match?

A. Yes.

34-2/2 Referee Authorizes Player to Infringe a Rule

Q. In error, a referee authorized a player to infringe a Rule of Golf. Is the player absolved from penalty in such a case?

A. Yes. Under Rule 34-2, a referee's decision is final, whether or not the decision is correct.

Imposition of Penalty by Referee After Any Player in Match Has Played from Next Tee — See 2-5/12.

34-2/3 Referee Warning Player About to Infringe Rule

Q. If the referee observes a player about to break a Rule, may he warn the player and thus prevent a breach?

A. Yes, but he is under no obligation to do so. If he volunteers information about the Rules, he should do so uniformly to both players.

34-2/4 Disagreement with Referee's Decision

Q. In match play, if a player disagrees with a referee's decision, may the player demand that the matter be considered by the Committee?

A. No. A referee's decision may be referred to the Committee only if the referee consents.

34-2/5 Referee Reverses Ruling Made at Last Hole of Match After Players Leave Putting Green

Q. In a match, A and B are all square playing the last hole. An incident occurs on the putting green and

34

the referee rules incorrectly that A loses the last hole and the match, whereas he should have ruled that B lost the last hole and the match. A and B walk off the putting green without disputing the ruling. Subsequently, the referee learns of his error, reverses his ruling and decided that B lost the last hole and the match. Did the referee act properly in reversing his ruling?

A. No. When the referee made his ruling on the putting green of the last hole, that ruling was final — Rule 34-2. It would not have been final if A or B had disputed the ruling before leaving the last green and the referee had agreed to refer the matter to the Committee.

The referee was in error in subsequently reversing the ruling. The error should have been corrected by reverting to the ruling made on the last green.

Procedure for Referee in Determining Ball Farther from Hole — See 10-1b/1.

Flagstick Attended by Referee — See 17-1/3.

34-3/1 Correction of Incorrect Ruling

Q. During the first round of a 36-hole stroke play competition a competitor plays a wrong ball from a bunker at the 6th hole and the ball comes to rest on the green. The competitor holes out with it. He then realizes that he has played a wrong ball and corrects his mistake. The competitor reports the facts to the Committee before returning his card and is incorrectly advised that he has incurred no penalty since the wrong ball was played from a hazard.

During the second round the Committee realizes that it made a mistake and retrospectively adds to the competitor's first-round score two penalty strokes at the 6th hole, but does not disqualify the competitor under Rule 6-6d.

The competitor objects on the ground that the Committee reached a decision on the matter the previous day and that, as Rule 34-3 states that the Committee's decision is final, it cannot now impose a penalty.

Was the Committee's procedure correct?

A. Yes.

Under Rule 34-3, a Committee's decision is final in that the competitor has no right to appeal. However, Rule 34-3 does not prevent a Committee from correcting an incorrect ruling and imposing or rescinding a penalty provided that no penalty is imposed or rescinded after the competition is closed except in the circumstances set forth in Rule 34-1b.

[34-3/2   Reserved]

34-3/3   Player Proceeds on Basis of Incorrect Ruling

Q. A player obtained a ruling from a member of the Committee and proceeded to play on the basis of that ruling, which involved dropping the ball at and playing from a wrong place. The Committee member then learns that he made an incorrect ruling. Should the Committee require the player to disregard the stroke or strokes played subsequent to the incorrect ruling and proceed correctly?

A. No. The strokes played subsequent to the incorrect ruling must stand. This applies whether or not the player has played from the next tee. The player incurs no penalty for having played from a wrong place.

Play of Wrong Ball Not Rectified Due to Incorrect Advice by Committee Member — See 33-7/5.

34-3/3.5   Player Lifts Ball Without Authority Due to Misunderstanding Committee Member's Instructions

Q. A player's ball comes to rest against a movable obstruction and he seeks relief. A member of the Committee correctly advises him that he may remove the obstruction under Rule 24-1 and that he should mark the position of the ball in case it moves during the removal of the obstruction. The player marks the position of the ball and lifts it before the member of the

34

Committee can stop him. The player was under the misapprehension that, having been requested to mark the position of the ball, he was entitled to lift it before the obstruction was removed. Should the player be penalized under Rule 18-2a in these circumstances?

A. No. Provided the Committee member is satisfied that the player misunderstood the instruction, the ball should be replaced without penalty.

34-3/4 Dispute as to Whether Competitor Played from Outside Teeing Ground

Q. In stroke play, B, A's fellow-competitor and marker, claimed at the completion of the round that A had played from outside the teeing ground at the 15th hole. A stated that he had played from within the teeing ground.

The Committee ruled that the claim was invalid because it was not made at the 15th tee and because A disputed the claim. Was the ruling correct?

It is a question of fact whether A played from outside the teeing ground. The matter should be resolved on the basis of the weight of evidence. The timing of a claim is not necessarily a factor.

In this case, it was B's word against A's and the weight of evidence did not favor either competitor. In such a case, the benefit of the doubt should be given to A, the player of the stroke.

34-3/5 True State of Match Not Determinable

Q. On completion of a match, A claims he is 1 up and B claims the match is all square. The matter is referred to the Committee. The Committee gathers all available evidence and is unable to determine the true state of the match. What should the Committee do?

A. It should resolve the matter in the fairest way. An equitable solution would be to order that the match be replayed.

Appendix I
LOCAL RULES;
CONDITIONS OF THE COMPETITION

Local Rules

Rule 33-8 provides:

"The Committee may make and publish Local Rules for abnormal conditions if they are consistent with the policy of the Governing Authority for the country concerned as set forth in Appendix I to these Rules.

"A penalty imposed by a Rule of Golf shall not be waived by a Local Rule."

Information regarding acceptable and prohibited Local Rules is provided in the Decisions on the Rules of Golf under Rule 33-8. Among the matters for which Local Rules may be advisable are the following:

1. Obstructions

Clarifying the status of objects which may be obstructions (Rule 24).

Declaring any construction to be an integral part of the course and, accordingly, not an obstruction, *e.g.*, built-up sides of teeing grounds, putting greens and bunkers (Rules 24 and 33-2a).

2. Roads and Paths

Providing relief of the type afforded under Rule 24-2b from roads and paths not having artificial surfaces and sides if they could unfairly affect play.

3. Preservation of Course

Preservation of the course by defining areas, including turf nurseries and other parts of the course under cultivation, as ground under repair from which play is prohibited.

4. Water Hazards

Lateral Water Hazards. Clarifying the status of sections of water hazards which may be lateral water hazards (Rule 26).

Provisional Ball. Permitting play of a provisional ball for a ball which may be in a water hazard of such character that it would be impracticable to determine whether the ball is in the hazard or to do so would unduly delay play. In such case, if a provisional ball is played and the original ball is in a water hazard, the player may play the original ball as it lies or continue the provisional ball in play, but he may not proceed under Rule 26-1.

5. Defining Bounds and Margins
Specifying means used to define out of bounds, hazards, water hazards, lateral water hazards and ground under repair.

6. Ball Drops
Establishment of special areas on which balls may be dropped when it is not feasible or practicable to proceed exactly in conformity with Rule 24-2b (immovable obstructions), Rule 25-1b or -1c (ground under repair), Rule 26-1 (water hazards and lateral water hazards) and Rule 28 (ball unplayable).

7. Temporary Conditions — Mud, Extreme Wetness
Temporary conditions which might interfere with proper playing of the game, including mud and extreme wetness warranting lifting an embedded ball anywhere through the green (see detailed recommendation below) or removal of mud from a ball through the green.

* * *

Following are the suggested texts for other Local Rules which are authorized by the USGA:

Lifting an Embedded Ball

Rule 25-2 provides relief without penalty for a ball embedded in its own pitch-mark in any closely mown area through the green.

On the putting green, a ball may be lifted and damage caused by the impact of a ball may be repaired (Rules 16-1b and c).

When permission to lift an embedded ball anywhere through the green would be warranted, the following Local Rule is suggested:

Anywhere "through the green," a ball which is embedded in its own pitch-mark in the ground, except in loose sand, may be lifted without penalty, cleaned and dropped as near as possible to the spot where it lay but not nearer the hole. (See Rule 20.)

("Through the green" is the whole area of the course except:

    a. Teeing ground and putting green of the hole being played;

    b. All hazards on the course.)

Exception: A player may not obtain relief under this Rule if it is clearly unreasonable for him to play a stroke because of interference by anything other than the condition covered by this Rule.

Practice Between Holes

When, between the play of two holes, it is desired to prohibit practice putting or chipping on or near the putting green of the hole last played, the following Local Rule is recommended:

    Between the play of two holes, a player shall not play any practice stroke on or near the putting green of the hole last played. (For other practice, see Rules 7 and 33-2c.)

PENALTY FOR BREACH OF LOCAL RULE:
Match play --- Loss of next hole; Stroke play --- Two strokes at next hole.

Marking Position of Lifted Ball

When it is desired to require a specific means of marking the position of a lifted ball on the putting green, the following Local Rule is recommended:

    Before a ball on the putting green is lifted, its position shall be marked by placing a small coin or some similar object immediately behind the ball; if the ball-marker interferes with another player, it should be moved one or more putterhead-lengths to one side. If the position of the ball is not so marked, *the player shall incur a penalty of one stroke* and the ball shall be replaced. If the ball is not replaced, *the player shall incur the penalty* for breach of Rule 20-3a, but no additional penalty under this Local Rule shall be applied. (This modifies Rule 20-1.)

Prohibition Against Touching Line of Putt with Club

When it is desired to prohibit touching the line of putt with a club in moving loose impediments, the following Local Rule is recommended:

    The line of putt shall not be touched with a club for any purpose except to repair old hole plugs or ball marks or during address. (This modifies Rule 16-1a.)

PENALTY FOR BREACH OF LOCAL RULE:
Match play --- Loss of hole; Stroke play --- Two strokes.

Protection of Young Trees

When it is desired to prevent damage to young trees, the following Local Rule is recommended:

Protection of young trees identified by _____ — If such a tree interferes with a player's stance or the area of his intended swing, the ball must be lifted, without penalty, and dropped in accordance with the procedure prescribed in Rule 24-2b(i) (Immovable Obstruction). The ball may be cleaned when so lifted.

Temporary Obstructions

When temporary obstructions are installed for a competition, the following Local Rule is recommended:

1. Definition

Temporary immovable obstructions include tents, scoreboards, grandstands, refreshment stands and lavatories. Any temporary equipment for photography, press, radio and television is also a temporary immovable obstruction, provided it is not mobile or otherwise readily movable.

Excluded are temporary power lines and cables and mats covering them and temporary telephone lines and stanchions supporting them (from which relief is provided in Clause 5) and mobile or otherwise readily movable equipment for photography, press, radio or television (from which relief is obtainable under Rule 24-1).

2. Interference

Interference by a temporary immovable obstruction occurs when (a) the ball lies in or on the obstruction or so close to the obstruction that the obstruction interferes with the player's stance or the area of his intended swing or (b) the obstruction intervenes between the player's ball and the hole or the ball lies within one club-length of a spot where such intervention would exist.

3. Relief

A player may obtain relief from interference by a temporary immovable obstruction as follows:

a. THROUGH THE GREEN

Through the green, the point on the course nearest to where the ball lies shall be determined which (a) is not nearer the hole, (b) avoids interference as defined in Clause 2 of this Local Rule and (c) is not in a hazard or on a putting green. He shall lift the ball and drop it without penalty within one club-length of the point thus determined on ground which fulfils (a), (b) and (c) above. The ball may be cleaned when so lifted.

b. IN A HAZARD

If the ball lies in a hazard, the player shall lift and drop the ball either:

(i) in the hazard, without penalty, on the nearest ground affording complete relief within the limits specified in Clause 3a above or, if complete relief is impossible, on ground within the hazard affording maximum relief, or

(ii) outside the hazard, *under penalty of one stroke*, as follows: The player shall determine the point on the course nearest to where the ball lies which (a) is not nearer the hole, (b) avoids interference as defined in Clause 2 of this Local Rule and (c) is not in a hazard. He shall drop the ball within one club-length of the point thus determined on ground which fulfils (a), (b) and (c) above.

The ball may be cleaned when so lifted.

Exception: A player may not obtain relief from a temporary immovable obstruction under Clause 3a or 3b if (a) it is clearly unreasonable for him to play a stroke, or in the case of intervention to play a stroke directly toward the obstruction, because of interference by anything other than the obstruction or (b) interference would occur only through use of an unnecessarily abnormal stance, swing or direction of play.

4. Ball Lost in Temporary Immovable Obstruction

If there is reasonable evidence that a ball is lost within the confines of a temporary immovable obstruction, the player may take relief without penalty as prescribed in Rule 24-2c.

5. Temporary Power Lines and Cables

The above Clauses do not apply to (1) temporary power lines or cables or mats covering them or (2) temporary telephone lines or stanchions supporting them. If such items are readily movable, the player may obtain relief under Rule 24-1. If they are not readily movable, the player may, if the ball lies through the green, obtain relief as provided in Rule 24-2b(i). If the ball lies in a bunker or a water hazard, the player may obtain relief under Rule 24-2b(i), except that the ball must be dropped in the bunker or water hazard.

Note: The prohibition in Rule 24-2b(i) against crossing over, through or under the obstruction does not apply.

If a ball strikes a temporary power line or cable which is elevated, it must be replayed, without penalty (see Rule 20-5). If the ball is not immediately recoverable, another ball may be substituted.

Exception: Ball striking elevated junction section of cable rising from the ground shall not be replayed.

6. Re-Dropping

If a dropped ball rolls into a position covered by this Local Rule, or nearer the hole than its original position, it shall be re-dropped without penalty. If it again rolls into such a position, it shall be placed where it first struck a part of the course when re-dropped.

PENALTY FOR BREACH OF LOCAL RULE:
Match play --- Loss of hole; Stroke play --- Two strokes.

"Preferred Lies" and "Winter Rules"

The USGA does not endorse "preferred lies" and "winter rules" and recommends that the Rules of Golf be observed uniformly. Ground under repair is provided for in Rule 25. Occasional abnormal conditions which might interfere with fair play and are not widespread should be defined accurately as ground under repair.

However, adverse conditions are sometimes so general throughout a course that the Committee believes "preferred lies" or "winter rules" would promote fair play or help protect the course. Heavy snows, spring thaws, prolonged rains or extreme heat can make fairways unsatisfactory and sometimes prevent use of heavy mowing equipment.

When a Committee adopts a Local Rule for "preferred lies" or "winter rules," it should be in detail and should be interpreted by the Committee, as there is no established code for"winter rules." Without a detailed Local Rule, it is meaningless for a Committee to post a notice merely saying "Winter Rules Today."

The following Local Rule would seem appropriate for the conditions in question, but the USGA will not interpret it:

> A ball lying on a "fairway" may be lifted and cleaned, without penalty, and placed within one club-length of where it originally lay, not nearer the hole, and so as to preserve as nearly as possible the stance required to play from the original lie. A ball so lifted is back in play when the player addresses it or, if he does not address it, when he makes his next stroke at it.

Before a Committee adopts a Local Rule permitting "preferred lies" or "winter rules," the following facts should be considered:

1. Such a Local Rule conflicts with the Rules of Golf and the fundamental principle of playing the ball as it lies.

2. "Winter rules" are sometimes adopted under the guise of protecting the course when, in fact, the practical effect is just the opposite — they permit moving the ball to the best turf, from which divots are then taken to injure the course further.

3. "Preferred lies" or "winter rules" tend generally to lower scores and handicaps, thus penalizing the players in competition with players whose scores for handicaps are made under the Rules of Golf.

4. Extended use or indiscriminate use of "preferred lies" or "winter rules" will place players at a disadvantage when competing at a course where the ball must be played as it lies.

Handicapping and "Preferred Lies"

Scores made under a Local Rule for "preferred lies" or "winter rules" may be accepted for handicapping if the Committee considers that conditions warrant. When such a Local Rule is adopted, the Committee should ensure that the course's normal scoring difficulty is maintained as nearly as possible through adjustment of tee-markers and related methods. However, if extreme conditions cause extended use of "preferred lies" or "winter rules" and the course management cannot adjust scoring difficulty properly, the club should obtain a Temporary Course Rating from its district golf association.

Conditions of the Competition

Rule 33-1 states: "The Committee shall lay down the conditions under which a competition is to be played." Conditions should include such matters as method of entry, eligibility requirements, format, the method of deciding ties, the method of determining the draw for match play and handicap allowances for a handicap competition.

How to Decide Ties

Rule 33-6 empowers the Committee to determine how and when a halved match or a stroke play tie shall be decided. The decision should be published in advance.

The USGA recommends:

1. Match Play

A match which ends all square should be played off hole by hole until one side wins a hole. The play-off should start on the hole where the match began. In a handicap match, handicap strokes should be allowed as in the prescribed round.

2. Stroke Play

(a) In the event of a tie in a scratch stroke play competition, an 18-hole play-off is recommended. If that is not feasible, a hole-by-hole play-off is recommended.

(b) In the event of a tie in a handicap stroke play competition, a play-off over 18 holes with handicaps is recommended. If a shorter play-off is necessary, the percentage of 18 holes to be played should be applied to the players' handicaps to determine their play-off handicaps. It is advisable to arrange for a percentage of holes that will result in whole numbers in handicaps; if this is not feasible, handicap stroke fractions of one-half stroke or more should count as a full stroke and any lesser fraction should be disregarded.

(c) In either a scratch or handicap stroke play competition, if a play-off of any type is not feasible, matching score cards is recommended. The method of matching cards should be announced in advance. An acceptable method of matching cards is to determine the winner on the basis of the best score for the last nine holes. If the tying players have the same score for the last nine, determine the winner on the basis of the last six holes, last three holes and finally the 18th hole. If such a method is used in a handicap stroke play competition, one-half, one-third, one-sixth, etc. of the handicaps should be deducted.

(d) If the conditions of the competition provide that ties shall be decided over the last nine, last six, last three and last hole, they should also provide what will happen if this procedure does not produce a winner.

Draw for Match Play

Although the draw for match play may be completely blind or certain players may be distributed through different quarters or eighths, the General Numerical Draw is recommended if flights are determined by a qualifying round.

General Numerical Draw

For purposes of determining places in the draw, ties in qualifying rounds other than those for the last qualifying place shall be decided by the order in which scores are returned, the first score to be returned receiving the lowest available number, etc. If it is impossible to determine the order in which scores are returned, ties shall be determined by a blind draw.

UPPER HALF	LOWER HALF	UPPER HALF	LOWER HALF
64 QUALIFIERS		**32 QUALIFIERS**	
1 vs. 64	2 vs. 63	1 vs. 32	2 vs. 31
32 vs. 33	31 vs. 34	16 vs. 17	15 vs. 18
16 vs. 49	15 vs. 50	8 vs. 25	7 vs. 26
17 vs. 48	18 vs. 47	9 vs. 24	10 vs. 23
8 vs. 57	7 vs. 58	4 vs. 29	3 vs. 30
25 vs. 40	26 vs. 39	13 vs. 20	14 vs. 19
9 vs. 56	10 vs. 55	5 vs. 28	6 vs. 27
24 vs. 41	23 vs. 42	12 vs. 21	11 vs. 22
4 vs. 61	3 vs. 62	**16 QUALIFIERS**	
29 vs. 36	30 vs. 35	1 vs. 16	2 vs. 15
13 vs. 52	14 vs. 51	8 vs. 9	7 vs. 10
20 vs. 45	19 vs. 46	4 vs. 13	3 vs. 14
5 vs. 60	6 vs. 59	5 vs. 12	6 vs. 11
28 vs. 37	27 vs. 38	**8 QUALIFIERS**	
12 vs. 53	11 vs. 54	1 vs. 8	2 vs. 7
21 vs. 44	22 vs. 43	4 vs. 5	3 vs. 6

Handicap Allowances

The USGA recommends the following handicap allowances in handicap competitions:

Singles match play: Allow the higher-handicapped player the full difference between the handicaps of the two players.

Four-ball match play: Reduce the handicaps of all four players by the handicap of the low-handicapped player, who shall then play from scratch. Allow each of the three other players 100 percent of the resulting difference.

Individual stroke play: Allow the full handicap.

Four-ball stroke play: Men — Allow each competitor 90 percent of his handicap. Women — Allow each competitor 95 percent of her handicap.

Best-ball-of-four, stroke play: Men — Allow each competitor 80 percent of his handicap. Women — Allow each competitor 90 percent of her handicap.

Optional Conditions

The following are some conditions which a Committee may wish to make:

List of Conforming Golf Balls

The USGA periodically issues a List of Conforming Golf Balls. If it is desired to require use of a brand of golf ball on the List, the List should be posted and the following issued as a condition of the competition:

> Only brands of golf balls on the USGA's latest List of Conforming Golf Balls may be used. Penalty for use of brand not on the List: Disqualification.

One-Ball Rule

If it is desired to prohibit changing brands of golf balls during a stipulated round, the following condition is recommended; it is suggested that it be considered only for competitions involving expert players:

Limitation on Golf Balls Used During Round
(Condition: Rules 5-1 and 33-1)

1. BALLS WITH IDENTICAL MARKINGS TO BE USED

Throughout a stipulated round, the player is limited to golf balls with identical markings, except that the player-identification numbers may differ by number only, not by color.

PENALTY FOR BREACH OF CONDITION:
Match play --- At the conclusion of the hole at which the breach is discovered, the state of the match shall be adjusted by deducting one hole for each hole at which a breach occurred. Maximum deduction per round: two holes. Stroke play --- Two strokes for each hole at which any breach occurred; maximum penalty per round: four strokes.

2. PROCEDURE WHEN BREACH DISCOVERED
When a player discovers that he has used a ball in breach of this condition, he shall abandon that ball before playing from the next teeing ground and complete the round using a proper ball; otherwise, *the player shall be disqualified.* If discovery is made during play of a hole and the player elects to substitute a proper ball before completing that hole, the player shall place a proper ball on the spot where the ball used in breach of this condition lay.

Time of Starting
If the Committee desires to adopt the condition in the Note under Rule 6-3a, the following wording is recommended:

> Rule 6-3a provides: "The player shall start at the time laid down by the Committee." The penalty for breach of Rule 6-3a is disqualification. However, it is a condition of the competition that, if the player arrives at his starting point, ready to play, within five minutes after his starting time, in the absence of circumstances which warrant waiving the penalty of disqualification as provided in Rule 33-7, the penalty for failure to start on time is loss of the first hole in match play or two strokes at the first hole in stroke play instead of disqualification.

Practice
The Committee may make regulations governing practice in accordance with the Note to Rule 7-1, Clause (c) of the Exception under Rule 7-2 and Rule 33-2c.

Advice in Team Competitions
If the Committee desires to adopt the condition in the Note under Rule 8, which applies to a team competition with or without concurrent individual competition, the following wording is recommended:

In accordance with the Note to Rule 8 of the Rules of Golf, each team may appoint one person (in addition to the persons from whom advice may be asked under Rule 8-1) who may give advice (including pointing out a line for putting) to members of that team. Such person [if it is desired to put a restriction on who may be appointed, insert such restriction here] shall be identified to the Committee prior to the start of the competition.

Automotive Transportation

If it is desired to prohibit automotive transportation in a competition, the following condition is suggested:

Players shall not use automotive transportation during play.

PENALTY FOR BREACH OF CONDITION:

Match play --- At the conclusion of the hole at which the breach is discovered, the state of the match shall be adjusted by deducting one hole for each hole at which a breach occurred. Maximum deduction per round: two holes.

Stroke play --- Two strokes for each hole at which any breach occurred; maximum penalty per round: four strokes.

Match or stroke play --- Use of any unauthorized automotive vehicle shall be discontinued immediately upon discovery that a breach has occurred. Otherwise, the player shall be disqualified.

Appendices II and III

Any design in a club or ball which is not covered by Rules 4 and 5 and Appendices II and III, or which might significantly change the nature of the game, will be ruled on by the United States Golf Association and the Royal and Ancient Golf Club of St. Andrews.

Note: Equipment approved for use or marketed prior to January 1, 1988 which conformed to the Rules in effect in 1987 but does not conform to the 1988 and subsequent Rules may be used until December 31, 1995; thereafter all equipment must conform to the current Rules.

Appendix II
DESIGN OF CLUBS

Rule 4-1 prescribes general regulations for the design of clubs. The following paragraphs, which provide some detailed specifications and clarify how Rule 4-1 is interpreted, should be read in conjunction with this Rule.

4-1a. General

ADJUSTABILITY — EXCEPTION FOR PUTTERS
Clubs other than putters shall not be designed to be adjustable except for weight.

Some other forms of adjustability are permitted in the design of a putter, provided that:

(i) the adjustment cannot be readily made;

(ii) all adjustable parts are firmly fixed and there is no reasonable likelihood of them working loose during a round; and

(iii) all configurations of adjustment conform with the Rules.

The disqualification penalty for purposely changing the playing characteristics of a club during a stipulated round (Rule 4-2) applies to all clubs, including a putter.

Note: It is recommended that all putters with adjustable parts be submitted to the United States Golf Association for a ruling.

4-1b. Shaft

GENERALLY STRAIGHT
The shaft shall be at least 18 inches (457mm) in length. It shall be straight from the top of the grip to a point not more than 5 inches (127mm) above the sole, measured along the axis of the shaft and the neck or socket.

BENDING AND TWISTING PROPERTIES
The shaft must be so designed and manufactured that at any point along its length:

(i) it bends in such a way that the deflection is the same regardless of how the shaft is rotated about its longitudinal axis; and

(ii) it twists the same amount in both directions.

App. II

CLUBS

GRIPS

GROOVES

EXAMPLES OF PERMISSIBLE GROOVE CROSS SECTIONS

ATTACHMENT TO CLUBHEAD

The neck or socket must not be more than 5 inches (127mm) in length, measured from the top of the neck or socket to the sole along its axis. The shaft and the neck or socket must remain in line with the heel, or with a point to the right or left of the heel, when the club is viewed in the address position. The distance between the axis of the shaft or the neck or socket and the back of the heel must not exceed 0.625 inches (16mm).

Exception for Putters: The shaft or neck or socket of a putter may be fixed at any point in the head and need not remain in line with the heel. The axis of the shaft from the top to a point not more than 5 inches (127mm) above the sole must diverge from the vertical in the toe-heel plane by at least 10 degrees when the club is in its normal address position.

4-1c. Grip

(i) For clubs other than putters the grip must be generally circular in cross-section, except that a continuous, straight, slightly raised rib may be incorporated along the full length of the grip.

(ii) A putter grip may have a non-circular cross-section, provided the cross-section has no concavity and remains generally similar throughout the length of the grip.

(iii) The grip may be tapered but must not have any bulge or waist.

(iv) For clubs other than putters the axis of the grip must coincide with the axis of the shaft.

(v) The cross-sectional dimension of a grip measured in any direction shall not exceed 1.75 inches (45mm).

(vi) A putter may have more than one grip, provided each is circular in cross-section and the axis of each coincides with the axis of the shaft.

Note: Putters approved for use or marketed prior to January 1, 1992 which are in breach of Clause (vi) may be used until December 31, 1992.

4-1d. Clubhead

DIMENSIONS

The dimensions of a clubhead (see diagram) are measured, with the clubhead in its normal address position, on horizontal lines between vertical projections of the outermost points of (i) the heel and the toe and (ii) the face and the back. If the outermost point of the heel is not clearly defined, it is deemed to be 0.625 inches (16mm) above the horizontal plane on which the club is resting in its normal address position.

PLAIN IN SHAPE

The clubhead shall be generally plain in shape. All parts shall be rigid, structural in nature and functional.

Features such as holes through the head, windows or transparencies, or appendages to the main body of the head such as plates, rods or fins for the purpose of meeting dimensional specifications, for aiming or for any other purpose are not permitted. Exceptions may be made for putters.

Any furrows in or runners on the sole shall not extend into the face.

4-1e. Club Face

GENERAL

Except for specified markings, the surface roughness must not exceed that of decorative sandblasting. Markings must not have sharp edges or raised lips, as determined by a finger test. The material and construction of the face shall not be designed or manufactured to have the effect at impact of a spring, or to impart significantly more spin to the ball than a standard steel face, or to have any other effect which would unduly influence the movement of the ball.

IMPACT AREA MARKINGS

Markings within the area where impact is intended (the "impact area") are governed by the following:

(i) *Grooves*. A series of straight grooves with diverging sides and a symmetrical cross-section may be used. (See diagram.) The width and cross-section must be generally consistent across the face of the club and along the length of the grooves. Any rounding of groove edges shall be in the form of a radius which does not exceed 0.020 inches (0.5mm). The width of the grooves shall not exceed 0.035 inches (0.9mm), using the 30 degree method of measurement on file with the United States Golf Association. The distance between edges of adjacent grooves must not be less than three times the width of a groove, and not less than 0.075 inches (1.9mm). The depth of a groove must not exceed 0.020 inches (0.5mm).

(ii) *Punch Marks.* Punch marks may be used. The area of any such mark must not exceed 0.0044 square inches (2.8 sq. mm). A mark must not be closer to an adjacent mark than 0.168 inches (4.3mm), measured from center to center. The depth of a punch mark must not exceed 0.040 inches (1.0mm). If punch marks are used in combination with grooves, a punch mark may not be closer to a groove than 0.168 inches (4.3mm), measured from center to center.

DECORATIVE MARKINGS
The center of the impact area may be indicated by a design within the boundary of a square whose sides are 0.375 inches (9.5mm) in length. Such a design must not unduly influence the movement of the ball. Decorative markings are permitted outside the impact area.

NON-METALLIC CLUB FACE MARKINGS
The above specifications do not apply to clubs on which the impact area of the face is non-metallic and whose loft angle is 24 degrees or less, but markings which could unduly influence the movement of the ball are prohibited. Clubs with this type of face and a loft angle exceeding 24 degrees may have grooves of maximum width 0.040 inches (1.0mm) and maximum depth 1« times the groove width, but must otherwise conform to the markings specifications above.

PUTTER FACE MARKINGS
The specifications above with regard to club face markings do not apply to putters.

Appendix III
THE BALL

a. WEIGHT
The weight of the ball shall not be greater than 1.620 ounces avoirdupois (45.93gm).

b. SIZE

The diameter of the ball shall be not less than 1.680 inches (42.67mm). This specification will be satisfied if, under its own weight, a ball falls through a 1.680 inches diameter ring gauge in fewer than 25 out of 100 randomly selected positions, the test being carried out at a temperature of 23 1 °C.

c. SPHERICAL SYMMETRY

The ball must not be designed, manufactured or intentionally modified to have flight properties which differ from those of a spherically symmetrical ball.

Furthermore the ball will not conform to the Rules of Golf if it fails to satisfy the performance specifications outlined below:

As described in procedures on file at the United States Golf Association, each ball type will be tested using 40 balls of that type, in 20 pairs. One ball of each pair will be launched spinning about one specified axis; the other ball of each pair will be launched spinning about a different, but also specified axis. Differences in carry and time of flight between the two balls of each pair will be recorded. If the mean of the differences in carry is greater than 3.0 yards, and that value is significant at the 5% level, OR if the mean of the differences in time of flight is greater than 0.20 seconds, and that value is significant at the 5% level, the ball type will not conform to the Rules of Golf.

Note: Methods of determining whether a ball performs as if it were generally spherically symmetrical may be subject to change as instrumentation becomes available to measure other properties accurately, such as aerodynamic coefficient of lift, coefficient of drag and moment of inertia.

d. INITIAL VELOCITY

The velocity of the ball shall not be greater than 250 feet (76.2m) per second when measured on apparatus approved by the United States Golf Association. A maximum tolerance of 2% will be allowed. The temperature of the ball when tested shall be 23±1°C.

e. OVERALL DISTANCE STANDARD

A brand of golf ball, when tested on apparatus approved by the USGA on the outdoor range at the USGA Headquarters under the conditions set forth in the Overall Distance Standard for golf balls on file with the USGA, shall not cover an average distance in carry and roll exceeding 280 yards plus a tolerance of 6%. Note: The 6% tolerance will be reduced to a minimum of 4% as test techniques are improved.

Appendix IV
MISCELLANEOUS

Par Computation

"Par" is the score that an expert golfer would be expected to make for a given hole. Par means error-less play without flukes and under ordinary weather conditions, allowing two strokes on the putting green.

Yardages for guidance in computing par are given below. They should not be applied arbitrarily; allowance should be made for the configuration of the ground, any difficult or unusual conditions and the severity of the hazards.

Each hole should be measured horizontally from the middle of the tee area to be used to the center of the green, following the line of play planned by the architect in laying out the hole. Thus, in a hole with a bend, the line at the elbow point should be centered in the fairway in accordance with the architect's intention.

YARDAGES FOR GUIDANCE

PAR	MEN	WOMEN
3	up to 250	up to 210
4	251 to 470	211 to 400
5	471 and over	401 to 575
6		576 and over

Flagstick Dimensions

The USGA recommends that the flagstick be at least seven feet in height and that its diameter be not greater than three-quarters of an inch from a point three inches above the ground to the bottom of the hole.

Protection of Persons Against Lightning

As there have been many deaths and injuries from lightning on golf courses, all clubs and sponsors of golf competitions are urged to take every precaution for the protection of persons against lightning.

Attention is called to Rules 6-8 and 33-2d.

The USGA suggests that players be informed that they have the right to stop play if they think lightning threatens them, even though the Committee may not have specifically authorized it by signal.

The USGA generally uses the following signals and recommends that all Committees do similarly:

Discontinue Play: Three consecutive notes of siren, repeated.

Resume Play: One prolonged note of siren, repeated.

Posters containing detailed information on protection from lightning are available from the USGA.

MISCELLANEOUS DECISIONS

Misc./1 Course Record

The term "course record" is not defined in the Rules of Golf. However, it is generally accepted that a record score should be recognized as the official "course record" only if made in an individual stroke play competition with the holes and tee-markers in their proper medal or championship positions.

It is recommended that a record score should not be recognized as the official "course record" if a Local Rule permitting preferred lies is in operation.

Misc./2 Whether Rakes Should be Placed In Or Outside Bunkers

Q. Should rakes be placed in or outside bunkers?

A. It is recommended that rakes be placed outside bunkers, as far away from the bunkers as is practical and in positions where they will be least likely to affect play.

DECISIONS APPLICABLE ONLY IN THE UNITED STATES OF AMERICA

US/2-3/100 Player Who Wins First Nine Holes in Nassau Match Withdraws During Second Nine

Q. The "Nassau" System of scoring is used in a team match, *i.e.*, in each match three points are awarded as follows: one point to the winning of the first nine holes, one point to the winner of the second nine and one point to the winner over 18 holes. In one match, a player who had defeated his opponent on the first nine holes withdrew due to illness during the second nine. Should the player retain the point he won on the first nine or, since he withdrew, should he lose all three points?

A. The players should be awarded one point; his opponent won the other two points by default.

US/4-1/100 Clubface Markings

Q. May a player in a USGA competition use a golf club with a groove spacing to groove width ratio of 2.3 to 1, if that club was manufactured before March 31, 1990, even though Appendix II 4-1e requires that the groove spacing to groove width ratio must be no less than 3 to 1.

A. Yes. It is, however, the responsibility of the player to provide proof of the date on which the club was manufactured. If the player cannot provide such proof, the club must conform with the specifications described in Appendix II 4-1e.

[US/5-1/100   Reserved]

US/5-1/101 Status of Ball Not on List of Conforming Golf Balls

Brands of balls not appearing on the current List of Conforming Golf Balls fall into three categories:
1. Brands which have never been tested.
2. Brands which appeared on a previous List but which have not been re-submitted for inclusion on the current List, and
3. Brands which have been tested and found not to conform to the Rules and specifications set forth in Appendix III.

Balls in categories 1 and 2 are presumed to conform and the onus of proof is on the person alleging that the ball does not.

All balls of brands in category 3 are deemed to be non-conforming.

US/5-1/102 Status of Ball to Be Removed from List of Conforming Golf Balls

Q. A brand of ball included on the current List of Conforming golf Balls is tested further and found not to conform to the specifications set forth in Appendix III. The brand will therefore be deleted from the next

List published. What is the status of the ball in the interim period?

A. Players are entitled to assume that all balls of a brand included on the current List of Conforming Golf Balls conform to the Rules and Appendix IIII. Accordingly, players may continue to use balls of the brand in question until the publication of the next List, unless by a condition of the competition the Committee has specifically excluded that brand. This applies whether or not it is a condition of the competition that only brands of golf balls on the List of Conforming Golf Balls may be used.

US/6-2a/100 Player in Match Uses Established Handicap But Handicap Too High Due to Player's Failure to Observe Provision of Handicap System

Q. A's handicap is 23 strokes and B's is 31. A and B play a handicap match and B receives 8 strokes, the difference between 31 and 23. B wins the match, 1 up. A questions B's handicap; B admits that he does not adjust his scores under the Equitable Stroke Control provision of the USGA Handicap System. It is determined that, if B had adjusted his scores, his handicap would be 29 strokes. The Committee disqualifies B under Rule 6-2a. Was the Committee correct?

A. Rule 6-2a provides:

> "Before starting a match in a handicap competition, the players should determine from one another their respective handicaps. If a player begins the match having declared a higher handicap which would affect the number of strokes given or received, he shall be disqualified; otherwise, the player shall play off the declared handicap."

B's handicap, although incorrect due to his failure to apply Equitable Stroke Control, was 31. Accordingly, B was not in breach of Rule 6-2a and the match should have stood as played.

As it is impracticable for a Committee conducting a competition to determine whether a player has correctly recorded each score, turned in all scores, etc., for handicap purposes, the Rules of Golf assume that he has done so. The solution to a situation such as this is for the Handicap Committee to take appropriate action against B because of his failure to apply Equitable Stroke Control to the scores he returned for handicap purposes.

US/20-1/100 Placing Ball-Marker to Side

Q. If a player is requested to mark the position of his ball to the side of where it lies, must he place a ball-marker behind the ball, measure a clubhead-length from the side of the ball and eliminate one step?

A. The player may measure from the side of the ball, unless the Local Rule entitled "Marking Position of Lifted Ball" in Appendix I of the Rules book is in effect. That Local Rule requires that a ball-marker be placed behind the ball and then moved to one side, if necessary.

US/29/100 Penalty in "Pinehurst" Foursome Not Related to Ball Holed Out

Q. In a foursome competition played under the so-called "Pinehurst" format, A and B were partners. In accordance with the format, A hit a second shot with B's ball. B then hit a second shot with a ball he thought was A's, but which in fact was a wrong ball. Since B's shot with the wrong ball was a poor one, B picked up the wrong ball and he and A proceeded to play out the hole with B's ball. It was then discovered that the ball B picked up was not A's ball, but rather a wrong ball.

Do A and B incur any penalty because B played a wrong ball in view of the fact that the hole was completed with B's ball which was not related to the play of the wrong ball?

A. The Rules of Golf do not cover this form of play.

It is recommended that a penalty in this form of play should be incurred only if related to the ball ultimately holed out by the side. Thus, as the ball played by B from the tee was ultimately holed out, the side should not have incurred a penalty because B played a stroke with a wrong ball instead of A's ball.

US/33-8/100 Local Rule of Lateral Water Hazard with Bunker Adjacent

Q. The 18th hole at the Pebble Beach Golf Links is bordered along the left side by Carmel Bay, and there is a sea wall which begins more than 100 yards short of the green and extends to the back of the green. There is a bunker approximately 12 feet wide between the sea wall and the fairway for much of this distance.

The bay is a lateral water hazard and the sea wall is the natural margin of the hazard. Accordingly, a player, when dropping a ball under Rule 26-1c(i), must drop in the bunker. The sand at this point is soft and a dropped ball usually plugs.

Would it be permissible to make a Local Rule to the effect that, when obtaining relief under the lateral water hazard Rule, the player may drop a ball to the right of the bunker, or alternatively, to place the line defining the lateral water hazard along the right edge of the bunker, making the bunker part of the lateral water hazard?

A. It is recommended:
1. that the hazard be marked along its natural boundary, *i.e.*, the sea wall; and
2. that a series of Ball Drops be established along the right-hand side of the bunker, and that there be a Local Rule stating that a player whose ball comes to rest in the water hazard may drop a ball, under penalty of one stroke, on the nearest Ball Drop which is not nearer the hole.

US/33-8/101 Local Rule for Breach of Sportsmanship Code

Q. A high school federation has a sportsmanship code for golfers who compete in high school matches.

May the federation make a Local Rule assessing a penalty for a breach of the code?

A. A Local Rule assessing a penalty for a breach of a sportsmanship code is not authorized. Penalties for a breach of a sportsmanship code should take a more generalized form, *e.g.*, subjection to censure, suspension or revocation of the privilege of playing in events.

US/33-8/102 Local Rule for Suspension of Play Due to Dangerous Situation

Q. In order to protect players and spectators, the Committee desires all players to stop play immediately upon notification of a suspension due to a dangerous situation such as lightning. Is this permissible?

A. Yes. The use of the following Local Rule is recommended:

> "When play is suspended for a dangerous situation, if the players in a match or group are between the play of two holes, they shall not resume play until the Committee has ordered a resumption of play. If they are in the process of playing a hole, they shall discontinue play immediately and shall not thereafter resume play until the Committee has ordered a resumption of play."

PENALTY FOR BREACH OF LOCAL RULE:

Disqualification

All practice areas shall be closed during suspension for a dangerous situation until the Committee has declared them open for use.

NOTE: A suspension for a dangerous situation shall be signalled by _____. All other types of suspension shall be signalled by _____. (The Committee should use different signals to distinguish suspensions for dangerous situations and suspensions for other reasons.)

US/34-3/100 Committee Intervention in Match Play

In the absence of a referee, a Committee has no authority to intervene in match play unless there is a reason to believe Rule 1-3 is being infringed or a breach of Rule 6-7 is involved. When there is no referee, the players must protect their own rights by invoking Rule 2-5 and by referring to the Committee any dispute they cannot resolve — see Rule 34-3.

US/34-3/101 Committee Intervention in Match Play When Search for Lost Ball Exceeds Five Minutes

Q. Decision US/34-3/100 permits a Committee member to intervene in a match to which a referee has not been assigned in case of a breach of Rule 6-7 (Undue Delay).

Would it be in order for a Committee member to intervene in such a match if he has observed that a player has looked for his ball for five minutes and is continuing to search?

A. Yes. It would be appropriate for a Committee member to intervene and advise the player that the ball is lost under the Rules and, if he does not resume play immediately, a penalty for undue delay will result.

PRINCIPAL CHANGES SINCE 1992

NEW DECISIONS

3-3/6.5 **Competitor Plays Second Ball Without Announcing Intention to Invoke Rule 3-3 and Fails to Report Facts to Committee**

6-3a/2 **Time of Starting; All Competitors Must Be Present**

6-4/4.5 **Another Caddie or Friend Carries Clubs While Player's Caddie Returns to Tee with Player's Glove**

7-1b/7 **Competitor Practices Putting on 3rd Green After Finishing Hole During First Round of 36-Hole Stroke Play Competition**

8/1 **Conditions of Team Competition Stipulate Who Is Authorized to Give Advice**

20-6/3 **Ball Mistakenly Substituted When Dropped; Correction of Error**

30-3a/3 **Determination of Handicap Allowances in Four-Ball Match If One Player Unable to Compete**

31-7a/2 **Lower Gross Score Attributed to Wrong Partner**

32-2a/2 **Four-Ball Stableford Competition on Handicap Basis; Side's Scores Transposed at a Hole to Side's Advantage**

REVISED DECISIONS

13-2/35 **Removal of Dew or Frost.** Amended to include frost.

16-1a/3 **Removing Dew of Frost from Line of Putt.** Amended to include frost.

17/4 **Adjustment of Flagstick; Player's Rights.** Amended to clarify that the flagstick may be adjusted by anyone.

18/7.5 **Player's Ball Moved by Ball Accidently Dropped by Opponent or Fellow-Competitor.** Amended to refer to the Note to the Definiton of "Equipment" rather than Decision 18/7.

19-5/1 **Player Lifts His Ball on Putting Green and Sets It Aside; Opponent's or Fellow-Competitor's Ball Played from Green Subsequently Strikes Player's Ball.** Amended to refer to the Note to the Definition of "Equipment" rather than Decision 18/7.

19-5/1.5 **After Player Putts Opponent or Fellow-Competitor Drops His Ball; Player's Ball Strikes Opponent's or Fellow-Competitor's Ball After It Is at Rest.** Amended to refer to the Note to the Definition of "Equipment" rather than Decision 18/7.

19-5/1.7 **Ball Dropped on Putting Green by Opponent or Fellow-Competitor Falls on Player's Moving Ball.** Amended to refer to the Note to the Definition of "Equipment" rather than Decision 18/7.

32-2a/1 **Four-Ball Stableford Competition on Handicap Basis; Side's Scores Transposed at a Hole But Not to Side's Advantage.** Amended to clarify the recorded score of each partner.

NOTES